Brief Contents

P9-CFG-903

7TH EDITION

SUCCESSFUL COLLEGE WRITING

SKILLS | STRATEGIES | LEARNING STYLES

KATHLEEN T. McWHORTER

Niagara County Community College

bedford/st.martin's
Macmillan Learning

Boston | New York

For Bedford/St. Martin's

Vice President, Editorial, Macmillan Learning Humanities: *Edwin Hill*
Senior Program Director for English: *Leasa Burton*
Program Manager: *Molly Parke*
Marketing Manager: *Vivian Garcia*
Director of Content Development: *Jane Knetzger*
Executive Developmental Editor: *Jane Carter*
Senior Content Project Manager: *Ryan Sullivan*
Senior Workflow Manager: *Jennifer Wetzel*
Production Assistant: *Brianna Lester*
Media Project Manager: *Melissa Skepko-Masi*
Editorial Services: *Lumina Datamatics, Inc.*
Composition: *Cenveo® Publisher Services*
Photo Editor: *Angela Boehler*
Permissions Manager: *Kalina Ingham*
Senior Art Director: *Anna Palchik*
Text Design: *Cenveo® Publisher Services*
Cover Design: *William Boardman*
Cover Photo: *Yagi Studios/nicolas_/Getty Images*
Printing and Binding: *LSC Communications*

Manufactured in the United States of America.

2 1 0
f e d c

For information, write: Bedford/St. Martin's, 75 Arlington Street, Boston, MA 02116

ISBN 978-1-319-05859-3 (Student Edition)

Acknowledgments

Text acknowledgments and copyrights appear at the back of the book on pages 817–18, which constitute an extension of the copyright page. Art acknowledgments and copyrights appear on the same page as the art selections they cover.

Contents

PART ONE

An Introduction to Reading, Writing, and Learning in College 1

Paul Bradbury/Getty Images

Just-in-Time Guide to Reading and Responding   81

PART TWO

Strategies for Writing Essays 97

mantinov/Shutterstock

4 Prewriting: How to Find and Focus Ideas 98

WRITING QUICK START 98

PART THREE

Patterns of Development 215

WILDLIFE GmbH/Alamy

10 An Introduction to Patterns of Development 216

11 Narration: Recounting Events 228

16 ▸ Classification and Division: Explaining Categories and Parts 400

17 ▸ Definition: Explaining What You Mean 426

PART FOUR

Reading and Writing Arguments 491

PART FIVE

Writing with Sources 547

Joelle Sedlmeyer/Getty Images

21 Planning a Research Project and Evaluating Sources 548

PART SIX

Academic and Business Applications   645

ThomasVogel/Getty Images

24   Reading and Writing about Literature   646

WRITING QUICK START   646

READING   The Bean Eaters, *Gwendolyn Brooks*   647

■ Literature in College and the Workplace   648

A General Approach to Reading Literature   648

Understand the Language of Literature   649

Similes, Metaphors, and Personification   649 | Symbols   650 | Irony   650

PART SEVEN

Handbook: Writing Problems and How to Correct Them 705

© THPStock/Getty Images

Thematic Contents

Preface

Other texts assume that first-year composition students already possess the basic skills they will need to succeed in college, but my own experience tells me that this is not true. That is why I wrote *Successful College Writing*. It uses a unique, highly visual, student-centered approach to teach students the reading and study skills they need while guiding them through the writing strategies and activities that form the core of composition instruction. The overwhelmingly positive response to the first six editions demonstrates that *Successful College Writing* fulfills an important need.

The seventh edition continues to meet students where they are and get them where they need to go by building on one of the text's core strengths: its integration of writing and reading instruction as two aspects of the same process. Through consultation with students and a complete redesign, the seventh edition is now more accessible and better than ever at helping instructors address the needs of first-year college students at a variety of levels of preparedness.

Proven Features of *Successful College Writing*

True to its goal of offering more coverage of essential skills, *Successful College Writing* provides abundant guidance and support for inexperienced writers along with thorough help with reading and study skills. Every chapter of *Successful College Writing* provides practical, student-oriented instruction, along with extra help for those students who need it.

Practical, Step-by-Step Writing Assignments

Successful College Writing provides the tools to approach writing as a flexible, multifaceted process, alleviating some of the frustration students often feel.

Part 1 begins this process by emphasizing the importance of reading and writing to students' success in college and career, not only as a way to communicate with others, but also as a way for mastering complex information and ideas, and applying them to new situations. It also alerts students to the expectations their college instructors will have for them as readers, thinkers, and writers, including how they read, think, and respond critically to texts and images.

A new **"Just-in-Time Guide to Reading and Responding"** provides students with the survival reading skills they need to understand and fully engage with college-level texts. The handbook format allows students to dip into the guide to find the support they need, and the bite-sized responses let them get back to their assigned reading quickly. This guide may be particularly useful for those students in first-year composition classrooms who, in past years, may have been assigned to a developmental writing or reading class.

Part 2 provides detailed coverage of the writing process—from choosing and narrowing a topic and generating ideas to developing and supporting a thesis, drafting essays and paragraphs, revising, editing, and proofreading. Each chapter in Part 2 includes the following:

- plenty of skill-building exercises, many of them collaborative
- essay-in-progress activities that lead students through each step in writing an essay
- writing-in-progress sample essays that follow student writers through the various stages of drafting and revision. Part 2 follows the writing process of one student, Latrisha Wilson, as she devises ideas and drafts, and revises her essay. Chapter 7 shows another student (Robin Ferguson) using an outline and a graphic organizer to plan, followed by the final essay. Chapter 8 shows a draft of a third student (Kate Atkinson) with comments from her instructor; a revised version of this essay appears in Chapter 17.

Parts 3 and **4** cover the patterns of development that students encounter most frequently in college and on the job. Graphic organizers offer students a visual guide to the structure of reading selections and offer a structure for students as they draft their own essays. Each Guided Writing Assignment emphasizes activities for generating and evaluating ideas, developing a thesis, organizing and drafting the essay, and revising and editing that essay.

Part 5 provides instruction for writing a research project, including information about finding useful and reliable sources, synthesizing information and ideas from sources to support the writer's ideas, and incorporating and documenting material borrowed from sources.

Part 6 covers writing in academic and business settings, from writing about literature, taking essay exams, and creating a portfolio to making presentations and writing résumés, job application letters, and business emails.

Appealing, Helpful Visuals

Because inexperienced writers are often more comfortable with images than with text, *Successful College Writing* employs a visual approach to writing instruction. Look for the following visual aids throughout the book.

- **Writing Quick Starts** jumpstart each chapter, providing engaging images for students to respond to in writing and introducing them to the main topic of the chapter.
- **Graphic Organizers**—charts that display relationships among ideas—offer tools both for analyzing readings and for planning and revising essays, and they present students with a more visual alternative to traditional outlines.
- **Guided Writing Assignments**—in a streamlined, step-by-step, visual format—walk students through the process of writing essays in each of the rhetorical modes.
- **Revision Flowcharts** help students read and revise their own essays systematically as well as review the essays of their peers.

- **Visualizing the Reading** activities give students a simple way to chart key features of the reading, with the first part of each chart done for them to provide guidance.
- Numerous **figures**, **photographs**, **boxes**, and **bulleted lists** throughout the text reinforce key points and summarize information.

Improving Reading Skills: A Five-Pronged Approach

Recognizing that students frequently enter first-year writing courses without the active and critical reading skills they need to succeed in first-year composition and other college courses, *Successful College Writing* supports students with a five-pronged approach to improving their reading skills that will also help students become better writers. This five-pronged approach includes:

1. **Overt reading instruction in Chapters 2 and 3, in the new "Just-in-Time Guide to Reading and Responding," and in the new "How Writers Read" boxes.** Chapter 2 includes a "Guide to Active Reading" and a "Guide to Responding to a Reading," and Chapter 3 offers detailed coverage of reading both text and visuals critically. The new "Just-in-Time Guide" offers support that students can dip into as needed and lets them get right back to their reading, and the new "How Writers Read" boxes throughout help students recognize that reading and writing are two sides of the same coin.
2. **Graphic Organizers** in Parts 2, 3, and 4 that help students recognize the structure of the essay
3. **Activities to foster critical reading** following readings in Parts 3 and 4 and in LearningCurve, Bedford/St. Martin's adaptive quizzing program. (Activities on eleven core topics are available in LaunchPad for *Successful College Writing*, which can be packaged with the textbook or purchased on its own; for more information, see p. xxxv.)
4. **Collaborative activities** to enhance critical reading
5. **Peer review–style activities and revision flowcharts**, which can be used alone or with classmates to emphasize reading and thinking critically

Over the years, my work with students has convinced me that skills taught in isolation are seldom learned well or applied, so each of the chapters on the patterns of development in Parts 3 and 4 reinforces the reading skills taught in Part 1 and elsewhere. As students develop their writing skills by producing a particular type of essay, they simultaneously learn practical strategies for reading that type of essay.

High-Interest Readings

In addition to guidelines for reading different types of texts, *Successful College Writing* includes reading selections from the diverse array of texts students are likely to encounter in their personal, academic, and professional lives. Since students who enjoy what they read become more proficient readers, the selections in this text were carefully chosen not only to function as strong rhetorical models but also to interest students. Selections come from such well-known writers as Paul Kalanithi, Deborah

Tannen, and Brent Staples, and address intriguing topics from junk-food addiction to police misconduct to how our possessions define us.

Comprehensive Coverage of Research and Documentation

Because finding and evaluating useful sources has become so challenging in the digital age and because of the ease with which writers can copy and paste information from sources into their own writing, *Successful College Writing* provides three full chapters (Part 5) on writing with sources, including a careful discussion of accidental plagiarism and paraphrasing without "patchwriting," using information and ideas from sources to support the writer's own ideas, and documenting sources in MLA and APA styles (including updated MLA citations using the new eighth edition of the *MLA Handbook*).

Thorough Reference Handbook

The handbook in Part 7 covers basic grammar, sentence problems, punctuation, mechanics, spelling, and ESL troublespots, and includes the following:

- hand-corrected examples to make needed revisions easy to understand
- key grammatical terms defined in the margin
- helpful revision flowcharts and summary boxes
- sentence and paragraph exercises

It also reinforces students' learning with plenty of opportunities for practice, with exercises in the text; additional exercises keyed to the handbook in A *Student's Companion for Successful College Writing*, a new supplement, and LaunchPad for *Successful College Writing*, an online course space; and supplemental practice through LearningCurve, Bedford/St. Martin's adaptive quizzing program (also available in LaunchPad for *Successful College Writing*).

A Unique Emphasis on Learning Styles

Students learn in different ways for different tasks and assignments, yet most writing texts do not take these differences in learning style into account. In this text, I focus on four learning styles that are relevant for writing:

- verbal versus spatial
- creative versus pragmatic
- concrete versus abstract
- social versus independent

A brief questionnaire in Chapter 1 enables students to assess their learning styles. Recognizing that no one strategy works for every student or every assignment, the text includes a variety of methods for generating ideas and revising an essay.

Attention to Outcomes

Successful College Writing helps students build proficiency in the four categories of learning that writing programs across the country use to assess student work.

- rhetorical knowledge
- critical thinking, reading, and composing
- processes
- knowledge of conventions

For a table that correlates the Council of Writing Program Administrators (WPA) outcomes to features of *Successful College Writing*, see pages xxxviii–xliii.

New to the Seventh Edition

The main goal of the revision—based on feedback from experienced instructors familiar with the needs of today's students—was to focus on three key areas: further integration of reading and writing instruction, concentration on the practical learning strategies students need to succeed in college, and enhancement of the accessibility of the text, in light of changes to first-year writing and developmental education in colleges and universities across the country. These new and enhanced features address all three of these needs.

NEW! **Now more accessible both in terms of design and readability.** A review by forty-three students from three different schools showed us what students are actually reading and how much of the assigned instructional content they are skipping. Since the content they are skipping is wasted space, I pared back the text and broke it into more easily absorbable chunks to make the prose more direct, with more scannable lists and useful boxes. The book was also redesigned, not only to make it more attractive but also to make it more accessible to students with visual impairments. Now, greater contrast between colors used for an instructional purpose makes the text easier to read and understand, and Bedford/St. Martin's new e-book format makes the text more accessible for students using screen readers and more readable for students accessing the text on mobile devices.

NEW! **Attention to proven learning strategies.** While *Successful College Writing* has long focused on learning styles, I recognize that what's comfortable isn't always what makes learning most effective, and learning styles that may be effective for learning one type of content may not work especially well in a different context. In response to new research, the seventh edition of *Successful College Writing* has added material on some of the most effective learning strategies for students in first-year composition and beyond. A new section in Chapter 1 (pp. 7–9) highlights learning strategies such as using metacognition (becoming aware of what is working and what's not), connecting new learning with what was learned before, and using writing to synthesize and extend ideas. New annotations in the Instructor's Annotated Edition also point out ways instructors can coach students to use challenging but effective learning strategies.

NEW! **Further attention to integrated reading and writing, with the new "Just-in-Time Guide to Reading and Responding" and "How Writers Read" boxes throughout the text.** In addition to Chapters 2 and 3 and the activities for reading actively and critically that follow the reading selections, the new seventh edition now also includes a "Just-in-Time Guide to Reading and Responding" (pp. 81–96). This guide allows students to dip in for the help they need to understand and fully engage with the assigned, college-level reading, without bogging them down in a detailed lesson. While this guide is designed to help students who, in past years, may have been assigned to a developmental writing or reading class, it can help any students adjusting to college-level expectations.

Also new to this edition are the "How Writers Read" boxes (see, for example, pp. 106 and 378), which appear throughout the text. These boxes strengthen the reading-writing connection emphasized throughout the book by offering concrete strategies students can apply to the professional and student essays in this book and to all their college reading assignments. These boxes showcase the application of writing skills and strategies to reading, demonstrating to students that what they are learning about writing will also help them read more effectively.

NEW! **Updated professional and student readings.** The seventh edition now includes eighteen new professional reading selections and three new essays by student writers. Reading selections such as excerpts from Sam Quinones's important book *Dreamland: The True Tales of America's Opium Epidemic* and Baratunde Thurston's *How to Be Black* as well as a pair of readings by Jenny Jarvie and Aaron Hanlon on trigger warnings will engage students and get them thinking and writing. Other notable additions include a classic selection by Deborah Tannen from her book *I Only Say This Because I Love You*, and new student essays: "Sometimes, We Give," about one student's response to a homeless peer; "Are Zoos the Best Answer for Animals?" an argument against keeping animals in zoos; and "The Short, Happy Life of Louise Mallard," an analysis of the classic "The Story of an Hour."

NEW! **Updated coverage of online presentations and business writing.** Chapter 26 has been updated to include a revised discussion of best practices for making presentations using PowerPoint and Prezi, and now includes an image of a Prezi overview slide. Coverage of business writing now includes a new résumé and cover letter.

Acknowledgments

I would like to express my gratitude to the following instructors and their students, who reviewed chapters from *Successful College Writing* and provided valuable feedback about its readability, usefulness, and features: Karen Engels (Waukesha County Technical College), Kimberly Murphy (Montgomery College), and Andrew Preslar (Lamar State College–Orange).

This edition also benefited from the experience of those instructors who reviewed the sixth edition and the manuscript for the seventh edition; I am grateful for their thoughtful comments and helpful advice: Raphael Bennett, Broward College; Lynda Brooks, Kilgore College; Patricia Campbell, Broward College; Sandra Cooper, College of Central Florida; Michel de Benedictis, Miami Dade College; Karen Engels, Waukesha County Technical College; Laura Fox, Harford Community College; Seonae Ha-Birdsong, Northeastern Oklahoma A&M College; Sheena Hernandez, Garden City Community College; Elizabeth (Dollie) Hudspeth, Northeast Lakeview College; Linda Iaccino,

Broward College; John Kitts, Mohave Community College; Dina Levitre, Community College of Rhode Island; Valrie Martin, Palm Beach State College; Rebecca Millan, South Texas College; Jason Morgan, Shaw University; Kimberly Murphy, Montgomery College; Andrew Preslar, Lamar State College–Orange; Melissa Reddish, Wor-Wic Community College; Kristin Redfield, Forsyth Technical Community College; Jim Richey, Tyler Junior College; and Marsha Wright, Garden City Community College.

I am indebted to the valuable research conducted by George Jensen, John DiTiberio, and Robert Sternberg on learning-style theory that informs the pedagogy of this book. For their comments on the coverage of learning styles in this text, I would like to thank John DiTiberio, Saint Louis University; Ronald A. Sudol, Oakland University; and Thomas C. Thompson, The Citadel. My thanks go to Mary Jane Feldman, Niagara County Community College, for designing the field test of the Learning Styles Inventory and conducting the statistical analysis of the results. I would also like to thank the instructors and students who participated in a field test of the Learning Styles Inventory: Laurie Warshal Cohen, Seattle Central Community College; Lee Brewer Jones, DeKalb College; Edwina Jordan, Illinois Central College; Jennifer Manning, John Jay College; Mildred Melendez, Sinclair Community College; Paul Resnick, Illinois Central College; and Deanna M. White, University of Texas at San Antonio.

I also want to thank Elizabeth Gruchala-Gilbert for her research assistance; Jamey Gallagher for writing material on teaching a co-requisite (or ALP) course alongside a freshman writing course; Carolyn Lengel for devising the activities and exercises and assembling the rest of the materials in *A Student's Companion for Successful College Writing*, a new supplement for students in co-requisite (or accelerated learning) classes or for anyone who needs a little extra help developing ideas, drafting, and revising an essay; and Andy Preslar, who wrote the assignment rubrics that appear in *A Student's Companion*. I especially want to thank Kathy Tyndall for her valuable assistance in helping me revise portions of the manuscript, including the apparatus following the readings, the annotations in the Instructor's Annotated Edition, and the reading quizzes for comprehension and summary.

Many people at Bedford/St. Martin's have contributed to the creation and development of *Successful College Writing*. Each person with whom I have worked is a true professional: Each demonstrates high standards and expertise, and each is committed to producing a book focused on student needs.

My thanks to Leasa Burton, senior program director for the English group at Bedford/St. Martin's, for overseeing the project and making valuable contributions to the revision. I value her editorial experience and appreciate her creative energy. I also thank Molly Parke, program director for rhetorics and business/tech writing, for her forthright advice and for valuable assistance in making some of the more difficult decisions about the book and her untiring efforts to champion this book. Special thanks to Melissa Skepko-Masi, new media production editor, and Will Stonefield, new media editor, for their careful and talented work on LaunchPad. I also appreciate the advice and guidance that marketing manager Vivian Garcia has provided at various junctures in the revision of this text. Suzanne Chouljian, assistant editor, has helped improve and prepare the manuscript in innumerable ways. Ryan Sullivan, senior content project manager, deserves special recognition for guiding this revision through the production process.

I owe the largest debt of gratitude to Jane Carter, my development editor, for her valuable guidance and assistance in preparing this revision. Her careful editing and attention to detail have strengthened the seventh edition significantly. She helped me to reinforce the book's strengths and to retain its focus on providing extra help to the student.

Finally, I must thank the many students who inspired me to write this book. From them I have learned how to teach, and they have shown me how they think and learn. My students, then, have made the largest contribution to this book, for without them I would have little to say and no reason to write.

Kathleen T. McWhorter

We're all in. As always.

Bedford/St. Martin's is as passionately committed to the discipline of English as ever, working hard to provide support and services that make it easier for you to teach your course your way.

You can find **community support** at the Bedford/St. Martin's English Community (**community.macmillan.com**), where you can follow our *Bits* blog for new teaching ideas, download titles from our professional resource series, and review other projects in the pipeline.

Choose **curriculum solutions** that offer flexible custom options, combining our carefully developed print and digital resources, acclaimed works from Macmillan's trade imprints, and your own course or program materials to provide the exact resources your students need.

Rely on **outstanding service** from your Bedford/St. Martin's sales representative and editorial team. Contact us or visit **macmillanlearning.com** to learn more about any of the options below.

LaunchPad for *Successful College Writing*: Where Students Learn

LaunchPad provides engaging content and new ways to get the most out of your book. Get an interactive e-book combined with assessment tools in a fully customizable course space, then assign and mix our resources with yours.

- **Reading quizzes** let you check your students' comprehension with an auto-graded, multiple-choice quiz.
- **Summary activities** provide your students with practice and offer them a model summary as feedback against which they can check their work.
- A *Student's Companion for Successful College Writing,* a new supplement for students taking a co-requisite (or accelerated learning) course in conjunction with first-year composition or for any students who need a little extra help making the transition to college, is included in full in LaunchPad for *Successful College Writing* and is available separately as a print supplement.
- **Diagnostics** provide opportunities to assess areas for improvement and assign additional exercises based on students' needs. Visual reports show performance by topic, class, and student as well as improvement over time.
- **Pre-built units**—including readings, videos, quizzes, and more—are easy to adapt and assign by adding your own materials and mixing them with our high-quality multimedia content and ready-made assessment options, such as **LearningCurve** adaptive quizzing and Exercise Central.
- Use LaunchPad on its own or **integrate it** with your school's learning management system so that your class is always on the same page.

LaunchPad for *Successful College Writing* can be purchased on its own or packaged with the print book at a significant discount. An activation code is required. To order

LaunchPad for *Successful College Writing* with the print book, use one of the following ISBNs:

- *Successful College Writing,* Seventh Edition (with Part 7: Handbook): ISBN 978-1-319-13852-3
- *Successful College Writing,* Brief Seventh Edition (without Part 7: Handbook): ISBN 978-1-319-13850-9

For more information, go to **launchpadworks.com**.

NEW! *A Student's Companion for Successful College Writing*

If your students need a little extra support, consider ordering *A Student's Companion for Successful College Writing* (ISBN 978-1-319-13029-9) by Carolyn Lengel, with rubrics by Andrew B. Preslar, Lamar State College–Orange. This text provides sentence templates and hands-on activities to help students develop writing assignments in each chapter of Parts 3 and 4 of *Successful College Writing.* It also includes guidance for key college success topics, such as time management and writing ethically; rubrics that students can use to assess their own writing or that of their peers; sentence templates for academic writing; and activities for grammar practice and application. This is the perfect text for students taking a co-requisite (or ALP section) or just for students who might need more support for developing their college writing projects fully. To order *A Student's Companion* packaged with *Successful College Writing,* Seventh Edition, use one of the following ISBNs:

- *Successful College Writing,* Seventh Edition (with Part 7: Handbook), plus *A Student's Companion for Successful College Writing:* ISBN 978-1-319-18226-7
- *Successful College Writing,* Brief Seventh Edition (without Part 7: Handbook), plus *A Student's Companion for Successful College Writing:* ISBN 978-1-319-18227-4

Choose from Alternative Formats of *Successful College Writing*

Bedford/St. Martin's offers a range of formats. Choose what works best for you and your students.

- To order the full edition of *Successful College Writing* (with Part 7: Handbook), use ISBN 978-1-319-05859-3; to order the brief edition (without Part 7: Handbook), use ISBN 978-1-319-09395-2.
- *Popular e-book formats*   For details of our e-book partners, visit **macmillanlearning .com/ebooks**.
- *A Student's Companion*   To order the full edition of *Successful College Writing* (with Part 7: Handbook) packaged with *A Student's Companion for Successful College Writing* and LaunchPad, use ISBN 978-1-319-16734-9; to order the brief edition (without Part 7: Handbook) packaged with *A Student's Companion for Successful College Writing* and LaunchPad, use ISBN 978-1-319-16738-7.

Select Value Packages

Add value to your text by packaging the following resource with *Successful College Writing*.

LaunchPad Solo for Readers and Writers allows students to work on what they need help with the most. At home or in class, students learn at their own pace, with instruction tailored to each student's unique needs. *LaunchPad Solo for Readers and Writers* features:

- **Prebuilt units that support a learning arc.** Each easy-to-assign unit is comprised of a pretest check, multimedia instruction and assessment, and a post-test that assesses what students have learned about critical reading, writing process, use of sources, grammar, style, and mechanics. Dedicated units also offer help for multilingual writers.
- **Diagnostics that help establish a baseline for instruction.** Assign diagnostics to identify areas of strength and areas that require improvement, helping students plan a course of study. Use visual reports to track performance by topic, class, and student as well as improvement over time.
- **A video introduction to many topics.** Introductions offer an overview of the unit's topic, and many include a brief, accessible video to illustrate the concepts at hand.
- **Twenty-five reading selections with comprehension quizzes.** Assign a range of classic and contemporary essays, each of which includes a label indicating Lexile level to help you scaffold instruction in critical reading.
- **Adaptive quizzing for targeted learning.** Most units include LearningCurve, game-like adaptive quizzing that focuses on the areas in which each student needs the most help.
- **Additional reading comprehension quizzes.** *Successful College Writing* includes multiple-choice quizzes, which help you quickly gauge your students' understanding of the assigned reading. These are available in *LaunchPad Solo for Readers and Writers*.

LaunchPad Solo for Readers and Writers can be packaged with *Successful College Writing* at a significant discount. For more information, contact your sales representative or visit **macmillanlearning.com/readwrite**.

Instructor Resources

You have a lot to do in your course. We want to make it easy for you to find the support you need—and to get it quickly.

- *Instructor's Resource Manual for Successful College Writing* (available as a PDF). In addition to advice for teaching with *Successful College Writing*, the instructor's manual includes suggestions for helping underprepared students successfully complete the course, advice for instructors teaching a co-requisite (or ALP) section, sample syllabi, suggestions for using the writing center at your school, and more.
- **Presentation slides for *Successful College Writing*.** Presentation slides are available for every chapter in the text.

Visit the instructor resources tab for *Successful College Writing* at **macmillanlearning.com**.

Features of *Successful College Writing*, Seventh Edition, Correlated to the Writing Program Administrators (WPA) Outcomes Statement (2014)

Desired Student Outcomes	Relevant Features of *Successful College Writing*
RHETORICAL KNOWLEDGE	
Learn and use key theoretical concepts through analyzing and composing a variety of texts.	• Chapter 1: Covers successful learning strategies in general and for the writing class in particular (pp. 7–15, 17–19), and expectations for reading and writing in college (pp. 15–16). • Chapter 2: Offers advice for reading academic and other challenging texts, including instruction on active reading (previewing, pp. 26–41) and reading to respond (annotating, summarizing, and keeping a response journal, pp. 41–54). • Chapter 3: Offers advice for reading texts and visuals critically, including analyzing the author's ideas (pp. 56–61), language (pp. 61–66), and assumptions, generalizations, or omissions (pp. 66–72), and reading photos and graphics actively and critically (pp. 72–80). • Chapters in Parts 3 and 4: Includes reading selections for a variety of audiences, from popular to more scholarly (see, for example, "The Psychology of Stuff and Things," pp. 350–55), followed by scaffolded apparatus to help students read actively and critically (pp. 355–57); writing essays using a variety of rhetorical modes (see the Guided Writing Assignment and student essay in Chapter 14, pp. 340–49, for example); "Using [Mode] in College and the Workplace" boxes (for example, on p. 329). • Part 5: Offers advice for writing using sources and citing sources in MLA and APA style. • Part 6: Offers advice about writing in specific academic contexts (Chapter 24, "Reading and Writing about Literature," and Chapter 25, "Essay Examinations and Portfolios"), and about writing in the workplace (Chapter 26, "Multimedia Presentations and Business Writing").
Gain experience reading and composing in several genres to understand how genre conventions shape and are shaped by readers' and writers' practices and purposes.	• Chapter 1: Covers reading a syllabus (pp. 9–11) and highlights the expectation that students will both read and produce writing in a variety of genres, from abstracts to research projects. • Chapters 19–20: Covers reading and writing arguments. • Chapter 23: Covers writing a research project, with example research projects in MLA and APA style (pp. 603–27, 628–44). • Chapter 24: Writing literary analyses, with a sample essay (pp. 671–73). • Chapter 25: Covers writing essay examinations and compiling portfolios, with a sample essay answer (p. 683), sample portfolio contents, and reflective letter (pp. 687–90). • Chapter 26: Covers creating multimedia presentations using PowerPoint and Prezi presentation slides (pp. 691–98); writing résumés and job application letters (pp. 698–702); and writing in electronic media for business (pp. 702–3).
Develop facility in responding to a variety of situations and contexts calling for purposeful shifts in voice, tone, level of formality, design, medium, and/or structure.	• Chapter 3: Covers reading critically, particularly by paying attention to the author's use of language (pp. 61–66). • Chapter 9: Offers instruction on editing words and sentences, including editing to create an appropriate tone and level of diction (pp. 205–8). • Chapter 23: Covers appropriate formats for writing a paper using sources, in MLA and APA style (pp. 596–97, 601–3, 621–28, 639–44). • Chapter 26: Covers appropriate business writing formats and styles for résumés, job application letters, and electronic business correspondence (pp. 698–703), and appropriate design and formatting of slides in presentation software, such as PowerPoint and Prezi (pp. 694–96). • LaunchPad*: Includes tutorials in critical reading and digital writing; LearningCurve activities in critical reading, topic sentences and supporting details, topics and main ideas, and issues of correctness.

*Additional resource, available free when packaged with the text. See p. xxxv for details.

Desired Student Outcomes	Relevant Features of *Successful College Writing*

RHETORICAL KNOWLEDGE

Understand and use a variety of technologies to address a range of audiences.	• Chapter 9: Discusses computer-aided proofreading (including the pitfall of relying too heavily on spell-check and grammar-check software (p. 212). • LaunchPad*: Offers tutorials in documenting and working with sources in both MLA and APA style, as well as tutorials in making multimedia presentations, job searching, and personal branding.
Match the capacities of different environments (e.g., print and electronic) to varying rhetorical situations.	• Chapter 22: Covers researching online (pp. 564–72). • Chapter 23: Covers using appropriate formats (MLA or APA) for writing a paper using sources (pp. 586–64). • Chapter 25: Covers using print and digital portfolios for assessment and learning (683–90). • Chapter 26: Covers planning, drafting, and delivering a multimedia presentation using visual aids (objects and presentation slides), whether face to face or via the Web (pp. 691–98); creating effective résumés and job application letters, whether printed or uploaded electronically; and using electronic media for business writing (pp. 698–703). • *Instructor's Resource Manual for Successful College Writing*, Seventh Edition (for instructors): Covers teaching and learning online. • LaunchPad*: Offers tutorials on digital writing, (including photo and audio editing), making presentations, word processing, using online research tools, and job search/personal branding.

CRITICAL THINKING, READING, AND COMPOSING

Use composing and reading for inquiry, learning, critical thinking, and communicating in various rhetorical contexts.	• The entire book is informed by the connection between reading critically and writing effectively. • Chapter 1: Covers the importance of reading and writing for college success and the distinctive qualities and demands of academic reading and writing. • Chapter 2: Covers reading actively (pp. 26–41) and understanding and responding to reading in writing (pp. 41–54). • Chapter 3: Covers thinking critically about text and images by analyzing the author's ideas (pp. 56–61), use of language (pp. 61–66), assumptions, generalizations, and omissions (pp. 66–70), synthesizing ideas (pp. 71–72), and analyzing photographs and graphics by reading them actively and critically (pp. 72–80). • "Just-in-Time Guide to Reading and Responding": Provides a useful reference for students who need help with reading, developing college-level vocabulary, highlighting appropriately, and preparing for a discussion of a reading selection (pp. 81–96). • Parts 3 and 4: Covers thinking critically about the features of the genre, including analyzing and evaluating a reading in the chapter's pattern (see the "How Writers Read" box on p. 338, for example), and synthesizing ideas across readings (see the "Synthesizing Ideas" box on p. 362). The activities following the reading selections in the latter part of each chapter provide activities that walk students through the process of analyzing the reading (see, for example, pp. 355–57). • LaunchPad*: Offers tutorials and activities in LearningCurve on reading critically.
Read a diverse range of texts, attending especially to relationships between assertion and evidence, to patterns of organization, to interplay between verbal and nonverbal elements, and to how these features function for different audiences and situations.	• Chapter 1: This chapter includes coverage of expectations for academic reading and writing and why improving one's reading and writing skills is crucial (pp. 16–17). • Chapter 2: The entire chapter (pp. 25–54) focuses on strategies for reading and responding to text and visuals. • Chapter 3: Includes coverage of assessing evidence (pp. 58–59), distinguishing between fact and opinion (pp. 60–61), and the roles patterns of development and synthesis (p. 71–72) and illustrations (photographs and graphics) play in writing (pp. 72–80). • Chapter 4: Includes coverage of the importance of purpose, audience, point of view, genre, and medium in reading and writing (pp. 102–6). • Chapter 5: Emphasizes the importance of supporting a thesis with evidence, including incorporating visuals as evidence (pp. 125–30). • Chapter 6: Focuses on the relationship between a paragraph's topic and use of supporting evidence (pp. 144–48).

*Additional resource, available free when packaged with the text. See p. xxxv for details.

Desired Student Outcomes	Relevant Features of *Successful College Writing*

CRITICAL THINKING, READING, AND COMPOSING

	• Parts 3 and 4: Each of the chapters in these parts focuses on a pattern of organization, with each including a section that asks students to consider the role of the audience and situation (see Chapter 12, p. 276, for example). Readings in these chapters range from popular (see "I'm Not Leaving until I Eat This Thing," pp. 285–88, and "How to Be the Black Employee," pp. 357–60) to accessible scholarly selections (see "The Psychology of Stuff and Things," pp. 350–55, and "His Marriage and Hers: Childhood Roots," pp. 387–91, for example). Where appropriate, activities following the readings also ask students to think critically about the relationship between text and visuals (see Chapter 14, pp. 356–57, for example). • Chapter 19: Covers supporting an arguable claim (p. 495), evidence and appeals (pp. 496–98), and responses to alternative views (p. 498). • Chapter 23: Addresses appropriate tone for essays written for academic audiences (pp. 591–92) and the role of reasons and evidence in supporting the writer's ideas (p. 593).
Locate and evaluate (for credibility, sufficiency, accuracy, timeliness, bias, and so on) primary and secondary research materials, including journal articles, essays, books, databases, and informal electronic networks and Internet sources.	• Chapter 3: Focuses on analyzing a selection critically, including assessing the quality of the evidence and the author's use of language to discover bias or faulty reasoning (pp. 58–59, 61–66). • Chapter 21: Emphasizes choosing appropriate source types for the project (primary vs. secondary sources, p. 556; scholarly, popular, and reference sources, pp. 556–58; books vs. articles vs. media sources, pp. 558–59); evaluating sources for relevance, including timeliness and appropriateness for the audience (pp. 559–60); and reliability, including fairness and objectivity, verifiability, and bias (pp. 560–61). • Chapter 22: Provides instruction on using library resources, including using key words effectively for searching catalogs and databases (pp. 565–68), using and choosing appropriate research tools such as subject guides and government documents (pp. 569–72), and conducting field research (pp. 573–74).
Use strategies—such as interpretation, synthesis, response, critique, and design/redesign—to compose texts that integrate the writer's ideas with those from appropriate sources.	• Chapter 2: Covers a variety of strategies, including synthesis, analysis, response, and critique in its "Guide to Responding to a Reading" (pp. 41–54). • Chapter 3: Covers using analysis of an author's ideas, language, and assumptions/generalizations/ omissions to read critically (pp. 56–72). • Chapters 11–18: Each chapter contains a "How Writers Read" box that challenges students to analyze and evaluate the readings in the chapter's rhetorical mode (see Ch. 15, "Comparison and Contrast," p. 378, for example) and a "Synthesizing Ideas" box (see Chapter 15, p. 399, for example) that asks students to make connections among readings. The apparatus following reading selections in the second half of each chapter also includes activities for analyzing the writer's technique, thinking critically about the rhetorical mode, and responding to the reading (see Ch. 15, pp. 391–92). • Chapter 22: Covers evaluating notes and synthesizing sources (pp. 580–83). • Chapter 23: Covers integrating information from sources with the students' own ideas (pp. 593–94) as well as integrating quotations, paraphrases, and summaries (pp. 594–99) while avoiding plagiarism (pp. 589–91). • LaunchPad* tutorials in documenting and working with sources are available.

PROCESSES

| Develop a writing project through multiple drafts. | • Part 2: Chapter 4 focuses on finding and focusing ideas; Chapter 5, on developing and supporting a thesis; Chapter 6, on writing focused, well-supported paragraphs; Chapter 7, on organizing and drafting an essay; Chapter 8, on revising an essay for content and organization, including benefits and processes of peer revising; Chapter 9, on reading and revising a draft critically. One student's writing process, from idea generation through revision, is depicted across the chapters in Part Two, while two other student essays (by Robin Ferguson and Kate Atkinson) show at least part of a student's writing process in Parts 2 and 3.
• Parts 3 and 4: The Guided Writing Assignments in each chapter walk students through the writing process for each of the rhetorical modes (see, for example, Chapter 15, pp. 379–83). |

*Additional resource, available free when packaged with the text. See p. xxxv for details.

Desired Student Outcomes	Relevant Features of *Successful College Writing*

	• Chapter 25: Coverage of developing a portfolio emphasizes the importance of demonstrating and reflecting on the writing process (pp. 683–90). • *Portfolio Keeping,* Second Edition (ISBN 978-1-4576-3285-3): Emphasizes the importance of portfolio keeping as a reflection of the writing process. *Portfolio Keeping* can be packaged with *Successful College Writing* at a discount. Contact your sales representative for details. • *A Student's Companion for Successful College Writing* (ISBN 978-1-319-13029-9), a new supplement, offers⋅ additional activities to help students build a fully developed essay in each of the modes covered by the parent text. *A Student's Companion* is available as a stand-alone or as a student-facing resource in LaunchPad*.
Develop flexible strategies for reading, drafting, reviewing, collaborating, revising, rewriting, rereading, and editing.	• Chapter 1: Introduces the idea of learning strategies (pp. 7–9) and styles (pp. 19–24). • Chapter 2: Offers a "Guide to Active Reading" (pp. 26–41) that asks students to preview, activate background knowledge and write guide questions, highlight key points, and make connections among ideas. It also includes a "Guide to Responding to a Reading" (pp. 41–54) that asks students to summarize to check their understanding, annotate and synthesize to connect the writer's ideas with their own, and analyze and evaluate the reading. The chapter also walks students through the process of writing a response essay (pp. 51–54), from devising ideas to revising, editing, and proofreading. • Part 2: Provides an overview of the writing process, with activities and student samples punctuating the process. • Parts 3 and 4: A Guided Writing Assignment in each chapter offers pattern-specific coverage of prewriting, drafting, revision, editing, and proofreading (for example, pp. 379–83). Learning styles options (see p. 379, for example) provide opportunities to tailor the writing process to the writer's needs. • Chapter 25: Coverage of developing a portfolio emphasizes the importance of demonstrating and reflecting on the student's writing process (pp. 683–90). • *A Student's Companion for Successful College Writing* (ISBN 978-1-319-13029-9), a new supplement, offers rubrics for each of the Guided Writing Assignments in the text. Students can use these rubrics to assess their own writing or the writing of their peers. • *Portfolio Keeping,* Second Edition (ISBN 978-1-4576-3285-3): Emphasizes the importance of portfolio keeping as a reflection of the writing process. *Portfolio Keeping* can be packaged with *Successful College Writing* at a discount. Contact your sales representative for details.
Use composing processes and tools as a means to discover and reconsider ideas.	• Chapter 2: Walks students through the process of writing a response essay based on techniques of active reading, critical reading, and reading-to-write strategies such as annotating an essay and keeping a response journal (pp. 51–54). • Chapter 3: Asks students to read, analyze, and evaluate the author's ideas, using strategies such as analyzing the author's language (denotation vs. connotation), figurative language, and tone (pp. 61–66), and analyzing generalizations and omissions (pp. 61–70). • Chapter 8: Focuses on revising for big-picture issues, the thesis, supporting evidence, organization, and development. The chapter also introduces peer revision and responding to the instructor's comments as strategies for revising. • Parts 3 and 4: Offer pattern-specific coverage of prewriting, drafting, revision, editing, and proofreading (for example, pp. 379–83). Learning styles options (see p. 379, for example) provide opportunities to tailor the writing process to the writer's needs. • Chapter 25: Coverage of developing a portfolio emphasizes the importance of demonstrating and reflecting on the student's writing process (pp. 683–90). • Part 5: Chapters in this part cover writing a research project, including planning (pp. 548–59), finding and evaluating sources (pp. 559–63, 565–72), drafting and synthesizing information to support the writer's own ideas (pp. 580–83, 593–99), revising the research project (pp. 599–601), and citing sources in a style that is appropriate to the discipline (pp. 603–39). Student samples in these chapters provide appropriate models for college-level research projects.

*Additional resource, available free when packaged with the text. See p. xxxv for details.

Desired Student Outcomes	Relevant Features of *Successful College Writing*
PROCESSES	
	• *Portfolio Keeping*, Second Edition (ISBN 978-1-4576-3285-3): Discusses portfolio keeping as a reflection of writing processes. *Portfolio Keeping* can be packaged with *Successful College Writing* at a discount. Contact your sales representative for details. • *Teaching Composition* (for instructors; 978-0-312-46933-7): Chapter 2 covers thinking about the writing process. *Teaching Composition* is available as a free download to instructors.
Experience the collaborative and social aspects of writing processes.	• Opportunities to work collaboratively appear in exercises throughout the book (see, for example, pp. 137–38), with additional ideas for collaboration available in the annotated instructor's edition. • Chapter 4: Provides instruction for brainstorming in groups (pp. 110–11). • Chapter 8: Includes coverage of peer review and tips for getting the best result from collaborative editing (pp. 182–84). • *Instructor's Resource Manual for Successful College Writing* (for instructors): Chapter 6 offers tips on managing the peer review process. The *Instructor's Resource Manual* is available as a free download from the instructor's tab on the *Successful College Writing* catalog page at **macmillanlearning.com**.
Learn to give and to act on productive feedback on works in progress.	• Chapter 8: Includes coverage of peer review and tips for getting the best result from collaborative editing (pp. 182–84) and using the instructor's comments (pp. 184–87). • Parts 3 and 4: The chapters in these parts provide Guided Writing Assignments, offering pattern- and genre-specific advice on peer review and revision (for example, pp. 414–16), with revision flowcharts that can be used to guide the peer-review process or revision by individual writers. • *Instructor's Resource Manual for Successful College Writing* (for instructors): Chapter 6 offers tips on managing the peer review process. • *A Student's Companion for Successful College Writing* (ISBN 978-1-319-13029-9), a new supplement, offers rubrics for each of the Guided Writing Assignments in the text. Students can use these rubrics to assess their own writing or the writing of their peers. For packaging options, see p. xxxvi.
Adapt composing processes to a variety of technologies and modalities.	• The entire book assumes that students will be using technology for writing and research. • Chapter 1: Emphasizes the importance of avoiding the distractions that can arise from multitasking (pp. 3–7) and provides advice for managing online courses responsibly (p. 15). • Part 5: Chapter 21 provides special tips for evaluating resources in a digital landscape (p. 561); Chapter 22 provides searching strategies for online research, including searching of catalogs and databases (pp. 569–70), searching the Web (pp. 570–72), and using citation managers for managing the research process (p. 576), and it also gives instruction on organizing notes regardless of the medium in which they were taken (pp. 575–76); Chapter 23 gives instruction on avoiding plagiarism by cutting and pasting carelessly (p. 590). • Chapter 26: Covers making multimedia presentations, using PowerPoint or Prezi (pp. 691–98), making a Web-based presentation (p. 698), submitting a résumé and cover letter online, and using electronic media (such as email, Twitter, Facebook) for business (pp. 698–703). • LaunchPad*: Offers tutorials on digital writing, including photo and audio editing, making presentations, word processing, using online research tools, and job search/personal branding.
KNOWLEDGE OF CONVENTIONS	
Develop knowledge of linguistic structures, including grammar, punctuation, and spelling, through practice in composing and revising.	• Chapter 9: Covers editing words and sentences, including writing concisely, varying sentences, editing to create an appropriate tone and level of diction, choosing appropriate words, and editing to avoid errors of grammar, punctuation, and mechanics (pp. 194–213). • Parts 3 and 4: Guided Writing Assignments offer pattern- and genre-specific advice about editing and proofreading (for example, see p. 416).

*Additional resource, available free when packaged with the text. See p. xxxv for details.

Desired Student Outcomes	Relevant Features of *Successful College Writing*

KNOWLEDGE OF CONVENTIONS

	• Part 7, Handbook (full edition): Provides instruction in correcting errors of grammar, punctuation, mechanics, and spelling. • LaunchPad*: Provides access to *LearningCurve for Readers and Writers*, adaptive game-like quizzing that provides opportunities for learning to identify and correct common writing problems. • Additional exercises for Chapters 6, 7, and 9 and the Handbook: Available in *A Student's Companion for Successful College Writing* (ISBN 978-1-319-13029-9) and in LaunchPad.
Understand why genre conventions for structure, paragraphing, tone, and mechanics vary.	• Chapter 1: Highlights differences in expectations for writing as students move from high school to college, including expecting to find differences among genres (pp. 15–16) and between disciplines (p. 16). • Chapter 9: Covers editing to create an appropriate tone and level of diction, whether the level is formal, popular, informal, or academic (pp. 206–8), and choosing appropriate words depending on the audience and purpose (pp. 209–11).
Gain experience negotiating variations in genre conventions.	• Parts 3 and 4: Each chapter in Parts 3 and 4 includes a box highlighting how the rhetorical mode could be used in college and in the workplace (see p. 261, for example); a range of readings so students gain experience reading selections written for sophisticated popular audiences as well as more academic audiences (see "The Psychology of Stuff and Things," by Christian Jarrett, pp. 350–55, for example); and apparatus following the readings in the second half of each chapter to help students gain experience in negotiating variations in the conventions. • Chapter 26: Highlights style choices that are appropriate for writing in a business context (pp. 698–703).
Learn common formats and/or design features for different kinds of texts.	• Chapter 23: Highlights variations in formatting depending on expectations in the discipline for which the text was created (pp. 601–2, 603–27, 628–44). • Chapter 26: Covers formatting expectations for PowerPoint and Prezi slides, business writing formats for résumés, job application letters, and other forms of electronic business writing. • LaunchPad*: Provides tutorials on photo and audio editing, creating presentations, and personal branding.
Explore the concepts of intellectual property (such as fair use and copyright) that motivate documentation conventions.	• Chapter 23: Covers concepts underlying plagiarism, including common knowledge (pp. 590–91, 602–3).
Practice applying systematic citation conventions to a range of source material in students' own work.	• Chapter 24: Covers documenting sources in MLA (pp. 603–21) and APA (pp. 628–38) style. • LaunchPad*: Offers tutorials in documentation and working with sources.

*Additional resource, available free when packaged with the text. See p. xxxv for details.

xliii

How Writers Read

How Readers Write

Paul Bradbury/Getty Images

PART ONE

An Introduction to Reading, Writing, and Learning in College

1

Reading and Writing for College Success

Hero Images Inc./Alamy

In this chapter you will learn to:

- discover the factors that contribute to college success

- develop learning strategies to improve your reading and writing skills

- understand what academic reading and writing involves

- grasp the importance of improving your reading and writing skills

- assess your learning style using a Learning Style Inventory

WRITING QUICK START   This photograph shows a college student studying. What factors might explain why the student does (or does not) excel academically?

Write a paragraph based on your experiences with education up to this point that explains which factors you think contribute to academic success and which lead to frustration. Be specific: You might discuss tasks that students need to know how to perform, offer tips, identify pitfalls, or consider nonacademic factors, such as jobs and family responsibilities.

What factors did you identify as contributing to college success? Some you may have mentioned include the following:

- being motivated and organized
- completing all assignments
- focusing on a task to study and learn
- having good instructors
- performing well in class and on exams
- knowing how to write papers and essay exams

All of these skills, and many others, contribute to academic success. This chapter begins with a reading that discusses several key factors that contribute to college success. The remainder of the chapter presents numerous strategies to help you develop the skills you need for success in all college courses and in your writing class in particular.

Factors That Contribute to Success

Read "The New Marshmallow Test," the article that follows. As you read, highlight the main points the writer is making about multitasking and academic success, and write notes, questions, and comments in the margin about your own media multitasking habits and your ability to devote your undivided attention to class lectures and course materials during your study time. You'll be glad you did!

READING

The New Marshmallow Test: Students Can't Resist Multitasking

Annie Murphy Paul

Annie Murphy Paul is a contributing writer for *Time* magazine and often writes about learning and its improvement. She also blogs about learning at CNN.com, Forbes .com, and HuffingtonPost.com and has written several books, including *The Cult of Personality*, which explores the historical quirks of how personality tests were developed and critiques their value; *Origins: How the Nine Months before Birth Shape the Rest of Our Lives*, a book about the science of prenatal influences; and *Brilliant: The New Science of Smart*.

1 Living rooms, dens, kitchens, even bedrooms: Investigators followed students into the spaces where homework gets done. Pens poised over their "study observation forms," the observers watched intently as the students—in middle school, high school, and college, 263 in all—opened their books and turned on their computers.

2 For a quarter of an hour, the investigators from the lab of Larry Rosen, a psychology professor at California State University–Dominguez Hills, marked down once a minute what the students were doing as they studied. A checklist on the form included: reading a book, writing on paper, typing on the computer— and also using email, looking at Facebook, texting, talking on the phone, watching television, listening to music, surfing the Web. Sitting unobtrusively at the back of the room, the observers counted the number of windows open on the students' screens and noted whether the students were wearing earbuds.

3 Although the students had been told at the outset that they should "study something important, including homework, an upcoming examination or project, or reading a book for a course," it wasn't long before their attention drifted: Students' "on-task behavior" started declining around the two-minute mark as they began responding to arriving texts or checking their Facebook feeds. By the time the

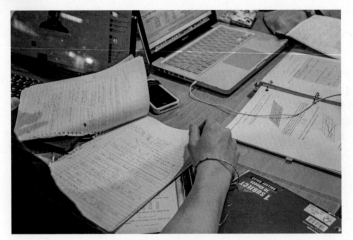

Attending to multiple streams of information and entertainment while studying, doing homework, or even sitting in class has become a common behavior among college students.   JHU Sheridan Libraries/Gado/Contributor/ Archive Photos/Getty Images

15 minutes were up, they had spent only about 65 percent of the observation period actually doing their schoolwork.

Rosen's study, published in the May 2013 issue of *Computers in Human Behavior*, is part of a growing body of research focused on a very particular use of technology: media multitasking *while learning*. Evidence from psychology, cognitive science, and neuroscience suggests that when students multitask while doing schoolwork, their learning is far spottier and shallower than if the work had their full attention. They understand and remember less, and they have greater difficulty transferring their learning to new contexts. So detrimental is this practice that some researchers are proposing that a new prerequisite for academic and even professional success—the new marshmallow test of self-discipline—is the ability to resist a blinking inbox or a buzzing phone.

The media multitasking habit extends into the classroom. While most middle and high school students don't have the opportunity to text, email, and surf the Internet during class, studies show the practice is nearly universal among students in college and professional school. One large survey found that 80 percent of college students admit to texting during class; 15 percent say they send 11 or more texts in a single class period.

During the first meeting of his courses, Rosen makes a practice of calling on a student who is busy with his phone. "I ask him, 'What was on the slide I just showed to the class?' The student always pulls a blank," Rosen reports. "Young people have a wildly inflated idea of how many things they can attend to at once, and this demonstration helps drive the point home: If you're paying attention to your phone, you're not paying attention to what's going on in class." Other professors have taken a more surreptitious approach, installing electronic spyware or planting human observers to record whether students are taking notes on their laptops or using them for other, unauthorized purposes.

In a study involving spyware, for example, two professors of business administration at the University of Vermont found that "students engage in substantial multitasking behavior with their laptops and have non-course-related software applications open and active about 42 percent of the time." Another study, carried out at St. John's University in New York, used human observers stationed at the back of the classroom to record the technological activities of law students. The spies reported that 58 percent of second- and third-year law students who had laptops in class were using them for "non-class purposes" more than half the time. Texting, emailing, and posting on Facebook and other social media sites are by far the most common digital activities students undertake while learning, according to Rosen. That's a problem, because these operations are actually quite mentally complex, and they draw on the same mental resources—using language, parsing meaning—demanded by schoolwork.

David Meyer, a psychology professor at the University of Michigan who's   8
studied the effects of divided attention on learning, takes a firm line on the
brain's ability to multitask: "Under most conditions, the brain simply cannot do
two complex tasks at the same time. It can happen only when the two tasks are
both very simple and when they don't compete with each other for the same
mental resources. An example would be folding laundry and listening to the
weather report on the radio. That's fine. But listening to a lecture while texting, or
doing homework and being on Facebook—each of these tasks is very demanding,
and each of them uses the same area of the brain, the prefrontal cortex."

Young people think they can perform two challenging tasks at once, Meyer   9
acknowledges, but "they are deluded," he declares. It's difficult for anyone to prop-
erly evaluate how well his or her own mental processes are operating, he points
out, because most of these processes are unconscious. And, Meyer adds, "there's
nothing magical about the brains of so-called 'digital natives' that keeps them
from suffering the inefficiencies of multitasking. They may like to do it, they may
even be addicted to it, but there's no getting around the fact that it's far better to
focus on one task from start to finish."

Researchers have documented a cascade of negative outcomes that occurs   10
when students multitask while doing schoolwork. First, the assignment takes longer to complete, because of the time spent on distracting activities and because,
upon returning to the assignment, the student has to refamiliarize himself with
the material.

Second, the mental fatigue caused by repeatedly dropping and picking up a   11
mental thread leads to more mistakes. Third, students' subsequent memory of
what they're working on will be impaired if their attention is divided. As the
unlucky student spotlighted by Rosen can attest, we can't remember something
that never really entered our consciousness in the first place. And a study last
month showed that students who multitask on laptops in class distract not just
themselves but also their peers who see what they're doing.

Fourth, some research has suggested that when we're distracted, our brains   12
actually process and store information in different, less useful ways. In a 2006
study in the *Proceedings of the National Academy of Sciences*, Karin Foerde of the
University of Texas–Austin and two colleagues asked participants to engage in a
learning activity on a computer while also carrying out a second task, counting
musical tones that sounded while they worked. Brain scans taken during
Foerde's experiment revealed that different regions of the brain were active under
the two conditions, indicating that the brain engages in a different form of memory when forced to pay attention to two streams of information at once. The
results suggest, the scientists wrote, that "even if distraction does not decrease the
overall level of learning, it can result in the acquisition of knowledge that can be
applied less flexibly in new situations."

Finally, researchers are beginning to demonstrate that media multitasking   13
while learning is negatively associated with students' grades. In Rosen's study,
students who used Facebook during the 15-minute observation period had lower
grade-point averages than those who didn't go on the site. Meyer, of the
University of Michigan, worries that the problem goes beyond poor grades.

"There's a definite possibility that we are raising a generation that is learning more shallowly than young people in the past," he says. "The depth of their processing of information is considerably less, because of all the distractions available to them as they learn."

Given that these distractions aren't going away, academic and even professional achievement may depend on the ability to ignore digital temptations while learning—a feat akin to the famous marshmallow test. In a series of experiments conducted more than forty years ago, psychologist Walter Mischel tempted young children with a marshmallow, telling them they could have two of the treats if they put off eating one right away. Follow-up studies performed years later found that the kids who were better able to delay gratification not only achieved higher grades and test scores but were also more likely to succeed in school and their careers.   14

Two years ago, Rosen and his colleagues conducted an information-age version of the marshmallow test. College students who participated in the study were asked to watch a 30-minute videotaped lecture, during which some were sent eight text messages while others were sent four or zero text messages. Those who were interrupted more often scored worse on a test of the lecture's content; more interestingly, those who responded to the experimenters' texts right away scored significantly worse than those participants who waited to reply until the lecture was over.   15

The ability to resist the lure of technology can be consciously cultivated, Rosen maintains. He advises students to take "tech breaks" to satisfy their cravings for electronic communication: After they've labored on their schoolwork uninterrupted for 15 minutes, they can allow themselves two minutes to text, check websites, and post to their hearts' content. Then the devices get turned off for another 15 minutes of academics. Over time, Rosen says, students are able to extend their working time to 20, 30, even 45 minutes, as long as they know that an opportunity to get online awaits. Device-checking is a compulsive behavior that must be managed, he says, if young people are to learn and perform at their best.   16

Understanding the Reading

1. **Main Idea** Explain the author's main point in your own words.
2. **Effects** According to the reading selection, what are some short-term effects of multitasking while studying? What may be some long-term effects?
3. **Comparison** What was the original marshmallow test, and what did it show? How would the new marshmallow test work?

Responding to the Reading

1. **Collecting Data** Explore your media multitasking habits by trying to replicate Larry Rosen's investigation. For one hour while you are studying, use the following categories to mark down once every fifteen minutes what you are doing as you study.

☐ reading a book
☐ writing on paper
☐ typing on the computer
☐ reading or writing email
☐ texting
☐ talking on the phone

☐ reading or writing on Facebook (or another social media site)
☐ watching television
☐ listening to music
☐ surfing the Web

2. **Analysis** At the end of the hour, analyze your findings.
   - What percentage of your one-hour study time did you devote to studying?
   - How long were you able to go without a distraction?
   - What was your primary distraction?
3. **Assessment** Write a paragraph or two explaining how well you think you "learned" what you were studying and what lessons you will take away from this exercise. What changes will you make in your study habits (if any), and how will you make them?

Adopt Success Strategies for All Your Courses

"The New Marshmallow Test" showed that focusing on what you're studying both inside and outside the classroom contributes significantly to your success in college. There are also other strategies for college success that will help you read, write, and learn more effectively and efficiently. These strategies are presented in this section.

Use Effective Learning Strategies

The more you know about how learning works, the easier learning becomes. The following section summarizes some tried-and-true, practical learning strategies based on verbal learning theory. Applying them will make many tasks you face in college easier—especially those in your writing classes.

Focus your attention. As you learned from reading "The New Marshmallow Test" at the beginning of the chapter, you cannot learn if your mind is wandering. Use the following strategies to direct your concentration to the task at hand.

- **Work at peak periods of attention.** Identify the time of day or night that you are most efficient and focused. Avoid working when you are tired, hungry, or distracted, if you can.
- **Vary your activities.** Do not complete, say, three reading assignments consecutively. Instead, alternate assignments: for example, read, then write, then work on math problems, then read another assignment, and so on. Use writing to keep you mentally alert and physically active. Highlight, annotate, and take notes as you read.
- **Don't work too long on any given task.** It is better to space out your study. Don't work on an essay draft for four hours. You will accomplish more if you spread out your work into two, two-hour sessions.

- **Challenge yourself with goals and deadlines.** Before beginning an assignment, estimate how long it should take and work toward completing it within that time limit.
- **Keep a to-do list.** When you are working on an assignment, stray thoughts about other pressing things (getting your car repaired, planning a birthday party for your mother) are bound to zip through your mind. When these thoughts occur to you, jot them down so that you can unclutter your mind and get back to work.

Reward yourself.   As Professor Rosen (in "The New Marshmallow Test") suggests, use a fun activity, such as texting a friend or getting a snack, as a reward for reaching your goal or completing your assignment.

See the Just-in-Time Guide to Reading and Responding (pp. 83–84) for more help with deciding what to learn.

Decide what to learn and how to learn it.   It is difficult to learn something unless you intend to. Try drawing the front of a one-dollar bill. Most likely you could not provide much detail. Why? You never intended to learn it, despite the many bills you have handled.

You cannot learn every detail in this or any other textbook. Learning will occur more easily if you decide what you need to focus on. Some instructors may help you decide what is important by providing grading rubrics that make the criteria of evaluation clear. Others may not, but you can develop your own sense of what strong and weak work looks like by asking your instructor for examples and then making a list of the features that make one piece of writing work better than another.

Learning theory shows that you shouldn't learn everything the same way. You shouldn't study mathematics the same way you study art history. Similarly, you may not write an essay for your composition class the same way you would write a lab report for your biology class. Analyze each writing assignment you are given; understand the *genre*, or type of writing, you are expected to produce; and decide the best strategies to complete it. The Learning Style Inventory (p. 19) may help you discover alternative learning strategies that work well for you or that usefully challenge your ways of thinking.

Use metacognition.   Metacognition is self-awareness of how your reading, writing, and learning is going. It involves monitoring and assessing what is working and what is not, and experimenting with approaches to learning. Writing is a gradual process, but you will learn to write better if you are aware of strategies that work and those that don't. While writing, take time to ask yourself whether what you are doing is producing the results you expect. If not, make changes. You may discover, for example, that when planning an essay, outlining is too rigid but free-flowing brainstorming works much better. The Learning Style Inventory (p. 19) will help you assess how you learn and show you alternative strategies for writing.

For more about mapping and outlining, see pp. 109 and 161–64.

Group and organize information.   New information is more easily learned if it is organized or grouped into chunks. The graphic organizers used throughout this book (see p. 24, for example) help you see an essay as a whole, rather than as numerous individual pieces. Outlining and mapping or clustering are also effective means of organizing information.

Practice, review, and respond. Rereading and rote memorization are two of the most ineffective ways to learn. Instead, interact with the information by applying it, discussing it, and evaluating it. The writing activities throughout this book (for example, on pp. 6–7) enable you to learn writing skills through practice, review, and response. Peer review (assessing your writing and that of your classmates) is another tool that can help you hone your skills for assessing your own writing.

For more about peer review, see pp. 182–84.

Activate prior knowledge. It is difficult to store and retrieve new, unfamiliar pieces of information from your memory. Activating prior knowledge can help you connect new learning to something that you already know. That's why previewing techniques such as asking and answering questions based on the headings in a reading selection aid learning. You can also connect a new essay you are reading with something you've experienced or learned about in another class. For example, if you are reading an essay on language change and the evolution of new words entering the English language, you might think of the new and recently coined terms you just learned in a computer science class. In this book, the headnotes that precede each reading provide background information that will help prepare you to read, understand, and remember the reading.

For more about previewing and synthesizing, see p. 28.

Synthesize your learning. **Synthesis** is a way to extend and reinforce your learning. It means pulling together ideas from your reading assignments, your class lectures, and your own experience. It involves analyzing similar or competing ideas and using them to extend or challenge your understanding. It may also involve connecting ideas to your own experience to see the practical consequences of an idea. For example, if after reading "The New Marshmallow Test" (pp. 3–6) you considered your own media multitasking or completed the checklist in the "Responding to the Reading" section, then you were synthesizing the reading with your own experience. During a biology class lecture on genetics, you might write a note connecting the topic of trait inheritance with your personal family history. In an American history class, you might read a letter from a freed slave, a diary of a plantation owner, and a speech by an abolitionist and then write about what life as an enslaved person was like prior to the Civil War.

Use Your Course Syllabus

The most important document you will receive in your first week of class is your course **syllabus,** a document that describes how the course operates and directs you through your class. A typical syllabus includes information on required texts, attendance and plagiarism policies, the grading system, course objectives, weekly assignments or readings, due dates, and dates of exams. A sample syllabus is shown in Figure 1.1 (pp. 10–11). Here are some tips for using a syllabus to maximize your learning and your course grade.

- **Read the syllabus carefully at the beginning of the course.** Check it regularly so that you are prepared for class.
- **Ask your instructor any questions you may have about the syllabus, course structure, deadlines, and expectations about course objectives.** Note the answers on the syllabus or in your course notebook.

- **Mark all deadlines on your planner, including the intermediate dates you will need to meet your deadlines.** For example, include not only the due date for a paper, but also the date by which you will need to complete the research and the date by which you will need to complete the first draft in order to have time to revise thoughtfully.
- **Pay close attention to the course objectives.** These outline what you are expected to learn in the course. Papers and exams will measure how well you meet them.
- **Make sure you can access the syllabus.** Print a copy and keep it in your notebook or save a copy on your computer, tablet, or smartphone.

FIGURE 1.1   Excerpted Sample Syllabus for a College Writing Course

I. General Information

Course Title:	English Composition I	*Course Number:*	ENG 161
Prerequisite:	English 070 or placement test	*Semester:*	Fall
Instructor:	John Gillam	*Phone:*	(724) 555-7890
Email:	gillam@indiana.edu	*Office Hours & Location:*	MWF 3–5 English Department offices in Ryan Hall

This is a good way to contact your instructor.

Important: Be sure to use them.

II. Text

McWhorter, Kathleen T. *Successful College Writing.* 7th ed. New York: Bedford, 2018.

III. General Course Objectives

Planning and organizing are expected.

1. The student will learn to organize his or her thoughts into a meaningful written work.

Grammar is important.

2. The student will easily recognize grammar mistakes.

3. The student will be familiar with different types of writing.

4. The student will be able to use several different writing styles.

You will be graded on these.

IV. General Course Objectives

Learn these strategies.

1. The student will write papers using the following strategies: description, illustration, process analysis, comparison and contrast, classification and division, and cause and effect.

Correctness counts: Allow time for proofreading.

2. The student will edit and proofread for errors in grammar, punctuation, mechanics, and spelling.

Read assignments carefully.

3. The student will be tested on reading comprehension.

Learn about documentation.

4. The student will write a research paper using appropriate documentation.

5. The student will critically analyze readings that use specific writing strategies.

6. The student will use the Internet as a tool for research.

> **EXERCISE 1.1**   GETTING THE MOST FROM YOUR SYLLABUS

Review the syllabus that your writing class instructor distributed. Write a paragraph describing your expectations and concerns about your writing course based on the syllabus. Be sure to answer the following questions.

1. What are you expected to learn in the course?
2. What kinds of essays will you write?
3. What are the grading and attendance policies?
4. Is class participation expected and required? Is it part of your grade?
5. Is research required? Is Internet use required or expected?

V. Classroom Procedures

Absences: The student is responsible for attendance. Attendance affects performance, and all students are expected to take part in class discussions and peer-review editing sessions. Each student is expected to be present and is responsible for class notes and assignments. If absent, the student is responsible for arranging an appointment with the instructor to discuss the notes and assignments missed.   — Attendance is essential.

Format for papers: Papers must be typed double-spaced using a 12-point font. Be sure to keep a copy of each assignment for yourself.

VI. Disability Statement

If you need to have special arrangements made due to a physical or learning disability, please notify the instructor as soon as possible. (Disclosure of the type of disability is not required.)   — Don't hesitate to ask for needed services.

VII. Grading

All papers must be turned in on the due date. Late papers will be lowered one letter grade. No papers will be accepted after the last day of class. If you do not understand the grade assigned to a paper, see me immediately. You are encouraged to save all papers in a folder to enable you to keep track of progress and compute your own grade.   — Meeting deadlines is essential. The instructor encourages questions. Keep a copy of assignments.

VIII. Tentative Schedule

Week of Sept. 3:	Course Introduction
	Ch. 1 (Reading and Writing for College Success)
	Ch. 2 (Active Reading and Responding)
Week of Sept. 10:	Writing Assessments
	Ch. 3 (Thinking, Reading, and Writing Critically)
	Ch. 4 (Prewriting)
	Ch. 5 (Developing and Supporting a Thesis)
Week of Sept. 17:	Ch. 7 (Drafting an Essay)
	Ch. 11 (Narration)
	Draft of Essay #1 due
Week of Sept. 24:	Ch. 13 (Illustration)
	Draft of Essay #2 due

Read these chapters the first week. Your instructor may not remind you of reading assignments, so check the syllabus weekly.

Assignment due dates are noted.

Avoid Procrastination

Procrastination is putting off things that need to be done; you know you should work on an assignment, but you do something else instead. To avoid procrastination, try these tips.

- Develop a schedule at the beginning of each week in which you allot time to complete each assignment due that week.
- Divide each task into manageable parts.
- Avoid making excuses. It is easy to say you don't have enough time to get everything done, but often that is not true.
- Avoid escaping into routine tasks such as shopping, cleaning, or doing your laundry rather than completing the task.

Demonstrate Academic Integrity

Demonstrating academic integrity means conducting yourself in an honest and ethical manner. It involves avoiding the obvious forms of classroom dishonesty such as copying homework, buying a paper on the Internet, and cheating on exams or helping others do so. It also means not plagiarizing, using the ideas or language of others—deliberately or unintentionally—without giving credit. An example of intentional plagiarism is cutting and pasting information into your paper from the Internet without indicating that it is borrowed. Unintentional plagiarism occurs when you use language too similar to that of the original source, inadvertently omit a citation, or forget to place quotation marks around a quotation.

To learn how to avoid unintentional plagiarism, see Chapter 23, p. 590.

Consult Your Instructors

Don't be afraid to take advantage of your instructor's office hours. Most instructors will happily work with you to understand a reading or an assignment and to provide information on research, academic decisions, and careers in their fields. But you need to take the initiative. Find out when your instructors hold office hours, and if invited, use their email addresses to communicate.

Listen Carefully, Take Notes, and Participate in Class

Classroom participation involves both listening and speaking. Because you learn so much through listening, learning to listen carefully and critically—grasping what is said and discussing, questioning, and responding to what you hear—is a crucial success strategy.

Listen carefully and critically.   Did you know that you can process information faster than speakers can speak? As a result, your mind has time to wander while listening. Try using the following suggestions to maintain your attention in the classroom and prepare to respond.

- **Focus on the lecture.** Arrive promptly for class, shut off distracting media (your phone and your Web applications), sit toward the front of the room (not among a group of friends), and maintain eye contact with the speaker—all will make you feel more involved and less likely to drift off mentally.

- **Try to anticipate the ideas the speaker will address next.** Doing so will keep your mind active.
- **Maintain an open mind.** It is easy to shut out ideas and opinions that do not conform to your own values and beliefs. Try to avoid evaluating a message as positive or negative until it is complete and understandable, and strive to understand the speaker's viewpoint, even if you think you disagree.
- **Identify and assess the speaker's main point and key supporting evidence.** Once you've identified the speaker's thesis, or main point—it is likely to be repeated in different forms throughout the presentation—consider the speaker's reasons and evidence: Has enough support been supplied? Is the evidence relevant? Are the reasons logical?
- **Take notes.** Create an informal outline to keep track of the key points and the main reasons and evidence the speaker offers. After class, flesh out your notes while your memory is fresh.

Participate in class. You can learn more from your classes if you participate fully in class. Ask questions when you need information and clarification, and answer questions posed by the instructor to demonstrate and evaluate your knowledge and express interest in the class. Use the following tips to strengthen your questioning and answering skills.

- **As you read assignments, jot down questions to ask in class—don't worry if they seem silly or unimportant.** Bring your list to class, and use it when your instructor invites questions. And don't apologize for asking; other students probably have the same questions but are reluctant to ask them.
- **Speak out.** Stop worrying about what your friends and classmates will think. If you're nervous about participating in class, composing your response before volunteering to answer may give you confidence.
- **Focus on critical questions.** Instead of asking factual questions, think about how the information can be used, how ideas fit together, how things work, what might be relevant problems and solutions, or what the long-term value and significance of the information are.

EXERCISE 1.2 ▶ **IMPROVING YOUR LISTENING AND CLASS-PARTICIPATION SKILLS**

Review the advice given above. Then choose at least three points to apply in the next two lectures you attend for one of your other courses. Finally, write a paragraph reflecting on what you learned from the experience.

EXERCISE 1.3 ▶ **WORKING TOGETHER**

Working with a classmate, brainstorm a list of questions you could ask about the content presented in this chapter.

Learn to Manage Stress

Stress is a natural reaction to the challenges of daily living, but if you are expected to accomplish more or perform better than you think you can, stress can become overwhelming. As a successful student, you need to monitor your stress. Take the "How Stressed Are You?" quiz on the next page to assess your stress level.

Quiz: How Stressed Are You?	Always	Sometimes	Never
1. I worry that I do not have enough time to get everything done.	☐	☐	☐
2. I regret that I have no time to do fun things each week.	☐	☐	☐
3. I find myself losing track of details and forgetting due dates, promises, and appointments.	☐	☐	☐
4. I worry about what I am doing.	☐	☐	☐
5. I have conflicts or disagreements with friends or family.	☐	☐	☐
6. I lose patience over small annoyances.	☐	☐	☐
7. I seem to be late, no matter how hard I try to arrive on time.	☐	☐	☐
8. I have difficulty sleeping.	☐	☐	☐
9. My eating habits have changed.	☐	☐	☐
10. I find myself needing a cigarette, drink, or prescription drug.	☐	☐	☐

You can use stress to motivate yourself to start a project or assignment, or you can let it interfere with your ability to function mentally and physically. If you answered "Always" or "Sometimes" to more than two or three items in the "How Stressed Are You?" quiz, you may be reacting to stress negatively. Here are some effective ways to change your thinking and habits to reduce stress.

- **Establish your priorities.** If college is more important than your part-time job, for example, request a work schedule to accommodate your study schedule. If someone asks you to take on an extra shift that will cut into study time, be selfish and say no.
- **Simplify your life by making fewer choices.** For example, instead of deciding what time to set your alarm clock each morning, get up at the same time each weekday.
- **Focus on the positive.** Instead of saying "I'll never be able to finish this assignment on time," ask yourself, "What do I have to do to finish this assignment on time?"
- **Separate work, school, and social problems.** Create mental compartments for your worries. Don't spend class time thinking about a work problem. Deal with problems at the appropriate time.
- **Keep a personal journal.** Relieve stress by writing down your worries, but include notes about how you can resolve those problems, too.

Manage Online Courses Responsibly

Online courses are convenient, but they require more self-direction and ability to work alone than face-to-face classes do. Here are some tips for succeeding in online courses.

- **Avoid taking online courses during your first term in college.** Once you are familiar with college expectations, you will be better prepared to take an online course.
- **Study for online courses as you do for face-to-face classes.** Most students who fail online courses do so because they fall hopelessly behind on reading and assignments. Even if a class does not meet at a specified time, build study time for the course into your schedule to avoid procrastinating on classwork.
- **Plan on doing a lot of reading and writing.** In addition to reading assignments and papers, you will also need to read posts from your professor and other students and contribute to written class "discussions."
- **Write thoughtful posts, and use appropriate language online.** Make it easy for classmates and your instructor to read your posts. Think through what you want to say, and use correct spelling and grammar. Besides adding your own ideas, respond to earlier posts, and be polite, even when you disagree with an earlier comment. Finally, be sure to reread your comments before posting them.

Don't Let Nonacademic Problems Interfere with Success

The reason large numbers of students drop out of college has nothing to do with academics. These students would be able to handle the work if only nonacademic problems—from erratic work schedules and child-care difficulties to financial problems and family conflicts—did not interfere. These kinds of problems can result in missing classes or coming to class unprepared and failing to turn in assignments on time (or at all), which can all lead to low grades.

Your campus does have resources to help you. If personal problems are interfering with your performance at school, the first thing to do is talk to your instructors. Once they understand your circumstances, most instructors will do everything they can to help you succeed. Then seek help from student services, such as the financial aid office, the health center, the counseling center, and commuter service centers. These services are usually free. (You are already paying for them through your tuition.) Your campus's Web site will list the services available and indicate where to find them.

Academic Reading and Writing: What Should You Expect?

An important part of doing well with any task is knowing ahead of time what it involves. The list below explains what you can expect about reading and writing in college.

- **Expect your reading and writing to become less personal and more academic.** Most of your reading and writing in college will be informative or persuasive.

Informative writing presents information in an objective, nonpersonal way; **persuasive writing** attempts to convince readers to act or to understand a text or an event in a certain way.

- **Expect to read and write in different forms, or genres.** Academic reading and writing assignments may include specialized types, or **genres**, from scholarly articles and scientific studies to abstracts and research projects. Each genre has its own conventions. For example, lab reports have a specific purpose (to report the results of a laboratory experiment), format (including sections with headings such as *Introduction*, *Materials and Methods*, *Results/Data*, and *Conclusions*), and style of writing (brief, factual, and concise). As you encounter new genres, study samples that can serve as models for your own writing.

For help with revising, see Chapter 8; for help with editing and proofreading, see Chapter 9 and, unless you are using the Brief Edition, the Handbook at the back of this book. See the Just-in-Time Guide, pp. 85–89, for suggestions on learning vocabulary.

- **Expect to use standard American English and the language of the discipline.** College students are generally expected to avoid slang, present their ideas clearly and accurately, and write in complete and grammatically correct sentences. They are also expected to understand and use the specialized vocabulary of the field, words like *photosynthesis* and *homeostasis* in biology, or *allegory* and *personification* in literature. You may need to consult a specialized dictionary, encyclopedia, or database for help with unfamiliar terms.

For more on reading actively and critically, see Chapters 2 and 3.

- **Expect to read, write, and think critically.** In college, instructors will expect you to go beyond merely repeating what you hear in class or read in the textbook; they'll expect you to demonstrate understanding by being able to draw your own inferences based on what you have learned; synthesize, or combine, information to support your ideas; and apply ideas to new situations.

For guidance in identifying, locating, using, and citing scholarly sources, see Part 5.

- **Expect to read, use, and document scholarly sources.** Instructors expect you to locate and use books and articles written by experts and published in scholarly journals and by university presses. Whether you quote, summarize, or paraphrase words and ideas from sources, your instructors will expect you to credit them by including an in-text citation and a list of works cited (or references).

Why Improve Your Reading and Writing Skills?

Most college students ask themselves these two questions:

1. How can I improve my grades?
2. How can I improve my chances of getting a good job after college?

The answer to both questions is the same: Improve your reading and writing skills. Here are three reasons why doing so will be worth the time and effort.

1. **Reading and writing help you learn and remember.** In general, the more senses you use in learning, the more easily you learn and the more you will remember. You take in information visually while reading, and you engage your sense of touch as you put your pen to paper while writing. (Evidence suggests that handwriting is more effective than typing at solidifying memory.) Taking notes, outlining, summarizing,

and annotating enhance learning by engaging your attention and getting you to think about the subject matter as you connect, define, and evaluate ideas.

2. **Reading and writing help you think and solve problems.** Reading makes the ideas of experts available to you, and writing forces you to think through issues in a sustained way, define issues or problems, and see new aspects of them. For example, one student had a father-in-law who seemed hostile and uncooperative. The student described her problem in an email to a friend: "He looks at me as if I'm going to take his son to the end of the earth and never bring him back." When she reread what she had written, she realized that her father-in-law might resent her because he was afraid of losing contact with his son. She looked for ways to reassure her father-in-law and strengthen their relationship. Writing about the problem helped the student define it and discover ways to solve it.

3. **Reading and writing skills enable you to communicate effectively.** Employers consistently want the "total package"—both technical knowledge *and* strong oral and written communication skills—in recent college graduates. Why? Because in almost all jobs, you can expect to read and write plenty of letters, email messages, and reports to customers, colleagues, and supervisors. Because your writing course offers both immediate and long-range benefits, it is one of the most important college courses you will take.

Adopt Success Strategies for Your Writing Class

You have already learned some general strategies for success in college. The section below presents strategies that help you in your writing class.

Start with a Positive Attitude toward Reading and Writing

You have the ability to be a strong reader and a successful writer. To approach your writing course with a positive attitude and get the most out of it, use the following suggestions.

1. **Think of reading and writing as processes.** Reading a complex text requires more than just reading it through once; it requires prereading, annotating, and critical analysis to understand it fully. Writing, too, is not a single act of getting words down on paper. It is a series of steps—planning, organizing, drafting, revising, and editing and proofreading—all of which can be done in whatever order makes sense and repeated as needed. (Most writers go back and forth among these steps.)

2. **Be patient.** Writing improves with practice. On some days, writing will be easier than on other days, but as you draft and revise your essays, your writing will improve in small ways that build on one another. Build in extra time for completing writing assignments.

3. **Understand how your instructor will assess your writing.** Some instructors may have a rubric, or list of characteristics with examples at different levels of success; others may be willing to share past examples of successful writing.

Use the College Writing Center

Writing centers generally provide trained student tutors and professional staff, who may help you do the following:

- understand an assignment
- analyze a reading selection
- organize your ideas
- revise a draft
- use appropriate format and documentation
- understand errors on a graded paper

However, do not expect them to interpret a reading, write your paper, or correct all of its errors. When you visit the writing center, be sure to bring the following:

- your assignment
- all drafts of your essay
- any articles or essays to which the assignment refers
- paper and pen or pencil

Get the Most out of Writing Conferences

Many writing instructors require writing conferences with individual students to discuss the student's work and his or her progress in the course. If the conferences are optional, be sure to schedule one.

The following tips will help you get the most out of a writing conference.

1. **Reread recently returned papers and notes from previous conferences ahead of time.** Your instructor's comments should be fresh in your mind.
2. **Arrive prepared and be on time or a few minutes early.** Bring copies of the essay you are currently working on, as well as previously graded papers.
3. **Allow your instructor to set the agenda.** Still, you should be prepared to ask questions.
4. **Take notes on your instructor's comments and suggestions.** Take them during the conference, if doing so is not distracting, or immediately after.
5. **Revise the draft essay you and your instructor discussed.** The revision will go most smoothly if you revise while your instructor's suggestions are still fresh in your mind.

Keep a Writing Journal

Keeping a **writing journal** will help you improve your writing by giving you a judgment-free place to practice and an opportunity to reflect on what you're learning. In your journal, you can experiment with voice, topics, or approaches to a topic; comment on a reading selection or assignment; record your impressions and observations; or explore relationships among people or ideas. It can also be a good source of topics for writing assignments. Here's how to get started.

1. **Write in a spiral-bound notebook or create a computer file.** Date each entry.
2. **Set aside five to ten minutes for journal writing each day.** You don't need a long block of time; instead, you can write while waiting for a bus or for class to start.
3. **Concentrate on capturing your ideas, not on being grammatically correct.** Try to write correct sentences, but don't focus on grammar and punctuation.

WRITING ACTIVITY 1

Write a journal entry describing your reaction to something you learned in one or more of your classes this term. For example, you might write about how you could apply it or how it relates to something else you already know about.

Understanding Learning Style

Each person has his or her own **learning style**, a unique approach to learning and writing based on experience, personality, and prior learning. Some may prefer instructors who provide real-life examples; others may prefer instructors who draw diagrams to show relationships. To assess your learning style, complete the Learning Style Inventory below. Of course, all learners, no matter what their preferred learning style, do best when they adapt their learning styles to what they are learning: Verbal learners adopt spatial strategies as they study geometry, and spatial learners adopt verbal learning styles when studying literature. And all learners benefit from using an array of strategies. In fact, understanding your learning style can help you push yourself toward strategies you might find uncomfortable, which can be more of an aid to learning than doing what comes easily to you.

Take the Learning Style Inventory

Directions: Each numbered item presents two choices. Select the alternative that describes you better. There are no right or wrong answers. In cases in which neither choice suits you, select the one closer to your preference. Check the letter of your choice next to the question number on the answer sheet on page 21.

1. In a class, I usually
   a. make friends with just a few students.
   b. get to know many of my classmates.

2. If I were required to act in a play, I would prefer to
   a. have the director tell me how to say my lines.
   b. read my lines the way I think they should be read.

3. Which would I find more helpful in studying the processes by which the U.S. Constitution can be amended?
   a. a one-paragraph summary
   b. a diagram

4. In making decisions, I am more concerned with
   a. whether I have all the available facts.
   b. how my decision will affect others.

5. When I have a difficult time understanding how something works, it helps most if I can
   a. see how it works several times.
   b. take time to think the process through and analyze it.

6. At a social event, I usually
   a. wait for people to speak to me.
   b. initiate conversation with others.

7. I prefer courses that have
   a. a traditional structure (lectures, assigned readings, periodic exams, and assignments with deadlines).
   b. an informal structure (class discussions, flexible assignments, and student-selected projects).

8. If I were studying one of the laws of motion in a physics course, I would prefer to have my instructor begin the class by
   a. stating the law and discussing examples.
   b. giving a demonstration of how the law works.

9. Which set of terms describes me better?
   a. fair and objective
   b. sympathetic and understanding

10. When I learn something new, I am more interested in
    a. the facts about it.
    b. the principles behind it.

11. As a volunteer for a community organization that is raising funds for a hospice, I would prefer
    a. stuffing envelopes for a mail campaign.
    b. making phone calls asking for contributions.

12. I would begin an ideal day by
    a. planning what I want to do during each hour of the day.
    b. doing whatever comes to mind.

13. If I wanted to learn the proper way to prune a rose-bush, I would prefer to
    a. have someone explain it to me.
    b. watch someone do it.

14. It is more important for me to be
    a. consistent in thought and action.
    b. responsive to the feelings of others.

15. If I kept a journal or diary, it would most likely contain entries about
    a. what happens to me each day.
    b. the insights and ideas that occur to me each day.

16. If I decided to learn a musical instrument, I would prefer to take
    a. one-on-one lessons.
    b. group lessons.

17. If I worked in a factory, I would prefer to be a
    a. machine operator.
    b. troubleshooter.

18. I learn best when I
    a. write down the information.
    b. form a mental picture of the information.

19. If I gave a wrong answer in class, my main concern would be
    a. finding out the correct answer.
    b. what others in class thought of me.

20. I prefer television news programs that
    a. summarize events through film footage and factual description.
    b. deal with the issues behind the events.

21. Whenever possible, I choose to
    a. study alone.
    b. study with a group.

22. In selecting a topic for a research paper, my more important concern is
    a. choosing a topic for which there is adequate information.
    b. choosing a topic I find interesting.

23. To help me reassemble a complicated toy or machine I took apart to repair, I would
    a. write a list of the steps I followed when taking the toy or machine apart.
    b. draw a diagram of the toy or machine.

24. As a member of a jury for a criminal trial, I would be primarily concerned with
    a. determining how witness testimony fits with the other evidence.
    b. judging the believability of witnesses.

25. If I were an author, I would most likely write
    a. biographies or how-to books.
    b. novels or poetry.

26. A career in which my work depends on that of others is
    a. less appealing than working alone.
    b. more appealing than working alone.

27. When I am able to solve a problem, it is usually because I
    a. worked through the solution step by step.
    b. brainstormed until I arrived at a solution.

28. I prefer to keep up with the news by
    a. reading a newspaper.
    b. watching television news programs.

29. If I witnessed a serious auto accident, my first impulse would be to
    a. assess the situation.
    b. comfort any injured people.

30. I pride myself on my ability to
    a. remember numbers and facts.
    b. see how ideas are related.

31. To solve a personal problem, I prefer to
    a. think about it myself.
    b. talk it through with friends.

32. If I had one last elective course to take before graduation, I would choose one that presents
    a. practical information that I can use immediately.
    b. ideas that make me think and stimulate my imagination.

33. For recreation, I would rather do a
    a. crossword puzzle.
    b. jigsaw puzzle.

34. I can best be described as
    a. reasonable and levelheaded.
    b. sensitive and caring.

35. When I read a story or watch a film, I prefer one with a plot that is
    a. clear and direct.
    b. intricate and complex.

Answer Sheet

Directions: Check either *a* or *b* in the boxes next to each question number.

	Column 1			Column 2			Column 3			Column 4			Column 5	
	a	b		a	b		a	b		a	b		a	b
1			2			3			4			5		
6			7			8			9			10		
11			12			13			14			15		
16			17			18			19			20		
21			22			23			24			25		
26			27			28			29			30		
31			32			33			34			35		
Total														

Directions for Scoring

1. On your answer sheet, add the checkmarks in each *a* and *b* column, counting first the number of *a*s checked and then the number of *b*s.
2. Enter the number of *a*s and *b*s you checked in the boxes at the bottom of each column.
3. Transfer these numbers to the Scoring Grid on page 22. Enter the number of *a* choices in Column 1 in the blank labeled "Independent," the number of *b* choices in Column 1 in the blank labeled "Social," and so on.

4. Circle your higher score in each row. For example, if you scored 2 for Independent and 5 for Social, circle "5" and "Social."
5. Your higher score in each row indicates a characteristic of your learning style. Scores that are close, such as 3 and 4, probably do not indicate a strong preference for either approach to learning. Scores that are far apart, such as 1 and 6, suggest a strong preference.

Scoring Grid	Number of Checkmarks	
Column	Choice *a*	Choice *b*
1		
	Independent	Social
2		
	Pragmatic	Creative
3		
	Verbal	Spatial
4		
	Rational	Emotional
5		
	Concrete	Abstract

Interpret Your Scores

Each question in the Learning Style Inventory assesses one of five aspects of your learning style. Here is how to interpret those aspects.

1. **Independent or social.** These scores indicate your preferred level of interaction with others. *Independent* learners prefer to work and study alone. They focus on the task at hand rather than on the people around them. Independent learners are often goal oriented and self-motivated. *Social* learners are more people oriented and prefer to learn and study with classmates. They often focus their attention on those around them and see a task as an opportunity for social interaction.
2. **Pragmatic or creative.** These scores suggest how you prefer to approach learning tasks. *Pragmatic* learners are practical and systematic. They approach tasks in an orderly, sequential manner. They like rules and learn step by step. *Creative* learners approach tasks imaginatively. They prefer to learn through discovery or experiment. They enjoy flexible, open-ended tasks and tend to dislike following rules.
3. **Verbal or spatial.** These scores indicate the way you prefer to take in and process information. *Verbal* learners rely on language, usually written text, to acquire information. They are skilled in the use of language and can work with other symbol systems (such as numbers) as well. *Spatial* learners prefer to take in information by studying graphics such as drawings, diagrams, films, or videos. They can visualize in their minds how things work or how they are positioned in space.
4. **Rational or emotional.** These scores suggest your preferred approach to decision making and problem solving. *Rational* learners are objective; they rely on facts and information when making decisions or solving problems. Rational learners are logical, often challenging or questioning a task. They enjoy prioritizing,

analyzing, and arguing. *Emotional* learners are subjective; they focus on feelings and values. Emotional learners are socially conscious and consider what others think. They seek harmony and may base a decision in part on its effect on others. Emotional decision makers are often skilled at persuasion.

5. **Concrete or abstract.** These scores indicate how you prefer to perceive information. *Concrete* learners pay attention to what is concrete and observable. They focus on details and tend to perceive tasks in parts or steps. Concrete learners prefer specific, tangible tasks and usually take a no-nonsense approach to learning. *Abstract* learners tend to focus on the "big picture"—large ideas, meanings, and relationships.

The results of the Learning Style Inventory probably confirmed things you already knew about yourself as a learner and provided you with some new insights as well. Keep in mind, though, that there are other ways to measure learning style.

- The inventory you completed is an informal measure of your learning style. Other, more formal measures may be available at your college's counseling or academic skills center.
- The inventory you completed measures the five aspects of learning style most relevant to the writing process, but many other aspects exist.
- You are the best judge of the accuracy of the results of this inventory and how they apply to you. If you think that one or more of the aspects of your learning style indicated by the inventory do not describe you, trust your instincts.

Use Your Learning Style When Reading and Writing

Because learning styles differ, this book presents alternative strategies for generating ideas and revising your writing. The following advice will help you take advantage of these learning style alternatives.

1. **Your learning style profile suggests your strengths as a writer.** Try to build on your strengths, which Graphic Organizer 1.1 can help you identify.
2. **Experiment with options.** Trying a new approach can challenge you and offer new insights. Sometimes choose activities that do not match your preferred learning style.
3. **Don't expect the option that is consistent with your learning style to require less attention or effort.** Even if you have social learner tendencies, an interview must still be carefully planned and well executed.

WRITING ACTIVITY 2

Write a two-page profile of yourself as a reader and a writer, describing your reactions to the results of the Learning Style Inventory. Explain how you expect to use the results in your writing course or other courses.

EXERCISE 1.4 **SELECTING LEARNING STRATEGIES**

Not all students study the same way, and most students study differently for different courses. List the courses you are taking this semester. For each, identify a study strategy that works for that course. Compare your list with those of other students and add useful techniques you learn from them.

GRAPHIC ORGANIZER 1.1 Your Strengths as a Writer

LEARNING STYLE CHARACTERISTIC	STRENGTHS AS A WRITER
Independent	You are willing to spend time thinking about a topic and are able to pull ideas together easily.
Social	You usually find it easy to write from experience. Writing realistic dialogue may be one of your strengths. You tend to have a good sense of whom you are writing for (your audience) and what you hope to accomplish (your purpose).
Pragmatic	You can meet deadlines easily. You recognize the need for organization in an essay. You tend to approach writing systematically and work through the steps in the writing process.
Creative	You tend to enjoy exploring a topic and often do so thoroughly and completely. Your writing is not usually hindered or restricted by rules or requirements.
Verbal	You may have a talent for generating ideas to write about and expressing them clearly.
Spatial	You can visualize or draw a map of the organization of your paper. Descriptions of physical objects, places, and people come easily.
Rational	You tend to write logically developed, well-organized essays. You usually analyze ideas objectively.
Emotional	Expressive and descriptive writing usually go well for you. You have a strong awareness of your audience.
Concrete	You find it easy to supply details to support an idea. You are able to write accurate, detailed descriptions and observations. You can organize facts effectively and present them clearly.
Abstract	You can develop unique approaches to a topic; you can grasp the point to which supporting ideas lead.

2
Active Reading and Responding

In this chapter you will learn to:

- develop an active approach to reading
- review and focus before reading
- think and interact while reading
- review and organize after reading
- respond to a reading assignment, using summary, annotation, synthesis, analysis, and evaluation
- write a focused response essay

WRITING QUICK START Assume you are taking a Mass Communication class and your instructor has asked you to complete the following assignment.

> Study the photograph on this page and write a paragraph explaining its relevance to our study of communication. Be sure to examine the photograph closely and then explain the point it makes about communication. Be detailed and specific in your response.

To explain the photograph, you had to think beyond the obvious. You had to identify and examine the details in the photograph that depict a shepherd using a mobile phone. Then you had to consider all the details together to decide what the main point of the photograph is. Finally, you had to consider why your instructor asked you to reflect on the photo.

Reading words involves a similar process of comprehension and evaluation. You must understand what the author *says*, and you must determine what the author *means*. Both parts of the process are essential. This chapter will focus on understanding, interpreting, and responding to what you read, while Chapter 3 will consider how to analyze, evaluate, and think critically about what you read (both print and visual selections).

A Guide to Active Reading

To read effectively, especially on the college level, students must engage words actively to understand how they work together to express ideas. To clarify the distinction between active and passive, think of sports fans watching a game. Diehard fans cheer some players and boo others, evaluate plays and calls, and shout out advice. By contrast, nonfans let the game take its course with little or no personal involvement or reaction and may well not even recall the score after the game is over.

HOW WRITERS READ ▶	ACTIVE VERSUS PASSIVE READING
PASSIVE READING	**ACTIVE READING**
Passive readers begin reading.	Active readers begin by reading the essay's title and thinking about what they already know about the author and subject. Then they decide what they need to know before they begin reading.
Passive readers read the essay only because it is assigned.	Active readers read the essay while looking for answers to questions and key elements.
Passive readers read but do not write.	Active readers highlight or underline, annotate, and write notes as they read.
Passive readers close the book when finished.	Active readers review, analyze, and evaluate the essay.

Like fans of a sports team, active readers get involved with the material they read. They become active participants by questioning, thinking about, and reacting to ideas using the process outlined in Graphic Organizer 2.1. In fact, it is this kind of active involvement in what they read that helps effective readers understand and remember a selection long after they finish the page. The sections that follow explain in detail each of the steps in reading actively.

Active readers achieve understanding and recall by engaging with the material *before* they read, *while* they read, and *after* they read. This chapter will explain what to do at each stage, and the readings throughout this book will guide you in applying these techniques at each stage.

GRAPHIC ORGANIZER 2.1 The Active Reading Process

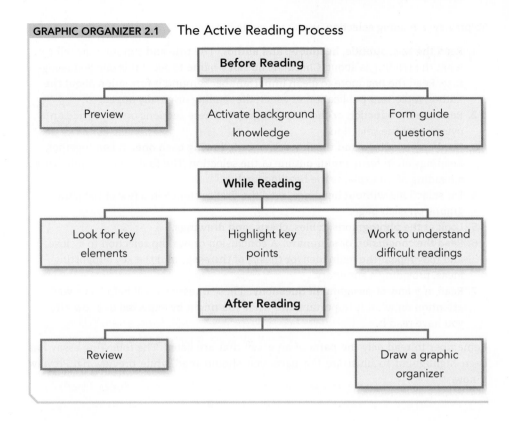

Before Reading: Write to Preview and Create Guide Questions

To read actively, start your reading by preparing your mind: Preview the selection and write guide questions to help you discover what the reading is about and focus your mind on the topic.

Preview

Previewing is a quick way of familiarizing yourself with an essay's content and organization. It helps you decide what you need to learn, and it has a number of other benefits as well.

- It helps you get interested in the material.
- It helps you concentrate on the material because you have a mental outline of it before you begin reading and therefore know what to expect.
- It helps you remember more of what you read.

To preview a reading selection, use these guidelines.

1. **Read the title, subtitle, headnote, and author.** The title and subtitle may tell you what the reading is about. Check the author's name to see if it is one you recognize. Read the headnote to glean important background information about the author, topic, and publication in which the reading originally appeared.

2. **Read the introduction or the first paragraph.** These sections often provide an overview of the selection.

3. **Read any headings and the first sentence following each one.** Taken together, headings often form a mini-outline of the selection. The first sentence following a heading often explains the heading further.

4. **For selections without headings, read the first sentence in a few of the paragraphs on each page.**

5. **Look at the photographs, tables, charts, and drawings.**

6. **Read the conclusion or summary.** A conclusion draws the selection to a close and may repeat the main idea (or thesis) of the essay and the key supporting ideas, providing a summary.

7. **Read any end-of-assignment questions.** These questions will help focus your attention on what is important and what you might be expected to know after you have read it.

Remember to read *only* the parts of an essay that are listed. The following essay has been highlighted to illustrate the parts you should read while previewing. Preview it now.

> READING

American Jerk: Be Civil, or I'll Beat You to a Pulp

Todd Schwartz

Todd Schwartz is a writer based in Portland, Oregon. A longer version of this essay originally appeared in the *Oregon Humanities Review* in 2008 under the title "the Great Civility War." The version below was published in 2009 in the *Utne Reader*.

It was the most civil of times, it was the least civil of times, it was the age of   1
politeness, it was the age of boorishness, it was the epoch of concern, it was the
epoch of who cares, it was the season of hybrid, it was the season of Hummer, it
was the spring of Obama, it was the winter of hate speech . . .

   With apologies to Mr. Dickens (or not: screw him), we have arrived at simulta-   2
neously the most and least civil moment in U.S. history. A moment when a roomful of even relatively evolved people will react with discomfort to an off-color
joke about people of color—and when those same people have no compunction
whatsoever about loudly ignoring one another as they blather into their cell
phones.

   We have never been more concerned about the feelings of minority groups, the   3
disabled, and the disadvantaged. Yet we have never been less concerned about the
feelings of anyone with whom we share the road, the Internet, or the movie theater.

Political correctness holds such sway that holidays go 4
unnamed for fear of insulting or excluding someone. Schools won't
let teachers use red pens to correct papers, because little Ethan's or
Emily's self-esteem might be bruised. No one is "poor," but many are
"socioeconomically disadvantaged." Civility and thoughtfulness in
speech have never been so complete or so codified.

All of which is well intentioned and mostly a wonderful thing. 5
I'm all for being polite and caring and Golden Rule-ish. Sadly, like a
lovely field of wildflowers—which in reality is filled with bloodsucking ticks and noxious pollen—we live oh-so-politely in what must
certainly be the rudest era in recorded history. Maybe even
prehistory.

Neanderthals were probably nicer to each other than we are. 6

Pick your poison: reality television, slasher movies, video 7
games, online porn, cell phones, automated answering systems,
giant assault vehicles for trips to the grocery store, car stereos
played at volumes easily heard on Jupiter, web-powered copyright
infringement, people who will not shut their inane traps in movie
theaters, and, lord help us, now even people who won't shut their
inane traps during live theater.

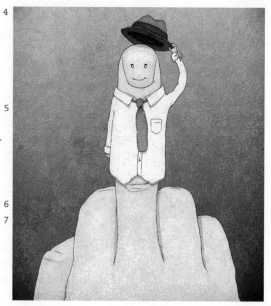

Jesse Kuhn/RawToast Design

We're all talking to someone all the time, but it's ever more rarely to the people we 8
are actually with. Our cell phones blare ringtones that no one else wants to hear. We
love to watch TV shows about the stunningly predictable results of hand-feeding a
grizzly bear or lighting a stick of dynamite with a cigarette. We also love shows where
people lie to others for money and programs where snarky, slightly talented folks say
vicious things to hopeful, and usually more talented, contestants.

Civility rules, friends. 9

Civility is dead, jerks. 10

Why? I have a few theories. 11

The first is that America is in the same position as Rome found itself in about 12
420 CE, meaning that we've reached the peak of our civilization and now everything is
going to Tartarus in a chariot. We're too far from our food and energy sources, and fewer
and fewer of the Druids and Visigoths like us anymore. So we desperately cling to a
patina of civility while we grab a snack and watch large, toothy predators devour people.

The second is that sunlight contains tiny spores that lodge in the cerebellum, 13
making the infected believe they are the center of the universe.

My final and somewhat less cutting edge theory is that a large percentage of people 14
are just clueless, distracted, and self-absorbed, unable to process concepts such as spatial
awareness (for example: when you are walking in the same direction with several hundred people in, say, an airport terminal, DON'T JUST STOP IN THE MIDDLE OF THE FLOW!).

But I digress. 15

I am not here to judge whether being civil and considerate is somehow better 16
than being a mindless dillweed. You must make that choice for yourself. We
inhabit the most civil of times and the least—and I completely honor and respect
your freedom to choose your side in the Great Civility War.

Just don't get in my way. I'm on my cell in the Escalade, and I can't be bothered. 17

EXERCISE 2.1 ▶   TESTING YOUR RECALL AFTER PREVIEWING

Based only on your preview of the essay "American Jerk," indicate whether each of the following statements is true or false. If most of your answers are correct, you will know that previewing helped you gain a sense of the essay's context and organization. (For the answers to this exercise, see p. 54.)

_____ 1. The reading is primarily about civility and the lack of it.

_____ 2. The author blames the Internet for our society's lack of civility.

_____ 3. The author suggests that political correctness does not go far enough.

_____ 4. People are often not intentionally rude but simply are distracted or unaware.

_____ 5. Society is unconcerned about minorities.

Activate Your Background Knowledge and Experience

After previewing, take time to discover what you already know or have experienced about the topic. For example, after previewing the essay in Chapter 1 on multitasking, think of how and when you multitask and whether it has helped you to be (or hindered you from being) productive and efficient. Think of situations when you have observed others multitasking and whether it seemed effective. Activating your prior knowledge will make the reading more meaningful, more interesting, and easier to remember.

EXERCISE 2.2 ▶   ACTIVATING YOUR KNOWLEDGE AND EXPERIENCE

Activate your knowledge and experience about ideas presented in "American Jerk" by listing three situations that demonstrate civility or the lack of it.

Form Questions to Guide Your Reading

Asking and answering questions will strengthen your comprehension and recall of the material. Before you begin reading, devise questions about the selection based on sections you previewed. Then, as you read, answer those questions. The following examples will help you start devising your questions.

Essay Titles	Questions
"Part-Time Employment Undermines Students' Commitment to School"	Why does part-time employment undermine commitment to school?
"Human Cloning: Don't Just Say 'No'"	What are good reasons to clone humans?

Headings	
"Types of Territoriality"	What are the types of territoriality?
"Territorial Encroachment"	What is territorial encroachment, and how does it occur?

Not all essays lend themselves to these techniques. In some essays, you may need to dig deeper into the introductory and final paragraphs to form questions. Look again at your preview of "American Jerk." Using the introductory paragraphs of that essay, you might decide to look for answers to this question: *Why is the author, Todd Schwartz, negative toward Americans?*

EXERCISE 2.3 ▸ FORMING GUIDE QUESTIONS

List three questions that you expect to be able to answer after reading "American Jerk."

HOW WRITERS READ ▸ ACTIVE READING ONLINE

Readers tend to read online material differently than they do print pages. For print pages, readers tend to progress linearly, moving across each line as they move down the page. Online readers tend to skim, looking for information or the interesting bits. They tend to use a pattern that follows the shape of the letter F, moving across the top of the page, skipping down to read another nearby horizontal section, and then moving their eyes vertically down the left edge of the page, noting what appears there.

These tendencies may work well when searching for information or interesting tidbits online, but they do not work for careful and complete reading. When you read college essays and assignments online, be sure to temper your inclination to skip and skim.

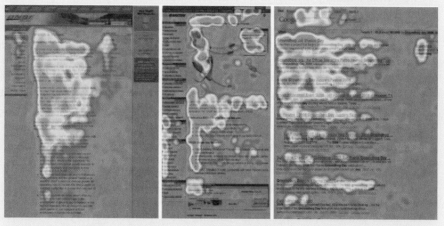

Heat maps from user eye-tracking studies of three Web sites. The areas where users looked the most are colored red; the yellow areas indicate fewer views, followed by the least-viewed blue areas. Gray areas didn't attract any fixations.   Nielsen Norman Group

While Reading: Write to Think and Interact with the Text

While you are reading, be sure to think about and interact with the reading, figuring out which ideas are important and which are less so by:

- identifying and examining key elements
- highlighting key points
- making marginal notes, called *annotations*, about any ideas that occur to you (annotation may be done more completely on a second read, after you have finished reading, understand the gist, and are ready to delve deeper)

For more about annotating, see pp. 44–45.

See the Just-in-Time Guide, pp. 85–89, for tips on mastering challenging words and expanding your vocabulary.

As you read, figure out the meaning of unfamiliar vocabulary and be prepared to strengthen your comprehension of challenging reading assignments.

Look for Key Elements

As you read assigned articles and essays, pay particular attention to the following key elements.

For more about introductions and conclusions, see Chapter 7.

For more about thesis statements, see Chapter 5.

To learn more about topic sentences and supporting details, see Chapter 6.

1. **The title and subtitle.** Although you read these while previewing, now examine them to determine how the title and subtitle relate to the subject and what they reveal about the author's point of view.
2. **The introduction.** The opening paragraph or paragraphs often provide background information, announce the topic, and grab the reader's attention.
3. **The author's main point.** Look for a **thesis statement** that directly expresses the one big idea that the essay explains, explores, or supports. Writers often place the thesis in the first or second paragraph to let readers know what lies ahead. But the thesis may appear at the end of an essay or may be implied or suggested rather than stated directly.
4. **The support and explanation.** Usually, each paragraph in the body of an essay supports the author's main point. Look at each paragraph to determine what it is about—the paragraph's main idea may be stated in a **topic sentence**—and consider how it relates to the thesis. Take note of the kinds of evidence the author supplies, such as facts and statistics, examples, anecdotes, or comparisons.
5. **The conclusion.** The essay's final paragraph or paragraphs often restate the author's main point or offer ideas for further thought.

The parts you examine when you read are those you use when you write. You'll learn much more about each part of an essay in Chapters 4–7.

Now read "American Jerk," paying attention to the marginal notes that identify and explain its various parts.

American Jerk: Be Civil, or I'll Beat You to a Pulp

Todd Schwartz

Todd Schwartz is a writer based in Portland, Oregon. A longer version of this essay originally appeared in the *Oregon Humanities Review* in 2008 under the title "The Great Civility War." The version below was published in 2009 in the *Utne Reader*.

It was the most civil of times, it was the least civil of times, it was the age of politeness, it was the age of boorishness, it was the epoch of concern, it was the epoch of who cares, it was the season of hybrid, it was the season of Hummer, it was the spring of Obama, it was the winter of hate speech . . .

With apologies to Mr. Dickens (or not: screw him), we have arrived at simultaneously the most and least civil moment in U.S. history. A moment when a roomful of even relatively evolved people will react with discomfort to an off-color joke about people of color—and when those same people have no compunction whatsoever about loudly ignoring one another as they blather into their cell phones.

We have never been more concerned about the feelings of minority groups, the disabled, and the disadvantaged. Yet we have never been less concerned about the feelings of anyone with whom we share the road, the Internet, or the movie theater.

Political correctness holds such sway that holidays go unnamed for fear of insulting or excluding someone. Schools won't let teachers use red pens to correct papers, because little Ethan's or Emily's self-esteem might be bruised. No one is "poor," but many are "socioeconomically disadvantaged." Civility and thoughtfulness in speech have never been so complete or so codified.

All of which is well intentioned and mostly a wonderful thing. I'm all for being polite and caring and Golden Rule-ish. Sadly, like a lovely field of wildflowers—which in reality is filled with bloodsucking ticks and noxious pollen—we live oh-so-politely in what must certainly be the rudest era in recorded history. Maybe even prehistory.

Neanderthals were probably nicer to each other than we are.

Pick your poison: reality television, slasher movies, video games, online porn, cell phones, automated answering systems, giant assault vehicles for trips to the grocery store, car stereos played at volumes easily heard on Jupiter, web-powered copyright infringement, people who will not shut their inane traps in movie theaters, and, lord help us, now even people who won't shut their inane traps during live theater.

We're all talking to someone all the time, but it's ever more rarely to the people we are actually with. Our cell phones blare ringtones that no one else wants to hear. We love to watch TV shows about the stunningly predictable results of hand-feeding a grizzly bear or lighting a stick of dynamite with a cigarette. We also love shows where people lie to others for money and programs where snarky, slightly talented folks say vicious things to hopeful, and usually more talented, contestants.

Civility rules, friends.

Civility is dead, jerks.

Why? I have a few theories.

**Side notes:**

Title and subtitle: Suggest idea of conflict over behavior

1 **Introduction:** Illustration suggest contradictory attitudes.

2 **Main idea:** Thesis states main idea and refers to Dickens, who used "It was the best of times, it was the worst of times" in his novel *A Tale of Two Cities*.

3 **Support:** Offers examples of contradictory attitudes toward groups

4

5

6

7 **Support:** Provides examples of rudeness

8 **Support:** More examples

9
10 **Contradictions:** Refer back to
11 information and introduce reasons to follow

Support: First reason

The first is that America is in the same position as Rome found itself in about 420 CE, meaning that we've reached the peak of our civilization and now everything is going to Tartarus in a chariot. We're too far from our food and energy sources, and fewer and fewer of the Druids and Visigoths like us anymore. So we desperately cling to a patina of civility while we grab a snack and watch large, toothy predators devour people. 12

Support: Second reason

The second is that sunlight contains tiny spores that lodge in the cerebellum, making the infected believe they are the center of the universe. 13

Support: Third reason

My final and somewhat less cutting edge theory is that a large percentage of people are just clueless, distracted, and self-absorbed, unable to process concepts such as spatial awareness (for example: when you are walking in the same direction with several hundred people in, say, an airport terminal, DON'T JUST STOP IN THE MIDDLE OF THE FLOW!). 14

But I digress. 15

Conclusion: Affirms thesis statement and ends on a humorous note

I am not here to judge whether being civil and considerate is somehow better than being a mindless dillweed. You must make that choice for yourself. We inhabit the most civil of times and the least—and I completely honor and respect your freedom to choose your side in the Great Civility War. 16

Just don't get in my way. I'm on my cell in the Escalade, and I can't be bothered. 17

Highlight Key Points

As you read, you will encounter many new ideas, some more important than others. You will agree with some and disagree with others. Later, as you write about what you have read, you will want to return to the main points to refresh your memory. To locate and remember these points easily, read with a highlighter or pen in hand. Caution: Highlighting is an active reading strategy *only* when you use it to distinguish important ideas from less important ideas, so be selective. (If you highlight every idea, none will stand out.) The following guidelines will make your highlighting as useful as possible.

1. **Before you begin reading, decide what kinds of information to highlight.** What types of tasks will you do as a result of your reading? Will you write a paper, participate in a class discussion, or take an exam? Think about what you need to know, and tailor your highlighting to the needs of the task.

2. **Read first; then highlight.** First read a paragraph or section; then go back and mark what is important within it. This approach will help you control the tendency to highlight too much.

3. **Highlight key elements, words, and phrases.** Mark the thesis statement, the topic sentence in each paragraph, important terms and definitions, and key words and phrases that relate to the thesis. While you read, you may also want to jot down any ideas that you do not understand or record your own thoughts about the author's ideas. These activities are part of the process of annotation, covered later in the chapter in the section on responding to reading (pp. 44–45).

> **EXERCISE 2.4** **HIGHLIGHTING KEY POINTS**
>
> Reread "American Jerk," highlighting as you read.

Work to Understand Difficult Readings

Some readings are straightforward, but much of the reading you'll do in college will be challenging. The subject matter may be complex, the sentences and paragraphs may be long or involved, or the writer *may* use difficult or unfamiliar vocabulary. Whatever the problem, however, you know you must complete the assignment. The Just-in-Time Guide to Reading and Responding on pages 81–96 provides tips for overcoming challenges in your reading. Dip into it to find useful solutions whenever you find yourself facing reading challenges.

After Reading: Review and Organize to Consolidate Understanding

When you finish reading an assignment, it may be tempting to close the book, periodical, or browser window and move immediately to another task. However, doing so increases the likelihood that you will forget most of what you have read because you will not have had time to process the material. The following strategies will help get you ready to write about what you have read.

Review to Consolidate Your Understanding

Review immediately after you finish reading to pull all the ideas in the reading together and make them stick in your mind. You will probably also discover more about how the ideas are connected. Reviewing should not take much time; your goal is to touch on each main point one more time, not to embark on a long and thorough study. To review material after reading, use the same steps you used to preview the reading. (See p. 28.) Pay particular attention to the following elements.

- the headings
- your highlighting
- your annotations
- the conclusion

Write new annotations about ideas or connections that come to you or become clearer as you review.

Draw a Graphic Organizer to Examine Relationships among Ideas

Think of a graphic organizer as a means of tracking the author's flow of ideas. Your graphic organizer should include all of the key elements of an essay listed on page 32. Graphic Organizer 2.2 (p. 36) shows a sample format of a graphic organizer.

GRAPHIC ORGANIZER 2.2 Graphic Organizer: Key Elements to Include

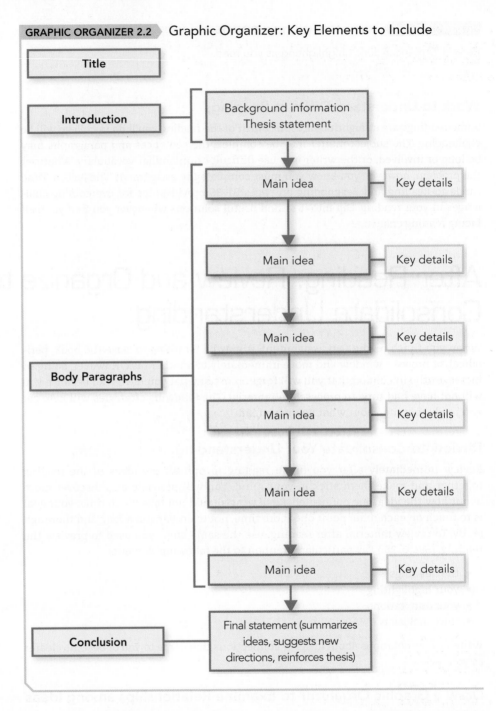

An example of a graphic organizer for "American Jerk" appears in Graphic Organizer 2.3 (p. 37). Work through the organizer, rereading the essay paragraph by paragraph at the same time.

GRAPHIC ORGANIZER 2.3   Graphic Organizer for "American Jerk"

"AMERICAN JERK"

There is a strange mixture of civility and incivility in today's society, with an emphasis on incivility.

- People are uncomfortable with jokes about people of color but rudely ignore each other.
- We are concerned about the feelings of groups yet are unconcerned about the feelings of individuals.
- Political correctness affects holidays, the way papers are graded, and the words used to describe the poor.

Politeness is practiced, but at the same time we are rude to each other.

- Entertainment and media highlight poor behavior.
- Cell phones are used rudely.

There are reasons for our rudeness.

- America has become too detached from food and energy sources.
- People are self-centered.
- People are distracted, self-absorbed, and unable to process basic concepts such as spatial awareness.

Everyone has a choice about whether to behave in a civil or an uncivil manner.

Apply Your Skills: Read a Selection Actively

The following reading selection will give you an opportunity to practice the active reading strategies you have just learned in this chapter. It will also be used as the reading assignment on which to base a response essay described in the following section.

Before Reading

1. **Preview.** Preview the reading using the steps listed on page 28, and answer the following questions.
   - What issue will the reading address?
   - Do you expect the author to take a position on the issue? Why or why not?

2. **Connect.** Activate your knowledge and experience on the topic by answering the following questions.
   - What figures, ideas, or images does the term *superhero* bring to mind?
   - What behaviors and characteristics are associated with supervillains?
   - In what possible ways could science create superheroes or supervillains?

While Reading

Highlight the key elements of the essay, as described on page 32. Make marginal notes of any ideas that come to mind as you read.

READING

Superhero or Supervillain? If Science Gives People Superpowers, Will They Use Them for Good or Evil?

Will Oremus

This essay originally appeared in the online magazine *Slate* in May 2013. *Slate's* Web site describes the magazine as a "general-interest publication offering analysis and commentary about politics, business, technology, and culture." Will Oremus is a staff writer for this magazine, writing about science and technology.

From invisibility to superhuman strength to telekinesis, a wave of emerging technologies promises to give people powers once reserved for comic-book characters. Which raises an important question: If humans become superhuman, will we turn out to be superheroes—or supervillains?   1

You might think the answer would depend on each individual's moral compass. Batman uses human-enhancement technologies to fight crime because he loathes injustice, while the Joker uses them to wreak mayhem because he's a   2 psychopath. In reality, though, most people possess the capacity for both good and evil. Which one wins out at any given time depends not only on our genes and our upbringing, but the circumstances in which we find ourselves. For Peter Parker, a shy and neurotic kid, the transformation into Spider-Man brings out a deep sense of social responsibility. For Otto Octavius, once a respected scientist, becoming Dr. Octopus means becoming a vengeful megalomaniac. Comic books typically provide pop-psychological back stories to explain the choices each character makes in response to the pressure of being extraordinary. But what if it also turns out that some types of powers inherently lend themselves to altruism, while others make us more likely to lie, cheat, steal, or kill?

Last year, Stanford researchers recruited 60 volunteers for an experiment on how virtual superpowers could influence moral decisions. In an immersive virtual-reality simulation, 30 of the subjects were granted the power of flight, like Superman, while the other 30 rode as passengers in a helicopter. Each volunteer had the same mission—to cruise over a city following an earthquake in search of a stranded child. The experiment was rigged so that everyone would find the boy in the same amount of time and save his life.   3

After the simulation, an experimenter sat down to debrief each subject. As they talked, the experimenter "accidentally" knocked over a canister full of pens, then waited five seconds before beginning to pick them up. The   4

(Top) Participant "flying" in virtual reality; (bottom) virtual child after being "rescued." (Top) Cody Karutz; (bottom) Robin Rosenberg/Stanford Virtual Human Interaction Lab

volunteers in the helicopter group took an average of six seconds to start helping clean up the spill, and some didn't pitch in at all. But those in the Superman group jumped right in, with most coming to the experimenter's aid even before she started gathering the pens herself.

The findings suggest that acquiring a superpower can spark benevolent tendencies. Give someone Superman's abilities, and she'll start to behave a little more like Superman. Clinical psychologist Robin Rosenberg, who helped design the experiment, said its outcome supported her hypothesis that people might treat an extraordinary ability as a sort of gift that brings with it a responsibility to help others. That's an encouraging finding, particularly in light of Lord Acton's maxim that power corrupts.   5

But wait—what if the researchers had given their subjects a different superpower? Rosenberg's co-author, Stanford communications professor Jeremy Bailenson, explained that they chose the power of flight partly because it seemed   6 like a classic "do-gooder" sort of ability. "We thought about giving them X-ray vision, but that would have been a little creepy," he noted.

It would be nice to think that morality emanates from the sheer goodness of people's souls, but research has consistently shown that people behave far better when they think they're being watched. In a 2010 study, Newcastle University researchers found that just hanging posters of a pair of staring eyes on the walls of a cafeteria was enough to cut littering in half. That's why Rosenberg, who has written a book on the psychology of superheroes, draws a distinction between visible powers and stealth powers. Soaring above the masses is a highly conspicuous activity, so it would behoove the flyer to be on his best behavior. X-ray vision is stealthier—you could use it for nefarious purposes without making a scene. 7

The ultimate stealth power, of course, is invisibility. Its promise is that of impunity—the ability to do things that would otherwise get you in trouble. In Plato's *Republic,* Glaucon recounts the story of an otherwise decent shepherd who came into possession of an invisibility ring. Unable to resist temptation, he used it to seduce the queen, kill the king, and claim the crown for himself. H.G. Wells's invisible man went on a similar spree. And in a classic episode of *This American Life,* John Hodgman went around asking people which superpower they'd prefer: flight or invisibility. Those who pondered invisibility couldn't resist premeditating a slew of illicit deeds. One fellow was so spooked by his own impulses that he ended up changing his answer to "flight" because the mere thought of invisibility "leads me down a dark path." 8

Powers that inherently violate other people's autonomy, like mind control, would also seem to lend themselves to abuse. A utilitarian might be able to dream up some applications that redound to the public welfare, but the German philosopher Immanuel Kant would argue that mind control is immoral no matter how it's used. Mind-reading would be similarly invasive. A form of telepathy that required both parties' active participation, on the other hand, might be stealthy, but it would be fundamentally social and consensual. That ups the odds that it would be used for virtuous ends. Other powers, like supreme intelligence, time travel, and indestructibility, are morality-agnostic and could be employed equally for good or ill. Likewise incredible strength, which Bruce Banner's Hulk uses mostly for good but which also bedevils him by amplifying the consequences of his rage. 9

That example suggests another way of looking at the risks and benefits of human-enhancement technologies. By definition, they enable people to transcend their natural limitations. That can obviously be a good thing, but it also carries heightened risks, because civil society and human morality have evolved against a background in which those constraints are taken for granted. That's why emerging technologies like drones and 3-D printing scare so many people—they enable behaviors that our laws and norms have not evolved to regulate. Imagine the panic that would ensue if hypothetical superpowers like mind-reading suddenly became widely available. 10

It's probably fortunate, then, that we're nowhere near as close to the technological singularity as Ray Kurzweil would have us believe. We have jet packs, but they're grossly impractical. Headlines about real-life invisibility cloaks tend to be exaggerated. Muscle suits so far are clunky enough that they're only really useful for people with disabilities. Brain-computer interfaces let you move things with your mind, but only if you're willing to undergo brain surgery and practice for 11 months just to feed yourself a bite of chocolate. Promises of super-longevity or immortality are premature.

That said, each of these human-enhancement technologies, and several more   12
that *Slate* will explore in the coming weeks, are progressing at various rates along a path that could someday lead to real-world viability. Before they do, it might be wise to take a little time to think about whether each one is likely to make people better—or just more potent.

After Reading

Working together.   Contact five people of varying ages (such as a child, a college student, a mature adult) and ask them the following question.

If you could have any superpower, what would it be, and how would you use it?

Record your responses in the chart below.

Age of Respondent	Desired Superpower	Proposed Use of Superpower

In class, join a small group of your peers to combine your charts and analyze the responses. Does your group's chart reveal any trends? Be prepared to share your results and any trends you noticed with the rest of the class.

A Guide to Responding to a Reading

Responding to a reading is usually the next step after careful, active reading. **Response** is a process of synthesizing, analyzing, evaluating ideas, reflecting on, and sometimes writing about what you read. When an instructor gives a reading assignment, some form of response is always required. For example, you might be expected to discuss it in class, analyze it on an essay exam, or research the topic further and report your findings. By responding to material, you understand and learn it better. Of course, you may go back and forth, returning to active reading as part of forming a response. A common assignment is a **response essay**, which requires you to read a selection, analyze it, and write about some aspect of it. Figure 2.1 shows the process of responding to an assignment. It begins with summarizing to check your understanding, moves to creating and organizing a response, and culminates in producing a response, often a written one.

For an example of a student's response essay, see Karen Vaccaro's "'American Jerk'? How Rude! (but True)" on pp. 52–54.

FIGURE 2.1   **Responding to a Reading**

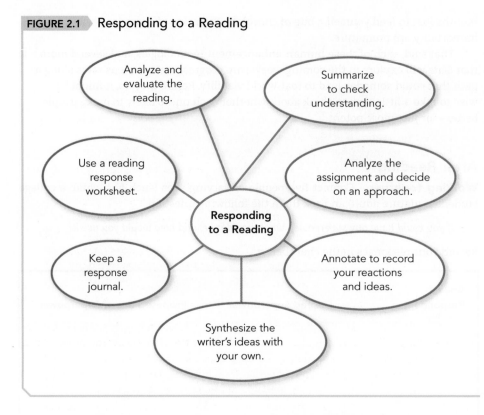

Many tools and strategies will help you create a reasoned and effective response to what you read. These include analyzing the assignment, annotating and synthesizing your ideas with those of the author, and using a response worksheet or a response journal to analyze and evaluate the reading. A good way to start is first to summarize the selection.

Summarize to Check Your Understanding

Before you respond to an assignment, be sure your understanding is thorough and complete. To prepare for discussing a reading in class or writing about it in a response paper or on an exam, writing a **summary** (a brief restatement of the major points) is a good first step. If you have difficulty writing a summary, you will know you do not fully understand the reading. Summarizing also requires you to make decisions about what is and is not important in a reading, and this can help improve your understanding and retention of the material. As you write, you will find that your own thoughts about the reading begin to take shape as well.

These guidelines will help you write an effective summary.

See the section on highlighting in the Guide to Active Reading, p. 34.

1. **Review your highlighting.**
2. **Start your summary with an opening sentence that states the author's thesis in your own words.** The thesis is the most important idea that the entire essay

addresses or explains. Include the author's name and the title of the selection you are summarizing.

3. **Include the author's most important supporting ideas.** Use either highlighted topic sentences or marginal summary notes as a guide for what to include. Be sure to use your own words and sentence patterns—not those of the author.

4. **Present the ideas in the order in which they appear in the original source.** Use transitions (connecting words and phrases, such as *first*, *next*, or *as a result*) as you move from one major supporting idea to the next.

5. **Reread your summary to determine whether it contains enough information.** Your summary should include the selection's main ideas and key supporting points. (Your opinions do not belong in a summary.) A good rule of thumb is that a summary should be about one-fifth the length of the original, but whether this will be too much or too little will depend on the source you are summarizing and your purpose in writing the summary. (A summary may be just one or two sentences in a response essay or research project but may be almost a third of the length of the original if you are using it as a study tool for a complex reading you will be tested on.)

Here is a sample summary by Karen Vaccaro, the student whose response to "American Jerk" appears on pages 52–54.

In "American Jerk," Todd Schwartz claims that, although people believe they are acting politely, rudeness and incivility are on the rise. We overdo political correctness, yet we behave rudely to everyone around us. The author believes that because our civilization has evolved to the point that we are no longer concerned with basic survival, we can act selfishly while pretending to be civil. The author also contends that people often are not intentionally rude but instead are simply distracted and self-absorbed. The bottom line is that people must choose their own behavior and decide how they will act.

> The writer expresses Schwartz's thesis in her own words.
>
> The order of ideas parallels the order in Schwartz's essay.
>
> The writer continues to use her own words—not those of Schwartz.

Many students keep a journal in which they write summaries and other responses to what they've read. These journal entries can serve as useful sources of ideas for writing papers.

ESSAY IN PROGRESS 1 ▶ WRITING A SUMMARY

This assignment is the first step of a five-part essay-in-progress assignment. The steps lead you through the process of developing and writing a response to the essay "Superhero or Supervillain?" (pp. 38–41) or another reading selection your instructor has chosen. The writing assignment is as follows:

> Write a two- to three-page paper in response to "Superhero or Supervillain?" (or an essay assigned by your instructor). Choose one question or issue that the essay addresses and detail your response to it.

As part of completing the above assignment, complete each of the following tasks.

1. **Review** Reread your highlighting for "Superhero or Supervillain?"
2. **Organize** Draw a graphic organizer of the essay.
3. **Summarize** Write a brief one-paragraph summary of "Superhero or Supervillain?"

Analyze the Assignment and Decide on an Approach

Before beginning your response, make sure you understand the parameters of the assignment.

- **The task.** Will you be discussing the reading selection in class to consolidate your understanding? Review your annotations and any notes you wrote while reading, and bring any ideas or questions you might have about the selection to class.
- **Your purpose.** Will you be analyzing it for an essay exam as a way of demonstrating your command of issues or themes you have studied in class? Consider themes or topics you have discussed in class or in other readings, and think about how the reading selection relates.
- **Instructor expectations.** Will you be writing a response to demonstrate your understanding and analysis as well as your ability to write a clear, cohesive essay? Consider the direction or approach you should take, the length your instructor expects, and whether you are expected (or allowed) to do additional research, as well as how best to organize and develop the response.

If you are uncertain about your instructor's expectations, be sure to ask.

ESSAY IN PROGRESS 2   **ANALYZING THE ASSIGNMENT**

Essay in Progress 1 gives the following assignment.

> Write a two- to three-page paper in response to "Superhero or Supervillain?" (or an essay assigned by your instructor). Choose one question or issue that the essay addresses and detail your response to it.

Write a paragraph in which you identify the task, your purpose, and your instructor's likely expectations.

Generate and Record Ideas: Annotating, Synthesizing, Analyzing, and Evaluating

Once you have created and organized ideas from the reading, it is time to generate and create your own ideas. This involves synthesizing, keeping a response journal, and analyzing and evaluating.

Annotate to Record Your Impressions

When you **annotate** a reading assignment, you jot down your questions and reactions to the reading in the margins or in a reading journal. Think of your annotations as a personal response to the author's ideas. You can annotate while you read, but your most useful annotations will often come after an initial reading, as you reread and review the material. You may want to go back to reread and annotate a selection once you have an idea of what you will be writing about. Your annotations can take many forms.

- important points (such as the thesis) to which you react intellectually or emotionally
- places where you want or need further information
- passages that reveal the author's reasons for writing
- passages that raise questions or that intrigue or puzzle you
- ideas you agree or disagree with or that seem inconsistent
- themes or ideas that relate to a topic you may want to write about

Later, as you write about or discuss the reading, your annotations will help you focus on major issues and questions. A portion of Karen Vaccaro's annotations on "American Jerk" are shown below.

For more about keeping a journal, see Chapter 1, p. 18.

Karen Vaccaro's response to "American Jerk" appears on pp. 52–54.

Sample Annotations

Civility rules, friends.
Civility is dead, jerks.
Why? I have a few theories.

A reference to A Tale of Two Cities, a novel about the French Revolution. Is Schwartz implying that Americans are ready to revolt?

The first is that America is in the same position as Rome found itself in about 420 CE, meaning that we've reached the peak of our civilization and now everything is going to Tartarus in a chariot. We're too far from our food and energy sources, and fewer and fewer of the Druids and Visigoths like us anymore. So we desperately cling to a patina of civility while we grab a snack and watch large, toothy predators devour people.

The second is that sunlight contains tiny spores that lodge in the cerebellum, making the infected believe they are the center of the universe.

My final and somewhat less cutting-edge theory is that a large percentage of people are just clueless, distracted, and self-absorbed, unable to process concepts such as spatial awareness (for example: when you are walking in the same direction with several hundred people in, say, an airport terminal, DON'T JUST STOP IN THE MIDDLE OF THE FLOW!).

Tartarus = Hell. Fall of Rome: Are things really so bad now? Romans kept slaves!

Is this such a bad thing? We have time to relax and think.

Rome's "neighbors"?

Patina = only on the surface

Schwartz's main point. My boyfriend gets distracted by his phone — a lot! (I do, too, sometimes.)

ESSAY IN PROGRESS 3 ▸ ANNOTATING

Reread "Superhero or Supervillain?" on pages 38–41. Annotate the essay as you reread.

Synthesize the Writer's Ideas with Your Own

One way to start ideas flowing for a response is to connect, or **synthesize**, the ideas expressed in the reading with your own ideas, knowledge, and experiences. Doing so builds a bridge between your ideas and the author's. You may have begun synthesizing ideas as you annotated, but to synthesize more formally, follow these steps.

1. **Look for useful information in the essay that you could apply or relate to other real-life situations.** Think of familiar situations or examples that illustrate the subject. For example, for "American Jerk," which considers incivility

in society, you might write a journal entry about incivility among college students.

2. **Think beyond the reading.** Recall other material you have read and events you have experienced that relate to the reading. In thinking about "American Jerk," for example, you might recall the behavior of students in the classroom, as described in the reading "The New Marshmallow Test" from Chapter 1 (pp. 3–6). How does student use of digital technology in the classroom relate to the topic of civility, for example?

3. **Use the key-word response method for generating ideas.** Choose one or more key words that describe your initial response, such as *angered, amused, surprised, confused, annoyed, curious,* or *shocked.* Then write for five to ten minutes without stopping in response to your word. You can explain your response or offer examples to support your reaction. Try approaching the reading from many different perspectives. Here is the result of Karen Vaccaro's key-word response to "American Jerk."

> **Possible topic 1:** How generations create their own values
>
> **Possible topic 2:** How behavior changes with changes in technology
>
> **Possible topic 3:** How bad is rudeness in comparison with evils of earlier times?

After reading "American Jerk," <u>I felt annoyed and insulted</u>. I agree that the world has changed because of cell phones, but I don't think that these changes have made people ruder. Each generation creates its own rules and values, and the cell-phone generation is doing that. If media and entertainment were horrible and insulting, then people wouldn't watch them. Humans are evolving, and our expectations have to evolve with technology. Some people do act like they are polite when they actually do rude things all the time. But really, are things as bad as he claims? Isn't enslaving people a lot worse than talking on the phone when out with a friend?

ESSAY IN PROGRESS 4 ▶ SYNTHESIZING IDEAS

Use synthesis to draw connections between the ideas expressed in "Superhero or Supervillain?" and your own ideas and experiences.

Analyze and Evaluate the Reading

After you see a movie, you ask a friend, "What did you think of it?" Your friend may praise the plot, criticize the acting, or comment on the characters' behavior. Your friend is analyzing the film, breaking the film down into its component parts and assessing how well they work together. When you analyze a reading, you may focus on any aspect of the selection, such as how the author tries to reach his or her intended readers by choosing evidence readers will respond to, offering reasons they can accept, or using a tone readers will find appealing. When you evaluate a reading, you consider the author's fairness or accuracy, the effectiveness of the presentation, the quality of the supporting evidence provided, and relevance of the selection to your purpose. Numerous techniques for both analysis and evaluation are explored in detail in Chapter 3.

An effective starting point for analysis and evaluation is to devise critical questions. Asking critical questions and then answering them is a useful method for analysis and for discovering ideas for a response, as well. Critical questions go beyond what the author said and explore what he or she meant. These questions may focus on the implications, practicality, accuracy, and application of the author's ideas, for example. Here are three sample questions and the answers that Karen Vaccaro wrote after reading "American Jerk."

> Can we turn the tide and find a way to return to a polite society?
>
> I think that adults emphasize politeness less than in the past. Parents and
>
> teachers hardly try to instill it in children. People no longer have to learn
>
> etiquette. To improve manners would require us to rethink how we raise and
>
> educate children.

Possible topic: How to teach politeness and effective methods

> Is technology causing people to be less civil, or is it just an excuse?
>
> Technology has changed the way that people communicate with one another.
>
> Technology makes it easier to have less personal contact with others, but it does
>
> not encourage rudeness. It's possible to use technology and still be civil to other
>
> people.

Possible topic: The effects of technology on human behavior

> Is American society actually worse than it used to be, as Schwartz seems to claim?
>
> While horrible things still happen here, we no longer have slavery or segregation;
>
> women, gay people, and nonwhites have much more freedom and opportunity.

Possible topic: The contrast between the evils of the past and the "evils" of present-day rudeness

ESSAY IN PROGRESS 5 ▶ **WRITING CRITICAL QUESTIONS**

Write critical questions in response to the reading you are preparing to write about. As you read the essay a second time, record additional reactions that occur to you. Some students prefer to use a different color of ink to record their second set of questions. (Refer to the sample student annotation shown on p. 45.)

Keep a Response Journal

A **response journal** is a section of your writing journal in which you record summaries of readings as well as your reactions to and questions about readings that arise as you annotate. Experiment with the following two ways to organize a response journal entry to discover the one that works better for you.

For more about keeping a journal, see Chapter 1, p. 18.

The open-page format.   On a blank page, write, outline, draw, or create a diagram to express your reactions to an essay. Because the open-page format encourages you to let your ideas flow freely, it may work well for creative and spatial learners. Figure 2.2 shows Karen Vaccaro's open-page response journal entry for "American Jerk." This entry suggests several possible topics to write about: identifying generational differences in defining civility, determining standards for civility, and recognizing subjectivity in evaluating behavior.

The two-column format.   Divide several pages of your journal into two columns or create a table with two columns. On the left, jot down five to ten quotations

FIGURE 2.2 Sample Open-Page Journal Format

People are always distracted because they are surrounded by many choices.

Who decides what is polite and what is rude? Where do the standards come from?

Changes in Civility and Politeness

People make choices about what is important to them, and they are always subjective.

What some people view as rude, others see as normal behavior.

Older generations always complain about a loss of civility in younger generations.

from the text. Choose remarks that seem important—that state an opinion, summarize a viewpoint, and so forth. On the right, write your response to each quotation. You might explain it, disagree with or question it, relate it to other information in the reading or in another reading, or tie it to your experiences. The two-column format forces you to think actively about an essay while you question what you have read and draw connections. Figure 2.3 provides an example of the two-column format.

FIGURE 2.3 Sample Two-Column Journal Format
Possible writing topics are noted

Topic: Types or degrees of rudeness

Topics: Contrast between/meaning of "socioeconomically disadvantaged" and "poor"

Quotations	Responses
"A moment when a roomful of even relatively evolved people will react with discomfort to an off-color joke about people of color—and when those same people have no compunction whatsoever about loudly ignoring one another as they blather into their cell phones."	This statement implies that racial jokes and talking on your cell phone are somehow on the same level of rudeness.
"No one is 'poor,' but many are 'socioeconomically disadvantaged.'"	There is a distinction between "poor" and "socioeconomically disadvantaged," and it's an important one. The first term has to do with money, but the second one also has to do with culture and opportunities.

You may find it useful to make a third column for a paraphrase of the quotation. Paraphrasing forces you to think about the meaning of the quotation, and ideas for writing may come to mind as a result.

For more on paraphrasing, see Chapter 22, p. 577.

ESSAY IN PROGRESS 6 ▸ WRITING A RESPONSE JOURNAL ENTRY

For "Superhero or Supervillain?" or another essay chosen by your instructor, write a response in your journal using the open-page or the two-column format.

Use a Reading-Response Worksheet

A reading-response worksheet guides and records your response while directing your thinking. Figure 2.4 shows the format of a response worksheet.

Try Alternative Learning Styles

The kinds of verbal strategies discussed in this chapter are important in engaging with reading selections, but other strategies may also help you read actively.

- **Spatial strategies.** Try enhancing your reading and writing by creating mental pictures of people and places. For example, while reading "American Jerk," create a mental image of a person behaving rudely. Graphic organizers and diagrams can help you organize the ideas in an essay.
- **Social strategies.** Try previewing a reading assignment with a classmate and discussing your reactions to it after reading. (Use the "Guide to Active Reading," pp. 26–41, and this "Guide to Responding to a Reading" to get started.)
- **Abstract strategies.** Try thinking about the patterns the author uses to persuade readers to accept his point of view. For example, does he tell stories (narration) or make comparisons? How effective are his methods?

LEARNING STYLE OPTIONS

- **Creative strategies.** Try imagining scenarios that confirm or challenge the author's points. Is he ignoring important considerations or overgeneralizing?
- **Concrete and pragmatic strategies.** Make the essay as "real" as possible by visualizing events occurring or by visualizing yourself interviewing the author, alone or with a panel of classmates. Or try connecting the ideas or examples in the reading with something you have experienced or read about in the news.
- **Emotional strategies.** Focus on the way the author uses the reader's feelings to convey an overall message and how he uses people or events in the essay to get his or her message across.
- **Rational strategies.** Focus on the logic of the ideas: How does the author argue for his conclusion? He uses many examples of rudeness, but are they all equally effective? Why or why not?

FIGURE 2.4   Reading-Response Worksheet

Reading-Response Worksheet

Title: *"American Jerk"*

Author: *Todd Schwartz*

First Impressions: *The article is funny, but a little extreme. I agree that some people are very concerned about political correctness, while others feel free to flaunt their racism, but are these the same people?*

Summary: *In "American Jerk," Todd Schwartz argues that people believe they are acting politely, while rudeness and incivility are on the rise. Schwartz claims that since we don't have to fight for our survival, we can act selfishly while pretending to be civil and that people are often rude because of their self-absorption. We can choose not to be rude.*

Connections to Your Own Experiences: *We've all experienced road rage, cell phones ringing/texting at the movies or with friends. On the other hand, political correctness has led to trigger warnings in school, teachers not using red pen for fear of hurting students' feelings, and parents even being afraid to discipline their kids and owners—their dogs.*

Analysis (issue, aspect, feature, problem)

1. *Schwartz seems to think we're ruder now than ever. But are we? Were slave holders polite to the people they "owned"? And is it the same people who are being overly politically correct and rude? I'm not sure his argument holds up*

2. *Is it really so bad to live in a place where people are politically correct? I like being able to walk down the street without men (generally) making comments about my body. That people can't make jokes about racial or ethnic groups is a good thing. Is that really too much political correctness?*

Write a Response Essay

A response essay presents an organized and focused discussion of the content of the reading assignment.

Determine the Content and Focus of Your Response Essay

Your response essay may include a brief summary of the reading assignment. However, most of your response should focus on interpreting and evaluating what you have read. Your essay should be focused; it should not present unrelated reactions to the reading or jump from idea to idea. Focus your response on:

- one key idea
- one primary question the essay raises
- one major issue it explores

For example, suppose your instructor asks you to read an article entitled "Advertising: A Form of Institutional Lying," which argues that advertisements deceive consumers by presenting half-truths, distortions, and misinformation. Your instructor then asks you to write a two-page paper responding to the essay but gives you no other directions. In writing this paper, you might take one of the following approaches.

- Discuss how you were once deceived by an advertisement, as a means of confirming the author's thesis and main points.
- Evaluate the evidence and examples the author provides, and determine whether the evidence is relevant and sufficient to support the claim.
- Discuss the causes or effects of deception in advertising that the author overlooks. (You may need to consult other sources to take this approach.)
- Evaluate the assumptions the author makes about advertising or consumers.

Follow the Steps for Writing a Response Essay

Use the following steps as a guide when writing response essays.

1. **Reread the writing you did in response to the selection.** Look for related ideas. Try to find ideas that fit together to produce a viewpoint or position toward the reading. (Do not attempt to cover all your ideas. Your essay should not analyze every aspect of the essay. Instead, you should focus on one feature or aspect.)
2. **Write a sentence that states your central point.** This sentence will become your thesis statement. It should state what your essay will assert or explain.
3. **Collect ideas and evidence from the reading to support your thesis.**
4. **Organize your ideas into essay form.** Your essay should have a title, introduction, body, and conclusion.
5. **Revise your essay.** Be sure that all your ideas support your thesis, you have explained your ideas clearly, and you have provided support from the reading for each one.
6. **Edit your sentences and words, and proofread for accuracy and correctness.**

For more about writing and supporting a thesis, see Chapter 5.

For more about drafting an essay, see Chapter 7.

For more about revising an essay, see Chapter 8.

Make sure your sentences are clear, concise, and varied, and your words are accurate, specific, and appropriate. Then use the suggestions in "Proofread Carefully" in Chapter 9 (pp. 211–13) to catch any remaining typos or formatting errors.

Write a two- to three-page paper in response to "Superhero or Supervillain?" (or whichever essay you've been writing about in previous Essay in Progress activities in this chapter). Choose one question or issue that the essay addresses and detail your response to it. Use the steps listed above and the ideas you generated in Essays in Progress 3–6 to develop your essay.

STUDENTS WRITE

"American Jerk"? How Rude! (but True)

Karen Vaccaro

Karen Vaccaro wrote the following essay in response to "American Jerk." As you read, notice how Vaccaro analyzes Schwartz's points about civility and the lack of it in our society.

Introduction: Identifies the article Vaccaro is responding to

Vaccaro's thesis statement indicates how her ideas differ from Schwartz's.

Vaccaro agrees with Schwartz.

Vaccaro offers examples of lack of concern.

In his article "American Jerk," Todd Schwartz claims that Americans today are both the most and the least civil we have ever been. Although the painful truth in these observations is a bit hard to take, Schwartz eases the reality by providing a great deal of humorous relief. Schwartz's claim is an apt one, and most of his observations about our current culture are accurate, but some of his observations and accusations are broad generalizations that don't always hold true.

"We have never been more concerned about the feelings of minority groups, the disabled, and the disadvantaged," Schwartz writes in paragraph 3, and he is right. We have become a culture obsessed with being PC (politically correct). I often carefully choose and often second-guess the words I use to describe anyone of a different race or physical or mental ability, for fear of offending anyone. And yet many people I encounter seem hardly concerned about offending me. Schwartz is right that "we have never been less concerned about the feelings of anyone with whom we share the road, the Internet, or the movie theater" (para. 3). Cyclists seem to have taken over city streets and even shout insults at me when I am walking in a crosswalk (and they are breaking the law by ignoring a red light). Despite many methods used to discourage theater goers from using their cell phones, cell phones ring during films, concerts, and plays.

1

2

In fact, last week I was at a live theater performance, and in the middle of an important scene, a cell phone rang in the audience—twice.

In another example of how (overly) civil we've become, Schwartz writes, "Schools won't let teachers use red pens to correct papers because . . . self-esteem might be bruised" (para. 4). This reminded me of the teaching internship I did while studying abroad in China one semester. I taught an English writing course to Chinese high school students. One day I was marking up the students' papers with a red pen (as I thought teachers were supposed to do). Another American teacher said, "I thought teachers weren't supposed to mark students' papers with red pens anymore." I asked if red was offensive to Chinese students. "No," she answered. "Some of my teachers back home in America said it's because red is a harsh color that really stands out from the black and white." "Well, yes, I thought that was the point," I said. "But it can make some students feel bad," she responded. "That's the silliest thing I've ever heard," I said as I went back to marking my students' papers with the red pen. Have we become so "civil" that we're afraid to teach students? Don't young men and women come to class expecting to learn something, knowing that at some point they will need to be corrected to see their mistakes so that they can truly learn?

Then there are the less civil aspects of our culture, as Schwartz so accurately points out. We Americans have become obsessed with reality television shows that often take advantage of the misfortune and embarrassment of others. In addition, "giant assault vehicles" (para. 7) dwarf other cars on the road, guzzle gas, often take up more than one parking space, and seem unnecessary on city streets in a time of environmental awareness and concern. Furthermore, we are so interested in our technological gadgets that we ignore real human-to-human interactions. "We're all talking to someone all the time," Schwartz writes, "but it's ever more rarely to the people we are actually with" (para. 8). I have noticed that my boyfriend often whips out his new iPhone. Even when we're walking and talking, catching up after days of not seeing one another, he's playing a new game, downloading a new app, or chatting with his friends. I myself can be guilty of this rude behavior. Sometimes I am spending time with one friend but will be texting another friend. I know it's rude, but I do it anyway (usually because the friend I'm with is doing the same thing and therefore it seems okay). We no

3

Vaccaro connects Schwartz's ideas to her own experience and affirms his ideas.

4

Vaccaro identifies another of Schwartz's points that she agrees with and admits that she is guilty of it as well.

longer realize how rude it is to divide our attention between two sources instead of giving our friend or loved one our full, undivided attention.

Where I must disagree with Schwartz, though, is his sweeping, unfounded statement that we are now living in "what must certainly be the rudest era in history" (para. 5). Really? Are we ruder than people who enslaved others and denied them any and all rights, including the right to be treated like human beings and not animals? Are people who refuse to "shut their inane traps" (para. 7) ruder than people in the time of segregation? It might be easy to convince ourselves that the present must be the rudest time in our history, since it is freshest in our minds, and we know it very well. But if Schwartz took time to flesh out his observations and accusations with concrete examples, he might rethink such a generalization.

Even if it doesn't fix the problems it calls attention to, Schwartz's entertaining and witty article forces us to stop and think about how contemporary American culture straddles the line between civility and rudeness. Many of his examples illustrate the hypocrisy of our behaviors and ways of thinking. Ultimately, Schwartz is correct in his claim that "we have arrived at simultaneously the most and least civil moment in U.S. history" (para. 2). I doubt, though, that Neanderthals — with their barbaric weapons and primitive hunting instincts — "were probably nicer to each other than we are" (para. 6).

Vaccaro moves to points with which she disagrees.

5

Conclusion: Vaccaro points out the value of Schwartz's article.

6

Analyzing the Writer's Technique

1. Express Vaccaro's thesis (central point) in your own words.
2. What kinds of information does Vaccaro include to support her thesis?
3. Where would additional examples help Vaccaro support her thesis?

Responding to the Reading

1. Vaccaro admits to texting one friend while spending time with another. Are you also guilty of acts of incivility? If so, describe one.
2. What steps or actions could be taken to build Americans' awareness of their lack of civility?
3. Do you agree or disagree that our culture is obsessed with political correctness? Give examples to support your answer.
4. Write a journal entry describing an act of incivility that you have observed or experienced that particularly disturbed or annoyed you.

Answers, Ex 3.1
1. T
2. F
3. F
4. T
5. F

3

Thinking, Reading, and Writing Critically

Thomas Imo/Getty Images

WRITING QUICK START Suppose your sociology instructor shows you this photo of a pile of old mobile phones in a scrap heap in Ghana; he asks you to write an analysis of what you see and what you think it means. Now imagine that your computer science instructor asks you to write an analysis of the same photograph. Write two paragraphs describing the photograph and analyzing its significance from these two different perspectives. How do your two paragraphs differ in word choice, content, and point of view?

As you analyzed and wrote about the photo, you not only had to question, evaluate, and respond critically, but you also chose words and ideas that helped to express your point of view. In this chapter you will learn strategies for thinking, reading, and writing critically that you can apply to reading essays, newspaper and magazine articles, textbook selections, works of literature, and visuals, including photographs and graphics, and that you can apply to essays and other college assignments you write.

In this chapter you will learn to:

- determine whether authors make reasonable inferences and use appropriate evidence
- analyze the author's tone, assumptions, generalizations, and omissions
- use critical thinking skills as you write
- interpret and think critically about photographs and graphics

Analyzing What You Read

We live in a world of overload, surrounded by news, opinions, advertisements, and other kinds of information everywhere we look (or listen). Sometimes the information we encounter presents ideas fully and fairly. More often, writers and speakers present only their own views on a topic, without fully exploring the range of positions. And sometimes writers and speakers present their positions in such a way as to make their viewpoint sound like the only logical option. So it is important to assess carefully the ideas and information we encounter. And since writers may not always be aware when unfair bias creeps in, it is also important to assess carefully the way you present your own ideas, making sure that you have presented them clearly and fairly. The sections that follow provide the tools you need to evaluate texts critically—both those you create and those you consume.

Analyze the Author's Ideas

To analyze an essay, begin by examining the author's ideas closely and critically. This involves knowing what the author *says*, and, more important, it involves making inferences about what the author *means*. It also involves examining the supporting evidence an author offers, distinguishing between fact and opinion, and identifying bias.

Make Reasonable Inferences

An **inference** is a reasonable guess based on the available facts and information, including content directly provided in the reading. Inferences are logical connections between what the writer states directly and what he or she implies. Consider the following situation.

> You have been attending your history class all semester; you participate in class and your interest in history is evident. Your scores on three exams were 95, 97, and 99, out of 100. You wrote one paper for the class and got an A on it. It is the end of the semester, your instructor has just announced the date of the final exam, and she asks you to stop and talk to her after class. During the class, the instructor also mentions some summer internships that she recently learned about.

In this situation, you are confident that you are passing the course. So what might she want to talk to you about? One reasonable inference is that it has something to do with the final exam, since it was just announced. Another possible inference is that she may want to encourage you to apply for one of the internships she mentioned. Here are some guidelines for making reasonable inferences.

1. **Understand the author's purpose and literal meanings.** Before you can make reasonable inferences, you need a clear understanding of the author's purpose and the reading's thesis statement, main ideas, and supporting details.
2. **Pay attention to details.** Sometimes details offer a hint regarding what the writer has implied or left unsaid. When you notice a striking or unusual detail, ask yourself: Why is this detail included? For example, read the following passage.

> Maria attends college, has a full-time job, takes care of her two children, cooks dinner for her family every night, and pays taxes. She doesn't *look* like an illegal immigrant, but this is how the U.S. government classifies her.

What is the writer's reason for including the detail about Maria's immigration status? Perhaps the writer is implying that undocumented workers are just like everyone else: They go to school, work, and have families. You might also reasonably infer that the writer disagrees with or questions this classification.

3. **Consider the facts.** Consider the complete set of facts provided in the reading. What is the writer trying to suggest with these facts? What conclusions do the complete set of facts support? Suppose a writer presents the following facts.

> Dr. Tannenbaum is an old-school doctor. His staff greets you by name and offers you a cup of coffee when you arrive for your appointment. A receptionist answers the phone and returns all calls promptly. Dr. Tannenbaum talks to you as if you're a human being, not just a medical chart, and he'll make house calls if you live alone and have no transportation to his office.

From these sentences, the conclusion is clear: The writer considers Dr. Tannenbaum an excellent doctor who treats his patients with respect.

4. **Examine word choices.** A writer's choice of words often conveys his or her feelings toward the topic. Look for words that are heavy with connotations (or associations) and ask yourself why the writer chose these words. For example, in the paragraph about Dr. Tannenbaum, the author uses the adjective *old-school* to imply a traditional doctor who cares about his patients.

5. **Support your inference with specific evidence.** Valid inferences are based on fact, context, and personal experiences. Be sure you have ample evidence to back up any inference you make. It would be incorrect to infer that Dr. Tannenbaum is highly skilled at diagnosing rare illnesses, for example, based on the information presented.

For more on connotation, see pages 61–62.

EXERCISE 3.1 ▸ MAKING REASONABLE INFERENCES

Read the following excerpt from "American Jerk" (p. 33) and answer the questions that follow.

> Pick your poison: reality television, slasher movies, video games, online porn, cell phones, automated answering systems, giant assault vehicles for trips to the grocery store, car stereos played at volumes easily heard on Jupiter, web-powered copyright infringement, people who will not shut their inane traps in movie theaters, and, lord help us, now even people who won't shut their inane traps during live theater.
>
> We're all talking to someone all the time, but it's ever more rarely to the people we are actually with. Our cell phones blare ringtones that no one else wants to hear. We love to watch TV shows about the stunningly predictable results of hand-feeding a grizzly bear or lighting a stick of dynamite with a cigarette. We also love shows where people lie to others for money and programs where snarky, slightly talented folks say vicious things to hopeful, and usually more talented, contestants.

1. What reasonable inferences can you make about the author's opinion of the typical American? Provide three adjectives that the author would use to describe Americans.
2. Which specific words or phrases in the selection provide hints regarding the author's attitude toward "American jerks"?
3. What details are particularly revealing about Americans' behavior?

HOW READERS WRITE   ▶   **IMPLIED MEANINGS**

Put yourself in your readers' position: As you write, consider the inferences your readers are likely to draw from what you write. To avoid confusion, misunderstanding, or misinterpretation, be sure to:

- **State accurately and precisely what you want readers to understand.** If you only suggest an idea, some writers may miss it. Others may misinterpret it. As a result, they may take away a meaning you did not intend.

- **Define your terms.** If a term, such as *masculinity*, has many possible shades of meaning, define the term as you intend to use it.

- **Choose your terms carefully.** Terms may convey not only their dictionary meaning (or denotation) but may also be associated with feelings. For example, both *slender* and *skinny* mean thin, but *slender* has positive overtones while *skinny* has negative ones.

- **Be careful when leaving readers to draw their own conclusions.** If you choose to leave an idea unstated, only implying what you mean, be sure that the examples or evidence you supply can lead only to the conclusion you intend.

For more about connotation versus denotation, see pages 61–62.

Assess the Evidence

In general, the most reliable information is based on solid *evidence*. When reading or writing, assess the evidence provided carefully.

- Is it reliable?
- Does the evidence support the writer's assertions?
- Has enough evidence been provided to make a strong case?

The following list of pros and cons will help you determine the reliability of some of the most common types of evidence.

Type	Pros	Cons
Personal experience or examples	• Can be powerful: No one understands an experience, for example, like a person who has lived it.	• Is subjective: Two people can experience the same event very differently. • May not offer enough examples to support a broad generalization.

Eyewitness reports	• May be powerful: Witnesses often have strong convictions that their memories are reliable.	• Are often inaccurate: Many studies have shown that memory is easily influenced. • May be subjective: If two people see a man running from a burning building, one may think, "What a lucky man! He escaped from the burning building," while the other may think, "That man started the fire."
Surveys	• May be highly reliable when conducted by experienced researchers who collect responses from a wide array of subjects.	• May be misleadingly worded or administered inconsistently, or may include responses from too narrow a spectrum of respondents.
Data and statistics	• Tend to be collected by academic researchers and members of professional research organizations who try to be as objective and accurate as possible.	• Can be used in ways that hide the truth. Example: A soda company may claim that "90% of the people in a taste test preferred our cola to the competitor's." This may be true, but consider how many subjects were tested, whether the test was run in a neutral location, and so on.
Evidence from scientific experiments and studies	• Usually considered highly reliable because they are based on the scientific method, a set of procedures that researchers follow to investigate their hypotheses and test the results of other experiments and studies.	• May apply to only a narrow range of cases. • Can be influenced by uncontrollable factors. Example: Studies on drug safety are often contradictory. • May reflect the economic or political biases of scientists conducting the study; occasionally, results may be falsified or outcomes misrepresented.

For more about analyzing data in graphics, see pp. 75–78.

HOW READERS WRITE ▶ EVIDENCE

One of your main responsibilities as a writer is to provide reliable and sufficient evidence to support your thesis. As you select data and evidence to support your ideas, think critically about:

• **Your audience.** Evidence that may convince one audience may be unconvincing to another. For example, a medical doctor may not be persuaded by anecdotal experiences of a remedy's effectiveness, while a group of patients may be more receptive to personal stories.

• **Your purpose.** Your purpose may influence the type of supporting evidence you provide in your essay. If your purpose is to explain the process of flying a drone, then you need accurate step-by-step facts and procedures. If your purpose, however, is to persuade readers that drones are a threat to safety, then you need reasons why drones can be hazardous and statistical evidence demonstrating that injuries and accidents have occurred as a result of the use of drones.

EXERCISE 3.2   **EVALUATING STATEMENTS**

Consider each of the following statements and the context in which it is made. List what types of information are missing that would help you weigh the evidence and evaluate the claim being made. What further types of evidence would you need to accept or reject the statement?

1. On the label of a bag of cookies: "CONTAINS 45% LESS FAT and 0 grams of TRANS FAT!"
2. In a printed campaign flyer for mayoral candidate Mary Johnson: "My opponent, Joe Smith, has been accused of serious conflicts of interest in the awarding of city contracts during his term as mayor."
3. In large print on the cover of a novel you see at the supermarket checkout: "'This novel is a . . . wild and exciting . . . ride through the rough-and-tumble days of the Gold Rush . . . full of . . . adventure and excitement. . . . Memorable.' — *New York Times*"

Distinguish Fact from Opinion

In order to determine whether an opinion has been adequately supported by facts, first you must be able to distinguish facts from opinions. The chart below will help.

Definition	Examples
Facts are objective statements of information that can be verified — that is, their truth can be established with evidence. Facts can be checked in trustworthy sources such as online dictionaries and Web reference sources such as refdesk.com.	• Many people who smoke marijuana do not go on to use more dangerous drugs. • Texting while driving has caused many accidents.
Opinions are subjective — that is, they differ by individual. They make a claim based on attitudes, feelings, or beliefs. These claims cannot be established definitely as either true or false, at least at the present time. Often they put forth a particular position or agenda.	• Marijuana use will probably be legalized in all fifty states by 2020. • People who text while driving should be fined and have their driver's licenses revoked.

When writers want to limit the extent of a claim, they often use qualifying words and phrases. For example, an expert on government debt may write, "It *seems likely* that Social Security payments will decline for future generations of Americans." Using such words and phrases limits the writer's responsibility for providing solid evidence to support the claim and allows other viewpoints to be acceptable.

HOW READERS WRITE ▸ **FACT AND OPINION IN ACADEMIC WRITING**

Facts are important to include in all types of academic writing. Including your opinions may or may not be appropriate, however.

Omit personal opinions from informative writing, unless they are specifically asked for. Examples of informative writing include summaries, paraphrases, lab reports, and research reports.

Include personal opinions in persuasive writing. Examples of persuasive writing include response papers, book or movie reviews, interpretations or analyses for history or literature classes, and proposals. When personal opinions are included, be sure to support them with evidence, reasons, or explanations.

EXERCISE 3.3 ▸ **DISTINGUISHING BETWEEN FACTS AND OPINIONS**

Label each of the following statements as fact (*F*) or opinion (*O*).

1. The best symphonies are shorter than twenty minutes.
2. About half the population of Uruguay lives in Montevideo.
3. More women earned doctoral degrees in engineering in 2016 than in 2000.
4. Private companies should not be allowed to operate concessions inside our national parks.
5. The mountains of northern Idaho contain the most scenic landscapes in the country.

EXERCISE 3.4 ▸ **WRITING FACTS AND OPINIONS**

For two of the following topics, write one statement of fact and one statement of opinion.

1. voter turnout rates in presidential elections
2. alternative energy solutions
3. the Super Bowl

Analyze the Author's Language

Authors often convey their message through the language they use, choosing words to create impressions, express feelings, even shape the readers' attitudes and feelings toward the topic. When analyzing language, be sure to consider denotative versus connotative meanings, figurative language, and euphemisms and doublespeak, as well as the writer's overall tone.

Consider Denotation versus Connotation

A **denotation** is the literal meaning of a word. For example, the denotation of the word *talking* is "expressing ideas using speech." A **connotation** is the set of additional meanings or associations that a word has taken on. Often a word's connotation has a much stronger effect on readers or listeners than its denotation does. The manner in which a politician talks to his or her audience might be described as "responding to ideas" (which carries a positive connotation), "discussing ideas" (which is an objective-sounding statement of fact), or "lecturing" or "ranting" (which give readers a negative impression). As you read, ask yourself, "What effect is the writer's word choice likely to have on readers?"

> **EXERCISE 3.5** **ANALYZING DENOTATION AND CONNOTATION**

For each of the following words, think of one word with a similar denotation but a positive connotation and another word with a similar denotation but a negative connotation.

> ▶ Group (of people): positive connotation, *audience*; negative connotation, *mob*

1. choosy
2. cheap
3. smart
4. bold
5. walk

Assess Figurative Language

Figurative language is language used in a nonliteral way to create a striking impression. For example, "The teenage boy tore into his sandwich like a hyena into a fallen zebra" creates a stronger image and conveys a more meaningful description than "He ate his sandwich quickly." The four common types of figurative expressions are:

1. **Personification.** Giving an object human qualities or characteristics. For example, in the sentence, "The urn glared at me from the mantelpiece," an urn (an inanimate object) is made to seem ominous.
2. **Symbolism.** Using one thing to represent something else. For instance, the White House is often considered a symbol of the United States. For many people, a car symbolizes freedom.
3. **Simile.** Comparing two items using the word *like* or *as*. For example, in *Peter Pan*, J. M. Barrie describes Mrs. Darling's mind with the following simile: "Her romantic mind was like the tiny boxes, one within the other, that come from the puzzling East."
4. **Metaphor.** Comparing two objects without using the word *like* or *as*. For example, Shakespeare wrote in *Romeo and Juliet*, "But soft, what light through yonder window breaks? / It is the east and Juliet is the sun." Here the speaker compares Juliet to the sun.

Most writers use figurative language to add color and shades of meaning to their writing. Carefully chosen, figurative language can persuade or convey a certain impression. For example, a political party may use powerful patriotic images, such as the White House or the bald eagle, to convey the idea that their agenda is "what's right for America." In the quote from *Peter Pan* above, the author uses figurative language to convey a strong impression of Mrs. Darling: Her mind is "romantic" (which may connote "unrealistic" or "out of touch"), and it is similar to tiny boxes within boxes from the "puzzling East." Through this simile, Barrie implies that Mrs. Darling's thought processes are puzzling, even to the people who know her.

When you encounter figurative language, ask yourself the following questions.

- How does it affect the writer's tone?
- Does it advance the author's agenda?
- Does it reveal bias?
- Is the author using figurative language to inform and delight or to hide something?

EXERCISE 3.6 ▶ RECOGNIZING SIMILES AND METAPHORS

Identify each of the following excerpts as a simile or metaphor and explain the items being compared. What is the tone of each excerpt? How does the figurative language help to convey a particular impression?

1. "She entered with ungainly struggle like some huge awkward chicken, torn, squawking, out of its coop." —Sir Arthur Conan Doyle, "The Adventure of the Three Gables"
2. "Her father had inherited that temper; and at times, like antelope fleeing before fire on the slope, his people fled from his red rages." —Zane Grey, *Riders of the Purple Sage*
3. "Shall I compare thee to a summer's day? / Thou art more lovely and more temperate." —William Shakespeare, Sonnet 18

HOW READERS WRITE ▶ FIGURATIVE LANGUAGE

Figurative language can freshen and energize your writing, or, if used inappropriately, confuse readers and lead to misunderstanding. When using figures of speech, consider your audience.

- **What meaning, detail, or nuance will the figure of speech add?** That is, how will the figure of speech enhance the reader's experience or understanding?

- **Will your audience understand the comparison or reference?** For the figure of speech to be effective, your readers will need a basic understanding of all terms used. For example, if you write a simile comparing an embarrassed friend with Hester Prynne (from Nathaniel Hawthorne's *The Scarlet Letter*), your point may be lost if your audience has never read this book.

- **Will the comparison appeal to your readers?** If you compare something sacred and valued by your audience to something commercial and entertaining, you may alienate them. For example, comparing a Gothic cathedral with a castle at Disneyland might offend some readers.

See Chapter 9, pp. 210–11, for more information about how to use figures of speech.

Identify Euphemisms and Doublespeak

A **euphemism** is a word or phrase that is used to avoid a word that is unpleasant, embarrassing, or otherwise objectionable. For example, many people think it is more considerate to say that a loved one "passed away" rather than "died." Many people prefer the terms *disabled* and *person with disabilities* to the word *handicapped*.

Doublespeak is a type of euphemism that uses deliberately unclear or evasive language to sugarcoat an unpleasant reality. As a critical thinker you should always be alert for it, particularly when reading about business and politics. For example, a government may say that it is engaging in "enhanced interrogation" when it is actually torturing prisoners; a corporation may tell employees that the company will be "downsizing" or "smartsizing" instead of saying that some of them will be laid off.

Euphemisms and doublespeak use roundabout, indirect, or neutralized language to avoid stating the facts directly. Any time you encounter such language, your critical-thinking skills should kick into gear. Ask yourself questions like these.

- What is the author trying to prevent me from knowing?
- Why is the author hiding something: to spare my feelings, avoid personal embarrassment, or hide something nasty about the author or the group the author represents?

EXERCISE 3.7 ▶ RECOGNIZING EUPHEMISMS AND DOUBLESPEAK

Answer each of the following questions.

1. The media often report about people from other countries who come to the United States without permission from the U.S. government or who stay here after their permission to visit has expired. Two terms are used to refer to these people: *illegal aliens* and *undocumented immigrants*. Discuss which term seems to have a more negative connotation and which seems more neutral. Why does each term carry the connotations it does? Is the more neutral term a euphemism? Why or why not?
2. Working with a classmate, brainstorm a list of euphemisms and doublespeak currently in use in the media. Be prepared to share your list with the class.

Analyze the Author's Tone

Tone refers to how a writer sounds to readers, and it is influenced by how the writer feels about his or her topic and readers and the language the writer uses to convey that attitude.

Tone is constructed primarily by:

- choosing words with the appropriate connotation
- using figurative language effectively
- using euphemism and doublespeak
- using stylistic features such as sentence patterns and length to lend emphasis

For more on sentence patterns and length, see Chapter 9, pp. 197–203.

Using these strategies effectively, a writer can communicate surprise, disapproval, disgust, admiration, gratitude, or amusement. These are just a few of the words commonly used to describe tone; Table 3.1 lists many others. Recognizing an author's tone will help you interpret and evaluate the message and its effect on you.

TABLE 3.1 Words Commonly Used to Describe Tone

angry	detached	impassioned	objective
arrogant	earnest	indignant	sarcastic
bitter	forgiving	informative	serious
compassionate	frustrated	joyful	sympathetic
condescending	hateful	mocking	worried

HOW READERS WRITE ▸ TONE

Finding the most appropriate and effective tone to use in a piece of writing requires you to think critically about the characteristics of your audience and determine what would be clear, understandable, and appealing to them. In choosing a tone, consider the following:

- **Knowledge of the subject.** A helpful, supportive tone may be best if your readers are unfamiliar with the subject. However, if your readers are knowledgeable about your subject, they may regard a helpful, supportive tone as demeaning or insulting.

- **Background and experience.** Consider your readers' gender, education, professional position, age, and so forth in analyzing what tone would be most appropriate. For example, a lighthearted, familiar tone might not be appropriate for an academic paper intended for your professor or other scholars in the field.

- **Attitudes and beliefs.** If your audience agrees with your position on an issue, a passionate, highly partisan tone may be welcome, but if your audience disagrees, a passionate tone may offend or alienate your readers.

EXERCISE 3.8 ▸ ANALYZING TONE

Read each of the following statements and describe its tone. Which words in the statement provide clues to the tone? (Refer to Table 3.1 if necessary.)

1. Do you eat canned tuna? Then you are at least partially responsible for the deaths of thousands of innocent dolphins, which are mercilessly slaughtered by fishermen in their quest for tuna.

2. The penalty for creating and launching a computer virus should include a personal apology to every person who was affected by the virus, and each apology should be typed—without errors!—on a manual typewriter.
3. Piles of solid waste threaten to ruin our environment, pointing to the urgent need for better disposal methods and strategies for lowering the rate of waste generation.
4. All poets seek to convey emotion and the complete range of human feeling, but the only poet who fully accomplished this goal was William Shakespeare.

> **EXERCISE 3.9** **EXPERIMENTING WITH TONE**
>
> Consider the following situation: A developer has received permission to bulldoze an entire city block filled with burned-out tenement buildings and abandoned factories. In their place, the developer is going to build a community of three hundred upscale condominiums for people who work in the city and want to live close to their jobs.
>
> Write three different sentences (or paragraphs) that react to this news. Make the tone of your first sentence *outraged*. Make the tone of your second sentence *joyful*. Make the tone of your third sentence *nostalgic*.

Analyze the Author's Assumptions, Generalizations, and Omissions

Authors make decisions or take shortcuts that can influence readers' understanding. For example, they make assumptions and generalizations, and they decide which information to include or exclude. As a critical reader and writer, analyze the author's assumptions and assess whether the generalizations the author makes are fair and whether he or she omits any information that is important to a full understanding of the subject.

Recognize the Author's Assumptions

An **assumption** is an idea or principle the writer accepts as true and makes no effort to prove. Often the writer implies assumptions rather than stating them directly.

Some assumptions are fair and reasonable; others are not. For example, it is reasonable to assume that most of the people who read *People* magazine are interested in celebrities. It is not reasonable to assume that readers of *People* magazine are Republicans.

Assumptions can be based on any combination of the following:

- anecdotal evidence
- facts
- opinions
- values and beliefs
- personal experiences
- background

Writers often make assumptions at the beginning of an essay and then base the rest of the essay on that assumption. If the assumption is false or cannot be proven, then the ideas that flow from it may also be incorrect. For instance, the following excerpt begins with an assumption (highlighted) that the writer makes no attempt to prove or justify.

> Childbirth is a painful experience, intolerable even with appropriate medications. In response to this pain, modern women should accept the painkillers offered to them by their doctors. Why be a martyr? You have to suffer sleepless nights because of your child for the rest of your life; bring them into this world on your terms—pain free. Women should not be embarrassed or reluctant to request anesthesia during labor.

The author assumes that all women find childbirth intolerably painful and then argues that women should request anesthesia during labor. But if the writer's initial assumption is false, much of the argument that follows should be questioned.

As you read, look for assumptions the author takes for granted, and then decide whether these assumptions are realistic and reasonable by asking questions like these.

- Are these assumptions supported by facts?
- Does the writer use terms that have more than one meaning or interpretation? Would the writer's preferred definition be acceptable to most readers?
- How do the writer's assumptions reinforce or challenge social norms (or standards)?
- What effects do these assumptions have on the essay? Whose interests are served?
- What information, beliefs, or values, if any, would raise doubts about this assumption?

The answers to these questions will help you determine whether arguments or opinions based on these assumptions make sense. If you disagree with some of the assumptions in a source, check other sources to obtain different viewpoints.

HOW READERS WRITE   ASSUMPTIONS

In your writing, you will undoubtedly make assumptions that reflect your own beliefs and traditions. But be on the lookout for assumptions that may not be shared.

- **Be sure your assumptions are reasonable and supportable.** You may assume, for example, in an essay on how to overcome rising college costs, that a college education is valuable and worthwhile. Recognize, however, that while most readers would agree with this assumption, some may not.

- **If readers are likely to disagree with your assumption, include evidence that validates your assumption.** You could offer statistics showing, for example, that on average a college education increases lifetime earnings.

For more about reasoning errors, see Chapter 19, p. 508.

EXERCISE 3.10 ▶ IDENTIFYING ASSUMPTIONS

Each of the following statements contains one or more assumptions. Identify the assumption(s) made in each statement.

1. Computer users expect Web sites to entertain them with graphics, sound, and video.
2. In response to the problem of ozone depletion, the U.S. Environmental Protection Agency has designed various programs to reduce harmful emissions. It wants to stop the production of certain substances so that the ozone layer can repair itself over the next fifty years.
3. Only the routine vaccination of all children can eliminate the threat of serious disease and ensure optimum public health. These shots should be administered without hesitation. Parents must have full confidence in their doctors on this matter.
4. Since so many athletes and coaches approve of the use of performance-enhancing drugs, these substances should be allowed without regulation.
5. Because they recognize that meat consumption is environmentally damaging, environmentalists are often vegetarians.

EXERCISE 3.11 ▶ IDENTIFYING ASSUMPTIONS IN A READING

Reread "American Jerk" on pages 33–34. What assumptions does the author make in the first four paragraphs of the essay?

Assess the Author's Generalizations

A **generalization** is a claim based on one or more specific examples and applied more widely. Many writers generalize to argue a point, and generalizations may be reasonable or not. They are unreasonable when they are based on too little evidence or when all the variables are not taken into consideration (hasty generalization) and also when the conclusion is applied more widely than the evidence supports (sweeping generalization). Here's an obvious example of sweeping generalization: A woman who feels unfulfilled in her emotional life divorces her husband, leaves her children, and decides to travel the world. As she travels, she learns more about herself and falls in love with a new man. Based on this one woman's experience, is it safe to assume that all women in search of a richer emotional life should leave their husbands and children and travel the world? Of course not.

Most generalizations, however, are not so clearly reasonable or unreasonable. Imagine you are reading an article by a writer who argues that cars should be prohibited in congested cities. To support this claim, the writer cites studies showing the benefits of banning cars in three European cities. Is such a generalization fair? The reader must decide whether these three case studies provide *sufficient* evidence for such a generalization.

When assessing generalizations, ask yourself the following questions to determine whether such generalizations are justified.

- How many examples has the author provided?
- Are these examples representative of the situation? That is, do the examples represent most people's experiences?

- Can the generalization be proved scientifically? In other words, is there a scientific consensus about the generalization?

Generalizations can provide many ideas for your own writing. An informative essay might look at the evidence supporting and contradicting a generalization. A persuasive essay might argue that an assumption is unreasonable or unfair.

HOW READERS WRITE > GENERALIZATIONS

Ask yourself these questions to analyze the generalizations you make in your own writing.

- **Is it logical?** Is your generalization one that most reasonable people would accept? For example, most would not accept the generalization "Because Dr. Harper is young, she is bound to be a good doctor," because age is not commonly associated with medical competence.

- **Is it supportable?** Can you provide concrete and convincing evidence that will encourage your readers to accept your generalization? For example, you would find it difficult if not impossible to support the claim "Every college student is primarily interested in obtaining a high-paying job," because you could not find out what every single college student's goals are.

For more about problems of logical reasoning, see Chapter 19, p. 508.

EXERCISE 3.12 > IDENTIFYING GENERALIZATIONS

Label each of the following statements fact (*F*) or generalization (*G*). Indicate what support or documentation would be necessary for you to evaluate its accuracy.

1. Many women want to become pilots.
2. Elephants can vocalize at frequencies below the range of human hearing.
3. In certain parts of the Red Sea, the temperature of the water can reach 138 degrees Fahrenheit.
4. Most people who live in San Diego are associated with the U.S. Navy.
5. People all over the world showed sympathy by donating money to Serbian refugees.

Look for Purposeful Omissions

Writers and speakers sometimes mislead by omission.

- They leave out essential information, background, or context, or include only the details that favor their position.
- They adopt the passive voice (*a decision was made*) to avoid taking or assigning responsibility for an action.

- They use vague nouns and pronouns (*they are bleeding our city's coffers dry*) to avoid specifying exactly what or whom they are referring to.

Consider an article written by a parent who has home-schooled her children. As an advocate of home schooling, she is likely to emphasize her children's educational progress and her own sense of personal fulfillment achieved by teaching her children. However, she may omit information—for example, that home-schooled children sometimes feel lonely or isolated from their peers. She also may refer to home schooling as "better" for children without specifying exactly what it is better than (her local public school, public schools in general, or any kind of school) or in what ways it is better.

Regardless of what you are reading, ask yourself the following questions to be sure you are getting full and complete information.

- Has any important information or contradictory evidence been omitted? What, if anything, am I not being told?
- Is it clear to whom actions or thoughts are being attributed? If not, why not?
- Is there another side to this argument or aspect to this topic that I should consider?
- Based on my own knowledge and experience, how do I evaluate this material?

To answer these questions, you may need to do some additional reading or research.

EXERCISE 3.13 ▸ **IDENTIFYING PURPOSEFUL OMISSIONS**

Read the following scenarios and determine what information is being withheld from you. What additional information do you need to determine whether you are being misled?

1. You see a TV ad for a fast-food restaurant that shows a huge hamburger topped with pickles, onions, and tomatoes. The announcer says, "For a limited time, get your favorite burger for only ninety-nine cents!"
2. You open your mailbox and find a letter from a credit-card company. The letter invites you to open a charge card with no annual fee and offers you instant credit if you return the attached card in a postage-paid envelope.
3. You are shopping online for an exercise bike and find one that appears to be a good deal. The site states that it requires some assembly, shipping and handling charges may apply, and seat cushion style may vary.

EXERCISE 3.14 ▸ **IDENTIFYING BIAS IN A READING SELECTION**

Reread the excerpt from "American Jerk" in Exercise 3.1. Using the techniques described in "Analyze the Author's Language," write a paragraph explaining whether you detect hidden bias in the selection or whether the writer makes clear that he is expressing only one viewpoint among others. If you detect bias, point to purposeful omissions or other strategies (such as his word choices) the writer uses to hide his biases. If you do not, explain why you feel the excerpt is not biased.

Use the Patterns of Development to Think and Read Critically

The patterns you will learn to identify and use in Part 3 suggest useful questions for critical reading, questions that highlight aspects of the reading selection you might not otherwise have considered. Each chapter in Part 3 includes a box called "How Writers Read." These boxes explore in depth the concerns critical readers and thinkers should address as they analyze and evaluate readings using each pattern.

Use Synthesis to Think and Read Critically

At times you may realize that you do not have sufficient knowledge or experience to analyze and evaluate an author's ideas. In such cases, you may need to locate additional sources to fill in the gaps, provide additional viewpoints, challenge the author's assumptions or speculations, or offer more detailed evidence. When you synthesize information from sources to assess or challenge a writer's assumptions or claims, you must do two things:

1. Synthesize, or merge, information from sources with your existing, but limited, knowledge and experience.
2. Test the evidence or claims from the original reading against your own experience and what you've learned from the new sources.

Use the following questions as guidelines.

- **On what do two or more of the sources agree?** On what, if anything, do they disagree?
- **What new information or perspectives did you encounter?** Did they reinforce or challenge information or ideas in the other source(s)?
- **In what ways do the new sources help you understand the original reading?** Do they provide context, expand upon a topic, or challenge the writer's interpretation, for example?

See Chapter 22, pp. 580–83, for more about synthesis.

EXERCISE 3.15 ▶ SYNTHESIZING YOUR SKILLS

As a cumulative activity and to synthesize all the critical-thinking strategies you have learned in this chapter, refer to the reading "Superhero or Supervillain?" (Chapter 2, pp. 38–41) to answer the following questions.

1. Using the information you find in the introduction to the reading and in the reading itself, evaluate Will Oremus's qualifications to write about human-enhancement technologies.
2. What types of evidence does Oremus use to support his ideas? Give several examples, and explain in a sentence or two whether the evidence is relevant.

3. List at least two inferences Oremus makes and at least one inference the researchers he discusses make. Identify at least three statements of fact and three statements of opinion.
4. Identify at least five words with positive or negative connotations.
5. Describe the author's tone. What effect does the tone have on you as a reader? How effective do you find it?
6. Identify at least one assumption the author makes.
7. What generalizations does the author make? List two.
8. What additional information would you need to evaluate Oremus's claims about the likelihood of certain kinds of superpowers being used for good or evil?
9. Based on your analysis, do you think Oremus seems fair or biased? Write a paragraph justifying your answer.

Reading Visuals Critically

Visuals appear everywhere—on television and in movies; in magazines, newspapers, textbooks, and presentation slides; on signs, flyers, and billboards; in print and online. They may appear on their own, but often they are combined with text to make a message even more effective. Visuals are used so widely because they can convey information and impressions, sell products and ideas, raise questions, and trigger emotions. Because they are so powerful, make sure you study them as carefully as you read, analyze, and evaluate written text. You should also choose them carefully when you use them in your own writing.

For more about how to incorporate a visual into an essay, refer to Chapter 5, pp. 128–30.

Consider, for example, the public service advertisement (PSA) from LoveIsRespect.org. What did you notice first? Perhaps you noticed the headline with its shocking statistic:

Courtesy of loveisrespect.org and the National Domestic Violence Hotline. LoveIsRespect.org

"Dating Abuse Affects 1 in 3 Young People." Or perhaps you noticed the photographs of hands holding speech bubbles telling viewers what love really is ("the closest thing we have to magic," "caring enough to ask," "respect," "playing fair"). Or maybe the white shape in the bottom-left corner caught your eye, with its message: "Connect NOW!"

Whatever you noticed first, second, or third, when you put the text and images together, you recognized the purpose of the ad: to help young people who may be involved in abusive relationships understand what a loving relationship should be all about and to provide them with help to "break the cycle." The design, the colors, and the headline contrasting with the photos arranged in the shape of a heart below—together these elements make a dramatic statement about love and self-respect. By combining words and images, this PSA makes the issue of abusive relationships much more compelling and engaging than it would have been with written text alone.

For more on using visuals in your writing, see Chapter 5, pp. 128–30.

Analyze Photographs

Use these guidelines when reading photographs and any words (a caption, labels, slogans, text) that accompany them.

1. **Preview the visual.** What is its main subject? What did you notice first, and how did it affect you?
2. **Study the visual as a whole, and then examine its parts.** What is its focal point? What details appear in the foreground and the background? (If you are a verbal learner, translating the photo into words may be helpful.) Is it a close-up or a distance shot? (Close-ups may reveal emotions; distance shots provide more context.)
3. **Read the caption and any accompanying text, consider the context, and make connections.** What information about time, place, or subject is provided? What does the author want to emphasize? How does the photo relate to the ideas presented in the surrounding text? What happened before or after the photo was taken? Is any other context provided?
4. **Determine the author's purpose and intended message.** Is the purpose to inform, amuse, shock, persuade, or some combination of these or other motives? Is the photo intended to elicit a powerful reaction from viewers or to provide information?

LEARNING STYLE OPTIONS

What do you learn when you apply these guidelines to the photograph in Figure 3.1, which is taken from a reading textbook?

FIGURE 3.1   **Reading Happens Anytime, Anywhere**

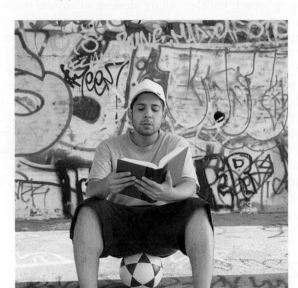

Glow - Hola/Glow - Hola/Superstock

EXERCISE 3.16   **ANALYZING A TEXTBOOK PHOTO**

Apply the guidelines for analyzing photos on page 73 to the photo in Figure 3.2, which is taken from an economics textbook. Then answer these questions.

1. Describe your first impression of the photo.
2. Summarize what is happening in the photo. What details convey this impression? Is it a close-up or distance shot? What is revealed (or hidden) about the subject of the photograph as a result?
3. What does the caption or any context contribute to your understanding of the photo? (This photograph appeared in an economics textbook in a chapter titled "Factor Markets and Distribution of Income.")
4. Why did the author include this photo? Does it reveal any assumptions or biases?
5. Does the photo look staged, edited, or touched up? If so, what details convey this impression?
6. Does the photo achieve the author's purpose? What other kinds of photos or visuals might the writer have used to make the same point? (Provide reasons or use details from the photograph to support your claim.)

FIGURE 3.2 ▶ The Value of a Degree

If you have doubts about completing college, consider this: Factory workers with high school diplomas earn much less than college graduates. The present discounted value of the difference in lifetime earnings is as much as $1 million. Monika Graff/The Image Works

EXERCISE 3.17 ▶ WRITING ABOUT PHOTOS

Examine one of the photographs that accompanies the reading "Superhero or Supervillain?" in Chapter 2 (pp. 38–41) or another reading chosen by your instructor. Then write a paragraph explaining what the photo shows and analyzing the factors that contribute to the impression it makes.

Analyze Graphics

Graphics organize and condense information, making lengthy or complicated data and concepts easier to understand. Writers use many types of graphics; the purpose of each of the common types is summarized in Table 3.2.

TABLE 3.2   **Graphics and Their Purposes**

Type of Graphic	Purpose	Example
Pie (circle) chart	To show the relationships among parts of a whole; to show how given parts of a unit are divided or classified	A chart showing the proportions of different racial and ethnic groups in the U.S. population
Bar graphs	To make comparisons between quantities or amounts	A graph comparing the number of calories needed by men and women leading sedentary lives
Line graphs	To show changes in a variable over time or to compare relationships between two or more variables	A graph showing variations in quiz scores
Tables	To organize and condense data; to compare and classify information	A table showing how many calories men and women need daily for various age groups with either an active or a sedentary lifestyle
Diagrams and flowcharts	To explain processes or procedures or show how things work	A diagram showing the parts of an essay

Use these guidelines when analyzing graphics and any words (a caption, labels, slogans, text) that accompany them.

1. **Preview the table or chart.** Read the title and caption (if any) and look quickly at the table or chart. What is it supposed to show?
2. **Look at the headings (of tables/charts), labels (of figures), and legends (of charts/ figures) to determine how the data are organized.** The headings and labels should indicate the variables. The legend (or guide to the colors, symbols, terms, or other information) should show what is being analyzed. A scale shows how measurements should be read.
3. **Read the caption (if any) and any discussion of the graphic in the text, and make connections.** Does the text explain why the graphic was included or what it is intended to show? (If not, make your own connections between the text and graphic.) To understand a complicated graphic, you may need to study the text

and graphic carefully several times. Read the whole explanation in the text before looking back at the graphic.

4. **Study the data to try to identify trends or patterns.** Note unexpected changes (such as sudden increases or decreases in amounts), surprising statistics, or unexplained variations. Summarize any trends and note any patterns you find. Writing will crystallize the idea in your mind, and your notes will be useful for review.

5. **Check the source of the data.** Are the data from a reliable source? Are they up to date?

EXERCISE 3.18 ANALYZING A TABLE

Use the guidelines above to analyze Table 3.3.

TABLE 3.3 U.S. Book Reading Habits, 2016

	18–29	30–49	50–64	65+
Read book in any format	80	73	70	67
Read a print book	75	65	64	61
Read an e-book	36	32	24	19
Listened to an audiobook	16	15	15	9
Read on a tablet	15	18	15	10
Read on an e-book reader	5	9	9	7
Read on a desktop/laptop	16	11	9	5
Read on a phone	22	18	9	4

SOURCE: Data from "Book Reading, 2016." Pew Research Center, 7 Mar.–4 Apr. 2016, pewinternet
.org/2016/09/01/book-reading-2016/.

EXERCISE 3.19 WORKING WITH TABLES AND FIGURES

Study the figure below, which converts some of the data from Table 3.3 into a line graph, and answer the following questions.

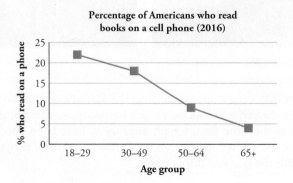

Percentage of Americans who read books on a cell phone (2016)

1. Compare this figure with Table 3.3. What variables does this figure use? Which data from that table were used to create this figure?
2. What title would you give this figure? The title should accurately describe the information conveyed by the figure.
3. Write a caption for this figure that accurately describes the trend(s) it shows.

Think Critically about Photos and Graphics

Just as you should critically examine all the words you read, you should also critically examine all visuals that accompany a reading. Photographs and graphics may reflect bias or distort information, either intentionally or unintentionally. For example, an author may choose more or less powerful or flattering photographs demonstrating support or criticism of a person or issue. (See Figure 3.3 below.)

FIGURE 3.3   The Power of Pictures

Featureflash Photo Agency/Shutterstock.com   JStone/Shutterstock.com

Or an author may crop a photo to distort the viewer's perception (see Figure 3.4). The first photo in the series shows only a gun barrel, apparently pointing at the head of the wounded soldier (the focal length appears to have been shortened); the last photo shows only the soldier being given water from a canteen; only the photo in the middle shows both the gun and the canteen.

FIGURE 3.4   Cropping Photographs to Affect Viewers' Reactions

AP Photo/Itsuo Inouye. Cropping information from Antonskarp, sci-ence.org/cropping/

When reading graphics, consider also whether showing the data in a different type of graphic would change the reader's perception of the information. Compare Figure 3.5 (below) with Exercise 3.19 (p. 77). How does showing the data in a bar graph change your perception of the data?

FIGURE 3.5   Shaping Readers' Perceptions through Depiction of the Data

Percentage of Americans who read books on a cell phone (2016)

% who read on a phone

Age group: 18–29, 30–49, 50–64, 65+

Finally, consider whether the scale or units of measurement are misleading in any way. Reducing the scale, for example, can make differences seem huge, and expanding the scale can make them seem tiny. Compare the bar graph in Figure 3.6 (on p. 80) with that in Figure 3.5. The data used in both charts are the same, but because the chart in Figure 3.5 reduces the scale, the difference between the groups appears more dramatic than it is.

FIGURE 3.6   Misleading by Adjusting the Scale

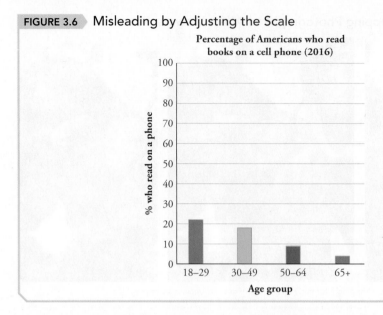

Percentage of Americans who read
books on a cell phone (2016)

Be especially careful when pictures are used in graphics instead of lines or bars (Figure 3.7). The labels in this graphic clearly indicate that more U.S. households own dogs (36.5%) than own cats (30.4%). But the relative size of the two animals suggests that the percentage difference is much greater than 6.1% (36.5–30.4%). If you looked only at the images, you might assume that dog ownership is much greater than it really is. You might also reasonably conclude that there are more pet dogs than pet cats in the United States, but the labels indicate that the pictures represent households that own *at least one* cat or dog. Some households may own two, six, or even ten cats. In fact, as of 2013 the American Pet Products Association estimates that there were over 10 million more pet cats than pet dogs in the United States. But you wouldn't know this from a glance at this graphic.

FIGURE 3.7   Cat and Dog Ownership in the United States

30.4% of U.S. households   36.5% of U.S. households
own at least one cat   own at least one dog

SOURCE: Data from American Pet Products Association, American Veterinary Medicine Association, and the Humane Society of the United States. humanesociety.org/issues/pet_overpopulation/facts/pet_ownership _statistics.html, avma.org/KB/Resources/Statistics/Pages/Market-research-statistics-US-pet-ownership.aspx. (*cat*) © Benjamin Simeneta/Shutterstock.com; (*dog*) © ARTSILENCE/Shutterstock.com

Just-in-Time Guide to Reading and Responding

Many of the reading assignments for your college courses will be straightforward. Some, however, may make you throw your up hands and say, "I can't handle this!" This guide will help you overcome the obstacles you face and find answers to the questions you have. This guide is the help you need, just in time. Because reading and writing are two sides of the same process, much of what you learn in this Just-in-Time Guide can be flipped and applied to issues you encounter as a writer.

1 ▶ Getting Started

Each time you begin a new reading, you are starting from scratch. What do you do if you're having difficulty getting started?

1a If I don't know anything about the subject, what should I do?

Having even a small amount of background knowledge will help you orient yourself to the reading, which will help you learn more. Use these two key strategies: Preview the reading, and Google the topic.

1. **Preview the reading.** You learned to preview in Chapter 2 (pp. 27–30). It is a fast and easy way to become familiar with the reading's content and organization, and it gives you a good sense of what the selection is about. If you're having trouble getting started (or even if you're not), begin by previewing.

For more about credibility, see Chapter 21, pp. 559–63.

2. **Google the topic, especially unfamiliar terminology.** To find needed background information, look for sources that are written for the beginner or novice and that come from a credible source. For example, suppose your biology instructor assigns a chapter titled "Biodiversity." A quick Web search will help you learn the basic meaning of *biodiversity* ("the variety of life in a particular habitat"). *Note:* Many other search engines can be as effective as Google. Try using Ask.com, WebCrawler, and Yahoo if Google doesn't return the results you want. Also, if you're a visual learner, try searching YouTube for videos that provide background information on your topic.

1b What can I do to keep my mind on an unappealing topic or selection?

All readings are not equally interesting. How do you stay focused on dry, technical reading assignments, especially when you're not particularly interested in the topic?

1. **Ask and answer questions.** Create a dialogue with the text. By asking and answering questions about the reading, you turn the reading into a quest for information. You can base your questions on titles or chapters or sections, like so:

Chapter Title or Section	Questions
Psychological Disorders	What is a psychological disorder?
Supply and Demand	What are supply and demand?
The Human Development Index	What is the human development index, and what does it measure?

2. **Be active: write, think, talk aloud, draw diagrams.** Read with a pencil in your hand. Take notes in the margins, sketch out important concepts, or write a response at the top or bottom of the page. Get up, walk around the room, and talk to yourself about what you've read to get ideas flowing.

3. **Predict what will come next.** Writers provide signals (transitions and repetition) to prepare you for what's coming next. Watch for these cues. When you see one, stop for a moment to predict what the author is about to say.

> Nonverbal communication means communication that takes place without words or sounds. Body language is a key form of nonverbal communication. For example, standing with your arms crossed can send a signal that you are feeling mistrustful, insecure, or uncomfortable.

Expect an illustration of body language to follow.

4. **Brainstorm with classmates.** Talk with your classmates to clarify concepts and form study groups. In your study group, prepare for exams by trying to figure out which questions will be on the exam. If a group member comes up with a question that you can't answer, write it down and ask your instructor during the next class session.

5. **Relate the author's ideas to your own experience.** You will learn the material more effectively and have a better sense of its relevance if you can relate the ideas you are reading about to your own life or experience. Consider this example from a sociology textbook.

> A dyad is a group of two people, the smallest possible social group.

My parents are a dyad. So is any couple.

1c How can I figure out what I am supposed to learn from an assignment?

Your instructor and your course materials (such as your syllabus or textbook) can help you determine what exactly you need to learn from each assignment.

1. **Take cues from your instructor.** Often your instructor will identify the goals for each assignment. If you're not sure of your instructor's expectations, ask.

Your Instructor Says . . .	Clue: What You Should Learn
"Read the excerpt from Maya Angelou's *I Know Why the Caged Bird Sings* and come to class prepared to discuss it."	A discussion generally centers on key ideas, so you know that you are not expected to memorize every detail in the reading selection.
"Read the chapter on sensation and perception, and be ready for a pop quiz."	Read for main ideas, because most pop quizzes test on major concepts, not tiny details.
"Come to the lab knowing all the bones in the human arm."	Memorize *all* the bones in the arm, not just a few of them.

2. **Refer to the syllabus.** Determine how each assignment matches the course goals or learning objectives on the syllabus, and spend more time on readings that directly relate to each of those objectives. If you are unsure of the goal of any

For more about how to use a syllabus, see Chapter 1, pp. 9–11.

given assignment, don't be shy about asking your instructor. Do *not* ask "Will this be on the test?"—which implies that you care only about the right answers and not about gaining knowledge or learning. Rather, ask "What should I be able to do after reading this assignment?"

3. **Use learning objectives.** Learning objectives often appear in textbooks, either at the beginning of the chapter (as in this text) or at the beginning of each new section. They often begin with imperative verbs (commands) like *describe, list, explain, define, compare, summarize,* or *analyze.* As you complete each section, make sure you can do exactly what the learning objective says you must do.

Learning Objective	What You Must Do
Apply broken windows theory to the experience of New York City in the 1980s.	Show *how* New York City used broken windows theory in the 1980s. Being able to *define* broken window theory is not enough to accomplish this objective.
List and *explain* the four key elements of management.	Identify each of the four key components of management (planning, organizing, leading, and controlling) *and* describe what each one is or does.

1d What should I do when an assignment has me feeling overwhelmed or completely lost?

Sometimes, despite your best efforts, you feel completely defeated by an assignment. No matter how hard you try, you can't make any progress—but you still have to complete it. What should you do?

1. **Read the headnote or chapter introduction.** Both provide invaluable pathways into the reading.
   - A *headnote* is brief information about the assignment that appears after the author and title, but before the reading itself. Headnotes are often included with essays or literature. They provide key biographical information about the author, along with some context about the reading.
   - A *chapter introduction* often includes a *vignette,* or story, or a visual that helps to set the stage for the chapter. Many students are tempted to skip the chapter introduction because they think, "I just want to get on with it." Skipping chapter introductions is a mistake, because they often include interesting examples that bring concepts to life.

2. **Read the items that follow the reading.** A highly effective way to prepare yourself for a reading assignment is to preview the end-of-chapter material.
   - Lists of **key terms** identify essential vocabulary.
   - **Summaries and comprehension, discussion, and critical-thinking questions** signal which material is most important in the chapter.

Core Concepts Summary

2.1 THE ATOM IS THE FUNDAMENTAL UNIT OF MATTER.

Atoms consist of positively charged protons and electrically neutral neutrons in the nucleus, and negatively charged electrons darting around the nucleus. page 2-1

The number of protons determines the identity of an atom. page 2-2

Protons and neutrons together determine the mass of an atom. page 2-2

Protons and electrons determine the charge of an atom. page 2-3

Negatively charged electrons travel around the nucleus in regions called orbitals. page 2-3

The periodic table of the elements reflects a regular and repeating pattern in the chemical behavior of elements. page 2-3

2.2 ATOMS CAN COMBINE TO FORM MOLECULES LINKED BY CHEMICAL BONDS.

Electrons that occupy the outermost energy level (shell) of an atom (valence electrons) determine its ability to combine with other atoms to form molecules. page 2-4

A covalent bond results from the sharing of electrons between atoms to form molecular orbitals. page 2-4

A polar covalent bond results when two atoms do not share electrons equally as a result of a difference in the ability of the atoms to attract electrons, a property called electronegativity. page 2-5

Core concepts summary, pp. 2-19, from Morris, James, et al., *How Life Works*, W. H. Freeman, 2013

3. **Talk to your instructor.** When all else fails, ask your instructor for help. He or she may be able to recommend background readings or study aids, refer you to the tutoring center, and offer other tools that will help you. Do not be afraid to approach your instructors; they are there to help you learn.

2 Learning Words

Words are the building blocks of language; they are the keys to both reading and writing more effectively. As a college student, you will encounter many unfamiliar words.

2a Do I need to learn every unfamiliar word?

The answer is no! (This is not the answer you expected, right?) It is impossible to learn all the words in the English language. Instead, focus on learning vocabulary that you will need to write effectively in your classes (including essay exams).

Each academic discipline has its own vocabulary, a set of terms that is unique to the field or that is used in a specific way. For example, in psychology, you may need to learn terms such as *placebo effect* ("improvement resulting from the belief that medicine is effective") or understand the specialized meaning of the word *extinction* ("the gradual weakening of conditioned behavior").

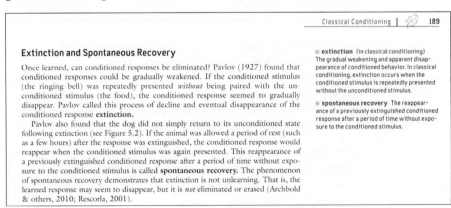

Classical Conditioning | 189

Extinction and Spontaneous Recovery

Once learned, can conditioned responses be eliminated? Pavlov (1927) found that conditioned responses could be gradually weakened. If the conditioned stimulus (the ringing bell) was repeatedly presented *without* being paired with the unconditioned stimulus (the food), the conditioned response seemed to gradually disappear. Pavlov called this process of decline and eventual disappearance of the conditioned response **extinction.**

Pavlov also found that the dog did not simply return to its unconditioned state following extinction (see Figure 5.2). If the animal was allowed a period of rest (such as a few hours) after the response was extinguished, the conditioned response would reappear when the conditioned stimulus was again presented. This reappearance of a previously extinguished conditioned response after a period of time without exposure to the conditioned stimulus is called **spontaneous recovery.** The phenomenon of spontaneous recovery demonstrates that extinction is not unlearning. That is, the learned response may seem to disappear, but it is *not* eliminated or erased (Archbold & others, 2010; Rescorla, 2001).

▪ **extinction** (in classical conditioning) The gradual weakening and apparent disappearance of conditioned behavior. In classical conditioning, extinction occurs when the conditioned stimulus is repeatedly presented without the unconditioned stimulus.

▪ **spontaneous recovery** The reappearance of a previously extinguished conditioned response after a period of time without exposure to the conditioned stimulus.

Extinction and spontaneous recovery definition; marginal definitions, p. 189, from Hockenbury & Hockenbury, *Psychology*, 6e, Worth, 2013

You can recognize the terms you need to learn because:

- **Your instructor will use them.** She may emphasize or define terms in class: "Make sure you understand the key elements of *Pavlovian conditioning*." Or she may simply repeat them or list them on a lecture slide. Record these new terms in your class notes and code them in a way that helps you find them easily for study and review.
- **Your textbook will define them.** These terms may appear in the text (in **boldface** or *italics*, as in the example on p. 85), in the margin, in a list of key terms at the end of the chapter, or in a glossary at the end of the book.
- **They appear in research articles or reports in scholarly journals.**

2b What should I do if I don't know the meaning of a word?

1. **Pronounce it.** By pronouncing the word *magnific* aloud, you may hear part of the word *magnify* and know that it has something do with enlargement. This general meaning may give you enough information to continue reading. (*Magnific* means "large, imposing, or impressive.")
2. **Look for context clues to meaning.** These clues may appear within the sentence or in surrounding sentences.

Type of Clue	Example
Definition or Synonym	*introduced* is a synonym for "prefaced" The poet *prefaced*, or <u>introduced</u>, her reading with a personal story.
Example	These examples suggest that opiates are painkilling drugs. *Opiates*, such as <u>methadone, oxycodone, and morphine</u>, are often misused and abused.
Contrast/ Opposites	This phrase provides a term opposite in meaning. In certain societies children are always *on the periphery,* <u>never the center</u>, of family life.
Inference	Your experience helps you understand that *fracas* means "scuffle" or "brawl." After the playoff game, a *fracas* broke out among hometown fans of the losing team.

Be sure to confirm that you have figured out the correct meaning by substituting the meaning in the sentence and checking that it makes sense.

3. **Use word parts.** Many words are made up of *prefixes* (beginnings), *roots* (middles), and *suffixes* (endings) that have specific meanings. By looking at its parts, you may be able to figure out the meaning of an unfamiliar word. Understanding the word parts will make the word easier to remember, too.

Prefix +	Root +	Suffix =	New Word
three	color	pertaining to	having three colors
tri	chrom	atic	trichromatic

If you are studying the sciences, you will find word parts essential in learning a vast number of new vocabulary words. In anatomy and physiology, for example, if you learn that *hypo* means "below" or "deficient," you can figure out words such as *hypodermis* (the lowest layer of the skin), *hypocalcemia* (calcium deficiency), *hypoglycemic* (low blood sugar), *hypotension* (low blood pressure), and so forth.

4. **Use a dictionary.** Dictionaries are no longer huge, clunky books that sit on library stands—they now appear online and as smartphone apps, and most of them are free. Many e-readers, including Amazon Kindle, have built-in dictionaries that allow you to click on a word and pull up its definition. Even Microsoft Word has a built-in dictionary that you can access by highlighting a word and right-clicking on it.

Some online dictionaries such as Merriam-Webster.com feature an audio button that you can "push" to hear the word pronounced out loud. Most dictionaries also provide the word's *etymology* (origin and history), which can be useful in helping you learn the word.

Because accessing a dictionary is now so easy, you might think a dictionary should be your first line of defense, but if you find many unfamiliar words in a passage, looking up every one may not be practical. You are also more likely to learn a word if you try pronouncing it, looking for context clues, or analyzing its parts before turning to a dictionary.

5. **Make marginal notes.** When you figure out the meaning of a new word or look it up, jot its meaning in the margin so you don't forget it. Writing down the word's meaning also helps to cement it in your memory.

2c Which online resources are useful for vocabulary development?

The following resources are reliable and trustworthy.

- Merriam-Webster.com is a reliable online dictionary that offers audio pronunciation and etymology, as well as definitions, synonyms, and antonyms.
- Refdesk.com is an online reference source that provides factual information about people, places, and events. (This site is chock-full of links, so stay focused on finding what you need.) You will find the links to dictionary.com and Merriam-Webster at the center of the page, under the category "More Word of the Day."

2d How can I learn the words I need to know?

The key to learning any new word is to use it. Experts estimate that you need to use a word five to ten times before you learn it, so practice using new vocabulary at every opportunity as you speak and write.

- **Be sure you know how to pronounce the word.** Use online dictionaries to hear the word's correct pronunciation. Many people are reluctant to use a word if they are uncertain about its pronunciation.
- **Think of two synonyms and one antonym for the word.**
- **Use the word in a sentence or two.** Write the sentences down.
- **Draw diagrams.** Creating diagrams that show relationships between terms may be helpful. For example, in biology, you might draw the following map to help you remember the three bodily sense systems.

- **For technical, specialized, or challenging terminology, use flash cards.** Write the word on the front of an index card, and write its meaning (and pronunciation) on the back, or use one of the many online sites that enable you to create electronic flash cards. (Note: Writing your own flash cards may work better than typing them or using preprinted ones.) The secret to success in using flash cards is to test yourself to determine which words you have learned and which need further study.

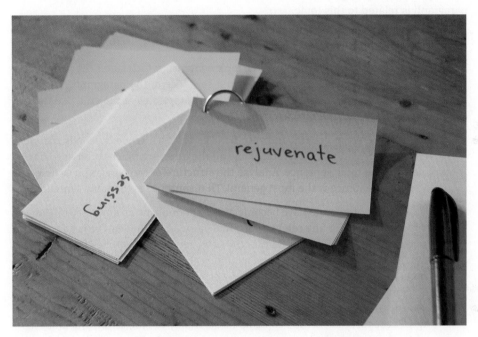

Mike Enright

3 Reading Paragraphs: Main Ideas

Paragraphs are the building blocks of good writing. Here are some strategies for understanding the key idea of any paragraph.

3a How do I identify the topic of a paragraph?

The one general subject discussed in the paragraph is its **topic**. Every sentence in the paragraph explains or discusses this topic. Consider this paragraph:

> Weather forecasts have become as sensationalistic as any story in *The National Enquirer* or on TMZ. Weather is a fact of life across the globe, and each year the TV news reports (sometimes for hours at a time) on bouts of severe weather, including thunderstorms, blizzards, hurricanes, and tornadoes.

Topic sentence

Meteorologists—especially those on TV—make a habit of acting as if every snowstorm, heavy rainstorm, or hurricane is going to destroy thousands of homes, kill millions of people, and cause billions in damage. These forecasts whip people up into a frenzy of fear when the truth is that most storms cause fairly little damage in isolated areas. The highest cost of these storms is the emotional toll that sensationalized forecasts take on people who stay glued to the TV set listening to the weatherpeople predicting the end of the world.

The topic of this paragraph is *sensationalistic weather forecasts*. Each sentence in the paragraph is related to this topic.

3b How do I find the topic sentence?

The topic of a paragraph is often found in a **topic sentence**, which states the paragraph's main idea. Often, the topic sentence is the first sentence of the paragraph, but sometimes it comes in the middle of the paragraph and sometimes at the end. Use the following strategies to find the topic sentence.

1. **Distinguish between general and specific.** The topic sentence is usually the most general sentence in the paragraph, while all the other sentences offer specific support for the topic sentence. Analyze the structure of the paragraph to determine which sentence is the most general. That sentence is the topic sentence.

General

Specific

   Weather forecasts have become as sensationalistic as any story in *The National Enquirer* or any celebrity-scandal story on TMZ. Weather is a fact of life across the globe, and each year the TV news reports (sometimes for hours at a time) on bouts of severe weather, including thunderstorms, blizzards, hurricanes, and tornadoes. Meteorologists—especially those on TV—make a habit of acting as if every snowstorm, heavy rainstorm, or hurricane is going to destroy thousands of homes, kill millions of people, and cause billions in damage. These forecasts whip people up into a frenzy of fear, terror, and anxiety when the truth is that most storms cause fairly little damage in isolated areas.

2. **Look for a sentence that introduces the topic.** When you read a how-to paragraph, for example, the sentence that precedes the first step is often the topic sentence, as in the following paragraph.

Topic sentence

   Buying a new car is a nerve-racking experience for many people, but it doesn't have to be. You can follow a few simple steps to get the car you want for the right price. First, do your research on the Internet. Find out the invoice price and whether the manufacturer is offering any special incentives to the dealer. Next, go to the dealership and announce, "I want to buy a car today." You will receive instant and close attention. Third, use the broken-record method of negotiating by saying the same thing over and over again: "I want to pay $X for this car."

3. **Ask questions.** You can ask two simple questions that together will help you identify the topic sentence.
   - *If I had to choose a title for this paragraph, which one or two words would I use?*
   - *What sentence in the paragraph makes the main point about the topic I identified in my title?*

3c How do I figure out the implied main idea of a paragraph?

Sometimes paragraphs do not include a topic sentence. In those paragraphs, you must infer the main idea from the content. Consider the following paragraph.

> The United States is a democracy, but almost half of the U.S. population (44% to be exact) does not vote in presidential elections. Data exist for voter turnout in 170 of the world's nations; the United States ranks at #120 on the list. Only 20% of young people (ages 18–24) bother to cast a vote in any election. In local (city) elections, as few as 10% of registered voters show up at the polls. Almost 25% of American adults have not even *registered* to vote.

Use repeated words and ideas to identify the implied main idea.

How can you determine the implied main idea?

1. **Find the topic.** Whether the paragraph states its main idea directly or not, a paragraph is always a collection of sentences on a single topic. To identify the topic, notice its frequent repetition of related terms or ideas. Then you ask yourself, "What is the one idea that is repeated in the paragraph?" The answer is clear: *Low voter turnout in the United States.*

2. **Decide what the writer wants you to know about the topic.** You can think of the implied main idea as the general idea that is supported by the specifics. In the paragraph about voter turnout, the author has provided shocking statistics about the lack of voter turnout in the United States. All of the sentences point to the general implied main idea: "Although the United States is a democracy in which voting is essential to the political process, there is widespread apathy among American voters, and many do not bother going to the polls."

4   Reading Paragraphs: Details

The sentences that support a paragraph's main idea are its **details**. Not all details are equally important.

4a How do I know which details are worth remembering?

Sometimes everything in a paragraph looks important; other times, nothing seems worth remembering. You may be right in both cases.

1. **Sometimes none of the details is essential to learn and remember.** In the following paragraph, all the detail sentences are just examples. Not any one is important in itself to remember, but together they do give you a better sense of the author's main point. You could highlight one to jog your memory, or just mark "ex" in the margin.

> *Criticism* refers to materials that respond to and evaluate a particular work. A film critic may write a movie review examining the plot and characterization, as well as the cinematography. A magazine review may evaluate a new mystery novel by comparing it to others of the same genre. A scientist may respond to a recently published research study on immunotherapy, challenging its methodology.

Topic (or main idea) sentence

Examples

2. **Sometimes the paragraph contains only important details, details that** *directly*
   explain **or** *support* **the main idea.** Pay attention to all of these.

Topic (or main idea) sentence

> McClelland, a well-known Harvard psychologist, hypothesized that human
> behavior is motivated by three distinct psychological needs. The need for affilia-
> tion involves seeking to be liked by others and held in high regard by them. The
> need for power urges people to influence or seek control over others. The need
> for achievement involves reaching both realistic and idealistic goals.

Key details

3. **Some paragraphs contain secondary details that explain more about the important details.** Secondary details are not essential to remember.

> McClelland, a well-known Harvard psychologist, hypothesized that human
> behavior is motivated by three distinct psychological needs. The need for affilia-
> tion involves seeking to be liked by others and held in high regard by them.
> Those motivated by the need for affiliation enjoy working with others and work
> well in groups. The need for power urges people to influence or seek control over
> others. For these individuals, status and prestige are important; some may tend
> to be showy and ruthless. The need for achievement involves reaching both real-
> istic and idealistic goals. Those motivated to achieve seek evaluation and feed-
> back about their ideas and skills and tend to seek challenge.

Secondary details

4. **Use transitions to guide you from primary detail to primary detail.** Notice how
   the writer uses the transitions "first," "second," and "finally" to lead you from one
   reason to the next.

Transitions

> Within human communication, silence is the absence of speech, but it,
> too, can carry meaning. First, silence can be a weapon used against others;
> think of it as a kind of punishment. After a quarrel, a spouse may refuse to
> speak to his or her partner, communicating anger or disappointment. Second,
> the lack of speech may express emotion. Refusing to speak may indicate lack
> of cooperation or defiance. Imagine a silent child pouting, for example. Finally,
> silence can suggest shyness or discomfort. A person new to a group may be
> silent until he or she learns what the group accepts and expects.

Other common transitions include *for example, in conclusion, meanwhile,* and *however.*
You can find a list of the most commonly used transitions in Table 6.1 (p. 149).

4b What should I do if I don't understand a sentence or a detail?

1. **Keep reading!** Sometimes the rest of the paragraph or selection will provide the
   clues you need to make sense of the confusing detail, or you may realize that you
   really don't need that particular detail to fulfill your purpose. If, after reading the
   whole selection, you still don't understand a detail that seems important, first
   figure out any unfamiliar words. (See 2. Learning Words.) Then try to express the
   detail in your own words.
2. **Look for and pay attention to examples.** Examples often make complicated or
   difficult concepts clear and easy to understand.

How will entry or exit by other firms affect the profits of a typical existing firm? Because the differentiated products offered by firms in a monopolistically competitive industry compete for the same set of customers, entry or exit by other firms will affect the demand curve facing every existing producer. If new gas stations open along a highway, each of the existing gas stations will no longer be able to sell as much gas as before at a given price.

Challenging text

Example that clarifies and explains

5 ▸ Reading Essays and Textbook Chapters

The two most common reading assignments in college courses are essays and textbook chapters. Use the following strategies to plan your reading schedule and complete your assignments on time.

5a What should I do if I just can't get started on the assignment?

Sometimes assignments are intimidating. The key to getting started is to make the assignment manageable.

1. **Divide the task into doable pieces, and work in time blocks.** A typical textbook chapter is twenty to thirty pages long. A long essay or journal article may be fifteen to twenty pages long. To make a long, complicated text more manageable, start by previewing the assignment, looking for breaks indicated by headings, numbers, or some other element. Then read one chunk at a time, perhaps over several days.
2. **Reward yourself when you complete the task.** Give yourself a small treat, such as a healthy snack or a half hour of YouTube, to motivate you to finish.

5b How can I keep from getting lost in a difficult and lengthy reading assignment?

1. **Review previously read material before beginning new material.** Take a moment to flip through the previous chapter or review your class notes. Doing so will activate your memory and orient you to the new assignment. This strategy is particularly helpful when you are moving from one discipline to another—for example, when you have just completed your philosophy reading and must now move on to your economics assignment.
2. **Look for patterns.** The author of your assignment may have used a specific pattern in each section of the chapter you are reading. For example, each major section in an economics textbook may be organized in this manner:

- heading
- key terms and definitions
- examples
- graphical analysis
- application to the real world
- comprehension questions

By identifying this pattern, you get into the flow of reading the chapter. You know what to expect, and you train your brain to learn the concepts according to the system the author has set up. Trust the author's system of organization! Most textbook authors are expert teachers, and they write their books to maximize students' ability to learn the material. Also look for patterns of text development and the transitions that signal them. For an overview of these patterns, see Chapter 10.

For more about creating an outline or graphic organizer, see Chapter 2, pp. 35–37, and Chapter 7, pp. 161–64.

3. **Create an overview (an outline, graphic organizer, or a diagram) and refer to it frequently.** Research shows that taking notes (especially by hand) while reading increases comprehension and learning. On a separate sheet of paper, draw a diagram of each main section or create a point-by-point outline or graphic organizer. If you are a visual learner, try drawing a branching diagram or idea map.

5c How can I be sure I am understanding what I read?

Have you ever finished reading an essay and thought, "What did I just read? My mind is a complete blank." Don't worry—it happens to everyone occasionally. Fortunately, two useful strategies can help.

1. **Express each idea in your own words.** After reading each main section of a textbook chapter or essay, write out the main idea in your own words. Do not simply copy topic sentences from the text. By restating the key idea in your own words, you test your own understanding of the material. If you can't accomplish this task, you didn't really understand what you read. Reread the section and try again to capture the main idea before moving on to the next section. (Essays may have no section breaks. In this case, stop every few pages to summarize what you've read.)

2. **Test yourself.** Use the textbook features—such as the learning objectives at the start of the chapter or the key concepts at the end of the chapter—to test yourself. If the book provides an answer key, use it to check your work, not to avoid doing the work. (The latter strategy will come back to bite you at exam time.) If your text lacks learning objectives or a list of key concepts, turn headings into questions and then make sure you can answer those questions correctly. Use the results of your self-testing to determine which materials need further study or review.

6 Reviewing

Students frequently think that rereading is a great tool for learning, but other strategies, like those listed below, often work better.

6a Should I reread assigned chapters or reading selections to review?

You may need to reread challenging assignments to understand them. But don't make a habit of rereading all of your assignments from start to finish to review.

1. **Reread only for a specific purpose.** Comprehension improves when you identify main ideas and key supporting details, not when you reread the entire assignment. To ensure that you have understood a difficult paragraph, it makes sense to reread the paragraph. But by the time you finish the assignment, you should reread only sections and only for a specific purpose—for example, to find a piece of information, to review a concept you find challenging, or to check your understanding of a particular topic.

2. **Use alternative strategies for review.** Rather than rereading the entire assignment, try these strategies.

   • **Test yourself by anticipating exam questions.** Make up questions based on headings or visual aids, and write the answers to them.

   • **Write, highlight, annotate, paraphrase, or summarize.** Take your pick; each can be useful, depending on the situation.

   • **Memorize key information when you have to.** Sometimes there is no substitute for simple memorization. Use flash cards to help you memorize key vocabulary. Also develop memory tricks, or *mnemonics*, to aid in recall. For example, many students use the name "Roy G. Biv" to remember the colors of the rainbow: red, orange, yellow, green, blue, indigo, and violet. Or they use the acronym HOMES to remember the names of the Great Lakes: Huron, Ontario, Michigan, Erie, Superior. Develop a set of mnemonics that work for you.

6b How can I remember what I just read?

Immediate review and periodic review are the keys to learning and then retaining information.

1. **Review right after you read.** When you're done reading the assignment, don't simply close the book and move on. Rather, spend five to ten minutes flipping through the selection, rereading your notes, and gauging your understanding of the material. Keep a list with two columns: "Material I Understand and Remember" and "Material I Need to Review and Practice." Use this list to aid in periodic review.

2. **Review what you've read periodically (say, once a week).** The best way to keep information in your memory is to review it periodically. If six weeks will elapse between your first reading of the assignment and the test, spend a bit of time (perhaps half an hour) in each of those six weeks reviewing your notes. Then, the night before the test, you will not need to cram in order to relearn the material.

3. **Write to consolidate information.** By writing out information, you will remember and learn it better. Research shows that writing by hand aids recall better than typing on a computer does.

6c How can I prepare for a quiz on a reading assignment?

Try these strategies.

1. **Highlight and annotate as you read, and review your highlighting and annotations.** For guidelines on how to highlight and annotate effectively, see Chapter 2, "Active Reading and Responding" (pp. 44–45).

2. **Outline or summarize the reading.** Draw a graphic organizer or create an outline to help you understand the reading's content, organization, and key points. Write a one-paragraph summary in your own words, and then evaluate your summary: Ask yourself, "Would this summary tell someone who has not read the essay what the essay is about?" For detailed instructions on outlining and drawing a graphic organizer, see Chapter 7 (pp. 161–64); for detailed instructions on summarizing, see Chapter 2 (pp. 42–43).

3. **Test yourself by predicting and answering questions.** Write actual questions and practice answering them within a certain period of time. Doing so not only gives you practice at writing a timed response, but it also pushes you to identify the ideas you've learned and those you need to brush up on. (Quizzes will most likely focus on key points rather than secondary or unimportant details.)

6d How can I prepare for class discussions based on a reading assignment?

Often, your instructor will use the reading assignment as the basis for a class or group discussion. The instructor will often say something like, "Be prepared to discuss this essay during our next class session."

1. **Make marginal notes as you read.** Jot down your reactions in the margins, engaging in a "conversation" with the assignment. Write not only about agreements, but also about disagreements, examples from your own life or other classes, and further thoughts on the topic. Then review your annotations after you've completed the assignment.

2. **Write in your journal.** A response journal is a section of your writing journal in which you record summaries of readings, along with your reactions to and questions about those readings. Chapter 2 (pp. 47–49) provides details about two useful formats: the open-page format and the two-column format.

6e What should I do if I highlight practically everything?

Too much highlighting is a common error. Here are some tips for highlighting just the right amount of your reading assignment.

1. **Determine what you need to know.** Highlight only main ideas and important details. If you have trouble identifying main ideas, see Section 4a of this guide, "How do I know which details are important and worth remembering?" As a general rule, do not highlight full sentences, and highlight no more than one-quarter of a page. Limiting your highlighting forces you to sort more important from less important ideas, and this sorting process enhances learning.

2. **Read a paragraph or short section first; then go back and highlight it.** By doing so, you give yourself time to identify what's important. Use headings and bold-faced key terms to help you determine what should be highlighted. Consider using different highlighting colors for different types of information—for example, use yellow for key vocabulary and definitions and green for key examples. (Make sure you use colors that are easy to read through.)

3. **Compare your highlighting with a classmate's.** Determine which of you has a more effective method of highlighting, and then adapt your highlighting methods accordingly.

Strategies for Writing Essays

PART TWO

4
Prewriting
How to Find and Focus Ideas

In this chapter you will learn to:

- choose and narrow a topic
- consider audience, purpose, point of view, genre, and medium
- discover ideas to write about

WRITING QUICK START   Study the photo on this page. What is happening? What do you think the man could be reacting to? Write whatever comes to mind. You might write about times when you've felt the same emotions you think the man is expressing, or about times when you've seen others express strong emotions in public. Try to write nonstop for at least five minutes. Don't stop to evaluate your writing or worry about grammar. Just record your thoughts.

You have just used **freewriting**, a method of discovering ideas about a topic by writing without stopping for a set period of time. Read over what you wrote. Suppose you are now asked to write an essay about joy or exuberance. Do you see some starting points and usable ideas in your freewriting?

Generating ideas, considering your writing situation (your purpose, audience, point of view, and genre), and choosing and narrowing a topic are all part of the writing process, as illustrated in Graphic Organizer 4.1 (p. 99). Although writing is often described as a step-by-step process, writers often move back and forth between the steps and return to an earlier step to cut and paste material they previously developed. This movement is designated by arrows pointing in both directions in the graphic organizer.

GRAPHIC ORGANIZER 4.1 An Overview of the Writing Process

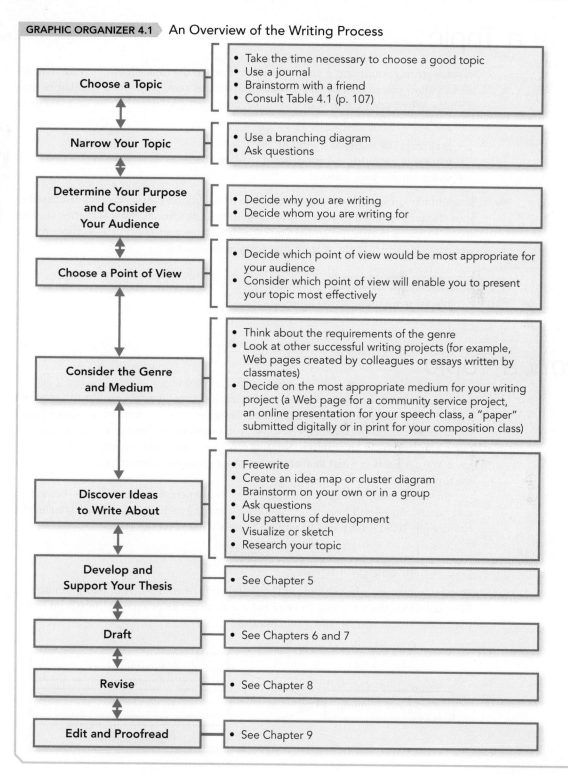

Choose a Topic
- Take the time necessary to choose a good topic
- Use a journal
- Brainstorm with a friend
- Consult Table 4.1 (p. 107)

Narrow Your Topic
- Use a branching diagram
- Ask questions

Determine Your Purpose and Consider Your Audience
- Decide why you are writing
- Decide whom you are writing for

Choose a Point of View
- Decide which point of view would be most appropriate for your audience
- Consider which point of view will enable you to present your topic most effectively

Consider the Genre and Medium
- Think about the requirements of the genre
- Look at other successful writing projects (for example, Web pages created by colleagues or essays written by classmates)
- Decide on the most appropriate medium for your writing project (a Web page for a community service project, an online presentation for your speech class, a "paper" submitted digitally or in print for your composition class)

Discover Ideas to Write About
- Freewrite
- Create an idea map or cluster diagram
- Brainstorm on your own or in a group
- Ask questions
- Use patterns of development
- Visualize or sketch
- Research your topic

Develop and Support Your Thesis
- See Chapter 5

Draft
- See Chapters 6 and 7

Revise
- See Chapter 8

Edit and Proofread
- See Chapter 9

Choose a Topic

In some writing situations, your instructor will assign the topic. In others, your instructor will allow you to choose your own topic, perhaps selecting from a number of possibilities. When you choose your own topic, don't just grab the first one that comes to mind. Rather, look for a topic that:

- is appropriate to the assignment
- you know something about or want to learn about
- will maintain your interest

For more on keeping a journal, see Chapter 1, p. 18.

In addition to Internet browsing to search for a topic, don't overlook topics discussed in your classes or related to your entries in your writing journal, daily activities such as sports or social events, programs you've heard or seen on radio or television, or the world around you: people, objects, and social interactions.

> **ESSAY IN PROGRESS 1**
>
> List at least three broad essay topics.

Narrow a Topic

Once you have chosen a topic, narrow it to make it manageable within the required length of your essay. For example, if you are assigned a two- to four-page essay, a broad topic such as divorce is too large. However, you might write about one specific cause of divorce or its effects on children. *Skipping this step is one of the biggest mistakes you can make.* You can waste a great deal of time working on an essay only to discover later that the topic is too broad.

To narrow a topic, limit it to a specific part or aspect. Two techniques—branching and questioning—will help you. The idea-generating techniques covered later in the chapter (pp. 107–17) may also be used to narrow a broad topic.

Use a Branching Diagram

Start by writing your broad topic at the far left side of your paper or computer screen. Then subdivide the topic into three or more subcategories or aspects. Here is an example for the broad topic of wild-game hunting.

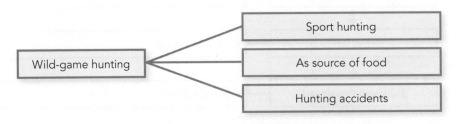

Then choose one subcategory and subdivide it further, as shown here.

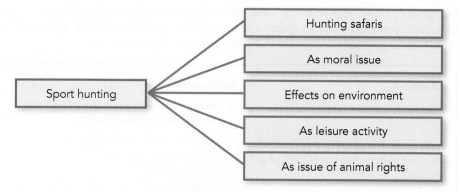

Continue narrowing the topic in this way until you feel you have found one that is interesting, appropriate to your assignment, and manageable. The following example shows narrowed topics that would be workable for a two- to four-page essay on the effects of sport hunting on the environment.

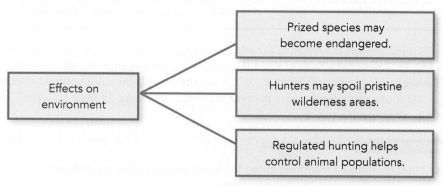

Note: Did you notice that as the narrowing progressed, the topics changed from words and phrases to statements of ideas?

Once you begin planning, researching, and drafting your essay, you may need to narrow your topic even further.

EXERCISE 4.1 ▶ BRANCHING

Use branching diagrams to narrow three of the following broad topics to more manageable topics for a two- to four-page essay.

1. Manned space travel
2. School lunches
3. Air travel safety measures
4. Campaign finance rules
5. Alternative energy sources

ESSAY IN PROGRESS 2 ▶

Narrow one of the broad topics you chose in Essay in Progress 1 to a topic manageable for a two- to four-page essay.

Ask Questions to Narrow a Broad Topic

Use questions that begin with *who, what, where, when, why,* and *how* to narrow your topic. Questioning will lead you to consider and focus your attention on specific aspects of the topic. Here is an example of questioning for the broad topic of divorce.

Questions	Narrowed Topics
Why does divorce occur?	• Lifestyle differences as a cause of divorce • Infidelity as a cause of divorce
How do couples divide their property?	• Division of assets after a divorce
Who can help couples work through a divorce?	• Role of friends and family • Role of mediator • Role of attorney
What are the effects of divorce on children?	• Emotional effects of divorce on children • Financial effects of divorce on children
When might it be advisable for a couple considering divorce to remain married?	• Couples who stay together for the sake of their children • Financial benefit of remaining married

Sometimes you may need to ask additional questions to limit the topic sufficiently. The topic "emotional effects of divorce on children," for example, is still too broad for an essay. Asking questions such as "What are the most common emotional effects?" and "How can divorcing parents prevent emotional problems in their children?" can lead to more specific topics.

EXERCISE 4.2   **QUESTIONING**

Use questioning to narrow three of the following subjects to topics that would be manageable within a two- to four-page essay.

1. Senior citizens
2. Mental illness
3. Environmental protection
4. Cyberbullying
5. Television programming

Think about Your Writing Situation

Once you have decided on a manageable topic, you are ready to consider your writing situation: your purpose, audience, point of view, genre, and medium.

Determine Your Purpose

A well-written essay should have a specific purpose or goal. There are three main purposes for writing.

1. **To *express* yourself:** For example, to express the writer's feelings about an incident of road rage that he or she observed

2. **To *inform* your reader:** For example, to inform readers about the primary causes of road rage
3. **To *persuade* your reader:** For example, to persuade readers to vote for funding to investigate the problem of road rage in the community

To identify your purpose, ask yourself the following questions.

1. Why am I writing this essay?
2. What do I want this essay to accomplish?

Some essays can have more than one purpose. An essay on snowboarding, for example, could be both informative and persuasive: It could explain the benefits of snowboarding and urge readers to take up the sport because it is good exercise.

Consider Your Audience

Considering your **audience** (the people who will read your essay) is an important part of the writing process. Many aspects of your writing—how you express yourself, which words you choose, which details and examples you include, which types of sentences you use, and what attitude you take toward your topic—depend on the audience. Your **tone** (how you sound to your audience) is especially important. If you want your audience to feel comfortable with your writing, you need to write in a manner that your readers can understand and that appeals to them.

For more on tone, see Chapter 3, pp. 64–66.

If you were describing a student orientation session to a friend, you would use a different tone and select different details than you would if you were describing the orientation in an article for the student newspaper.

Telling a Friend	Writing for the Student Newspaper
Remember I told you how nervous I am about attending college in the fall? Well, guess what? I went to my student orientation over the weekend, and it was much better than I expected! I even met one of my teachers, and he was so nice and down-to-earth that now I'm starting to get excited about going to college.	College student orientations are often thought to be stuffy affairs where prospective students attempt to mix with aloof professors. For this reason, I am pleased to report that the college orientation held on campus last weekend was a major success and not a pointless endeavor after all. Along with my fellow incoming first-year students, I was impressed with the friendliness of instructors and the camaraderie that developed between students and faculty.
Language: casual	**Language:** more formal
Sentence structure: shorter sentences	**Sentence structure:** longer sentences
Tone: familiar, friendly	**Tone:** serious, formal

How to consider your audience. As you consider your audience, keep the following points in mind.

- **Your readers are not present and cannot observe or participate in what you are writing about.** If you are writing about your apartment, for example, they cannot visualize it unless you describe it in detail.
- **Your readers do not know everything you know.** They may not have the same knowledge about and experience with the topic that you do, so you will have to define specialized terms, for example, if readers are unlikely to know what they mean.
- **Your readers may not share your opinions and values.** If you are writing about raising children and assume that strict discipline is undesirable, for example, some readers may not agree with you.
- **Your readers may not respond in the same way you do to situations or issues.** Some readers may not see any humor in a situation that you find funny. An issue that you consider only mildly disturbing may upset or anger some readers.

For a helpful list of questions you can ask to analyze your audience, consult the box below.

Analyzing Your Audience

When analyzing your audience, ask yourself the following questions.

- **What does my audience know (or not know) about my topic?** If you are proposing a community garden project to an audience of city residents who know little about gardening, you will need to describe the pleasures and benefits of gardening to capture their interest.
- **What is the education, background, and experience of my audience?** If you are writing your garden-project proposal for an audience of low-income residents, you might emphasize how much money they could save by growing vegetables, and if you are proposing the project to middle-income residents, you might stress how relaxing gardening can be and how a garden can beautify a neighborhood.
- **What attitudes, beliefs, opinions, or biases are my audience likely to hold?** Suppose your audience believes that most development is harmful to the environment. If you are writing an essay urging your audience to sponsor a new community garden, consider emphasizing how the garden will benefit the environment and decrease development.
- **What tone do my readers expect?** Suppose you are writing to your local city council urging council members to approve the community garden. Although the council has been stalling on the issue, your tone should be serious and not accusatory. As community leaders, the council members expect to be treated with respect.
- **What tone will help me achieve my purpose?** If you are writing to your city counselor to urge her to support the community garden, a respectful tone is more likely to achieve your goal than a hostile one.

Considering your audience when it is composed of one person: your instructor. Instructors occasionally direct students to write for a particular audience, such as readers of a certain magazine or newspaper, but you can often assume that your main audience is your instructor. In most cases, it is best to write as if your instructor were unfamiliar with your topic. He or she wants to see if you understand the topic and can write and think clearly about it. For academic papers, provide enough information to demonstrate your knowledge of the subject (including background information, definitions of technical terms, and relevant details), make sure your essay is clear and understandable, maintain a reasonable tone, provide evidence from sources that are appropriate to your discipline, and treat alternative views fairly.

EXERCISE 4.3 ▶ **CONSIDERING YOUR AUDIENCE**

1. Write a one-paragraph description of a current television commercial for a particular product. Your audience is another college student.
2. Write a description of the same commercial for one of the following writing situations.
   a. An assignment in a business marketing class: Analyze the factors that make the advertisement interesting and appealing. Your audience is a marketing instructor.
   b. A letter to the company that produces the product: Describe your response to the advertisement. Your audience is the consumer relations director of the company.
   c. A letter to your local television station: Comment favorably on or complain about the advertisement. Your audience is the station director.

Choose a Point of View

Point of view is the perspective from which you write an essay. There are three types: first, second, and third person. In choosing a point of view, consider your topic, your purpose, and your audience.

Think of point of view as the "person" you become as you write.

- **First person** uses first-person pronouns (*I, me, mine, we, ours*). First person is often effective and appropriate in an essay narrating an event in which you participated. For formal essays, many instructors prefer that you not write in the first person.
- **Second person** uses second-person pronouns (*you, your, yours*). Second person is appropriate when giving directions, as in an essay explaining how to build a fence: "First, *you* should measure . . ." Sometimes the word *you* may be understood but not directly stated, as in, "First, measure . . ." Many textbooks, including this one, use the second person to address student readers; however, many instructors prefer that you avoid using the second person in formal essays.
- **Third person** uses people's names and third-person pronouns (*he, she, it*). Third person is prevalent in academic writing. It is less personal and more formal than first person and second person. Think of the third person as public rather than private or personal. The writer reports what he or she sees.

EXERCISE 4.4   **POINT OF VIEW**

Working with a classmate, discuss which point of view (first, second, or third person) would be most appropriate in each of the following writing situations.

1. An essay urging students to participate in a march against hunger to support a local food drive
2. A description of a car accident on a form that your insurance company requires you to submit in order to collect benefits
3. A paper for an ecology course on the effects of air pollution caused by a local industry

---

Consider the Genre and Medium

Genre is a term used to classify types of text—for example, laboratory reports, proposals, or blog posts. Each genre has its own conventions, or ways of doing things. A laboratory report, for example, has a specific purpose: To inform readers about how an experiment was conducted so that it can be repeated and to tell readers the results. It takes the third-person point of view, uses technical language, and includes the sections *Introduction, Methods, Results,* and *Discussion.*

To write effectively you need to understand the conventions of the genre and follow them closely. Reviewing samples of effective writing in the genre, either by classmates or those posted on reliable Web pages, can be helpful.

Medium refers to the means through which ideas are expressed and information conveyed. In your writing class, your primary medium will be printed text, but your essays may include visuals, and if assignments are submitted or viewed electronically, you may also include audio or visual files, animations, or hyperlinks to Web sites. Be sure to choose a medium that suits your purpose and your audience. (For example, consider whether your readers will have high-speed Internet access when reading your assignment.) Also consider the conventions of the genre in which you are writing.

HOW WRITERS READ   ANALYZING THE AUTHOR'S GENRE, PURPOSE, AUDIENCE, AND POINT OF VIEW

Considering the author's purpose, audience, point of view, and genre can help you read effectively and sharpen your critical-thinking skills.

BEFORE READING	• Previewing to determine the selection's **genre** will help you decide which sections are most important. Knowing what you're expected to know or write about will allow you to read to find that information.
WHILE READING	• Pay attention to **purpose**, **audience**, and **point of view**. Depending on the purpose and audience, a writer may not always feel the need to provide complete information. Point of view may hint at the writer's slant or bias.
AFTER READING	• Identify the author's **purpose** and the **audience** for whom an essay is written and use this information to evaluate the reliability and sufficiency of the evidence provided and to identify possible biases.

Discover Ideas to Write About

Discovering ideas to write about is a process of gathering all of your separate but related ideas on a topic and fitting them together. For example, you may know a lot about biking, but all your knowledge is not stored in one place in your brain: Verbal information is stored in one place; sensory impressions are stored in another. Be sure to draw on both. Table 4.1 shows the ideas one student developed on bicycling, providing a wealth of ideas to write about on the topic.

TABLE 4.1 ▶ Synthesizing Your Ideas on a Topic

To Discover Ideas, Draw Upon Your . . .	Example Topic: Bicycling
Verbal knowledge: facts, dates, numbers, concepts, definitions, reasons, and so forth	Types of bikes, costs, speeds, repairs, convenience, bike races
Personal knowledge: events you have experienced	A bike trip to Yellowstone National Park, pedaling to school
Mental images: pictures in your mind, recollections of images on television, videos	A mental image of the first bike you rode; a video of the Tour de France
Sensory impressions: recollections of tastes, smells, touch, and sound	The feel of wind in your face as you ride, the roar of a truck coming up behind you
Motor skills: memory of physical actions	Keeping your balance, steering, braking, changing gears

In the following sections, you will learn a number of specific strategies for discovering and recording ideas to write about. Depending on your learning style, you will probably find that some strategies work better than others. Experiment with each before deciding which will work for you. You may also find that the technique you choose for a given essay may depend on your topic.

Freewrite

When you use freewriting, you write for a specific period of time, usually five to ten minutes. Freewriting allows you to explore ideas and make associations, jumping from one idea to another. If nothing comes to mind, just write the topic, your name, or "I can't think of anything to write" until something occurs to you. The following tips will help you.

- **Write or type nonstop.** Writing often forces thought, so keep going, even after you think you have nothing more to say.
- **Don't be concerned with grammar, punctuation, or spelling.**
- **Write or type fast!** Try to keep up with your thinking. (Most people can think faster than they can write or type.)
- **Record ideas as they come to you** and in whatever form they appear—words, phrases, questions, sentences—or pictures and doodles.

- **If you are freewriting on a computer, darken the screen** so that you are not distracted by errors, formatting issues, and the words you have already written.

When you are done, reread your freewriting, and highlight or underline ideas that seem useful. Look for patterns and connections: Do several ideas together make a point, reflect a sequence, or suggest a larger, unifying idea? Here is an excerpt from one student's freewriting on the broad topic of violence in the media.

> There seems to be a lot of violence in the media these days, particularly on TV. For example, last night when I watched the news, the camera man showed people getting shot in the street. What kind of people watch this stuff? I'd rather watch a movie. It really bothered me because people get so turned off by such an ugly, gruesome scene that they won't want to watch the news anymore. Then we'll have a lot of uninformed citizens. There are too many already. Some people do not even know who the vice president of the U.S. is. A negative thing—the media has a negative impact on any person or group who wants to do something about violence in the inner city. And they create negative impressions of minority and ethnic groups, too. If the media shows one Latino man committing a crime, viewers falsely assume all Latinos are criminals. It's difficult to think of something positive that can be done when you're surrounded by so much violence. It's all so overwhelming. What we need in the inner city is not more coverage of violence but viable solutions to the violence we have. The media coverage of violent acts only serves to make people think that this violence is a normal state of affairs and nothing can be done about it.

A number of subtopics surfaced from this student's freewriting.

- the media's graphic portrayal of violence
- the negative effect of media violence on viewers
- the media's portrayal of minority and ethnic groups

LEARNING STYLE OPTIONS

Any one of these topics could be narrowed to a manageable topic for an essay. If you are a creative learner or feel restricted by organization and structure, freewriting may appeal to you because it allows you to give your imagination free rein.

EXERCISE 4.5 **FREEWRITING**

Set a clock or timer for five minutes and freewrite on one of the following broad topics. Then review and highlight your freewriting, identifying usable ideas with a common theme that might serve as a topic for an essay. Starting with one of the potential topics from your freewriting, freewrite for another five minutes to narrow your topic further and develop your ideas.

1. Hip-hop music
2. Instagram
3. How to be self-sufficient
4. Pressures on college students
5. Job interviews

Draw a Map or Cluster Diagram

Mapping, or **clustering**, is a visual way to discover ideas and relationships. Here is how to create a map.

1. Write your topic in the middle of a blank sheet of paper, and draw a box or circle around it. (Consider using a graphics program such as bubbl.us or smartdraw.com.)
2. Think of ideas that are related to or suggested by your topic. As you think of them, write them down in clusters around the topic, connecting them to the topic with lines (Figure 4.1). Think of your topic as a tree trunk and the related ideas as branches.
3. Draw arrows and lines or use highlighting to show relationships and connect groups of related ideas.
4. Think of still more ideas, clustering them around the ideas already on your map.

The sample map in Figure 4.1 was done by a student working on the topic of the costs of higher education. In this map, the student compared attending a local community college and attending an out-of-town four-year college. A number of different subtopics evolved, including the following:

- transportation costs
- social life
- availability of degree programs
- room and board costs

Mapping may appeal to you if you prefer a spatial method of dealing with information and ideas. It also appeals to creative learners who like to devise their own structure or framework within which to work.

LEARNING STYLE OPTIONS

FIGURE 4.1   Sample Map

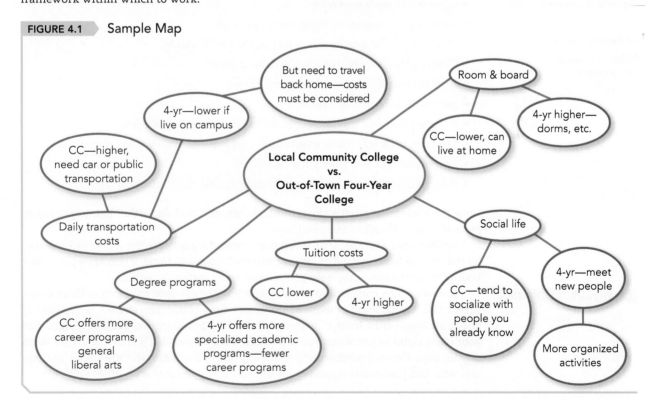

EXERCISE 4.6   **MAPPING**

Narrow one of the following topics. Then draw a map of related ideas as they come to mind.

1. Presidential politics
2. Daydreaming
3. Tattoos
4. Cable TV
5. Year-round schooling

Brainstorm

When you **brainstorm**, you list everything that comes to mind when you think about your topic: facts, impressions, emotions, and reactions. Record words or phrases rather than sentences, and give yourself a time limit; this will force ideas to come to your mind faster. If you use a computer, you might use bullets or the indent function to brainstorm.

The following example shows a student's brainstorming on the narrowed topic of the disadvantages of home schooling. Three clusters of topics are evident.

Topic: Disadvantages of Home Schooling

- Parent may not be an expert in every subject
- Libraries not easily accessible
- Wide range of equipment, resources not available
- Child may be confused by parent playing the role of teacher
- Child does not learn to interact with other children
- Child does not learn to compete against others
- Parents may not enforce standards
- Parents may not be objective about child's strengths and weaknesses
- Child may learn only parent's viewpoint—not exposed to wide range of opinions
- Special programs (art, music) may be omitted
- Services of school nurse, counselors, reading specialists not available

Unavailable services/resources

Limitations of parents

Problems of social development

Once the student selected a cluster to focus on, he could do further brainstorming to generate ideas about his narrowed topic.

Brainstorming is more structured than freewriting because the writer focuses only on the topic at hand instead of writing whatever comes to mind. If you are a pragmatic learner, brainstorming may help you release your creative potential.

LEARNING STYLE OPTIONS

Brainstorming can also work well when it is done in groups of two or three classmates. Use a chalkboard or whiteboard in an empty classroom, share a large sheet of paper, sit together in front of a computer screen, or use networked computers. Say your ideas aloud as you write. You'll find that your classmates' ideas will trigger more of your own. Group brainstorming often appeals to students who are social learners and who find it stimulating and enjoyable to exchange ideas with other students.

EXERCISE 4.7	BRAINSTORMING

Choose one of the following subjects and narrow it to a manageable topic for a two- to four-page paper. Then brainstorm, either alone or with one or two classmates, to generate ideas to write about.

1. Value of music
2. National parks
3. Credit-card fraud
4. Texting
5. Web advertising

Ask Questions

Questioning is another way to discover ideas about a narrowed topic. Working either alone or with a classmate, write down every question you can think of about your topic. Focus on ideas, not correctness. Don't judge or evaluate ideas as you write. It may help to imagine that you are asking an expert on your topic anything that comes to mind.

Here is a partial list of questions one student generated on the narrow topic of the financial problems that single parents face.

> *How can single parents afford to pay for day care?*
>
> *How do single parents find time to attend college to improve their employability and earning power?*
>
> *How can women force their former husbands to keep up with child support payments?*

Beginning a question with "What if . . ." is a particularly good way to extend your thinking and look at a topic from a fresh perspective. Here are a few challenging "What if . . ." questions about the financial situation of single parents.

> *What if the government provided national day care or paid for day care?*
>
> *What if single parents were not allowed to deduct more than one child on their income tax?*
>
> *What if single parents were entitled to special tax rebates?*

Another way to stimulate your thinking is to ask questions that approach the topic from a number of different perspectives. For the topic of the increased popularity of health foods, you could write questions about human motivation to purchase, marketing strategies, or nutritional value, for instance.

You may find questioning effective if you are an analytical, inquisitive person. Social learners will enjoy using this technique with classmates. Because questions often tend to focus on specifics and details, questioning is also an appealing strategy for concrete learners.

After devising a number of questions, you may want to write tentative answers, or hypotheses. If you need to conduct research, you can use these hypotheses as a guide.

LEARNING STYLE OPTIONS

To learn more about using research questions and hypotheses, see Chapter 21, pp. 554–55.

Working either alone or with a classmate, choose one of the following topics, narrow it, and write a series of questions to discover ideas about it.

1. The campus newspaper
2. Learning a foreign language
3. Financial aid regulations
4. The minimum wage
5. Government aid to developing countries

Use the Patterns of Development

In Parts 3 and 4 of this book, you will learn nine ways to develop an essay or a paragraph.

- narration
- description
- illustration
- process analysis
- comparison and contrast
- classification and division
- definition
- cause and effect
- argument

These methods are often called *patterns of development*.

In addition to providing ways to develop an essay or a paragraph, the patterns of development may be used to generate ideas about a topic. Think of the patterns as doors through which you gain access to your topic. The list of questions in Table 4.2 (p. 113) will help you approach your topic through these different "doors." For any given topic, some questions work better than others. If your topic is voter registration, for example, the questions listed for definition and process analysis would be more helpful than those listed for description. (You might choose the definition or process analysis pattern if you are a pragmatic learner who enjoys structured tasks or a creative learner who likes to analyze ideas from different viewpoints.)

LEARNING STYLE OPTIONS

Use the patterns of development to generate ideas on one of the following topics. Refer to Table 4.2 (p. 113) to form questions based on the patterns.

1. Buying only American-made products
2. Community gardens in urban areas
3. How high-speed trains would change travel
4. Cell-phone usage
5. Effects of a computer virus

Visualize or Sketch

Visualizing or **sketching** may be effective ways to discover ideas about your topic. To visualize a person, for example, close your eyes and picture that person in your mind. Imagine what he or she is wearing and what his or her facial expressions and gestures might look like.

TABLE 4.2 Using the Patterns of Development to Explore a Topic

Pattern of Development	Questions to Ask
Narration (Chapter 11)	What stories or events does this topic remind you of?
Description (Chapter 12)	What does the topic look, smell, taste, feel, or sound like?
Illustration (Chapter 13)	What examples of this topic are particularly helpful in explaining it?
Process Analysis (Chapter 14)	How does this topic work? How do you do this topic?
Comparison and Contrast (Chapter 15)	To what is the topic similar? In what ways? Is the topic more or less desirable than those things to which it is similar?
Classification and Division (Chapter 16)	Of what larger group of things is this topic a member? What are its parts? How can the topic be subdivided? Are there certain types or kinds of the topic?
Definition (Chapter 17)	How do you define the topic? How does the dictionary define it? What is the history of the term? Does everyone agree on its definition? Why or why not? If not, what points are in dispute?
Cause and Effect (Chapter 18)	What causes the topic? How often does it happen? What might prevent it from happening? What are its effects? What may happen because of it in the short term? What may happen as a result of it over time?
Argument (Chapters 19 and 20)	What issues surround this topic?

One student who was investigating the topic of extrasensory perception (ESP) decided to use the questions for definition and cause and effect. Here are the answers she wrote.

Definition (How can my topic be defined?)

- ESP, or extrasensory perception, is the ability to perceive information not through the ordinary senses but as a result of a "sixth sense" (as yet undeveloped in most people).
- Scientists disagree on whether ESP exists and how it should be tested.

Cause and Effect (What causes my topic? What may happen because of it?)

- Scientists do not know the cause of ESP and have not confirmed its existence, just the possibility of its existence.
- Some people with ESP claim to have avoided disasters such as airplane crashes.

Here is what one student "saw" when visualizing a shopping mall. Possible subtopics are annotated.

Possible subtopics:
Tour-group shopping

Teenage behavior

Body piercing

As I walked through the local mall, I crossed the walkway to get to Target and noticed a large group of excited women all dressed in jogging suits; they were part of a shopping tour, I think. I saw a tour bus parked outside. Across the walkway was a bunch of teenagers, shouting and laughing and commenting on each other's hairstyles. They all wore T-shirts and jeans; some had body adornments — pierced noses and lips. They seemed to have no interest in shopping. Their focus was on one another. Along the walkway came an obvious mother-daughter pair. They seemed to be on an outing, escaping from their day-to-day routine for some shopping, joking, and laughing.

LEARNING STYLE OPTIONS

Visualization is a technique particularly well suited to spatial and creative learners.

The technique of sketching, or storyboarding, uses a series of sketches to show the sequence of events or relationships among ideas. Visual learners may find it easier to draw sketches than to formulate ideas in words, and once the ideas are on paper in sketch form, they can be converted to text.

EXERCISE 4.10   VISUALIZING AND SKETCHING

Visualize one of the following situations. Make notes on or sketch what you "see." Include as many details as possible.

1. A couple obviously "in love"
2. A class you recently attended
3. The campus snack bar
4. A traffic jam
5. A sporting event

Research Your Topic

For more about finding, using, and citing sources, see Chapters 21 and 22.

To learn more about avoiding plagiarism, see Chapter 23, pp. 589–91.

Do some preliminary research on your topic. Reading what others have written about your topic may suggest new approaches, reveal issues or controversies, and help you determine what you already know (or do not know) about the topic.

Take notes while reading sources, and be sure to record the publication data you will need to cite each source (author, title, publisher, page numbers, and so on). If you use ideas or information from sources in your essay, you must give credit to those sources of the borrowed material. Make sure to avoid simply cutting and pasting material from your sources directly into your notes to avoid plagiarizing inadvertently. Plagiarism, even by accident, carries serious penalties.

LEARNING STYLE OPTIONS

While research may be particularly appealing to concrete or rational learners, all students may need to use it at one time or another depending on their topic.

HOW WRITERS READ ▶	USING PREWRITING STRATEGIES TO STRENGTHEN UNDERSTANDING
	The numerous prewriting strategies you use as a writer can also help you understand and remember more of what you read.
BEFORE READING	• Use **freewriting** or **brainstorming** to discover what you already know about the subject of the essay you are about to read.
WHILE READING	• Use **questioning** to interact with the author and read critically. • **Look for patterns** to help you interact with the text and connect ideas.
AFTER READING	• **Draw a map or graphic organizer** to help you organize and consolidate the content of the essay. It is also a useful strategy for study and review.

EXERCISE 4.11 ▶ RESEARCHING A TOPIC

Do library or Internet research to generate ideas on one of the narrowed topics listed here.

1. Reducing the federal deficit
2. Preventing terrorism in public areas
3. Controlling children's access to television programs
4. A recent local disaster (flood, earthquake)
5. Buying clothing on eBay

EXERCISE 4.12 ▶ PREWRITING

Choose two prewriting techniques discussed in this chapter that appeal to you. Experiment with each method by generating ideas about one of the topics from the previous exercises in the chapter. Use a different topic for each prewriting technique you choose.

ESSAY IN PROGRESS 3 ▶

Keeping your audience and purpose in mind, use one of the prewriting strategies discussed in this chapter to generate details about the topic you narrowed in Essay in Progress 2.

◀ STUDENTS WRITE

In this and the remaining five chapters of Part 2, we will follow the work of Latrisha Wilson, a student in a first-year writing course who was assigned to write about surveillance and loss of privacy.

Wilson decided to use questioning to narrow her topic and freewriting to generate ideas about her narrowed topic. Here is an example of her questioning.

Latrisha Wilson's Questioning

What are some examples of surveillance in the US?

Cameras in retail stores and at bank cash machines

Cell-phone surveillance and tracking

Airport security checkpoints

Online surveillance

Nanny cams

Traffic cameras and street corners

GPS devices worn by people on probation

Undercover police

Cameras in government buildings

Cameras on school buses

Wilson decided to explore further the types of surveillance commonly conducted in the United States. She did so by asking another question:

Which of these types of surveillance are the least "obvious"?

1. Undercover police

They disguise their identity.

They often become friends with the people they are investigating.

They participate in drug deals.

Oftentimes, their family members do not even know about their assignments.

They become the "bad guy" in order to get the "bad guy."

2. Online surveillance

Who is hiding behind our computer screens?

Valuable information about us is gathered from the Web.

Lots of information is gathered without our consent.

Google studies Gmail accounts for key words and sells the information to companies.

Information on Facebook is also sold to marketers.

After looking over the answers to her questions, Wilson decided to focus on types of surveillance. The following excerpt from her freewriting shows how she started to develop her topic.

Latrisha Wilson's Freewriting

I feel like I have no privacy. Just the other day I read how the mayor of my city brags of his new plan to put surveillance cameras on all the big street corners. There are already lots of traffic and security cameras. Soon there won't be anywhere I can walk without being monitored by some government employee sitting behind his desk. My life is like a movie anybody can watch. A reality tv show. If I'm not breaking the rules, what right does anyone have to track me? I'm not even safe going online. Netflix and YouTube keep suggesting movies to me. Stores where I have only shopped once keep emailing me about their new products. I get so much junk mail that Gmail just created a folder in my inbox just for "promotions." And right beside my inbox I see all those ads targeted specifically to me. If I write my mom "happy birthday," the next day I see ads for places to buy birthday hats. That's really creepy. I use Google for everything but that doesn't give them the right to pour through all my messages in search of information they can sell. I thought Google was a free service. To the mayor I'm just a potential criminal and to Google I'm just a potential consumer. What happened to my right to privacy?

As you work through the remaining chapters of Part 2, you will see how Wilson develops her tentative thesis statement in Chapter 5, a specific paragraph in Chapter 6, her first draft in Chapter 7, and her final draft in Chapter 8. In Chapter 9, you will see a paragraph from her final draft, edited and proofread to correct sentence-level errors.

5

Developing and Supporting a Thesis

"*The story is all over the Internet—I saved two little kids from drowning an hour ago. It's the latest thing: D.I.Y. news.*"

David Sipress/The New Yorker Collection/The Cartoon Bank

In this chapter you will learn to:

- write effective thesis statements
- support your thesis statement with evidence

WRITING QUICK START ▷ Study the cartoon on this page, which humorously depicts a serious situation. Working alone or with one or two classmates, write a statement that expresses the main point of the cartoon. Your statement should not only describe what is happening in the cartoon but also state the idea that the cartoonist is trying to communicate to his audience.

The statement you have just written is an assertion around which you could build an essay. Such an assertion is called a *thesis statement*. Developing a thesis is an important part of the writing process shown in Graphic Organizer 5.1 (p. 120), which lists the skills presented in this chapter while placing them within the larger context of the writing process.

What Is a Thesis Statement?

A **thesis statement** is the main point of an essay. It is usually expressed in a single sentence. An effective thesis statement should accomplish three goals. It should:

1. introduce your narrowed topic
2. reveal what your essay is about
3. state the point you will make about that topic

It may also forecast how the essay will be organized.

Here is a sample thesis statement.

┌────── Topic ──────┐   ┌────────── Position ──────────┐
Playing team sports, especially football and baseball, develops skills

and qualities that can make you successful in life because these sports

┌────────── Forecast ──────────┐
demand communication, teamwork, and responsibility.

When you write, think of a thesis statement as a promise to your reader. The rest of your essay delivers on your promise. The example thesis promises the audience that by reading this essay, they will discover how football and baseball players learn communication, teamwork, and responsibility and how these skills and qualities contribute to the players' success in life.

Develop Your Thesis Statement

Keep the following guidelines in mind as you develop your thesis statement.

- **Expect your thesis statement to evolve during prewriting.** Exploring your topic may lead you to discover a new focus or a more interesting way to approach your topic.

- **Expect to do research to revise your thesis.** You may need to do some reading or research to learn more about your topic or tentative thesis.

- **Expect to revise your thesis as you draft and revise your essay.** You may write several versions of a thesis statement before you find one that works, and you may revise your thesis as you gather and organize supporting evidence, draft, and revise your essay.

For more on prewriting, see Chapter 4.

For more on conducting research, see Chapter 22.

For more on drafting and revision, see Chapters 7 and 8.

LEARNING STYLE OPTIONS

Your learning style can influence how you develop a thesis statement. Pragmatic and concrete learners find it helpful to generate facts and details about a narrow topic and then write a thesis statement that reveals a large idea that is demonstrated by the details. Creative and abstract learners find it easier to begin with a broad idea, focus it in a thesis statement, and then generate details to support the thesis.

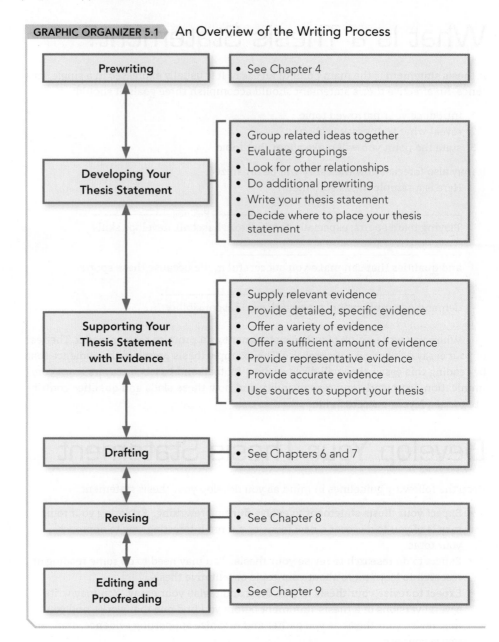

GRAPHIC ORGANIZER 5.1   An Overview of the Writing Process

Prewriting — • See Chapter 4

Developing Your Thesis Statement
- Group related ideas together
- Evaluate groupings
- Look for other relationships
- Do additional prewriting
- Write your thesis statement
- Decide where to place your thesis statement

Supporting Your Thesis Statement with Evidence
- Supply relevant evidence
- Provide detailed, specific evidence
- Offer a variety of evidence
- Offer a sufficient amount of evidence
- Provide representative evidence
- Provide accurate evidence
- Use sources to support your thesis

Drafting — • See Chapters 6 and 7

Revising — • See Chapter 8

Editing and Proofreading — • See Chapter 9

Synthesize Ideas to Generate a Working Thesis Statement

Coming up with a working thesis statement involves reviewing your prewriting to determine how some or all of the ideas you discovered fit together. It is a process of looking for similarities among ideas and grouping them in related categories. Use the following steps, adapting the process to your learning style.

1. **Review your prewriting, group together details on the same topic, and write a one- or two-word headline for each group.** A student working on the topic of intelligence in dogs noticed in her brainstormed list that the details could be grouped into two general categories: (1) details about learning and (2) details about instinct. Here is how she arranged her ideas.

Learning	Instinct
follow commands	females deliver and care for puppies
read human emotions	avoid danger and predators
get housebroken	seek shelter
serve as guide dogs for blind people	automatically raise hair on back in response to aggression

2. **Decide which group(s) of ideas best represents the focus your paper should take.** Sometimes, one group of details will be enough to develop a working thesis. Other times, you'll need to use the details in two or three groups. The student working on a thesis for the topic of intelligence in dogs evaluated her grouped details and decided that learning provided enough material to write about.

3. **Consider whether you have enough relevant details.** If your list of details is thin, you may not have enough details to come up with a good working thesis. Delete any details that do not work, and use prewriting to generate more ideas, trying a different prewriting strategy from the one you used previously. A new strategy may help you see your narrowed topic from a different perspective. If your second prewriting does not produce better results, consider refocusing or changing your topic.

ESSAY IN PROGRESS 1

If you used a prewriting strategy to generate details about your topic in response to Essay in Progress 3 in Chapter 4 (p. 115), review your prewriting, highlight useful ideas, and identify several sets of related details among those you have highlighted.

Write an Effective Thesis Statement

Use the following guidelines to write an effective thesis statement or to evaluate and revise your working thesis.

1. **An effective thesis makes an assertion.** Rather than stating a fact, a thesis should take a position, express a viewpoint, or suggest your approach toward the topic.

Lacks an Assertion	Hollywood movies, like *Sully* and *Loving*, are frequently based on true stories.
Revised Assertive	Hollywood movies, like *Sully* and *Loving*, manipulate true stories to cater to the tastes of the audience.

2. **An effective thesis is specific.** Provide as much information as possible about your main point.

Too General	I learned a great deal from my experiences as a teenage parent.
Revised	From my experiences as a teenage parent, I learned to accept responsibility for my own life and for that of my son.

EXERCISE 5.1   IDENTIFYING AND REVISING THESIS STATEMENTS THAT LACK ASSERTIONS

First, determine which of the following is a statement of fact and which is an assertion. Then revise each statement of fact, making it an assertion that could be an effective thesis statement for a brief (two- to four-page) college writing assignment.

1. By budgeting time and money, students can avoid stress and enjoy the holidays.
2. The viewers were moved by pictures of the devastation in Haiti following Hurricane Matthew.
3. Levying a fine on college students who cheat on an assignment might help improve academic integrity.
4. Taking a class online can be convenient, but succeeding in online classes requires self-discipline and motivation.
5. As a result of taking care of her family's dog, Adrian developed a strong desire to rescue abandoned pit bulls.

EXERCISE 5.2   IDENTIFYING AND REVISING OVERLY GENERAL THESIS STATEMENTS

First, determine which of the following thesis statements are too general for a brief (two- to four-page), college-level writing assignment. Then narrow the overly general thesis statements using the strategies for narrowing topics discussed above and in Chapter 4 (pp. 100–102).

1. Unfortunately, discrimination exists in many forms in today's society.
2. The demands of my job undermined my relationship with my family.
3. The experience of living in a dorm provides students with opportunities to develop valuable people skills that will serve them well throughout their lives.
4. Violent storms can have devastating effects on communities.
5. Although it seemed unwise at the time, postponing college was one of the wisest decisions I ever made.

3. **Focus on one central point.** Limit your essay to one major idea.

Focuses on Several Points	This college should improve its tutoring services, sponsor more activities of interest to Latino students, and speed up the registration process for students.
Revised	To better represent the student population it serves, this college should sponsor more activities of interest to Latino students.

4. **Offer an original perspective on your topic.** If your thesis seems dull or ordinary, it probably needs revision. Search your prewriting for an interesting angle on your topic.

Too Ordinary	Many traffic accidents are a result of carelessness.
Revised: More Interesting	An automobile accident can change a driver's entire approach to driving.

EXERCISE 5.3   IDENTIFYING AND REVISING THESIS STATEMENTS THAT FOCUS ON SEVERAL POINTS

The following thesis statements focus on more than one central point. Revise them so that each focuses clearly on only one point.

1. In order to be more successful in college, students must learn time management strategies, curtail their social life during the week, and learn to balance work and school obligations so that they are able to enjoy all parts of their life.
2. The Internet has revolutionized the way friends communicate, but it has also made children more sedentary, which has had negative health effects, and it has also made people in the workforce more solitary, which has undermined teamwork.
3. Movie theaters continue to attract viewers to new releases although many of them are simply remakes of older movies and ones that appeal only to those who like graphic violence.
4. Although the tornado destroyed the entire town and seriously injured hundreds of people, the local townspeople grew closer as they tended to the injured, helped to rebuild houses, and shared their financial resources with one another.
5. Although the company has made strides in repairing its reputation in the community, it still needs to pay its employees a fair salary, restructure management, and conduct business with more reputable vendors.

---

5. **Avoid making an announcement.** Don't use phrases such as "This essay will discuss" or "The subject of my paper is." Instead, state your main point directly.

Makes an Announcement	The point I am trying to make is that people should not be allowed to smoke on campus.
Revised: Main Point Stated Directly	The college should prohibit smoking on campus.

6. **Use your thesis to preview the organization of the essay.** Consider using your thesis to mention the two or three key concepts on which your essay will focus, in the order in which you will discuss them.

EXERCISE 5.4   EVALUATING THESIS STATEMENTS

Working in a group of two or three students, discuss what is wrong with each of the following thesis statements. Then revise each thesis to make it more effective.

1. In this paper, I will discuss the causes of asthma, which include exposure to smoke, chemicals, and allergic reactions.

2. Jogging is an enjoyable aerobic sport.
3. The crime rate is increasing in U.S. cities.
4. Living in an apartment has many advantages.
5. Children's toys can be dangerous, instructional, or creative.

ESSAY IN PROGRESS 2

Keeping your audience in mind, select one or more of the groups of ideas you identified in Essay in Progress 1. Write a working thesis statement based on these ideas.

Place the Thesis Statement Effectively

Your thesis statement can appear anywhere in your essay, but it is usually best to place it in the first paragraph as part of your introduction. When your thesis appears at the beginning of the essay, your readers will know what to pay attention to and what to expect in the rest of the essay. If you place your thesis later in the essay, you need to build up to it gradually in order to prepare readers for it.

Use an Implied Thesis

In some professional writing, especially in narrative or descriptive essays, the writer may not state the thesis directly. Instead, the thesis may be strongly implied by the details the writer chose and the way he or she organized them. Although some professional writers use an implied thesis, academic writers, including professors and students, generally state their thesis. You should always include a clear statement of your thesis in your college papers.

HOW WRITERS READ **IDENTIFYING AND USING THE THESIS STATEMENT**

Just as you express the main point of an essay you are writing in a thesis statement, so do most of the writers you will read in this text and in your other assigned reading. The strategies here will help you identify the thesis statement and use it to guide your reading.

BEFORE READING
- Preview the title, introduction, and conclusion to identify the subject of the reading, and then predict the thesis the writer may develop.

WHILE READING
- Identify the actual thesis. Does it confirm your prediction? If you have trouble identifying the thesis, ask yourself, "What is the most important idea the writer wants to express about the subject?" Then look for a sentence that states this point.
- Use the thesis statement to help you draw a blueprint of the essay: Think of the thesis statement as the roof; how do the reasons and key evidence the writer supplies support the thesis?

AFTER READING
- Paraphrase the thesis. If you cannot, this is a sign that you do not really understand the essay. (You may suffer from what psychologists of learning call the "illusion of knowing.") Reread the selection, or consult the "Just-in-Time Guide to Reading and Responding" (p. 94) for help.

Support Your Thesis Statement with Evidence

After you have written a working thesis statement, the next step is to develop evidence that supports your thesis. **Evidence** is any type of information, such as examples and anecdotes, facts and statistics, or expert opinion, that will convince your reader that your thesis is reasonable or correct. This evidence, organized into well-developed paragraphs, makes up the body of your essay. To visualize the basic structure of an essay, look ahead to Graphic Organizer 7.2 on page 157.

Tailor the Evidence to Your Writing Situation

Your writing situation—that is your purpose, audience, point of view, genre, and medium—will determine which types of evidence will be most effective. For example:

- If your purpose is to persuade, using comparison and contrast to highlight advantages and disadvantages, giving examples of problems, citing statistics to support your claim, and using quotations from experts may help make your argument convincing.
- If your audience is unfamiliar with your topic, providing definitions, historical background, an explanation of a process, and factual and descriptive details may be necessary.

Table 5.1 (p. 126) lists various types of evidence and gives examples of how each type could be used to support a working thesis on acupuncture. **Note:** Many of the types of evidence correspond to the patterns of development discussed in Parts 3 and 4.

| EXERCISE 5.5 | CHOOSING THE BEST EVIDENCE FOR YOUR WRITING SITUATION |

1. In groups of two or three students, discuss and list the types of evidence that could be used to support the following thesis statement for an informative essay.

   The need to become financially independent is a challenge for many young adults and often causes them to develop social and emotional problems.

2. For each audience, discuss and record the types of evidence that would offer the best support for the preceding thesis.
   a. Young adults
   b. Parents of young adults
   c. Counselors of young adults

Collect Evidence to Support Your Thesis

Select one or more of the following suggestions to generate evidence that supports your thesis.

LEARNING STYLE OPTIONS

TABLE 5.1 ▸ Types of Evidence Used to Support a Thesis

Working Thesis:	Acupuncture, a form of alternative medicine, is becoming more widely accepted in the United States.
Types of Evidence	**Example**
Definitions	Explain that in acupuncture, needles are inserted into specific points of the body to control pain or relieve symptoms.
Historical Background	Explain that acupuncture is a medical treatment that originated in ancient China.
Explanation of a Process	Explain the principles on which acupuncture is based and how scientists think it works.
Factual Details	Explain who uses acupuncture, on what parts of the body it is used, and under what circumstances it is applied.
Descriptive Details	Explain what acupuncture needles look and feel like.
Narrative Story	Relate a personal experience that illustrates the use of acupuncture.
Causes or Effects	Discuss one or two theories that explain why acupuncture works. Offer reasons for its increasing popularity.
Classification	Explain types of acupuncture treatments.
Comparison and Contrast	Compare acupuncture with other forms of alternative medicine, such as massage and herbal medicines. Explain how acupuncture differs from these other treatments.
Advantages and Disadvantages	Describe the pros (nonsurgical, relatively painless) and cons (fear of needles) of acupuncture.
Examples	Describe situations in which acupuncture has been used successfully—by dentists, in treating alcoholism, for pain control.
Problems	Explain that acupuncture is not always practiced by medical doctors; licensing and oversight of acupuncturists may thus be lax.
Statistics	Indicate how many acupuncturists practice in the United States.
Quotations	Quote medical experts who attest to the effectiveness of acupuncture as well as those who question its value.

1. Create a two-column worksheet; list types of evidence in the left column and provide examples that support your thesis in the right column. Collect evidence only for the types that are appropriate for your thesis.
2. Picture yourself speaking to your audience. What would you say to convince your audience of your thesis? Jot down ideas as they come to you.
3. Develop a skeletal outline of major headings. Leave plenty of blank space under each heading, and fill in ideas about each heading as they come to you.
4. Draw a graphic organizer of your essay, filling in supporting evidence as you think of it.
5. Discuss your thesis statement with a classmate; try to explain why he or she should accept your thesis as valid.

For more on outlining and drawing a graphic organizer, see Chapter 7.

Using the preceding list of suggestions and Table 5.1, generate at least three differ- ent types of evidence to support the working thesis statement you wrote in Essay in Progress 2.

Choose the Best Evidence

In collecting evidence in support of a thesis, you will probably generate more than you need. Consequently, you will need to identify the evidence that (1) best supports your thesis and (2) best suits your purpose and audience. Your learning style can influence the way you select evidence and the kinds of evidence you favor. If you are a creative or an abstract learner, for example, you may tend to focus on large ideas and overlook the need for supporting detail. If you are a pragmatic or concrete learner, you may tend to include too many details or fail to organize them logically.

LEARNING STYLE OPTIONS

The following guidelines will help you select the types of evidence that will best support your thesis.

1. **Make sure the evidence is relevant.** All of your evidence must clearly and directly support your thesis. Irrelevant evidence will distract and puzzle (or annoy) your readers. If your thesis is that acupuncture is useful for controlling pain, you would not need to describe other alternative therapies.

2. **Provide specific evidence.** Avoid general statements that will not help you make a convincing case for your thesis. For instance, to support the thesis that acupuncture is becoming more widely accepted by patients in the United States, citing statistics that demonstrate an increase in the number of practicing acupuncturists in the United States over the past five years would be most convincing. (You may need to return to your prewriting or conduct research to find evidence for your thesis.)

For more on conducting, incor- porating, and citing research, see Chapters 21 and 22.

3. **Offer a variety of evidence.** Using different kinds of evidence increases the likeli- hood that your evidence will convince your readers. If you provide only four exam- ples of people who have found acupuncture helpful, for instance, your readers may conclude that four people's experiences do not mean that acupuncture is becom- ing more popular nationally. If you also provide statistics and quotations from experts, however, more readers will be likely to accept your thesis. Using different types of evidence also enhances your credibility, showing readers you are well informed about your topic. The checklist on page 128 lists a number of evidence types. Use it to determine whether the evidence you are offering is varied enough.

4. **Provide a sufficient amount of evidence.** The amount of evidence you need var- ies according to your audience and your topic. To discover whether you have pro- vided enough evidence, ask a classmate to read your essay and tell you whether he or she is convinced. If your reader is not convinced, ask him or her what addi- tional evidence is needed.

5. **Provide representative evidence.** Do not provide unusual, rare, or exceptional sit- uations as evidence. Suppose your thesis is that acupuncture is widely used for various types of surgery. An example of one person who underwent painless heart surgery using only acupuncture will not support your thesis unless the use

For more about choosing reliable evidence, see Chapter 20.

of acupuncture in heart surgery is common. Including such an example would mislead your reader and may bring your credibility into question.

6. **Provide accurate evidence from reliable sources.** Do not make vague statements, guess at statistics, or make estimates. For example, do not simply say that many medical doctors are licensed to practice acupuncture in the United States or estimate the number. Instead, find out exactly how many U.S. physicians are licensed for this practice.

Checklist: Types of Evidence

Use this checklist to make sure you are offering a variety of evidence in support of your thesis.

- ☐ Historical background
- ☐ Factual details (facts, statistics)
- ☐ Narration (a story or anecdote)
- ☐ Descriptive details (details that appeal to the senses)
- ☐ Examples
- ☐ Explanation of a process
- ☐ Comparison and contrast
- ☐ Classification
- ☐ Definitions
- ☐ Causes or effects
- ☐ Advantages/disadvantages
- ☐ Problems
- ☐ Quotations

Choose Evidence for Academic Writing

For most kinds of academic writing, certain types of evidence are preferred over others. In general, your personal experiences and opinions are not considered as useful as more objective evidence such as facts, statistics, historical background, and expert testimony.

Suppose you are writing an academic paper on the effects of global warming. Your observations about climate changes in your city would not be considered adequate or appropriate evidence to support the idea of climatic change as an effect of global warming. To support your thesis, you would need to provide facts, statistics, and expert testimony on climatic change in a wide geographic area and demonstrate their relationship to global warming.

ESSAY IN PROGRESS 4

Evaluate the evidence you generated in Essay in Progress 3. Select the evidence that you could use to support your thesis in a two- to four-page essay.

Incorporate Visuals into an Essay

Today's readers are used to seeing more than words on a page, and since your task is to engage readers and communicate meaning effectively, using appropriate visuals may help. Visuals can enhance your essay and contribute to its meaning by:

- offering an example
- conveying information more clearly or concisely than you could in words
- eliciting a response or reaction from readers
- providing emphasis
- sparking interest

Of course, including visuals is not appropriate in every writing situation, nor is a visual a substitute for an explanation. And including a visual that is merely decorative is rarely appropriate, especially in academic writing. (Your instructor can advise you if you are unsure about whether including a visual is appropriate.)

The excerpt from a student essay on the next page illustrates how to use a visual effectively and how to integrate it into an essay.

The photograph of the horse and goat achieves several purposes.

- It offers an example of altruism among animals of different species.
- It creates visual interest.
- It lends emphasis to the essay's thesis—that animals exhibit emotions, including altruism.

Select Appropriate Visuals

Use the following guidelines to choose effective and reliable visuals.

See Chapter 3, pp. 72–80, for more about reading visuals actively and critically.

1. **Use visuals to illustrate important ideas in your essay.** Illustrations should offer support for your thesis or the topic sentence of the paragraph in which they appear. For example, you might include a photograph of a painting you are analyzing or a visual example that supports the point you are making in a paragraph (as above). You may also include a chart, table, or graph that allows you to convey a large amount of data clearly and succinctly.

2. **Use visuals that are appropriate given your audience.** Use visuals that are appropriate to your writing situation and that your audience will understand and appreciate. (For example, it would be inappropriate to include visuals that are merely decorative in a college essay.) Visuals should be avoided if they require prior knowledge your audience lacks or they make a point that could be more easily conveyed in words.

3. **Use visuals that are consistent with your method of development.** For example, a descriptive essay might include a photograph, a comparison-and-contrast essay might include a bar graph, a classification or division essay might include a table or pie chart, and a process essay might feature a diagram or flowchart.

4. **Avoid misleading visuals.** Make sure the data used to create charts and graphs are reliable and that photographs do not distort or misrepresent the subjects. Visuals from sources such as well-respected news organizations or government agencies are generally reliable.

To incorporate a visual effectively within your essay, reference the visual (*for example, see fig. 1*) and briefly explain its intended message. Place the visual as close after the reference in the text as possible to ensure readers can connect the visual with the part of the text in which it is discussed. Include the figure number and a brief explanatory caption below.

One final word of caution: Unless the visual is a photograph you took or a graphic created from data you collected, you must credit the source. For academic papers, include complete source information at the end of the caption (unless your instructor provides other instructions).

Destino 4

Sympathy and caring have been noted in non-primate species as well. Researchers have found that young barn owls are "impressively generous" towards each other, saving portions of their food for smaller and hungrier owls (Angier). Likewise, the *Nature* episode "Animal Odd Couples" documents a number of instances in which animals of one species have cared for animals of another. In one example, Jack, a goat, led Charlie, a blind horse, around the ranch where they lived *every day for sixteen years*, until Jack's death (Fig. 1). The animals' caretaker even compared Jack to the television character Lassie, describing how Jack got human help to rescue Charlie after he became trapped in a grove of trees following a microburst of wind.

Fig. 1. Seeing is believing: Jack leading Charlie (a blind horse). Film still from "Animal Odd Couples" (27:23), *Nature* (PBS, 7 Nov. 2012).

What makes this example particularly noteworthy is that the animals were of different species. Had the goat been helping another goat, it would be easy to assume that the act of caring was the result of what scientists call *genetic altruism,* animals helping others of their own species because there is something in it for them—namely, the assurance that their kin (and, therefore, their genes) will continue. This theory certainly provides an adequate, unbiased scientific explanation for why animals might care for others. However, if

Identifies the source

Introduces and explains the visual

Includes a figure number in the text and caption, and numbers figures consecutively; places the visual as close after the figure callout as possible

Includes a caption that explains the visual and includes source information

Topic sentence supports the thesis and references the example

Use Sources to Support Your Thesis

For many topics, you will need to conduct research to collect enough evidence to support your thesis. Chapter 22 provides a thorough guide to finding reliable sources by using library catalogs and databases and Internet search engines (pp. 565–72), and it also includes tips for accomplishing firsthand (or primary) research by conducting interviews, surveys, and observations (pp. 573–74). Chapter 23 provides guidelines for integrating and documenting sources (pp. 593–99). Also see "Write from Sources: Use Sources to Make Your Own Ideas Convincing," in Chapter 21, pp. 550–51. As you use sources, be sure to record complete source information so you can credit them.

Note: Cutting and pasting information directly from sources into your notes and papers can lead to accidental plagiarism, so always be sure to put borrowed material in quotation marks or to rephrase it in your own words.

> ### ESSAY IN PROGRESS 5

Locate and consult at least two sources to find evidence that supports the working thesis statement you wrote in Essay in Progress 2.

> ### STUDENTS WRITE

In the Students Write section of Chapter 4, you saw how Latrisha Wilson narrowed her topic and generated ideas for her essay on surveillance. You also saw how she explored types of surveillance as they affect her privacy. After reviewing her responses to questions about her topic and her freewriting, Wilson drafted the following working thesis.

> These new digital technologies have both benefits and drawbacks.

She realized that her thesis was overly general and too broad, so she did more freewriting and brainstorming to help her recall details about types of surveillance. Here's an excerpt from her brainstorming.

- Spies like James Bond are no longer necessary. Movies and video games fool us into believing they are, but mainly spying is done by computers.
- The National Security Agency (NSA) watches everything we do on the Internet and everything we say on our phones.
- Edward Snowden, the NSA whistleblower, was a newsmaker. He exposed the NSA's secret surveillance.
- Google has access to everything about us, and they sell the information to other companies.
- If we want to communicate through a screen or a phone, we have to give up our privacy.
- We seldom are asked for our consent to share information about ourselves.

- Twitter, Flickr, YouTube, Facebook, and other new media also provide lots of information about our daily lives, and not just to our "friends."
- Because we enjoy sharing our lives and learning about the lives of others, we forget about where the information is going.
- In reality, we have very little privacy if we use digital devices.

After brainstorming, she decided that she should focus on the drawbacks of digital communications technology. She narrowed her thesis even further to focus on the subtle forms of surveillance new communications technology enable.

> Often advertised as free services, new ways of communicating put us under more invasive but less obvious forms of surveillance.

READING

Internet Addiction

Greg Beato

The following essay by Greg Beato was first published in 2010 in *Reason*, a magazine that offers updates on current developments in politics and culture from a libertarian perspective. Beato, a contributing editor for *Reason*, supports the essay's thesis with a variety of evidence. As you read, highlight the thesis statement and notice the types of evidence used to support it.

Before Reading

1. **Preview** Use the steps listed on page 28.
2. **Connect** What does *addiction* mean in this context, and what kinds of Internet use does Beato mean?

While Reading Pay particular attention to Beato's thesis and the evidence he provides to support it.

In 1995, in an effort to parody the way the American Psychiatric Association's hugely influential *Diagnostic and Statistical Manual of Mental Disorders* medicalizes every excessive behavior, psychiatrist Ivan Goldberg introduced on his website the concept of "Internet Addiction Disorder." Last summer Ben Alexander, a 19-year-old college student obsessed with the online multiplayer game *World of Warcraft*, was profiled by CBS News, NPR, the Associated Press, and countless other media outlets because of his status as client No. 1 at reSTART, the first residential treatment center in America for individuals trying to get themselves clean from Azeroth, iPhones, and all the other digital narcotics of our age.   1

At reSTART's five-acre haven in the woods near Seattle, clients pay big bucks to detox from pathological computer use by building chicken coops, cooking hamburgers, and engaging in daily therapy sessions with the program's two founders,   2 psychologist Hilarie Cash and clinical social worker and life coach Cosette Rae. With room for just six addicts at a time and a $14,500 program fee, reSTART isn't designed for the masses, and so far it seems to have attracted more reporters than paying clients. When I spoke with Rae in May, she said "10 to 15" people had participated in the 45-day program to date.

Still, the fact that reSTART exists at all shows how far we've progressed in   3
taking Dr. Goldberg's spoof seriously. You may have been too busy monitoring

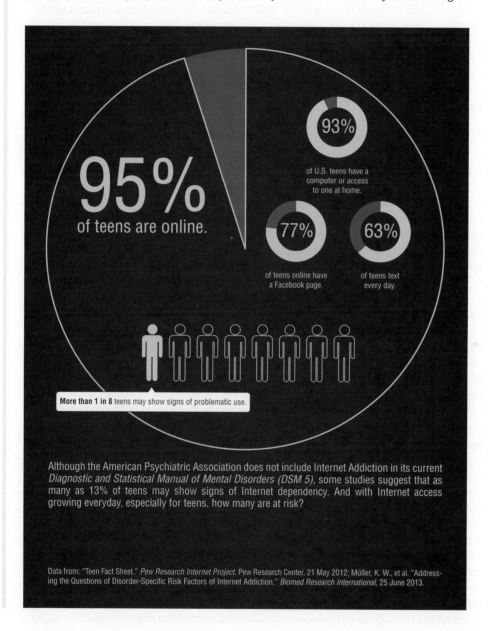

95%
of teens are online.

93%
of U.S. teens have a computer or access to one at home.

77%
of teens online have a Facebook page.

63%
of teens text every day.

More than 1 in 8 teens may show signs of problematic use.

Although the American Psychiatric Association does not include Internet Addiction in its current *Diagnostic and Statistical Manual of Mental Disorders (DSM 5)*, some studies suggest that as many as 13% of teens may show signs of Internet dependency. And with Internet access growing everyday, especially for teens, how many are at risk?

Data from: "Teen Fact Sheet." *Pew Research Internet Project*. Pew Research Center, 21 May 2012; Müller, K. W., et al. "Addressing the Questions of Disorder-Specific Risk Factors of Internet Addiction." *Biomed Research International*, 25 June 2013.

Kim Kardashian's every passing thought-like thing on Twitter to notice, but Digital Detox Week took place in April, and Video Game Addiction Awareness Week followed on its heels in June. Internet addiction disorder has yet to claim a Tiger Woods of its own, but the sad, silly evidence of our worldwide cyber-bingeing mounts on a daily basis. A councilman in the Bulgarian city of Plovdiv is ousted from his position for playing *Farmville* during budget meetings. There are now at least three apps that use the iPhone's camera to show the world right in front of you so you can keep texting while walking down the street, confident in your ability to avoid sinkholes, telephone poles, and traffic. Earlier this year, 200 students taking a class in media literacy at the University of Maryland went on a 24-hour media fast for a group study, then described how "jittery," "anxious," "miserable," and "crazy" they felt without Twitter, Facebook, iPods, and laptops. "I clearly am addicted," one student concluded, "and the dependency is sickening."

In the early days of the Web, dirty talk was exchanged at the excruciatingly slow rate of 14.4 bits per second, connectivity charges accrued by the hour instead of the month, and the only stuff for sale online was some overpriced hot sauce from a tiny store in Pasadena. It took the patience of a Buddhist monk, thousands of dollars, and really bad TV reception to overuse the Web in a self-destructive manner. Yet even then, many people felt Ivan Goldberg's notes on Internet addiction worked better as psychiatry than comedy. A year before Goldberg posted his spoof, Kimberly Young, a psychologist at the University of Pittsburgh, had already begun conducting formal research into online addiction. By 1996 the Harvard-affiliated McLean Hospital had established a computer addiction clinic, a professor at the University of Maryland had created an Internet addiction support group, and *The New York Times* was running op-eds about the divorce epidemic that Internet addiction was about to unleash.

Fifteen years down the line, you'd think we'd all be introverted philanderers by now, isolating ourselves in the virtual Snuggie of *World of Warcraft* by day and stepping out at night to destroy our marriages with our latest hook-ups from AshleyMadison.com. But the introduction of flat monthly fees, online gaming, widespread pornography, MySpace, YouTube, Facebook, WiFi, iPhones, netbooks, and free return shipping on designer shoes with substantial markdowns does not seem to have made the Internet any more addictive than it was a decade ago.

In 1998 Young told the Riverside *Press-Enterprise* that "5 to 10 percent of the 52 million Internet users [were] addicted or 'potentially addicted.'" Doctors today use similar numbers when estimating the number of online junkies. In 2009 David Greenfield, a psychiatrist at the University of Connecticut, told the *San Francisco Chronicle* that studies have shown 3 percent to 6 percent of Internet users "have a problem." Is it possible that the ability to keep extremely close tabs on Ashton Kutcher actually has reduced the Internet's addictive power?

Granted, 3 percent is an awful lot of people. Argue all you like that a real addiction should require needles, or spending time in seedy bars with people who drink vodka through their eyeballs, or at least the overwhelming and nihilistic urge to invest thousands of dollars in a broken public school system through the purchase of lottery tickets. Those working on the front lines of technology overuse have plenty of casualties to point to. In our brief conversation, Cosette Rae tells me about a Harvard student who lost a scholarship because he spent too much time playing games, a guy who spent so many sedentary hours at his computer that he developed blood clots in his leg and had to have it amputated, and an 18-year-old who chose homelessness over gamelessness when his parents told him he either had to quit playing computer games or move out.

A few minutes on Google yields even more lurid anecdotes. In 2007 an Ohio   8
teenager shot his parents, killing his mother and wounding his father, after they took away his Xbox. This year a South Korean couple let their real baby starve to death because they were spending so much time caring for their virtual baby in a role-playing game called *Prius Online*.

On a pound-for-pound basis, the average *World of Warcraft* junkie undoubtedly   9
represents a much less destructive social force than the average meth head. But it's not extreme anecdotes that make the specter of Internet addiction so threatening; it's the fact that Internet overuse has the potential to scale in a way that few other addictions do. Even if Steve Jobs designed a really cool-looking syringe and started distributing free heroin on street corners, not everyone would try it. But who among us doesn't already check his email more often than necessary? As the Internet weaves itself more and more tightly into our lives, only the Amish are completely safe.

As early as 1996, Kimberly Young was promoting the idea that the American   10
Psychiatric Association (APA) should add Internet addiction disorder to the *Diagnostic and Statistical Manual of Mental Disorders* (DSM). In February, the APA announced that its coming edition of the *DSM*, the first major revision since 1994, will for the first time classify a behavior-related condition—pathological gambling—as an "addiction" rather than an "impulse control disorder." Internet addiction disorder is not being included in this new category of "behavioral addictions," but the APA said it will consider it as a "potential addition . . . as research data accumulate."

If the APA does add excessive Internet use to the *DSM*, the consequences will   11
be wide-ranging. Health insurance companies will start offering at least partial coverage for treatment programs such as reSTART. People who suffer from Internet addiction disorder will receive protection under the Americans with Disabilities Act if their impairment "substantially limits one or more major life activities." Criminal lawyers will use their clients' online habits to fashion diminished capacity defenses.

Which means that what started as a parody in 1995 could eventually turn   12
more darkly comic than ever imagined. Picture a world where the health care system goes bankrupt because insurers have to pay for millions of people determined to kick their Twitter addictions once and for all. Where employees who view porn at work are legally protected from termination. Where killing elves in cyberspace could help absolve you for killing people in real life. Is it too late to revert to our older, healthier, more balanced ways of living and just spend all our leisure hours watching *Love Boat* reruns?

Examining the Reading

1. **Definition** Define the term *Internet addiction*.
2. **Examples** What are some examples of dangerous behavior caused by Internet addiction?
3. **Meaning** Why does adding Internet addiction to the *DSM* have important social consequences?
4. **Vocabulary** Define each of the following words as they are used in the essay: *parody* (para. 1), *pathological* (2), *nihilistic* (7), *lurid* (8), and *specter* (9).

Analyzing the Writer's Technique

1. **Thesis** State the author's thesis in your own words. Then, using the guidelines on pages 121–23, evaluate the effectiveness of the thesis.
2. **Rhetorical Situation** To what audience does Beato address this essay? What purpose does the essay fulfill? How do you think the writing situation affects the author's choice of evidence?
3. **Support** Cite one paragraph from the essay in which you think the author provides detailed, specific information. Explain why you chose that paragraph. Does it support the thesis? Why or why not?

Visualizing the Reading

In the chart below, supply an example of each type of evidence the author has used in the reading. The first one has been done for you.

Type of Evidence	Example
Historical Background	Website parody of the *DSM* in 1995 included Internet addiction and 1996 McLean Hospital program for Internet addiction
Descriptive Details	
Statistics	
Examples	
Comparison and Contrast	
Quotations	

Thinking Critically about the Reading

1. **Sources** Evaluate the sources that Beato uses to support his thesis. Are they trustworthy and reliable?
2. **Tone** Describe the author's tone. How does the tone affect your response to the reading?
3. **Opinion** Identify at least one statement of opinion in paragraph 9. Does the author offer evidence to support the opinion?
4. **Connotation** What is the connotation of the word *junkies* in paragraph 6? Identify at least four other words in the selection with strong positive or negative connotations.
5. **Evaluation** How useful are the anecdotes in paragraphs 7 and 8 as evidence?

For more about connotation and tone, see Chapters 3 and 9, pp. 61–62, 64–66, 206, 209; for more about distinguishing between facts and opinions, see Chapter 3, pp. 60–61.

Interpreting a Graphic

1. **Meaning** The text below the large pie chart on page 133 reports that "13% of teens show signs of Internet dependency," and the pictogram says that "more than 1 in 8 teens may show signs of problematic use." What is the difference between the terms *dependency* and *problematic use*?
2. **Source** How reliable do the sources for this graphic seem? What other sources might you use for a paper on Internet dependency among teens?

Responding to the Reading

1. **Audience** How do you think this essay would change if the author wrote it for *Parents* magazine?
2. **Discussion** Why do you think the number of people addicted to the Internet has actually lessened since 1998? What might it mean that the American Psychological Association is not ready to include Internet addiction in the *DSM*? What does this say about the disorder?
3. **Journal** In your journal, write about ways you use the Internet that may not be healthy. How does it negatively affect your life? Do you feel it has more positive than negative effects on your life? Explain.

Working Together

1. Imagine that you and a classmate are authors of an advice column for your college newspaper. Write a letter responding to a reader who asked for advice about kicking her Internet addiction. Working with your partner, draft a one-paragraph reply, suggesting steps the person can take to break free of her addiction. Be creative in your response. Be prepared to share your advice with the class.
2. Working with two or three of your classmates, spend five to ten minutes brainstorming a list of positive and negative effects of Internet use among college students. Then write a thesis statement based on the ideas you generated. Compare your list with the lists of other groups in the class.

3. In groups of two or three, examine the cartoon below. Together, come up with a one-sentence thesis statement (or punch line) that expresses the main point of the cartoon. Do not describe the cartoon. Rather, convey the underlying message the cartoonist is trying to communicate—humorously, if you can. (To see the caption the cartoonist supplied, turn to the Acknowledgments page at the end of the book.)

Michael Crawford, The New Yorker Collection/The Cartoon Bank

Thesis/punch line: _____

DON EMMERT/AFP/Getty Images

6
Writing Effective Paragraphs

WRITING QUICK START   The photograph above shows a phenomenon called "santa crowding." Study the photograph and write a sentence that describes the mood or feelings of those participating in the event. Then write several more sentences that explain what details in the photograph reveal the feelings exhibited by the crowd.

In much the same way as a photograph does, a paragraph makes an overall impression, or main point, and includes details that support this main point. Your first sentence, or **topic sentence**, states the main idea, and the other sentences you write provide the details that support it.

Structure Your Paragraphs Effectively

A paragraph is a group of connected sentences that develop a single idea about a topic. Each paragraph in your essay should support your thesis and contribute to the overall meaning and effectiveness of your essay. A well-developed paragraph contains:

- a well-focused topic sentence
- specific supporting details (definitions, examples, facts and statistics, explanations, or other evidence)
- transitions and strategic repetition that show how the ideas are related, within and across paragraphs

For a paragraph to develop a single idea, it must have **unity**: It must stay focused on one idea, without switching or wandering from topic to topic. A paragraph also should be of a reasonable length, neither too short nor too long. Short paragraphs are often underdeveloped; long paragraphs may be difficult for readers to follow. Note that what is an appropriate length may change across genres (or types) of writing—college essays usually have longer paragraphs than newspaper articles, and scholarly articles usually have longer paragraphs than college essays.

Here is a sample paragraph from a college textbook with its parts labeled.

Topic sentence: Main idea

Repetition: Key terms

Transitions: Guideposts

Audiences gather with varying degrees of willingness to hear a speaker. Some are anxious to hear the speaker, and may even have paid a substantial admission price. The "lecture circuit," for example, is a most lucrative aspect of public life. But whereas some audiences are willing to pay to hear a speaker, others don't seem to care one way or the other. Other audiences need to be persuaded to listen (or at least to sit in the audience). Still other audiences gather because they have to. For example, negotiations on a union contract may require members to attend meetings where officers give speeches.

DeVito, *The Essential Elements of Public Speaking*

Notice also how the writer repeats the words *audience(s)* and *speaker*, along with the synonyms *lecture* and *speeches*, to help tie the paragraph to the idea in the topic sentence. To visualize the structure of a well-developed paragraph, see Graphic Organizer 6.1.

GRAPHIC ORGANIZER 6.1   The Structure of a Paragraph

Topic Sentence
- Identifies what the paragraph is about
- Makes a point about the topic
- Connects to the previous paragraph

Supporting Details
- Explain the topic sentence
- Support the topic sentence with evidence, such as examples, facts, statistics, personal experience, and definitions

Concluding or Transitional Sentence
- Draws the paragraph to a close, *or*
- Leads to the next paragraph

Write Effective Topic Sentences

A **topic sentence** is to a paragraph what a thesis statement is to an essay. Just as a thesis announces the main point of an essay, a topic sentence states the main point of a paragraph. In addition, each paragraph's topic sentence must support the thesis of the essay. An effective topic sentence should be focused, support the thesis, and be placed appropriately (usually at the beginning of the paragraph).

A Topic Sentence Should Be Focused

A topic sentence should make clear what the paragraph is about (its topic) and express a view or make a point about the topic.

> ┌─────── topic ───────┐
> Shocking behavior by fans, including rudeness and violent language,
>
> ┌─────────── point about topic ───────────┐
> has become common at many sporting events.

It should use specific and detailed language to tell readers what the paragraph is about. Avoid vague, general, or unfocused statements.

Unfocused	Some members of minority groups do not approve of affirmative action.
Focused	Some members of minority groups disapprove of affirmative action because it implies that they are not capable of obtaining employment based on their own accomplishments.
Unfocused	Many students believe that hate groups shouldn't be allowed on campus.
Focused	The neo-Nazis, a group that promotes hate crimes, should not be permitted to speak in our local community college because most students find its members' views objectionable.

If you have trouble focusing your topic sentences, review the guidelines for writing an effective thesis statement in Chapter 5 (pp. 121–24), many of which also apply to writing effective topic sentences.

A Topic Sentence May Preview the Organization of the Paragraph

A topic sentence may suggest the order in which details are discussed in the paragraph, so readers know what to expect.

> Teaching employees how to handle conflicts through both
> ┌─── detail 1 ───┐   ┌─ detail 2 ─┐
> anger management and mediation is essential in high-stress jobs.

Readers can expect a discussion of anger management first, followed by a discussion of mediation.

EXERCISE 6.1 **WORKING WITH TOPIC SENTENCES**

Revise each of the following topic sentences to make it focused and specific. At least two of your revised topic sentences should also preview the organization of the paragraph.

1. In society today, there is always a new fad or fashion in clothing.
2. People watch television talk shows because they find them irresistible.
3. Tattoos are a popular trend.
4. Procrastinating can have a negative effect on your success in college.
5. In our state, the lottery is a big issue.

A Topic Sentence Should Support Your Thesis

Each topic sentence must in some way explain the thesis or show why the thesis is believable or correct. For example, this sample thesis could be supported by the topic sentences that follow it.

Thesis   Adoption files should not be made available to adult children who are seeking their biological parents.

Topic Sentences

- Research has shown that not all biological parents want to meet with the sons or daughters they gave up many years before.
- If a woman gives up a child for adoption, it is probable that she does not ever intend to have a relationship with that child.
- Adult children who try to contact their biological parents often meet resistance and even hostility, which can cause them to feel hurt and rejected.
- A woman who gave up her biological child because she became pregnant as a result of rape or incest should not have to live in fear that her child will one day confront her.

All of these topic sentences support the thesis because they offer valid reasons for keeping adoption files closed.

EXERCISE 6.2 **USING TOPIC SENTENCES TO SUPPORT A THESIS**

For each of the following thesis statements, identify the topic sentence in the list below it that does not support the thesis.

1. To make a marriage work, a couple must build trust, communication, and understanding.
   a. Knowing why a spouse behaves as he or she does can improve a relationship.
   b. People get married for reasons other than love.

    c. The ability to talk about feelings, problems, likes, and dislikes should grow as a marriage develops.

    d. Marital partners must rely on each other to make sensible decisions that benefit both of them.

2. Internet sales are capturing a larger market share relative to in-store sales.

    a. Internet retailers that target a specific audience tend to be most successful.

    b. The convenience of ordering any time of day or night accounts, in part, for increased Internet sales.

    c. Many customers use PayPal for online purchases.

    d. Websites that locate and compare prices for a specified item make comparison shopping easier on the Internet than in retail stores.

A Topic Sentence Should Be Strategically Placed

The beginning of the paragraph is the most common and often the best position for a topic sentence: You state your main point, and then you explain it. The topic sentence tells readers what to expect in the rest of the paragraph, making it clear and easy for them to follow.

> Advertising is first and foremost based on the principle of visibility—the customer must notice the product. Manufacturers often package products in glitzy, even garish, containers to grab the consumer's attention. For example, one candy company always packages its candy in reflective wrappers. When the hurried and hungry consumer glances at the candy counter, the reflective wrappers are easy to spot. It is only natural for the impatient customer to grab the candy and go.

Topic sentence: Appears at beginning of paragraph

When one or two sentences are needed at the beginning of a paragraph to smooth the transition from one paragraph to the next, the topic sentence may follow these transitional sentences.

> However, visibility is not the only principle in advertising; it is simply the first. A second and perhaps more subtle principle is identity: The manufacturer attempts to lure the consumer into buying a product by linking it to a concept with which the consumer can identify. For instance, Boundaries perfume is advertised on television as the choice of "independent" women. Since independent women are admired in our culture, women identify with the concept and therefore are attracted to the perfume. Once the consumer identifies with the product, a sale is more likely to occur.

Topic sentence: Appears after transitional sentence, before example

If you want to present convincing evidence before stating your point about the issue, you may want to save your topic sentence until the end of the paragraph. This allows readers to draw their own conclusions based on the details you have provided. This strategy is common in argumentative writing (especially when readers may not be sympathetic to the writer's position).

> The saying "Guns don't kill people; people kill people" is deceptive in the same way that the statement "Heroin doesn't kill people; people kill themselves" is deceptive. Naturally, people need to pull the trigger of a gun to make the gun kill other

people, just as it is necessary for a person to use heroin for it to kill him or her. However, these facts do not excuse us from the responsibility of keeping guns (or heroin) out of people's hands as much as possible. People cannot shoot people unless they have a gun. This fact alone should persuade the government to institute stiff gun control laws.

Topic sentence: Follows evidence

See the Just-in-Time Guide to Reading and Responding for help determining the implied main point of a paragraph (p. 91) and which supporting details are most important to remember (pp. 91–92).

ESSAY IN PROGRESS 1

For an essay that you have written for this or another class, evaluate each of your topic sentences for content and placement. Revise as needed to make each more effective.

HOW WRITERS READ **PARAGRAPHS**

Use these strategies to understand and remember what you read.

WHILE READING
- Identify the paragraph's topic, or main idea, and the position or point of view the writer wants to express about the topic. (This is usually conveyed by the topic sentence, but may be implied.)
- Use transitional words and phrases to guide you from one detail to another and to alert you when the author moves on to a new idea. Transitions may even signal what kind of idea (an example, a contradictory fact, a further explanation) is to follow and which supporting ideas are most important.

AFTER READING
- Test your understanding and recall of the paragraph's main point by paraphrasing the topic sentence (expressing it in your own words) without looking at the paragraph.

Include Supporting Details

In addition to including well-focused topic sentences, effective paragraphs are unified and well developed—they provide relevant details that support the main point.

Effective Paragraphs Have Unity

A paragraph has unity when all of the sentences directly support the topic sentence. Including details that are not relevant to the topic sentence makes your paragraph unclear and distracts your reader from the point you are making. To identify irrelevant details, evaluate each sentence by asking the following questions.

1. Does this sentence directly explain the topic sentence? What new information does it add?
2. Would any essential information be lost if this sentence were deleted? (If not, delete it.)
3. Is this information distracting or unimportant? (If so, delete it.)

The following sample paragraph lacks unity. As you read it, try to identify the sentences that do not support the topic sentence.

Paragraph Lacking Unity

(1) Much of the violence we see in the world today may be caused by the emphasis on violence in the media. (2) More often than not, the front page of the local newspaper contains stories involving violence. (3) In fact, one recent issue of my local newspaper contained seven references to violent acts. (4) There is also violence in public school systems. (5) Television reporters frequently hasten to crime and accident scenes and film every grim, violent detail. (6) The other day, there was a drive-by shooting downtown. (7) If the media were a little more careful about the ways in which they glamorize violence, there might be less violence in the world today and children would be less influenced by it.

Topic sentence: Main idea

Although sentences 4 and 6 deal with the broad topic of violence, neither is directly related to the main point stated in the topic sentence. Both should be deleted.

| EXERCISE 6.3 | **PRACTICING PARAGRAPH UNITY** |

Alone or in a group of two or three students, read each paragraph and identify the sentences that do not support the highlighted topic sentence.

1. (a) Today many options and services for the elderly are available that did not exist years ago. (b) My grandmother is eighty-five years old now. (c) Adult care for the elderly is now provided in many parts of the country. (d) Similar to day care, adult care provides places where the elderly can go for meals and social activities. (e) Retirement homes for the elderly, where they can live fairly independently with minimal supervision, are another option. (f) My grandfather is also among the elderly at eighty-two. (g) Even many nursing homes have changed so that residents are afforded some level of privacy and independence while their needs are being met.

2. (a) Just as history repeats itself, fashions have a tendency to do the same. (b) In the late 1960s, for example, women wore miniskirts that came several inches above the knee; some forty years later, the fashion magazines are featuring this same type of dress, and many teenagers are wearing them. (c) The miniskirt has always been flattering on slender women. (d) I wonder if the fashion industry deliberately recycles fashions. (e) Men wore their hair long in the hippie period of the late 1960s and 1970s. (f) Today, some men are again letting their hair grow. (g) Beards, considered "in" during the 1970s, have once again made an appearance.

Effective Paragraphs Are Well Developed

A well-developed paragraph should include enough supporting details to demonstrate that the topic sentence is accurate and believable. Compare the two paragraphs below.

Underdeveloped Paragraph

Email and texting are important technological advances, but they have hidden limitations, even dangers. It is too easy to avoid talking to people face to face.

Does not explain why email and text messaging are important

Emailing and texting can be addictive, too. Plus, they encourage ordinary people to ignore others while typing on a keyboard.

Developed Paragraph

Email and texting are important technological advances, but they have hidden limitations, even dangers. While email and texting allow fast and efficient communication and exchange of information, they provide a different quality of human interaction. It is too easy to avoid talking to people. It is easier to click on a phone number and text a friend to see if she wants to meet for dinner than it would be actually to talk to her. In fact, using these services can become addictive. For example, some students on campus are obsessed with checking their email and sending, reading, or checking for texts many times throughout the day, even during class lectures and small group discussions. They spend their free time texting with acquaintances across the country while ignoring interesting people right in the same room. There is something to be said for talking with a person who is sitting next to you and responding to his or her expressions, gestures, and tone of voice.

The first paragraph has skeletal ideas that support the topic sentence, but it does not explain those ideas. The second paragraph fleshes out the ideas by providing examples and explanations.

To discover if your paragraphs are well developed, ask yourself the following questions.

- Have I provided enough evidence to achieve my purpose?
- Have I given my readers enough information to make my ideas understandable and believable?
- Have I provided the amount and type of evidence that readers of a college essay will expect?
- Do I jump quickly from one idea to another without explaining each idea first? (Reading your essay aloud, or asking a friend to do so, can help you hear gaps.)

To develop your paragraphs further, you can use a prewriting strategy or do some research to find supporting evidence for your topic sentence. The same types of evidence that can be used to support a thesis can be used to develop a paragraph.

EXERCISE 6.4 ▸ USING EVIDENCE TO DEVELOP A PARAGRAPH

Use Table 5.1 (p. 126) to suggest the type or types of evidence that might be used to develop a paragraph based on each of the following topic sentences.

1. Many people have fallen prey to fad diets, risking their health and jeopardizing their mental well-being.
2. One can distinguish experienced soccer players from rookies by obvious signs.
3. To begin a jogging routine, take a relaxed but deliberate approach.
4. The interlibrary loan system is a fast and convenient method for obtaining print materials from libraries affiliated with the campus library.
5. Southwest Florida's rapid population growth poses a serious threat to its freshwater supply.

Margin annotations:

Does not provide any evidence of how or why they can be addictive

States reason that emailing and texting are disadvantageous

Provides further information about the addictive qualities of texting and email

Explains the qualities of face-to-face interaction that are absent from email and texting

To learn more about prewriting strategies, see Chapter 4; for more on research, see Part 5; for a list of evidence that can be used to support a paragraph, see Table 5.1, p. 126.

EXERCISE 6.5 ▸ USING DETAILS TO DEVELOP A PARAGRAPH

Create a well-developed paragraph by adding details to the following paragraph.

> Although it is convenient, online shopping is a different experience than shopping in an actual store. You don't get the same opportunity to see and feel objects. Also, you can miss out on other important information. There is much that you miss. If you enjoy shopping, turn off your computer and support your local merchants.

Effective Paragraphs Provide Supporting Details and Arrange Them Logically

The evidence you provide to support your topic sentences should be concrete and specific. Specific details interest your readers and make your meaning clear and forceful. Compare the following two examples.

Vague

Many people are confused about the difference between a psychologist and a psychiatrist. Both have a license, but a psychiatrist has more education than a psychologist. Also, a psychiatrist can prescribe medication.

General statements that do not completely explain the topic sentence

Concrete and Specific

Many people are confused about the difference between psychiatrists and psychologists. Both are licensed by the state to practice psychotherapy. However, a psychiatrist has earned a degree from medical school and can also practice medicine. Additionally, a psychiatrist can prescribe psychotropic medications. A psychologist, on the other hand, usually has earned a Ph.D. but has not attended medical school and therefore cannot prescribe medication of any type.

Concrete details make clear the distinction between the two terms

To make your paragraphs concrete and specific, use the following guidelines.

1. **Focus on *who, what, when, where, how,* and *why* questions.** Ask yourself these questions about your supporting details, and use the answers to expand and revise your paragraph.

   Vague   Some animals hibernate for part of the year. (What animals? When do they hibernate?)

   Specific   Some bears hibernate for three to four months each winter.

2. **Name names.** Include the names of people, places, brands, and objects.

   Vague   When my sixty-three-year-old aunt was refused a job, she became an angry victim of age discrimination.

   Specific   When my sixty-three-year-old Aunt Angela was refused a job at Vicki's Nail Salon, she became an angry victim of age discrimination.

3. **Use action verbs.** Select strong verbs that help your readers visualize the action.

Vague	When Silina came on stage, the audience became excited.
Specific	When Silina burst onto the stage, the audience screamed, cheered, and chanted, "Silina, Silina!"

4. **Use descriptive language that appeals to the senses (smell, touch, taste, sound, sight).** Words that appeal to the senses help your readers feel as if they are observing or participating in the experience you are describing.

Vague	It's relaxing to walk on the beach.
Specific	I walked in the sand next to the ocean, breathing in the smell of the salt water and listening to the rhythmic sound of the waves.

5. **Use adjectives and adverbs.** Carefully chosen adjectives and adverbs in your description of a person, place, or experience can make your writing more concrete.

Vague	As I weeded my garden, I let my eyes wander over the meadow sweets and hydrangeas, all the while listening to the chirping of a cardinal.
Specific	As I slowly weeded my perennial garden, I let my eyes wander over the pink meadow sweets and blue hydrangeas, all the while listening absent-mindedly to the chirping of a bright red cardinal.

For more on organization, see Chapter 7, pp. 156–64.

The details in a paragraph should also follow a logical order. You might arrange the details from most to least (or least to most) important, in chronological order, or in spatial order.

EXERCISE 6.6 ▸ PROVIDING CONCRETE, SPECIFIC DETAILS

Alone or in a group of two or three students, revise and expand each sentence in the following paragraph to make it specific and concrete. Feel free to add new information and new sentences, and be sure to arrange the supporting details logically.

> I saw a great concert the other night in Dallas. Two groups were performing. The music was great, and there was a large crowd. In fact, the crowd was so enthusiastic that the second group performed an hour longer than scheduled.

ESSAY IN PROGRESS 2 ▸

For the essay you worked with in Essay in Progress 1 (p. 144), evaluate the supporting details you used in each paragraph. Revise as necessary to make each paragraph unified and logically organized. Make sure you have provided concrete, specific details.

Use Transitions and Repetition

All the details in a paragraph must fit together and function as a connected unit of information. When a paragraph has **coherence**, its ideas flow smoothly, allowing readers to follow its progression with ease. Two useful devices for linking details are transitions between sentences and repetition of key terms.

Transitions are words, phrases, or clauses that lead your reader from one idea to another. Think of transitions as guideposts, or signals, of what is coming next in a paragraph. Some commonly used transitions are shown in Table 6.1, which groups transitions according to the type of connections they show.

TABLE 6.1 ▶ Commonly Used Transitional Expressions

Type of Connection	Transitions
Logical Connections	
Items in a series	then, first, second, next, another, furthermore, finally, as well as
Illustration	for instance, for example, namely, that is
Result or cause	consequently, therefore, so, hence, thus, then, as a result
Restatement	in other words, that is, in simpler terms
Summary or conclusion	finally, in conclusion, to sum up, all in all, evidently, actually
Similarity/agreement	similarly, likewise, in the same way
Difference/opposition	but, however, on the contrary, nevertheless, neither, nor, on the one/other hand, still, yet
Spatial Connections	
Direction	inside/outside, along, above/below, up/down, across, to the right/left, in front of/behind
Nearness	next to, near, nearby, facing, adjacent to
Distance	beyond, in the distance, away, over there
Time Connections	
Frequency	often, frequently, now and then, gradually, week by week, occasionally, daily, rarely
Duration	during, briefly, hour by hour
Reference to a particular time	at two o'clock, on April 27, in 2010, last Thanksgiving, three days ago
Beginning	before then, at the beginning, at first
Middle	meanwhile, simultaneously, next, then, at that time
End	finally, at last, eventually, later, at the end, subsequently, afterward

In the two examples that follow, notice that the first paragraph is disjointed and choppy because it lacks transitions. The revised version is more coherent and therefore easier to follow.

Without Transitions

Most films are structured much like a short story. The film begins with an opening scene that captures the audience's attention. The writers build up tension, preparing for the climax of the story. They complicate the situation by revealing other elements of the plot, perhaps by introducing a surprise or additional characters. They introduce a problem. It will be solved either for the betterment or to the detriment of the characters and the situation. A resolution brings the film to a close.

With Transitions

Repetition: Key words and pronouns

Transitions: Guideposts

Most films are structured much like a short story. The film begins with an opening scene that captures the audience's attention. Gradually the writers build up tension, preparing for the climax of the story. Soon after the first scene, they complicate the situation by revealing other elements of the plot, perhaps by introducing a surprise or additional characters. Next, they introduce a problem. Eventually the problem will be solved either for the betterment or to the detriment of the characters and the situation. Finally, a resolution brings the film to a close.

Notice that the repetition of key terms (*film(s)*, *writers*), as well as pronouns that stand in for the key terms (*they* for *writers*), also lends coherence to the paragraph.

> **ESSAY IN PROGRESS 3**

For the essay you worked with in Essay in Progress 2 (p. 148), evaluate your use of transitions within each paragraph, adding them where needed to make the relationship among your ideas clearer.

> **STUDENTS WRITE**

Chapters 4 to 7 show Latrisha Wilson's progress in planning and drafting an essay on surveillance. Below you can see her first-draft paragraph (also included in Chapter 7 as part of her first draft essay, pp. 171–72) and her revision to strengthen the paragraph.

First-Draft Paragraph

Transition needed

Need to explain who Snowden is, what he did, and when; also add transition to make connection clear

Snowden's travels irrelevant

Need to explain what NSA is, what it did

Surveillance can refer to a thrilling activity, like the kind of spying on foreign terrorists that goes on in James Bond movies. But the truth is that most spying is done by surveillance computers. And then there is surveillance by drones. Edward Snowden bounced around for weeks from one airport to another, and lived for a while in the Moscow airport, eating who knows what and sleeping who knows where. The NSA seems to be able to do whatever it wants without having to answer to anyone or suffer any consequences. But we can't say the same for whistleblowers. Just look what they did to Bradley Manning! The US government aggressively pursued Snowden. The NSA is more and more aggressively protecting its own secrecy, by punishing whistleblowers, and lying to Congress, and it seems as if they are more concerned about themselves than the people they are spying on.

Revised Paragraph

When the word *surveillance* comes up, people think of some thrilling and dangerous activity, like the spying on foreign terrorists that goes on in James Bond movies. But in the U.S. today, most spying isn't done by handsome secret agents out to save the world; it's done by surveillance computers, and they monitor U.S. citizens, not just foreign terrorists. For example, consider what we learned from the whistleblower Edward Snowden, who sacrificed his career as a contractor for the National Security Agency (NSA) to alert the public to the deals the NSA makes with companies like Microsoft, Facebook, and Verizon to collect personal information and monitor everything their customers do on the Internet or speak into a telephone.

> Relevance of Bradley Manning not made clear; explain or delete
>
> Detail needed to support claim about spying by surveillance computers in topic sentence

Analyzing the Writer's Technique

1. **Topic Sentence** Identify Wilson's topic sentence. How did she strengthen it in her revision?
2. **Details** What irrelevant details did she delete?
3. **Transitions** What transitions did she add to provide coherence?
4. **Repetition** What words are repeated, thus contributing to coherence?
5. **Further Revision** What further revisions do you recommend?

▸ READING

Black Men and Public Space

Brent Staples

Brent Staples is a journalist who has written numerous articles and editorials as well as a memoir, *Parallel Time: Growing Up in Black and White* (1994). He holds a Ph.D. in psychology and is a member of *The New York Times* editorial board and a regular contributor to its Commentary section. This essay, first published in *Harper's* magazine in 1986, is a good model of a well-structured essay. As you read the selection, highlight or underline the author's thesis.

Before Reading

1. **Preview** Use the steps listed on page 28.
2. **Connect** What is public space, and how does our society expect us to behave there?

While Reading Pay particular attention to how Staples structures his paragraphs.

My first victim was a woman—white, well dressed, probably in her early twenties. I came upon her late one evening on a deserted street in Hyde Park, a relatively affluent neighborhood in an otherwise mean, impoverished section of Chicago. As I swung onto the avenue behind her, there seemed to be a discreet, uninflammatory distance between us. Not so. She cast back a worried glance. To her, the youngish black man—a broad six feet two inches with a beard and billowing hair, both hands shoved into the pockets of a bulky military jacket—seemed menacingly close. After a few more quick glimpses, she picked up her pace and was soon running in earnest. Within seconds she disappeared into a cross street.

That was more than a decade ago. I was twenty-two years old, a graduate student newly arrived at the University of Chicago. It was in the echo of that terrified woman's footfalls that I first began to know the unwieldy inheritance I'd come into—the ability to alter public space in ugly ways. It was clear that she thought herself the quarry of a mugger, a rapist, or worse. Suffering a bout of insomnia, however, I was stalking sleep, not defenseless wayfarers. As a softy who is scarcely able to take a knife to a raw chicken—let alone hold one to a person's throat—I was surprised, embarrassed, and dismayed all at once. Her flight made me feel like an accomplice in tyranny. It also made it clear that I was indistinguishable from the muggers who occasionally seeped into the area from the surrounding ghetto. That first encounter, and those that followed, signified that a vast, unnerving gulf lay between nighttime pedestrians—particularly women—and me. And I soon gathered that being perceived as dangerous is a hazard in itself. I only needed to turn a corner into a dicey situation, or crowd some frightened, armed person in a foyer somewhere, or make an errant move after being pulled over by a policeman. Where fear and weapons meet—and they often do in urban America—there is always the possibility of death.

In that first year, my first away from my hometown, I was to become thoroughly familiar with the language of fear. At dark, shadowy intersections, I could cross in front of a car stopped at a traffic light and elicit the *thunk, thunk, thunk, thunk* of the driver—black, white, male, or female—hammering down the door locks. On less traveled streets after dark, I grew accustomed to but never comfortable with people crossing to the other side of the street rather than pass me. Then there were the standard unpleasantries with policemen, doormen, bouncers, cabdrivers, and others whose business it is to screen out troublesome individuals *before* there is any nastiness.

I moved to New York nearly two years ago and I have remained an avid night walker. In central Manhattan, the near-constant crowd cover minimizes tense one-on-one street encounters. Elsewhere—in SoHo, for example, where sidewalks are narrow and tightly spaced buildings shut out the sky—things can get very taut indeed.

After dark, on the warrenlike streets of Brooklyn where I live, I often see women who fear the worst from me. They seem to have set their faces on neutral, and with their purse straps strung across their chests bandolier-style, they forge ahead as though bracing themselves against being tackled. I understand, of course, that the danger they perceive is not a hallucination. Women are particularly vulnerable to street violence, and young black males are drastically overrepresented among the perpetrators of that violence. Yet these truths are no solace against the kind of alienation that comes of being ever the suspect, a fearsome entity with whom pedestrians avoid making eye contact.

It is not altogether clear to me how I reached the ripe old age of twenty-two   6
without being conscious of the lethality nighttime pedestrians attributed to me.
Perhaps it was because in Chester, Pennsylvania, the small, angry industrial town
where I came of age in the 1960s, I was scarcely noticeable against a backdrop of
gang warfare, street knifings, and murders. I grew up one of the good boys, had perhaps a half-dozen fistfights. In retrospect, my shyness of combat has clear sources.

As a boy, I saw countless tough guys locked away; I have since buried several,   7
too. They were babies, really—a teenage cousin, a brother of twenty-two, a childhood friend in his mid-twenties—all gone down in episodes of bravado played out
in the streets. I came to doubt the virtues of intimidation early on. I chose, perhaps
unconsciously, to remain a shadow—timid, but a survivor.

The fearsomeness mistakenly attributed to me in public places often has a peril-   8
ous flavor. The most frightening of these confusions occurred in the late 1970s and
early 1980s, when I worked as a journalist in Chicago. One day, rushing into the office
of a magazine I was writing for with a deadline story in hand, I was mistaken for a
burglar. The office manager called security and, with an ad hoc posse, pursued me
through the labyrinthine halls, nearly to my editor's door. I had no way of proving
who I was. I could only move briskly toward the company of someone who knew me.

Another time I was on assignment for a local paper and killing time before an   9
interview. I entered a jewelry store on the city's affluent Near North Side. The proprietor excused herself and returned with an enormous red Doberman pinscher straining at the end of a leash. She stood, the dog extended toward me, silent to my
questions, her eyes bulging nearly out of her head. I took a cursory look around, nodded, and bade her good night.

Relatively speaking, however, I never fared as badly as another black male jour-   10
nalist. He went to nearby Waukegan, Illinois, a couple of summers ago to work on a
story about a murderer who was born there. Mistaking the reporter for the killer,
police officers hauled him from his car at gunpoint and but for his press credentials
would probably have tried to book him. Such episodes are not uncommon. Black men
trade tales like this all the time.

Over the years, I learned to smother the rage I felt at so often being taken for a   11
criminal. Not to do so would surely have led to madness. I now take precautions to
make myself less threatening. I move about with care, particularly late in the evening.
I give a wide berth to nervous people on subway platforms during the wee hours, particularly when I have exchanged business clothes for jeans. If I happen to be entering
a building behind some people who appear skittish, I may walk by, letting them clear
the lobby before I return, so as not to seem to be following them. I have been calm and
extremely congenial on those rare occasions when I've been pulled over by the police.

And on late-evening constitutionals I employ what has proved to be an excel-   12
lent tension-reducing measure: I whistle melodies from Beethoven and Vivaldi and
the more popular classical composers. Even steely New Yorkers hunching toward
nighttime destinations seem to relax, and occasionally they even join in the tune.
Virtually everybody seems to sense that a mugger wouldn't be warbling bright
sunny selections from Vivaldi's *Four Seasons*. It is my equivalent of the cowbell that
hikers wear when they know they are in bear country.

Examining the Reading

1. **Paraphrase** Explain what Staples means by "the ability to alter public space" (para. 2).
2. **Details** Staples considers himself a "survivor" (para. 7). To what does he attribute his survival?
3. **Examples** What does Staples do to make himself seem less threatening to others?
4. **Vocabulary** Explain the meaning of each of the following words as it is used in the reading: *uninflammatory* (para. 1), *unwieldy* (2), *vulnerable* (5), *retrospect* (6), and *constitutionals* (12).

Analyzing the Writer's Technique

1. **Unity** Analyze paragraph 3 of "Black Men and Public Space." Does it have a topic sentence, and if so, where is the topic sentence placed? Does this paragraph effectively support Staples's thesis? Do all the supporting details seem concrete and specific? Why or why not?
2. **Supporting Details** Identify several places in the essay where Staples uses specific, concrete supporting details effectively. Explain your choices.
3. **Transitions and Repetition** Cite several examples of effective transitional strategies. Write a paragraph explaining how they lend coherence to the essay. Identify any places in the essay where you think Staples could have made connections between paragraphs clearer.

Thinking Critically about the Reading

1. **Word Choice** Why did Staples choose the word *victim* in paragraph 1? What connotations does it have? What images does he create through its use?
2. **Fact and Opinion** Highlight the facts about what Staples sees during his night walks, and underline his opinions about what he sees. Evaluate the evidence for his interpretations and opinions and consider the following question: Is he also prejudging people?
3. **Sources** What other kinds of sources might Staples have considered in formulating his views? How would including such sources have changed his essay?
4. **Tone** Describe the tone of the essay. What effect does the tone have on you as a reader? How effective do you find it?
5. **Omissions** What information has Staples omitted that would help you further understand his thesis, if any?

Responding to the Reading

1. **Reaction** Why is Staples's whistling of classical music similar to hikers wearing cowbells in bear country?
2. **Discussion** In what other ways can an individual "alter public space"?
3. **Journal** Do you think Staples should alter his behavior in public to accommodate the reactions of others? Write a journal entry explaining whether you agree or disagree with Staples's actions.
4. **Essay** Staples describes himself as a "survivor" (para. 7) of the streets he grew up on. In a sense, everyone is a survivor of certain decisions or circumstances that, if played out differently, might have resulted in misfortune. Write an essay that explains how and why you or someone you know is a survivor.

7
Drafting an Essay

In this chapter you will learn to:

- structure an essay effectively
- organize supporting details
- write effective introductions, conclusions, and titles

WRITING QUICK START The photograph here shows people using a bike-sharing program. A number of such programs have sprouted up across the country and even on some college campuses. Working alone or with a classmate, write a sentence that states your opinion of this type of initiative and how likely a bike-sharing program would be to succeed in your area or on your campus. Then brainstorm evidence to support your opinion. Number your best evidence 1, your second-best evidence 2, and so on. Finally, write a paragraph that begins with the sentence you wrote and includes your evidence.

The paragraph you just wrote could be part of an essay on how cities and towns are trying to become more environmentally sustainable. To write an essay you would need to do the following:

- Do additional prewriting and research to learn more about this topic.
- Write a thesis statement and develop supporting paragraphs.
- Write an effective introduction and conclusion.
- Choose a good title.

This chapter will guide you through the process of developing an essay as part of the writing process shown in Graphic Organizer 7.1.

GRAPHIC ORGANIZER 7.1 An Overview of the Writing Process

Prewriting to Find and Focus Ideas
- See Chapter 4

Developing and Supporting Your Thesis
- See Chapter 5

Writing Effective Paragraphs
- See Chapter 6

Drafting Your Essay
- Organize your supporting details
- Write a strong introduction, conclusion, and title

Revising Your Essay
- See Chapter 8

Editing and Proofreading Your Essay
- See Chapter 9

Structure Your Essay Effectively

Think of an essay as a complete piece of writing, with a title, an introduction and thesis statement, several paragraphs supporting the thesis, and a conclusion. (See Graphic Organizer 7.2.)

Organize Your Supporting Details

For more on developing a thesis and selecting evidence to support it, see Chapter 5.

The body of your essay contains the paragraphs that support your thesis. Before you begin writing these paragraphs, decide on the supporting evidence you will use and the order in which you will present your evidence.

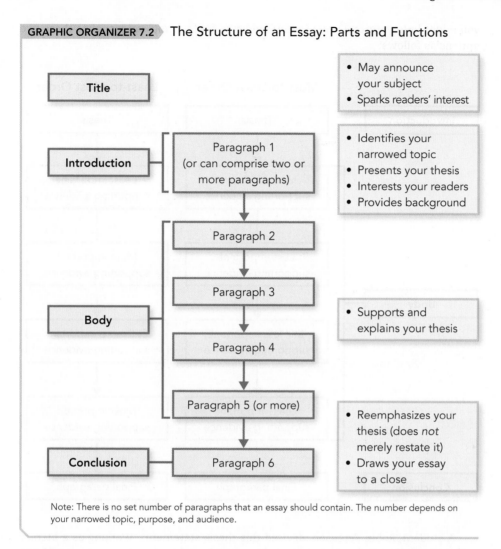

GRAPHIC ORGANIZER 7.2   The Structure of an Essay: Parts and Functions

Title

- May announce your subject
- Sparks readers' interest

Introduction — Paragraph 1 (or can comprise two or more paragraphs)

- Identifies your narrowed topic
- Presents your thesis
- Interests your readers
- Provides background

Body

Paragraph 2

Paragraph 3

Paragraph 4

Paragraph 5 (or more)

- Supports and explains your thesis

Conclusion — Paragraph 6

- Reemphasizes your thesis (does *not* merely restate it)
- Draws your essay to a close

Note: There is no set number of paragraphs that an essay should contain. The number depends on your narrowed topic, purpose, and audience.

Select a Method of Organization

Three common ways to organize ideas are most-to-least (or least-to-most) order, chronological order, and spatial order. To decide which to use, consider your topic and how it can be most logically and most compellingly presented.

Most-to-least (or least-to-most) order. When you choose this method of organizing an essay, you arrange your supporting details moving gradually from most to least (or least to most) important, familiar, or interesting. If you need to entice readers or expect they will read only the beginning of your essay, you might include your strongest evidence first. If readers are interested in the topic and likely to read on, you might hold your most memorable evidence for last. You can visualize these two options as follows:

The revised draft of Robin Ferguson's essay appears on pp. 169–70.

A student, Robin Ferguson, devised this thesis statement: "Working as a literacy volunteer taught me more about learning and friendship than I ever expected." She identified four primary benefits related to her thesis.

- I learned about the learning process.
- I developed a permanent friendship with my student, Marie.
- Marie built self-confidence.
- I discovered the importance of reading for Marie.

Ferguson then chose to arrange the supporting evidence from least to most important.

Least
to Most
Important

Paragraph 1: Learned about the learning process
Paragraph 2: Discovered the importance of reading for Marie
Paragraph 3: Marie increased her self-confidence
Paragraph 4: Developed a permanent friendship with Marie

EXERCISE 7.1 ▸ **WORKING WITH MOST-TO-LEAST AND LEAST-TO-MOST ORDER**

For each of the following narrowed topics, identify several qualities or characteristics that you could use to organize details in most-to-least or least-to-most order. For each, would you choose most-to-least or least-to-most order? Why?

1. Three stores in which you shop
2. Three friends
3. Three members of a sports team
4. Three fast-food restaurants
5. Three television shows

Chronological order.   When you arrange your supporting details in **chronological** (or time) **order**, you put them in the order in which they happened, beginning the body of your essay with the first event and progressing through the others as they occurred. Chronological order is commonly used in narrative essays (essays that tell a story or recount events) and process analyses (essays that explain how something works or is done). You can visualize chronological order as follows.

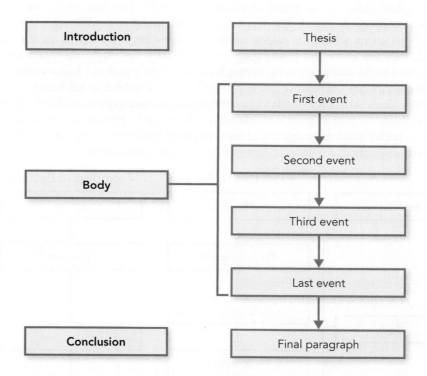

Suppose that Robin Ferguson, writing about her experiences as a literacy volunteer, decides to demonstrate her thesis by relating the events of a typical tutoring session. In this case, she might organize her essay by narrating the events in the order in which they usually occur, using each detail about the session to demonstrate what tutoring taught her about learning and friendship.

EXERCISE 7.2 ▸ **WORKING WITH CHRONOLOGICAL ORDER**

Alone or with a classmate, identify at least one thesis statement from those listed below that could be supported with paragraphs organized in chronological order. Explain how you would use chronological order to support this thesis.

1. European mealtimes differ from those expected by many American visitors, much to the visitors' surprise and discomfort.
2. Despite the many pitfalls that await those who shop at auctions, people can find bargains if they prepare in advance.
3. My first day of kindergarten was the most traumatic [or exhilarating] experience of my childhood, one that permanently shaped my view of education.
4. Learning how to drive a car increases a teenager's freedom and responsibility.

Spatial order. When you use **spatial order**, you organize details about your subject by location. Spatial organization is commonly used in descriptive essays (essays that portray people, places, and things) as well as in classification and division essays (essays that explain categories or parts). Consider, for example, how you might use spatial order to support the thesis that movie theaters are designed to shut out the outside world and create a separate reality within. You could begin by describing the ticket booth, then the lobby, and finally the theater. Similarly, you might describe a person from head to toe. Robin Ferguson, writing about her experiences as a literacy volunteer, could describe her classroom or meeting area from front to back or left to right.

Visualize spatial organization by picturing your subject in your mind or by sketching it. "Look" at your subject systematically—from top to bottom, inside to outside, front to back. Cut it into imaginary sections or pieces and describe each piece. Here are two possible options for visualizing an essay that uses spatial order.

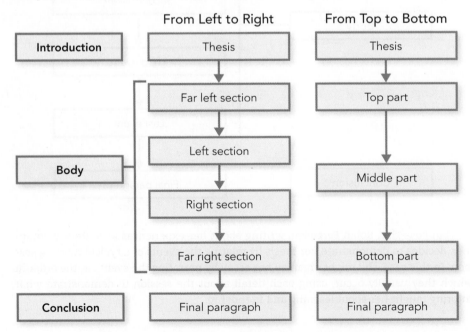

	From Left to Right	From Top to Bottom
Introduction	Thesis	Thesis
Body	Far left section	Top part
	Left section	Middle part
	Right section	
	Far right section	Bottom part
Conclusion	Final paragraph	Final paragraph

EXERCISE 7.3 ▶ **WORKING WITH SPATIAL ORDER**

Alone or with a classmate, identify one thesis statement listed below that could be supported by means of spatial organization. Explain how you would use spatial order to support this thesis.

1. Our family's yearly vacation at a cabin in Maine provides us with a much-needed opportunity to renew family ties.
2. The Civic Theatre of Allentown's set for Tennessee Williams's play *A Streetcar Named Desire* was simple yet striking and effective.
3. Although a pond in winter may seem frozen and lifeless, this appearance is deceptive.
4. A clear study space can cut down on time-wasting distractions.

ESSAY IN PROGRESS 1 ▶

Choose one of the following activities.

1. Using the thesis statement and evidence you gathered for the Essay in Progress activities in Chapter 5, choose a method for organizing your essay.
2. Choose one of the following narrowed topics:
   a. Positive or negative experiences with computers
   b. Stricter (or more lenient) regulations for teenage drivers
   c. Factors that account for the popularity of action films
   d. Discipline in public elementary schools
   e. Advantages or disadvantages of instant messaging

Then, using the steps in Graphic Organizer 7.1 (p. 156), prewrite to produce ideas, develop a thesis, and generate evidence to support the thesis. Next, choose a method for organizing your essay. Explain briefly how you will use that method of organization.

Prepare an Outline or a Graphic Organizer

After you have written a thesis statement and chosen a method of organization, take a few minutes to create an outline or graphic organizer of the essay's main points in the order you plan to discuss them. This is especially important when your essay is long or complex. Outlining or drawing a graphic organizer can help you see how ideas fit together and may reveal places where you need to add supporting information.

Outlining. There are two types of outlines: informal and formal. An **informal** (or **scratch**) **outline** uses key words and phrases to list main points and subpoints. Below is an informal outline of Robin Ferguson's essay (pp. 169–70). Recall that Ferguson chose to use the least-to-most-important method of organization.

Sample Informal Outline

<u>Thesis</u>: Working as a literacy volunteer taught me more about learning and friendship than I ever expected.

<u>Paragraph 1</u>: Learned about the learning process
- Went through staff training program
- Learned about words "in context"

<u>Paragraph 2</u>: Discovered the importance of reading for Marie
- Couldn't take bus, walked to grocery store
- Couldn't buy certain products
- Couldn't write out grocery lists

<u>Paragraph 3</u>: Marie increased her self-confidence
- Made rapid progress
- Began taking bus
- Helped son with reading

<u>Paragraph 4</u>: Developed a permanent friendship with Marie
- Saw each other often
- Both single parents
- Baby-sat each other's children

<u>Conclusion</u>: I benefited more than Marie did.

Formal outlines use Roman numerals (I, II), capital letters (A, B), Arabic numbers (1, 2), and lowercase letters (a, b) and indentation to designate levels of importance. Formal outlines fall into two categories.

- *Sentence outlines* use complete sentences.
- *Topic outlines* use only key words and phrases.

Here is a sample topic outline that a student wrote for an essay for her interpersonal communication class.

Sample Formal (Topic) Outline

First Topic	I. Types of listening
First Subtopic	A. Participatory
First Detail	1. Involves the listener responding to the speaker
Second Detail	2. Has expressive quality
Detail or Example	a. Maintain eye contact
Detail or Example	b. Express feelings using facial expressions
Second Topic	B. Nonparticipatory
First Detail	1. Involves the listener listening without talking or responding
Second Detail	2. Allows speaker to develop his or her thoughts without interruption

All items at the same level should be equally important, explain or support the topic or subtopic under which they are placed, and be grammatically parallel.

For more on parallel structure, see Chapter 9.

Not Parallel	**Parallel**
I. Dietary Problems	I. Dietary Problems
A. Consuming too much fat	A. Consuming too much fat
B. High refined-sugar consumption	B. Consuming too much refined sugar

If your instructor allows, you can use both phrases and sentences within an outline, as long as you do so consistently. You might write all subtopics (designated by capital letters A, B, and so on) as sentences and all supporting details (designated by 1, 2, and so on) as phrases, for instance.

Preparing a graphic organizer. If you have a pragmatic learning style, a verbal learning style, or both, preparing an outline will probably appeal to you. If you are a creative or spatial learner, however, you may prefer to draw a graphic organizer. Graphic Organizer 7.3

LEARNING STYLE OPTIONS

GRAPHIC ORGANIZER 7.3 Sample Graphic Organizer

To learn more about creating a graphic organizer, see Chapter 2.

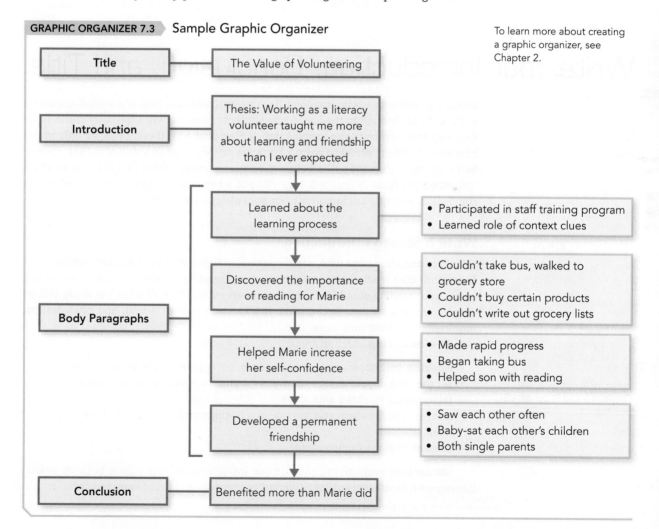

shows the graphic organizer that Robin Ferguson created for her essay (pp. 169–70). Notice that it follows the least-to-most-important method of organization, as did her informal outline on page 162.

Whichever method you find more appealing, begin by putting your working thesis statement at the top of a page and listing your main points below. Leave plenty of space between main points. While you are filling in details that support one main point, you will often think of details or examples to use in support of a different one. As these details or examples occur to you, jot them down under or next to the appropriate main point on your outline or graphic organizer.

ESSAY IN PROGRESS 2

For the topic you chose in Essay in Progress 1, prepare an outline or draw a graphic organizer to show your essay's organizational plan.

Write Your Introduction, Conclusion, and Title

When you write an essay, you don't have to start with the title and introduction and write straight through to the end. Some students prefer to write the body of the essay first and then return to the introduction. (Often your true thesis emerges only in the conclusion.) Others prefer to write a tentative introduction as a way of getting started. Some students think of a title before they start writing; others find it easier to add a title when the essay is finished. Regardless of when you write them, the introduction, conclusion, and title are important components of a well-written essay.

Write a Strong Introduction

Introductions often start with a fairly general statement of the topic and narrow their focus until they reach the thesis statement at the end of the paragraph. However you begin, your readers should be able to form an expectation of what the essay will be about from this section. Because the introduction creates a first, and often lasting, impression, take the time to get it right.

An effective introduction should:

For more about tone, see Chapters 3 and 9, pp. 64–65 and 206.

- establish your topic and indicate your focus, approach, and point of view
- set the tone of your essay—how you "sound" to your readers and what relationship you have with them
- interest your readers and provide any background information they may need
- present your thesis statement

Notice how each of the two sample introductions that follow, both on sexual harassment, creates an entirely different impression and set of expectations.

Introduction 1

Sexual harassment has received a great deal of attention in recent years. From the highest offices of government and the military to factories in small towns, sexual harassment cases have been tried in court and publicized on national television for all Americans to witness. This focus on sexual harassment has been, in and of itself, a good and necessary thing. However, when a first-grade boy makes national headlines because he kissed a little girl of the same age and is accused of "sexual harassment," the American public needs to take a serious look at the definition of sexual harassment.

Sets tone: Tone is reasonable yet with mild sense of disbelief

Engages readers/provides background: Grabs readers' attention with provocative example

Thesis: Thesis prepares readers for an essay that examines definitions of sexual harassment and perhaps offers one.

Introduction 2

Sexual harassment in the workplace seems to happen with alarming frequency. As a woman who works part time in a male-dominated office, I have witnessed at least six incidents of sexual harassment aimed at me and my female colleagues on various occasions during the past three months alone. For example, in one incident, a male coworker repeatedly made kissing sounds whenever I passed his desk, even after I explained that his actions made me uncomfortable. A female coworker was invited to dinner several times by her male supervisor; each time she refused. The last time she refused, he made a veiled threat: "You obviously aren't happy working with me. Perhaps a transfer is in order." These incidents were not isolated, did not happen to only one woman, and were initiated by more than one man. My colleagues and I are not the only victims. Sexual harassment is on the rise and will continue to increase unless women speak out against it loudly and to a receptive audience.

Sets tone: Tone is outraged, angry

Engages readers/provides background: Provides specific, distressing examples

Thesis: Thesis prepares readers for an essay that suggests ways women can speak out against sexual harassment.

An introduction can be difficult to write. If you have trouble, return to it later, once you have written the body of your essay. As you draft, you may think of a better way to grab your readers, set your tone, and establish your focus.

The following suggestions for writing a strong introduction will help you capture your readers' interest:

1. **Ask a provocative or disturbing question, or pose a series of related questions to direct readers' attention to your key points.**

   Should health insurance companies pay for more than one stay in a drug rehabilitation center? Should insurance continue to pay for rehab services when patients consistently put themselves back into danger by using drugs again?

2. **Begin with a dramatic or engaging anecdote or an example that is relevant to your thesis.**

   The penal system sometimes protects the rights of the criminal instead of those of the victim. For example, during a rape trial, the defense attorney can question the victim about his or her sexual history, but the prosecuting attorney is forbidden by law to mention that the defendant was charged with rape in a previous trial. In fact, if the prosecution even hints at the defendant's sexual history, the defense can request a mistrial.

3. **Offer a quotation that illustrates or emphasizes your thesis.**

As Indira Gandhi once said, "You cannot shake hands with a clenched fist." This truism is important to remember whenever people communicate with one another but particularly when they are attempting to resolve a conflict. Both parties need to agree that there is a problem and then agree to listen to each other with an open mind. Shaking hands is a productive way to begin working toward a resolution.

4. **Cite a little-known fact or shocking statistic.**

Recent research has shown that the color pink has a calming effect on people. In fact, a prison detention center in western New York was recently painted pink to make prisoners more controllable in the days following their arrest.

5. **State a commonly held misconception, and correct this misconception in your thesis.**

Many people have the mistaken notion that only homosexuals and drug users are in danger of contracting AIDS. In fact, many heterosexuals also suffer from this debilitating disease. Furthermore, the number of heterosexuals who test HIV-positive has increased substantially over the past decade. It is time the American public became better informed about the prevention and treatment of AIDS.

6. **Describe a hypothetical situation.**

Suppose you were in a serious car accident and became unconscious. Suppose further that you slipped into a coma, with little hope for recovery. Unless you had a prewritten health-care proxy that designated someone familiar with your wishes to act on your behalf, your fate would be left in the hands of doctors who knew nothing about you or your preferences for treatment.

7. **Compare your topic with one that is familiar or of special interest to your readers.**

The process a researcher uses to locate a specific piece of information in the library is similar to the process an investigator follows in tracking a criminal; both pose a series of questions and follow clues to answer them.

Write an Effective Conclusion

Write a **conclusion** that brings your essay to a satisfying close. For most essays, your conclusion should reaffirm your thesis without directly restating it. For lengthy essays, you may want to summarize your main points. Shorter essays can be ended more memorably and forcefully by using one of the following suggestions.

1. **Take your readers beyond the scope and time frame of your essay.**

For now, then, the present system for policing the Internet appears to be working. In the future, though, it may be necessary to put a more formal, structured procedure in place.

2. Remind readers of the relevance of the issue or suggest why your thesis is important.

> As stated earlier, research has shown that the seat-belt law has saved thousands of lives. These lives would almost certainly have been lost had this law not been enacted.

3. Offer a recommendation or urge your readers to take action.

> To convince the local cable company to eliminate pornographic material, concerned citizens should organize, contact their local cable station, and threaten to cancel their subscriptions.

4. Discuss broader implications not fully addressed in the essay (but do not introduce a completely new issue).

> When fair-minded people consider whether the FBI should be allowed to tap private phone lines, the issue inevitably leads them to the larger issue of First Amendment rights.

5. Conclude with a fact, quotation, anecdote, or example that emphasizes your thesis.

> The next time you are tempted to send a strongly worded email, consider this fact: Your friends and your enemies can forward those messages, with unforeseen consequences to you.

Introductions and Conclusions: Four Common Mistakes to Avoid

In your introduction, don't . . .

make an announcement. Avoid opening comments such as "I am writing to explain . . ." or "This essay will discuss . . ."

prolong your introduction unnecessarily. An introduction that is longer than two paragraphs will probably sound long-winded and make your readers impatient.

discourage your readers from continuing. Statements such as "This process may seem complicated, but . . ." may make your readers apprehensive.

use a casual, overly familiar, or chatty tone, especially in academic writing. Openings such as "You'll never in a million years believe what happened . . ." are generally not appropriate for college essays.

In your conclusion, don't . . .

make an announcement or a restate your thesis directly. Statements like "In my essay I have shown. . . ." are dull and mechanical.

introduce major points or supporting evidence. Reasons and evidence that support your thesis belong in the body of your essay.

apologize or weaken your stance. Do not say, for example, "Although I am only twenty-one, . . ." or back down after criticizing someone by saying "After all, she's only human."

use standard phrases. Don't use phrases such as "To sum up," "In conclusion," or "It can be seen, then." They are routine and tiresome.

Write a Good Title

The title of your essay should indicate your topic and prepare readers for what follows. Titles such as "Baseball Fans" or "Gun Control," which just indicate the topic, provide readers with little information or incentive to continue reading. For academic essays, write straightforward titles that accurately describe your topic and approach.

Topic   Position

<u>Why</u> State Lotteries Are an <u>Unfair</u> Tax on the Poor

           ↑

Suggests a cause-effect analysis   Suggests an argument

For other writing situations—depending on your purpose, audience, stance, genre, and medium—your title may be direct, informative, witty, intriguing, or a combination of these. The following suggestions will help you write effective titles.

- **Ask a question that your essay answers.**

   Who Plays the Lottery?

- **Use alliteration.** Repeating initial sounds often produces a catchy title.

   Lotteries: Dreaming about Dollars

- **Use a play on words or a catchy or humorous expression.** This technique may work well for less formal essays.

   Playing to Lose

- **Use a brief quotation.** You will likely need to mention the quotation in your essay and indicate there who said it and where.

   The Lottery: "A Surtax on Desperation"?

EXERCISE 7.4   **WRITING TITLES**

For each of the following essays, suggest a title. Use each of the above suggestions at least once.

1. An essay explaining tenants' legal rights
2. An essay opposing drug testing on animals
3. An essay on the causes and effects of road rage
4. An essay comparing fitness routines
5. An essay explaining how to choose a primary care physician

EXERCISE 7.5   **EVALUATING INTRODUCTIONS, CONCLUSIONS, AND TITLES**

The following student essay by Robin Ferguson on volunteering in a literacy program was written using Graphic Organizer 7.3 (p. 163). Read the essay and answer the questions that follow.

The Value of Volunteering

Robin Ferguson

I began working as a literacy volunteer as part of a community service course I was   1
taking last semester. The course required a community service project, and I chose
literacy volunteers simply as a means of fulfilling a course requirement. Now I realize
that working as a literacy volunteer taught me more about learning and friendship
than I ever expected.

When I first went through the training program to become a literacy volunteer,   2
I learned about the process of learning—that is, the way in which people learn
new words most effectively. To illustrate this concept, the person who trained me
wrote a brief list of simple words on the left side of a chalkboard and wrote
phrases using the same words on the right side of the chalkboard. She instructed
us to read the words and then asked which words we would be most likely to
remember. We all said the words on the right because they made more sense. In
other words, we could remember the words in the phrases more easily because
they made more sense in context. The trainer showed us several more examples of
words in context so we could get a grasp of how people learn new information by
connecting it to what they already know.

The training I received, though excellent, was no substitute for working with a   3
real student, however. When I began to discover what other people's lives are like
because they cannot read, I realized the true importance of reading. For example,
when I had my first tutoring session with my client, Marie, a forty-four-year-old
single mother of three, I found out she walked two miles to the nearest grocery
store twice a week because she didn't know which bus to take. When I told her I
would get her a bus schedule, she confided to me that it would not help because
she could not read it and therefore wouldn't know which bus to take. She also said
she had difficulty once she got to the grocery store because she couldn't always
remember what she needed. Since she did not know words, she could not write
out a grocery list. Also, she identified items by sight, so if the manufacturer
changed a label, she could not recognize it as the product she wanted.

As we worked together, learning how to read built Marie's self-confidence,   4
which gave her an incentive to continue in her studies. She began to make rapid
progress and was even able to take the bus to the grocery store. After this successful trip, she reported how self-assured she felt. Eventually, she began helping her
youngest son, Mark, a shy first grader, with his reading. She sat with him before
he went to sleep, and together they would read bedtime stories. When his eyes
became wide with excitement as she read, her pride swelled, and she began to see
how her own hard work in learning to read paid off. As she described this experience, I swelled with pride as well. I found that helping Marie to build her self-
confidence was more rewarding than anything I had ever done before.

As time went by, Marie and I developed a friendship that became permanent.   5
Because we saw each other several times a week, we spent a lot of time getting
to know each other, and we discovered we had certain things in common. For

instance, I'm also a single parent. So we began to share our similar experiences with each other. In fact, we have even baby-sat for each other's children. I would drop my children off at her house while I taught an evening adult class, and in return, I watched her children while she worked on Saturday mornings.

As a literacy volunteer, I learned a great deal about learning, teaching, and helping others. I also established what I hope will be a lifelong friendship. In fact, I may have benefited more from the experience than Marie did.

6

Analyzing the Writer's Technique

1. Assess Ferguson's introduction: How effectively does it prepare the reader for the balance of the essay? Does it capture your interest as a reader? Why or why not?
2. Highlight Ferguson's thesis statement. What assertion does it make? What angle on the topic does it offer?
3. What method(s) does Ferguson use to arrange her details logically within paragraphs?
4. Assess Ferguson's conclusion. Does it effectively draw Ferguson's essay to a close? Why or why not?
5. Assess Ferguson's title. Does it provide you with enough incentive to want to keep reading (assuming that the fact that it was assigned is not sufficient)? How could you change it to make it more compelling to you and your classmates?

ESSAY IN PROGRESS 3

Using the outline or graphic organizer you created in Essay in Progress 2, write a first draft of your essay.

Chapter 1 outlines some key learning strategies. Chapter 2 walks you through the process of reading actively to respond. Chapter 3 offers help with analyzing and evaluating what you read.

HOW WRITERS READ	ESSAYS
	Seeing a reading assignment as a whole, rather than as a series of individual sentences and paragraphs, makes it easier to recall and make sense of what you just read. Use these strategies to get the most out of what you read.
BEFORE READING	• Activate your prior knowledge, establish an intent to remember, and prepare your brain to learn by previewing the essay, reading the headnote, brainstorming to discover what you already know about the topic, and reading the questions or assignments that follow the essay.
WHILE READING	• Read actively and critically by highlighting key ideas and making notes in the margins about your questions and reactions, analyzing how the essay is organized, and assessing the author's purpose and perspective on the topic. (This may require you to reread the selection.)
AFTER READING	• Reinforce and extend your learning by drawing a graphic organizer or outlining the selection (this will confirm your understanding and consolidate your memory) and devising critical questions that will help you analyze the author's language, assess the evidence he or she provides, recognize assumptions or omissions, and synthesize the author's ideas with your own.

The Threats of Surveillance (Draft)

Latrisha Wilson

The first draft of an essay by Latrisha Wilson follows. Wilson used her freewriting (pp. 115–17) and her working thesis (p. 131) as the basis for her draft, adding details that she came up with by doing additional brainstorming (p. 131). Because she was writing a first draft, Wilson did not worry about correcting the errors in grammar, punctuation, and mechanics. (You will see an excerpt from her revised draft and her final draft in Chapter 8, pp. 191–93, and an excerpt that shows Wilson's final editing and proofreading in Chapter 9, p. 213.)

The Threats of Surveillance

There are plenty of new ways to talk to friends and family. We can communicate by talking on our iPhones, but there are dangers there. Our conversations can be recorded, and the GPS function on the phone allows our whereabouts to be tracked. We can chat on Skype, Gmail, Facebook message, read each other's Twitter or Blog posts. And then there are security cameras that record our every move. These new digital technologies are incredibly useful; however, they also come at a hidden cost.

Surveillance can refer to a thrilling activity, like the kind of spying on foreign terrorists that goes on in James Bond movies. Bond used high-tech devices and gadgetry to carry out his missions. But the truth is that most spying is done by surveillance computers. And then there is surveillance using drones. Edward Snowden bounced around for weeks from one airport to another, and lived for a while in the Moscow airport, eating who knows what and sleeping who knows where. The NSA seems to be able to do whatever it wants without having to answer to anyone or suffer any consequences. But we can't say the same for whistleblowers. Just look what they did to Chelsea Manning! The US government aggressively pursued Snowden. The NSA is more and more aggressively protecting its own secrecy, by punishing whistleblowers, and lying to Congress and, it seems as if they are more concerned about themselves than the people they are spying on.

The NSA isn't the only organization to be spying on us. You got companies like Google and other companies doing it to. The next time you pull up your Gmail account, go to your inbox and click on a message. Do you see all those advertisements to the right of your inbox? There directly related to the message you are reading. (I wish my mom "Happy Birthday!" and now I see ads for places to buy birthday hats. This creepy connection is because Google is a major online marketing business, and it automatically scans all of our e-mails for keywords and phrases all at the same time. Companies are paying Google tons of money to record our search histories and pore over our personal messages. Spokesmen for Google reassure us that only computers, no human beings, are reading our e-mails.

Google and other corporations could do more do inform it's users   4
about privacy concerns. How much personal information are we giving away when we make an account with G-mail, Facebook, or Netflix? What kind of controls keep employees at this companies from accessing our viewing histories, profiles, or private communications? Its never easy to tell. The terms are long legal documents written in a lingo your everyday person doesn't want to bother to decipher. We just check a box.

Well, what's the big deal? I have nothing to hide from neither the   5
government nor companies like Google and Facebook. Neither do I, I would say in response. But I don't like the idea of having people I don't know constantly looking over my shoulder. When I'm writing a Facebook message to my boyfriend, do I need to worry about getting blackmailed by some Facebook employee, who got bored on a break and decided to do some browsing? Less and less is there any kind of privacy, online or in real life.

Analyzing the First Draft

1. **Title and Introduction** Evaluate Wilson's title and introduction.
2. **Thesis** Evaluate Wilson's thesis statement.
3. **Support** Does Wilson provide adequate details in her essay? If not, which paragraphs need more detail? What additional information might she include?
4. **Organization** How does Wilson organize her ideas?
5. **Conclusion** Evaluate the conclusion.

Working Together

Working in a group with two or three of your classmates, complete the graphic organizer for the article "Black Men and Public Space" (pp. 151–53). Then come up with an alternate title (one that will spark your readers' interest). Be prepared to share your title and explain the reason your group chose it.

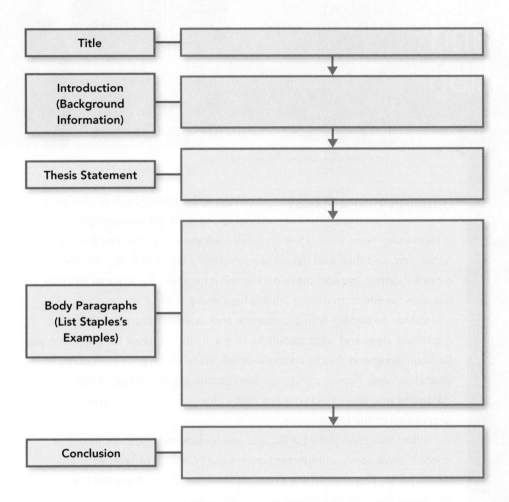

Title	
Introduction (Background Information)	
Thesis Statement	
Body Paragraphs (List Staples's Examples)	
Conclusion	

8

Revising Content and Organization

Roberto Westbrook/Blend Images/Getty Images

In this chapter you will learn to:

- ask key questions to revise
- work with your classmates to revise
- use your instructor comments to revise
- consider your learning style when revising

WRITING QUICK START Looking at the photograph on this page from left to right, list everything that is happening. Now, write a few sentences summarizing what you think is happening, and then add details to your original list to describe the photo more fully. After you add these details, will it be easier for a reader who has not seen the photo to picture what is happening in it?

Exchange papers with a classmate and examine how your classmate organized ideas and what details he or she included. Look for parts that you find confusing and that need more detail. Write down your comments for your classmate. Finally, using your own comments and those of the classmate who examined your list, make changes to improve your own description of the photograph.

When you changed your list, did you include more details from the photo? Leave some unimportant details out? Change or rearrange any details? If so, you *revised* the description of the photo. **Revision** is a process of making changes to improve what your essay says and how you say it. Revising an essay works in much the same way as the revision of your list did. As Graphic Organizer 8.1 shows, revision is an essential part of the writing process.

GRAPHIC ORGANIZER 8.1 An Overview of the Writing Process

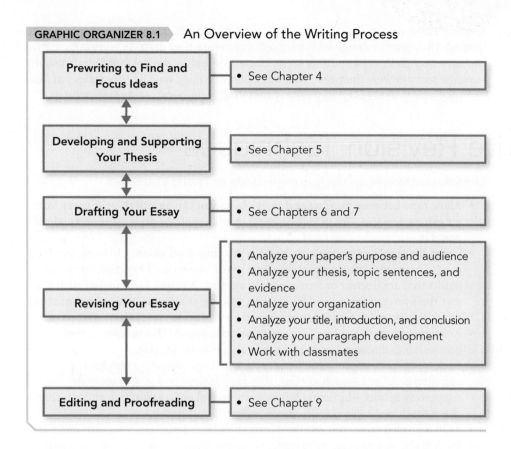

Why Revise?

A thorough, thoughtful revision can change a C paper to an A paper! Revising can make a significant difference in how well your paper:

- achieves your purpose,
- expresses your ideas to your intended audience, and
- reflects your reader's expectations of your genre.

This difference is why most professional writers—and successful student writers—revise frequently and thoroughly.

Revising is not a process of correcting surface errors, such as spelling mistakes or punctuation errors. Rather, it is a process of looking at your *ideas* and finding ways to make them clearer and easier to understand. This may mean adding, eliminating, or reorganizing key elements within the essay, even revising your thesis statement and refocusing the entire essay.

The amount of revision you need to do depends in part on how you approach the task of writing. Some writers spend more time planning; others spend more time revising. For example, pragmatic learners tend to take a highly structured approach to writing. They plan in detail what they will say before they draft. In contrast, creative learners may dash off a draft as ideas come to mind. A well-planned draft usually requires less revision than one that was spontaneously written. Regardless of how carefully planned an essay may be, any first draft requires at least some revision.

Use Effective Revision Techniques

The following techniques will help you evaluate and revise your essays.

- **Allow time between drafting and revising, so you can approach your essay from a fresh perspective.** Try to leave enough time to set your draft aside overnight if possible.
- **Listen for problems as you or a friend reads your draft aloud.** Listening carefully can help you identify awkward wording, vague or overused expressions, or main points that are unclear or lack adequate support. A reader less familiar with the text than you may also slow down when reading or misread confusing passages, providing a hint for areas that need revision.
- **Ask a classmate to read and comment on your paper.** This process, called *peer review*, is discussed in detail later in this chapter (p. 182).
- **Look for consistent problem areas in your writing.** Develop a checklist of common problems—such as confusing organization or a lack of concrete supporting details—by listing issues from several essays you have written; then check for these problem areas as you revise.
- **Read a printed copy.** You will be able to analyze and evaluate your writing more impartially, and you can write marginal annotations, circle troublesome words or sentences, and draw arrows to connect details more easily.
- **Draw a graphic organizer or outline your draft.** A graphic organizer or outline allows you to see how your thesis and topic sentences relate to one another and helps you evaluate content and organization. If you spot a problem, such as a detail or an example that does not support a topic sentence, write notes to the right of your organizer (or outline), as shown in Graphic Organizer 8.2.

For more about creating a graphic organizer, see Chapter 2, pp. 35–37; for more on outlining, see Chapter 7, pp. 161–64.

Ask Key Questions for Revision

To identify broad areas of weakness in your essay, ask yourself these five key questions.

1. Does my essay clearly convey a purpose, address an appropriate audience, and follow the conventions of the genre?
2. Does my essay state a clear, well-focused thesis and provide enough reasons and evidence to support the thesis?
3. Does each paragraph include a clear main idea (usually stated in a topic sentence) and enough details to develop the idea fully?
4. Do the ideas in my essay fit together logically?
5. Does my essay have a strong introduction and conclusion, and an appropriate title?

GRAPHIC ORGANIZER 8.2 Sample Graphic Organizer for Revision

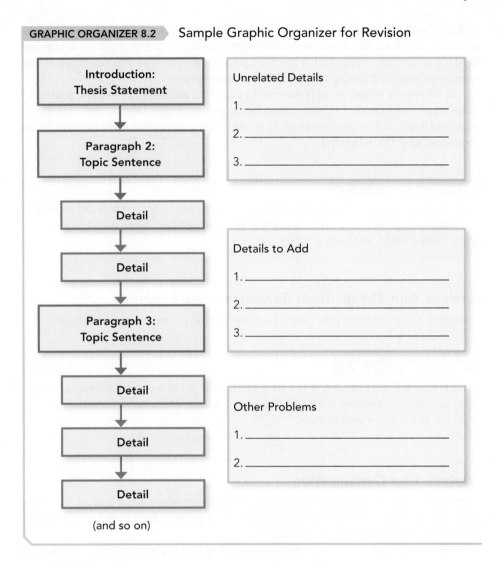

After you have identified areas that need reworking, refer to the self-help flow-charts that follow.

Analyze Your Purpose and Audience

First drafts often lack focus. They may go off in several directions rather than have a clear purpose. For instance, one section of an essay on divorce may inform readers of its causes, and another section may argue that it harms children. A first draft may also contain sections that appeal to different audiences. For instance, one section of an essay on counseling teenagers about drug abuse might seem to be written for parents; other sections might be more appropriate for teenagers.

To determine if your paper has a clear focus, write a sentence stating what your essay is supposed to accomplish. If you cannot write such a sentence, your paper

For more about purpose and audience, see Chapter 4; for more about developing a thesis, see Chapter 5.

probably lacks a clear purpose. To find a purpose, reread your draft. Does one purpose predominate? If so, revise the sections that do not fit in. If not, do some additional thinking or brainstorming, listing as many possible purposes as you can think of and revising to address the purpose you find most appropriate.

To determine if your essay is directed to a specific audience, write a few sentences describing your intended readers. Describe their knowledge, beliefs, and experience with your topic. If you are unable to do so, focus on a particular audience and revise your essay with them in mind.

ESSAY IN PROGRESS 1

Evaluate the purpose and audience of the draft essay you wrote in Essay in Progress 3 in Chapter 7 (p. 170) or another essay that you have written. Make notes on your graphic organizer or annotate your outline.

Analyze Your Thesis, Topic Sentences, and Evidence

Use Figure 8.1 to examine your thesis statement, topic sentences, and evidence.

ESSAY IN PROGRESS 2

Using Figure 8.1, evaluate the thesis statement, topic sentences, and evidence of the essay you began assessing in Essay in Progress 1 above. Make notes on your graphic organizer or annotate your outline.

Analyze Your Organization

Your readers will not be able to follow your ideas if your essay is not unified. To assess your essay's unity, examine its organization. Your graphic organizer or outline (see pp. 163–64) will help you discover any flaws.

You can also ask a classmate to read your essay and explain how it is organized. If your classmate cannot describe your essay's organization, it probably needs further work. Use one of the methods in Chapter 7 (pp. 156–61) or one of the patterns of development described in Parts 3 and 4 to reorganize your ideas.

Analyze Your Introduction, Conclusion, and Title

The following questions can help you evaluate your introduction, conclusion, and title.

1. **Will your introduction interest your readers and provide needed background information?** If your essay jumps into the topic without preparing readers for it, your introduction needs to be revised. Ask the questions *who, what, when, where, why,* and *how* to determine the background information your readers will need. Then use the suggestions in Chapter 7 (pp. 164–66) to create interest.

FIGURE 8.1 Flowchart for Evaluating Your Thesis Statement, Topic Sentences, and Evidence

QUESTIONS   REVISION STRATEGIES

1. Does your essay have a thesis that identifies your topic and position and suggests your slant? (To find out, state your thesis; then highlight the sentence in your draft that comes closest to what you just said. If you cannot find such a sentence, you probably do not have a well-focused thesis).

NO ▶

- Reread your essay and answer this question: What is the essay's one main point?
- Write a thesis statement that expresses that main point.
- Revise your paper to focus on that main point.
- Delete parts of the essay that do not support your thesis statement.

YES
▼

2. Do your readers have the background they need to understand your thesis? (To find out, ask someone unfamiliar with your topic to read your essay, and get feedback.)

NO ▶

- Answer *who, what, when, where, why,* and *how* questions to discover more background information.

YES
▼

3. Have you presented enough evidence to support your thesis? (Place a ✔ beside the evidence that supports your thesis. For paragraphs with few ✔ s, ask yourself: Do they need more evidence to be convincing?)

NO ▶

- Use prewriting strategies or do additional research to discover more supporting evidence.
- Evaluate this new evidence and add the most convincing evidence to your essay.

YES
▼

4. Does each topic sentence logically connect to and support the thesis? Read the thesis, and then read each topic sentence. Revise when the connection is not obvious.

NO ▶

- Rewrite the topic sentence so that it clearly supports the thesis.
- If necessary, broaden your thesis so that it encompasses all your supporting points.

YES
▼

5. Is your evidence specific and detailed? Reread paragraphs where you placed ✔ s. Does each item answer one of these questions: *Who? What? When? Where? Why? How?* For paragraphs with few or no ✔ s, add more detailed evidence.

NO ▶

- Answer *who, what, when, where, why,* and *how* questions to discover more detailed evidence. Name names, give dates, specify places.
- Use action verbs and descriptive language, including carefully chosen adjectives and adverbs.

2. **Does your conclusion draw your essay to a satisfactory close, reinforce your thesis statement, and follow logically from the introduction?** If not, try imagining yourself explaining the significance or importance of your essay to a friend, and use this explanation to rewrite your conclusion. Then use the suggestions for writing conclusions in Chapter 7 (pp. 166–67) to add interest.

3. **Does your title accurately reflect the content of your essay?** Write a few words that "label" your essay. Mine your thesis for a few key words that can serve as part of your title. Finally, use the suggestions in Chapter 7 (p. 168) to help you write a title.

HOW WRITERS READ ▷ **YOUR OWN WRITING**

When you are revising, you are expected to analyze and evaluate your own writing. The most effective way to do this is to treat your own writing as if it were someone else's. These steps can help.

BEFORE READING
- Take a break: You will be better able to create the distance you need to be objective.
- Preview your essay: Do the title, introduction, headings (if any), and conclusion together provide an effective overview?

WHILE READING
Assume you know nothing more about the subject than what you have written in the essay.
- Are there points where you would be confused?
- Would you need more information to be convinced?

AFTER READING
Ask yourself these "so what?" questions.
- Did the essay enrich your understanding of the topic? (If not, you may need to provide more or better evidence.)
- Did the essay show that the topic matters—to you and to your readers? (If not, you may need to reconsider your tone or even your thesis.)

▷ **ESSAY IN PROGRESS 3**

Evaluate the organization of your essay in progress. Make notes on your draft copy.

Analyze Your Paragraph Development

See Chapter 6 for more on paragraph development.

Each paragraph in your essay must fully develop a single idea that supports your thesis. (Exception: Each paragraph of a narrative essay focuses on a separate part of the action; see Chapter 10). In a typical first draft, paragraphs are often weak or loosely structured. They may contain irrelevant information or lack a clearly focused topic sentence.

Study each paragraph in conjunction with your thesis statement. Then, consider whether your topic sentence supports your thesis and whether the reasons and evidence in the paragraph support the topic sentence. You may need to delete or combine some paragraphs, rework or reorganize others, or move paragraphs to more appropriate placement in the essay. If you need to supply additional information to support your thesis, you may need to add paragraphs to the draft. Use Figure 8.2 to analyze and revise your paragraphs.

ESSAY IN PROGRESS 4

Using Figure 8.2, examine each paragraph of your essay in progress, and make notes on your draft.

FIGURE 8.2 Flowchart for Evaluating Your Paragraphs

QUESTIONS   REVISION STRATEGIES

1. Does each paragraph have a clear topic sentence that supports the thesis? <u>Underline</u> the topic sentence in each paragraph. Then evaluate whether the topic sentence makes a statement that supports the main idea of the essay.

- Revise a sentence within the paragraph so that it clearly states the main point.
- Write a new sentence that supports the thesis and states the main point of the paragraph.

 YES

2. Do all sentences in each paragraph support the topic sentence? To find out, read the topic sentence and each supporting sentence in turn.

- Revise supporting sentences to make their connection to the topic sentence clear.
- Delete any sentences that do not support the topic sentence.

YES

3. Does the paragraph offer adequate explanation and supporting details? Place ✔ s beside supporting details. Then ask yourself: Will readers want or need to know anything else?

- Add more details if your paragraph seems skimpy.
- Use either the *who, what, when, where, why,* and *how* questions or the prewriting strategies in Chapter 4 to generate the details you need.

YES

4. Will it be clear to your reader how each sentence and each paragraph connects to those before and after it? (To find out, read your paper aloud to see if it flows smoothly or sounds choppy.)

- Add transitions where they are needed. Refer to the list of common transitions on page 149.

Work with Classmates to Revise Your Essay

Many instructors ask students to use **peer review**, a process in which two or more students read and comment on one another's papers. Working with classmates is an excellent way to get ideas for improving your essays and your approach to the writing process. Peer review can also hone your critical-reading skills. The following suggestions will help writers and reviewers get the most from peer review.

Find a Good Reviewer

Your instructor may pair you with another class member or let you find your own reviewer, either a classmate or someone outside class. If you can select your own reviewer, use these tips.

- Select a classmate who is attentive in class, so he or she will be familiar with the assignment and with what you have learned so far in the course. If you need to find someone outside of class, choose a person who has already taken the course, preferably someone who did well in it.
- Avoid choosing close friends; they are not necessarily the best reviewers because they may be reluctant to offer criticism or may be too critical. Instead, choose someone who is serious, skillful, objective, and willing to spend the time needed to provide useful comments.
- If your college has a writing center, ask a tutor in the center to read and comment on your draft.
- Use more than one reviewer if possible, so you can get several perspectives.

Get Helpful Advice

To get the greatest benefit from peer review, use the following suggestions.

1. **Provide readable copy.** A typed, double-spaced draft is best.
2. **Do some revision yourself first.** Think through your draft, and try to fix obvious problems. The more developed your draft is, the more helpful your reviewer's comments will be.
3. **Offer specific questions or guidelines.** Give your reviewer a copy of the "Questions for Peer Reviewers" below, and add other questions that you want answered. You might also give your reviewer one of the revision flowcharts in this (or another) chapter.
4. **Be open to criticism and new ideas.** Try not to be defensive. Look at your essay objectively, seeing it from your reader's perspective.
5. **Don't feel obligated to accept all of the advice you are given.** A reviewer might suggest a change that will not work well in your paper or wrongly identify something as an error. If you are uncertain about a suggestion, discuss it with your instructor or other reviewers.

Questions for Peer Reviewers

1. What is the purpose of the essay?
2. Who is the intended audience?
3. What expectations are associated with this genre?
4. Is the introduction fully developed?
5. What is the main point or thesis? Is it easy to identify?
6. Does each paragraph offer a clear topic sentence and relevant and convincing evidence to support the main point? Where is more evidence needed? (Identify specific paragraphs.)
7. Is each paragraph clear and well organized? Are transitions needed to connect ideas within paragraphs?
8. Is the organization easy to follow? Where might it be improved, and how? Are transitions needed to connect ideas between paragraphs?
9. Does the conclusion draw the essay to a satisfying close?
10. What do you like about the draft? What could be improved? Underline or highlight passages that are unclear or confusing.

Give Helpful Advice

Reviewers should be honest but tactful. Criticism is never easy to accept, so keep your reader's feelings in mind. These tips will help you provide useful comments.

1. **Read the draft through twice before making any judgments or comments.**
2. **Focus on the main points and how clearly they are expressed.** If you notice a misspelling or a grammatical error, you can circle it, but correcting errors is not your primary task.
3. **Offer praise.** It will help the writer to know what works as well as what needs improvement.
4. **Be specific.** For instance, instead of saying that more examples are needed, tell the writer which ideas in which paragraphs are unclear or unconvincing without examples. Suggest useful examples in each case.
5. **Use the Questions for Peer Reviewers above as well as any additional questions that the writer provides to guide your review.** If the essay was written in response to an assignment in one of the chapters in Part 3 or 4, consult the revision flowchart in that chapter.
6. **Write notes and comments directly on the draft.** At the end of the essay, write a note that summarizes your overall reaction, pointing out both strengths and weaknesses. Here is one reviewer's sample final note.

> Overall, I think your paper has great ideas. It definitely held my interest, and the example about the judge proved your point well. But it could be organized better. The last three paragraphs don't seem connected to the rest of the essay. Maybe better transitions would help. Also the conclusion just repeats your thesis statement. It needs to be developed more.

7. **Use the Comments feature or insert comments in brackets or in a different color following the passage.** Make it easy for the writer to find and delete your comments after reading them.

8. **Do not rewrite paragraphs or sections of the essay.** Instead, suggest how the writer might revise them.

ESSAY IN PROGRESS 5

Give your essay in progress to a classmate to read and review. Ask your reviewer to respond to the Questions for Peer Reviewers (p. 183). Revise your essay using your revision outline, Figures 8.1 and 8.2, and your reviewer's suggestions.

Use Your Instructor's Comments

The comments your instructor provides are an important resource to use in revising your essays. You can use them not only to revise an essay but also to improve your writing throughout the course.

Revise an Essay Using Your Instructor's Comments

Often your instructor's comments provide a road map for you to begin your revision. An essay by a student, Kate Atkinson, appears in Figure 8.3. Her assignment was to write an essay defining a specialized term, and Kate chose "guerrilla street art" as her subject. In the margin, Kate's instructor comments on a range of elements in the essay, including the effectiveness of the introduction, paragraph unity and development, word choice, and source citations. (Because this was a draft, Kate's instructor did not comment on errors, such as misspellings and capitalization mistakes, that Kate will correct while editing and proofreading.) Kate read the comments carefully and used them to revise her essay. Her final draft appears in Chapter 17 (pp. 445–48).

FIGURE 8.3   Using Your Instructor's Comments to Revise Your Essay

Guerrilla Street Art: Definition Essay Rough Draft

Comment [KM1]: Good opening sentence. It gives readers a reason for wanting to know more about it and challenges them to look for it.

Guerrilla street art is everywhere, if you look for it. There are countless   1
examples in the small college town where I grew up, where the dense population of college students and artists breeds creativity. Just around the corner from my school there are stickers littering sign posts, colorful graffiti tags on exposed

Comment [KM2]: This term is not yet defined. I know it is defined later, but readers will wonder what it is now. Perhaps choose a different example here?

brick walls, homemade posters advertising local bands at the bus stop, and a cheerful Dr. Seuss character stencilled on the sidewalk. These small works of art can go easily unnoticed, but they bring an unexpected vibrancy to the city that is unique. Guerrilla street art is any unauthorized art in a public space. By taking art out of the traditional context, guerrilla street artists create controversy and intrigue by making art free and accessible to a broad audience.

> **Comment [KM3]:** This is your thesis, but it is not very detailed. What about combining it with the following sentence to create a stronger thesis?

Graffiti is unauthorized writing or drawing on a public surface. It dates back centuries and artists have been know to use chalk, markers, paint, and even carving tools to inscribe their messages on public property. Common techniques used by street artists today include graffiti, stenciling, poster art, sticker art, and wheat pasting. Graffiti is so common that it is difficult to travel far in most urban settings without coming across a word or image scrawled in spray paint on a public a surface. Stenciling is a form of graffitti in which artists use pre-cut stencils to guide their work, and pre-made stickers and posters are popular because they can be quickly appled and are easy to mass produce. "Wheat pasting" refers to the use of a vegetable-based adhesive to adhere posters to walls. Using a less common technique called "yarn bombing," crafty artists knit colorful sheaths of wool and acrylic and wrap them around telephone poles and park benches. The finished pieces are eye-catching and unusual, but not permanent or damaging to public property.

2

> **Comment [KM4]:** This sentence defining graffiti is almost the same definition as your definition of guerrilla street art in para. 1.

> **Comment [KM5]:** The paragraph is about graffiti-writing or drawing. Do wheat pasting and yarn bombing fall into this category? If so, can you expand the definition to fit them? Or are they other forms of guerrilla street art? If so, I'd put them in a separate paragraph. Right now you only mention one form of guerrilla art—graffiti—yet your title suggests the essay is about street art. Are there other forms you haven't mentioned?

The various motives behind guerilla street art are as diverse as the artwork itself and range from social and political activism to self-promotion of the artist. Artist embellish telephone poles with colorful yarn or train carriges with ornate murals as a way to reclaim and beautify public space. Others use public space as a billboard for to advocate for a cause. An example of street art as propaganda is artist Shepard Fairey's iconic image of Barack Obama. The simple design combines a striking red, white, and blue portrait of Obama with the word "Hope." With the nod of approval from Obama's campaign team, Fairey and his team dispersed and glue, stencilled, and tacked the image onto countless public surfaces across the US until it became an important facet of the campaign. The picture itself is powerful, but what made it even more effective as a campaign tool was the distribution of the image by supporters and the youth appeal that it garnered as a result.

3

> **Comment [KM6]:** This is a strong topic sentence.

> **Deleted:** a

> **Comment [KM7]:** Are all causes propaganda? You might want to chose a different word here or introduce propaganda and a separate motive first.

> **Comment [KM8]:** Add source citation

Street Art is also an easy way for new artists to gain notoriety withouth revealing who they really are. A tag, which is an artists signature or symbol, is the most prevalent type of graffitti. Before the Obama campaign, Shepard Fairey gained international acclaim for a sticker depicting wrestler Andre the Giant and the word "Obey." The image soon became his tag and can be found in almost all of his work, making it instantly recognizable. The anonymity of street art also gives artists the freedom to express themselves without fearing the judgement of their peers. At worst, this freedom can result in crude or offensice inscriptions on public property but at best, it can produce bold statements.

4

(continued on next page)

(Figure 8.3 continued)

> **Comment [KM9]:** This sentence leads me to believe that the para. will be about secrecy, but midway through the topic seems to switch to reasons for street art's appeal. Maybe make this part into a separate paragraph?

> **Comment [KM10]:** Add source citation

> **Comment [KM11]:** I am glad you raised this question. I kept wondering about it all along as I read the essay. Can you raise it earlier? And should you try to answer this knotty question of "What is art"? Maybe just recognize that the question exists?

Due to the illicit nature of their art, the street artist community is shrouded in secrecy. In the film "Exit through the Gift Shop," a documentary by notorious British street artist Banksy, hooded figures in ski masks are shown scaling buildings and perched precariously on ledges, armed with spray cans and buckets of industrial paste and always on the lookout for the police. Despite his celebrity, Banksy has managed to keep his identity anonymous and his face is never shown in the film. It is common for street artists to be arrested for trespassing and vandalism, and the risk and intentional disobience involved in street art adds to its appeal, especially amoung young people. Another appeal of guerrilla street art is that it is comtemporary and can be enjoyed without a visit to a museum. It is free and encourages the belief that art should be accessible and available to everyone. It is also a movement that anyone can take part in and that challenges traditional standards of art. 5

Guerrilla street art has blossomed from and underground movement to a cultural phenomenon. At the very least, it brings up the controversial questions of what constitutes art, and whether public space is an appropriate place for it. It brings beauty and intrigue to urban spaces that would otherwise go unnoticed and it is a tool for artists to exercise freedom of speech and expression. 6

EXERCISE 8.1 ▶ **COMPARING A FIRST DRAFT AND A FINAL DRAFT**

Either alone or in small groups, compare Kate Atkinson's first draft (pp. 184–86) with her final draft on pages 445–48. Make a list of the changes she made to her essay in response to her instructor's comments. Also, put a checkmark next to any problems that recur throughout the first draft of the essay.

Use Your Instructor's Comments to Improve Future Essays

When you receive a graded essay back from an instructor, it is tempting to note the grade and then file away the essay without reading any accompanying notes or suggestions. To improve your writing, however, take time to study each comment. Use the following suggestions to improve future essays.

- **Reread your essay at least twice.** It takes more than one reading to process numerous comments on a wide range of topics. Read your essay once to note grammatical corrections. Then read it a second time to study comments about organization or content.

- **If you did not get a high grade, try to determine why.** Was the essay weak in content, organization, or development?
- **Make sure you understand (and can correct) each grammatical error.** If you cannot, check a grammar handbook or ask a classmate. If you still do not understand your error, check with your instructor.
- **Record grammar errors in an error log.** When you proofread your next essay, look carefully for each type of error.
- **Using Figures 8.1 (p. 179) and 8.2 (p. 181), highlight or mark weaknesses that your instructor identified.** When writing your next essay, refer back to these flowcharts. Pay close attention to the areas you had trouble with as you revise your next paper.
- **If any comments are unclear, first ask a classmate if he or she understands them.** If not, talk to your instructor, who will be pleased that you are taking time to study the comments.

EXERCISE 8.2 ▶ **USING YOUR INSTRUCTOR'S COMMENTS ON A DRAFT**

If your instructor has returned a marked-up first draft to you, read the comments carefully. Then draw a line down the middle of a blank sheet of paper. On the left, write the instructor's comments; on the right, jot down ways you might revise the essay in response to each comment. Put a checkmark next to any problems that recur throughout your essay; these are areas to which you will want to pay particular attention in your future writing.

Consider Your Learning Style When You Revise

Depending on your learning style, you may need to address specific kinds of problems in your drafts. The following revision tips for various learning styles may help.

LEARNING STYLE OPTIONS

- *Creative* learners sometimes write drafts that lack organization, so they will benefit greatly from preparing outlines and graphic organizers.

- *Independent* learners often need time for reflection, so they should allow extra time between drafting and revising.

- *Verbal* learners may prefer to outline drafts to check the organization.

- *Pragmatic* learners tend to write tightly organized drafts that may lack interest, originality, or content, so they should make sure their draft offers interesting and relevant supporting details.

- *Social* learners often find discussing revision plans with classmates helpful, so they should add time to get feedback from classmates.

- *Spatial* learners may prefer to draw a graphic organizer to check the organization.

- *Rational* learners should be sure their drafts do not seem dull or impersonal, adding vivid descriptions and personal examples where appropriate.

- *Concrete* learners tend to focus on specifics, so they should check that their thesis and topic sentences are clearly stated.

- *Emotional* learners should check to make sure they have stated their ideas directly, without hedging or showing undue concern for those who disagree.

- *Abstract* learners tend to focus on general ideas, so they should be sure their essay has enough supporting details.

STUDENTS WRITE

After writing her first draft, which appears in Chapter 7 (pp. 171–72), Latrisha Wilson used the guidelines and revision flowcharts in this chapter to guide her revision. For example, she decided that she needed to focus more on how communications technologies allow greater surveillance. She added details and examples, including a visual to show what she was describing.

Wilson asked a classmate to review her essay. A portion of his comments is shown below.

Reviewer's Comments

I like your topic. It's current and interesting, but maybe your thesis could be more specific? Maybe it should focus on how new ways of communicating put us at risk of surveillance? Or you could revise your intro to focus on whistleblowers (that's what your first body paragraph talks about), but you'd need to add a lot of information.

Since I have a gmail account and a Facebook page, I'd like to know more about how those sites use our personal information to make money, and maybe you could include a screenshot of a gmail page to show where the ads are. That might be helpful for the 5 people in the world (like the teacher?) who don't have gmail accounts. The only other thing that I think may be a problem is the tone. It's kind of casual for an essay for class. Maybe you could make your tone more formal?

Using her own analysis and her classmate's suggestions, Wilson created a graphic organizer (Graphic Organizer 8.3) to help her decide how to revise her draft. She used the format for an illustration essay provided in Chapter 13 (p. 305).

After creating the graphic organizer, Wilson revised her first draft. A portion of her revised draft, with her revisions indicated using the Track Changes function of Microsoft Word, follows.

GRAPHIC ORGANIZER 8.3 Graphic Organizer for Latrisha Wilson's Revision Plans

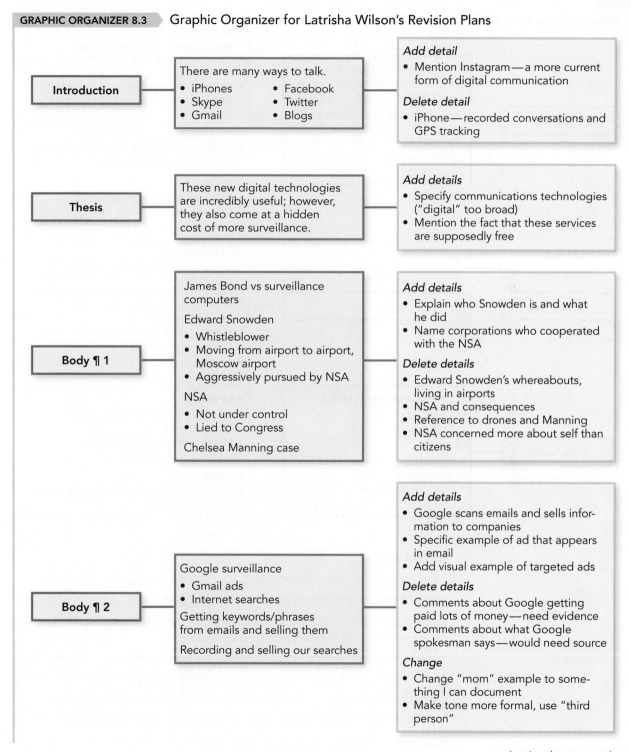

Introduction

There are many ways to talk.
- iPhones
- Skype
- Gmail
- Facebook
- Twitter
- Blogs

Add detail
- Mention Instagram—a more current form of digital communication

Delete detail
- iPhone—recorded conversations and GPS tracking

Thesis

These new digital technologies are incredibly useful; however, they also come at a hidden cost of more surveillance.

Add details
- Specify communications technologies ("digital" too broad)
- Mention the fact that these services are supposedly free

Body ¶ 1

James Bond vs surveillance computers

Edward Snowden
- Whistleblower
- Moving from airport to airport, Moscow airport
- Aggressively pursued by NSA

NSA
- Not under control
- Lied to Congress

Chelsea Manning case

Add details
- Explain who Snowden is and what he did
- Name corporations who cooperated with the NSA

Delete details
- Edward Snowden's whereabouts, living in airports
- NSA and consequences
- Reference to drones and Manning
- NSA concerned more about self than citizens

Body ¶ 2

Google surveillance
- Gmail ads
- Internet searches

Getting keywords/phrases from emails and selling them

Recording and selling our searches

Add details
- Google scans emails and sells information to companies
- Specific example of ad that appears in email
- Add visual example of targeted ads

Delete details
- Comments about Google getting paid lots of money—need evidence
- Comments about what Google spokesman says—would need source

Change
- Change "mom" example to something I can document
- Make tone more formal, use "third person"

(continued on next page)

(Graphic Organizer 8.3 continued)

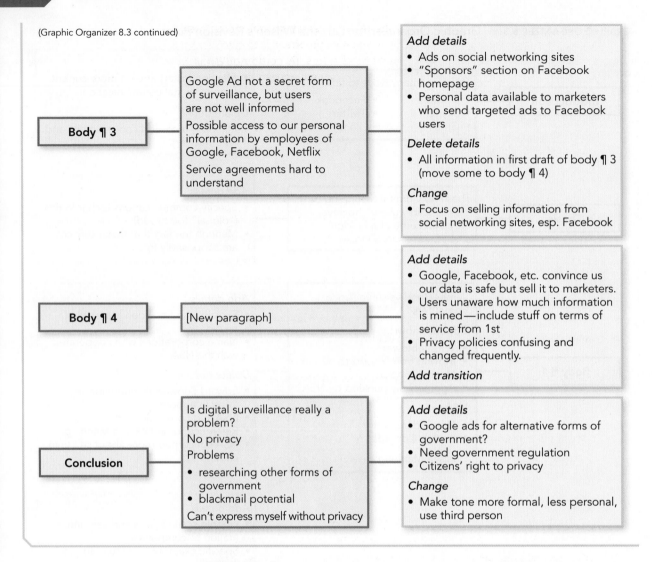

Body ¶ 3	Google Ad not a secret form of surveillance, but users are not well informed Possible access to our personal information by employees of Google, Facebook, Netflix Service agreements hard to understand	*Add details* • Ads on social networking sites • "Sponsors" section on Facebook homepage • Personal data available to marketers who send targeted ads to Facebook users *Delete details* • All information in first draft of body ¶ 3 (move some to body ¶ 4) *Change* • Focus on selling information from social networking sites, esp. Facebook
Body ¶ 4	[New paragraph]	*Add details* • Google, Facebook, etc. convince us our data is safe but sell it to marketers. • Users unaware how much information is mined—include stuff on terms of service from 1st • Privacy policies confusing and changed frequently. *Add transition*
Conclusion	Is digital surveillance really a problem? No privacy Problems • researching other forms of government • blackmail potential Can't express myself without privacy	*Add details* • Google ads for alternative forms of government? • Need government regulation • Citizens' right to privacy *Change* • Make tone more formal, less personal, use third person

Revised draft

Do we need to talk? There are plenty of exciting new ways to do it. We can ~~communicate by talking on~~ use our iPhones, chat on Skype, Gmail, Facebook message or read each other's Twitter, or blog posts, or share pictures on Instagram. ~~but there are dangers there. Our conversations can be recorded, and the GPS function on the phone allows our whereabouts to be tracked. We can chat on Skype, Gmail, Facebook message, or read each other's Twitter or blog posts. And then there are security cameras that record our every move.~~ These new digital technologies are incredibly useful; however, they also come at a hidden cost. Often advertised as free services, new ways of communicating put us under more invasive but less obvious forms of surveillance.

Before Wilson submitted her final draft, she read her essay several more times, editing it for sentence structure and word choice. She also proofread it to catch errors in grammar and punctuation as well as typographical errors. (A portion of Wilson's revised essay, with editing and proofreading changes marked, appears in Chapter 9, p. 213.) The final version of Wilson's essay follows.

Final Draft

No Place Left for Privacy

Do we need to talk? There are plenty of exciting new ways to do it. We can use our iPhones, chat on Skype, Gmail, Facebook message, or read each other's Twitter feed or blog posts, or share pictures on Instagram. These new digital technologies are incredibly useful; however, they also come at a hidden cost. Often advertised as free services, new ways of communicating put us under more invasive but less obvious forms of surveillance.   1

When the word *surveillance* comes up, people think of some thrilling and dangerous activity, like the spying on foreign terrorists that goes on in James Bond movies. But in the U.S. today, most spying isn't done by handsome secret agents out to save the world; it's done by surveillance computers, and they monitor U.S. citizens, not just foreign terrorists. For example, consider what we learned from the whistleblower Edward Snowden, who sacrificed his career as a contractor for the National Security Agency (NSA) to alert the public to the deals the NSA makes with companies like Microsoft, Facebook, and Verizon to collect personal information and monitor everything their customers do on the Internet or speak into a telephone.   2

The NSA, of course, isn't the only organization spying on us. Another kind of surveillance, which doesn't make top press, is the eavesdropping that Google and other communication service providers regularly do on their users. Google software, for example, automatically scans the content of all Gmail for keywords and phrases that then must get sold or rented to other companies because users of Gmail regularly see targeted advertisements related to what they've written about: If a user wishes her friend "Happy Birthday!" she now sees advertisements for party clowns and birthday packages. (See fig. 1.)   3

Advertisers pay social networking sites to do something similar, which is why users might have noticed that section of "sponsors" to the right of your   4

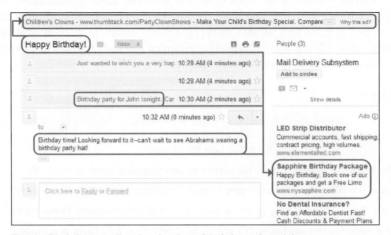

Fig. 1. Birthday email string leads to birthday advertising

Facebook homepage. Everything public on a typical person's profile page—their age, relationship status, favorite music, education history—is available to marketers (for a price), so they can send their ads to specific people.

In this way, Facebook, Google, and other digital service providers sell advertisers intimate data about us, while also attempting to convince us that all our personal data is safe. Most people have little to no idea how much data they give up when they get on the Internet. How would they? Facebook and Google constantly change their privacy policies, and the terms-of-service agreements are long legal documents written in a language which your everyday person doesn't have the time or energy to decipher. So they just check a box.

"What's the problem?" you might say. "I have nothing to hide from either the government or companies like Google and Facebook." But think about it for a few minutes: When researching a political science paper on alternate forms of government, will typing words like "anarchism" or "Marxism" into a search box set off warning signals at the NSA or trigger Google to send advertisements for *The Anarchist's Handbook* (which might set off warning signals)? To honestly express ourselves, we need privacy. But less and less is there any kind of space for it online,

5

6

> where most of us read, write, and communicate. There needs to be some space online where all our activity is not recorded and sold (or taken by government agencies). But unless more rules and regulations are put in place to govern the behavior of Internet service providers and governmental data miners, privacy will become a thing of the past, and people will forget that they are not just consumers, but also citizens with rights, like the right to privacy.

Analyzing the Revision

1. **Revision** Identify the major revisions that Wilson made from the earlier draft in Chapter 7. Explain why you think she made the changes she did. Are there other changes she could have made to make the final draft even better?
2. **Introduction and Conclusion** Examine Wilson's introduction and conclusion. In what ways are they more effective than the introduction and conclusion in her first draft? What additional improvements could she make?
3. **Details** Choose one paragraph, and compare the details provided in it with those in the corresponding paragraph of the first draft. Which added details are particularly effective, and why?
4. **Tone** Consider the differences in tone between Wilson's first draft and her revised draft. What changes affected her tone? (List three.) Given that she was writing this essay for a college course and that her instructor was her main audience, how effective is the tone of the revised essay?

Working Together

In groups of two or three classmates, use the questions below to analyze paragraph 6 (or another paragraph) from the essay "The New Marshmallow Test: Students Can't Resist Multitasking" (p. 4) or another essay.

- What is the topic sentence of this paragraph?
- How is the paragraph organized?
- What transitions does the author use in the paragraph?
- What action verbs (if any) does the author use in the paragraph? (Give an example.)
- Does the author use descriptive language (language that appeals to the senses)? If so, give an example of such language.

Be prepared to share your responses with the rest of the class.

9
Editing Sentences and Words

NO FISHING/NO ADMITTANCE TO NON – SYNDICAT MEMBERS TACKLE WILL BE SEIZED TRESSPASSERS PROSERCUTED ZERO TOLLERANCE

© Geogphotos/Alamy Stock Photo

In this chapter you will learn to:

- analyze and edit your sentences for wordiness; repetition of type, length, and pattern; parallelism; and weak verbs

- analyze and edit your word choice for tone, level of diction, overly general word choice, and use of clichés

- proofread effectively

WRITING QUICK START ▸ The photo on this page shows a sign with errors of grammar and punctuation. First, correct the errors. Then write a few sentences describing how errors like these affect viewers' reaction to the message and their opinion of the sign's creator.

When you identified errors in the sign and corrected them, you edited and proofread it. **Editing** and **proofreading** are processes of examining individual sentences and words and correcting them as needed so that each conveys the intended meaning accurately, concisely, and in an interesting and appropriate way. These are the last steps in the writing process (see Graphic Organizer 9.1), and they are crucial. Because you are almost finished with your assignment, you may be tempted to hurry through or skip the editing and proofreading stage altogether. But as this Writing Quick Start demonstrates, careful editing and proofreading will always pay off in the end because an error-free essay is important to conveying your message effectively and establishing a positive relationship with your reader. This chapter will help you sharpen your sentences and refine your word choice.

GRAPHIC ORGANIZER 9.1 An Overview of the Writing Process

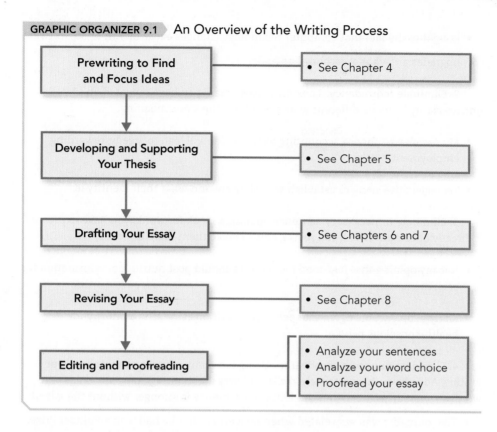

Analyze Your Sentences

Effective sentences should have four important characteristics.

1. They should be clear and concise.
2. They should be varied.
3. They should use parallel structure for similar ideas.
4. They should contain strong, active verbs.

Are Your Sentences Concise?

Concise sentences convey their meaning in as few words as possible. Use the following suggestions to make your sentences concise.

　1. Avoid wordy expressions. Omit words and phrases that contribute little or no meaning. If a sentence is clear without a particular phrase or if the phrase can be replaced by a more direct word or phrase, take it out or replace it.

- ~~In the near future,~~ ̭another revolution in computer technology is bound to
   　　　soon.
   occur̭.

- ~~In light of the fact that~~ ^{Since} computer technology changes ~~every month or so,~~ ^{monthly,} software upgrades are ~~what everybody has to do.~~ ^{necessary.}

2. Eliminate redundancy. Look for places where you have repeated an idea unnecessarily by using different words that have the same meaning.

- ~~My decision to choose~~ ^{Choosing} accounting as my major will lead to steady, rewarding employment.

- Teenagers use slang to establish ~~who they are and what~~ their identity ~~is~~.

3. Eliminate unnecessary sentence openings. Look for words you have expressed indirectly or tentatively. As you revise, edit to make them more direct.

- ~~It is my opinion that~~ ^Ffast-food restaurants should post nutritional information for each menu item.

- ~~Many people would agree that~~ ^Sselecting nutritious snacks is a priority for health-conscious people.

An **adverb** modifies a verb, an adjective, or another adverb.

4. Eliminate unnecessary adverbs. Using too many **adverbs** can weaken your writing. Adverbs such as *extremely*, *really*, and *very* add nothing and can weaken the words they modify. Notice that the following sentence is stronger without the adverb.

- The journalist was ~~very~~ elated when he learned that he had won a Pulitzer Prize.

Other adverbs, such as *somewhat*, *rather*, and *quite* also add little or no meaning and are often unnecessary.

- The college president was ~~quite~~ disturbed by the findings of the Presidential Panel on Sex Equity.

A **prepositional phrase** is a group of words that begins with a preposition and includes the object or objects of the preposition and all their modifiers: *above the low wooden table.*

5. Eliminate unnecessary phrases and clauses. Wordy phrases and clauses make it difficult for readers to find and understand the main point of your sentence. This problem often occurs when you use too many **prepositional phrases** and clauses that begin with *who*, *which*, or *that*.

- The ^{students'}complaints ~~of students in the college~~ encouraged the dean to create additional parking spaces.

- The ~~teenagers who were~~ ^{teenage}mall walkers disagreed with the ^{newspaper}editorial ~~in the newspaper that supported the~~ ^{supporting}shopping mall regulations.

6. Avoid weak verb-noun combinations. Weak verb-noun combinations such as *wrote a draft* instead of *drafted* or *made a change* instead of *changed* tend to make sentences wordy.

- The attorney ~~made an assessment of~~ the company's liability in the accident.

  (assessed)

- The professor ~~gave a lecture~~ on Asian American relations.

  (lectured)

Edit the following sentences to make them concise.

1. Due to the fact that Professor Wu assigned twenty-five math problems for tomorrow, I am forced to make the decision to miss this evening's lecture to be given by the vice president of the United States.
2. In many cases, workers are forced to use old equipment that needs replacing despite the fact that equipment malfunctions cost the company more than the price of new machines.
3. Miley Cyrus is one of the best examples of an entertainment celebrity being given too much publicity.
4. The president of Warehouse Industries has the ability and power to decide who should and who should not be hired and who should and who should not be fired.
5. The soccer league's sponsor, as a matter of fact, purchased league jerseys for the purpose of advertisement and publicity.

HOW WRITERS READ   SENTENCES AND PARAGRAPHS

Sentences and paragraphs that are unclear, vague, or repetitious can be confusing (and annoying). Fortunately, most of your college reading assignments will have been carefully edited, but you may encounter poor writing on the job, on personal Web sites, and even in some periodicals.

When you encounter material that contains numerous grammatical or spelling errors or that uses dull, stilted, or unclear language, take the time to check the reliability of the content carefully: Lack of care in writing and editing can often be a sign of sloppy thinking, and authors who do not take the time to present their ideas in clear, correct prose may not have taken the time to think through or research their topic fully.

Are Your Sentences Varied?

Sentences that are varied will help hold your reader's interest and make your writing flow more smoothly. Vary the type, length, and pattern of your sentences.

How to vary sentence type.   There are four types of sentences: *simple, compound, complex,* and *compound-complex.* Each type consists of one or more clauses. A **clause** is a group of words with both a subject and a verb. There are two types of clauses.

- An **independent clause** can stand alone as a complete sentence.
- A **dependent clause** cannot stand alone as a complete sentence. It begins with a subordinating conjunction (for example, *because* or *although*) or a relative pronoun (for example, *when, which,* or *that*).

A brief summary of each sentence type and its clauses appears in Table 9.1.

TABLE 9.1 ▸ **Sentence Types**

Sentence Type	Clauses	Example
Simple	One independent clause and no dependent clauses	Credit-card fraud is increasing in the United States.
Compound	Two or more independent clauses and no dependent clauses	Credit-card fraud is increasing in the United States; it is a violation of financial privacy.
Complex	One or more dependent clauses and one independent clause	Because credit-card fraud is increasing in America, consumers must become more cautious.
Compound-complex	One or more dependent clauses and two or more independent clauses	Because credit-card fraud is increasing in America, consumers must be cautious, and retailers must take steps to protect consumers.

Use the following suggestions to vary your sentence types.

1. Use simple sentences for emphasis and clarity. A **simple sentence** contains only one independent clause, but it is not necessarily short. It can have more than one subject, more than one verb, and several modifiers.

- ⌜subject⌝ ⌜subject⌝ ⌜verb⌝ ⌜verb⌝
  Both retailers and consumers have and must exercise the responsibility
  ⌜modifier⌝ ⌜modifier⌝
  to curtail fraud by reporting suspicious use of credit cards.

A short, simple sentence can be used to emphasize an important point or to make a dramatic statement.

- Credit-card fraud is rampant.

If you use too many simple sentences, however, your writing will sound choppy and disjointed.

Disjointed	It was a cold, drizzly spring morning. I was driving to school. A teenage hitchhiker stood alongside the road. He seemed distraught.
Better	I was driving to school on a cold, drizzly spring morning when I saw a teenage hitchhiker standing alongside the road. He seemed distraught.

2. Use compound sentences to show relationships among equally important ideas. A **compound sentence** consists of two or more independent clauses joined in one of the following ways.

- With a comma and **coordinating conjunction**:

  - Leon asked a question, *and* the whole class was surprised.

- With a semicolon:

  - Graffiti had been scrawled on the subway walls; passersby ignored it.

- With a semicolon and a **conjunctive adverb**:

  - Each year thousands of children are adopted; *consequently*, adoption service agencies have increased in number.

- With a **correlative conjunction**:

  - *Either* the jury will reach a verdict tonight, *or* it will recess until Monday morning.

In each example, both clauses are equally important and receive equal emphasis.

You can also use compound sentences to explain *how* equally important ideas are related. For example, you can use different coordinating conjunctions to show the relationship between two important related ideas. (See Table 9.2 below.)

Coordinating conjunctions (*and, but, or, nor, for, so, yet*) connect sentence elements that are of equal importance.

A **conjunctive adverb** is a word (such as *also, however,* or *still*) that links two independent clauses.

A **correlative conjunction** is a word pair (such as *not only . . . but also*) that works together to join elements within a sentence.

TABLE 9.2 Selecting Coordinating Conjunctions to Convey Relationships

Coordinating Conjunction	Relationship	Example
and	Additional information	The three teenage vandals were apprehended, *and* their parents were required to pay damages.
but, yet	Contrast or opposition	No one wants to pay more taxes, *yet* taxes are necessary to support vital public services.
for, so	Causes or effects	Text messages can disrupt a student's concentration, *so* turning your cell phone off in class is essential to learning.
or, nor	Choices or options	Quebec may become a separate country, *or* it may settle its differences with the Canadian government.

3. **Use complex sentences to show that one or more ideas are less important than (or subordinate to) another idea.** A **complex sentence** consists of one independent clause and at least one dependent clause. Either type of clause may come first. When the dependent clause comes first, it is usually followed by a comma. When the independent clause comes first, a comma is usually not used.

- Because the dam broke, the village flooded.
- The village flooded because the dam broke.

| TABLE 9.3 | Selecting Subordinating Conjunctions to Convey Relationships |

Subordinating Conjunction	Relationship	Example
as, as far as, as soon as, as if, as though, although, even though, even if, in order to	Circumstance	*Even though* cable television has expanded, it is still unavailable in some rural areas.
because, since, so that	Causes or effects	*Because* the movie industry has changed, the way theaters are built has changed.
before, after, while, until, when	Time	*When* prices rise, demand falls.
whether, if, unless, even if	Condition	More people will purchase hybrid cars *if* these cars become less expensive.

In the preceding sentences, the main point is that the village flooded. The dependent clause explains *why* the flood happened. A dependent clause often begins with a *subordinating conjunction* that indicates how the less important (dependent) idea is related to the more important (independent) idea. Table 9.3 lists some subordinating conjunctions and the relationships they suggest.

Dependent clauses can also begin with a relative pronoun (*that, who, which*).

- Many medical doctors *who are affiliated with a teaching hospital* use interns in their practices.

To see how complex sentences can improve your writing, study the following two paragraphs.

Original

Are you one of the many people who has tried to quit smoking? Well, don't give up trying. Help is here in the form of a nonprescription drug. A new nicotine patch has been developed. This patch will help you quit gradually. That way, you will experience less severe withdrawal symptoms. Quitting will be easier than ever before, but you need to be psychologically ready to quit smoking. Otherwise, you may not be successful.

Monotonous use of simple and compound sentences

Revised

If you are one of the many people who has tried to quit smoking, don't give up trying. Help is now here in the form of a nonprescription nicotine patch, which has been developed to help you quit gradually. Because you experience less severe withdrawal symptoms, quitting is easier than ever before. However, for this patch to be successful, you need to be psychologically ready to quit.

Varied sentence types convey relationships among ideas.

4. Use compound-complex sentences occasionally to express complicated relationships. A **compound-complex sentence** contains one or more dependent clauses and two or more independent clauses.

- If you expect to study medicine, you must take courses in biology and chemistry, and you must prepare for four more years of study after college.

Use compound-complex sentences sparingly. When overused, they make your writing hard to follow.

Combine each of the following sentence pairs into a single compound or complex sentence.

1. A day-care center may look respectable. Parents assume a day-care center is safe and run well.
2. In some states, the training required to become a day-care worker is minimal. On-the-job supervision and evaluation of day-care workers are infrequent.
3. Restaurants are often fined or shut down for minor hygiene violations. Day-care centers are rarely fined or closed down for hygiene violations.
4. More and more mothers have entered the workforce. The need for quality day care has increased dramatically.
5. Naturally, day-care workers provide emotional support for children. Few day-care workers are trained to provide intellectual stimulation.

How to vary sentence length.   If you vary sentence type, you often automatically vary sentence length as well. Simple sentences tend to be short, while compound and complex sentences tend to be longer. Compound-complex sentences tend to be the longest.

You can use sentence length to achieve a specific effect: Short sentences tend to be sharp and emphatic; they move ideas along quickly, creating a fast-paced essay. In the following example, a series of short sentences creates a dramatic pace.

- The jurors had little to debate. The incriminating evidence was clear and incontrovertible. The jury announced its verdict with astonishing speed.

Longer sentences, in contrast, move the reader more slowly through the essay. Notice that the lengthy sentence in this example suggests a leisurely, unhurried pace.

- While standing in line, impatient to ride the antique steam-powered train, the child begins to imagine how the train will crawl deliberately, endlessly, along the tracks, slowly gathering speed as it spews grayish steam and emits hissing noises.

How to vary sentence pattern.   A sentence is usually made up of one or more subjects, verbs, and modifiers. **Modifiers** are words (adjectives or adverbs), phrases, or clauses that describe or limit another part of the sentence (a noun, pronoun, verb, phrase, or clause). Here are some examples of modifiers in sentences.

Words as Modifiers	The *empty* classroom was unlocked. [adjective]
	The office runs *smoothly*. [adverb]
Phrases as Modifiers	The student *in the back* raised his hand.
	Schools should not have the right *to mandate community service*.
Clauses as Modifiers	The baseball *that flew into the stands* was caught by a fan.
	When the exam was over, I knew I had earned an A.

As you can see, the placement of modifiers may vary, depending on the pattern of the sentence.

1. Modifier last: subject-verb-modifier. The main message (expressed in the subject and verb) comes first, followed by information that clarifies or explains the message.

- The instructor walked into the room.

In some cases, a string of modifiers follows the subject and verb.

- The salesperson demonstrated the word-processing software, creating and deleting files, moving text, creating directories, and formatting tables.

2. Modifier first: modifier-subject-verb (periodic sentences). Information in the modifier precedes the main message, elaborating the main message but slowing the overall pace. The emphasis is on the main message at the end of the sentence.

- Tired and depressed from hours of work, the divers left the scene of the accident.

Use periodic sentences sparingly: Too many will make your writing sound stiff and unnatural.

3. Modifier in the middle: subject-modifier-verb. The modifier interrupts the main message and tends to slow the pace of the sentence. The emphasis is on the subject because it comes first in the sentence.

- The paramedic, trained and experienced in water rescue, was first on the scene of the boating accident.

Avoid placing too many modifiers between the subject and verb in a sentence. Doing so may cause your reader to miss the sentence's key idea.

4. Modifiers used throughout.

- Because human organs are in short supply, awarding an organ transplant, especially hearts and kidneys, to patients has become a controversial issue, requiring difficult medical and ethical decisions.

By varying the order of subjects, verbs, and modifiers, you can give emphasis where it is needed as well as vary sentence patterns as shown in the paragraphs that follow:

Original

Theme parks are growing in number and popularity. Theme parks have a single purpose—to provide family entertainment centered around high-action activities. The most famous theme parks are Disney World and Disneyland. They serve as models for other, smaller parks. Theme parks always have amusement rides. Theme parks can offer other activities such as swimming. Theme parks will probably continue to be popular.

Monotonous use of same subject-verb-modifier pattern

Revised

Theme parks are growing in number and popularity. Offering high-action activities, theme parks fulfill a single purpose—to provide family entertainment. The most famous parks, Disney World and Disneyland, serve as models for other, smaller parks. Parks always offer amusement rides, which appeal to both children and adults. Added attractions such as swimming, water slides, and boat rides provide thrills and recreation. Because of their family focus, theme parks are likely to grow in popularity.

Ideas come alive through use of varied sentence patterns

EXERCISE 9.3

Add modifiers to the following sentences to create varied sentence patterns.

1. The divers jumped into the chilly waters.
2. The beach was closed because of pollution.
3. Coffee-flavored drinks are becoming popular.
4. The dorm was crowded and noisy.
5. The exam was more challenging than we expected.

Are Your Sentences Parallel in Structure?

Parallelism means that similar ideas in a sentence are expressed in similar grammatical form. It means balancing words with words, phrases with phrases, and clauses with clauses. Parallel sentences flow smoothly and make your thoughts easy to follow. Study the following sentence pairs. Which sentence in each pair is easier to read?

- The horse was large, had a bony frame, and it was friendly.
- The horse was large, bony, and friendly.

- Maria enjoys swimming and sailboats.
- Maria enjoys swimming and sailing.

In each pair, the second sentence sounds better because it is balanced grammatically. *Large, bony,* and *friendly* are all adjectives. *Swimming* and *sailing* are nouns ending in *-ing*.

The following sentence elements should be parallel in structure.

1. **Nouns in a series**

   - A thesis statement, ~~that is clear,~~ ^clear^ strong supporting paragraphs, and ~~a~~ ^an interesting^ conclusion ~~that should be interesting~~ are all elements of a well-written essay.

2. **Adjectives in a series**

   - The concertgoers were rowdy and ~~making a great deal of noise.~~ ^noisy.^

3. **Verbs in a series**

   - The sports fans jumped and ~~were applauding.~~ ^applauded.^

4. **Phrases and clauses within a sentence**

   - The parents who supervised the new playground were pleased ~~about~~ ^that^ the preschoolers ~~playing~~ ^played^ congenially and that everyone enjoyed the sandbox.

5. **Items being compared**

   - It is usually better to study for an exam over a period of time than ~~cramming~~ ^to cram^ the night before.

EXERCISE 9.4

Edit the following sentences to eliminate problems with parallelism.

1. The biology student spent Saturday morning reviewing his weekly textbook assignments, writing a research report, and with lab reports.
2. The career counselor advised Althea to take several math courses and that she should also register for at least one computer course.
3. Three reasons for the popularity of fast-food restaurants are that they are efficient, offer reasonable prices, and most people like the food they serve.
4. Driving to Boston is as expensive as it is to take the train.
5. While at a stop sign, it is important first to look both ways and then proceeding with caution is wise.

Do Your Sentences Have Strong, Active Verbs?

Strong, active verbs make your writing lively and vivid. By contrast, *to be* verbs (*is, was, were, has been,* and so on) and other **linking verbs** (*feels, became, seems, appears*)—which connect a noun or pronoun to words that describe it—can make your writing sound dull. Linking verbs often contribute little meaning to a sentence. Whenever possible, use stronger, more active verbs.

"To Be" Verb	The puppy *was* afraid of thunder.
Action Verbs	The puppy *whimpered* and *quivered* during the thunderstorm.
Linking Verb	The child *looked* frightened as she boarded the bus for her first day of kindergarten.
Action Verbs	The child *trembled* and *clung* to her sister as she boarded the bus for her first day of kindergarten.

To strengthen your writing, use active verbs rather than passive verbs as much as possible. A **passive verb** is a form of the verb *to be* combined with a past participle (*killed*, *chosen*, *elected*). In a sentence with a passive verb, the subject does not perform the action of the verb but instead receives the action. By contrast, in a sentence with an **active verb**, the subject performs the action.

Passive	It *was claimed* by the cyclist that the motorist failed to yield the right of way.
Active	The cyclist *claimed* that the motorist failed to yield the right of way.

Notice that the first sentence emphasizes the action of claiming, not the person who made the claim. In the second sentence, the person who made the claim is the subject.

Unless you decide deliberately to deemphasize the subject, try to avoid using passive verbs. On occasion, you may need to use passive verbs, however, to emphasize the object or person receiving the action.

For more about possible problems with using passive voice, see pp. 69–70.

- The Johnsons' house *was destroyed* by the flood.

Passive verbs may also be appropriate if you do not know or choose not to reveal who performed an action. Journalists often use passive verbs for this reason.

- It *was confirmed* late Tuesday that Senator Kraemer is resigning.

EXERCISE 9.5

Edit the following sentences by changing passive verbs to active ones, adding a subject when necessary.

1. Songs about peace were composed by folk singers in the 1960s.
2. The exam was thought to be difficult because it covered thirteen chapters.
3. For water conservation, it is recommended that low-water-consumption dishwashers be purchased.
4. The new satellite center was opened by the university so that students could attend classes nearer their homes.
5. In aggressive telemarketing sales calls, the consumer is urged by the caller to make an immediate decision before prices change.

ESSAY IN PROGRESS 1

For your essay in progress (the one you worked on in Chapters 6–8) or any essay you are working on, evaluate and edit your sentences.

Analyze Your Word Choice

Each word in your essay contributes to your essay's meaning. Consequently, when you are revising, be sure to analyze your word choice, or **diction**. The words you choose should suit your purpose, audience, tone, and genre. This section describes four aspects of word choice to consider as you evaluate and revise your essay:

1. Tone and level of diction
2. Word connotations
3. Concrete and specific language
4. Figures of speech

Are Your Tone and Level of Diction Appropriate?

Imagine that as a technician at a computer software company, you discover a time-saving shortcut for installing the company's best-selling software program. Your supervisor asks you to describe your discovery and how it works for two audiences—your fellow technicians at the company and customers who might purchase the program. Would you say the same thing in the same way? Definitely not. Your writing would differ not only in content but also in tone and level of diction. The writing addressed to the other technicians would be technical and concise, explaining how to use the shortcut and why it works. The writing directed to customers would praise the discovery, mention the time customers will save, and explain in nontechnical terms how to use the shortcut.

For more about tone, see pp. 64–66.

Tone refers to how you sound to your readers. Your word choice should be consistent with your tone. When writing to the technicians, you would use a direct, matter-of-fact tone. When writing to the customers, your tone would be enthusiastic. There are three common **levels of diction**: formal, popular, and informal.

HOW WRITERS READ ▶ **TONE**

Tone contributes to and affects meaning, and the author's tone can be a sign of her or his approach or attitude toward the subject. Use these strategies to identify tone.

BEFORE READING

- Read the headnote to get a sense of where the writer commonly publishes; academic writers and writers who contribute to serious newspapers (like *The New York Times*) often strive for a serious, neutral tone.

WHILE READING

- Pay attention to the title, which often sets or at least provides a clue to the author's tone.
- Read the introduction with care. Writers often try to capture the reader's attention in the introduction, so it is often a place where the writer's attitude toward the topic is clearest.
- If you see a word, phrase, or sentence that clearly establishes the tone (because, for example, it uses words with rich connotations), highlight or annotate it for later reference.

AFTER READING

- Think about how the selection's tone shaped your response to the essay. Did the tone make the reading seem trustworthy, sarcastic, concerned, or mean-spirited, for example? Did it enhance or undermine your trust for the author?
- Consider how tone and purpose are related. Given the author's purpose, did the tone seem appropriate?

Formal diction.   The **formal** level of diction is serious and dignified. Think of it as the kind of language that judges use in interpreting laws, presidents employ when greeting foreign dignitaries, or speakers choose for commencement addresses. Formal diction is often written in the third person, tends to include long sentences and multisyllabic words, and contains no slang or contractions. It has a slow, rhythmic flow and an authoritative, distant, and impersonal tone. Here is an example taken from *The Federalist, No. 51*, a political tract written by James Madison in 1788 to explain constitutional theory.

> It is of great importance in a republic, not only to guard the society against the oppression of its rulers, but to guard one part of the society against the injustice of the other part. Different interests necessarily exist in different classes of citizens. If a majority be united by a common interest, the rights of the minority will be insecure.

Formal diction is also used in scholarly publications, operation manuals, and most academic fields. Notice in the following excerpt from a chemistry textbook that the language is concise, exact, and marked by specialized terms, called *jargon*, used within the particular field of study. The examples of jargon are in italics.

> A *catalyst* is classified as *homogeneous* if it is present in the same *phase* as that of the *reactants*. For reactants that are *gases*, a *homogeneous catalyst* is also a *gas*.
>
> Atkins and Perkins, *Chemistry: Molecules, Matter, and Change*

Popular diction.   **Popular**, or casual, diction is common in magazines and newspapers. It sounds more conversational and personal than formal diction. In popular diction, sentences tend to be shorter and less varied than in formal diction. The first person (*I, me, mine, we*) or second person (*you, your*) may be used. Consider this example taken from a popular arts magazine, *Paste Magazine*.

> "Concert for George" pays tribute to not only one of the greatest musicians in history, but one of the freakin' Beatles. The performance took place in honor of the first anniversary of George Harrison's death, with Eric Clapton and Jeff Lynne serving as musical directors.
>
> Wyndham Wyeth, "The 11 Best Concert Films"

Informal diction.   **Informal** diction, also known as *colloquial language*, is the language of everyday speech and conversation. It is friendly and casual. Contractions (*wasn't, I'll*), slang expressions (*selfie, YOLO, tat*), sentence fragments, and first-person and second-person pronouns are all common. Informal diction should not be used in essays and academic writing, except when it is part of a quotation or a block of dialogue. Also inappropriate for essays and academic writing is the use of language shortcuts typically used in email and texting. These include abbreviations (*u* for *you, r* for *are*) and emoticons (☺). Here is an example of informal diction. Notice the use of the first person, slang expressions, and a loose sentence structure.

> This guy in my history class is a psycho. He doesn't let anybody talk but him. I mean, this guy interrupts all the time. Never raises his hand. He drives us nuts—what a loser.

Contractions are acceptable

Diction in academic writing.   When you write academic papers, essays, and exams, you should use formal diction and avoid flowery or wordy language. Here are some guidelines.

- Use the third person (*he, she, it*) rather than the first person (*I, we*), unless you are expressing a personal opinion.
- Use standard vocabulary, not slang or a regional or ethnic dialect.
- Use correct grammar, spelling, and punctuation.
- Aim for a clear, direct, and forthright tone.

One of the most common mistakes students make in academic writing is trying too hard to sound "academic." Be sure to avoid writing stiff, overly formal sentences, using big words just for the sake of it, and expressing ideas indirectly.

Inappropriate Diction

Who among us would be so bold as to venture to deny that inequities are rampant in our ailing health- and medical-care system? People of multiethnic composition overwhelmingly receive health care that is not only beneath the standard one would expect, but even in some cases threatening to their very lives. An abundance of research studies and clinical trials prove beyond a doubt that a person of non-European descent residing in the United States of America cannot rely on doctors, nurses, physician assistants, nurse practitioners, and other health-care workers to provide treatment free of invidious discrimination.

Language is stiff, pompous

Revised Diction

Who can deny that inequities are common in our ailing medical care system? Racial and ethnic minorities receive health care that is substandard and in some cases life-threatening. Many research studies and clinical trials demonstrate that minorities in the United States cannot rely on doctors, nurses, physician assistants, nurse practitioners, and other health-care workers to provide unbiased treatment.

Language is formal but clear

EXERCISE 9.6

Revise the following informal statement by giving it a more formal level of diction.

It hadn't occurred to me that I might be exercising wrong, though I suppose the signs were there. I would drag myself to the gym semi-regularly and go through the motions of walking (sometimes jogging) on the treadmill and doing light weight training. But I rarely broke a sweat. I just didn't have the energy. "Just doing it" wasn't cutting it. My body wasn't improving. In fact, certain areas were getting bigger, overly muscular. I needed someone to kick my butt—and reduce it too.

Wendy Schmid, "Roped In," *Vogue*

Do You Use Words with Appropriate Connotations?

Many words have two levels of meaning—a denotative meaning and a connotative meaning. A word's **denotation** is its precise dictionary definition. For example, the denotative meaning of the word *mother* is "female parent." A word's **connotation** is the collection of feelings and attitudes the word evokes—its emotional colorings or shades of meaning. A word's connotation may vary from one person to another. One common connotation of *mother* is a warm, caring person. Some people, however, may think of a mother as someone with strong authoritarian control. Similarly, the phrase *horror films* may conjure up memories of scary but fun-filled evenings for some people and terrifying experiences for others.

For more about analyzing connotative meanings, see pp. 61–62.

Since the connotations of words can elicit a wide range of responses, be sure the words you choose convey only the meanings you intend. In each pair of words that follows, notice that the two words have a similar denotation but different connotations.

artificial/fake   firm/stubborn   lasting/endless

EXERCISE 9.7

Describe the different connotations of the three words in each group of words.

1. crowd/mob/gathering
2. proverb/motto/saying
3. prudent/penny-pinching/frugal
4. token/gift/keepsake
5. display/show/expose

Do You Use Concrete Language?

Specific words convey much more information than general words. The following examples show how you might move from general to specific word choices.

General	Less General	More Specific	Specific
store	department store	Sears	Sears at the Galleria Mall
music	popular music	country rock music	Taylor Swift's "Eyes Open"

Concrete words add life and meaning to your writing. In each of the following sentence pairs, notice how the underlined words in the first sentence provide little information, whereas those in the second sentence provide interesting details.

General   Our <u>vacation</u> was <u>great fun</u>.

Concrete   Our <u>rafting trip</u> was filled with <u>adventure</u>.

General   The <u>red and white flowers</u> were blooming in our yard.

Concrete   <u>Crimson and white petunias</u> were blooming in our yard.

Suppose you are writing about a shopping mall that has outlived its usefulness. Instead of saying "a number of stores were unoccupied, and those that were still in business were shabby," you could describe the mall in concrete, specific terms that would enable your readers to visualize it.

The vacant storefronts with "For Rent" signs plastered across the glass, the half-empty racks in the stores that were still open, and the empty corridors suggested that the mall was soon to close.

EXERCISE 9.8

Revise the following sentences by adding concrete, specific details.

1. The book I took on vacation was exciting reading.
2. The students watched as the instructor entered the lecture hall.
3. The vase in the museum was an antique.
4. At the crime scene, the reporter questioned the witnesses.
5. Although the shop was closed, we expected someone to return at any moment.

Do You Use Fresh, Appropriate Figures of Speech?

For more on figures of speech, see Chapter 12, p. 265.

A **figure of speech** is a word or phrase that makes sense imaginatively or creatively but not literally. For example, if you say "the movie was *a roller coaster ride*," you do not mean the movie was an actual ride. Rather, you mean it was thrilling, just like a ride on a roller coaster. This figure of speech, like many others, compares two seemingly unlike objects or situations by finding one point of similarity.

Fresh and imaginative figures of speech can help you create vivid images for your readers. However, overused figures of speech can detract from your essay. Be sure to avoid **clichés** (trite or overused expressions) such as *blind as a bat, green with envy, bite the bullet,* or *sick as a dog.*

Three common figures of speech are simile, metaphor, and personification. A **simile** uses words such as *like* or *as* to make a direct comparison of two unlike things.

The child acts *like a tiger.*

The noise in a crowded high school cafeteria is as deafening *as a caucus of crows.*

A **metaphor** also compares unlike things but does not use *like* or *as.* Instead, the comparison is implied.

That child is a tiger.

If you're born in America with black skin, you're born in prison.

Malcolm X, "Interview"

Personification describes an idea or object by giving it human qualities.

A sailboat devours money.

In this example, the ability to eat is ascribed to an inanimate object, the sailboat.

When you edit an essay, look for and eliminate overused figures of speech, replacing them with creative, fresh images. If you have not used any figures of speech, look for descriptions that could be improved by using a simile, a metaphor, or personification.

EXERCISE 9.9

Invent fresh figures of speech for two items in the following list.

1. Parents of a newborn baby
2. A lengthy supermarket line or a traffic jam
3. A relative's old refrigerator
4. A man and woman obviously in love
5. Your team's star quarterback or important player

Evaluate Your Word Choice

Use Figure 9.1 (p. 212) to help you evaluate your word choice. If you have difficulty identifying which words to revise, ask a classmate or friend to evaluate your essay by using the flowchart as a guide and marking any words that may need revision.

ESSAY IN PROGRESS 2

For the essay you worked on in Essay in Progress 1, use Figure 9.1 to evaluate and edit your word choice.

Proofread Carefully

When you are satisfied with your edited words and sentences, you are ready for the final step of the writing process—*proofreading*. By proofreading, you make sure your essay is error free and presented in acceptable manuscript format. Your goals are to catch and correct surface errors—such as errors in grammar, punctuation, spelling, and mechanics—as well as keyboarding or typographical errors. An essay that is free of surface errors gives readers a favorable impression of the essay and of you as its writer.

Spotting errors is easier when working with a clean, printed copy, so start with a fresh printout. Do not attempt to work with a previously marked-up copy or on a computer screen. Be sure to double-space the copy to allow room to mark corrections between lines.

Use the following suggestions to produce an error-free essay.

1. **Review your paper once for each type of error.** Because it is difficult to spot all types of surface errors simultaneously, read your essay several times, each time focusing on *one* error type—errors in spelling, punctuation, grammar, mechanics, and so on. Then read once more, focusing on just the errors you make most often. (Keep a list of your most common errors in your writing journal, and update it as each assignment is returned.)

FIGURE 9.1 Flowchart for Evaluating Your Word Choice

QUESTIONS	REVISION STRATEGIES
1. Have you used an appropriate tone and level of diction? (To find out, imagine that you are talking to a member of your audience. Look for and circle any words or phrases that seem too formal or too informal, especially any slang or jargon.) **NO** ▶	• Replace circled words and phrases with language appropriate for your audience.

YES ▼

2. Have you chosen words with appropriate connotations? (To find out, look for and circle any words whose connotations do not fit your intended meaning and whose connotations you are unsure of.) **NO** ▶	• Check a dictionary, if necessary, and replace circled words with words that have more appropriate connotations.

YES ▼

3. Is your language concrete and specific? (To find out, look for and circle any general, vague words that contribute little or no meaning.) **NO** ▶	• Replace circled words with more concrete, specific words.

YES ▼

4. Have you used fresh, appropriate figures of speech? (To find out, look for and underline any expressions that sound trite or overused.) **NO** ▶	• Replace the underlined expressions with fresh and appropriate figures of speech.

2. **Read your essay backward, from the last sentence to the first.** Reading in this way will help you spot errors without being distracted by the flow of ideas.

3. **Use the spell-check and grammar-check functions cautiously.** The spell-check function can help you spot some — but not all — spelling and keyboarding errors. For example, it cannot detect the difference in meaning between *there* and *their* or *to* and *too*. Similarly, the grammar-check function can identify only certain kinds of errors and is not a reliable substitute for a careful proofreading.

4. **Read your essay aloud.** By reading aloud slowly, you can catch certain errors that sound awkward, such as missing words, errors in verb tense, and errors in the singular or plural forms of nouns.

5. **Ask a classmate to proofread your paper.** Another reader may spot errors you have overlooked.

Recall that Latrisha Wilson's essay, "No Place Left for Privacy," was developed, drafted, and revised in the Students Write sections of Chapters 5 to 8. Below is a body paragraph from a second draft of Wilson's essay with her final editing and proofreading changes shown. The reasons for each change, identified by number, are noted in the margin. The final draft of Wilson's essay, with these changes incorporated into it, appears in Chapter 8 (pp. 191–93).

❶ Added transition
❷ Edited for wordiness
❸ Fixed run-on
❹ Edited for repetition
❺ Deleted unnecessary comma
❻ Revised to make more specific
❼ Revised to avoid 1st person (/)
❽ Corrected misspelling

(See fig. 1.)

WILDLIFE GmbH/Alamy

10

An Introduction to Patterns of Development

Vova Pomortzeff/Alamy Stock Photo

In this chapter you will learn to:

- recognize common patterns of development
- identify patterns of development in essays that use more than one pattern
- write an essay using more than one pattern

WRITING QUICK START   Suppose your instructor asks you to write a paragraph about the photo on this page.

To write your paragraph, you have to decide on an approach to the topic that would be appropriate to your writing situation, which includes your purpose, audience, genre, and medium. For example, if you wanted to write a blog post to express your thoughts and feelings to your friends, you might have chosen to tell a story about what the people in the photograph are doing or how they got there (*narration*). If you were writing an exam for your biology instructor, you might have described the changes in the physiology of the woman in response to environmental cues (*process analysis*) or analyzed the differences in responses of the woman and the group of people observing her (*comparison and contrast*). If you were writing a response to the photograph for a composition class, you might have described how the winter scene looked, felt, and sounded from the perspective of the scantily clad woman or one of the furred and booted group of observers.

Many paragraphs and essays use specific **patterns of development** (also called **rhetorical modes**, or just **modes**) like narration, process analysis, and comparison or contrast, because they help the writer:

To learn more about the writing situation, see Chapter 4, pp. 102–6.

- devise a strong thesis or topic sentence
- select appropriate evidence
- create a unified paragraph or essay

The patterns also help readers learn and remember by comparing something they know well with something unfamiliar, or by describing a place they've never been so that they can picture it, for example.

While some authors write essays that focus mainly on a single mode, many others create essays from paragraphs in a variety of patterns, choosing among the patterns that will best help them achieve their goals.

In Chapters 10 to 19, you will read and write essays that focus mainly on one mode. In this chapter, you will find one mixed-mode reading, and the chapters in Parts 3 and 4 also include a reading that uses a variety of patterns to supplement the main one. As you read these essays and write your own mixed-mode essay later in this chapter, think about how writers use patterns to achieve their goals.

Understand the Patterns of Development

The most common patterns are:

- narration
- description
- illustration (or exemplification)
- process analysis
- comparison and contrast

- classification and division
- definition
- cause and effect
- argument

Narration Tells a Story

Narration uses a sequence of events—a story—to make a point. The following excerpt from a narrative essay tells the story of one man's experience with the police.

> **Example**   Friday for me usually means a trip to the bank, errands, the gym, dinner, and then off to the theater. On this particular day, I decided to break my pattern of getting up and running right out of the house. Instead, I took my time, slowed my pace, and splurged by making strawberry pancakes. Before I knew it, it was 2:45; my bank closes at 3:30, leaving me less than 45 minutes to get to midtown Manhattan on the train. I was pressed for time but in a relaxed, blessed state of mind. When I walked through the lobby of my building, I noticed two light-skinned Hispanic men I'd never seen before. Not thinking much of it, I continued on to the vestibule, which is separated from the lobby by a locked door.
>
> —Alton Fitzgerald White, "Right Place, Wrong Face" (para. 5, p. 236)

When to use it. Use narration when you want readers to learn something by experiencing an episode or sequence of events from your life. In the Writing Quick Start, you could use narration to tell a story of how the people in the photos got to their location. You might begin with their trip to the airport and end at the moment the photo was taken.

Description Creates a Word Picture

Description uses words that appeal to the five senses. The following excerpt from a descriptive essay uses words that appeal to the senses to convey the appearance of a homeless man.

> **Example**   He sat on the sidewalk, leaning with his back against the side of a brick building, wearing a filthy, gray tank-top and dingy cargo pants with rips in the knees. His hair was dirty and wild, barely restrained by a flimsy elastic tie. He wasn't begging; his exposed knees were pulled up to his chest and his head was cradled in his arms, hidden from view. His shoulders shook slightly from quiet sobs but he didn't bother anyone passing him on the sidewalk.
>
> —Maia Nault, "Sometimes, We Give" (para. 6, p. 281)

When to use it. Use description when you want to emphasize the sensory aspects of an object or experience. In the Writing Quick Start, you could use description to convey in detail what the winter landscape looked, smelled, or felt like.

Illustration Explains with Examples

Illustration uses examples to explain unfamiliar topics, concepts, or terms. In the following excerpt from an illustration essay, the author provides a specific example (*illustration*) to support his thesis that road rage represents a decline in civilized society.

> **Example**   A most amazing example of driver rage occurred recently at the Manhattan end of the Lincoln Tunnel. We were four cars abreast, stopped at a traffic light. And there was no moving even when the light had changed. A bus had stopped in the cross traffic, blocking our paths: it was a normal-for-New-York-City gridlock. Perhaps impatient, perhaps late for important appointments, three of us nonetheless accepted what, after all, we could not alter. One, however, would not. He would not be helpless. He would go where he was going even if he couldn't get there. A Wall Street type in suit and tie, he got out of his car and strode toward the bus, rapping smartly on its doors. When they opened, he exchanged words with the driver. The doors folded shut. He then stepped in front of the bus, took hold of one of its large windshield wipers and broke it.
>
> —Martin Gottfried, "Rambos of the Road" (para. 8, p. 307)

When to use it. Use illustration when you want to provide specific, sometimes extended, examples to support your thesis statement. You could use the photo in the Writing Quick Start as inspiration for an essay about how global warming is changing the environment; you might cite average temperatures over the last fifty years and provide examples of how changes have affected plants and animals.

Process Analysis Explains How Something Works or Is Done

Process analysis explains step by step how something works, is done, or is made. In the following how-to essay, the writer describes the process of writing a second draft.

Example   The next day, I'd sit down, go through it all with a colored pen, take out everything I possibly could, find a new lead somewhere on the second page, figure out a kicky place to end it, and then write a second draft. It always turned out fine, sometimes even funny and weird and helpful. I'd go over it one more time and mail it in.

—Anne Lamott, "Shitty First Drafts" (para. 8, p. 338)

When to use it. Use process analysis when you want to provide step-by-step instructions or a part-by-part analysis. In the Writing Quick Start, you might discuss the physiological changes a swimmer in the polar bear club would experience before, during, and after an icy plunge.

Comparison and Contrast Shows Similarities and Differences

Writers compare or contrast to examine closely what two things have in common or what their differences are. Many essays use both comparison and contrast. In the following excerpt, the author compares the effects of alcohol and marijuana.

Example   I think about which substance might put young people at risk for being hurt by others. That's where things become even more stark. In 1995 alone, college students reported more than 460,000 alcohol-related incidents of violence in the United States ("Alcohol"). A 2011 prospective study found that mental and physical dating abuse were more common on drinking days among college students. On the other hand, a 2014 study looking at marijuana use and intimate partner violence in the first nine years of marriage found that those who used marijuana had lower rates of such violence (Smith et al.). Indeed, the men who used marijuana the most were least likely to commit violence against a partner.

—Aaron E. Carroll, "Alcohol or Marijuana? A Pediatrician
Faces the Question" (para. 10, p. 369)

When to use it. Use comparison and contrast to provide an in-depth analysis that explores the similarities and/or differences between two things. In the Writing Quick Start, there is opportunity to compare physiological differences between the woman in the swimsuit and her companions in heavy coats and hats.

Classification Categorizes Items, and Division Separates an Item into Parts

Classification groups things into categories; division breaks a single item down into its component parts. In the following excerpt from a classification essay, the writer classifies bystanders of bullying into three categories.

Example   Together with colleagues from Boston College in the United States (V. Paul Poteat) and York St. John University in the United Kingdom (Nathalie Noret), I have attempted to better understand the "mind-set" of the bystander, in the hope that it will provide me with further clues as to why bullying continues, despite forty years of research and intervention. In essence, this research has resulted in a recasting of the role of the bystander into three very distinct types of pupil: the confederate, the co-victim, and the isolate. These three types are very different from the pupil who does not engage; these are pupils who are desperate to avoid the torment being meted out on their classmate. This is not rocket science, but it does highlight a flaw in much of the research that has gone before: Without taking into account the experiences of bystanders, we may have underplayed the lasting impact that bullying can have on individuals and the school community.

—Ian Rivers, "Empower Pupils to Beat the Bullies" (para. 2, pp. 421–22)

When to use it.   Use classification or division when you want to look closely at the subcategories or parts of a particular topic. In the Writing Quick Start, you might classify people in terms of how likely they are to indulge in extreme sports, such as swimming in icy waters.

Extended Definition Explains How a Term Is Used or What It Means

An extended definition explains in detail how a term is used or differentiates among its shades of meaning. The following excerpt from an extended definition begins the process of explaining what the word *dude* means by showing how it is used and how its meaning has changed over time.

Example   Originally meaning "old rags," a "dudesman" was a scarecrow. In the late 1800s, a "dude" was akin to a dandy, a meticulously dressed man, especially in the western United States. *Dude* became a slang term in the 1930s and 1940s among black zoot suiters and Mexican American pachucos. The term began its rise in the teenage lexicon with the 1982 movie *Fast Times at Ridgemont High*. Around the same time, it became an exclamation as well as a noun. Pronunciation purists say it should sound like "duhd"; "dood" is an alternative, but it is considered "uncool" or old.

—Mike Crissey, "Dude, Do You Know What You Just Said?" (para. 2, p. 436)

When to use it.   Use an extended definition when you want to conduct a close analysis of a complicated word, phrase, or phenomenon. In the Writing Quick Start, you might use the photo as a jumping-off point to define the term *adventure tourism*, which means traveling to participate in physically challenging outdoor activities.

Cause and Effect Uses Reasons or Results to Explain

Causes are the reasons that an event or phenomenon happens, and effects are what happen because of the event or phenomenon. Often, causes and effects are discussed together. The following excerpt points to a single cause (counting calories while dieting) leading to a single effect (reduced mental capacity).

Example   Many diets also require constant calculations to determine calorie counts. All this clogs up the brain. Psychologists measure the impact of this clogging on various tasks: logical and spatial reasoning, self-control, problem solving, and absorption and retention of new information. Together these tasks measure "bandwidth," the resource that underlies all higher-order mental activity. Inevitably, dieters do worse than nondieters on all these tasks; they have less bandwidth.

—Sendhil Mullainathan, "The Mental Strain of Making Do with Less"
(para. 7, p. 486)

When to use it.   Use cause and effect to show how one (or more) thing(s) leads to another or many other things. In the Writing Quick Start, you might use the photo as inspiration for writing about what motivates some people to join the polar bear club on its annual New Year's plunge.

Argument Takes and Supports a Position

Writers use arguments to persuade readers to adopt (or at least to consider) their position on an issue. In the following excerpt from an argument essay, the author tries to persuade readers that the size of the tip does not correspond to the quality of service a customer receives. This is one reason that tipping, which is supposed to motivate wait staff to provide good service, should be abolished.

Example   Tipping does not incentivize hard work. The factors that correlate most strongly to tip size have virtually nothing to do with the quality of service. Credit card tips are larger than cash tips. Large parties with sizable bills leave disproportionately small tips. We tip servers more if they tell us their names, touch us on the arm, or draw smiley faces on our checks. Quality of service has a laughably small impact on tip size. According to a 2000 study, a customer's assessment of the server's work only accounts for between 1 and 5 percent of the variation in tips at a restaurant.

—Brian Palmer, "Tipping Is an Abomination" (para. 3, p. 503)

When to use it.   Use argumentation when you are trying to convince your readers that your point of view is correct or when you want them to take action. In the Writing Quick Start, you might argue that taking a swim in freezing water in winter is a challenge more people should experience.

Combine the Patterns

Some essays use only one major pattern, but many writers combine several patterns to engage their readers and support their ideas. For example, an essay may mainly tell a story (the primary pattern), but it may also include description and illustration (secondary patterns). The following excerpt is from an essay that mainly uses cause and effect but also uses several other patterns of development.

Narration: The writer tells the story of restaurant meals.

Description: The writer helps you picture the child's behavior.

Process: The writer explains how they proceeded through a meal.

Comparison-Contrast: The writer contrasts her child's behavior with that of French children.

We ate breakfast at the hotel, but we had to eat lunch and dinner at the little seafood restaurants around the old port. We quickly discovered that having two restaurant meals a day with a toddler deserved to be its own circle of hell.

Bean would take a brief interest in the food, but within minutes she was spilling salt shakers and tearing apart sugar packets. Then she demanded to be sprung from her high chair so she could dash around the restaurant and bolt dangerously toward the docks.

Our strategy was to finish the meal quickly. We ordered while being seated, then begged the server to rush out some bread and bring us our appetizers and main courses at the same time. While my husband took a few bites of fish, I made sure Bean didn't get kicked by a waiter or lost at sea. Then we switched. We left enormous, apologetic tips to compensate for the arc of torn napkins and calamari around the table.

After a few more harrowing restaurant visits, I started noticing that the French families around us didn't look like they were sharing our mealtime agony. Weirdly, they looked like they were on vacation. French toddlers were sitting contentedly in their high chairs, waiting for their food, or eating fish and even vegetables. There was not shrieking or whining. And there was no debris around their tables.

—Pamela Druckerman, *Bringing Up Bébé*

Recognizing that many writers combine patterns, Chapters 11–20 offer not only detailed instructions on how to write an effective essay in each pattern but how to combine the patterns into a **mixed-mode** essay. Each of these chapters also offers readings that show multiple patterns at work in a single essay. Use the following guidelines, along with the detailed instructions on writing in each mode in the chapters that follow, to plan and write a mixed-mode essay.

PREWRITING   DRAFTING   REVISING   EDITING & PROOFREADING

A Guided Writing Assignment*

MULTIPLE PATTERNS OF DEVELOPMENT

1 Choose and narrow a topic, and select a main pattern of organization.

Chapter 4 can help you narrow your topic. Many essays benefit from following **one dominant pattern** of organization. Select the major pattern of organization that best fits your **purpose**.

2 Write a preliminary thesis, and generate details to support it.

Chapter 5 can help with devising a thesis and generating details. You may also want to consult the chapter in Part 3 or 4 that corresponds to your main mode of development.

3 Determine which secondary patterns will help you support your thesis.

The idea-generating strategies from **Chapter 4**, especially using the modes of development, can help you flesh out your ideas with specific evidence. Be cautious about using too many patterns of organization, though, because doing so can make your essay difficult to follow.

4 Prepare a graphic organizer or an outline of your essay.

Make sure your graphic organizer or outline:

- clearly indicates the essay's **organization** and each paragraph's **relationship to the thesis statement**
- includes only details that **support your thesis**

The chapter in Part 3 or 4 that corresponds to your main mode of development can provide a model graphic organizer.

5 Keep your purpose and audience in mind.

Do not worry about grammar or spelling at this point. Instead, focus on the following:

- using **supporting details** that help you achieve your purpose with your readers
- making sure your **introduction** and **conclusion signal your primary pattern** of organization, so readers know what to expect or experience a satisfying sense of closure
- using **transitions** to signal that you are moving from one pattern to another, so readers can follow your train of thought

* The writing process is *recursive*; that is, you may find yourself revising as you draft or prewriting as you revise. This is especially true when writing on a computer. Your writing process may also differ from that of your classmates, depending on your preferred learning style.

PREWRITING

DRAFTING

6 **Evaluate your draft and revise as necessary.**

As you reread your essay, ask yourself questions like these.

- Have I **fully developed** my primary pattern?
- Have I **effectively used secondary patterns** to support my thesis?

Then ask a classmate or friend to read your essay and answer your questions. Refer to **Chapter 8** for help with revising, and use the **flowchart for revising essays** from **Chapters 11 to 20** that corresponds to your main pattern of development.

7 **Edit the words and sentences of your essay, and then proofread carefully.**

As you edit your essay, ask yourself questions like these.

- Are my sentences **concise**, **varied** (in type, length, and sentence pattern), and **parallel**?
- Do they use **strong active verbs**?
- Are my words at an appropriate **level of diction** for my readers?
- Do I use concrete language, with appropriate **connotations** and fresh **figures of speech**?

As you **proofread**, look for errors in **grammar**, **punctuation**, and **spelling**. Look for the kinds of errors you regularly make, and do not rely too heavily on spell- or grammar-checkers, which can lead you astray.

For additional help, refer to **Chapter 9**, "Editing Sentences and Words," and to the guided writing assignment in the chapter that corresponds to your main pattern of development.

In the following reading, note how the author effectively combines multiple patterns of organization.

READING

Against Forgetting: Where Have All the Animals Gone?

Derrick Jensen

Derrick Jensen writes about environmental issues for a number of publications, including *Audubon* and *The Sun Magazine*. He is the author of *Resistance against Empire* (2010), *Truths among Us: Conversations on Building a New Culture* (2011), and *The Myth of Human Supremacy* (2016). This article originally appeared in *Orion* (July/August 2013). According to the magazine's mission statement, "It is *Orion's* fundamental conviction that humans are morally responsible for the world in which we live and that the individual comes to sense this responsibility as he or she develops a personal bond with nature."

Before Reading

1. **Preview:** Use the steps listed on page 28.
2. **Connect:** Ask yourself questions, such as "Why do you think animal species are declining?"

While Reading Notice how the author uses a variety of patterns and consider why he is doing so.

Last night a host of nonhuman neighbors paid me a visit. First, two gray foxes sauntered up, including an older female who lost her tail to a leghold trap six or seven years ago. They trotted back into a thicker part of the forest, and a few minutes later a raccoon ambled forward. After he left I saw the two foxes again. Later, they went around the right side of a redwood tree as a black bear approached around the left. He sat on the porch for a while, and then walked off into the night. Then the foxes returned, hung out, and, when I looked away for a moment then looked back, they were gone. It wasn't too long before the bear returned to lie on the porch. After a brief nap, he went away. The raccoon came back and brought two friends. When they left the foxes returned, and after the foxes came the bear. The evening was like a French farce: As one character exited stage left, another entered stage right.

Although I see some of these nonhuman neighbors daily, I was entranced and delighted to see so many of them over the span of just one evening. I remained delighted until sometime the next day, when I remembered reading that, prior to conquest by the Europeans, people in this region could expect to see a grizzly bear every 15 minutes.

This phenomenon is something we all encounter daily, even if some of us rarely notice it. It happens often enough to have a name: declining baselines. The phrase describes the process of becoming accustomed to and accepting as normal worsening conditions. Along with normalization can come a forgetting that things were not always this way. And this can lead to further acceptance and further normalization, which leads to further amnesia, and so on. Meanwhile the world is killed, species by species, biome by biome. And we are happy when we see the ever-dwindling number of survivors.

I've gone on the salmon-spawning tours that local environmentalists give, and I'm not the only person who by the end is openly weeping. If we're lucky, we see 15 fish. Prior to conquest there were so many fish the rivers were described as "black and roiling." And it's not just salmon. Only five years ago, whenever I'd pick up a piece of firewood, I'd have to take off a half-dozen sowbugs. It's taken me all winter this year to see as many. And I used to go on spider patrol before I took a shower, in order to remove them to safety before the deluge. I still go on spider patrol, but now it's mostly pro forma. The spiders are gone. My mother used to put up five hummingbird feeders, and the birds would fight over those. Now she puts up two, and as often as not the sugar ferments before anyone eats it. I used to routinely see bats in the summer. Last year I saw one.

1

Narration: Tells a story in chronological (time) order, to establish baseline

Description: Uses concrete details to help readers picture animal parade

2

Comparison-contrast: Contrasts number of animals today with number in the past

3

Definition: Provides definition of key term to be used in his thesis/argument

Cause-effect: Explains a chain of causes and effects to explain declining baselines

4

Comparison-contrast: Contrasts number of animals today with number at various times in the past to dramatize declining

Process analysis: Shows process of decline in songbird populations

Cause-effect: Shows causes of huge declines in songbird populations (effects)

Comparison-contrast: Contrasts number of animals today with number at various times in the past to dramatize declining

Cause-effect: Effects of declining baselines

Illustration: Examples to help readers understand how baselines decline

Comparison-contrast: Contrasting responses today with responses previously

Argument: Thesis states author's position

Cause-effect

You can transpose this story to wherever you live and whatever members of the nonhuman community live there with you. I was horrified a few years ago to read that many songbird populations on the Atlantic Seaboard have collapsed by up to 80 percent over the last 40 years. But, and this is precisely the point, I was even more horrified when I realized that *Silent Spring* came out more than 40 years ago, so this 80 percent decline followed an already huge decline caused by pesticides, which followed another undoubtedly huge decline caused by the deforestation, conversion to agriculture, and urbanization that followed conquest.

My great-grandmother grew up in a sod house in Nebraska. When she was a tiny girl—in other words, only four human generations ago—there were still enough wild bison on the Plains that she was afraid lightning storms would spook them and they would trample her home. Who in Nebraska today worries about being trampled by bison? For that matter, who in Nebraska today even thinks about bison on a monthly, much less daily, basis?

This state of affairs is problematic for many reasons, not the least of which is that it's harder to fight for what you don't love than for what you do, and it's hard to love what you don't know you're missing. *It's harder still to fight an injustice you do not perceive as an injustice* but rather as just the way things are. How can you fight an injustice you never think about because it never occurs to you that things have ever been any different?

Declining baselines apply not only to the environment but to many fields. Take surveillance. Back in the 1930s, there were people who freaked out at the notion of being assigned a Social Security number, as it was "a number that will follow you from cradle to grave." But since 9/11, according to former National Security Agency official William Binney, the U.S. government has been retaining every email sent, in case any of us ever does anything the government doesn't like. How many people complain about that? And it's not just the government. I received spam birthday greetings this year from all sorts of commercial websites. How and why does ESPN .com have my birth date? And remember the fight about GMOs? They were perceived as scary (because they are), and now they're all over the place, but most people don't know or don't care. The same goes for nanotechnology.

Yesterday I ate a strawberry. Or rather, I ate a strawberry-shaped object that didn't have much taste. When did we stop noticing that strawberries/plums/tomatoes no longer taste like what they resemble? In my 20s I rented a house where a previous resident's cat had pooped all over the dirt basement, which happened to be where the air intakes for the furnace were located. The house smelled like cat feces. After I'd been there a few months, I wrote to a friend, "At first the smell really got to me, but then, as with everything, I got used to the stench and it just doesn't bother me anymore."

This is a process we need to stop. Milan Kundera famously wrote, "The struggle of man against power is the struggle of memory against forgetting." Everything in this culture is aimed at helping to distract us from—or better, help us to forget—the injustices, the pain. And it is completely normal for us to want to be distracted from or to forget pain. *Pain hurts.* Which is why on every level from somatic reflex to socially constructed means of denial we have pathways to avoid it.

5

6

7

8

9

10

But here is what I want you to do: I want you to go outside. I want you to   11
listen to the (disappearing) frogs, to watch the (disappearing) fireflies. Even if
you're in a city—especially if you're in a city—I want you to picture the land as it
was before the land was built over. I want you to research who lived there. I want
you to feel how it was then, feel how it wants to be. I want you to begin keeping a
calendar of who you see and when: the first day each year you see buttercups, the
first day frogs start singing, the last day you see robins in the fall, the first day for
grasshoppers. In short, I want you to pay attention. If you do this, your baseline
will stop declining, because you'll have a record of what's being lost.

Do not go numb in the face of this data. Do not turn away. I want you to feel   12
the pain. Keep it like a coal inside your coat, a coal that burns and burns. I want all
of us to do this, because we should all want the pain of injustice to stop. We should
want this pain to stop not because we get used to it and it just doesn't bother us
anymore, but because we stop the injustices and destruction that are causing the
pain in the first place. I want us to feel how awful the destruction is, and then act
from this feeling.

And I promise you two things. One: Feeling this pain won't kill you. And two: 13
Not feeling this pain, continuing to go numb and avoid it, will.

Argument: Uses repetition
to persuade readers to take steps

Cause-effect

Argument: Urges readers to take
steps

11
Narration
Recounting Events

REUTERS/Yuriko Nakao YN/FA

WRITING QUICK START   The photograph here shows an event in Tokyo in which 300 Japanese women donned identical blonde wigs. Working alone or with a classmate, imagine the series of events that led up to the gathering. What happened, who was involved, and what did the participants do to get them to the scene shown in the photograph? Then write a brief summary of the events you imagined.

As you imagined the events that led up to the scene in the photograph, you probably described a series of events or turning points in the order in which they occurred. In short, you constructed a **narrative**: a chronological series of events, real or imaginary, that tells a story to make a point.

Narratives provide human interest and entertainment, spark our curiosity, and draw us close to the storyteller. They can also create a sense of shared history or provide instruction in proper behavior or conduct.

In this chapter, you will read narratives; you will also write narrative essays or use narrative in essays that rely on one or more of the other patterns of development.

- Each student in your *business law course* must attend a court trial and complete the following written assignment: "Describe what happened and how the proceedings illustrate the judicial process."

- Your *sociology instructor* announces that the class session will focus on the nature and types of authority figures in U.S. society. She begins by asking class members to describe situations in which they found themselves in conflict with an authority figure.

- Your *job in sales* involves frequent business travel, and your company requires you to submit a report for each trip. You are expected to recount the meetings you attended, your contacts with current clients, and the new sales leads you developed.

What Are the Characteristics of a Narrative?

A narrative does not merely report events; it is *not* a transcript of a conversation or a news report. Instead, it is a story that conveys a particular meaning. It presents actions and details that build toward a *climax*, the point at which the conflict of the narrative is resolved. Most narratives also use dialogue to present portions of conversations that move the story along.

Narratives Make a Point

A narrative makes a point by telling readers about an event or a series of events. The point may be to describe the significance of the event(s), make an observation, or present new information. The writer may state the point directly, using an explicit thesis statement, or leave it unstated, using an implied thesis. Either way, the point should always be clear to the audience by the details selected and the way they are presented.

The following excerpt comes from "Chop Suey " (p. 253). Ira Sukrungruang tells the story of a moment in time that was forever etched in his mind—a time that taught him things about his mother that he had never known. Through the story of a trip to a bowling alley with his mom, he recounts what he learned about her strength as a woman and her prowess as a champion bowler. Notice how he chooses vocabulary to describe the strength of character of his mother and the way she handled the rude and disrespectful man.

> My mother grabbed my hand and took one step toward the man. In that instant, I saw in her face the same resolve she had when she spanked, the same resolve when she scolded. In that instant, I thought my mother was going to hit the man. And for a moment, I thought the man saw the same thing in her eyes, and his smile disappeared from his face. Quickly, she smiled—too bright, too large—and said, "You're welcome." (para. 18)

Details that reinforce the main point

Narratives Convey Action and Detail

Narratives present a detailed account of an event or a series of events, using *dialogue*, *physical description*, and *action verbs* to make readers feel as if they are watching the scene or experiencing the action.

Action verbs

Physical description

Dialogue

> The attending scrubbed in, and together we completed the <u>bony removal</u>. He began to pick away at the ligaments, beneath which lay the dura, which contained <u>spinal fluid</u> and the <u>nerve roots</u>. The most common error at this stage is tearing a hole in the dura. I worked on the opposite side. Out of the corner of my eye, I saw near his instrument a <u>flash of blue</u>—the dura starting to peek through.
>
> "Watch out!" I said, just as the mouth of his instrument bit into the dura. <u>Clear spinal fluid</u> began to fill the wound. I hadn't had a leak in one of my cases in more than a year. Repairing it would take another hour.
>
> "Get the micro set out," I said. "We have a leak."
>
> ("My Last Day as a Surgeon," pp. 233–34)

Narratives Present a Conflict and Create Tension

An effective narrative presents a **conflict**—such as a struggle, question, or problem—and works toward its resolution. The conflict can be between participants or between a participant and some external force, such as a law, value, tradition, or act of nature. (In the first reading, the conflict is between the narrator and his cancer diagnosis.) **Tension** is the suspense created as the story unfolds and the reader wonders how the conflict will be resolved. The height of the action—the point just before the resolution of the conflict—is the **climax**.

EXERCISE 11.1 ▶ BUILDING CONFLICT

Working alone or with a classmate, complete each of the following statements by setting up a conflict. Then, for one of the completed statements, write three to four sentences that build tension through action, physical description, or dialogue (or some combination of the three).

1. You are ready to leave the house when . . .
2. You have just turned in your math exam when you realize that . . .
3. Your spouse suddenly becomes seriously ill . . .
4. Your child just told you that . . .
5. Your best friend phones you in the middle of the night to tell you . . .

Narratives Sequence Events

A narrative often presents events in **chronological order**—the order in which they happened. Some narratives use flashback and foreshadowing to add tension and drama. A **flashback** returns readers to events that took place in the past; **foreshadowing** hints at events that will occur in the future. Both techniques are used frequently in fiction and film. For example, an episode of a soap opera might open with a woman lying in a hospital bed, flash back to a scene showing the accident that put her there, and then return to the scene in the hospital. When used sparingly, flashback and foreshadowing can build interest and add variety to a narrative, especially a lengthy chronological account.

Narratives Use Dialogue

Just as people reveal much about themselves by what they say and how they say it, dialogue can reveal much about the characters in a narrative. The use of dialogue can also dramatize the action, emphasize the conflict, and reveal the personalities or motives of the key participants in a narrative. Dialogue can be strategically inserted to heighten the drama and help characterize the people depicted.

Narratives Are Told from a Particular Point of View

Most narratives use either the first-person or third-person point of view.

- The **first-person** point of view ("I first realized the problem when . . .") allows you to assume a personal tone and speak directly to your audience, permitting you to express your attitudes and feelings and offer your interpretation and commentary. A drawback to using the first person is that you cannot easily convey the inner thoughts of other participants (unless they have shared their thoughts with you). When you narrate an event that occurred in your life, the first person is probably your best choice.
- The **third-person** point of view ("The problem began when Saul Overtone . . .") gives the narrator more distance from the action and often provides a broader, more objective perspective. When you narrate an event that occurred in someone else's life, the third person is likely to be the natural choice.

EXERCISE 11.2 ▶ CHOOSING A POINT OF VIEW

Discuss the advantages and disadvantages of using the first- and third-person points of view for each of the following situations, and then decide which point of view would work better.

1. The day you and several friends played a practical joke on another friend
2. An incident of sexual or racial discrimination that happened to you or someone you know
3. An incident at work that a coworker told you about

The following readings demonstrate the techniques discussed above for writing effective narratives. The first reading is annotated to point out how Paul Kalanithi uses these techniques to help readers understand the experience of his last day as a surgeon. As you read the second essay, try to identify how the writer uses the techniques of narrative writing to help readers understand how his encounter with the police changed his life.

My Last Day as a Surgeon

Paul Kalanithi

Paul Kalanithi, a writer and neurosurgeon, died of lung cancer in 2015 at age thirty-seven. While completing his neurosurgical residency, he wrote articles for several newspapers, magazines, and other media outlets about his experiences as a doctor and a patient. *My Last Day as a Surgeon* is an excerpt from his memoir, *When Breath Becomes Air*, which was published in 2016, after his death.

Before Reading

1. **Preview** Preview the reading using the steps listed on page 28.
2. **Connect** Activate your knowledge and experience on the topic by answering the following questions.
   - What comes to mind when you hear the word *cancer*?
   - How would you live your life if you knew you only had a year to live?

While Reading Study the annotations that accompany the reading to discover how the essay illustrates the characteristics of narration as presented on pages 229–31.

Point of view: Uses first person for this personal essay

I hopped out of the CT scanner, seven months since I had returned to surgery. This   1
would be my last scan before finishing residency, before becoming a father, before
my future became real.

"Wanna take a look, Doc?" the tech said.   2

"Not right now," I said. "I've got a lot of work to do today."   3

Provides background readers need to understand his normal day-to-day life

It was already 6 P.M. I had to go see patients, organize tomorrow's O.R. sched-   4
ule, review films, dictate my clinic notes, check on my post-ops, and so on. Around
8 P.M., I sat down in the neurosurgery office, next to a radiology viewing station. I
turned it on, looked at my patients' scans for the next day—two simple spine
cases—and, finally, typed in my own name. I zipped through the images as if they
were a kid's flip-book, comparing the new scan to the last. Everything looked the
same; the old tumors remained exactly the same . . . except, wait.

Details: Includes a description of the tumor, uses comparison, metaphor

I rolled back the images and looked again. There it was. A new tumor, large,   5
was filling my right middle lobe. It looked, oddly, like a full moon having almost
cleared the horizon. Going back to the old images, I could make out the faintest
trace of it, a ghostly harbinger now brought fully into the world.

Provides background readers need to understand his predicament and to build tension

I was neither angry nor scared. It simply was. It was a fact about the world,   6
like the distance from the sun to the Earth. I drove home and told [my wife,] Lucy.
It was a Thursday night, and we wouldn't see [my oncologist] Emma again until
Monday, but Lucy and I sat down in the living room, with our laptops, and mapped
out the next steps: biopsies, tests, chemotherapy. The treatments this time around
would be tougher to endure, the possibility of a long life more remote. T. S. Eliot
once wrote, "But at my back in a cold blast I hear / the rattle of the bones, and
chuckle spread from ear to ear." Neurosurgery would be impossible for a couple of

weeks, perhaps months, perhaps forever. But we decided that all of that could wait to be real until Monday. Today was Thursday, and I'd already made tomorrow's O.R. assignments; I planned on having one last day as a resident.

As I stepped out of my car at the hospital, at five twenty the next morning, I inhaled deeply, smelling the eucalyptus and . . . was that pine? I hadn't noticed that before. I met the resident team, assembled for morning rounds. We reviewed overnight events, new admissions, new scans, then went to see our patients before M. & M., or morbidity and mortality conference, a regular meeting in which the neurosurgeons gathered to review mistakes that had been made and cases that had gone wrong. Afterward, I spent an extra couple of minutes with a patient, Mr. R. He had developed a rare syndrome, called Gerstmann's, where, after I'd removed his brain tumor, he'd begun showing several specific deficits: an inability to write, to name fingers, to do arithmetic, to tell left from right. I'd seen it only once before, as a medical student, eight years ago, on one of the first patients I'd followed on the neurosurgical service. Like him, Mr. R. was euphoric—I wondered if that was part of the syndrome that no one had described before. Mr. R. was getting better, though: His speech had returned almost to normal, and his arithmetic was only slightly off. He'd likely make a full recovery.

The morning passed, and I scrubbed for my last case. Suddenly the moment felt enormous. Was this my last time scrubbing? Perhaps this was it. I watched the suds drip off my arms, then down the drain. I entered the O.R., gowned up, and draped the patient, making sure the corners were sharp and neat. I wanted this case to be perfect. I opened the skin of his lower back. He was an elderly man whose spine had degenerated, compressing his nerve roots and causing severe pain. I pulled away the fat until the fascia appeared and I could feel the tips of his vertebrae. I opened the fascia and smoothly dissected the muscle away, until only the wide, glistening vertebrae showed up through the wound, clean and bloodless. The attending wandered in as I began to remove the lamina, the back wall of the vertebrae, whose bony overgrowths, along with ligaments beneath, were compressing the nerves.

"Looks good," he said. "If you want to go to today's conference, I can have the fellow come in and finish."

My back was beginning to ache. Why hadn't I taken an extra dose of NSAIDs beforehand? This case should be quick, though. I was almost there.

"Naw," I said. "I want to finish the case."

The attending scrubbed in, and together we completed the bony removal. He began to pick away at the ligaments, beneath which lay the dura, which contained spinal fluid and the nerve roots. The most common error at this stage is tearing a hole in the dura. I worked on the opposite side. Out of the corner of my eye, I saw near his instrument a flash of blue—the dura starting to peek through.

"Watch out!" I said, just as the mouth of his instrument bit into the dura. Clear spinal fluid began to fill the wound. I hadn't had a leak in one of my cases in more than a year. Repairing it would take another hour.

"Get the micro set out," I said. "We have a leak."

By the time we finished the repair and removed the compressive soft tissue, my shoulders burned. The attending broke scrub, offered his apologies and said his thanks, and left me to close. The layers came together nicely. I began to suture

---

Thesis: Main point

7 **Organization:** Narrates events in chronological order; uses transitions of time

8 **Action and detail:** Uses detailed descriptions and action verbs to involve readers, heighten drama

9 **Dialogue:** Uses dialogue to reveal character and dramatize the action

10

11

12 **Action and detail:** Uses details to reinforce the main point and build tension

13

14

15 **Action and detail:** Details make readers feel as if they are watching the scene

the skin, using a running nylon stitch. Most surgeons used staples, but I was convinced that nylon had lower infection rates, and we would do this one, this final closure, my way. The skin came together perfectly, without tension, as if there had been no surgery at all.

That's one good thing.   16

As we uncovered the patient, the scrub nurse, one with whom I hadn't worked   17
before, said, "You on call this weekend, Doc?"

Climax

"Nope." *And possibly never again.*   18

"Got any more cases today?" "Nope." *And possibly never again.*   19

"Shit, well, I guess that means this is a happy ending! Work's done. I like happy   20
endings, don't you, Doc?"

"Yeah. Yeah, I like happy endings."   21

I sat down by the computer to enter orders as the nurses cleaned and the   22
anesthesiologists began to wake the patient. I had always jokingly threatened that
when I was in charge, instead of the high-energy pop music everyone liked to play
in the O.R., we'd listen exclusively to bossa nova. I put "Getz/Gilberto" on the radio,
and the soft, sonorous sounds of a saxophone filled the room.

I left the O.R. shortly after, then gathered my things, which had accumulated   23
over seven years of work—extra sets of clothes for the nights you don't leave,
toothbrushes, bars of soap, phone chargers, snacks, my skull model and collection
of neurosurgery books, and so on.

On second thought, I left my books behind. They'd be of more use here.   24

On my way out to the parking lot, a fellow approached to ask me something,   25
but his pager went off. He looked at it, waved, turned, and ran back in to the hospital—"I'll catch you later!" he called over his shoulder. Tears welled up as I sat in the
car, turned the key, and slowly pulled out into the street. I drove home, walked
through the front door, hung up my white coat, and took off my ID badge. I pulled
the battery out of my pager. I peeled off my scrubs and took a long shower.

Resolution: Tension is relieved when Victoria regretfully receives her co-resident's news and acknowledges his perseverance.

Later that night, I called [my co-resident] Victoria and told her I wouldn't be in   26
on Monday, or possibly ever again, and wouldn't be setting the O.R. schedule.

"You know, I've been having this recurring nightmare that this day was coming,"   27
ing," she said. "I don't know how you did this for so long."

Visualize a Narrative: Create a Graphic Organizer

For more on creating a graphic organizer, see pp. 35–37.

Seeing the content and structure of an essay in simplified, visual form can help you analyze a reading, recall key events as you generate ideas for an essay, and structure your own writing. Graphic Organizer 11.1 diagrams the basic structure of a narrative. You can use this graphic organizer as a basic model of a narrative, but keep in mind that narrative essays vary widely in organization and therefore may lack one or more of the elements included in the model.

GRAPHIC ORGANIZER 11.1 The Basic Structure of a Narrative Essay

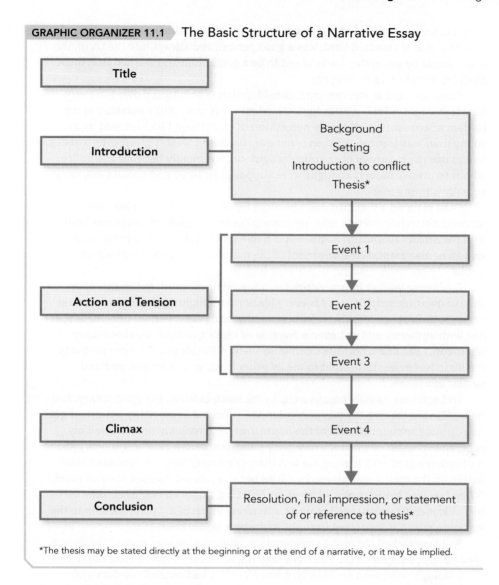

Title

Introduction — Background / Setting / Introduction to conflict / Thesis*

Action and Tension — Event 1 → Event 2 → Event 3

Climax — Event 4

Conclusion — Resolution, final impression, or statement of or reference to thesis*

*The thesis may be stated directly at the beginning or at the end of a narrative, or it may be implied.

READING

Right Place, Wrong Face

Alton Fitzgerald White

Alton Fitzgerald White is an actor, singer, and dancer and has appeared in several Broadway shows. He is also the author of *Uncovering the Heart Light*, a collection of poems and short stories. **Before reading**, preview the selection and make connections by thinking of incidents of racial profiling you have heard about or experienced. **While reading**, pay attention to the essay's organization. Once you have finished the selection, study Graphic Organizer 11.2 on page 238.

As the youngest of five girls and two boys growing up in Cincinnati, I was raised   1
to believe that if I worked hard, was a good person, and always told the truth, the
world would be my oyster. I was raised to be a gentleman and learned that these
qualities would bring me respect.

While one has to earn respect, consideration is something owed to every   2
human being. On Friday, June 16, 1999, when I was wrongfully arrested at my
Harlem apartment building, my perception of everything I had learned as a
young man was forever changed — not only because I wasn't given even a second to use the manners my parents taught me, but mostly because the police,
whom I'd always naively thought were supposed to serve and protect me, were
actually hunting me.

I had planned a pleasant day. The night before was a payday, plus I had   3
received a standing ovation after portraying the starring role of Coalhouse Walker
Jr. in the Broadway musical *Ragtime*. It is a role that requires not only talent but
also an honest emotional investment of the morals and lessons I learned as
a child.

Coalhouse Walker Jr. is a victim (an often misused word, but in this case   4
true) of overt racism. His story is every black man's nightmare. He is hardwork-
ing, successful, talented, charismatic, friendly, and polite. Perfect prey for someone with authority and not even a fraction of those qualities. On that Friday
afternoon, I became a real-life Coalhouse Walker. Nothing could have prepared
me for it. Not even stories told to me by other black men who had suffered
similar injustices.

Friday for me usually means a trip to the bank, errands, the gym, dinner, and   5
then off to the theater. On this particular day, I decided to break my pattern of getting up and running right out of the house. Instead, I took my time, slowed my
pace, and splurged by making strawberry pancakes. Before I knew it, it was 2:45;
my bank closes at 3:30, leaving me less than 45 minutes to get to midtown Manhattan on the train. I was pressed for time but in a relaxed, blessed state of mind.
When I walked through the lobby of my building, I noticed two light-skinned
Hispanic men I'd never seen before. Not thinking much of it, I continued on to the
vestibule, which is separated from the lobby by a locked door.

As I approached the exit, I saw people in uniforms rushing toward the door. I   6
sped up to open it for them. I thought they might be paramedics, since many of
the building's occupants are elderly. It wasn't until I had opened the door and
greeted them that I recognized that they were police officers. Within seconds, I
was told to "hold it"; they had received a call about young Hispanics with guns. I
was told to get against the wall. I was searched, stripped of my backpack, put on
my knees, handcuffed, and told to be quiet when I tried to ask questions.

With me were three other innocent black men who had been on their way to   7
their U-Haul. They were moving into the apartment beneath mine, and I had just
bragged to them about how safe the building was. One of these gentlemen got
off his knees, still handcuffed, and unlocked the door for the officers to get into
the lobby where the two strangers were standing. Instead of thanking or even
acknowledging us, they led us out the door past our neighbors, who were all but
begging the police in our defense.

The four of us were put into cars with the two strangers and taken to the pre-   8
cinct station at 165th and Amsterdam. The police automatically linked us, with no
questions and no regard for our character or our lives. No consideration was given
to where we were going or why. Suppose an ailing relative was waiting upstairs,
while I ran out for her medication? Or young children, who'd been told that Daddy
was running to the corner store for milk and would be right back? My new neighbors weren't even allowed to lock their apartment or check on the U-Haul.

After we were lined up in the station, the younger of the two Hispanic men   9
was identified as an experienced criminal, and drug residue was found in a pocket
of the other. I now realize how naive I was to think that the police would then
uncuff me, apologize for their mistake, and let me go. Instead, they continued to
search my backpack, questioned me, and put me in jail with the criminals.

The rest of the nearly five-hour ordeal was like a horrible dream. I was hand-   10
cuffed, strip-searched, taken in and out for questioning. The officers told me that
they knew exactly who I was, knew I was in *Ragtime*, and that in fact they already
had the men they wanted.

How then could they keep me there, or have brought me there in the first   11
place? I was told it was standard procedure. As if the average law-abiding citizen
knows what that is and can dispute it. From what I now know, "standard procedure" is something that every citizen, black and white, needs to learn, and fast.

I felt completely powerless. Why, do you think? Here I was, young, pleasant,   12
and successful, in good physical shape, dressed in clean athletic attire. I was carrying a backpack containing a substantial paycheck and a deposit slip, on my way to
the bank. Yet after hours and hours I was sitting at a desk with two officers who
not only couldn't tell me why I was there but seemed determined to find something on me, to the point of making me miss my performance.

It was because I am a black man!   13

I sat in that cell crying silent tears of disappointment and injustice with the   14
realization of how many innocent black men are convicted for no reason. When I
was handcuffed, my first instinct had been to pull away out of pure insult and violation as a human being. Thank God I was calm enough to do what they said.
When I was thrown in jail with the criminals and strip-searched, I somehow knew
to put my pride aside, be quiet, and do exactly what I was told, hating it but coming to terms with the fact that in this situation I was a victim. They had guns!

Before I was finally let go, exhausted, humiliated, embarrassed, and still in   15
shock, I was led to a room and given a pseudo-apology. I was told that I was at the
wrong place at the wrong time. My reply? "I was where I live."

Everything I learned growing up in Cincinnati has been shattered. Life will   16
never be the same.

EXERCISE 11.3 ▶ DRAWING A GRAPHIC ORGANIZER

Using Graphic Organizer 11.1 or 11.2 as a basis, draw a graphic organizer for "My Last
Day as a Surgeon" (pp. 232–34).

GRAPHIC ORGANIZER 11.2 The Structure of "Right Place, Wrong Face"

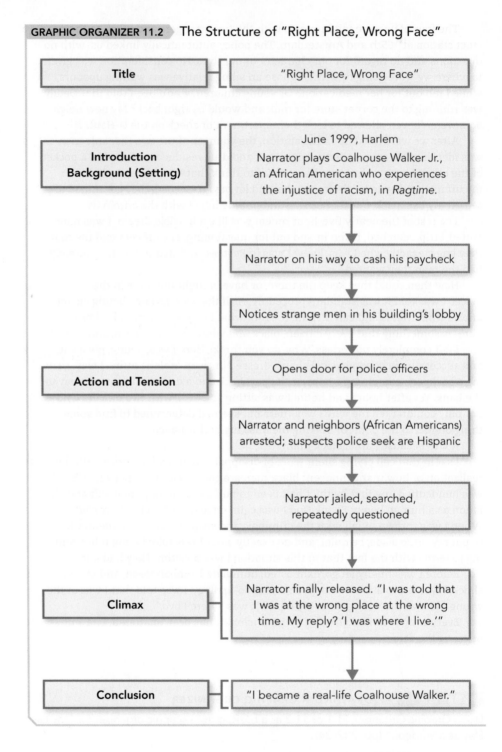

Title — "Right Place, Wrong Face"

Introduction Background (Setting) — June 1999, Harlem
Narrator plays Coalhouse Walker Jr., an African American who experiences the injustice of racism, in *Ragtime*.

Action and Tension —
Narrator on his way to cash his paycheck

Notices strange men in his building's lobby

Opens door for police officers

Narrator and neighbors (African Americans) arrested; suspects police seek are Hispanic

Narrator jailed, searched, repeatedly questioned

Climax — Narrator finally released. "I was told that I was at the wrong place at the wrong time. My reply? 'I was where I live.'"

Conclusion — "I became a real-life Coalhouse Walker."

HOW WRITERS READ ▶ NARRATION	
THE READING PROCESS	**STRATEGIES**
BEFORE READING	**Preview** the essay to get an overview of the content and organization.

Make connections by thinking about what the title means.

Read the headnote (if one is provided) for background information about the author and the reading. |
| **WHILE READING** | **Identify the characteristics of a narrative** (pp. 229–34). Be sure you can answer the following questions.

• What is the **sequence of events**? (Number them in the margin.)
• What is the writer's **thesis**? Is it stated or implied?
• Who are the **characters**, and what are their **relationships** to one another?
• How does the **dialogue** reveal character?
• What is the **conflict**, and how is it resolved? How does the writer create **tension**?
• What is the author's **purpose**? Who is the intended **audience**? |
| **AFTER READING** | Draw a **graphic organizer** listing the main events of the plot. (Use your graphic organizer for review and study.)

Analyze and evaluate the reading by answering the following questions.

• What broader issue is the essay concerned with? That is, what is its **theme**? Does the theme **follow logically** and **clearly** from the events in the narrative? (Express the theme in a sentence or two.)
• Is the **resolution** of the conflict **believable** and **well explained**?
• What is your **reaction** (positive, negative, mixed) to the narration? (Explain your reaction in detail.)
• How **objective** is the writer? How is the information in the essay influenced by the author's **beliefs** and **values**?
• What is the writer's **tone**? (Describe the tone with two or three adjectives.)
• What are the **writer's feelings** about the incident or events?
• What does the writer **leave unspoken** or **unreported**? Are any relevant **details omitted**? If so, why?
• What is the **lasting merit** of the essay? |

EXERCISE 11.4   THINKING CRITICALLY

Apply the questions in the "How Writers Read" box to the selection "Right Place, Wrong Face" (pp. 235–37).

Integrate Narration into an Essay

The essay "Writing about What Haunts Us," later in this chapter (pp. 254–56), uses multiple patterns of development to convey the author's ideas.

In many of your essays, you will want to use both narration and one or more other patterns of development to support your thesis. For example, although "My Last Day as a Surgeon" is primarily a narrative, it also uses description to present detailed information about the surgery the author performed on his last day. Similarly, "Right Place, Wrong Face" is a narrative that uses cause and effect to explain why the author was detained despite evidence that he was a respectable, law-abiding citizen. Similarly, "Writing about What Haunts Us" is a narrative that also uses cause and effect to explain why the author stole from his dad and how this act affected him.

Although most of your college essays will not be primarily narrative, you can use stories—to illustrate a point, clarify an idea, support an argument, or capture readers' interest—in essays that rely mainly on another pattern of development or use several patterns. Here are a few suggestions for combining narration effectively with other patterns of development.

1. **Use a story.** It should illustrate your main point (or thesis) accurately and well (not just because it's funny or interesting).
2. **Keep the narrative short.** Include only the details readers need to understand the events you are describing.
3. **Introduce the story with a transitional sentence or clause.** It should indicate that you are about to shift to a narrative and make clear the connection between the story and the point it illustrates.
4. **Use descriptive language, dialogue, and action.** These will make your narrative vivid, lively, and interesting.

PREWRITING	DRAFTING	REVISING	EDITING & PROOFREADING

A Guided Writing Assignment*

NARRATION

Your Essay Assignment

Write a narrative essay about an experience that had a significant effect on you or that changed your views in some important way. You can choose an experience that:

- taught you something about yourself
- revealed the true character of someone you know
- helped you discover a principle to live by
- helped you appreciate your ethnic identity
- has become a family legend (one that reveals the character of a family member or illustrates a clash of generations or cultures)
- explains the personal significance of a particular object

* The writing process is *recursive*; that is, you may find yourself revising as you draft or prewriting as you revise. This is especially true when writing on a computer. Your writing process may also differ from project to project or from that of your classmates.

1 Select a topic from the list on page 240, or create your own.

Use one or more of the following suggestions to choose an experience to write about.

1. Alone or with another student, **list one or more broad topics**—for example, *Learn about Self, A Principle to Live By, Family Legend*—and then **brainstorm** to come up with **specific experiences** in your life for each category. (Rational and pragmatic learners may prefer this kind of listing.)

2. Flip through a **family photo album**, or page through a **scrapbook**, **diary**, or **yearbook** to remind yourself of events from the past. Other prewriting strategies, like freewriting or questioning, may also help trigger memories of experiences. (Spatial and emotional learners may prefer reviewing memorabilia.)

3. **Work backward:** Think of a principle you live by, an object you value, or a family legend. How did it become so? (Abstract and independent learners may prefer working backward.)

After you have chosen your topic, make sure that it is **memorable and vivid** and that you can develop your main idea into a **working thesis.**

2 Consider your purpose and audience, and choose a point of view.

Ask yourself these questions.

- Will my essay's **purpose** be to **express myself**, **inform**, or **persuade**?

- Who is my **audience**? Will readers need any **background information** to understand my essay? Am I **comfortable writing about my experience** for this audience?

- What **point of view** best suits my purpose and audience? (In most cases, you will use **first person** to relate a personal experience.)

3 Gather details about the experience or incident.

Use idea-generating strategies to recollect as many details about the experience or incident as possible.

1. **Replay** the experience or incident in your mind's eye. Jot down what you see, hear, smell, and feel—colors, dialogue, sounds, odors, and sensations—and how these details make you feel. (A broad range of learners—spatial, concrete, creative, and emotional—may prefer to generate ideas using mental imaging.)

2. Write down the following headings: *Scene, Key Actions, Key Participants, Key Lines of Dialogue, Feelings.* Then **brainstorm** ideas for each and list them. (Pragmatic and rational learners may prefer to use brainstorming.)

3. **Describe** the incident or experience to a friend. Have your friend ask you questions as you tell the story. Jot down the details that the telling and questioning helped you recall. (Social and verbal learners may prefer to use storytelling.)

As you gather details for your narrative, be sure to include those that are essential to an effective narrative.

- **Describe the scene:** Include relevant **sensory details** to allow your readers to feel as if they are there. (Looking at a photograph or video might help.) Choose details that point to or hint at the narrative's main point, and avoid those that distract readers from the main point.

- **Include key actions:** Choose actions that **create tension, build it to a climax**, and **resolve it**. Answer questions like these.

  Why did the experience or incident occur?

  What events led up to it, what was the turning point, and how was it resolved?

  What were its short- and long-term outcomes? What is its significance?

- **Describe key participants:** Concentrate on the **appearance** and **actions** of only those people who were directly involved, and include details that help highlight relevant character traits.

- **Quote key lines of dialogue:** Include dialogue that is **interesting, revealing**, and **related to the main point** of the narrative. To make sure the dialogue sounds natural, read the lines aloud or ask a friend to do so.

- **Capture feelings:** How did you feel during the incident, how did you reveal your feelings, and how did others react to you? How do you feel about the incident now? What have you learned from the experience?

Use at least two idea-generating strategies, and then work with a classmate to evaluate your ideas.

4 Evaluate your ideas to make sure they describe your experience or incident vividly and meaningfully.

Try these suggestions to help you evaluate your ideas.

- **Reread** everything you have written. (Sometimes reading your notes aloud is helpful.)

- **Highlight** the most relevant material, and **cross out** any material that does not directly support your main point. Then **copy** and **paste** the usable ideas to a new document to consult while drafting.

- **Collaborate** in small groups, take turns **narrating your experience** and **stating its main point** and having classmates tell you:

  1. how they react to the story

  2. what more they need to know about it

  3. how effectively the events and details support your main point

5 Focus and place your thesis effectively.

Make the main point of your narrative clear and effective by focusing your thesis. For example, a student who decided to write about a robbery at her family's home devised the following focused thesis statement for her narrative.

Example:

┌─ focuses on 1 object ─┐ ┌────── explains value ──────┐

The silver serving platter, originally owned by my great-grandmother,

┌────── introduces experience & expresses main point ──────┐

became our most prized family heirloom after a robbery terrorized our family.

Team up with classmates to test your thesis. Is it clear? Is it interesting? Provide feedback to help your partner focus the thesis more effectively.

Consider the best placement for your thesis. A thesis statement may be placed at the beginning (as in "Right Place, Wrong Face," p. 235) or at the end of a narrative, or it may be implied. (Even if you don't state your thesis explicitly in your essay, having a focused thesis written down can help you craft your narrative.)

(**Note:** Once you have a focused thesis, you may need to do some additional prewriting, or you may need to revise your thesis as you draft. Return to the steps above as needed.)

 Choose a narrative sequence.

Organize your narrative. You may use **chronological order** from beginning to end or present some events using **flashbacks** or **foreshadowing** for dramatic effect. To help you determine the best sequence for your narrative, try the following.

1. Write a **brief description** of each event on an index card. Highlight the card that contains the climax. Experiment with various ways of arranging your details by rearranging the cards. (Pragmatic learners may benefit from using index cards this way.)
2. Create an **outline** or draw a **graphic organizer** of the experience or incident using Graphic Organizer 11.1 on page 235 as a model. (Spatial learners in particular may benefit from drawing a graphic organizer.)
3. Create a **list** of the events, and then cut and paste them to experiment with different sequences. (Verbal learners may benefit from creating a list.)

7 Write a first draft of your narrative essay.

Use the following guidelines to keep your narrative on track.

- The **introduction** should set up the sequence of events. It may also contain your **thesis**.
- The **body paragraphs** should **build tension** and follow a clear order of progression. Use **transitional words and phrases**, such as *during*, *after*, and *finally*, to guide readers. Most narratives use the past tense ("Yolanda discovered the platter . . ."), but fast-paced, short narratives may use the present ("Yolanda discovers the platter . . ."). Avoid switching between the two unless the context clearly requires it. Consider whether including a photograph (or a video or audio file if the writing project is presented online) could help engage readers by depicting the setting or a key character.
- The **conclusion** is unlikely to require a summary. Instead, try . . .
  - **making a final observation about the experience or incident**. (Example: "Overall, I learned a lot more about getting along with people than I did about how to prepare fast food.")
  - **asking a probing question**. (Example: "Although the visit to Nepal was enlightening for me, do the native people really want or need us there?")
  - **suggesting a new but related direction of thought**. (Example: An essay on racial profiling might conclude by suggesting that police sensitivity training might have changed the outcome of the situation.)
  - **referring to the beginning of the essay** (example: "Right Place, Wrong Face," para. 16, p. 237) or **restating the thesis in different words** (example: "Being Double," para. 22, p. 250).

8 Evaluate your draft and revise as necessary.

Use **Figure 11.1, "Flowchart for Revising a Narrative Essay,"** to evaluate and revise your draft.

FIGURE 11.1 Flowchart for Revising a Narrative Essay

QUESTIONS		REVISION STRATEGIES

1. Highlight the sentence(s) that express the main point of your narrative. Is the main point clear?

 NO ▶

- Rework your thesis to make it more explicit.

 YES ▼

2. Summarize the conflict of your narrative in one brief sentence. Is the conflict clear? Does it relate directly to the main point?

 NO ▶

- Add events and dialogue to clarify or dramatize the conflict.
- Rework your thesis to make it better relate to the conflict.

 YES ▼

3. Place an ✘ by each important scene, person, or action. Does each clearly relate to both the main point and the *conflict*?

 NO ▶

- Delete scenes, people, or actions that don't help you make your main point or establish conflict.

 YES ▼

4. Place a checkmark ✔ by each descriptive word or phrase. Is each important scene, person, or action vividly described?

 NO ▶

- Brainstorm to discover more vivid details.
- Consider adding dialogue to bring people and events to life.

 YES ▼

5. *Number* the major events in chronological order. Is the sequence clear? If you use foreshadowing or flashbacks, is the shift from present to past or future clear?

 NO ▶

- Look for gaps in the sequence, and add any missing events.
- Consider rearranging the events.
- Use transitions to clarify the sequence of events.

 YES ▼

6. Underline the topic sentence of each paragraph. Is each paragraph focused on a separate part of the action?

 NO ▶

- Be sure each paragraph has a topic sentence and supporting details. (See Chapter 6.)
- Combine closely related paragraphs.
- Split paragraphs that cover more than one event.

 YES ▼

QUESTIONS		REVISION STRATEGIES

7. Highlight the dialogue. Does it sound realistic? Does it directly relate to the *conflict*?

 NO ▶

- Act out your dialogue, and record what you say.
- Cut dialogue that does not help you make your main point or add drama.

YES
▼

8. Circle each personal pronoun and each verb. Do you use a consistent point of view and verb tense?

 NO ▶

- Revise places where your point of view shifts for no reason.
- Check for places where the tense changes for no reason, and revise to make it consistent.

YES
▼

9. Look at your introduction and conclusion. Do they address each other and the main point? Does the conclusion resolve the *conflict*?

 NO ▶

- Revise your introduction and conclusion. (See pp. 164–67.)

REVISING

---

 9 **Edit and proofread your essay.**

Refer to Chapter 9 for help with:

- **editing sentences** to avoid wordiness, make your verb choices strong and active, and make your sentences clear, varied, and parallel, and
- **editing words** for tone and diction, connotation, and concrete and specific language.

Pay particular attention to **dialogue.**

- Each quotation by a new speaker should start a **new paragraph**.
- Use **commas** to separate each quotation from the phrase that introduces it unless the quotation is integrated into your sentence. If your sentence ends with a quotation, the **period** should be inside the quotation marks.

> **Example:** The wildlife refuge guide noted,"American crocodiles are an endangered species and
>
> must be protected."

> **Example:** The wildlife refuge guide noted that/"American crocodiles are an endangered species
>
> and must be protected."/

EDITING & PROOFREADING

Readings: Narrative in Action

> **STUDENTS WRITE**
>
> ## Being Double
>
> **Santiago Quintana**
>
> Santiago Quintana, a junior literature major, wrote this essay for an assignment given by his first-year writing instructor. He had to describe a situation that challenged him and taught him a valuable lesson. As you read the essay, notice how Quintana's narrative creates conflict and tension and builds to a climax and resolution. Highlight the sections(s) where you think the tension is particularly intense.

Details: Exact details help readers imagine the scene.

Dialogue: Quotations sound natural and capture the relationship between mother and son.

Conflict: Description of Quintana's feelings introduces conflict and foreshadows the process he will undergo during his first year in college.

Background: Provides background about his English skills

A summer sun shone on the Wisconsin Indian mounds and the grass poked its little blades through my sandaled toes. "College, finally," said Mom, and her hand fell slowly on my hair. I couldn't stop the shaking. It was inside me though; outside I was as still as a statue, with a smile frozen on my lips. "Hey, should we leave some stuff in the car and come get it later, or should we all help you carry it to the building?" asked my brother as he held two crates, one with my sheets in it and the other with books. The idea of having my family parade around campus yelling in Spanish, being "those loud Mexicans" I'd seen in American movies, and carrying all my stuff with me sounded terrifying. At the same time, I thought, why not? I didn't know anyone on campus, so there was no reason for me to be concerned about what others thought of me or my family. In Mexico City, I would have been mortified to be seen walking around high school with my whole family. Then again, that was high school, that was teenage Santiago, and that was Mexico City. I was in college now, in America; it was the time to read more, stop smoking, make friends, and do all those things that I had postponed beyond the imaginary line of "when I go to college." 1

With Wisconsin as our final destination, my family and I had been traveling around the Midwest for a week. I spoke the best English, so for the whole trip, I had been translating directions and ordering food for all. In my bilingual high school, I had the top grades in English, and hours 2 watching YouTube videos and standing in front of a mirror had made my accent one of the least recognizable among my friends. Now, in America, all that obsession with language was paying off. My lighter skin and over rehearsed accent baffled many a waiter and cab driver when they discovered I was Mexican. My English was the reason I had chosen and been able to get into an American college. Now, here I was, my accent and lexicon ready to be put to the test.

The room was larger than I thought it would be, and my roommate quieter. My parents and I set the room up and left for coffee.

"Your roommate seems nice," said my mom.

"Yeah, a little quiet," I said, "and way younger than me."

"Everyone will be younger than you here," said my dad, "and you didn't really talk much either. You're usually so talkative."

"He's nervous dad," said my brother.

"I'm not. It's just, I don't know, weird. I don't know what to say to them," I said.

"Them? As in?" asked my dad.

"As in Americans. I don't know what to say to them, what they think is funny, and what is too much. You know my humor; I can go way overboard sometimes, and I don't want to mess up," I said.

"I see. Well, I'm sure it'll come with time. You'll get used to it," said my mom.

After my parents left I sat on my dorm bed for two or three hours and had three cups of tea. I then decided to go out for a walk and try to talk to people. I closed the door behind me and was greeted by a long, empty hallway in muted colors with doors on both sides. I walked quietly down the hallway to the stairs without meeting anyone. I went down the stairs and out the back door of the building. The air was more humid that I had ever felt, and the sun burnt my skin. I eventually found my way to the Office of International Education, where I saw a crowd of similarly terrified students standing at the door. I approached them, not sure how I would introduce myself, or what excuse I'd have for talking to them. In the end, I didn't need an excuse. One of the students recognized me from orientation and called out to me. "Hey! You're from Mexico aren't you?"

"Yeah," I answered.

3
4
5
6
7
8
9
10
11
12
13

Details: Exact details help readers imagine the writer's appearance and language.

Tension: Quintana anticipates the challenge of putting his English skills to work and builds tension.

Tension: Dialogue helps build tension.

Transitions: Transitions of time help sequence events.

Details: Exact details help readers visualize situation.

Tension: Dialogue reinforces Santiago's struggle and builds tension.

Transitions: Transitions of time help sequence events.

Details: Detailed description helps build tension.

"Come, I'm from El Salvador. We were just talking about how different it is to learn English in class and have to speak it all the time with other Americans and also in class. I mean, you haven't had class yet, but you'll see. It's different," he said.   14

"I've already gotten lost like three times because I couldn't understand directions," said Amy, from Japan.   15

"It's the intonation. It's all wrong," said Matej from the Czech Republic.   16

"Also, they go too fast." All of the international students had stories of struggling with English, and they all had theories for the difference.   17

Finally, the time came for my first class—Mythology. I nervously entered the classroom, took a seat, and with pen and notebook ready, prepared to take notes. As I looked around, I noticed that there were only about ten students in the class. This only added to my nervousness; I would not be able to hide. I knew college in America would be difficult, but I could not have ever imagined how difficult it would actually be. Before class, I had made myself the promise that I would ask at least one question, or participate at least once. By the end of class, I had, at the most, one sentence scribbled on the page, and I had participated much more than once. I had asked the professor to explain terms and phrases, and sometimes even to repeat himself. I knew this was annoying for the rest of the students, and I apologized profusely through my blush. The professor assured me that it was fine, that he'd rather have us know the first half of the material really well, than go through the whole of it with only a vague inkling of what we were talking about. After he let us out of class, I stopped another student, a junior, and asked him to repeat what the homework assignment was, because I hadn't understood the professor. He smiled and said I didn't need to apologize, that it was only natural I would struggle with the language for the first week or so.   18

At the end of class, I was physically, mentally, and emotionally exhausted. Wanting to be alone, I went back to my room, lay down for a bit, and then made some tea. It was early afternoon now, and I had another class after lunch. I tried to relax. My head thumped from the adrenaline,   19 and my heart hurt from the loneliness. My roommate came in and asked if I was doing fine and if I wanted to have lunch with him and his friends. "Friends, friends, how can he have friends already?" I thought, "We've been here for less than a week and you call them friends." I said yes anyway. I knew I had to get out and walk it off, so to speak. Lunch was equally stressful, but being a less formal situation, I couldn't raise my hand and ask my roommate's friends to define terms and explain phrases and repeat themselves. So I just smiled and let most of the conversation go without participating. One of my roommate's friends must have seen confusion written on my face for she took her food and sat across from me and started talking to me. I asked her to go slowly, and told her that I was just getting used to English and that I was sorry for being a nuisance. She laughed. "The first thing you need to do is stop apologizing. We are not cold, heartless people. Well, most of us aren't. We understand. I can enunciate more clearly and speak more slowly, and it won't be a problem. Tell me, you went to high school in Mexico City?"

I was hesitant at first and thought about every word and whether it was appropriate. My new friend was incredibly patient with me, and she made me feel fine about my English. I don't know when or how, but eventually I was laughing at her jokes and the others joined in on our conversation, and I stopped thinking about every word I said. The words seemed to fall effortlessly out of my mouth, already strung into phrases. I told them about Mexico City and how crazy everything is, and no it's not nearly as dangerous as reporters make it seem in the news. I learned about their home towns, their interests, and what they did for fun. I was thinking about the conversation rather than the words. I forgot myself and only then did the English that I knew finally make an appearance.

It wasn't permanent though. It still took me a while to switch from translating to talking. I still struggled in class for the rest of the month, but the moments when I forgot myself and flowed with the conversation began happening more often. They happened when I didn't apologize for my "bad English," when I didn't talk myself down, when I knew myself capable, and when I trusted the years and years of English lessons behind me, rather than searching for words like papers in a file cabinet.

20

Details: Exact details help readers understand Quintana's experience.

Climax

21

Conclusion: Transitions highlight what Quintana has learned—that he must relearn confidence each year.

> Now, I am about to start my third year of college. I have increased my   22
> vocabulary and improved my style immensely. Nevertheless, there is
> always a week or two at the beginning of school when I have to tell
> myself to find that confidence again, to not apologize, and to trust my
> knowledge. Sometimes I still apologize and struggle when choosing
> words, but it has become easier and easier to find those moments when I
> forget it's me talking, and I just let the talking happen.

Analyzing the Writer's Technique

1. **Thesis** Evaluate the strength of Quintana's thesis. How clear and specific is it?
2. **Details** How effectively does Quintana use details to reinforce his main point and to help readers visualize key people and places? Did you feel more details were needed? If so, where? Which details, if any, would you suggest he add or delete?
3. **Conflict and Tension** How does Quintana establish conflict and create tension?
4. **Foreshadowing** Where does Quintana use foreshadowing? How effective is it?
5. **Title, Introduction, and Conclusion** Evaluate the title, introduction, and conclusion of the essay.

Thinking Critically about Narration

1. **Tone** Describe Quintana's tone. What words convey his attitude or perspective? Does the tone change over the course of the essay? If so, how? Does it seem appropriate for the topic?
2. **Connotation** What connotation does the phrase "those loud Mexicans" (para. 1) have in the context of the paragraph?
3. **Fact and Opinion** In paragraph 2, Quintana writes, "My English was the reason I had chosen and been able to get into an American college." Is this statement a fact or an opinion? How do you know?

Responding to the Reading

1. **Reaction** Quintana mentions one experience with other international students, but he ends up bonding with a group of Americans. Why do you think this happened?
2. **Discussion** International students have a sizable presence on most college campuses in America. What can American colleges do to better meet the needs of these students?
3. **Journal** Write a journal entry about someone you befriended when others may have brushed him or her aside. How did you reach out to the individual, and what were the results?
4. **Essay** Quintana felt lonely and anxious as he began college in a new country with a new language. Write a narrative essay about a time when you felt like an outsider, lonely and anxious about making friends and fitting in.

Chop Suey

Ira Sukrungruang

Ira Sukrungruang, a professor at the University of South Florida, writes in many different genres: essays, stories, poetry, and memoir. His memoir *Southside Buddhist* won the 2015 American Book Award. The author calls "Chop Suey," which follows, a "flash essay" because it captures a moment in memory that he feels compelled to record in writing; it captures the first time Sukrungruang saw his mother bowl and recognized her power. **Before reading**, preview the selection and make connections by thinking of a time when you experienced or witnessed someone making an unfair assumption about you or your culture. **While reading**, consider how Sukrungruang presents the conflict and creates tension as well as how he presents his relationship with his mother.

My mother was a champion bowler in Thailand. This was not what I knew of   1
her. I knew only her expectations of me to be the perfect Thai boy. I knew her distaste for blonde American women she feared would seduce her son. I knew her distrust of the world she found herself in, a world of white faces and mackerel in a

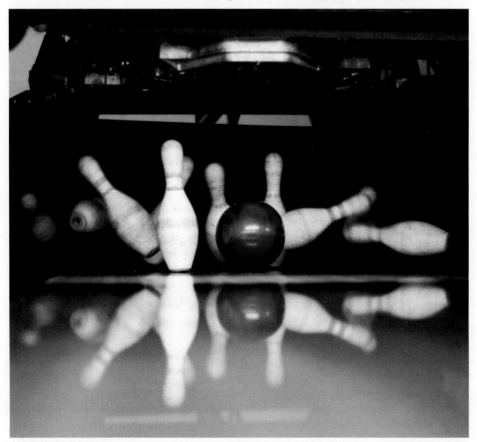

lkpgfoto/E+/Getty Images

can. There were many things I didn't know about my mother when I was ten. She was what she was supposed to be. My mother.

At El-Mar Bowling Alley, I wanted to show her what I could do with the pins.   2
I had bowled once before, at Dan Braun's birthday party. There, I had rolled the ball off the bumpers, knocking the pins over in a thunderous crash. I liked the sound of a bowling alley. I felt in control of the weather, the rumble of the ball on the wood floor like the coming of a storm, and the hollow explosion of the pins, distant lightning. At the bowling alley, men swore and smoked and drank.

My mother wore a light pink polo, jeans, and a golf visor. She put on a lot of   3
powder to cover up the acne she got at 50. She poured Vapex, a strong smelling vapor rub, into her handkerchief, and covered her nose, complaining of the haze of smoke that floated over the lanes. My mother was the only woman in the place. We were the only non-white patrons.

I told her to watch me. I told her I was good. I set up, took sloppy and uneven   4
steps, and lobbed my orange ball onto the lane with a loud thud. This time there were no bumpers. My ball veered straight for the gutter.

My mother said to try again. I did, and for the next nine frames, not one ball   5
hit one pin. Embarrassed, I sat next to her. I put my head on her shoulder. She patted it for a while and said bowling wasn't an easy game.

My mother rose from her chair and said she wanted to try. She changed her   6
shoes. She picked a ball from the rack, one splattered with colors. When she was ready, she lined herself up to the pins, the ball at eye level. In five concise steps, she brought the ball back, dipped her knees, and released it smoothly, as if her hand was an extension of the floor. The ball started on the right side of the lane and curled into the center. Strike.

She bowled again and knocked down more pins. She told me about her nearly   7
perfect game, how in Thailand she was unbeatable.

I listened, amazed that my mother could bowl a 200, that she was good at   8
something beyond what mothers were supposed to be good at, like cooking and punishing and sewing. I clapped. I said she should stop being a mother and become a bowler.

As she changed her shoes, a man with dark hair and a mustache approached   9
our lane. In one hand he had a cigarette and a beer. He kept looking back at his buddies a few lanes over, all huddling and whispering. I stood beside my mother, wary of any stranger. My mother's smile disappeared. She rose off the chair.

"Hi," said the man.   10

My mother nodded.   11

"My friends over there," he pointed behind him, "well, we would like to thank   12
you." His mustache twitched.

My mother pulled me closer to her leg, hugging her purse to her chest.   13

He began to talk slower, over-enunciating his words, repeating again. "We . . .   14
would . . . like . . . to . . . thank . . ."

I tugged on my mother's arm, but she stood frozen.   15

". . . you . . . for . . . making . . . a . . . good . . . chop . . . suey. You people make   16
good food."

The man looked back again, toasted his beer at his friends, laughing smoke   17
from his lips.

My mother grabbed my hand and took one step toward the man. In that 18
instant, I saw in her face the same resolve she had when she spanked, the same
resolve when she scolded. In that instant, I thought my mother was going to hit
the man. And for a moment, I thought the man saw the same thing in her eyes,
and his smile disappeared from his face. Quickly, she smiled—too bright, too
large—and said, "You're welcome."

Understanding the Reading

1. **Reasons** Why did the author's mother distrust the world she lived in?
2. **Thesis** What is Sukrungruang's thesis? Is it stated or implied?
3. **Details** What detail in paragraph 1 compels the young boy to want to show his mother what he "could do with pins"?
4. **Details** Contrast the description of how the boy bowled with the description of how his mother bowled.

Analyzing the Writer's Technique

1. **Opening and Conclusion** How does the concluding paragraph connect with the opening paragraph?
2. **Description** How does Sukrungruang use description and other strategies to make his experience vivid and engaging. Cite several examples.
3. **Patterns of Organization** Identify at least two other patterns of organization Sukrungruang uses and explain the benefit of including these other patterns.
4. **Details** How well do you think Sukrungruang describes his mother? What details do you find most effective? Are there any aspects of his mother about which you would like to learn more?

Thinking Critically

1. **Tone** Describe the tone of Sukrungruang's essay. Highlight words or phrases that reveal his attitude.
2. **Inference** What can readers infer about what the American man in the bowling alley thinks of Sukrungruang's mother?
3. **Fact or Opinion** In paragraph 1, the author writes: "She was what she was supposed to be. My mother." Is this statement a fact or an opinion?
4. **Discussion** Discuss why Sukrungruang describes his mother's smile as "too bright, too large." What does this description convey about his mother's attitude toward the man?
5. **Title** Consider the title in relation to the essay as a whole. Does it effectively capture the main idea? Why or why not?

Responding to the Reading

1. **Discussion** Why does the author make such a point of the fact that his mother was what she was supposed to be? What *are* mothers supposed to be? Does this type of mindset or these expectations present problems in our society today? Why or why not?

2. **Journal** Try to put yourself in the shoes of Sukrungruang's mother. How would the encounter with the man at the bowling alley have made you feel? How do you think you would have responded? What do you learn from this encounter, and how could it possibly affect your interaction with others who are different from you? Write a journal entry in which you speculate about these questions.

3. **Essay** Sukrungruang's trip with his mom to the bowling alley was a turning point in his relationship with his mother and possibly his life. His experiences there gave him a new respect for his mother and also a taste of the rudeness and disrespect that people can have for those who are different. Write a narrative essay about an event in your life that made a lasting impression on you. Be sure to follow the basic structure of a narrative essay (see Graphic Organizer 11.1) and include dialogue, description, and action verbs.

Working Together

Ira Sukrungruang learned several things about his mom when they went to the bowling alley. Working in small groups, create a motto that captures the essence of what Sukrungruang learned that day. You may focus on one or all of the things he learned. Be prepared to share your motto and explain the significance of it to the class.

READING ▶ NARRATION COMBINED WITH OTHER PATTERNS

Writing about What Haunts Us

Peter Orner

Peter Orner, a professor of creative writing at San Francisco State University, is an award-winning author and essayist whose works have appeared in publications such as *The Southern Review*, *The Atlantic*, and *The New York Times*. He is the author of two novels: *Love and Shame and Love* (2011) and *The Second Coming of Mavala Shikongo* (2006). This memoir, which appeared in *The New York Times* online, is about a secret Orner kept from his parents for years. **Before reading**, preview and make connections by thinking about the kinds of secrets children might keep from their parents (or parents from their children). **While reading**, look for patterns other than narration that the author uses to tell his story.

I've been trying to lie about this story for years. As a fiction writer, I feel an almost   1
righteous obligation to the untruth. Fabrication is my livelihood, and so telling something straight, for me, is the mark of failure. Yet in many attempts over the years I've not been able to make out of this tiny—but weirdly soul-defining—episode in my life anything more than a plain recounting of the facts, as best as I can remember them. Dressing them up into fiction, in this case, wrecked what is essentially a long overdue confession.

    Here's the nonfiction version.   2

    I watched my father in the front hall putting on his new, lambskin leather   3
gloves. It was a sort of private ceremony. This was in early November, 1982, in Highland Park, Ill., a town north of Chicago along Lake Michigan. My father had

just returned from a business trip to Paris. He'd bought the gloves at a place called Hermès, a mythical wonderland of a store. He pulled one on slowly, then the other, and held them up in the mirror to see how his hands looked in such gloves.

A week later, I stole them. 4

I remember the day. I was home from school. Nobody else was around. I opened 5 the left-hand drawer of the front hall table and there they were. I learned for the first time how easy it is to just grab something. I stuffed the gloves in my pants and sprinted upstairs to my room. I hid them in the back of my closet under the wicker basket that held my license plate collection. Then I braced myself, for days. It was a warm November.

When we finally left that house—my mother, my brother and me—I took the 6 gloves with me to our new place. I took them with me to college. To Boston, to Cincinnati, to North Carolina, to California. I even took them with me to Namibia for two years. I have them now, on my desk, 30 years later.

I've never worn them, not once, although my father and I have the same small 7 hands. I didn't want the gloves. I never wanted the gloves. I only wanted my father not to have them.

Now that he is older and far milder, it is hard to believe how scared I used 8 to be of my father. Back then he was so full of anger. Was he unhappy in his marriage? No doubt. He and my mother never had much in common. But his anger—sometimes it was rage—went beyond this not so unusual disappointment. My own totally unscientific, armchair diagnosis is that like other chronically unsatisfied people, the daily business of living caused my father despair. At no time did this manifest itself more powerfully than when he came home from work. A rug askew, a jacket not hung up, a window left open—all could set off a fury. My brother once spilled a pot of ink on the snowy white carpet of my parents' bedroom: Armageddon.

His unpredictability is what made his explosions so potent. Sometimes the 9 bomb wouldn't go off, and he'd act like my idea of a normal dad. When he finally noticed those precious gloves were missing, he seemed only confused.

"Maybe they're in the glove compartment," my mother said. 10

"Impossible. I never put gloves in the glove compartment. The glove compart- 11 ment is for maps."

"Oh, well," my mother said. 12

He kept searching the front hall table, as if he had somehow overlooked them 13 amid all the cheap imitation leather gloves, mismatched mittens and tasseled Bears hats. I am certain the notion that one of us had taken the gloves never crossed his mind.

Haunted by my guilt, a frequent motivation for my fiction in general, I've tried 14 to contort my theft into a story, a made-up story.

In my failed attempts, the thief is always trying to give the gloves back. In one 15 abandoned version, the son character (sometimes he's a daughter) mails the gloves back to the father, along with a forged letter, purportedly written by a long-dead friend of the father, a man the father had once betrayed. I liked the idea of a package arriving, out of the blue, from an aggrieved ghost. I'm returning your gloves, Phil. Now at least one of us may be absolved.

The problem was that it palmed off responsibility on a third party. And it   16
muddied the story by pulling the thief out of the center of what little action there
was.

In a simpler but equally bad version, the son character, home for Thanksgiv-   17
ing, slips the gloves back in the top left-hand drawer of the front hall table of the
house he grew up in, the house where the father still lives. This attempt was
marred not only by cooked-up dialogue but also by a dead end.

"Dad! How about we take a walk by the lake?"   18

"It's been years, Son, since we've taken a walk."   19

"Pretty brisk out. Maybe you need your gloves?"   20

The moment arrives: the father slides open the drawer. Voilà! (Note the   21
French.) Cut to the father's face. Describe his bewilderment. I must have
checked this drawer a hundred thousand times. Decades drop from the father's
eyes, and both father and son face each other as they never faced each other
when both were years younger. The son stammers out a confession I could
somehow never get right. He tries to explain himself, but can't. Why did he take
the gloves? My character could never express it in words and the story kept
collapsing.

This is where the truth of this always derails the fiction. I can't give the gloves   22
back, in fiction or in this thing we call reality. If I did, I'd have to confront something I've known all along but have never wanted to express, even to myself alone.
My father would have given me his gloves. All I had to do was ask. He would have
been so pleased that for once we shared a common interest. This happened so few
times in our lives. All the years I've been trying to write this, maybe I've always
known that this essential fact would stick me in the heart.

Our imaginations sometimes fail us for a reason. Not because it is cathartic to   23
tell the truth (I finally told my father last year) but because coming clean may also
be a better, if smaller, story. A scared (and angry) kid rips off his father's gloves,
carries them around for decades. Sometimes he takes them out and feels them but
never puts them on. When I see my father these days, we graze each other's
cheeks, a form of kissing in my family. I love my father. I suppose I did even then,
in the worst moments of fear.

Well-made things eventually deteriorate. The Hermès gloves are no longer   24
baby-soft. All the handless years have dried them up.

In 1982, my father wasn't much older than I am at this moment. I think of him   25
now, standing in the front hall. He's holding his hands up in the mirror, pulling on
his beautiful gloves, a rare stillness on his face, a kind of hopeful calm. Was this
what I wanted to steal?

Understanding the Reading

1. **Reasons** Why does Orner say that he had such a hard time writing the truth about
   the glove incident?
2. **Thesis** What is Orner's thesis?
3. **Detail** In paragraph 6, what do you find out about Orner's father?

4. **Vocabulary** Explain the meaning of each of the following words as it is used in the reading: *askew* (para. 8), *marred* (17), *stammers* (21), *cathartic* (23). Refer to your dictionary as needed.

Analyzing the Writer's Technique

1. **Details** How well do you think Orner describes his father? What details do you find most effective? Are there any aspects of his father about which you would like to learn more?
2. **Patterns of Organization** Identify at least two other patterns of organization Orner uses and explain the benefit of including these other patterns.
3. **Climax** What is the climax of the story, and when and how is tension resolved, providing the narrative with its climax?
4. **Conclusion** Is Orner's final question, "Was this what I wanted to steal?" an effective conclusion? Why or why not?

Thinking Critically

1. **Tone** Based on the language the author uses and the style of his writing, what do you think the tone of the essay is? Explain your answer.
2. **Inference** What can you infer about the mother's level of concern over the missing gloves (para. 12)?
3. **Fact or Opinion** In paragraph 13, Orner writes, "I am certain the notion that one of us had taken the gloves never crossed his mind." Is this statement fact or opinion?
4. **Author's Attitude** What attitude is the writer trying to convey about himself and his father?

Responding to the Reading

1. **Discussion** Why do you think that Orner paints such an unflattering picture of his father when Orner was a child? Do you think Orner was justified in taking the gloves because of his father's disposition?
2. **Journal** Stealing the gloves started out as an impulsive act that ended up weighing on Orner's mind for thirty years. Write a journal entry in which you discuss an event or conflict that grew and festered in your mind the longer you let it go unresolved.
3. **Essay** Do you have a past action that haunts you or an incident from your childhood that you have kept from your parent(s) for years? Brainstorm to recollect the details of this incident, and then write a narrative essay about this memorable event in your life. Be sure to follow the basic structure of a narrative essay (see Graphic Organizer 11.1), and include dialogue, description, and action verbs as Orner did.

Working Together

Peter Orner does not tell his readers what he said to his father or what happened when he told him about the gloves. Working in small groups, create a script of that encounter. Be prepared to role-play the meeting between Peter and his father.

Apply Your Skills: Additional Essay Assignments

For more on locating and documenting sources, see Part 5.

Write a narrative on one of the topics listed below, using the elements and techniques of narration you learned in this chapter. Depending on the topic you choose, you may need to do research to gather support for your ideas.

To Express Your Ideas

1. Write a narrative about an incident or experience that you see differently now than you did when it happened.
2. In "Right Place, Wrong Face," Alton Fitzgerald White says he always believed that the police "were supposed to serve and protect" him (para. 2). After the incident he describes in the essay, he feels otherwise. Write a narrative describing an incident involving police officers or law enforcement agents that you may have experienced, observed, or read about. Did the incident change your attitude about police or law enforcement or confirm opinions you already held?

To Inform Your Reader

3. Write an essay informing your reader about the characteristics of a strong (or weak) relationship, the habits of successful (or unsuccessful) students, or the ways of keeping (or losing) a job. Use a narrative to support one or more of your main points.

To Persuade Your Reader

4. At one time, America was described as a melting pot, where newcomers shed their cultural identity in favor of becoming an American. Critics of this loss of cultural identity would prefer to think of America as a tossed salad in which all the "ingredients" retain their distinctive identities. Write an essay taking a position on whether immigrants to the United States should attempt to blend in or strive to retain their culture, language, and other unique cultural characteristics. Support your position, drawing on your own experiences, the experiences of friends and family members, or the experience of the mother and son in "Chop Suey."
5. In "Right Place, Wrong Face," White takes a position on racial profiling. Write an essay persuading your reader to take a particular stand on an issue of your choice. Use a story from your experience to support your position or tell how you arrived at it.

Cases Using Narration

6. Write a paper for a sociology course on the advantages of an urban, suburban, or rural lifestyle. Support some of your main points with events and examples from your own experiences.

7. Write a draft of the presentation you will give as the new human resource director of a nursing care facility in charge of training new employees. You plan to hold your first orientation session next week, and you want to emphasize the importance of teamwork and communication by telling related stories from your previous job experiences.

SYNTHESIZING IDEAS   HARSH TREATMENT OF OUTCASTS

Both "Right Place, Wrong Face" (pp. 235–37) and "Chop Suey" (pp. 251–53) describe the harsh treatment of someone seen as an outcast—a person who does not deserve respect or courtesy.

Analyzing the Readings

1. Compare the situations of each disrespected person. Then consider how each one responded to those who treated him harshly.
2. Compare the social issues that each author addresses in the narrative of his experience.

Essay Idea

Write an essay describing a situation in which you feel you or someone you know was treated as an outcast. Describe the background to the situation, the treatment received, and the response to the treatment.

12

Description

Portraying People, Places, and Things

Marianna Massey/DigitalVision/Getty Images

In this chapter you will learn to:

- understand the purpose and function of descriptive essays

- use graphic organizers to visualize descriptive essays

- integrate description into an essay

- read and think critically about description

- plan, organize, draft, revise, and edit essays using description

WRITING QUICK START   Suppose the owner of a local restaurant that you go to often asks you to increase the restaurant's presence on social media by praising the restaurant in a Facebook post or giving the restaurant a positive review on Yelp. You decide to include several photos of menu items, including the one shown here. Write an appealing description to accompany this photograph. Use words that will appeal to the readers' senses of sight and smell, but also their senses of sound and even touch. You may even want to include a comparison that will help readers understand the dining experience.

As you write your post or review, be sure to include lots of details that will make readers' mouths water. Include details about how scrumptious the dish looks, its delicious aroma, the creamy texture of the dish's sauce, and its delectable taste. You may also choose to include details about how the dining room looks, feels, and smells; how the waitstaff behaves with customers; and how customers react to the food, the service, and the ambience. Include any details that you think will help readers come away with a pleasant impression.

Description presents information in a way that appeals to one or more of the five senses (sight, sound, smell, taste, and touch) by creating an overall (dominant) impression or feeling. If you included concrete details and maybe an effective comparison in your Writing Quick Start, you wrote a successful **description**.

You use description every day—to describe a pair of shoes you bought, a flavor of ice cream you tasted, or a concert you attended recently. If you were an eyewitness to a car theft, the detective investigating the crime would ask you to describe what you saw.

Writers rely on description to present detailed information about people, places, and things and to grab and sustain their readers' interest. When you write vivid descriptions, you not only make your writing livelier and more interesting but also indicate your attitude toward the subject through your choice of concrete words and specific details.

USING DESCRIPTION ▸ **IN COLLEGE AND THE WORKPLACE**

- In a *chemistry lab report,* you describe the odor and appearance of a substance made by combining two chemicals.
- In an *art history class,* you visit a local gallery, choose a painting, and describe in a two-page paper the artist's use of line or color.
- As a *nurse* at a local treatment center for burn victims, you record on each patient's medical chart the overall appearance of and change in second- and third-degree burns.

What Are the Characteristics of a Description?

Successful descriptions offer readers more than just a list of sensory details or a catalog of characteristics. In a good description, the details work together to create a dominant effect or impression.

Description Uses Sensory Details

Sensory details appeal to one or more of the five senses—sight, sound, smell, taste, and touch—and help your readers experience the object, sensation, event, or person you are describing.

Sight. When you describe what something looks like, you help your reader create a mental picture of the subject. In the following excerpt, notice how Loren Eiseley uses visual detail—shape, color, action—and specific nouns and noun phrases to describe what he comes across in a field.

One day as I cut across the field which at that time extended on one side

noun phrase

Noun and noun phrases   of our suburban shopping center, I found a giant slug feeding from a

noun   adjective   noun phrase

Descriptive adjectives of   funnel of pink ice cream in an abandoned Dixie cup. I could see his
shape and color

active verbs   noun   adjective

Active verbs and adverbs   eyes telescope and protrude in a kind of dim, uncertain ecstasy as his dark
depicting motion

active verbs   adjective

body bunched and elongated in the curve of the cup.

—Loren Eiseley, "The Brown Wasps"

This description allows the reader to imagine the slug eating the ice cream in a way that a bare statement of the facts—"On my way to the mall, I saw a slug in a paper cup"—would not.

Sound. Sound can also be a powerful descriptive tool. Can you "hear" the engines in the following description?

adjective   adjective   adjective

Descriptive adjectives   They were one-cylinder and two-cylinder engines, and some were make-and-

adjective   adjective

break and some were jump-spark, but they all made a sleepy sound across the

active verbs   adjective   active verb

Active verbs used to evoke   lake. The one-lungers throbbed and fluttered, and the twin-cylinder ones *purred*
specific sounds; some are
onomatopoetic—they sound   active verb
like what they describe   and *purred*, and that was a quiet sound too.

—E. B. White, "Once More to the Lake"

Smell. Smells are sometimes difficult to describe, partly because the English language does not have as many adjectives for smells as it does for sights and sounds. Smell can be an effective descriptive device, however, as shown here.

Driving through farm country at summer sunset provides a cavalcade

nouns

of smells: manure, cut grass, honeysuckle, spearmint, wheat

Nouns used to evoke distinct   chaff, scallions, chicory, tar from the macadam road.
odors

—Diane Ackerman, *A Natural History of the Senses*

Notice how Diane Ackerman lists nouns that evoke distinct odors and leaves it to the reader to imagine how they smell.

Taste.   Words that evoke the sense of taste can make descriptions lively. Consider this restaurant critic's description of Vietnamese cuisine.

adjectives

In addition to balancing the primary flavors—the sweet, sour, bitter, salty   Descriptive adjectives of taste

and peppery tastes whose sensations are, in the ancient Chinese system,

directly related to physical and spiritual health—medicinal herbs were used in

most dishes. . . . For instance, the orange-red annatto seed is used for its "cooling"

adjective

effect as well as for the mildly tangy flavor it lends and the orange color it

imparts.

—Molly O'Neill, "Vietnam's Cuisine: Echoes of Empires"

Touch.   Annie Dillard's descriptions of texture, temperature, and weight allow a reader not only to visualize but also to experience what it feels like to hold a Polyphemus moth cocoon:

adjective

We passed the cocoon around; it was heavy. As we held it in our hands, the   Descriptive adjectives of weight and texture

active verbs

creature within warmed and squirmed. We were delighted, and wrapped it   Active verbs conveying temperature and motion

active verb & adverb   adjective   noun

tighter in our fists. The pupa began to jerk violently, in heart-stopping knocks.   Nouns and noun phrases

noun   adjective   nouns and noun phrases

Who's there? I can still feel those thumps, urgent through a muffling of spun

noun   noun

silk and leaf, urgent through the swaddling of many years, against the curve of

my palm.

—Annie Dillard, *Pilgrim at Tinker Creek*

Description Uses Active Verbs and Varied Sentences

Sensory details are often best presented through active, vivid verbs. In fact, active verbs are often more effective than adverbs in creating striking and lasting impressions, as the following example demonstrates.

For more on using active verbs, see Chapter 9.

adverb

Original   The team captain *proudly* accepted the award.

verb   verb

Revised   The team captain marched to the podium, grasped the trophy,

verb

and saluted his teammates.

Using varied sentences also contributes to the effective expression of sensory details. Be sure to use different types and patterns of sentences and to vary their lengths.

EXERCISE 12.1	USING SENSORY DETAILS, ACTIVE VERBS, AND VARIED SENTENCES

Using sensory details, active verbs, and varied sentences, describe one of the common objects in the following list or one of your own choosing. Do not name the object in your description. Exchange papers with a classmate. Your reader should be able to guess the item you are describing from the details you provide.

1. A piece of clothing
2. A food item
3. An appliance
4. A plant
5. An animal

Description Creates a Dominant Impression

For more on thesis statements, see Chapter 5.

An effective description leaves the reader with a **dominant impression**—an overall attitude, mood, or feeling about the subject. The impression may be awe, inspiration, anger, or distaste, for example.

Let's suppose that you are writing about an old storage box you found in your parents' attic. The aspect of the box you want to emphasize (your *slant*, *angle*, or *perspective*) is memories of childhood. Given this slant, you might describe the box in several ways, each of which would convey a different dominant impression.

- "A box filled with treasures from my childhood brought back memories of long, sunny afternoons playing in our backyard."
- "Opening the box was like lifting the lid of a time machine, revealing toys and games from another era."
- "When I opened the box, I was eight years old again, fighting over my favorite doll with my twin sister, Erica."

Notice that each example provides a different impression of the box's contents and would require a different type of support. That is, only selected objects from within the box would be relevant to each impression. Note, too, that in all of these examples, the dominant impression is stated directly in a thesis statement rather than implied.

To write an effective description, select details carefully, including only those that contribute to the dominant impression you are trying to create. Notice that Dillard, in the paragraph above, does not clutter her description by describing the physical appearance of the cocoon. Instead, she focuses on its movement and how it feels in her hand.

EXERCISE 12.2 ▶ **FOCUSING THE DOMINANT IMPRESSION**

As you read the following paragraph, cross out details that do not contribute to the dominant impression.

> All morning I had had a vague sense that bad news was on its way. As I stepped outside, the heat of the summer sun, unusually oppressive for ten o'clock, seemed to sear right through me. In fact, now that I think about it, everything seemed slightly out of kilter that morning. The car, which had been newly painted the week before, had stalled several times. The flowers in the garden, planted for me by my husband, purchased from a nursery down the road, were drooping. It was as though they were wilting before they even had a chance to grow. Even my two cats, who look like furry puffballs, moved listlessly across the room, ignoring my invitation to play. It was then that I received the phone call from the emergency room telling me about my son's accident.

Description Uses Connotative Language Effectively

As noted in Chapter 3, most words have two levels of meaning: denotative and connotative. The *denotation* of a word is its precise dictionary meaning. Often, however, feelings and attitudes—emotional colorings or shades of meaning—are also associated with a word. These are the word's *connotations*.

Word	Denotation	Connotations
Flag	A piece of cloth used as a national emblem	patriotism, love, and respect for one's country

As you write, be careful to select words with connotations that strengthen the dominant impression you are creating.

For more on connotation versus denotation, see Chapter 3.

Description Uses Comparisons

Comparing the person or object you are describing to something your readers are familiar with can help them visualize your subject. Several types of comparisons are used in descriptive writing: similes, metaphors, personification, and analogies.

For more on simile, metaphor, personification, and analogy, see Chapter 3.

Figure of Speech	Definition	Example
Simile	a direct comparison introduced by words such as *like* or *as*	*His lips were as soft as a rosebud's petals.*
Metaphor	an indirect comparison describing one thing as if it were another	*. . . his rosebud lips . . .*
Personification	a comparison that gives human qualities or characteristics to an inanimate object	*The television screen stared back at me.*

> **EXERCISE 12.3**   APPEALING TO THE SENSES
>
> Write a paragraph describing an animal or pet. Focus on one sense or appeal to several. If possible, include a simile or a metaphor.

Description Follows a Method of Organization

For more on methods of organization, see Chapter 7.

Effective descriptions must follow a clear method of organization. Three common methods of organization used in descriptive writing are spatial order, chronological order, and most-to-least or least-to-most order.

- When you use **spatial order**, you describe a subject from top to bottom, from left to right, from near to far away, or from a central point outward. For example, if you are describing a college campus, you might start by describing a building at the center of the campus—the library, perhaps—and then move to surrounding buildings.

  In writing a description using spatial order, you can use either a fixed or a moving **vantage point**. With a fixed vantage point, you describe what you see from a particular position. With a moving vantage point, you describe your subject from different positions. A fixed vantage point is like a stationary camera trained on a subject from one direction. A moving vantage point is like a hand-held camera that captures the subject from many directions.
- **Chronological order** works well when you need to describe events or changes that occur over a period of time. You might use chronological order to describe the changes in a puppy's behavior as it grows or to relate changing patterns of light and shadow as the sun sets.
- You might use either **most-to-least** or **least-to-most order** to describe the smells in a flower garden or the sounds of an orchestra tuning up for a concert.
- Clustering details by the **five senses**—how your subject looks, sounds, smells, tastes, and feels—might make sense for a topic such as a hot fudge sundae or a delicious meal at a restaurant.

The following readings demonstrate the techniques discussed above for writing effective descriptive essays. The first reading is annotated to point out how Rachel Maizes uses these techniques to make the depiction of her dog, Chance, come alive. As you read the second essay, try to identify for yourself how the writer uses the techniques of descriptive writing to help readers imagine the Dreamland pool as it was to residents of Portsmouth, Ohio, in its prosperous past.

Bad Dog

Rachel Maizes

Rachel Maizes is an attorney, a writer, and a dog lover who currently lives in Boulder, Colorado. Her essay "Bad Dog" was published in the "My Story" section of *The New York Times* online in September 2013.

Before Reading

1. **Preview:** Use the steps listed on page 28.
2. **Connect:** Have you ever had a bad dog or known someone who did? What behaviors made the dog bad?

While Reading Pay close attention to how the writer appeals to the senses in the description of her "bad dog."

© Jill Bielawski

1 My dog, Chance, is old. White fur circles his eyes, coats his muzzle, sprouts between his toes. Although still alive, he looks like a ghost. He used to stand like a champion, his chest and muzzle forward, his hind legs back. Now he can hardly support himself when he sits, balancing precariously like a pile of kindling propped against itself.

Sensory details: Appeals to the reader's sense of sight

Comparisons: Uses similes to compare Chance with a ghost, a champion

2 He takes an anti-inflammatory medication for arthritis and pumpkin for constipation and fish oil and glucosamine for his joints and mind, though it may be too late for the latter. He walks an endless circuit between the guest room and bedroom and master bath searching for what I don't know. When he tires, he lies next to me as I work. Sometimes he groans.

3 I think about what it means to have cared for Chance for most of his life. It confirms that I, too, am growing older. I turned 50 a few months ago. Overnight, wiry gray hair has sprouted at my temples. Always a theater buff, now I attend matinees. My back stiffens after weeding. In the mirror, I see a face rearranged by gravity's heavy hand. I remember Chance as a gangly puppy with floppy ears. I keep a picture of myself as a young woman, a 20-something with spiky hair, my arm around my mother, now dead 10 years. A dog's life is shorter than ours, but ours is, as the Talmud says, "k'heref aiyen," like the blink of an eye.

Comparison: Uses comparison to highlight author's identification with Chance

4 Chance's fur is long and mats easily. I brush it, collecting thick, webby piles. My second husband, Steve, saved the fur of a dog he once owned and a friend wove it into cloth. It's one of the things I love about Steve, the over-the-top affection he

Sensory details: Appeals to reader's sense of sight, touch bestows on animals. I toss Chance's hair into the trash or scatter it outside for birds to install in their nests.

Fourteen years ago my ex-husband and I adopted Chance from a shelter. He was a 4-month-old puppy, an Australian Shepherd mix, with brindle fur. We had another dog, Tilly, a 2-year-old black Lab, who trained him. When we told Chance to sit, he glanced at Tilly and followed her lead. We crated Chance, as the shelter recommended, keeping him in an enclosure for brief periods of time to housebreak him and give him a sense of security. Once I left him in the crate for several hours. I returned to find him trembling, squeezed into a corner of the crate to avoid the puddles and piles he had made. No emergency had kept me. I had been chatting with a friend and time got away. It wasn't the only time I failed Chance. It was easy to fail him, a mere dog, who couldn't insist that I return, who couldn't even embarrass me by telling the story.

When Chance turned 2 he became aggressive. He growled at other dogs and bared his teeth. He flattened puppies under his heavy paws. He chased children and cyclists, clamped down on their ankles and knocked them over. He even bit Tilly in a scuffle over my bed.

When I tired of apologizing for him, I hired a trainer. She told me his aggression was set off by fear. She said to keep him away from unfamiliar dogs and people, for their sake and his.

I fled when other dogs approached. If I was distracted and we crossed paths with another dog, I ordered Chance to sit and rewarded him with meaty treats if he stayed calm. Most days he preferred the fight. He hurled himself at the other dog, barely restrained by the leash. He barked furiously, drowning out my attempt to explain to the other dog's owner, "Chance doesn't like to socialize."

I didn't know when I adopted Chance that puppies need to interact with other dogs to learn social cues. A well-socialized dog employs a soft growl to tell another dog "you're in my space." A puppy who interacts with a variety of other dogs learns to roughhouse in a playful, rather than a threatening, way. Chance had Tilly for company and I mistakenly thought that was enough. I was depressed and in a bad marriage. Nothing got me off the couch. By the time I started taking better care of myself and walking the dogs every day, it was too late.

I divorced my first husband and the dogs took care of me. Chance made me feel safe in a large, empty house. Tilly shared my bed, resting her head on my ex-husband's pillow. But I hated being the owner of a bad dog. I felt ashamed turning away someone whose dog wanted to play and telling a schoolchild she couldn't pet Chance. I lived in constant fear of him attacking someone.

Yet in some ways, I am the perfect owner for Chance. An introvert, I identify with his desire to be left alone. I empathize with his feelings of jealousy. When Steve and I married and Tilly transferred her loyalty to him, lying at his feet instead of mine, I could hardly suppress my rage.

It's easy to love a well-behaved dog. It's harder to love Chance, with his bristly personality and tendency toward violence. Yet in the end, I measure the success of my relationship with Chance by its challenges, because if I can't love him at his most imperfect what use is love?

Margin annotations:

Dominant impression: Uses anecdote to reinforce main idea

Organization: Uses transition to suggest chronological organization

Sensory details: Appeals to reader's sense of sound, sight, touch

Active verbs: Uses striking verbs to present details

Dominant impression: Uses anecdote to reinforce main idea

Paragraph numbers: 5, 6, 7, 8, 9, 10, 11, 12

A few years ago, an old yellow Lab got loose. The dog lunged at Chance, sinking 13
his teeth into the soft flesh of his throat. He bit his head and tore at his face. The
Lab foamed, reveling in the attack. I kept hold of Chance's leash and screamed at
the owner, but she was frozen. I didn't see how Chance could survive multiple,
vicious bites.

Connotation: Chooses words with powerful connotations

Finally, the owner pulled the Lab off by his hind legs. Chance whimpered. He 14
hadn't fought back. What saved him were the other dog's teeth, so worn by age
they were mostly ineffective. Chance's teeth were sharp and he was young and
strong. Why had he held back? Perhaps he wasn't such a bad dog after all.

In his old age Chance has mellowed. When we walk, he attends to what is 15
directly in front of him, a flagpole or a mailbox, barely sensing other dogs. It takes
us 40 minutes to go around the block, but when I look at him he grins. It's his
favorite time of day and mine.

I try to be gentle with Chance, hoping when the time comes others will be 16
gentle with me. When I catch myself tugging his leash, I remind myself these are
his last days and to enjoy them. The night before Tilly died she tried to get my
attention, resting her muzzle on my keyboard. I moved her aside. I was busy writing and I thought there would be time to play, not knowing her cancer would take
a dramatic turn in the morning and we would have to euthanize her.

Comparison: Uses comparison to show that the author identifies with Chance

Dominant impression: Uses anecdote to reinforce main idea

I often think back to that night, wishing I had cuddled and cradled my girl. I 17
hope not to make the same mistake with Chance. Steve scratches his belly every
night before we go to bed. Chance deserves at least as much from me.

He is, after all, my good dog. 18

Visualize a Description: Create a Graphic Organizer

Seeing the content and structure of an essay in simplified, visual form can help you
analyze a reading, recall key images as you generate ideas for an essay, and structure
your own writing. Graphic Organizer 12.1 (p. 270) diagrams the basic structure of a
descriptive essay. When you write an essay in which your primary purpose is to describe
something, you will need to follow the standard essay format—title, introduction,
body, and conclusion—with slight adaptations and adjustments.

For more on creating a graphic organizer, see pp. 35–37.

- The **introduction** should provide a context for the description and present the
  thesis statement, which states or suggests the dominant impression.
- The **body** of the essay should present sensory details that support the dominant
  impression.
- The **conclusion** draws the description to a close and makes a final reference to
  the dominant impression. It may offer a final detail or make a closing statement.

When you incorporate a description into an essay in which you also use other patterns of development, you will probably need to condense or eliminate one or more of
the elements of your descriptive essay.

GRAPHIC ORGANIZER 12.1 The Basic Structure of a Descriptive Essay

Title

Introduction → Background / Setting / Dominant impression (stated or suggested in thesis)

↓

Supporting details

↓

Sensory Details and Comparisons → Supporting details

↓

Supporting details

↓

Conclusion → Reference to a dominant impression / Draws essay to a close

READING

Dreamland, Portsmouth, Ohio

Sam Quinones

Sam Quinones is a freelance journalist, a former *Los Angeles Times* reporter, and a storyteller. The selection here is from his most recent book, *Dreamland: The True Tale of America's Opiate Epidemic* (2015). **Before reading,** preview and make connections by thinking of a special place or experience that lives within your memory. What makes it so special? **While reading,** highlight the details that help you visualize Dreamland, and study Graphic Organizer 12.2 on page 273.

In 1929, three decades into what were the great years for the blue-collar town of Portsmouth, on the Ohio River, a private swimming pool opened and they called it Dreamland. The pool was the size of a football field. Over the decades, generations of the town grew up at the edge of its crystal-blue water.

Dreamland was the summer babysitter. Parents left their children at the pool every day. Townsfolk found respite from the thick humidity at Dreamland and then went across the street to the A&W stand for hot dogs and root beer. The pool's french fries were the best around. Kids took the bus to the pool in the morning,

1

2

and back home in the afternoon. They came from schools all over Scioto County and met each other and learned to swim. Some of them competed on the Dreamland Dolphins swim team, which practiced every morning and evening. WIOI, the local radio station, knowing so many of its listeners were sunbathing next to their transistor radios at Dreamland, would broadcast a jingle—"Time to turn so you won't burn"—every half hour.

The vast pool had room in the middle for two concrete platforms, from which   3
kids sunned themselves then dove back in. Poles topped with floodlights rose from the platforms for swimming at night. On one side of the pool was an immense lawn where families set their towels. On the opposite side were locker rooms and a restaurant.

Dreamland could fit hundreds of people, and yet, magically, the space around   4
it kept growing and there was always room for more. Jaime Williams, the city treasurer, owned the pool for years. Williams was part owner of one of the shoe factories that were at the core of Portsmouth's industrial might. He bought more and more land, and for years Dreamland seemed to just get better. A large picnic area was added, and playgrounds for young children. Then fields for softball and football, and courts for basketball and shuffleboard, and a video arcade.

For a while, to remain white only, the pool became a private club and the   5
name changed to the Terrace Club. But Portsmouth was a largely integrated town. Its chief of police was black. Black and white kids went to the same schools. Only the pool remained segregated. Then, in the summer of 1961, a black boy named Eugene McKinley drowned in the Scioto River, where he was swimming because he was kept out of the pool. The Portsmouth NAACP pushed back, held a wade-in, and quietly they integrated the pool. With integration, the pool was rechristened Dreamland, though blacks were never made to feel particularly comfortable there.

Dreamland did wash away class distinctions, though. In a swimming suit, a   6
factory worker looked no different from the factory manager or clothing-shop owner. Wealthy families on Portsmouth's hilltop donated money to a fund that would go to pay for summer passes for families from the town's East End, down between the tracks and the Ohio River. East End river rats and upscale hilltoppers all met at Dreamland.

California had its beaches. Heartland America spent its summers at swim-   7
ming pools, and, down at a far end of Ohio, Dreamland took on an outsized importance to the town of Portsmouth. A family's season pass was only twenty-five dollars, and this was a prized possession often given as a Christmas present. Kids whose families couldn't afford that could cut a neighbor's grass for the fifteen cents that a daily pool pass cost.

Friday swim dances began at midnight. They hauled out a jukebox and kids   8
spent the night twisting by the pool. Couples announced new romances by walking hand in hand around Dreamland. Girls walked home from those dances and families left their doors unlocked. "The heat of the evening combined with the cool water was wonderful," one woman remembered. "It was my entire world. I did nothing else. As I grew up and had my own children, I took them, too."

In fact, the cycle of life in Portsmouth was repeated over and over at Dream- 9
land. A toddler spent her first years at the shallow end watched by her parents,
particularly her mother, who sat on a towel on the concrete near the water
with other young moms. When the child left elementary school, she migrated
out to the middle section of Dreamland as her parents retreated to the grass.
By high school, she was hanging out on the grass around the pool's ten-foot
deep end, near the high dive and the head lifeguard's chair, and her parents
were far away. When she married and had children, she returned to the shallow
end of Dreamland to watch over her own children, and the whole thing began
again.

"My father, a Navy Vet from World War II, insisted that his four children learn 10
not only how to swim but how not to be afraid of water," one man wrote. "My
younger sister jumped off the fifteen-foot high diving board at age three. Yes, my
father, myself and brother were in the water just in case. Sister pops up out of the
water and screams . . . 'Again!'"

For many years, Dreamland's manager, Chuck Lorentz, a Portsmouth High 11
School coach and strict disciplinarian, walked the grounds with a yardstick, making sure teenagers minded his "three-foot rule" and stayed that far apart. He
wasn't that successful. It seems half the town got their first kiss at the pool, and
plenty lost their virginity in Dreamland's endless grass.

Lorentz's son, meanwhile, learned to swim before he could walk and 12
became a Dreamland lifeguard in high school. "To be the lifeguard in that chair,
you were right in the center of all the action, all the strutting, all the flirting,"
said John Lorentz, now a retired history professor. "You were like a king on a
throne."

sbk_20d pictures/Moment Select/Getty Images

Memories of Dream- 13
land, drenched in the smell
of chlorine, Coppertone,
and french fries, were what
almost everyone who grew
up in Portsmouth took with
them as the town declined.

Two Portsmouths 14
exist today. One is a town
of abandoned buildings at
the edge of the Ohio River.
The other resides in the
memories of thousands in
the town's diaspora who
grew up during its better
years and return to the
actual Portsmouth rarely, if
at all. When you ask them
what the town was back
then, it was Dreamland.

EXERCISE 12.4   DRAWING A GRAPHIC ORGANIZER

Using Graphic Organizer 12.1 or 12.2 as a basis, draw a graphic organizer for "Bad Dog" (pp. 267–69).

GRAPHIC ORGANIZER 12.2   The Structure of "Dreamland, Portsmouth, Ohio"

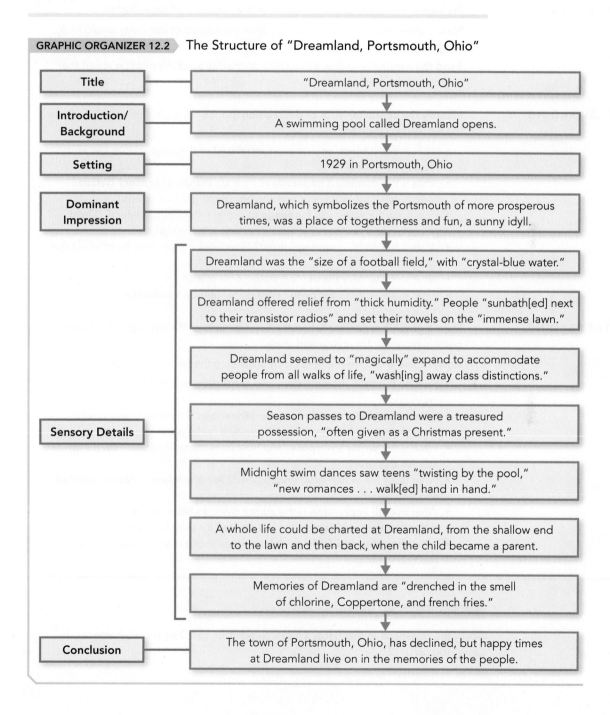

Title	"Dreamland, Portsmouth, Ohio"
Introduction/Background	A swimming pool called Dreamland opens.
Setting	1929 in Portsmouth, Ohio
Dominant Impression	Dreamland, which symbolizes the Portsmouth of more prosperous times, was a place of togetherness and fun, a sunny idyll.
Sensory Details	Dreamland was the "size of a football field," with "crystal-blue water."
	Dreamland offered relief from "thick humidity." People "sunbath[ed] next to their transistor radios" and set their towels on the "immense lawn."
	Dreamland seemed to "magically" expand to accommodate people from all walks of life, "wash[ing] away class distinctions."
	Season passes to Dreamland were a treasured possession, "often given as a Christmas present."
	Midnight swim dances saw teens "twisting by the pool," "new romances . . . walk[ed] hand in hand."
	A whole life could be charted at Dreamland, from the shallow end to the lawn and then back, when the child became a parent.
	Memories of Dreamland are "drenched in the smell of chlorine, Coppertone, and french fries."
Conclusion	The town of Portsmouth, Ohio, has declined, but happy times at Dreamland live on in the memories of the people.

THE READING PROCESS	STRATEGIES
BEFORE READING	**Preview** the essay to get an overview of the content and organization.
	Make connections by thinking about what the subject of the essay would look, sound, taste, smell, or feel like.
	Read the headnote (if one is provided) for background information about the author and the reading.
WHILE READING	**Identify the characteristics of description** (pp. 261–66). Be sure you can answer the following questions:
	• What is the **subject**, and on what **aspects(s)** of the subject does the essay focus?
	• What is the **dominant impression**? How do individual **sensory details** contribute to the dominant impression? (Highlight key details.)
	• How does the writer use **language** to achieve the desired effect? (Circle powerful word choices or place a checkmark in the margin.)
	• What is the author's **vantage point**? How does the vantage point affect the description?
	• What is the writer's **thesis**? Is it stated or implied?
	• What is the author's **purpose**? Who is the intended **audience**?
AFTER READING	Draw a **graphic organizer** listing the key elements of the description. (Use your graphic organizer for review and study.)
	Analyze and evaluate the reading by answering the following questions.
	• How do the **title**, **introduction**, and **conclusion** hint at the dominant impression?
	• What is the **writer's attitude** toward the subject? (Highlight words with strong connotations that reveal the writer's feelings.)
	• What is the **writer's purpose**, and how does the description help the writer achieve this goal?
	• What does the writer leave undescribed? Are any relevant **details omitted**, and if so, why?
	• What **overall impression** is the author trying to leave readers with?
	• Is the description **objective**, or is it **slanted** (or even biased)?
	• What **thoughts and feelings** did the essay evoke in you? (Explain your reaction in detail.)

EXERCISE 12.5 ▶ READING CRITICALLY

Apply the questions in the "How Writers Read" box to "Dreamland, Portsmouth, Ohio" (pp. 270–72).

Integrate Description into an Essay

Sometimes description alone fulfills the purpose of an essay. In most cases, however, you will use description in essays that mainly rely on a different mode. For instance, in a narrative essay, description helps readers experience events, reconstruct scenes, and visualize action. Although most of your college essays will not be primarily descriptive, you can use description in essays that explain the causes or effects of a phenomenon, compare or contrast animal species, or illustrate defensive behavior in children, for example.

The essay "Underground Lair: Inside a Chicken Processing Plant" later in this chapter (pp. 289–93) uses multiple patterns of development to convey the author's ideas.

Here are a few suggestions for combining description effectively with other patterns of development.

1. **Include only relevant details.** Whether you describe an event, a person, or a scene, the sensory details you choose should enhance the reader's understanding of your subject.
2. **Keep the description focused.** Select enough details to make your essential points and dominant impression clear. Readers may become impatient if you include too many descriptive details.
3. **Make sure the description fits the essay's tone and point of view.** A personal description, for example, is not appropriate in an essay explaining a technical process.

PREWRITING 〉 ORGANIZING & DRAFTING 〉 **REVISING**   EDITING & PROOFREADING

A Guided Writing Assignment *

> ## DESCRIPTION

Your Essay Assignment

Write a descriptive essay about something you can picture clearly or that you can readily observe. Choose one of the following to describe in detail.

- an unusual, striking, or surprising object
- a place that has significance to you, your family, or your cultural group
- a person who influenced you (for good or ill)

Examples: A robot you built from a kit; a playground you hung around in as a child; a teacher who changed your expectations about school or learning.

---

* The writing process is *recursive*; that is, you may find yourself revising as you draft or prewriting as you revise. This is especially true when writing on a computer. Your writing process may also differ from project to project or from that of your classmates.

1 Select a topic from the list on the previous page, or create your own.

Use one or more of the following suggestions to choose a subject to describe.

1. **List one or more broad topics**, such as *An Unusual Object, A Place with Personal Significance*, or *An Influential Person*. Then alone or with another student, **brainstorm a list of objects, activities,** or **people** that fit the assignment. Other prewriting strategies, like freewriting or questioning, may also help you generate topic ideas. (Rational, pragmatic, and concrete learners may prefer listing. Creative, emotional, and abstract learners may prefer freewriting or questioning.)

2. **Picture the objects in your room** or on your desk and ask yourself questions, such as, "Who gave me that object?" or "Why did I buy [or make] it?" (Spatial, creative, or emotional learners may prefer picturing.)

3. **Work backward:** Think about the most influential people or most important values in your life, and then think about a place or object that represents them in your mind. (Abstract and independent learners may prefer working backward.)

2 Consider your purpose and audience, and choose a perspective and point of view.

Ask yourself these questions.

• Will my essay's **purpose** be to **express myself**, **inform**, or **persuade**?

• Who is my **audience**? Will readers need any **background information** to understand my essay? Have I chosen a person, place, or thing that I can write about honestly for this audience?

• What **point of view** best suits my purpose and audience? The first person (*I, we*) will work best if describing an object with personal significance or if your purpose is expressive; third person (*it, they, he/she*) will be most appropriate if describing something objectively, of if your purpose is informative.

3 Choose an aspect of your subject to emphasize, and collect sensory details.

Choose one trait or aspect of your subject to focus on.

If it's a . . .	try focusing on . . .
person	a character trait
thing	its usefulness, value, or beauty

Then record details that support the slant you have chosen.

1. **Describe your subject to a friend**, concentrating on the slant you have chosen, and make notes on your comments and your friend's response.

2. **Draw a quick sketch** of your subject and label the parts.

3. **Make a table** and label each section with one of the senses. Then list the sensory details associated with your subject.

Generate comparisons. Think of appropriate comparisons—**similes**, **metaphors**, **personifications**—for as many details in your list as possible. Then select the one or two strongest comparisons and try to use them in your essay. Use at least two prewriting strategies to generate details. (More prewriting strategies appear in Chapter 4, pp. 107–17.)

Evaluate your details.

Reread your notes, highlighting the **vivid**, **concrete details** that will create pictures in your reader's mind. Cross out the following.

- vague details
- irrelevant details
- details that do not support your slant

Then copy and paste the remaining details into a new document for easy access when drafting.

In small groups, share your ideas and details.

1. Have each writer **explain her or his slant** on the subject and **provide a list of details**.
2. As a group, **evaluate each writer's details** in terms of her or his slant and suggest improvements.

5 Create a dominant impression.

Your **dominant impression** should:

- appeal to **your audience**
- offer an **unusual perspective**
- provide **new insights** on your subject

Description often includes an element of surprise; a description with an unexpected slant and new insights is more likely to engage the readers' imagination.

Think of the dominant impression as:

1. **a thesis** that conveys your main point and pulls your details together.
2. **a mood or feeling about the subject**, which all the details in your essay explain or support.

Team up with a classmate to evaluate each other's dominant impression. Underline or highlight any problematic wording and give feedback.

Choose a method of organization.

Select the **method of organization** that will best support your dominant impression. For example:

- If you are focusing on a person's slovenly appearance, then a **spatial** (top to bottom, left to right) organization may be effective. If using spatial organization, also consider what **vantage point(s)** will provide the most useful information or from which vantage point(s) you can provide the most revealing or striking details.
- If you are describing a visit to a wildlife preserve, **chronological** order might be a useful method of organization.
- A **most-to-least** or **least-to-most** arrangement might work best for a description of the symptoms of pneumonia.
- If you are describing a chocolate chip cookie, you may want to organize by the **five senses**, clustering details about how it looks, smells, tastes, and feels in your mouth.

7 Write a first draft of your descriptive essay.

Use the following guidelines to keep your narrative on track.

- The **introduction** should set up your **dominant impression**, which you may choose to state in a thesis.
- The **body paragraphs** should include **striking sensory details** that support your **dominant impression**. Be sure to include **enough details** that readers can picture your subject but not so many that readers will get bored. Try to work your one or two strongest comparisons into your draft. Organize each body paragraph so that it focuses on a **single topic**, and use **transitions** (*first, next, above, below, before, after*) to make relationships among details clear. You may want to include a **photograph** (or video or audio file if presenting your description online), but remember that an illustration cannot substitute for a detailed, sensory description.
- The **conclusion** should **revisit your dominant impression**. You may also want to refer to the beginning of your essay or make a final observation about the significance of your subject.

8 Evaluate your draft and revise as necessary.

Use **Figure 12.1, "Flowchart for Revising a Descriptive Essay,"** to help you discover the strengths and weaknesses of your descriptive essay.

FIGURE 12.1 Flowchart for Revising a Descriptive Essay

QUESTIONS		REVISION STRATEGIES

1. Without looking at your essay, *state* the dominant impression in a sentence. Then highlight the sentences that express the *dominant impression*. Do they successfully convey the impression?

 NO ▶

- Reread your essay. Make a list of the different impressions it conveys.
- Choose one impression that you have the most to say about, and brainstorm to develop additional details that support it.

 YES ▼

2. Place a ✔ by each sensory detail. Does each detail support your *dominant impression*?

 NO ▶

- Eliminate irrelevant sensory details.

 YES ▼

3. Highlight your sensory details. Is your language vivid enough to help readers visualize the topic? Are the connotations of your language appropriate?

 NO ▶

- Brainstorm additional sensory details.
- Replace passive verbs with active ones.
- Vary your sentences.
- Replace vague or inappropriate words with words that better support your dominant impression.

 YES ▼

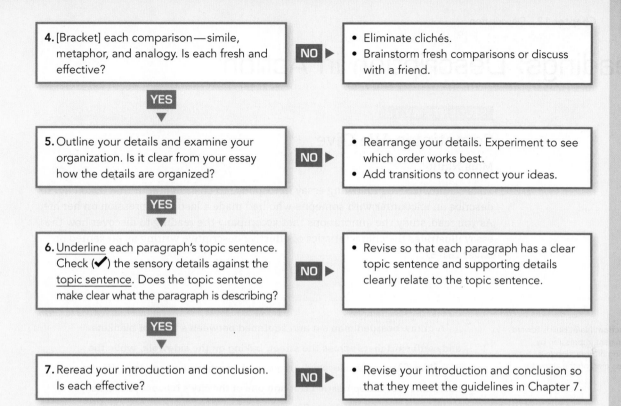

4. [Bracket] each comparison—simile, metaphor, and analogy. Is each fresh and effective?

NO ▶
- Eliminate clichés.
- Brainstorm fresh comparisons or discuss with a friend.

YES ▼

5. Outline your details and examine your organization. Is it clear from your essay how the details are organized?

NO ▶
- Rearrange your details. Experiment to see which order works best.
- Add transitions to connect your ideas.

YES ▼

6. <u>Underline</u> each paragraph's topic sentence. Check (✔) the sensory details against the <u>topic sentence</u>. Does the topic sentence make clear what the paragraph is describing?

NO ▶
- Revise so that each paragraph has a clear topic sentence and supporting details clearly relate to the topic sentence.

YES ▼

7. Reread your introduction and conclusion. Is each effective?

NO ▶
- Revise your introduction and conclusion so that they meet the guidelines in Chapter 7.

9 Edit and proofread your essay.

Refer to Chapter 9 for help with:

- **editing sentences** to avoid wordiness, making your verb choices strong and active, and making your sentences clear, varied, and parallel
- **editing words** for tone and diction, connotation, and concrete and specific language

Pay particular attention to the **punctuation of adjectives.**

1. Use a comma between **coordinate adjectives** that are not joined by *and*.

   – **Singh was a *confident, skilled* pianist.**

   Coordinate adjectives are a series of adjectives whose order can be changed (*skilled, confident* pianist or *confident, skilled* pianist).

2. Do not use commas between **cumulative adjectives** whose order cannot be changed.

   – **Two *frightened brown* eyes peered at us from under the sofa.**

   You would not write *frightened two brown* eyes.

3. Use a hyphen to connect two words that work together as an adjective before a noun *unless* the first word is an adverb ending in *-ly*.

   – **well-used** book

   – **foil-wrapped** pizza

   – **perfectly thrown** pass

Readings: Description in Action

Sometimes, We Give

Maia Nault

Maia Nault wrote the following essay in response to an assignment that asked her to describe an encounter with someone who had made a lasting impression on her life. As you read, study the annotations that accompany the reading to discover how the essay illustrates the characteristics of effective descriptive writing as presented on pages 261–67.

Introduction: Nault builds toward her dominant impression by describing her reaction to a homeless man on the sidewalk

Dominant impression: Thesis identifies the topic of the description.

Sensory details: Appeals to the reader's sense of sight and touch

Comparison: Uses comparison and simile to add humor and realism to visual details.

A grimy, bearded man sat and squirmed between a heap of blankets and cardboard mats across the street, baking on the sidewalk, while the sun glared down mercilessly during one of summer's hottest days. Heavy, lunchtime foot traffic bustled through one of the city's busiest plazas as everyone hurried from their offices to the chilled, air-conditioned relief of their destinations. The air was thick and uncomfortable, full of car exhaust fumes and the smell of sweat, but I stood unmoving in the middle of the plaza. I ignored the people shoving past me, and stared worriedly at the homeless man across the street. No one was stopping to help him. I had never interacted with a homeless person before—what was the right thing to do? My options swam in panicked circles through my mind, and my eyes darted nervously from the homeless man to the passing crowds. That day, I was called upon to make decisions that would test my character. 1

From the minute I clambered out of bed, I knew that it was going to be a difficult day. I slept through my alarm, didn't have time for breakfast, and forgot to pack my lunch the night before. On top of that, I managed to set myself up for a wardrobe malfunction. My pencil skirt was wrinkled, a hole the size of my dog's face had somehow materialized in the armpit of my blouse, and I donned my go-to black flats without putting on a pair of socks to help my feet breathe. It was the fourth day of my internship, and I was desperate to make a good impression, though I 2 seemed to be failing miserably. My sweaty toes squelched together in my flats, which were more like swimming pools by the time I got to work that morning. I could feel the makeup melting on my face, and my hair felt like a frizzy rat's nest on top of my head. I was a disheveled mess.

I left the office around noon to buy lunch and spotted the homeless man a block away. One look at this crumpled soul in his threadbare, filthy clothes halted my pity party and put things into perspective; I looked and felt like a wreck, but the sunburnt man across the street was surely having a worse day than I was.

Person after person walked past the homeless man, ignoring him completely. I pleaded with myself to do something, but the best I could manage was to drag my slippery feet around the block three times just to end up in the same spot again. I was nervous, stalling for time, and I couldn't figure out why. A different kind of sweat broke out across the nape of my neck and slid down my back as I chewed my nail anxiously. Was I scared of standing out from the crowd? Would people judge me? Did any of that even matter?

Then suddenly a wave of calmness washed over me. I took a slow, steady breath. *No*, I told myself. *None of that matters.* As my jittery mind became still, my legs mobilized. I wanted to do the right thing; I knew what that was because I knew myself.

I am kind. I walked into a nearby grocery store and hoisted a plastic basket onto my shoulder. *I am generous.* I filled my basket with water bottles, bananas, peanut butter, bagels, vitamins, and sunscreen. *I am resolute.* I paid, marched out of the store, clenched my fists tightly around my shopping bags, turned on my sweaty heel, and didn't stop until I was standing half a block from the homeless man. He sat on the sidewalk, leaning with his back against the side of a brick building, wearing a filthy, gray tank-top and dingy cargo pants with rips in the knees. His hair was dirty and wild, barely restrained by a flimsy elastic tie. He wasn't begging; his exposed knees were pulled up to his chest and his head was cradled in his arms, hidden from view. His shoulders shook slightly from quiet sobs but he didn't bother anyone passing him on the sidewalk.

3

Comparison: Uses metaphor and contrast to highlight author's connection with the homeless man

4

Sensory details: Appeals to reader's touch

Dominant impression: Uses questions to support main idea

5   **Comparison:** Uses metaphor

6   **Active verbs:** Uses striking verbs to present details

Dominant impression: Uses adjectives that appeal to the senses to support main idea.

Connotation: Chooses words with powerful connotations

Comparison: Uses personification

Sensory details: Appeals to reader's sense of touch, sight, and sound

I glanced up and down the sidewalk, assuring myself that there weren't any creeps around and that this wasn't going to turn into an ambush. My strategy was a simple one: approach target, complete a quick drop-off, leave target. No chit-chat, no surprises, no wasting time. Unfortunately, that plan dissolved as soon as he dragged his face up from his arms, scrubbed his dusty knuckles across his eyes, and fixed me with a watery gaze. His tears had cut paths through the grime on his face, leaving dark smudges on his cheeks. I imagined that, at some point, he may have had an attractive face. His eyes were tired but a pretty light green color, his long hair was greasy but blonde, and if it weren't for the red, splotchy sunburn, he would have had clear, fair skin. 7

I took a moment to process his features as we looked at one another, when an odd realization struck me. "You're so young," I blurted. I could feel my melting face light up with embarrassment, and he cracked a dry-lipped smile that revealed perfectly straight teeth. "Hello to you, too," he responded. "My name is Michael." His voice sounded a little congested from crying but was mellow and warm, with a pleasant tone that made me believe he enjoyed talking to people. From far away he looked old, grizzly, and emaciated, clinging to the ragged clothes that he must have filled out before hunger took its toll. I realized now that those assumptions were only based on a stereotype. Up close, he looked so different—not quite what I expected a homeless man to look like. He had no wrinkles, and he wasn't skin-and-bones skinny. His face was youthful, though his unkempt beard covered quite a bit of it, and while he was a little on the thin side, he looked healthy and lean. There were no hard lines around his eyes or mouth, and he had big, bright eyes that shone through the sweat and caked-on dirt with a depth of intelligence and curiosity that I didn't expect to see. 8

I learned a little more about Michael each time I visited, every couple of weeks, to drop off more essentials. He was pleasant, with an easygoing disposition and a genuine smile. Our conversations were brief, as I was reluctant to delve too deeply into his life and even more reluctant to give away anything about myself, but he expressed his gratitude for the visits nonetheless. On my third visit, as I was leaving, I learned that Michael was a student about a year ago. His voice quavered 9 as he told me about his studies; he used to be a history student, a junior in college, and he really loved to read. I remember watching his nose turn red and his eyes well up as he told me these things, and I was reminded of the first time I saw him, crying with his knees curled up to his chest. I walked away from him that day realizing that I could have been talking to one of my friends from school. He was my age—a college student—and in another life, he could have been just a regular guy on campus that I bumped into now and then. The thought made my chest tighten and my eyes sting; I couldn't comprehend how this could happen to somebody so young and full of potential.

On my fourth visit, I brought with me a couple of novels from the giveaway pile in our office's kitchen. Michael's smile stretched across his face when I presented him with the books, along with another bag of food, and he reached for them eagerly. His happiness was palpable; tears sprang to his green eyes again and this time, I couldn't help but to cry with him a little bit. He thanked me, so many times, and I waved goodbye as I turned to walk away. My heart felt light and happy, and I was proud of myself for being brave enough to help somebody.

I was a few steps away from Michael when a strong grip on my upper arm and a rough, gravelly voice stopped me. "What about me? Where's my bag?" I craned my head back and stared wide-eyed into the wild, bloodshot eyes of another homeless man. This man was older, more wrinkled and worn down than Michael. He was wearing layer upon layer of ripped, dusty clothes the color of wet cement, and the strong smell of body odor sprung to my nose. I always checked before approaching Michael. How did I not see him? What did I miss? What should I do now?

Before I knew it, I was being pushed aside and shielded from the intruder. In one quick movement, Michael had managed to wedge himself between me and the other man, breaking his hold on my arm. "Leave her alone," he warned firmly.

At least, I think it was a firm warning.

When I think about it now, I try very hard not to romanticize this encounter. Michael was certainly brave to put himself in harm's way for me, but his voice trembled and his eyes and posture lacked the strength

---

Sensory details: Appeals to reader's sense of sight

10 **Organization:** Uses transition to suggest chronological order

Dominant impression: Uses description of feeling to support main idea

11 **Active verbs:** Uses striking verbs to present details

Sensory details: Appeals to reader's sense of sight, smell, and touch

12 **Connotation:** Chooses words with powerful connotations

13

14 **Dominant impression:** Topic sentence focuses on author's feelings about the encounter

and durability that we expect from strong, heroic characters. Michael's voice shook and broke as he told me to leave, to find a cop, and to not come back to this spot for a while. In truth, he didn't seem at all confident in his decision to jump up and rescue me. Michael was not sure how to handle himself, and neither of these men were prepared to fight each other; the intruder had the same scared look on his face that Michael had. In the end, I was protected from one hungry, frightened man by another, equally hungry, frightened man. This wasn't a climactic scene between a hero, villain, and innocent; we were three ordinary people caught in a very sad, confusing situation.

I never saw Michael again. I waited a couple of weeks before one day   15
returning to his spot at lunchtime, but he wasn't there. I left a bag of water bottles and bread on the spot where his cardboard mats and blankets used to be; I came back the following day to see that the bag was gone, but I have no way of knowing whether or not he found it. I think about Michael whenever I pass through that part of town, and I think about all the choices I made that led to that last encounter. We are sometimes called upon to make decisions, and in those weeks, I decided to be so many things: kind, generous, unwavering, frightened, flawed, and brave. I chose to be true to my character and in the end my decision to give, when others wouldn't, helped me, too.

Dominant impression: Uses adjectives to reinforce main idea

Analyzing the Writer's Technique

1. **Dominant Impression** Describe Nault's dominant impression. Is it stated or implied?
2. **Sensory Language** Which examples of sensory language did you find particularly strong and engaging? What makes them effective? Which, if any, are weak, and how can they be improved?
3. **Comparisons** The annotations point out some of the comparisons Nault uses to explain her topic. Identify several others. Which ones are particularly effective? Do any seem ineffective? If so, why?
4. **Patterns** In addition to description, what other patterns of development does the writer use? How do these patterns make the description more effective?

Thinking Critically about Description

1. **Omissions** Nault leaves out the name of the place where she works. What other information is omitted that might have given you a fuller understanding of her encounters with the homeless man?
2. **Tone** What is Nault's tone? How does it affect your attitude toward the information that is contained in the essay?
3. **Connotation** One of the annotations (para. 7) points out a couple of Nault's word choices with particularly rich connotations. What connotation does the phrase "drag my slippery feet" have in the context of paragraph 4?
4. **Metaphor** The phrase "crumpled soul" (3) offers a vivid metaphor. What does Nault seem to be comparing? What would it lose if you were to translate the metaphor into less figurative language?

Responding to the Reading

1. **Reaction** In paragraph 4, Nault wonders why she was nervous when she first noticed the homeless man and ignored him by walking around the block. How do you react when you come face to face with a homeless person? Why do you think you respond as you do?
2. **Discussion** Nault notes that Michael did not look like the stereotypical homeless person to her. What other groups of people do you stereotype? Have you ever had your stereotype exploded by getting to know a member of the group?
3. **Journal** Write a journal entry about someone you befriended when others ignored him or her. How did you reach out to the individual, and what were the results?
4. **Essay** Nault's personal encounter with Michael tested her character. Write an essay describing a time when you were called upon to make a decision that tested your character.

READING

I'm Not Leaving until I Eat This Thing

John T. Edge

John Edge is the director of the Southern Foodways Symposium at University of Mississippi and the editor of the *Encyclopedia of Southern Culture*. A James Beard Foundation award winner, Edge has written several books, including the *Truck Food Cookbook* (2012), and written for numerous newspapers and magazines, including the *Oxford American*, a literary magazine featuring southern writers. **Before reading**, preview and make connections by thinking about the most unusual food you have ever eaten. **While reading**, highlight the descriptive words and phrases that best convey the experience of eating pickled pig lips.

It's just past 4:00 on a Thursday afternoon in June at Jesse's Place, a country juke   1
17 miles south of the Mississippi line and three miles west of Amite, Louisiana. The
air conditioner hacks and spits forth torrents of Arctic air, but the heat of summer

can't be kept at bay. It seeps around the splintered doorjambs and settles in, transforming the squat particleboard-plastered roadhouse into a sauna. Slowly, the dank barroom fills with grease-smeared mechanics from the truck stop up the road and farmers straight from the fields, the soles of their brogans thick with dirt clods. A few weary souls make their way over from the nearby sawmill. I sit alone at the bar, one empty bottle of Bud in front of me, a second in my hand. I drain the beer, order a third, and stare down at the pink juice spreading outward from a crumpled foil pouch and onto the bar.

I'm not leaving until I eat this thing, I tell myself.   2

Half a mile down the road, behind a fence coiled with razor wire, Lionel   3
Dufour, proprietor of Farm Fresh Food Supplier, is loading up the last truck of the day, wheeling case after case of pickled pork offal out of his cinder-block processing plant and into a semitrailer bound for Hattiesburg, Mississippi.

His crew packed lips today. Yesterday, it was pickled sausage; the day before   4
that, pig feet. Tomorrow, it's pickled pig lips again. Lionel has been on the job since 2:45 in the morning, when he came in to light the boilers. Damon Landry, chief cook and maintenance man, came in at 4:30. By 7:30, the production line was at full tilt: six women in white smocks and blue bouffant caps, slicing ragged white fat from the lips, tossing the good parts in glass jars, the bad parts in barrels bound for the rendering plant. Across the aisle, filled jars clatter by on a conveyor belt as a worker tops them off with a Kool-Aid-red slurry of hot sauce, vinegar, salt, and food coloring. Around the corner, the jars are capped, affixed with a label, and stored in pasteboard boxes to await shipping.

Unlike most offal—euphemistically called "variety meats"—lips belie their   5
provenance. Brains, milky white and globular, look like brains. Feet, the ghosts of their cloven hoofs protruding, look like feet. Testicles look like, well, testicles. But lips are different. Loosed from the snout, trimmed of their fat, and dyed a preternatural pink, they look more like candy than like carrion.

At Farm Fresh, no swine root in an adjacent feedlot. No viscera-strewn killing   6
floor lurks just out of sight, down a darkened hallway. These pigs died long ago at some Midwestern abattoir. By the time the lips arrive in Amite, they are, in essence, pig Popsicles, 50-pound blocks of offal and ice.

"Lips are all meat," Lionel told me earlier in the day. "No gristle, no bone, no   7
nothing. They're bar food, hot and vinegary, great with a beer. Used to be the lips ended up in sausages, headcheese, those sorts of things. A lot of them still do."

Lionel, a 50-year-old father of three with quick, intelligent eyes set deep in a   8
face the color of cordovan, is a veteran of nearly 40 years in the pickled pig lips business. "I started out with my daddy when I wasn't much more than 10," Lionel told me, his shy smile framed by a coarse black mustache flecked with whispers of gray. "The meatpacking business he owned had gone broke back when I was 6, and he was peddling out of the back of his car, selling dried shrimp, napkins, straws, tubes of plastic cups, pig feet, pig lips, whatever the bar owners needed. He sold to black bars, white bars, sweet shops, snowball stands, you name it. We made the rounds together after I got out of school, sometimes staying out till two or three in the morning. I remember bringing my toy cars to this one joint and racing them around the floor with the bar owner's son while my daddy and his father did business."

For years after the demise of that first meatpacking company, the Dufour fam-   9
ily sold someone else's product. "We used to buy lips from Dennis Di Salvo's company down in Belle Chasse," recalled Lionel. "As far as I can tell, his mother was the
one who came up with the idea to pickle and pack lips back in the '50s, back when
she was working for a company called Three Little Pigs over in Houma. But pretty
soon, we were selling so many lips that we had to almost beg Di Salvo's for product. That's when we started cooking up our own," he told me, gesturing toward the
castiron kettle that hangs from the rafters by the front door of the plant. "My
daddy started cooking lips in that very pot."

Lionel now cooks lips in 11 retrofitted milk tanks, dull stainless-steel caul-   10
drons shaped like oversized cradles. But little else has changed. Though Lionel's
father has passed away, Farm Fresh remains a family-focused company. His wife,
Kathy, keeps the books. His daughter, Dana, a button-cute college student who has
won numerous beauty titles, takes to the road in the summer, selling lips to convenience stores and wholesalers. Soon, after he graduates from business school, Lionel's younger son, Matt, will take over operations at the plant. And his older son, a
veterinarian, lent his name to one of Farm Fresh's top sellers, Jason's Pickled Pig
Lips.

"We do our best to corner the market on lips," Lionel told me, his voice tinged   11
with bravado. "Sometimes they're hard to get from the packing houses. You gotta
kill a lot of pigs to get enough lips to keep us going. I've got new customers calling
every day; it's all I can do to keep up with demand, but I bust my ass to keep up. I
do what I can for my family—and for my customers.

"When my customers tell me something," he continued, "just like when my   12
daddy told me something, I listen. If my customers wanted me to dye the lips
green, I'd ask, 'What shade?' As it is, every few years we'll do some red and some
blue for the Fourth of July. This year we did jars full of Mardi Gras lips—half purple,
half gold," Lionel recalled with a chuckle. "I guess we'd had a few beers when we
came up with that one."

Meanwhile, back at Jesse's Place, I finish my third Bud, order my fourth. *Now, I*   13
tell myself, my courage bolstered by booze, *I'm ready to eat a lip.*

They may have looked like candy in the plant, but in the barroom they're car-   14
rion once again. I poke and prod the six-inch arc of pink flesh, peering up from my
reverie just in time to catch the barkeep's wife, Audrey, staring straight at me. She
fixes me with a look just this side of pity and asks, "You gonna eat that thing or
make love to it?"

Her nephew, Jerry, sidles up to a bar stool on my left. "A lot of people like 'em   15
with chips," he says with a nod toward the pink juice pooling on the bar in front of
me. I offer to buy him a lip, and Audrey fishes one from a jar behind the counter,
wraps it in tinfoil, and places the whole affair on a paper towel in front of him.

I take stock of my own cowardice, and, following Jerry's lead, reach for a bag of   16
potato chips, tear open the top with my teeth, and toss the quivering hunk of hog
flesh into the shiny interior of the bag, slick with grease and dusted with salt. Vinegar vapors tickle my nostrils. I stifle a gag that rolls from the back of my throat,
swallow hard, and pray that the urge to vomit passes.

With a smash of my hand, the potato chips are reduced to a pulp, and I feel   17
the cold lump of the lip beneath my fist. I clasp the bag shut and shake it hard in
an effort to ensure chip coverage in all the nooks and crannies of the lip. The technique that Jerry uses—and I mimic—is not unlike that employed by home cooks
mixing up a mess of Shake 'n Bake chicken.

I pull from the bag a coral crescent of meat now crusted with blond bits of   18
potato chips. When I chomp down, the soft flesh dissolves between my teeth. It
tastes like a flaccid cracklin', unmistakably porcine, and not altogether bad. The
chips help, providing texture where there was none. Slowly, my brow unfurrows,
my stomach ceases its fluttering.

Sensing my relief, Jerry leans over and peers into my bag. "Kind of look like   19
Frosted Flakes, don't they?" he says, by way of describing the chips rapidly turning
to mush in the pickling juice. I offer the bag to Jerry, order yet another beer, and
turn to eye the pig feet floating in a murky jar by the cash register, their blunt tips
bobbing up through a pasty white film.

Understanding the Reading

1. **Reasons** According to the author, why are there no live pigs at Farm Fresh Food
   Supplier?
2. **Details** What are the ingredients in the "Kool-Aid-red slurry"?
3. **Explanation** How are pig lips different from pork brains, feet, and testicles?
4. **Thesis** What is the author's thesis? Is it stated or implied?
5. **Vocabulary** Explain the meaning of each of the following words as it is used in the
   reading: *carrion* (para. 5), *demise* (9), *cauldrons* (10), *bravado* (11), and *flaccid* (18).

Analyzing the Writer's Technique

1. **Dominant Impression** Express the essay's dominant impression in your own
   words.
2. **Comparison** Explain the comparison between the contents of the potato chip bag
   and Frosted Flakes.
3. **Conclusion** Evaluate the essay's conclusion. If the essay had ended with paragraph 12 instead of paragraph 19, would the conclusion have been more effective
   or less so? Why?
4. **Audience** What audience is the author addressing? What details help you determine the audience?
5. **Title** The title of Edge's essay is very vague. Why do you think the author chose
   this title? If you had to create a clever title for this essay, what would it be?

Thinking Critically about Description

1. **Omitted Details** What details are omitted from this essay that might have been included?
2. **Connotation** What is the connotation of the phrase "quivering hunk of hog flesh" (para. 16)?
3. **Details** How does the way in which the author describes eating a pig lip affect the way that you might view eating one?
4. **Sensory Detail** Which examples of sensory language did you find particularly powerful and engaging? What makes them effective?
5. **Attitude** What is the author's attitude toward those who eat at Jesse's Place?

Responding to the Reading

1. **Reaction** How would you react if a waiter accidentally served you the wrong dish—a plate of pig lips—and you unsuspectingly took a big bite?
2. **Journal** Do you have a favorite food? Write a journal entry that describes the food in vivid detail.
3. **Discussion** In small groups, discuss the nastiest, most disgusting foods that you have ever eaten and your reaction.
4. **Essay** Lionel Dufour's daughter spends her summers selling pig lips to convenience stores and wholesalers. Suppose you were asked to spend next summer selling a food product that many people might find distasteful or repulsive. Write an essay in which you describe the three most important selling features of this food. Be sure to use words that appeal to the senses.

Working Together

Collaboration Suppose you were to open a restaurant that specialized in dishes featuring beef tongue, chitlins (hog intestines), brains, chicken feet, or mountain oysters (pork testicles). Working with a partner, create a name for the restaurant and a thirty-second radio advertisement for its grand opening.

DESCRIPTION COMBINED WITH OTHER PATTERNS ‹ READING

Underground Lair: Inside a Chicken Processing Plant

Gabriel Thompson

This selection is from the book *Working in the Shadows: A Year of Doing the Jobs (Most) Americans Won't Do* (2010). The book (and this excerpt from it) describes Thompson's experiences working undercover at jobs staffed mostly by undocumented immigrants. Thompson has also published three other books: *There's No José Here* (2006), *Calling All Radicals* (2007), and *America's Social Arsonist* (2016), as well as numerous articles in publications including *New York* magazine, *The Nation,* and *The New York Times.*

Before reading, preview and make connections by thinking about your experiences, or those of a friend or family member, working a low-paying job. **While reading**, identify the dominant impressions Thompson creates and the strategies he uses to reinforce it.

Superhero comics aren't complete without an evil genius. Often he seeks to construct the ultimate weapon to hold the world hostage; if he's really deranged he simply wants to use it to end human civilization. Since the construction of the weapon must be clandestine, work goes on belowground or behind hidden doors. Walk through the door and an immense world of nameless and undoubtedly evil scientists are at work, tinkering with mysterious equipment while wearing smocks and continuously checking devices.

That's the image that immediately comes to mind when I push through the double doors that separate the break room from the plant floor. This isn't a workplace: This is an underground lair. In the first room, workers scurry around in plastic blue smocks akin to a surgeon's, carrying buckets of chicken pieces. Others lean over a long conveyor belt that moves a continuous stream of meat, their feet planted as they arrange the pieces in a line. We weave our way around large metal machinery and step through a frothy puddle of foam that spews from a thick hose on the cement floor. The smell is a mixture of strong industrial cleaner and fresh meat. To my left is a chest-high cylinder filled to the brim with chicken bits; while it captures my attention, I step on what feels like a sponge and lift my foot to find a piece of pink meat, now flattened. Up ahead, I can see from the puffs of condensation coming from his mouth that Lonnie is saying something to our group—the temperature is frigid, probably in the low forties—but I can't hear anything. I remove my earplugs and am greeted by the roar of machinery. It's not a piercing noise, more of a loud, all-encompassing rumble: Think of the sound you hear when putting your ear to a seashell and multiply by a hundred. I put my earplugs back in.

We walk beneath a doorway and the full scale of the processing floor is revealed. I see no walls in front of me, just open space filled with workers standing in various areas without moving their feet. Hundreds of dead and featherless chickens are hanging upside down from stainless steel hooks, moving rapidly across my field of vision. I hear a beeping sound and step aside from a man driving a scooter-like contraption, which is carrying a container of steaming chicken meat (the contraption turns out to be a pallet truck, and the steam is actually from dry ice). As we cross the plant floor we pass beneath a line of chickens, whirling along more steel hooks; liquid falls from their carcasses and lands with chilly plops on my scalp. Hopefully water. In front of us dozens of workers are slicing up chickens—the debone department—but we proceed further, until we're standing aside a blond-haired woman in her forties who, like Lonnie, is wearing a hard hat.

"This is your supervisor, Barbara," Lonnie tells us, "but she won't be needing you tonight." He tells Ben and Diane to follow him and motions me to stay put. When he returns he leads me through another doorway. "You're going to work in a different department today, but check in with DSI tomorrow," he says. Lonnie deposits me at the end of a line where boxes are being stacked.

The nearest person is a skinny white man with the hood of his Alabama football sweatshirt pulled tight over his head. I stay quiet, feeling slightly intimidated by my new coworker, who has deep lines cutting across his gaunt face and is missing a few front teeth. But when he turns to me he flashes a friendly smile. "How long you been here?" he asks.

"About five minutes."   6

He lets loose a squeaking chuckle, his shoulders bouncing up and down. "I've   7 only been here two weeks." Kyle, it turns out, is my neighbor. He lives in a trailer with his wife and two kids about half a mile from where I'm staying. "Been right at that trailer for eighteen years, on land that was my granddaddy's. I worked in the plant four years, then quit. Now I'm back . . . don't know exactly why."*

Kyle normally works in DSI, but he says that today they're short people in the   8 IQF department, another mysterious trio of initials. In IQF, bags of chicken wings are stuffed into boxes, taped, and shoved down on rollers to us. Our task is to stack the forty-pound boxes onto pallets. Once a pallet is stacked with forty-nine boxes—seven boxes to a row, seven rows high—a pallet driver whisks it away and we start loading up another. This is almost identical to the stacking of lettuce boxes completed by loaders on the machine, except that the pace here is much slower. I help Kyle do this for twenty minutes, until the machine at the front of the line breaks. A black woman with short blond hair, who has been taping the boxes shut, lets out a good-natured curse. It takes several minutes for a group of men to fix the machine; several minutes later it breaks down again. Over the coming month, I'll occasionally be asked to help out in IQF, and during almost every shift the machine breaks down—hourly. For this reason alone, it's considered a good place to work (as one of the "good" jobs, it also doesn't have a single immigrant working in the department).

With nothing to do, Kyle and I take a seat on the rollers. "You ever work in   9 debone?" I ask him.

"Way back when I started, they tried to get me on there. Stayed a month. They   10 told me I couldn't work fast enough so they shifted me out. I made sure I wasn't working fast enough too. Run you like slaves over there. I already knew how they did, though, 'cause my old lady was on the debone line for years." Now, he tells me, she's working at Wal-Mart.

The machine is finally fixed and we return to stacking boxes. After thirty   11 minutes the black woman who was cursing the contraption asks me to come up and tape boxes. I'm happy for the change in scenery, but this task soon becomes tedious. My job is to shake the box so that the bags lie flat, then pull the two top flaps together and shove it through a machine that tapes it shut. Cutting lettuce confirmed in my mind that much of what we call "low-skilled labor" is in fact quite difficult. But at the chicken plant, I'm already learning, many of the jobs are

---

* A note here on accents. Kyle, like many native Alabamans at the plant, speaks in a very heavy and melodic drawl. It was beautiful to hear, but that beauty soon becomes distracting when I attempt to render it accurately on the page. For example, when he told me he had been at the trailer for eighteen years, it sounded to my ears like: "Been rahht at tha-yat trawla' for eightee-yin years." For the sake of readability, I will not try to capture every nuance of the local dialect. One final point to illustrate the strength of the country accent: It took me a week of hanging out with Kyle before I finally realized that his name wasn't, in fact, Kyle. It was Gil. Later, when I listened repeatedly to a message he left on my cell phone, I realized that it wasn't Gil, but another name entirely. Here, he will remain Kyle. [Thompson's note.]

designed so that a person off the street, with minimal instruction, can do them correctly the very first time. I'm sure this is considered a "breakthrough" by the managerial class, but all it does is leave me bored within fifteen minutes.

Sometime after 2:00 a.m., I'm told to take a break. I hang up my gloves and white   12
smock on a hook and walk away from IQF. A minute later I've pushed through one swinging door and walked beneath two other doorways, and I'm watching an endless line of carved-up carcasses fall into a large container. I have no idea where I am. To my left, dozens of immigrant men and women are cutting up chickens with knives and scissors. I approach one woman who can't be much taller than four feet, and ask her in Spanish if she can tell me how to get to the break room. She looks at me and shakes her head.

"She doesn't speak Spanish," another woman says, in Spanish. "You go straight   13
down that row and make a left." I hear the two speak in what sounds like an Indian dialect, thank them both, and follow her directions.

The break room is mostly empty, but I notice Ben sitting alone in a corner   14
booth. We're both struck by how disorganized everything seems to be. Like me, Ben has been hired for one department (debone), transferred to another (DSI), and then relocated once more, with unclear instructions along they way. He doesn't even know the name of the department that he's in. "Whatever it is, they have me standing and watching chickens go by."

"That's it?" I ask. "Are you supposed to *do* anything?"   15

"Uh, I think like maybe they said to look for mold."   16

"Mold? The chickens have mold?"   17

"Not yet anyway. I haven't seen any. I'm looking for green stuff."   18

"And if they have mold, what do you do?"   19

"I dunno." Ben pushes his sliding glasses up, beginning to look concerned. "I   20
hope that's what I heard. I'm pretty sure somebody said something about mold." He looks at his watch and stands up. "I gotto go."

By now there are perhaps fifty people sitting in nearby booths, with about an   21
equal number of whites, blacks, and Latinos, who are mostly gathered in self-segregated groups. One wall is plastered with what are meant to be inspiring corporate messages in Spanish and English, illustrated with geometric shapes and arrows. The "Cornerstones of Continuous Improvement" are written at each point of a large triangle: "Quality, Process Improvement, Teamwork." Next to this diagram is a more detailed "14 Points of Continuous Improvement," which include quizzical tips like "Drive Out Fear." Workers pass these grand pronouncements without pause, but they take note of a yellow flyer taped to the wall that reads "Taco Soup Wednesday Night."

I'm joined a few minutes later by a white man in a flannel coat who tells me   22
that he's been on the debone line for five months. He snorts when I tell him that I'm impressed he's lasting so long.

"It's work release," he says. "The only reason I'm here is 'cause they locked my   23
ass up." I don't ask what landed him in prison, but he does reveal that after the death of his father, he went on a number of epic alcohol binges. "Can't do that any-more 'cause I'm locked up and got myself a bleeding ulcer. But I'll tell you one

thing," he says before I depart, "once I'm free you ain't never gonna see me step foot inside a chicken plant again."

I use the bathroom and manage to find my way back to Kyle and the boxes. He   24
is seated on the rollers, hood pulled even lower on his head to ward off the cold, while a mechanic tries to get the machine back up and working.

For reasons that aren't explained, IQF is released earlier than other departments.   25
As I walk toward the break room at 7:40 a.m., I meet a stream of men and women heading in the other direction, getting ready to begin the day shift. I swipe my ID card to sign out, am hit by the bright sunshine of another scorching day, hop on my bike, and pedal home. Kyle has agreed to pick me up tonight, so I don't have to worry about getting run over by a chicken truck. Back in my trailer I eat a quick breakfast of cereal and a peanut butter and jelly sandwich, type up my notes, and lay down. The sun is streaming through the window, my trailer shakes each time a truck loaded with live chickens passes, and my neighbor's roosters are engaged with a dog in some sort of noise competition. I can't be bothered; I fall asleep instantly.

Understanding the Reading

1. **Reasons** Why does Thompson mention and describe the two posters in paragraph 21? What is the significance of the poster describing the food?
2. **Details** In paragraph 8, Thompson mentions stacking lettuce boxes. How would he know about this job?
3. **Reasons** Why is the IQF a good place to work?
4. **Details** What erroneous assumption does the author make about the woman of whom he asks directions to the break room (para. 12)? Why did he assume this about her?
5. **Vocabulary** Explain the meaning of each of the following words or phrases as it is used in the reading: *deranged* (para. 1), *clandestine* (1), *lair* (2), *gaunt* (5), and *pronouncement* (21). Refer to a dictionary as needed.

Analyzing the Writer's Technique

1. **Dominant Impression** What dominant impression does Thompson convey in this essay? Is it stated or implied? Explain your answers.
2. **Title** What is the significance of the essay's title?
3. **Descriptive Language** How does Thompson's descriptive language allow you to understand and picture the processing floor (para. 3)? What words and phrases are most descriptive in this section?
4. **Patterns** What patterns other than description does Thompson use in this essay? What purposes do they serve?

Visualizing the Reading

Thompson conveys information about his job and surroundings by using many of the characteristics of descriptive essays. Analyze his use of these characteristics by completing the following chart. Give several examples for each type of characteristic used, including the paragraph numbers for reference. The first one has been done for you.

Descriptive Characteristic	Examples
Active verbs	1. "workers scurry around" (para. 2) 2. "I've pushed through a swinging door" (12)
Sensory details (sound, smell, touch, sight, taste)	3.
Varied sentences	4.
Comparisons	5.
Connotative language	6.

Thinking Critically about Description

1. **Connotation** What connotation does the word *lair* suggest (para. 2)?
2. **Detail** Why does the author make a point to say that Kyle's wife left the plant and went to work for Walmart?
3. **Connotation** Why does the author put the word *breakthrough* (para. 11) in quotations?
4. **Objective/Subjective** Is the essay objective, subjective, or a mixture of both? Explain your answer.
5. **Tone** Describe Thompson's tone in this essay. What information does his tone convey that is not directly stated?

Responding to the Reading

1. **Reaction** The author attempts to blend in with the other workers at the plant. Do you think that he is successful in doing so? Why or why not? Give examples from his behavior or his words that support your answer.
2. **Discussion** What do you think Thompson learned as a result of his undercover experience in the chicken processing plant?
3. **Journal** Thompson writes that much of what we call "low-skilled labor" is actually very difficult. Discuss some low-skilled jobs that you know about and explain what makes them so difficult.
4. **Essay** Write an essay in which you describe the worst job you or someone you know has ever had. In addition to describing the job, explain why the job was so bad.

Working Together

1. The poster in the break room of the chicken plant was entitled "14 Points of Continuous Improvement." Working with a small group of your peers, list fourteen changes that could be implemented in that plant in order to create a better work environment.
2. Many businesses have a catchy advertising slogan that draws the public's attention to their company. Working with a small group of your peers, brainstorm slogans that you hear on TV or radio. Then assume that you are Gabriel Thompson, and you want to create a slogan for the chicken plant that will "tell it like it is." Make sure your slogan is simple, catchy, and honest. Be prepared to share your slogan with the class and explain its significance.

Apply Your Skills: Additional Essay Assignments

Using what you learned about description in this chapter, write a descriptive essay on one of the topics listed below. Depending on the topic you choose, you may need to conduct research.

For more on locating and documenting sources, see Part 5.

To Express Your Ideas

1. Suppose a famous person, living or dead, visited your house for dinner. Write an essay describing the person and the evening and expressing your feelings about the occasion.
2. In "Dreamland, Portsmouth, Ohio," the author describes a place and what it meant to the townspeople of Portsmouth. Write an essay for your classmates describing a place that you visited as a child that still evokes fond memories.

To Inform Your Reader

3. Write an essay describing destruction or devastation you have observed as a result of a natural disaster (hurricane, flood), an accident, or a form of violence.
4. Write a report for your local newspaper on a local sporting event you recently observed or participated in.

To Persuade Your Reader

5. Write a letter to persuade your parents to lend you money. The loan may be to purchase a used car or to rent a more expensive apartment, for example. Include a description of your current car or apartment.
6. "Sometimes, We Give" describes a homeless man and one woman's response to him. Write a persuasive essay taking a position on the responsibility Americans (or their government) have toward the homeless.

Cases Using Description

7. Imagine that you are a product buyer for a cosmetics distributor, a food company, or a furniture dealership. Write a descriptive review of a product recommending to the board of directors whether to distribute it. Use something that you are familiar with or come up with your own product (such as a new cosmetic, an advice book on nutrition, or an electronic gadget for the home). Describe the product in a way that will help convince the company to accept your recommendation.

8. Write a brief description of your ideal internship. Then write an essay to accompany your application for your ideal summer internship. The sponsoring agency requires every applicant to submit an essay that describes the knowledge and experience the applicant can bring to the internship and the ways that the position would benefit the applicant personally and professionally.

SYNTHESIZING IDEAS   WORKING LOW-PAYING JOBS

Both "Underground Lair: Inside a Chicken Processing Plant" (pp. 289–93) and "I'm Not Leaving until I Eat This Thing" (pp. 285–88) describe food-processing plants. Thompson works in a chicken processing plant, and Edge reports on a plant producing pickled meat products.

Analyzing the Readings

1. Compare how Thompson and Edge feel about the processing plants. How does each author reveal his or her attitudes? How are they the same, and how do they differ?

2. As a writer who is researching jobs that most Americans won't do, Thompson works "undercover," but Edge merely visits the plant. How do you think these differences affect the essays and the authors' reported experiences?

Essay Idea

Write an essay describing a workplace you know well, and describe it to create a dominant impression. Then explain whether your experiences were more similar to those of Thompson or Edge—or why they did not resemble those of either.

13
Illustration

Explaining with Examples

WRITING QUICK START In an environmental science class, the instructor projects the photograph on this page onto a screen and makes the following statement: "Environmental pollution is a growing global problem." She asks the class to think of several examples, similar to the one shown in the photograph, that support this statement. Using the instructor's statement as your topic sentence, write a paragraph with examples of different types of environmental pollution that you have either observed or read about.

In this chapter you will learn to:

- understand the purpose and function of illustration essays
- use graphic organizers to visualize illustration essays
- integrate illustration into an essay
- read and think critically about illustration
- plan, organize, draft, revise, and edit essays using illustration

The sentences you just wrote could be part of an illustration essay. An **illustration** essay uses examples to reveal a topic's essential characteristics and reinforce the thesis statement. By providing specific examples that make abstract ideas concrete, you help readers connect these abstract ideas to their own experience.

USING ILLUSTRATION   **IN COLLEGE AND THE WORKPLACE**

- Your *literature instructor* assigns an analysis of metaphor and simile in the poems of Emily Dickinson. To explain your point about Dickinson's use of animal metaphors, you provide specific examples from several of her poems.

- You are studying sexual dimorphism (differences in appearance between the sexes) in a *biology course*. The following question appears on an exam: "Define sexual dimorphism and illustrate its occurrence in several different species." In your answer, you give examples of peacocks, geese, and chickens, explaining how the males and females in each species differ in physical appearance.

- As an *elementary school reading teacher*, you are writing a letter to the school board justifying the cost of the new computer software you have requested. In your letter, you provide several examples of the software's benefits to students.

What Are the Characteristics of Illustration Essays?

Effective illustration essays support a generalization, explain, and clarify by providing examples that maintain readers' interest and achieve the author's purpose. Because a good illustration essay is more than a list of examples, a well-thought-out organization is essential.

Illustration Supports Generalizations

Examples are an effective way to support a **generalization**—a broad statement about a topic. Thesis statements often contain a generalization, and the body of an illustration essay contains examples that support it.

The following statements are generalizations because they make assertions about an entire group or category.

- Most college students are energetic, ambitious, and eager to get ahead in life.
- Gestures play an important role in nonverbal communication.
- Boys are more willing to participate in class discussions than girls are.

To explain and support any of these generalizations, you could provide specific examples, along with other types of evidence (facts, statistics, expert opinions), to show how or why the statement is accurate. For instance, in addition to providing relevant facts and statistics, you could also support the first generalization by providing examples of several college students who demonstrate energy and ambition.

For more about idea-generating strategies, see Chapter 4.

> **EXERCISE 13.1** ▸ **DEVELOPING EXAMPLES TO SUPPORT GENERALIZATIONS**

Using one or more prewriting strategies for generating ideas, provide at least two examples that support each of the following general statements.

1. Television offers some programs with educational or social value.
2. Today's parents are not strict enough with their children.
3. The favorite pastime of most men is watching sports on television.

Illustration Explains or Clarifies

Examples are useful when you need to explain an unfamiliar topic, a difficult concept, or an abstract term.

Unfamiliar topics.   Use examples to help readers understand a topic about which they know little or nothing. An instructor of abnormal psychology, for example, might provide case studies of patients with schizophrenia and other disorders to help make the characteristics of each disorder easier to understand and remember.

Difficult concepts.   Many concepts are difficult to grasp by definition alone. For instance, a reader might guess that the term *urbanization*, a key concept in sociology, has something to do with cities. Defining the concept as "the process by which an area becomes part of a city" gives readers a place to begin. Providing examples of formerly suburban areas that have become urban makes the concept even more understandable.

Abstract terms.   Abstract terms refer to ideas rather than to concrete things you can see and touch. Terms such as *truth* and *justice* are abstract. Because abstractions are difficult to understand, examples help clarify them. In many cases, however, abstract terms mean different things to different people. By providing examples, you can clarify what *you* mean by an abstract term. Suppose you use the term *unfair* to describe your employer's treatment of workers. Readers might have different ideas of fairness. Providing examples of the employer's unfair treatment would make your meaning clear.

> **EXERCISE 13.2** ▸ **PROVIDING EXAMPLES TO EXPLAIN AND CLARIFY**

The following list contains a mix of unfamiliar topics, difficult concepts, and abstract terms. Choose three items from the list, and provide at least two examples of each that illustrate their meanings.

1. Phobia
2. Conformity
3. Gender role
4. Self-fulfilling prophecy
5. Sexual harassment

Illustration Considers Purpose and Audience

The number of examples a writer should include depends on his or her purpose and audience. For example, in an essay arguing that one car is a better buy than another, a series of examples explaining the various models, years, and options available to potential car buyers might be most persuasive. But if you are writing an essay for an audience of high school students about the consequences of dropping out of school, a single poignant example might be more compelling.

A careful analysis of your audience should play a key role in deciding what types of examples to include in your essay. For an expert audience, technical examples might be more appropriate; for novice readers, personal or everyday examples might be more effective. For instance, suppose you want to persuade readers that the Food and Drug Administration should approve a new cancer drug. If your audience is composed of doctors, your examples would likely include the results of scientific studies regarding the drug's effectiveness. But if your audience is the general public, your examples might focus on personal anecdotes about lives being saved.

It can be useful to provide examples that represent different aspects of or view-points on your topic. In writing about the new drug, for instance, you might include expert opinion from researchers as well as the opinions of doctors, patients, and a representative of the company that manufactures the drug.

EXERCISE 13.3   **DEVELOPING EXAMPLES FOR A SPECIFIC AUDIENCE**

For one of the following topics, suggest examples that would suit the different audiences listed.

1. Your college's policy on student on-campus employment
   a. First-year students attending a college orientation session
   b. Students already working on campus
   c. Parents or spouses of students who work on campus
2. A proposal recommending that drivers over age sixty-five undergo periodic assessment of their ability to operate a motor vehicle safely
   a. Senior citizens
   b. State senators
   c. Adult children of elderly drivers

Illustration Uses Carefully Selected Examples

Examples must be relevant, representative, accurate, and striking.

- *Relevant* examples have a direct and clear relationship to your thesis. If your essay advocates publicly funded preschool programs, support your case with examples of successful publicly funded programs, not privately operated programs.
- *Representative* examples show a typical or real-life situation, not a rare or unusual one. In an essay arguing that preschool programs advance children's reading skills, one example of an all-day, year-round preschool would not be representative of all or most other programs.

- *Accurate* and *specific* examples provide readers with enough information to evaluate their reliability. Notice how the second example below provides better (more specific) detail for the reader.

Overly General	Most students in preschool programs have better language skills than children who don't attend such programs.
Specific, Detailed	According to an independent evaluator, 73 percent of children who attended the Head Start program in Clearwater had better language skills after one year of attendance than students who did not attend the program.

Striking and dramatic examples make a strong, lasting impression on readers. For example, in an essay about identity theft, a writer might relate shocking incidents of how victims' lives are drastically changed with the swipe of a credit card.

Sometimes it is necessary to conduct research to find examples outside your knowledge and experience. For the essay on preschool programs, you would need to do research to obtain statistical information. You might also interview a preschool administrator or teacher to gather firsthand anecdotes and opinions or visit a preschool classroom to observe the program in action.

Illustration Uses Subexamples to Add Detail

When providing examples that are broad general categories, you will often find it helpful to include **subexamples**—specific examples that help explain the general examples. Suppose you are writing an essay about the problems that new immigrants to America face and you use three examples: problems with the language, with the culture, and with technology. For the broad culture example, you might give subexamples of how some immigrants do not understand certain American holidays, ways of socializing, and methods of doing business.

Illustration Organizes Details Effectively

When supporting a thesis with examples, organize the examples and the details that accompany them so readers can follow them easily. Often one of the methods of organization discussed in Chapter 6 will be useful:

- spatial order,
- chronological order, and
- most-to-least or least-to-most order.

For example, in an essay explaining why people wear unconventional dress, you might arrange the examples spatially, starting with outlandish footwear and continuing upward to headgear. For other writing assignments, you may want to organize your examples according to another pattern of development, such as comparison and contrast or cause and effect. For example, to support the thesis that a local department store needs to improve its customer service, you might begin by contrasting the department store with several other retailers that provide better service, offering examples of the services that each provides.

The following readings demonstrate the techniques for writing effective illustration essays. The first is annotated to point out how Deborah Tannen uses these techniques to help readers understand how families communicate. As you read the second essay, try to identify how the writer uses the techniques of illustration to help readers understand road rage.

What's That Supposed to Mean?

Deborah Tannen

Deborah Tannen, a professor of linguistics at Georgetown University, has published numerous scholarly articles and several popular books about interpersonal communication, including *You Were Always Mom's Favorite, You're Wearing That?*, and *I Only Say This Because I Love You,* from which this excerpt was taken.

Before Reading

1. **Preview:** Use the steps listed on page 28.
2. **Connect:** Think of a conversation between members of your own family in which a conflict or misunderstanding occurred. Why do you think it occurred? Could it have been avoided?

While Reading Study the examples Tannen offers and read the annotations provided.

Introduction: Uses a familiar situation to engage readers

Elizabeth, a college professor in her thirties, is making Thanksgiving dinner for her extended family in her own home. Her mother, who is visiting, is helping out in the kitchen. As Elizabeth prepares the turkey, her mother remarks, "Oh, you put onions in the stuffing?"   1

Feeling suddenly as if she were sixteen years old again, Elizabeth turns on her mother. "Why do you have to criticize everything I do?"   2

"I didn't criticize," her mother replies. "I just asked a question. What's got into you? I can't even open my mouth!"   3

Transition: Moves readers from example to explanation

Because family members have a shared history, everything we say echoes with meanings from the past. We develop a sixth sense for sniffing out criticism in almost anything a loved one says—even an innocent question about the ingredients in holiday stuffing.   4

Topic sentence

When family members talk to one another, there are often two meanings to what they say. The *message* is the meaning of the words and sentences spoken, what anyone with a dictionary and a grammar book could figure out. Two people in a conversation usually agree on what the message is. The *metamessage* (the prefix *meta* means, among other things, going beyond or higher) is meaning that is not stated—at least not in so many words—but that is gleaned from every aspect of context; the way something is said, who is saying it, or the fact that it is said at all. You might say that the message is the "word meaning," while the metamessage is the "heart meaning"—the meaning we react to most strongly, that triggers emotion.   5

Concept to be explained through examples

As in the case of Elizabeth and her mother, grown children often seem to take every remark of a parent as criticism. They become attuned to any hint—any metamessage—of disapproval. Understanding this, Elizabeth's mother might refrain from offering advice or even making helpful suggestions unless asked. Sometimes, smoother family talk is a simple matter of tongue-biting.

Sometimes, however, it's more complex. The following situations show ways to stop your nearest and dearest from pushing your buttons in conversation, as well as ways to avoid pushing theirs.

6

First of several ways to improve family communication

7

Thesis: There are ways to improve the communication that occurs in families.

Diet Police

Irene and David, a married couple from Vermont, are looking over menus in a restaurant. David says he will order a steak.

"Did you notice they also have salmon?" Irene asks.

"Will you please stop criticizing what I eat?" David protests.

"I didn't criticize," says Irene. "I just pointed out something I thought you might like."

David was reacting to what he saw as Irene's metamessage: that he eats too much red meat. It's possible that Irene really was not feeling disapproval when she pointed out the salmon on the menu. But most likely she was, and preferred to raise her concern as a question to avoid a fight.

When David reacted with annoyance, Irene cried literal meaning. Every one of us does that when we want to avoid discord. As a result, the deeper meanings of the conversation often are left unaddressed.

It might help to "metacommunicate"—that is, to talk about ways of talking. David might explain that Irene's suggestion made him feel like he was living with the diet police. If Irene actually did mean to express concern about David's health, she should admit that. By clarifying the meaning each person intended and perceived, the couple could build a bridge of understanding.

8

Relevant and representative example to illustrate *metamessage*

9

10

11

12

Topic sentence: Moves readers from example to explanation

13

14

Topic sentence: 2nd way to improve family communication

"Don't Call Us . . ."

There is another aspect of communication complicating everything we say to each other, and it's especially powerful in families. That is our simultaneous but conflicting desires for connection and control. We all seek connection: it makes us feel safe and loved. But being close gives family members a kind of power to control our actions that can limit our freedom and make us feel hemmed in. "Don't tell me what to do. Don't try to control me," are frequent protests within families. It is automatic for many of us to see others' incursions on our freedom as control maneuvers. We are less likely to think of them as connection maneuvers, but they often are that too.

Nathan and Joan, a couple in their late twenties, were leaving Joan's parents after a family visit. Holding the hand of her three-year-old daughter, Joan wobbled under the weight of a pregnancy nearing its term. As everyone said their good-byes, Joan's mother, Nora, said, "I'll see you when you give birth. I can't wait to get that call when you go into labor!"

15

2nd concept to be explained through example

Transition: Transitional sentence moves readers from explanation to example

16

Relevant and representative example to illustrate *conflicting desire for connection and control*

Joan and Nathan stiffened. When Joan was about to give birth to their first   17
child, Nora and her husband drove to the couple's town so they would be close to
the hospital. This had annoyed Nathan, who had expected his in-laws to wait until
they were asked to come.

"We're not going to call you when she goes into labor," Nathan said to his   18
mother-in-law. "I'll call to tell you when the baby is born."

Nora instantly protested that he had no right to keep such crucial knowledge   19
from her. He retorted that they had a right to keep the birth private and quiet, as
their daughter's birth had *not* been—because of Nora's showing up.

Nora defended herself: it had not been her idea to come ahead in that case,   20
but her husband's. She promised to abide by any rules they set, insisting that not
telling her when her daughter went into labor was too cruel an exclusion.

Nathan and Nora were both struggling to find their footing on the connection/   21
control continuum. He was feeling an assault on his sense of control over
his family, and she was feeling an assault on her sense of connection with her
daughter. But Nora was also feeling a loss of control, as if her hands would be
tied at a crucial moment—and Nathan was also feeling a loss of connection,
with his wife.

There are a few communication keys that would have helped them. Timing is   22
one. Nora could have avoided putting Nathan on the defensive by making her case
to be present at the birth in a calmer setting—by letter, or in a carefully thought-
out conversation about how she felt and what she would be willing to promise. It
probably also would have helped to say she was sorry she had come uninvited the
first time. Nathan could have avoided committing himself one way or the other
about calling Nora when Joan went into labor. Then later he could just not have
done it, and soothed hurt feelings by explaining, "Things happened so fast I wasn't
able to call."

"Didn't I Tell You?"

Even though you're related, it's easy to feel at times like you're talking to a   23
stranger. Age and gender differences are among the obstacles that can get in the
way. Cindy, a small-business owner, was increasingly distressed because her grown
son continued living at home after graduating from college and beginning a full-
time job. His upkeep was straining her tight budget. After about three months, she
said to him, "I think it would be fair for you to pay rent."

He replied, "I'm leaving soon."   24

Cindy was relieved that she had finally spoken up and settled the matter. But   25
time passed and no rent appeared. After several more months, her anger erupted.
During this quarrel it emerged that her son had felt that the issue of paying rent,
though raised, had been left in abeyance for a little while longer. Cindy, on the
other hand, had assumed that expressing her opinion implied a request for action,
that all she had to do was make her wishes known and her son would feel obligated to honor them.

Her son's interpretation was similar to the way many men react to women's   26
indirect requests. Since he himself would ask directly, he did not recognize Cindy's
statement of preferences as a request for action. Because men often honestly miss

Topic sentence: Moves readers from example to explanation

Topic sentence: Prepares readers for list of ways to improve communication

Topic sentence: 3rd issue in family communication

Transition: Highlights that explanation of example is coming indirect requests, Cindy would have done better to end her first talk with a direct statement, such as, "Then we agree you'll start paying rent next month." Or she could have finished with a question like, "When can I expect a check?"

3rd way to improve communication

Conversation with our family is an ongoing balancing act as we try to clarify meanings that did not get across or dispel misunderstandings—and at the same time interpret what is being said to us. Staying aware of all the subtleties of family talk can give us the power to improve the most important relationships in our lives.   27

Conclusion: Restates thesis in different words

Visualize an Illustration Essay: Create a Graphic Organizer

Graphic Organizer 13.1 will help you visualize the components of an illustration essay. The structure is straightforward.

For more on creating a graphic organizer, see pp. 35–37.

- The introduction contains background information and usually includes the thesis.

GRAPHIC ORGANIZER 13.1   The Basic Structure of an Illustration Essay

*In some essays, the thesis statement may be implied or may appear in a different position.

- The body paragraphs provide one or more related examples. For an essay using one extended example, such as a highly descriptive account of an auto accident intended to persuade readers to wear seat belts, the body of the essay will focus on the details of that one example.
- The conclusion presents a final statement.

READING >

Rambos of the Road

Martin Gottfried

Martin Gottfried has been a drama critic for such publications as the *New York Post* and *New York* magazine. He has also written several books, including biographies of Stephen Sondheim, Arthur Miller, and Angela Lansbury. This essay was first published in *Newsweek,* the weekly news magazine, in 1986. **Before reading**, preview the reading and make connections by thinking of overly aggressive drivers you have encountered. **While reading**, notice where Gottfried employs compelling examples to support his thesis, and highlight those you find particularly striking. Read the illustration essay first, and then study Graphic Organizer 13.2 (p. 310). What parts of the reading are included in the graphic organizer and why?

The car pulled up and its driver glared at us with such sullen intensity, such 1
hatred, that I was truly afraid for our lives. Except for the Mohawk haircut he didn't
have, he looked like Robert De Niro in *Taxi Driver,* the sort of young man who, delirious
for notoriety, might kill a president.

He was glaring because we had passed him and for that affront he pursued 2
us to the next stoplight so as to express his indignation and affirm his masculinity.
I was with two women and, believe it, was afraid for all three of us. It was
nearly midnight and we were in a small, sleeping town with no other cars on
the road.

When the light turned green, I raced ahead, knowing it was foolish and that 3
I was not in a movie. He didn't merely follow, he chased, and with his headlights
turned off. No matter what sudden turn I took, he followed. My passengers were
silent. I knew they were alarmed, and I prayed that I wouldn't be called upon to
protect them. In that cheerful frame of mind, I turned off my own lights so I
couldn't be followed. It was lunacy. I was responding to a crazy *as* a crazy.

"I'll just drive to the police station," I finally said, and as if those were the magic 4
words, he disappeared.

It seems to me that there has recently been an epidemic of auto macho—a 5
competition perceived and expressed in driving. People fight it out over parking spaces.
They bully into line at the gas pump. A toll booth becomes a signal for elbowing fend-
ers. And beetle-eyed drivers hunch over their steering wheels, squeezing the rims,
glowering, preparing the excuse of not having seen you as they muscle you off the
road. Approaching a highway on an entrance ramp recently, I was strong-armed by a
trailer truck, so immense that its driver all but blew me away by blasting his horn. The

behemoth was just inches from my hopelessly mismatched coupe when I fled for the safety of the shoulder.

And this is happening on city streets, too. A New York taxi driver told me that "intimidation is the name of the game. Drive as if you're deaf and blind. You don't hear the other guy's horn and you sure as hell don't see him." 6

The odd thing is that long before I was even able to drive, it seemed to me that people were at their finest and most civilized when in their cars. They seemed so orderly and considerate, so reasonable, staying in the right-hand lane unless passing, signaling all intentions. In those days you really eased into highway traffic, and the long, neat rows of cars seemed mobile testimony to the sanity of most people. Perhaps memory fails, perhaps there were always testy drivers, perhaps—but everyone didn't give you the finger. 7

A most amazing example of driver rage occurred recently at the Manhattan end of the Lincoln Tunnel. We were four cars abreast, stopped at a traffic light. And there was no moving even when the light had changed. A bus had stopped in the cross traffic, blocking our paths: it was a normal-for-New-York-City grid-lock. Perhaps impatient, perhaps late for important appointments, three of us nonetheless accepted what, after all, we could not alter. One, however, would not. He would not be helpless. He would go where he was going even if he couldn't get there. A Wall Street type in suit and tie, he got out of his car and strode toward the bus, rapping smartly on its doors. When they opened, he exchanged words with the driver. The doors folded shut. He then stepped in front of the bus, took hold of one of its large windshield wipers and broke it. 8

The bus doors reopened and the driver appeared, apparently giving the fellow a good piece of his mind. If so, the lecture was wasted, for the man started his car and proceeded to drive directly *into the bus*. He rammed it. Even though the point at which he struck the bus, the folding doors, was its most vulnerable point, ramming the side of a bus with your car has to rank very high on a futility index. My first thought was that it had to be a rental car. 9

To tell the truth, I could not believe my eyes. The bus driver opened his doors as much as they could be opened and he stepped directly onto the hood of the attacking car, jumping up and down with both his feet. He then retreated into the bus, closing the doors behind him. Obviously a man of action, the car driver backed up and rammed the bus again. How this exercise in absurdity would have been resolved none of us will ever know for at that point the traffic unclogged and the bus moved on. And the rest of us, we passives of the world, proceeded, our cars crossing a field of battle as if nothing untoward had happened. 10

It is tempting to blame such belligerent, uncivil and even neurotic behavior on the nuts of the world, but in our cars we all become a little crazy. How many of us speed up when a driver signals his intention of pulling in front of us? Are we resentful and anxious to pass him? How many of us try to squeeze in, or race along the shoulder of a lane merger? We may not jump on hoods, but driving the gantlet, we seethe, cursing not so silently in the safety of our steel bodies on wheels—fortresses for cowards. 11

What is it within us that gives birth to such antisocial behavior and why, all of   12
a sudden, have so many drivers gone around the bend? My friend Joel Katz, a Manhattan psychiatrist, calls it "a Rambo pattern. People are running around thinking
the American way is to take the law into your own hands when anyone does anything wrong. And what constitutes 'wrong'? Anything that cramps your style."

It seems to me that it is a new America we see on the road now. It has the   13
mentality of a hoodlum and the backbone of a coward. The car is its weapon and
hiding place, and it is still a symbol even in this. Road Rambos no longer bespeak
a self-reliant, civil people tooling around in family cruisers. In fact, there aren't
families in these machines that charge headlong with their brights on in broad
daylight, demanding we get out of their way. Bullies are loners, and they have
perverted our liberty of the open road into drivers' license. They represent an
America that derides the values of decency and good manners, then roam the
highways riding shotgun and shrieking freedom. By allowing this to happen, the
rest of us approve.

EXERCISE 13.4 ▶ DRAWING A GRAPHIC ORGANIZER

Using Graphic Organizer 13.1 or 13.2 as a basis, draw a graphic organizer for "What's
That Supposed to Mean?" (pp. 302–5).

HOW WRITERS READ ▶	ILLUSTRATION
THE READING PROCESS	**STRATEGIES**
BEFORE READING	**Preview** the essay to get an overview of the content and organization.
	Make connections by thinking about what the title means and considering what examples from your personal experience would be relevant.
	Read the headnote (if one is provided) for background information about the author and the reading.
WHILE READING	**Identify the characteristics of illustration** (pp. 298–302). Be sure you can answer the following questions.
	• What is the writer's **thesis**? Is it stated or implied? (If the thesis is unstated, ask yourself what one major point all of the examples illustrate.)
	• What are the **main points**, and how does each example illustrate them? (Make notes in the margin.)
	• How are the examples **organized**—chronologically, spatially, or in some other way?
	• What is the author's **purpose**? Who is the intended **audience**?
	• How does the writer use **language** to achieve the desired effect? (Circle strong word choices or place a checkmark in the margin.)

AFTER READING

Draw a **graphic organizer** showing the key examples and identifying how they are organized. (Use your graphic organizer for review and study.)

Analyze and evaluate the reading by answering the following questions.

- How well do the examples **explain or clarify the thesis**?
- After reading the essay, are you **convinced by the writer's thesis**? How could the author have done a better job of convincing you?
- What is the **emotional impact** of the examples and any **visual aids**? (Explain your reaction in detail.)
- Are the examples **fair, accurate, representative**, and **relevant**? Would **other types of evidence** have strengthened the essay?
- What is the **writer's attitude** toward the subject? (Highlight words with strong connotations that reveal the writer's feelings.)
- What is the writer's **tone**? (Describe the tone with two or three adjectives.)
- What **types of evidence**, other than examples, does the author offer to support the thesis?
- Does the author **omit** examples that would contradict or weaken the thesis?

EXERCISE 13.5 ▸ READING CRITICALLY

Apply the questions in the "How Writers Read" box to the selection "Rambos of the Road" (pp. 306–8).

Integrate Illustration into an Essay

Examples are an effective way to support a thesis that relies on one or more other patterns of development. For instance, you might use examples in the following ways.

For a reading that uses illustration as well as other patterns of development, see "Why Walking Helps Us Think" (pp. 322–25).

- to *define* a particular advertising ploy,
- to *compare* two types of small businesses,
- to *classify* types of movies,
- to *show the effects* of aerobic exercise, and
- to *argue* that junk food is unhealthy because of its high fat and salt content.

When using examples in an essay where illustration is not the main pattern of development, keep the following tips in mind.

1. **Choose effective examples.** They should be relevant, representative, accurate, specific, and striking.
2. **Use transitions such as "for instance" or "for example."** They make it obvious that an example follows.
3. **Provide enough details to help your readers understand how an example supports your point.** Do not overwhelm your readers with too many details.

GRAPHIC ORGANIZER 13.2 The Structure of "Rambos of the Road"

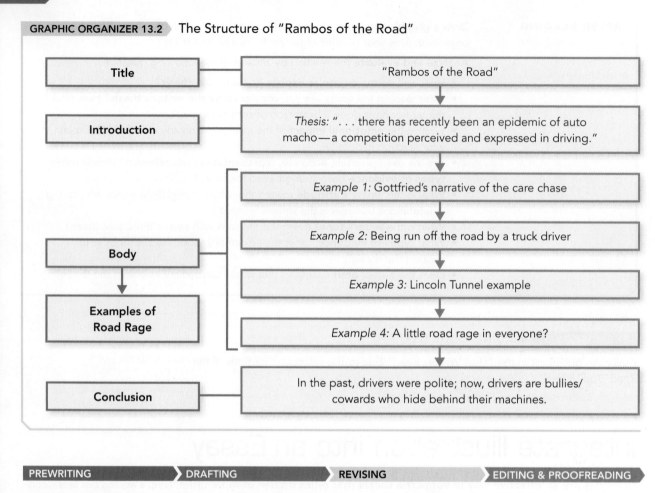

Title	"Rambos of the Road"
Introduction	*Thesis:* ". . . there has recently been an epidemic of auto macho—a competition perceived and expressed in driving."
Body → **Examples of Road Rage**	*Example 1:* Gottfried's narrative of the care chase
	Example 2: Being run off the road by a truck driver
	Example 3: Lincoln Tunnel example
	Example 4: A little road rage in everyone?
Conclusion	In the past, drivers were polite; now, drivers are bullies/cowards who hide behind their machines.

PREWRITING ⟩ DRAFTING ⟩ **REVISING** ⟩ EDITING & PROOFREADING

A Guided Writing Assignment*

ILLUSTRATION

Your Essay Assignment

Write an illustration essay explaining a topic your readers might find unfamiliar or challenging and that you can illustrate effectively with examples. Imagine you are writing for your campus newspaper, and choose a topic that you think might interest your readers. Below are some options.

- the popularity of a certain type of sport, television show, or hobby
- the connection between clothing and personality

* The writing process is *recursive*; that is, you may find yourself revising as you draft or prewriting as you revise. This is especially true when writing on a computer. Your writing process may also differ from essay to essay or from that of your classmates.

- the problems of balancing school, work, and family
- effective (or ineffective) parenting
- a concept from one of your courses, such as stress management or ergonomic design

1 Select a topic from the list on pages 310–11, or create your own.

Use one or more of the following suggestions to generate topic ideas.

1. **Peruse your textbooks**, looking for boldfaced terms that you find interesting or want to learn about. List several and then, alone or with another student, brainstorm examples that would help to illustrate or explain the concept. You may need to read your textbook for models. (If you are an abstract thinker, starting from a generalization and then coming up with examples may work better for you.)

2. **Work backward:** Make a list of the things you do for fun or find challenging and then consider what they have in common. Use that common thread as your topic.

After you have chosen your topic, make sure that you can **develop your main idea into a well-focused working thesis**.

2 Consider your purpose, audience, and point of view.

Ask yourself these questions.

- Will my essay's **purpose** be to **express myself**, **inform**, or **persuade**? Several examples may be needed to persuade. One extended example may be sufficient to inform readers about a very narrow topic (for example, how to select an educational toy for a child).

- Who is my **audience**? Will readers need any **background information** to understand my essay? **What types of examples** will be most effective with these readers? Straightforward examples, based on everyday experience, may be appropriate for an audience unfamiliar with your topic; more technical examples may be appropriate for an expert audience.

- What **other evidence** (such as facts and statistics, expert opinion) will I need to make my case with my audience? Do I have enough information to write about this topic, or must I consult additional sources? How might I use **additional patterns of development** within my illustration essay? (For example, you might use narration to present an extended example from your own life.)

- What **point of view** best suits my purpose and audience? (Unless the examples you use are all drawn from your personal experience, you will probably use the **third person** when using examples to explain.)

PREWRITING

3 Narrow your topic and generate examples.

Narrow your topic. Use prewriting to make your topic manageable. Be sure you can support your topic with one or more examples.

Use idea-generating strategies to come up with a wide variety of examples.

1. Write down the generalizations your essay will make, and then **brainstorm** examples that support them.
2. **Freewrite** to bring to mind relevant personal experiences or stories told by friends and relatives.
3. **Conduct research** to find examples used by experts and relevant news reports and to locate other supporting information, like facts and statistics.
4. **Review textbooks** for examples used there.

Creative and abstract learners may have trouble focusing on details. If you have trouble, try teaming up with a classmate who has a pragmatic or concrete learning style for help.

Hint: Keep track of where you found each example so that you can cite your sources accurately.

4 Evaluate your examples.

Try these suggestions to help you evaluate your examples.

- **Reread everything you have written.** (Sometimes reading your notes aloud is helpful.)
- **Highlight examples** that are **representative** (or typical) yet **striking**. Make sure they are **relevant** (they clearly illustrate your point). Unless you are using just one extended example, make sure your examples are **varied**. Then **copy and paste** the usable ideas to a new document to consult while drafting.
- **Collaborate.** In small groups, take turns **giving examples** and having classmates tell you:
  1. what they think your **main idea** is. (If they don't get it, rethink your examples.)
  2. what **additional information** they need to find your main idea convincing.

Classmates can also help narrow your topic or think of more effective examples.

5 Draft your thesis statement.

Try one or more of the following strategies to **develop a generalization** that your examples support. (Your generalization will become your working thesis.)

1. Systematically **review your examples** asking yourself what they have in common.
2. **Discuss your thesis with a classmate.** Do the examples support the thesis? If not, try to improve on each other's examples or revise the thesis.
3. In a **two-column list**, write words in the left column describing how you feel about your narrowed topic. (For example, the topic *cheating on college exams* might generate such feelings as anger, surprise, and confusion.) In the right column, add details about specific situations in which these feelings arose. (For example, your thesis might focus on your surprise on discovering that a good friend cheated on an exam.)
4. **Research** your topic in the library or on the Internet to uncover examples outside your own experience. Then ask yourself what the examples from your experience and your research have in common.

Note: As you draft, you may think of situations or examples that illustrate a different or more interesting thesis. Don't hesitate to revise your thesis as you discover more about your topic.

Collaborate with classmates to make sure your examples support your thesis statement.

Select a method of organization.

- If you are using a **single, extended example**, you are most likely to use **chronological order** to relate events in the sequence in which they happened.
- If you are using **several examples**, you are most likely to organize the examples from most to least or least to most important.
- If you are using **many examples**, you may want to **group them into categories**. For instance, in an essay about the use of slang, you might classify examples according to regions or age groups in which they are used.

Hint: An outline or graphic organizer will allow you to experiment to find the best order for supporting paragraphs. (Spatial learners may prefer to draw a graphic organizer, while verbal learners may prefer to write an outline.)

 Write a first draft of your illustration essay.

Use the following guidelines to keep your illustration essay on track.

- The **introduction** should spark readers' interest and include background information (if needed by readers). Most illustration essays include a **thesis** near the beginning to help readers understand the point of upcoming examples.
- The **body paragraphs** should include **topic sentences** to focus each paragraph (or paragraph cluster) on one key idea. Craft **one or more examples** for each paragraph (or cluster) to illustrate that key idea. Use **vivid descriptive language** to make readers feel as if they are experiencing or observing the situation. Include **transitions**, such as *for example* or *in particular*, to guide readers from one example to another. (Consult Chapter 8 for help with crafting effective descriptions.)
- The **conclusion** should **include a final statement** that pulls together your ideas and reminds readers of your thesis.

 Evaluate your draft, and revise as necessary.

Use **Figure 13.1, "Flowchart for Revising an Illustration Essay,"** to evaluate and revise your draft.

FIGURE 13.1 Flowchart for Revising an Illustration Essay

QUESTIONS | REVISION STRATEGIES

1. Highlight your thesis statement. Place a ✔ by each example. Do your examples clearly support the generalization your thesis makes?

NO ▶
- Revise your thesis, changing your generalization so that it fits your examples.

YES ▼

(continued on next page) ▶

(Figure 13.1 continued)

QUESTIONS		REVISION STRATEGIES

2. *Write* a sentence describing your readers. ~~Cross out~~ any examples that won't appeal to them. Do you have enough examples left?

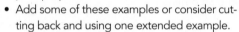

- Brainstorm more appealing examples.
- Add examples that represent different aspects of or viewpoints on your topic.

 YES

3. Write a sentence stating the purpose of your essay. ~~Cross out~~ any examples that don't fulfill your purpose. Do you have enough examples left?

- Brainstorm examples more appropriate to your purpose.
- Add some of these examples or consider cutting back and using one extended example.

 YES

4. Reread your examples. Is each one accurate, relevant, striking, representative, and specific? Are the examples varied?

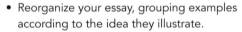

- Brainstorm to replace dull, irrelevant, or misleading examples.
- Conduct research to discover facts, expert opinion, or statistics.

 YES

5. Reread your supporting paragraphs. Does each one have a topic sentence? Does each topic sentence clearly make a point that the example(s) in that paragraph illustrate?

- Add or revise the topic sentence to clearly indicate the point each example or group of examples illustrates.
- Reorganize your essay, grouping examples according to the idea they illustrate.

 YES

6. Outline your essay. [Bracket] each transition. Is your organization clear and effective?

- Add transitions or use a different organizing strategy. (See Chapter 6.)

YES

7. Reread your introduction and conclusion. Is each effective?

- Revise your introduction to engage readers and provide background.
- Revise your conclusion to remind readers of your thesis and create a satisfying ending.

Edit and proofread your essay.

Refer to Chapter 9 for help with . . .

- **editing sentences** to avoid wordiness, making your verb choices strong and active, and making your sentences clear, varied, and parallel, and
- **editing words** for tone and diction, connotation, and concrete and specific language.

Pay particular attention to the following.

1. Keep **verb tenses** consistent in your extended examples. When using an event from the past as an example, however, always use the past tense to describe it.

   Example: Special events **are** an important part of children's lives. Parent visitation day at school **was** an event my daughter **talked** about for an entire week. Children **are** also excited by . . .

2. Use **first person** (*I, me, we, us*), **second person** (*you*), or **third person** (*he, she, it, him, her, they, them*) consistently.

   Example: I visited my daughter's first-grade classroom during parents' week last month. Each parent was invited to read a story to the class, and ~~you~~ we were encouraged to ask the children questions afterward.

3. Avoid **sentence fragments** when introducing examples. Each sentence must have both a subject and a verb.

   Example: Technology has become part of teenagers' daily lives. ~~For example, high~~ High school students who carry iPhones, are one example.

Readings: Illustration in Action

Conforming to Stand Out: A Look at American Beauty

Nick Ruggia

Nick Ruggia, a student at the University of Maryland at College Park, wrote this essay in response to an assignment in which he was asked to examine an American obsession.

Title: Ruggia identifies his topic and suggests his thesis.

He chose to write about Americans' obsession with physical appearance. As you read his illustration essay, notice how he supports his thesis with a variety of examples.

Introduction: Ruggia offers a biological reason for focusing on women. In his thesis statement, he makes a generalization about American women, and previews his organization by presenting his three examples in the order in which he will discuss them.

Organization: A topic sentence introduces example 1, the thin craze. In this paragraph and the next two, Ruggia uses specific celebrities and detailed statistics to support his claims.

Supporting evidence: Ruggia cites the sources for his subexamples using MLA style. The statistics suggest that the celebrities are representative of Americans in general.

Organization: A transitional sentence leads into the topic sentence for example 2, the plastic surgery craze, supported by detailed statistics from reliable sources.

In nature, two factors largely determine survival of the species: access to resources and physical attraction (necessary for the ability to mate). Humans function under the same basic rules. In modern America, where almost everyone can acquire the basic resources to live, humans are striving harder than ever to be physically attractive. Although men are increasingly caught up in its grip, the pressure to be beautiful falls most intensely on women. The thin craze, the plastic surgery craze, and the body art craze represent some of the increasingly drastic lengths American women are being driven to in their quest for physical perfection.

Since Kate Moss's wafer-thin frame took the modeling industry by storm, skinny has driven America's aesthetics. Hollywood is a mirror for our desires, and our stars are shrinking. Nicole Ritchie and Angelina Jolie, among others, have publicly struggled with eating disorders. Jennifer Anniston and Reese Witherspoon are rumored to be following a diet of baby food to keep weight off (Crawford A1). And the stars aren't alone. According to the United States National Institutes of Mental Health, about 0.9 percent of American women will suffer from anorexia in their lifetimes, while another 1.5 percent will be bulimic and 3.5 percent will binge. These numbers exclude the disordered eaters who do not meet all the criteria necessary for diagnosis or do not accurately self-report. In a population of 300 million, these statistics represent millions of women struggling with eating disorders. Men are not immune either, with 0.2 to 0.3 percent of men diagnosed with bulimia or anorexia and 2 percent diagnosed with binge eating (*The Numbers*).

But for every Kate Moss idolizer, there's a would-be Pamela Anderson. This ideal, fed by porn and Hollywood, is plastic perfection: instead of anorexically denying their curves, many women choose to enhance their features through surgery. The American Society of Aesthetic Plastic Surgery (ASAPS) reported that in 2015, cosmetic surgeries were up 7 percent, with an overall increase of nearly 40 percent since 2011. While

1

2

3

it must be remembered that some people have more than one surgery, still, the scope of this practice is staggering nonetheless. Further evidence is provided by the surgically enhanced lips, stomachs, buttocks, and breasts that cover the pages of men's magazines all over the country. Strippers, porn stars like Jenna Jameson, and *Playboy* models like Anderson and the late Anna Nicole Smith flaunt enormous fake breasts. Clearly there is a disconnect between the sexless anorexic standard that so many women strive for and the bottle blonde bombshell that so many men favor. What everyone seems to agree on, though, is that plastic surgery is a response to the fear of aging. And in this way as well, men too are increasingly vulnerable to the superficial, with the ASAPS reporting that they accounted for 9.5 percent of plastic surgeries in 2015.

Body art, in the form of piercing and tattoos, also illustrates (literally) Americans' obsession with physical appearance. The pierced and tattooed once jarred on public sensibilities, but now these body modifications have gone mainstream. Even "alternative" piercings are now accepted: the late Amy Winehouse, a heavily tattooed popular musician, has added to the popularity of the "Monroe" piercing, located above the lip where Marilyn Monroe had a mole. About 40 percent of the millennial generation has at least one tattoo, and nearly a quarter have pierced something other than their ears (*Millennials*). Once largely limited to sailors, criminals, and punk rockers — and to men — body art has become big business, drawing in more women as it spreads.

Maybe Americans have gone too far in basing their self-worth on physical appearance. Every visible part of the human body has been marketed as a fixable flaw or an opportunity for more adornment. Of course, Americans have always cared about their looks and made great efforts to improve them, but once most people kept the issue in perspective. Today, appearance rules. And men increasingly are joining women in obedience to its commands. Both sexes, though, will find that basing self-esteem on physical appearance, a fleeting commodity at best, is a recipe for misery.

Supporting evidence: Ruggia cites striking subexamples and detailed statistics.

4   **Organization:** A topic sentence introduces example 3, the body art craze.

Conclusion: Ruggia acknowledges that attention to appearance is nothing new, but suggests that Americans today place too much emphasis on it.

5

Sources: Ruggia lists his sources in MLA style, with the entries in alphabetical order. Notice the style for listing documents from Web sites sponsored by organizations and government agencies.

Works Cited

Crawford, Trish. "Celebrity 'Baby Food Diet' Recipe for Eating Disorder."
Toronto Star, 18 May 2010, p. A1.

Millennials: Confident, Connected, Open to Change. Pew Research Center
for the People and the Press, 24 Feb. 2010, www.pewsocialtrends
.org/2010/02/24/millennials-confident-connected-open-to-change/
#the-millennial-identity.

"2015 Quick Facts." American Society of Aesthetic Plastic Surgery, 2016,
www.surgery.org/sites/default/files/2015-quick-facts.pdf.

The Numbers Count: Mental Disorders in America. United States, Department
of Health and Human Services, National Institutes of Mental Health. 2013,
www.lb7.uscourts.gov/documents/12-cv-1072url2.pdf.

Analyzing the Writer's Technique

1. **Examples** Evaluate the three main examples Ruggia provides. How well do they illustrate his thesis? What other examples could he have used?
2. **Sources** Ruggia used four sources in writing the essay. What kinds of sources are they? How does his use of these sources strengthen his essay?
3. **Evidence** Ruggia uses celebrities and statistics as evidence to support each of the topic sentences about his three main examples. What other types of evidence could he have used?

Thinking Critically about Illustration

1. **Emotional Response** Do any of Ruggia's examples or pieces of evidence create an emotional impact? If so, choose several and explain their effects.
2. **Connotation** What are the connotations of "bottle blonde bombshell" (para. 3)?
3. **Alternative Viewpoints** What other types of sources could Ruggia have consulted to research and discuss alternative viewpoints?
4. **Generalization** Is the generalization in the essay's last sentence well-supported and well-explained in the essay?

Responding to the Essay

1. **Discussion** Discuss the meaning and effectiveness of Ruggia's title.
2. **Journal** In your journal, respond to the following question: To what extent do you agree that piercings and tattoos are widely accepted?
3. **Thinking Critically** What do you think is the reason for the "disconnect" that Ruggia mentions in paragraph 3? Is the problem that women don't understand

what men want? That men don't understand what women want? Both? Something else?

4. **Essay** Are Americans obsessed with appearances in other ways? Write an essay explaining another American obsession. Use examples to support your thesis.

Mascots

Brian Doyle

Brian Doyle is the editor of *Portland* magazine at the University of Portland, in Oregon. He is also a bestselling novelist as well as the author of collections of stories, essays, and poems. In the following piece, Doyle describes the wide variety of animals used as symbols for sports teams and explores the reasons we choose animals as mascots. **Before reading**, preview and make connections by thinking about the mascots you have been associated with as a student, an athlete, or a fan. **While reading**, highlight descriptive language and interesting word choices that reveal the author's feelings about his subject and his audience.

The first sports team I remember loving as a child, in the dim dewy days when I was two or three years old and just waking up to things that were not milk and mama or dirt and dogs, was the Fighting Irish of the University of Notre Dame. They were on television every day, it seemed, in our bustling brick Irish Catholic house. Inasmuch as I was hatched and coddled near Manhattan, there were also Metropolitans and Knickerbockers and Rangers and Islanders, and as I shuffled shyly into high school, I met snarling and roaring mammalian mascots, notably the Cougars of my own alma mater, which was plopped in marshlands where I doubt a cougar had been seen for 300 years.

1

Right about then I started paying attention to how we fetishize animals as symbols for our athletic adventures, and I have become more attentive since. For nearly 30 years now I have worked for colleges and universities; you could earn a degree in zoology just by reading the college sports news, where animals from anteater to wasp roar and fly and sprint and lope and canter and gallop and prowl. Among them, interestingly, are armadillos, bees, boll weevils, herons, owls, koalas, turtles, moose, penguins, gulls, sea lions, and squirrels, none of which seems especially intimidating or prepossessing—although I know a man in North Carolina who once lost a fistfight with a heron, and certainly many of us have run away from angry bees and moose, and surely there are some among us who could relate stories of furious boll weevils. But perhaps this is not the time, although anyone who *has* a story like that should see me right after class.

2

Mascottishly, there are vast numbers of canids (coyotes, foxes, huskies, salukis, great danes), felids (lions, tigers, panthers, lynx, bobcats), ruminants (bulls, chargers, broncs, broncos, and bronchoes, though no bronchials), mustelids (badgers, wolverine, otters), and denizens of sea and swamp (dolphins, gators, sharks, sailfish, and "seawolves," or orca). There are two colleges that have an aggrieved

3

Hero Images/Getty Images

camel as their mascot. There are schools represented by snakes and tomcats. There is a school whose symbol is a frog and one whose mascot is a large clam and one whose mascot famously is a slug. There is a school whose mascot is the black fly. There are the Fighting Turtles of the College of Insurance in New York. There are schools represented by lemmings and scorpions and spiders. There are the Stormy Petrels of Oglethorpe University in Georgia. There is a school represented by an animal that has never yet been seen in the Americas, the bearcat of Asia, although perhaps it is meant to be a wolverine, which did once inhabit southern Ohio, and may still live in Cincinnati, which has tough neighborhoods. The most popular mascot appears to be the eagle, especially if you count the 15 schools represented by golden eagles, which brings us to a round total of approximately 82 schools symbolized by the eagle, a creature Benjamin Franklin considered "a Bird of bad moral Character . . . too lazy to fish for himself . . . like those among Men who live by Sharping & Robbing he is generally poor and often very lousy. Besides he is a rank Coward." But the two schools that Franklin helped establish are nicknamed the Quakers and the Diplomats, so we can safely ignore Ben on this matter.

This is not even to delve into the mysterious world of fantastical fauna—blue bears and blue tigers, crimson hawks, trolls, dragons and firebirds, griffins and griffons and gryphons, delta devils and jersey devils (there are *a lot* of devils, which makes you wonder about American character), jayhawks and kohawks and duhawks, green eagles and phoenixes, thunderhawks and thunderwolves—the mind reels; and then there is the whole subset of nicknamery that has to do with botany, as evidenced most memorably by the fighting Violets of New York

4

University, on which image we had better pull this whole essay to the side of the road and sit silently for a moment, moaning gently.

Beyond all the obvious reasons we choose animals as symbols for our sporting teams—their incredible energy and muscle, grace and intelligence and verve, our ancient conviction of their power and magic, ancient associations as clan signs and tribal totems, even more ancient shivers perhaps of fear at animals who hunted and ate us, plus the way their images look cool on letterheads and sweatshirts and pennants and fundraising appeals—there is something else, something so deep and revelatory about human beings that I think we do not admit it because it is too sad.

I think we love animals as images because we miss them in the flesh, and I think we love them as images because they matter to us spiritually in ways we cannot hope to articulate. The vast majority of us will never see a cougar or a wolverine, never mind a boll weevil, but even wearing a riveting creature on a shirt, or shouting the miracle of its name in a stadium, or grinning to see its rippling beauty on the window of a car, gives us a tiny subtle crucial electric jolt in the heart, connects us somehow to what we used to be with animals: thrilled and terrified. We've lost the salt of that feeling forever, but even a hint of it matters immensely to us as animals too. Maybe that's what we miss the most—the feeling that they are our cousins and not just clans of creatures who once filled the earth and now are shreds of memory, mere symbols, beings who used to be.

Understanding the Reading

1. **Summarizing** What are the main points Doyle makes about why we choose animals as mascots?
2. **Details** What mascot does the author say is most popular? How many schools are symbolized by this animal?
3. **Examples** Explain what types of animals are considered "fantastical fauna."
4. **Vocabulary** Explain the meaning of each of the following words as it is used in the reading: *mammalian* (para. 1), *fetishize* (2), *prepossessing* (2), *denizens* (3), and *revelatory* (5).

Analyzing the Writer's Technique

1. **Introduction** The essay opens with a description of the author's childhood and his first awareness of the use of animals as mascots. Why is this an effective introduction?
2. **Abstractions** When the author explores why he thinks we choose animals as mascots, he uses the abstract phrases "we miss them in the flesh" and "they matter to us spiritually" (para. 6). How does Doyle make these ideas real and understandable?
3. **Conclusion** Doyle's poignant conclusion seems somewhat at odds with the playful tone of the rest of the essay. Is this change in tone appropriate, given what he says at the end of the essay?

Thinking Critically about Illustration

1. **Generalization** What generalization does Doyle make? How effectively is the generalization stated and supported through the examples he chooses? Are the examples relevant and representative? Does Doyle provide enough examples to support his claim? Why or why not?

2. **Details** Why did Doyle include a quote from Benjamin Franklin (para. 3)?

3. **Connotation** What impression does the author create through his choice of words in paragraph 5? Consider the connotative meanings of words such as *energy, muscle, grace, verve, power, magic, ancient, tribal.*

4. **Alternative Examples** How would the essay be different if Doyle had included other types of evidence to support his thesis? What other types of evidence might he have included?

Responding to the Reading

1. **Discussion** Why do you think we choose animals as mascots for our sports teams? Which of the author's reasons do you think are more compelling, the "obvious reasons," or the deeper, more spiritual reasons? Why does the author think the reasons are sad?

2. **Journal** How did the author organize and present his examples and details? Write a journal entry evaluating the effectiveness of the examples presented.

3. **Essay** The author refers to ancient "clan signs and tribal totems" as part of the connection we have with animals. What animals would you choose to represent yourself (or your family) as a sign or totem? What specific qualities of this animal reflect who you are or who you aspire to be? Write an essay describing the animal you would choose as your mascot and giving examples of the characteristics that make this animal a fitting symbol for you.

Working Together

Although the title of this essay, "Mascots," accurately reflects the content, a different title could do more to spark readers' interest. In small groups, come up with a list of at least three alternative titles for this selection. (Hint: Recall the suggestions for writing a good title on p. 168, such as asking a question that the essay answers, using alliteration, and creating a play on words.)

READING ILLUSTRATION COMBINED WITH OTHER PATTERNS

Why Walking Helps Us Think

Ferris Jabr

Ferris Jabr is a writer based in Portland, Oregon. His work has been anthologized in *The Best American Science and Nature Writing* series, and he has worked as a staff editor at *Scientific American*, where he is now a contributing writer. He has also written for publications including *The New York Times Magazine, Outside, Slate,* and

The New Yorker, where this essay originally appeared. **Before reading**, preview the essay and make connections by thinking about benefits you notice when you go for a walk. **While reading**, identify the examples Jabr uses to support his thesis and consider how effectively they support his generalization.

Since at least the time of peripatetic Greek philosophers, many other writers have discovered a deep, intuitive connection between walking, thinking, and writing. "How vain it is to sit down to write when you have not stood up to live!" Henry David Thoreau penned in his journal. "Methinks that the moment my legs begin to move, my thoughts begin to flow." Thomas DeQuincey has calculated that William Wordsworth—whose poetry is filled with tramps up mountains, through forests, and along public roads—walked as many as a hundred and eighty thousand miles in his lifetime, which comes to an average of six and a half miles a day starting from age five.   1

What is it about walking, in particular, that makes it so amenable to thinking and writing? The answer begins with changes to our chemistry. When we go for a walk, the heart pumps faster, circulating more blood and oxygen not just to the muscles but to all the organs—including the brain. Many experiments have shown that after or during exercise, even very mild exertion, people perform better on tests of memory and attention (Voss et al.). Walking on a regular basis also promotes new connections (Erickson, Mark I., et al.) between brain cells, staves off the usual withering of brain tissue that comes with age (Erickson, K. I., et al.), increases the volume of the hippocampus (a brain region crucial for memory), and elevates levels of molecules that both stimulate the growth of new neurons and transmit messages between them (Segal, S. K., et al.).   2

The way we move our bodies further changes the nature of our thoughts, and vice versa. Psychologists who specialize in exercise music have quantified what many of us already know (Karageorghis and Priest): listening to songs with high tempos motivates us to run faster, and the swifter we move, the quicker we prefer our music (Barney et al.). Likewise, when drivers hear loud, fast music, they unconsciously step a bit harder on the gas pedal (Warren). Walking at our own pace creates an unadulterated feedback loop between the rhythm of our bodies and our mental state that we cannot experience as easily when we're jogging at the gym, steering a car, biking, or during any other kind of locomotion. When we stroll, the pace of our feet naturally vacillates with our moods and the cadence of our inner speech; at the same time, we can actively change the pace of our thoughts by deliberately walking more briskly or by slowing down.   3

Because we don't have to devote much conscious effort to the act of walking, our attention is free to wander—to overlay the world before us with a parade of images from the mind's theatre. This is precisely the kind of mental state that studies have linked to innovative ideas and strokes of insight. Earlier this year, Marily Oppezzo and Daniel Schwartz of Stanford published what is likely the first set of studies that directly measure the way walking changes creativity in the moment. They got the idea for the studies while on a walk. "My doctoral advisor had the habit of going for walks with his students to brainstorm," Oppezzo says of Schwartz. "One day we got kind of meta."   4

In a series of four experiments, Oppezzo and Schwartz asked a hundred and   5
seventy-six college students to complete different tests of creative thinking
while either sitting, walking on a treadmill, or sauntering through Stanford's
campus. In one test, for example, volunteers had to come up with atypical uses
for everyday objects, such as a button or a tire. On average, the students thought
of between four and six more novel uses for the objects while they were walking
than when they were seated. Another experiment required volunteers to con-
template a metaphor, such as "a budding cocoon," and generate a unique but
equivalent metaphor, such as "an egg hatching." Ninety-five percent of students
who went for a walk were able to do so, compared to only fifty percent of those
who never stood up. But walking actually worsened people's performance on a
different type of test, in which students had to find the one word that united a
set of three, like "cheese" for "cottage, cream, and cake." Oppezzo speculates
that, by setting the mind adrift on a frothing sea of thought, walking is counter-
productive to such laser-focused thinking: "If you're looking for a single correct
answer to a question, you probably don't want all of these different ideas bub-
bling up."

Where we walk matters as well. In a study led by Marc Berman of the Univer-   6
sity of South Carolina, students who ambled through an arboretum improved their
performance on a memory test more than students who walked along city streets.
A small but growing collection of studies suggests that spending time in green
spaces — gardens, parks, forests — can rejuvenate the mental resources that man-
made environments deplete.

Psychologists have learned that attention is a limited resource that continu-   7
ally drains throughout the day. A crowded intersection — rife with pedestrians,
cars, and billboards — bats our attention around. In contrast, walking past a pond
in a park allows our mind to drift casually from one sensory experience to another,
from wrinkling water to rustling reeds.

Still, urban and pastoral walks likely offer unique advantages for the mind. A   8
walk through a city provides more immediate stimulation — a greater variety of
sensations for the mind to play with. But, if we are already at the brink of over-
stimulation, we can turn to nature instead. Virginia Woolf relished the creative
energy of London's streets, describing it in her diary as "being on the highest crest
of the biggest wave, right in the centre & swim of things." But she also depended
on her walks through England's South Downs to "have space to spread my mind
out in" (Dobbs). And, in her youth, she often travelled to Cornwall for the summer,
where she loved to "spend my afternoons in solitary trampling" through the countryside (Dobbs).

Perhaps the most profound relationship between walking, thinking, and   9
writing reveals itself at the end of a stroll, back at the desk. There, it becomes
apparent that writing and walking are extremely similar feats, equal parts
physical and mental. When we choose a path through a city or forest, our brain
must survey the surrounding environment, construct a mental map of the
world, settle on a way forward, and translate that plan into a series of footsteps.
Likewise, writing forces the brain to review its own landscape, plot a course

through that mental terrain, and transcribe the resulting trail of thoughts by guiding the hands. Walking organizes the world around us; writing organizes our thoughts.

Links

Barney, David, et al. "College Students' Usage of Personal Music Players (PMP) during Exercise." *ICHPER-SD Journal of Research*, vol. 7, no. 1 (2012), pp. 23–26, eric.ed.gov/?id=EJ973952.

Berman, Marc G., et al. "The Cognitive Benefits of Interacting with Nature." *Psychological Science*, vol. 19, no. 12 (Dec. 2008), pp. 1207–12, doi:10.1111/j.1467-9280.2008.02225.x.

Dobbs, David. "Virginia Woolf Takes a Walk, Finds a Novel." *Neuron Culture*, 4 June 2014, daviddobb .net/smoothpebbles/virginia-woolf-takes-a-walk-finds-a-novel.

Erickson, K. I., et al. "Physical Activity Predicts Gray Matter Volume in Late Adulthood." *Neurology*, vol. 75, no. 16 (2010), pp. 1415–22, doi:10.1212/WNL.0b013e3181f88359.

Erickson, Mark I., et al. "Exercise Training Increases Size of Hippocampus and Improves Memory." *Proceedings of the National Academy of Sciences of the United States of America*, vol. 108, no. 7, pp. 3017–22, doi:10.1073/pnas.1015950108.

Karageorghis, Costas I., and David-Lee Priest. "Music in the Exercise Domain: A Review and Synthesis." *International Review of Sport Exercise Psychology*, vol. 5, no. 1, pp. 67–84, doi:10.1080/1750984X.2011.631027.

Oppezzo, Marily, and Daniel L. Schwartz. "Give Your Ideas Some Legs: The Positive Effect of Walking on Creative Thinking." *Journal of Experimental Psychology: Learning, Memory, and Cognition*, vol. 40, no. 4 (2014), pp. 1142–52, doi: 10.1037/a0036577.

Segal, S. K., et al. "Exercise-Induced Noradrenergic Activation Enhances Memory Consolidation in Both Normal Aging Patients with Amnestic Mild Cognitive Impairment." *Journal of Alzheimers Disease*, vol. 32, no. 4 (2012), pp. 1011–18, doi:10.3233/JAD-2012-121078.

Voss, M. W., et al. "Plasticity of Brain Networks in a Randomized Intervention Trial of Exercise Training in Older Adults." *Front Aging Neuroscience*, vol. 32 (2010), doi:10.3389/fnagi.2010.00032.

Warren, Brodsky. "The Effects of Music Tempo on Simulated Driving Performance and Vehicular Control." *Transportation Research Part F: Traffic Psychology and Behaviour*, vol. 4, no. 4 (2001), pp. 219–41, doi:10.1016/S1369-8478(01)00025-0.

Woolf, Virginia. "[Sunday 5 September 1926.]" *Woolf Online*, edited by Pamela L. Caughie, et al., 2016, www.woolfonline.com.

Understanding the Reading

1. **Summarizing** Briefly explain the changes to our body chemistry that result from walking.
2. **Detail** What have psychologists discovered about the effects of music?
3. **Detail** How does location affect our thinking when we walk?
4. **Vocabulary** Explain the meaning of each of the following words as it is used in the reading: *peripatetic* (para. 1), *amenable* (2), *vacillates* (3), *cadence* (3), and *rejuvenate* (6).

Analyzing the Writer's Technique

1. **Introduction** Why does the author mention Thoreau and Wordsworth in the introduction?

2. **Thesis** Express Jabr's thesis in your own words. Is it stated directly in the essay or only implied?
3. **Audience** What audience do you think Jabr is addressing in this selection? How do his examples address or appeal to this audience?

Visualizing the Reading

Jabr uses cause and effect in addition to illustration in his essay. Use the chart below to identify the causes and effects discussed in each paragraph listed. The first one has been done for you.

Paragraph Number	Cause or Effect Discussed
Paragraph 2	Walking causes several changes to our body chemistry (heart pumps faster, more blood and oxygen circulated to organs, etc.).
Paragraph 3	
Paragraph 7	
Paragraph 8	

Thinking Critically about Illustration

1. **Connotation** What is the connotation of *ambled* (para. 6)? Is Jabr using it to mean something positive or negative?
2. **Sources** Jabr's examples are drawn primarily from university studies. How trustworthy do you consider these sources of information? What other source types could Jabr have used to give alternative viewpoints?
3. **Examples** Evaluate the effectiveness of the examples in this selection. Does Jabr provide a variety of relevant and useful examples to support his thesis?
4. **Meaning** What does the author mean when he says that walking "creates an unadulterated feedback loop between the rhythm of our bodies and our mental state"? How is it possible to change the pace of our thoughts?

Responding to the Reading

1. **Reaction** Jabr quotes the writer Virginia Woolf (para. 8) as relishing the "creative energy" of the city while depending on walks in the countryside for "space to spread my mind out in." Where do you go to find creative energy or mental stimulation? Where do you go to rejuvenate your mental resources?
2. **Journal** Aside from the physical effects of walking described in the selection, how does walking affect you? If you typically do not walk, how do other forms of exercise affect your mental state? Write a journal entry describing the effects of walking or exercise on your thinking and your writing.
3. **Essay** Jabr compares writing and walking as "equal parts physical and mental." Consider the mental map you create when you walk from class to home, then

write an essay giving examples of that landscape. Describe your path from your starting point to your destination, and give examples of landmarks and points of interest along the way.

Working Together

Imagine that you have been asked to help promote a walking trail system that goes around and through your campus or your town. Working with a partner, create a list of "talking points" to highlight the benefits of walking in both green spaces and urban environments. If you know the area well enough, suggest pathways that would offer stimulation and/or rejuvenation for people walking along the trail. Be prepared to share your work with the class.

Apply Your Skills: Additional Essay Assignments

Using what you learned about illustration in this chapter, write an illustration essay on one of the topics below. Depending on the topic you choose, you may need to conduct library or Internet research.

For more on locating and documenting sources, see Part 5.

To Express Your Ideas

1. In an article for the campus newspaper, explain what you consider to be the three most important qualities of a college instructor. Support your opinion with vivid examples from your experience.
2. Explain to a general audience the role played by grandparents within a family, citing examples from your own family or other families you know well.

To Inform Your Reader

3. In "Rambos of the Road," Martin Gottfried explains the concept of "auto macho," also known as "road rage," using examples from his own experience. Explain the concept of *peer pressure*, using examples from your experience.
4. Describe to an audience of college students the qualities or achievements you think should be emphasized during job interviews. Give examples that show why the qualities or achievements you choose are important to potential employers.

To Persuade Your Reader

5. Argue for or against an increased emphasis on physical education in public schools. Your audience is your local school committee.
6. In a letter to the editor of a local newspaper, argue for or against the establishment of a neighborhood watch group.

Cases Using Illustration

7. Prepare the oral presentation you will give to your local town board to convince board members to lower the speed limit on your street. Use examples as well as other types of evidence.

8. Write a letter to the parents of three-year-old children who will begin attending your day care center this year, explaining how they can prepare their children for the day care experience. Support your advice with brief but relevant examples.

SYNTHESIZING IDEAS   CIVILITY

Both "American Jerk: Be Civil, or I'll Beat You to a Pulp" (pp. 28–29) and "Rambos of the Road" (pp. 306–8) deal with bad behavior and incivility.

Analyzing the Readings

1. What types of behaviors does each reading address? Compare the authors' attitudes toward these behaviors.

2. Write a journal entry comparing the techniques that each author uses to support his thesis, especially considering the tone of each. Which is more effective? Explain your choice.

Essay Idea

Choose a public setting or forum in which selfish behavior and a lack of civility are evident to you. Write an essay illustrating the behavior.

14

Process Analysis

Explaining How Something Works or Is Done

WRITING QUICK START The photograph on this page shows a person assembling a piece of furniture from a kit. Write a brief paragraph describing how to assemble furniture so that you don't end up with any extra parts or forgotten pieces. Your audience is people who need to assemble furniture from a kit for the first time.

In this chapter you will learn to:

- understand the purpose and function of process analysis essays

- use graphic organizers to visualize process analysis essays

- integrate process analysis into an essay

- read and think critically about process analysis

- plan, organize, draft, revise, and edit essays using process analysis

To describe the steps involved in assembling furniture, you had to explain a process. A **process analysis** explains step by step how something works, is done, or is made. Process analyses provide people with practical information—directions for assembling equipment, instructions for registering for classes, an explanation of how a medication works. Whatever the purpose, the information in a process analysis must be accurate, clear, and easy to follow. In this chapter, you will read process analyses; you will also write a process analysis essay or use process analysis in essays that rely on one or more of the other patterns of development.

USING PROCESS ANALYSIS **IN COLLEGE AND THE WORKPLACE**

- For a *child development course*, your assignment is to visit a day care center, observe one confrontation between a child and a teacher, and explain how the teacher resolved the conflict.

- As part of a *chemistry lab report*, you need to summarize the procedure you followed in preparing a solution or conducting an experiment.

- While working as an *engineer* at a water treatment plant, you are asked to describe how the city's drinking water is tested and treated for contamination.

What Are the Characteristics of a Process Analysis Essay?

Most process analysis essays fall into two categories.

- A **how-to essay** explains how to do something to readers who want or need to perform the process. It may explain how to teach a child the alphabet, for instance. Your primary purpose in writing a how-to essay is to present the steps in the process clearly and completely so that your readers can perform the task you describe.
- A **how-it-works essay** explains how something works to readers who want to understand the process but not actually perform it. For example, you might explain how a popular radio talk show screens its callers. Your primary purpose in writing a how-it-works essay is to present the steps in the process clearly enough so that your readers can fully understand it.

Some essays contain elements of both types of process analysis. In writing about how a car alarm system works, for example, you might find it necessary to explain how to activate and deactivate the system as well as how it works.

A process analysis essay should include everything your reader needs to know to understand or perform the process. This usually means providing:

- an explicit thesis statement
- a clear, step-by-step description of the process in chronological order
- definitions of key terms, descriptions of needed equipment, and any other important background information
- enough detail for readers to follow the process
- help with avoiding potential problems

Process Analyses Usually Include an Explicit Thesis Statement

A process analysis usually contains a clear thesis that identifies the process to be discussed and suggests why the process is important or useful to the reader.

                                            process

How To   By carefully preparing for a vacation in a foreign country,

                 why it's useful
you can save time and prevent hassles.

                                         process

How It Works   Although understanding the grieving process will not lessen the grief

that you experience after the death of a loved one, knowing that your

                     why it's useful
experiences are normal does provide some comfort.

Process Analysis Is Organized Chronologically

The steps or events in a process analysis are usually organized in chronological order—that is, the order in which the steps are normally completed. For essays that explain lengthy processes, the steps may be grouped into categories or divided into substeps, with headings such as *Preparing for the Interview*, *During the Interview*, and

After the Interview. Transitions, such as *Before you are called for an interview* or *Once the interview is over*, are often used to make the order of steps and substeps clear.

Sometimes the steps of a process do not have to occur in any particular order. For example, in an essay on how to resolve a dispute between two coworkers, the order of the recommended actions may depend on the nature of the dispute. In this situation, some logical progression of recommended actions should be used, such as starting with informal or simple steps and progressing to more formal or complex ones.

EXERCISE 14.1   **WRITING A THESIS STATEMENT FOR PROCESS ANALYSIS**

Choose one of the following processes. The process should be one you are familiar with and can explain to others. Draft a working thesis statement and a chronological list of the steps or stages of the process.

1. How to use a specific computer program
2. How to study for an exam
3. How to end a relationship with a friend or partner
4. How to get an A in your writing class
5. How to complete an application (for college, a job, a credit card)

Process Analysis Provides Background Information Helpful to Readers

In some process analysis essays, readers may need additional information to understand the process. For example, in an essay explaining how scuba diving works to readers who are unfamiliar with the topic, you might need to define unfamiliar terms, such as *oxygen toxicity* or *decompression sickness*; you might need to provide background information about risks of injury or a history of the sport; and you would need to describe equipment such as dive masks, buoyancy compensators, and dive gauges. In a how-to essay, you might also need to explain where to obtain the equipment or training.

For more on defining terms, see Chapter 17.

EXERCISE 14.2   **PROVIDING BACKGROUND INFORMATION IN A PROCESS ESSAY**

For one of the following processes, list (a) the technical terms that you need to define in order to explain the process, (b) useful background information you might include in the essay, and (c) the types of equipment needed to perform the task.

1. How to perform a task at home or at work (such as changing the oil in a car or taking notes during a court hearing)
2. How a piece of equipment or a machine works (such as a treadmill or a lawn mower)
3. How to repair an object (such as a leaky faucet or a ripped piece of clothing)

Process Analysis Provides an Appropriate Level of Detail

In deciding what to include in a process analysis essay, be careful not to overwhelm your readers with too many details. An explanation of how to perform CPR written by and for physicians could be highly technical, but the same description should be much simpler when written for volunteers in the local ambulance corps.

For a process involving many complex steps or highly specialized equipment, consider including a drawing or diagram to help your readers visualize the steps they need to follow or understand. For example, in an essay explaining how to detect a wiring problem in an electric stove, you might include a diagram of the stove's circuitry.

To keep your writing lively and interesting when explaining technical or scientific processes, use sensory details and figures of speech. Rather than giving dry technical details, try using descriptive language.

Process Analysis Anticipates Difficulties and Offers Solutions

A how-to essay should anticipate potential trouble spots or areas of confusion and offer advice on how to avoid or resolve problems. It should also warn readers of any difficult, complicated, or critical steps, encouraging them to pay special attention or take extra care. For instance, in a how-to essay on hanging wallpaper, you would warn readers about the difficulties of handling sheets of wallpaper and suggest folding the sheets to make them easier to work with.

EXERCISE 14.3 **IDENTIFYING POTENTIAL DIFFICULTIES IN A PROCESS**

For one of the processes listed in Exercise 14.1 or Exercise 14.2, identify potential trouble spots in the process and describe how to avoid or resolve them.

The following readings demonstrate the techniques for writing effective process analyses as discussed above. The first reading is annotated to point out how Susan Silk and Barry Goldman use these techniques to help readers avoid saying the wrong thing to a suffering friend or relative. As you read the second essay, try to identify for yourself how the writer uses the techniques of process analysis to help readers understand how to transform a "shitty first draft" into a compelling piece of writing.

READING **HOW-TO ESSAY**

How Not to Say the Wrong Thing

Susan Silk and Barry Goldman

Susan Silk is the founder and CEO of MSI Strategic Communication, a company that provides communication consulting services. Barry Goldman is an arbitrator, mediator, and author. Using their experience, they have written an essay to help readers avoid saying the wrong thing when trying to provide comfort to someone who needs it.

Before Reading

1. **Preview:** Use the steps listed on page 28.
2. **Connect:** Think about a time you (or someone you know) said the wrong thing. How did you (or the other person) try to repair the relationship?

While Reading Study the annotations to identify the characteristics of process analysis.

When Susan had breast cancer, we heard a lot of lame remarks, but our favorite came from one of Susan's colleagues. She wanted, she needed, to visit Susan after the surgery, but Susan didn't feel like having visitors, and she said so. Her colleague's response? "This isn't just about you."

"It's not?" Susan wondered. "My breast cancer is not about me? It's about you?"

The same theme came up again when our friend Katie had a brain aneurysm. She was in intensive care for a long time and finally got out and into a step-down unit. She was no longer covered with tubes and lines and monitors, but she was still in rough shape. A friend came and saw her and then stepped into the hall with Katie's husband, Pat. "I wasn't prepared for this," she told him. "I don't know if I can handle it."

This woman loves Katie, and she said what she did because the sight of Katie in this condition moved her so deeply. But it was the wrong thing to say. And it was wrong in the same way Susan's colleague's remark was wrong.

Susan has since developed a simple technique to help people avoid this mistake. It works for all kinds of crises: medical, legal, financial, romantic, even existential. She calls it the Ring Theory.

1	**Introduction:** Presents an anecdote to help readers identify with the situation
2	
3	**Background:** Provides another anecdote to show problem is widespread
4	
5	**Thesis:** Thesis identifies process and indicates why it is important to learn.

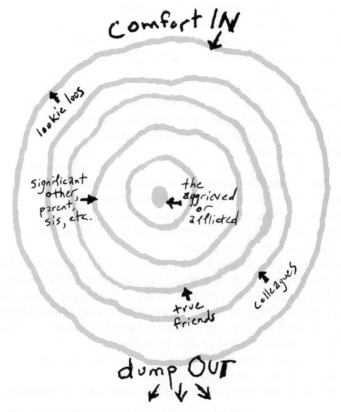

Copyright Wes Bausmith, Los Angeles Times, April 7, 2013

Organization: Transitional words and phrases signal chronological stages of process.

Draw a circle. This is the center ring. In it, put the name of the person at the center of the current trauma. For Katie's aneurysm, that's Katie. Now draw a larger circle around the first one. In that ring put the name of the person next closest to the trauma. In the case of Katie's aneurysm, that was Katie's husband, Pat. Repeat the process as many times as you need to. In each larger ring put the next closest people. Parents and children before more distant relatives. Intimate friends in smaller rings, less intimate friends in larger ones. When you are done you have a Kvetching Order. One of Susan's patients found it useful to tape it to her refrigerator. 6

Here are the rules. The person in the center ring can say anything she wants to anyone, anywhere. She can kvetch and complain and whine and moan and curse the heavens and say, "Life is unfair" and "Why me?" That's the one payoff for being in the center ring. 7

Everyone else can say those things too, but only to people in larger rings. 8

Anticipation of trouble spots: The author explains what people should avoid doing and saying.

When you are talking to a person in a ring smaller than yours, someone closer to the center of the crisis, the goal is to help. Listening is often more helpful than talking. But if you're going to open your mouth, ask yourself if what you are about to say is likely to provide comfort and support. If it isn't, don't say it. Don't, for example, give advice. People who are suffering from trauma don't need advice. They need comfort and support. So say, "I'm sorry" or "This must really be hard for you" or "Can I bring you a pot roast?" Don't say, "You should hear what happened to me" or "Here's what I would do if I were you." And don't say, "This is really bringing me down." 9

Point of view: Second person (*you*) is commonly used in how-to essays, though it may be frowned on in academic writing.

If you want to scream or cry or complain, if you want to tell someone how shocked you are or how icky you feel, or whine about how it reminds you of all the terrible things that have happened to you lately, that's fine. It's a perfectly normal response. Just do it to someone in a bigger ring. 10

Comfort IN, dump OUT. 11

There was nothing wrong with Katie's friend saying she was not prepared for how horrible Katie looked, or even that she didn't think she could handle it. The mistake was that she said those things to Pat. She dumped IN. 12

Complaining to someone in a smaller ring than yours doesn't do either of you any good. On the other hand, being supportive to her principal caregiver may be the best thing you can do for the patient. 13

Most of us know this. Almost nobody would complain to the patient about how rotten she looks. Almost no one would say that looking at her makes them think of the fragility of life and their own closeness to death. In other words, we know enough not to dump into the center ring. Ring Theory merely expands that intuition and makes it more concrete: Don't just avoid dumping into the center ring, avoid dumping into any ring smaller than your own. 14

Conclusion: Final paragraph cleverly connects to the introduction and speaks directly to the reader.

Remember, you can say whatever you want if you just wait until you're talking to someone in a larger ring than yours. 15

And don't worry. You'll get your turn in the center ring. You can count on that. 16

Visualize a Process Analysis Essay: Create a Graphic Organizer

Seeing the content and structure of an essay in simplified, visual form can help you analyze a reading, recall key steps as you generate ideas for an essay, and structure your own writing. Graphic Organizer 14.1 shows the basic structure of a process analysis essay. When your main purpose is to explain a process, follow this standard format. When you incorporate process analysis into an essay using one or more other patterns of development, briefly introduce the process and then move directly to the steps involved. If the process is complex, you may want to add a brief summary of it before the transition back to the main topic of the essay.

For more on creating a graphic organizer, see pp. 35–37.

GRAPHIC ORGANIZER 14.1   The Basic Structure of a Process Analysis Essay

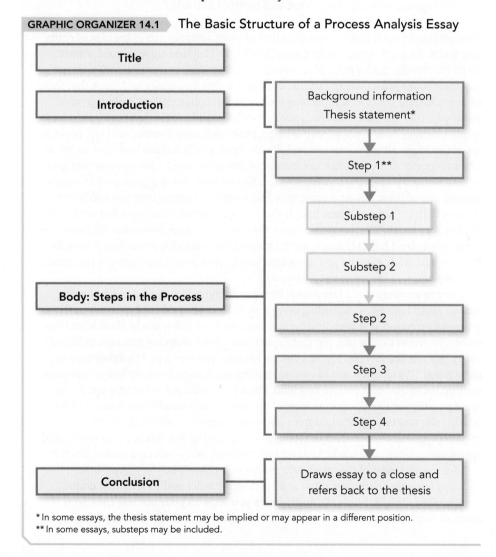

* In some essays, the thesis statement may be implied or may appear in a different position.
** In some essays, substeps may be included.

READING ▸ HOW-IT-WORKS ESSAY

Shitty First Drafts

Anne Lamott

Anne Lamott has published several nonfiction works, including *Bird by Bird: Instructions on Writing and Life* (1995), from which this essay is taken; *Help, Thanks, Wow: The Three Essential Prayers* (2012); and *Stitches: A Handbook on Meaning, Hope, and Repair* (2013). She is also the author of several novels, including *Blue Shoe* (2002) and *Imperfect Birds* (2010). **Before reading**, preview the selection and make connections by thinking about first drafts you have written. Were you satisfied with them? Why or why not? **While reading**, paraphrase each step of the process, and think about how Lamott reveals her attitude toward writing. Read the essay first, and then compare it to Graphic Organizer 14.2 (p. 339). What was omitted and why?

1   Now, practically even better news than that of short assignments is the idea of shitty first drafts. All good writers write them. This is how they end up with good second drafts and terrific third drafts. People tend to look at successful writers who are getting their books published and maybe even doing well financially and think that they sit down at their desks every morning feeling like a million dollars, feeling great about who they are and how much talent they have and what a great story they have to tell; that they take in a few deep breaths, push back their sleeves, roll their necks a few times to get all the cricks out, and dive in, typing fully formed passages as fast as a court reporter. But this is just the fantasy of the uninitiated. I know some very great writers, writers you love who write beautifully and have made a great deal of money, and not one of them sits down routinely feeling wildly enthusiastic and confident. Not one of them writes elegant first drafts. All right, one of them does, but we do not like her very much. We do not think that she has a rich inner life or that God likes her or can even stand her. (Although when I mentioned this to my priest friend Tom, he said you can safely assume you've created God in your own image when it turns out that God hates all the same people you do.)

2   Very few writers really know what they are doing until they've done it. Nor do they go about their business feeling dewy and thrilled. They do not type a few stiff warm-up sentences and then find themselves bounding along like huskies across the snow. One writer I know tells me that he sits down every morning and says to himself nicely, "It's not like you don't have a choice, because you do—you can either type, or kill yourself." We all often feel like we are pulling teeth, even those writers whose prose ends up being the most natural and fluid. The right words and sentences just do not come pouring out like ticker tape most of the time. Now, Muriel Spark is said to have felt that she was taking dictation from God every morning—sitting there, one supposes, plugged into a Dictaphone, typing away, humming. But this is a very hostile and aggressive position. One might hope for bad things to rain down on a person like this.

3   For me and most of the other writers I know, writing is not rapturous. In fact, the only way I can get anything written at all is to write really, really shitty first drafts.

4   The first draft is the child's draft, where you let it all pour out and then let it romp all over the place, knowing that no one is going to see it and that you can

shape it later. You just let this childlike part of you channel whatever voices and visions come through and onto the page. If one of the characters wants to say, "Well, so what, Mr. Poopy Pants?" you let her. No one is going to see it. If the kid wants to get into really sentimental, weepy, emotional territory, you let him. Just get it all down on paper because there may be something great in those six crazy pages that you would never have gotten to by more rational, grown-up means. There may be something in the very last line of the very last paragraph on page six that you just love, that is so beautiful or wild that you now know what you're supposed to be writing about, more or less, or in what direction you might go—but there was no way to get to this without first getting through the first five and a half pages.

I used to write food reviews for *California* magazine before it folded. (My writing   5
food reviews had nothing to do with the magazine folding, although every single review did cause a couple of canceled subscriptions. Some readers took umbrage at my comparing mounds of vegetable puree with various ex-presidents' brains.) These reviews always took two days to write. First I'd go to a restaurant several times with a few opinionated, articulate friends in tow. I'd sit there writing down everything anyone said that was at all interesting or funny. Then on the following Monday I'd sit down at my desk with my notes and try to write the review. Even after I'd been doing this for years, panic would set in. I'd try to write a lead, but instead I'd write a couple of dreadful sentences, XX them out, try again, XX everything out, and then feel despair and worry settle on my chest like an x-ray apron. It's over, I'd think calmly. I'm not going to be able to get the magic to work this time. I'm ruined. I'm through. I'm toast. Maybe, I'd think, I can get my old job back as a clerk-typist. But probably not. I'd get up and study my teeth in the mirror for a while. Then I'd stop, remember to breathe, make a few phone calls, hit the kitchen and chow down. Eventually I'd go back and sit down at my desk, and sigh for the next ten minutes. Finally I would pick up my one-inch picture frame, stare into it as if for the answer, and every time the answer would come: all I had to do was to write a really shitty first draft of, say, the opening paragraph. And no one was going to see it.

So I'd start writing without reining myself in. It was almost just typing, just mak-   6
ing my fingers move. And the writing would be terrible. I'd write a lead paragraph that was a whole page, even though the entire review could only be three pages long, and then I'd start writing up descriptions of the food, one dish at a time, bird by bird, and the critics would be sitting on my shoulders, commenting like cartoon characters. They'd be pretending to snore, or rolling their eyes at my overwrought descriptions, no matter how hard I tried to tone those descriptions down, no matter how conscious I was of what a friend said to me gently in my early days of restaurant reviewing. "Annie," she said, "it is just a piece of *chicken*. It is just a bit of *cake*."

But because by then I had been writing for so long, I would eventually let   7
myself trust the process—sort of, more or less. I'd write a first draft that was maybe twice as long as it should be, with a self-indulgent and boring beginning, stupefying descriptions of the meal, lots of quotes from my black-humored friends that made them sound more like the Manson girls than food lovers, and no ending to speak of. The whole thing would be so long and incoherent and hideous that for the rest of the day I'd obsess about getting creamed by a car before I could write a decent second draft. I'd worry that people would read what I'd written and believe that the

accident had really been a suicide, that I had panicked because my talent was waning and my mind was shot.

The next day, I'd sit down, go through it all with a colored pen, take out everything I possibly could, find a new lead somewhere on the second page, figure out a kicky place to end it, and then write a second draft. It always turned out fine, sometimes even funny and weird and helpful. I'd go over it one more time and mail it in.   8

Then, a month later, when it was time for another review, the whole process would start again, complete with the fears that people would find my first draft before I could rewrite it.   9

Almost all good writing begins with terrible first efforts. You need to start somewhere. Start by getting something—anything—down on paper. A friend of mine says that the first draft is the down draft—you just get it down. The second draft is the up draft—you fix it up. You try to say what you have to say more accurately. And the third draft is the dental draft, where you check every tooth, to see if it's loose or cramped or decayed, or even, God help us, healthy.   10

EXERCISE 14.4 ▶ **DRAWING A GRAPHIC ORGANIZER**

Using Graphic Organizer 14.1 or 14.2 as a basis, draw a graphic organizer for "How Not to Say the Wrong Thing" (pp. 332–34).

HOW WRITERS READ ▶	PROCESS ANALYSIS
THE READING PROCESS	**STRATEGIES**
BEFORE READING	**Preview** the essay to get an overview of its content and organization. **Make connections** by thinking about any experience you might have with this or a similar process.
AFTER READING	**Analyze and evaluate** the reading by answering the following questions. • Is the author **experienced and knowledgeable** about the process? (Check the writer's credentials.) • Are the steps in the process **clear**, **sequential**, **distinct**, and **sufficiently detailed**? (Can you visualize them or explain them in your own words?) Have any steps been left out? • Are there **other, similar processes**? If so, how are they similar to or different from the process explained in the essay? • Can you **apply** this information to your own life? • What was the **author's purpose** for writing the essay? Is it overt, or are the motives hidden? • Can the steps be **grouped into larger categories** to help you remember how to carry out the process correctly or effectively? • Does the essay provide **warnings about troublesome steps**? Should it?

Apply the questions in the "How Writers Read" box to the selection "Shitty First Drafts" (pp. 336–38).

GRAPHIC ORGANIZER 14.2 ▸ The Structure of "Shitty First Drafts"

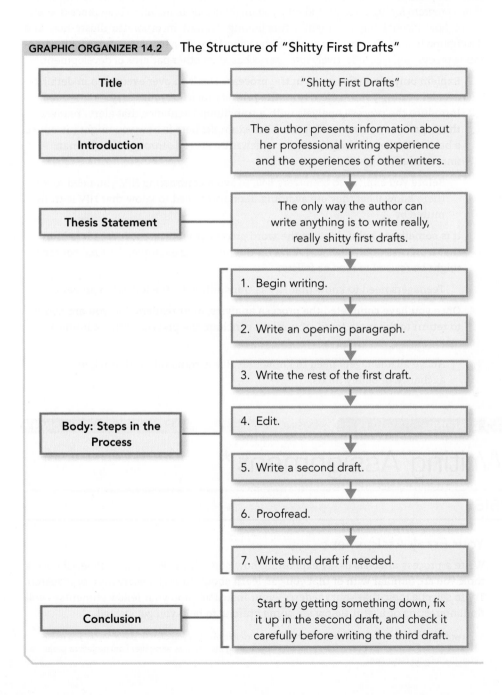

| Title | "Shitty First Drafts" |

| Introduction | The author presents information about her professional writing experience and the experiences of other writers. |

| Thesis Statement | The only way the author can write anything is to write really, really shitty first drafts. |

Body: Steps in the Process	1. Begin writing.
	2. Write an opening paragraph.
	3. Write the rest of the first draft.
	4. Edit.
	5. Write a second draft.
	6. Proofread.
	7. Write third draft if needed.

| Conclusion | Start by getting something down, fix it up in the second draft, and check it carefully before writing the third draft. |

Integrate Process Analysis into an Essay

The essay "The Psychology of Stuff and Things" later in this chapter (pp. 350–55) uses multiple patterns of development to explain how our stuff defines us across the life span.

You may find it helpful to incorporate a process analysis into a discussion that relies on a different pattern of development. For instance, in a descriptive essay about an alcohol abuse program for high school students, you might decide to include a brief process analysis of how alcohol impairs mental functioning. Lamott incorporates illustration and description to make her process analysis engaging. Here are a few suggestions for incorporating process analysis effectively into essays based on other patterns of development.

1. **Explain only the major steps in the process.** Don't go over every step in detail, to avoid diverting your readers from the primary focus of your essay.

2. **Introduce the process analysis with a transitional sentence that alerts readers that a process analysis will follow.** For example, here is how you might introduce a brief summary of the process by which AIDS spreads through HIV (human immunodeficiency virus).

   > Before you explain to teenagers *how* to avoid contracting HIV, you need to let them know *what* they are avoiding. Teenagers need to know that HIV is transmitted by . . .

3. **It is sometimes helpful to use the word *process* or *procedure* to let readers know that a process analysis is to follow.** In the preceding example, the final sentence might be revised to read as follows.

   > Teenagers need to know that HIV is transmitted by the following process.

4. **Once you have completed the process analysis, alert readers that you are about to return to the main topic.** You might conclude the process with a summary statement.

   > Above all, teenagers need to know that HIV is transmitted through an exchange of bodily fluids.

PREWRITING > DRAFTING > **REVISING** > EDITING & PROOFREADING

A Guided Writing Assignment *

PROCESS ANALYSIS

Your Essay Assignment

Write a process analysis essay explaining how something works or is done. Choose a topic you are familiar with or that you can learn about through observation or research. Try to select a topic that your readers—your instructor and your fellow students—will find interesting or useful. Below are some options to help you get started.

* The writing process is *recursive*; that is, you may find yourself revising as you draft or prewriting as you revise. This is especially true when writing on a computer. Your writing process may also differ from project to project or from that of your classmates.

How-To Essay Topics

- How to improve your _____ (study habits, wardrobe, batting average)
- How to be a successful _____ (diver, parent, gardener)
- How to make or buy _____ (an object for personal use or enjoyment)

How-It-Works Essay Topics

- How a decision is made to _____ (accept a student at a college, add or eliminate a state agency)
- How _____ (a quilt, a news broadcast, a Web site, a football team) is put together
- How your college _____ (spends tuition revenues, hires professors, raises money)

1 Select a topic from the list above, or create one of your own.

Use the following tips to select a process to write about.

- For a **how-to essay**, choose a process that you can **visualize or perform** as you write. Keep the equipment nearby for easy reference. For example, if you are writing an essay about how to scuba dive, it may be helpful to have your scuba equipment in front of you.
- For a **how-it-works essay**, choose a topic about which you **have background knowledge** or for which you can **find reliable information readily**.
- Choose a topic that is **useful** and **interesting** to your readers. Unless you can find a way to make an essay about how to do laundry interesting, do not write about it.

2 Consider your purpose, audience, and point of view.

Ask yourself these questions.

- Will my **purpose** be to **express myself, inform,** or **persuade**? (Process analyses tend to be informative.)
- Who is my **audience**? Will readers need any **background information** to understand my essay? Will they need me to **define terms** or **describe (or diagram) equipment**? How much **detail** do I need to go into for them to follow the steps or understand the process? Where will they need **special help** or **warnings**? (Check whether your readers will need background or definitions by asking a classmate to tell you how he or she would explain key terms to a novice.)
- What **point of view** best suits my purpose and audience? **How-to** essays commonly use the **second person**, addressing the reader directly as *you*. (Hint: Second person is often considered inappropriate in college writing.) **How-it-works** essays commonly use the **third person** (*he, she, it*).

3 Explore your subject and generate details.

Use idea-generating strategies to come up with the details your process analysis essay will use.

1. **List the steps** or **diagram the process**, keeping these questions in mind.
   - What separate actions are involved?
   - What steps are obvious to me but may not be obvious to someone unfamiliar with the process?
   - What steps, if omitted, will lead to problems or failure?

   (Listing is especially useful for pragmatic and concrete learners.)

2. Ask a friend or classmate to **act out your process**. What problems did this person encounter? What additional details did you need to tell him or her? (Acting out the process is especially useful for verbal, social, and emotional learners.)

3. Do some research to see **how others have described the process**. What details do other writers include? Do they generally add steps you've omitted or omit steps you've included? Be sure to keep track of any information you borrow from sources. (Research is useful for all learners.)

4. Alone or in pairs, list the words *looks like, sounds like, smells like,* and *feels like* across the top of a page and then **list as many words or comparisons** below as you can think of in 10 or 15 minutes. (Description is especially useful for verbal and concrete learners.)

Try taking an approach that challenges your learning style. For example, **pragmatic** and **abstract** learners—visualize steps in how-to essays; **creative learners**—slow down and set out detailed steps; **concrete learners**—convey the big picture of a social process in a how-it-works essay.

4 Draft your thesis statement.

Tell readers why the process is **important**, **beneficial**, or **relevant** to them.

_____ is important/beneficial/relevant because _____.
Name process   **State reasons audience can relate to**

Be sure to consider what *your* audience will find compelling.

5 Organize your essay.

Organize your ideas logically.

- For a process with **fewer than ten steps**, you can usually arrange the steps **chronologically**, devoting **one paragraph per step**.
- For a **more complicated process**, **group the steps** into three or four categories; use **one paragraph per group**, including **a topic sentence** to introduce the group and the **rest of the paragraph** to explain the individual steps involved. For an essay on how to run a garage sale, the steps might be grouped as follows:

   Group 1: Locating and collecting merchandise
   Group 2: Advertising
   Group 3: Pricing and setting up
   Group 4: Conducting the sale

Hint: An outline or graphic organizer will allow you to experiment to find the best order for supporting paragraphs.

To determine how usable your instructions are, ask a classmate to try them out.

Write a first draft of your process analysis essay.

Use the following guidelines to keep your process analysis on track.

- The **introduction** should present your **thesis statement**, include necessary **background information**, and convince readers the process is **relevant** to them. For lengthy or complex processes, consider including an **overview** of the steps.

- The **body paragraphs** should **identify each step** and make clear why it is important to the process. If the process is complex, including **a drawing or diagram** to outline steps can be helpful. (If including a graphic, introduce it in your essay and refer to it by its title.)

  - Use **headings** that name your main topics and signal changes in topic, whether your essay is brief or lengthy.

  - Use **transitions,** such as *before, next,* and *finally,* to signal steps in the process.

  - Make sure your **tone** is appropriate to your audience and purpose. In some situations, a matter-of-fact tone is appropriate; in others, an emotional or humorous tone may be suitable.

- The **conclusion** might emphasize the **value or importance** of the process, describe **particular situations** in which it is useful, or offer **a final amusing or emphatic comment or anecdote**. An essay that ends with the final step in the process may sound incomplete.

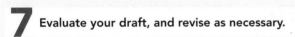 **Evaluate your draft, and revise as necessary.**

Use Figure 14.1, "Flowchart for Revising a Process Analysis Essay," to evaluate and revise your draft.

FIGURE 14.1 Flowchart for Revising a Process Analysis

QUESTIONS | REVISION STRATEGIES

1. Highlight your thesis statement. Does it make clear the importance of your process?

 NO ▶
- Ask yourself: Why would readers want or need to know this process? Incorporate the answers into your thesis statement.

 YES ▼

2. *Number* the steps of your process. Are they in chronological order (or some other logical progression)? Is the order clear?

 NO ▶
- Create a graphic organizer or outline to determine the best order.
- Visualize or carry out the process to determine if steps are missing.
- Rearrange steps and add transitions.

 YES ▼

(continued on next page) ▶

(Figure 14.1 continued)

REVISING

| QUESTIONS | | REVISION STRATEGIES |

3. [Bracket] any background information in your introduction. Is it sufficient? Have you provided an overview or shown the importance of the process?

 NO ▶

- Add an overview, if necessary.
- Give an example of a situation in which the process might be used.
- Explain that related processes and ideas depend on the process you are describing.

YES ▼

4. Place an ✗ beside any technical terms you have used. Have you defined them? Are your definitions clear?

 NO ▶

- Ask a classmate to read your draft and identify any other terms that need to be defined or clarified.
- Add or revise definitions as needed.

YES ▼

5. (Circle) any equipment you have mentioned. Have you included all necessary equipment? Will all of it be familiar to readers?

 NO ▶

- Add equipment you have overlooked.
- Describe equipment that might be unfamiliar to readers.

YES ▼

6. Place ✔s beside key details of the process. Have you included an appropriate level of detail for your readers?

 NO ▶

- Add or delete background information.
- Add or delete definitions of technical terms.
- Add or delete other detail.

YES ▼

7. For a how-to essay, <u>underline</u> sections where you have anticipated potential difficulties for your readers. Have you anticipated all likely trouble spots? Are these sections clear and reassuring?

 NO ▶

- Add more detail about critical steps.
- Add warnings about confusing or difficult steps.
- Offer advice on what to do if things go wrong.

YES ▼

8. Reread your introduction and conclusion. Is each effective?

 NO ▶

- Revise your introduction and conclusion so that they meet the guidelines in Chapter 7.

8 Edit and proofread your essay.

Refer to Chapter 9 for help with:

- **editing sentences** to avoid wordiness, making your verb choices strong and active, and making your sentences clear, varied, and parallel
- **editing words** for tone and diction, connotation, and concrete and specific language

Look out especially for **comma splices**.

A **comma splice** occurs when two independent clauses are joined only by a comma. To correct a comma splice:

- add a coordinating conjunction (*and*, *but*, *for*, *nor*, *or*, *so*, or *yet*)

  Example: The first step in creating a flower arrangement is to choose an attractive container, the ^but^ container should not be the focal point of the arrangement.

- change the comma to a semicolon

  Example: Following signs is one way to navigate a busy airport^;^ looking for a map is another.

- divide the sentence into two sentences

  Example: To lower fat consumption in your diet, first learn to read food product labels^. Next^ next eliminate those products that contain trans fats or unsaturated fats.

- subordinate one clause to the other

  Example: ^After you have placed^ Place the pill on the cat's tongue, hold its mouth closed, rubbing its chin until it swallows the pill.

Readings: Process Analysis in Action

Going Vegan: How to Have Your Eggless Cake, and Eat It, Too!

Justine Appel

Justine Appel wrote the following essay in response to an assignment that asked her to explain a process that she had mastered. As you read the essay, consider whether the steps described in the essay clearly explain the process of adopting a vegan lifestyle.

Introduction: Appel grabs readers' attention with an anecdote that provides background on her decision.

When I finally found the courage to tell my mom I had decided to go vegan, it was in a grocery store. We were shopping for Thanksgiving dinner, and I wordlessly grabbed a carton of soy milk and stuck it in the shopping cart. My mom shot me a weary look. "Are you vegan now?" I nodded. "Well, you'll have to be in charge of your own food," she said, continuing down the aisle. "I just can't keep track of all that."

Background: Defines *veganism*

Vegans, or people who adhere to a lifestyle free of animal products, face remarks like this all the time. Although the vegetarian diet, which excludes meat, fish, and poultry, is widely accepted in many parts of the world, the idea of avoiding all foods, fabrics, and substances derived from animals often seems absurd or highly difficult in the United States. Nonetheless, for those who feel passionately about animal welfare and environmental health, adopting a vegan lifestyle doesn't have to be difficult. With some research, preparation, and the right attitude, veganism can become second nature.

Thesis: Her thesis reveals the relevance of her topic for readers who might be considering "going vegan."

Organization: Uses a transition to keep readers on track and a topic sentence to identify step 1: think about the reasons for making a change.

As with all major lifestyle changes, the very first step is to think about the reasons for making a change. While there is a standard concept of veganism, all vegans have their own reasons for abstaining from animal products, which govern their individual choices. Some people are vegan for health reasons, and thus probably wouldn't turn down a pair of wool socks. Some are only opposed to industrial farming, and would feel comfortable eating eggs from a small, local farm. Still others don't believe in using animals for human consumption at all, and stay away from honey, glue, silk, and refined sugar (which is sometimes processed with animal bone char) on top of the usual list of animal-based food.

Organization: Transition provides segue to step 2; topic sentence identifies main idea.

Once you have considered the grounds for your veganism, it is important to maintain a critical mindset towards these issues. Being vegan is a deliberate ethical choice, but that doesn't mean your ethics as a vegan cannot evolve. Staying conscious about the effects of your lifestyle is a process, so consider this first step "repeat as needed." Several months after I stopped eating animal products for environmental reasons, I realized that chowing down on bananas shipped from Ecuador is not a very environmentally conscious choice, either. Now when choosing fruit to go in my vegan breakfast smoothies, I try to use what is more locally grown. While matching up your philosophy with your day-to-day eating habits can be hard,

Support: Offers an example to make the concept of the "critical mindset" concrete

1

2

3

4

looking at veganism as a process rather than a finish line will help you to know your limits and engage in behaviors that you feel are right.

The next step is a little easier, though it requires some investigation. Start to become familiar with the many forms of animal products and learn how to distinguish them on ingredient labels. While some animal ingredients are obvious (butter, milk, eggs), others are disguised by unfamiliar vocabulary. Gelatin, a substance used in marshmallows, jello, and gummy candy, usually comes from animal bones and cartilage. Lecithin is a common food additive that can come from animal tissue. Don't be afraid of these sneaky ingredients! A quick online search will procure several lists of hidden animal products. Fortunately, milk and eggs are common allergens, and will usually be listed in bold in the allergy warning below the ingredients list, which is much faster to find.

Once you know what to avoid, it's just as important to learn what to seek out. Since animal-based foods are good sources of several important nutrients, take the time to research some adequate substitutes to keep yourself well-fed and healthy. It is especially important to find good sources of protein and iron, since these nutrients are most easily available in animal products. Foods made from nuts, beans, or soy have high levels of protein and are usually quite filling. Meanwhile, nuts, beans, and whole grains are good sources of iron. Many fruits and vegetables are rich in other important dietary nutrients. All bodies have different needs, so if you are unsure, consult a doctor or nutritionist about how to get a healthy amount of vitamins, minerals, and other nutrients. In the meantime, eating a diverse array of foods is always a good measure.

Now that you've figured out what to eat, it's time to go food shopping. If you have a kitchen, proceed to stock it with food you like to eat. Vegan food can be found all over an average grocery store, and you will gradually learn the aisles with good vegan staples. While one of the many exciting aspects of going vegan is discovering new ingredients and dishes, forcing yourself to eat food you don't like is not a sustainable practice. For example, tempeh is a healthy soy product filled with protein, fiber, and vitamins that many vegans rely on for filling sandwiches and stir-fries, but I can't stand the texture of tempeh, so I stick to my favorite forms of protein, like lentils and peanut butter. There

5   **Organization:** Transition introduces step 3; topic sentence identifies it.

Background: Defines terms that may be unfamiliar to the reader

6   **Organization:** Transition introduces step 4; topic sentence, again, identifies it.

Support: Offers specific details to help readers maintain healthy protein and iron levels

7   **Organization:** Another transitional sentence introduces step 5: Go food shopping.

Support: An anecdote from her own experience supports discussion of the importance of figuring out what to buy are countless vegan meals and snacks out there, so don't waste time and energy buying or preparing food you won't feel like eating.

Next, polish your cooking skills. Knowing how to cook is an empowering tool for vegans, since it allows them to make dishes they will love and can share with friends and family. The Internet has tons of great cooking tutorials and blogs, which are often more personal and helpful than standard recipes. Use the Internet as a resource for tips on vegan cooking, and if you wish, supplement with a few vegan cookbooks. Finding one night a week to practice cooking not only will help you improve over time, but also can result in many dinners' worth of leftovers.

As useful as it is to know how to cook, going vegan should not mean the end of going out to eat. Familiarize yourself with the good restaurants in town that have vegan options, so you can recommend them when a group of friends is going out for lunch or dinner. Once there, don't be afraid to ask the waiter about the ingredients. It's easy for them to find out, and soon you'll gain a shrewd sense of what is vegan and what isn't. For example, naan, a type of Indian bread, usually comes with butter, whereas roti, another type, does not. When in an unfamiliar city, look for Thai, Chinese, Indian, or Middle Eastern restaurants, as they are usually the most accommodating to vegan diets.

Unfortunately, you will not always find enough vegan food to satisfy your hunger, particularly if you live in or are visiting a suburban or rural region where most locals are omnivorous. While American cities and coastal regions usually contain a wider diversity of ethnic food, I have found it especially difficult to find vegan fare in southeastern, central, and Midwestern states. Make sure to carry high-protein snacks when traveling to avoid feeling starved. Being prepared with trail mix and other travel-hardy food can save the day if the grandparents you're visiting take you to a steakhouse for dinner.

Once you've successfully established a vegan lifestyle that suits you, it is time to develop your vegan etiquette. By now, you will have noticed that your veganism sometimes interferes in social situations. Perhaps someone who has graciously invited you to dinner is serving lamb, or your grandmother gives you a pair of leather shoes for your birthday. It can be upsetting to refuse kind gestures such as these, but luckily there

8

9

10

11

Organization: Transitional word introduces step 6: polishing cooking skills.

Organization: Transitional clause prepares readers for step 7: going out to eat.

Offers several alternatives from which the reader may choose

Organization: Transition introduces step 8—satisfying your hunger

Organization: Transitional clause prepares readers for step 9: how to handle potentially difficult situations

Support: Specific examples of awkward situations

are ways to preempt them. When invited to eat in a social setting, inform the host of your dietary restrictions ahead of time, and ask if they would like you to bring a dish that you will be able to eat. When your birthday or a gift-giving holiday rolls around, make sure to specify what you do or don't eat, wear, and use, so relatives and friends will not give you non-vegan gifts. They may forget or make mistakes, which is okay. If anything, take it as an opportunity to discuss why you make the choices you do. Although preaching about the moral superiority of your diet will most certainly be unwelcome, a polite explanation about the motives behind your veganism might make for interesting, friendly debate.

Trouble spots: Practical advice for avoiding pitfalls

To that end, be prepared to answer many questions. Some of them may seem silly ("Is goat cheese vegan?"), but it is necessary to remember that everyone comes from a different background and therefore will have a unique set of values and beliefs. Recognize that food and clothing are political, but they also can be deeply personal or important in different cultural atmospheres. If you remain open to new thoughts and ideas and refrain from passing moral judgment on other peoples' lifestyle choices, you will find veganism much easier in social settings.

12   **Final step:** Be prepared to answer questions about the vegan lifestyle.

As the twenty-first century progresses, the political, social, and environmental effects of our day-to-day decisions are becoming more evident. There is no single issue that takes precedence over another, and being vegan is just one way to live consciously in an imperfect world. However, overcoming the doubts and suspicions surrounding veganism is an important first step in challenging norms and recognizing the connections between people, animals, and the earth. Finding veganism achievable makes other positive change seem achievable, too. And, for the record, my mom has become a master at identifying vegan ingredients, and surprised me by cooking a delicious dairy-less lasagna the last time I was home.

13   **Conclusion:** Transition emphasizes reason to go vegan: it's an ethical choice for today.

Emphasizes the value of the process

Ends the essay with a final, amusing anecdote

Analyzing the Writer's Technique

1. **Introduction** How successful are the first two paragraphs at providing a reason for learning the process?
2. **Style** Appel uses dialogue in her opening paragraph. What effect does this create?
3. **Organization** Explain how Appel has organized the steps in the process.
4. **Conclusion** Does Appel's conclusion bring the essay to a satisfying close? Why or why not?

5. **Opinion** Appel says that going vegan is an ethical choice. How does she convey her opinion? What reasons does she give?

Thinking Critically about Process Analysis

1. **Response** How does Appel's use of phrases such as "gelatin . . . usually comes from animal bones" (para. 5) and "lecithin . . . can come from animal tissue" (5) affect you as a reader? Do they increase or decrease the essay's effectiveness?

2. **Tone** How would you describe Appel's tone? What words or ideas help establish the tone?

3. **Audience** Who is the intended audience for this essay? How do you know? Is the essay appropriate for this audience? Why or why not?

4. **Omissions** What has Appel omitted from her process analysis, if anything? What additional information or advice might someone who is totally ignorant about the vegan lifestyle need? Would you need any additional information?

Responding to the Essay

1. **Reaction** Appel made a major lifestyle change when she chose to adhere to a vegan lifestyle. Do you think you could make the same lifestyle change? Why or why not? What would be the most difficult food for you to give up? How do you think your family and friends would respond to your lifestyle change? What would be your primary reason for making the change?

2. **Discussion** How important is it to follow the steps in the order Appel presents them? What are some other processes in which following the steps in order is especially important? List two or three.

3. **Essay** Appel sees her choice of a vegan lifestyle to be a positive change for herself. Write an essay explaining a change you have made or would like to make in your life that would change some facet of your life (your health, your sense of accomplishment) for the better. Describe the process that you would have to follow in order to make the change.

READING

The Psychology of Stuff and Things

Christian Jarrett

Dr. Christian Jarrett is a psychologist and a staff writer for the British Psychological Society's magazine *The Psychologist*. He also blogs for both the British Psychological Society and *Psychology Today*. He has published essays in numerous magazines such as *The Times* (London), *The Guardian*, and *Outdoor Fitness*. He has also published several books, including *The Rough Guide to Psychology* (2010) and *Great Myths of the Brain* (2015). At the end of his essay, Jarrett includes a list of references. Because he is writing in a journal for and by psychologists, he uses the citation style of the American Psychological Association (or APA). **Before reading**, preview and make connections by thinking about which possessions you are most attached to. **While reading**, highlight each step in the process. Because the process he describes occurs over a lifetime, underline transitions that signal chronological order or the next step in the process.

A man's Self is the sum total of all that he can call his.

—William James, *The Principles of Psychology* (1890)

Stuff everywhere. Bags, books, clothes, cars, toys, jewelry, furniture, iPads. If we're relatively affluent, we'll consider a lot of it ours. More than mere tools, luxuries or junk, our possessions become extensions of the self. We use them to signal to ourselves, and others, who we want to be and where we want to belong. And long after we're gone, they become our legacy. Some might even say our essence lives on in what once we made or owned.

Childhood and Adolescence

Our relationship with stuff starts early. The idea that we can own something, possess it as if a part of ourselves, is one that children grasp by the age of two. And by six, they exhibit the "endowment effect," placing extra value on an object simply by virtue of it being, or having been, theirs. Although children understand ownership from a very young age, they think about it in a more simplistic way than adults. A study by Ori Friedman and Karen Neary in 2008 showed that aged between two and four, kids make the assumption that whoever is first in possession of the object is the owner, regardless of whether they later give it away.

With ownership comes envy. When youngsters play with friends, they soon discover other people's toys they'd like to get their hands on. Or they experience the injustice of being forced to share what they had assumed was theirs alone. In his 1932 book *The Moral Judgment of the Child*, Jean Piaget observed that even babies express jealousy over objects, giving signs of "violent rage" when a toy is taken from them and given to another. When Batya Licht and her colleagues in 2008 filmed 22-month-olds playing with their peers in day-care, nearly a quarter of all sources of conflict were over possessions—where the "child either defended his or her objects from another child, or wanted to take an object from another child."

Most children have an unusually intense relationship with a specific "attachment object," usually a favorite blanket or a soft toy. In an intriguing study by Bruce Hood and Paul Bloom, the majority of three- to six-year-old children preferred to take home their original attachment object, as opposed to a duplicate made by a "copying machine." To the prospect of taking a copy, "the most common response was horror," says Nathalia Gjersoe, who helped run the studies. "A few very sweet and obedient children said okay but then burst into tears." Four of the children even refused for their attachment toy or object to be copied in the first place. That's despite the fact they were happy enough to take a copy of an experimenter's toy. It's as if the children believed their special object had a unique essence, a form of magical thinking that re-appears in adulthood in our treatment of heirlooms, celebrity memorabilia and artwork.

As children mature into teens, we see possessions starting to act as a crutch for the self. In 2007, Lan Chaplin and her colleagues interviewed participants aged between eight and 18 and found that "materialism" (identified by choosing material goods in answer to "What makes me happy?") peaked at middle adolescence, just when self-esteem tended to be lowest. In a follow-up, materialism was reduced in teens who were given flattering feedback from peers to boost their self-esteem.

Through adolescence, possessions increasingly reflect who people are, or at least how they would like to see themselves. In his seminal paper "Possessions and the Extended Self" Russell Belk quotes from novelist Alison Lurie's book *The Language of Clothes*, in which she observes: ". . . when adolescent girls exchange clothing they share not only friendship, but also identities—they become soulmates." Similarly, in interviews with teens, Ruthie Segev at Jerusalem College of Technology found evidence that selecting and buying gifts for their friends helps adolescents achieve a sense of identity independent from their parents, and that the mutual exchange of the same or similar gifts between friends helps them to create a feeling of overlapping identities.

In the transition from adolescence to adulthood, it's the first car that often becomes the ultimate symbol of a person's emerging identity. Interviews with car owners conducted by Graham Fraine and colleagues in 2007 found that young drivers, aged 18 to 25, were particularly likely to make the effort to personalize their cars with stickers, unusual number plates and seat covers, as if marking out their territory.

Adulthood

As our lives unfold, our things embody our sense of self-hood and identity still further, becoming external receptacles for our memories, relationships and travels. "My house is not 'just a thing,'" wrote Karen Lollar in 2010. "The house is not merely a possession or a structure of unfeeling walls. It is an extension of my physical body and my sense of self that reflects who I was, am, and want to be."

As our belongings accumulate, becoming more infused with our identities, so their preciousness increases. People whose things are destroyed in a disaster are traumatized, almost as if grieving the loss of their identities. Photographs from the aftermath of Hurricane Sandy, which struck the US East coast in 2012, show people standing bereft, staring in shock and bewilderment at all they've lost. Reflecting on the fire that took her home, Lollar says it was like "a form of death." Alexandra Kovach, who also lost her home in a fire, wrote in *The Washington Post* in 2007: "It isn't just a house. It's not the contents, or the walls, but the true feeling of that home—and all that it represents."

Later Life and Beyond

Older people don't just form bonds with their specific belongings, they seem to have an affection for brands from their youth too. Usually this manifests in a taste for music, books, films and other entertainment from yesteryear, but the same has been shown for fashions and hairstyles, it has been hinted at for perfumes, and in a study published in 2003 by Robert Schindler and Morris Holbrook, it was found that it also extends to the car.

Dozens of participants aged 16 to 92 rated their preference for the appearance of 80 cars, ranging from the 1915 Dodge Model 30-35 to the 1994 Chrysler Concorde. Among men, but not women, there was a clear preference for cars that dated from the participants' youth (peaking around age 26). This was particularly the case for men who were more nostalgic and who believed that things were better in the old days. What other examples might there be? "Children of both sexes tend to have strong feelings about foods they like as they grow up," says Schindler. "Although we haven't studied food, I would expect both men and women to have a lifetime fondness for foods they enjoyed during their youth."

How Mercury's new 161-horsepower engine makes <u>any</u> driving easy

GET IN AND TRY IT—You'll find Mercury's entirely new V-161 engine *smoother, quieter.* And with new ball-joint suspension, you'll enjoy greater handling ease.

PASSING—Extra power is provided instantly, whenever needed, by unique new 4-barrel carburetor.

HILL CLIMBING—V-161 power is *eager* power. And there's plenty in reserve to do the job effortlessly.

MAKE DRIVING AS EASY AS YOU WISH with optional 4-way power seat, power steering, power brakes, power windows, Merc-O-Matic Drive.

How often have you wished for more "go" from the car you now drive—especially when passing or hill climbing? How often have you been annoyed by sluggishness in traffic, stiff handling when parking, or wheel tug on curves?

Now—you can solve driving problems like these with Mercury's completely new V-161 engine teamed with new ball-joint front wheel suspension. The combination gives you a new feeling of safety in driving—smoother, easier power, unique in a popular-priced car. Road test a 1954 Mercury.

THE CAR THAT MAKES <u>ANY</u> DRIVING EASY

New 1954 **MERCURY**

MERCURY DIVISION • FORD MOTOR COMPANY

"Older people don't just form bonds with their specific belongings, they seem to have an affection for brands from their youth too." Jeff Morgan 11/Alamy Stock Photo

As with human relationships, the attachments to our things deepen with the   12
passage of time. Elderly people are often surrounded by possessions that have followed them through good times and bad, across continents and back. In 2000,
Linda Price at the University of Arizona and her colleagues interviewed 80 older
people about their decisions regarding these "special possessions." A common
theme was the way cherished objects come to represent particular memories. "I
can look at anything [in this house] and remember special occasions," recalled
Diane, aged 70. "It's almost like a history of our life."

After a person dies, many of their most meaningful possessions become fam-   13
ily heirlooms, seen by those left behind as forever containing the lost person's
essence. This idea is also seen in the behaviors that follow the death of a celebrity.
In a process that Belk calls "sacralization," possessions owned by a deceased star
can acquire astonishing value overnight, both sentimental and monetary. This is
often true even for exceedingly mundane items such as President Kennedy's tape
measure, auctioned for $48,875 in 1996. A study by George Newman and colleagues
in 2011 provided a clue about the beliefs underlying these effects. They showed
that people place more value on celebrity-owned items, the more physical contact
the celebrity had with the object, as if their essence somehow contaminated the
item through use.

The Future

Our relationship with our stuff is in the midst of great change. Dusty music and lit-   14
erary collections are being rehoused in the digital cloud. Where once we expressed
our identity through fashion preferences and props, today we can cultivate an
online identity with a carefully constructed homepage. We no longer have to purchase an item to associate ourselves with it, we can simply tell the world via Twitter or Facebook about our preferences. The self has become extended, almost
literally, into technology, with Google acting like a memory prosthetic. In short, our
relationship with our things, possessions and brands remains as important as ever,
it's just the nature of the relationship is changing. Researchers and people in general are gradually adjusting. The psychology of our stuff is becoming more interdisciplinary, with new generations building on the established research conducted by
consumer psychologists.

Twenty-five years after he published his seminal work on objects and the   15
"extended self," Russell Belk has composed an update: "The extended self in a digital world," currently under review. "The possibilities for self extensions have never
been so extensive," he says.

Bibliography

Belk, R. W. (1988). Possessions and the extended self. *Journal of Consumer Research, 15*, 139–168.
Belk, R. W. (2013). The extended self in a digital world. *Journal of Consumer Research, 40*(3), 477–500.
Carver, C. S. & Baird, E. (1998). The American dream revisited: Is it what you want or why you want
    it that matters? *Psychological Science, 9*(4), 289–292.
Chaplin, L. N. & John, D. R. (2007). Growing up in a material world: Age differences in materialism
    in children and adolescents. *Journal of Consumer Research, 34*(4), 480–493.
Cockrill, A. (2012). Does an iPod make you happy? An exploration of the effects of iPod ownership
    on life satisfaction. *Journal of Consumer Behaviour, 11*, 406–414.

Cova, B., Kozinets, R. & Shankar, A. (2007). *Consumer tribes.* Oxford: Butterworth-Heinemann.

Cushing, A. L. (2012). *Possessions and self extension in digital environments: Implications for maintaining personal information.* PhD thesis, University of North Carolina at Chapel Hill.

Fraine, G., Smith, S. G., Zinkiewicz, L., Chapman, R. & Sheehan, M. (2007). At home on the road? Can drivers' relationships with their cars be associated with territoriality? *Journal of Environmental Psychology, 27*(3), 204–214.

Friedman, O. & Neary, K. R. (2008). Determining who owns what: Do children infer ownership from first possession? *Cognition, 107*(3), 829–849.

Hood, B. M. & Bloom, P. (2008). Children prefer certain individuals over perfect duplicates. *Cognition, 106*(1), 455–462.

Kasser, T. (2003). *The high price of materialism.* Cambridge, MA: MIT Press.

Kovach, A. (2007, 27 October). What fire couldn't destroy. *Washington Post.* Retrieved 4 June 2013 from: www.washingtonpost.com/wp-dyn/content/article/2007/10/26/AR2007102601774.html

Lollar, K. (2010). The liminal experience: Loss of extended self after the fire. *Qualitative Inquiry, 16*(4), 262–270.

Newman, G. E., Diesendruck, G. & Bloom, P. (2011). Celebrity contagion and the value of objects. *Journal of Consumer Research, 38*(2), 215–228.

Nordsletten, A. E., Fernández de la Cruz, L., Billotti, D. & Mataix-Cols, D. (2012). Finders keepers: The features differentiating hoarding disorder from normative collecting. *Comprehensive Psychiatry.* doi:10.1016/j.comppsych.2012.07.063.

Piaget, J. (1965). *The moral judgment of the child.* New York: The Free Press. (Original work published 1932).

Price, L. L., Arnould, E. J. & Curasi, C. F. (2000). Older consumers' disposition of special possessions. *Journal of Consumer Research, 27*(2), 179–201.

Radford, S. K. & Bloch, P. H. (2012). Grief, commiseration, and consumption following the death of a celebrity. *Journal of Consumer Culture, 12*(2), 137–155.

Schindler, R. M. & Holbrook, M. B. (2003). Nostalgia for early experience as a determinant of consumer preferences. *Psychology and Marketing, 20*(4), 275–302.

Segev, R., Shoham, A. & Ruvio, A. (2012). What does this gift say about me, you, and us? The role of adolescents' gift giving in managing their impressions among their peers. *Psychology & Marketing, 29*(10), 752–764.

Shrum, L. J., Wong, N., Arif, F. et al. (2012). Reconceptualizing materialism as identity goal pursuits: Functions, processes, and consequences. *Journal of Business Research.* doi:10.1016/j.jbusres.2012.08.010

Srivastava, A., Locke, E. A. & Bartol, K. M. (2001). Money and subjective wellbeing. *Journal of Personality and Social Psychology, 80*(6), 959–971.

Steketee, G., Frost, R. O. & Kyrios, M. (2003). Cognitive aspects of compulsive hoarding. *Cognitive Therapy and Research, 27*(4), 463–479.

Van Boven, L., Campbell, M. C. & Gilovich, T. (2010). Stigmatizing materialism: On stereotypes and impressions of materialistic and experiential pursuits. *Personality and Social Psychology Bulletin, 36*(4), 551–563.

Van Boven, L. & Gilovich, T. (2003). To do or to have? That is the question. *Journal of Personality and Social Psychology, 85*(6), 1193–1202.

Understanding the Reading

1. **Summarizing** What are the steps in the process that Jarrett describes?
2. **Meaning** What does the author mean when he says that "our essence lives on in what once we made or owned" (para. 1)?

3. **Details** Explain the importance to sports fans of collecting paraphernalia and wearing team colors. To what part of the process does this relate?
4. **Vocabulary** Explain the meaning of each of the following words as it is used in the reading: *essence* (para. 1), *memorabilia* (4), *materialism* (5), *seminal* (6), *receptacles* (8), and *prosthetic* (14).

Analyzing the Writer's Technique

1. **Thesis** Identify Jarrett's thesis statement. What background information does he provide to support it?
2. **Conclusion** Does Jarrett's conclusion bring the essay to a satisfying close? Why or why not?
3. **Purpose** Explain how Jarrett's citation of research supports his purpose in writing the essay.
4. **Audience** Who is Jarrett's audience? Does his advice apply to others outside this group?
5. **Patterns** What methods of development, in addition to process, does Jarrett use in this essay? What does each add to your understanding of Jarrett's explanation of how our possessions become an extension of our selves?

Visualizing the Reading

Jarrett uses examples and details to explain how we come to identify with our possessions. List the steps in the process and provide an example or detail for each. The first one has been done for you.

Step	Example or Detail
Childhood	Children understand ownership early; between ages two and four, children assume that the person who possesses the object owns it even if he or she gives it away later.
Adolescence	
Adulthood	
Late adulthood	

Thinking Critically about Text and Images

1. **Tone** How would you describe Jarrett's tone? The essay appears to have been written for students of psychology and other psychologists. How could Jarrett have made the essay easier to read for a more general audience?

2. **Conclusion** What is Jarrett suggesting about how we will identify with our possessions in the digital age?

3. **Visuals** What does the visual near the end of the essay contribute to the reader's understanding of how older adults relate to their belongings?

4. **Additional Evidence** What additional evidence could Jarrett have included to make his claim about our relationship with our possessions more convincing?

Responding to the Reading

1. **Discussion** Do you believe that your essence lives on in what you once made or owned? Why or why not? What do you believe your possessions say about you?

2. **Journal** How does this essay make you feel about the possessions you have accumulated? Will it make any difference in what you do with your accumulated possessions in the future?

3. **Essay** Jarrett says that "most children have an unusually intense relationship with a specific 'attachment object,' usually a favorite blanket or soft toy." Reflect on your childhood and try to remember what your favorite toy or "attachment object" was. Write an essay in which you describe this object, explain how your attachment to it developed, and include a story or two about it.

Working Together

If Christian Jarrett were to design a bumper sticker based on the information in this essay, what would it say? In small groups, devise a brief motto that captures the essence of this essay.

PROCESS ANALYSIS COMBINED WITH OTHER PATTERNS ◀ READING

How to Be the Black Employee

Baratunde Thurston

Baratunde Thurston is a comedian and cultural critic interested in issues of race and media. He recently oversaw digital expansion for *The Daily Show*, he is the cofounder of Panoply's podcast *About Race*, and he is the cohost of the PBS podcast *Our National Conversation about Conversations about Race*. The excerpt below is from Thurston's satirical memoir *How to Be Black* (2012). **Before reading**, preview and make connections by thinking about how employees may represent any racial, ethnic, or cultural groups to which they belong. **While reading**, identify patterns other than process analysis that are used in this essay. Keep in mind that, although this reading is intended to be humorous, it also addresses serious issues about race and the workplace.

So you got a job in an office; you're one of the few minorities and possibly the only   1
black person. First of all, congratulations on having obtained a job. In this economy, that is amazing and makes you a superhero. Protect the job at all costs! Second, I'm so sorry for the awkwardness you have endured or will endure in this

environment. Hopefully this guide will help you weather the scenarios ahead or give you a different perspective on those you've already managed.

The truth is, you have two jobs.   2

The first is the explicit job for which you were hired. This is the job you saw   3
posted on the Web or heard about through a friend. It's the job title printed on your
business card and in the company directory. It's what you put on your LinkedIn
profile.

For the sake of argument, let's say the job was research associate at Optimus   4
Research Group. When you heard about this position, you were excited. Why?
Because you love research, and you're good at it. You prepared yourself. You
updated your résumé. You boosted your past research experience and added personal details that connect you to the type of research this job requires. You read
the company's Web site thoroughly. You Googled the business and its customers.
You may even have done your own research on particular employees, especially
management. You are prepared to be an excellent research associate, and when
you get the job, and sign the papers, and show up for your first day, that's a role
you are excited to play.

The thing is, you were also hired for another job: your blackness. That's not to   5
say you were merely accepted due to some affirmative action quota. If that were
the case, nothing more would be expected of you than simply being black and
doing Job #1 above. That would make you a research associate who happens to be
black. No, you have another job with specific responsibilities far beyond inhabiting
your skin. The people who hired you likely weren't even conscious of this extra job.
It's not as if they had one meeting about your research skills and another about
your blackness talents. Nevertheless, they expect great things from you, even if
subconsciously. In Job #2, you will be expected to:

- Part A: Represent the black community.
- Part B: Defend the company against charges of racism or lack of diversity.
- Part C: Increase the coolness of the office environment by enthusiastically
  participating in company events.

If you interpret this job description a certain way, you might conclude that you   6
have two, three, or even four jobs because your blackness duty combines the roles
of politician, lawyer, and entertainer. Now you're Jamaican! For the sake of simplicity and sanity, however, we will keep these jobs consolidated under the umbrella of
Job #2.

Also of note, it is not a requirement that you fully embrace all parts of the sec-   7
ond job. I'm merely informing you of the expectations. It's up to you to decide how
good of a Black Employee you really want to be.

During your first days on the job, before diving into Parts A, B, and C of Job #2,   8
there's something urgent you must do: *Spot the Negro.*

Like vampires and extremely rich people, black folk can sense one another. Use   9
your Spidey Sense (Blacky Sense?). Use your blackdar to inspect the workplace for
signs of Other Negroes. They may be working security for the building. They may be
in administrative support. They may be among the associate pool, or they may even

be in upper management. Black folk can be anywhere. After all, *you're* here. But one of the biggest mistakes you can make as The Black Employee is to assume you are the only one. You were hired as a research associate, remember? So do some research!

If you find that there is another Black Employee, do not panic. Employ the CARS system, as in *Collect* information, *Analyze* the data, *Review* your options, and *Set* your strategy. Like dogs sniffing each other's butts, you will need to figure out what your relationship to this other black person will be. How black do you expect him or her to be, and vice versa? Is this the type of person who feels threatened by your presence? Does this person even acknowledge that he or she is black? You must find answers to all of these questions. Your career may depend on it. For example, if you sit in the middle of the corporate ladder and the other black person is a blue-collar employee, the last thing you want to do is alienate this person. He or she probably knows lots of office secrets, has read discarded memos, and can either make your life easier or make sure your office always smells like rotten fish. On the other hand, if The Other Negro is above you and older, she may see you as a small version of herself and offer mentorship, advance warning on promotions, or just good information about what to avoid in the cafeteria. These and all other black-on-black intra-office interactions can be plotted on the Inter-Negro Spectrum of Hostility. Whether you gain or lose in these relationships depends heavily on where the other black employee falls on the INSH.

The Inter-Negro Spectrum of Hostility

On one end, you have **The Chill One**.   11

This other black employee takes everything in stride. She acknowledges you   12 in subtle ways, occasionally offers advice, and is overall an easygoing presence in the office and in your professional life. At a company meeting, when there's a mildly embarrassing racial moment, the two of you subtly smile at each other, connect eyes briefly, knowingly, and then return to business. Sometimes The Chill One will display light hints of subversion, but it's nothing over-the-top. For example, when the two of you are in the coffee room, she might say to you, "Hey, we should just take all these white people's shit and burn it." But then she laughs, and you laugh, and another coworker enters the room, asking, "What's so funny?" and without missing a beat you both say, "Tina Fey!"

My advice: if you encounter someone on the Chill end of the spectrum, be   13 natural. This is the best type of other black employee to have.

At the other extreme of the Inter-Negro Spectrum of Hostility, you have **The**   14 **Nemesis**.

This other black employee feels threatened by you. Everything is a competi-   15 tion. If you sign up for the community service committee, he brags about how much they got done last year. If you stay an hour late, he stays ninety minutes. He probably brandishes his education more than necessary, and he laughs too loud. He is naturally insecure, and your presence there serves to elevate his self-doubt further.

Do not respond directly to the competitive energy from The Nemesis. The best 16
defense in this case is simply to do your job. You will probably find many opportunities to publicly undermine him, but don't. That's cruel. He's probably just scared
because he's never not been the only black person before, and he's afraid you'll
take his place. Take the high road. Be inclusive. Hopefully, with time, he will learn
that there is room enough for two, maybe even three black people at this company.

At the very center of the spectrum you may encounter a type of black 17
employee known as **The Denier**. This person simply does not acknowledge her race
at all, perhaps hoping that by ignoring it, she'll never have to deal with any nega-
tivity associated with her race. While not explicitly combative with you, she's also
unlikely to be a useful ally, especially if she ranks above you. It's not that she feels
threatened by you. It's that she feels nothing. So she won't act to improve the situation at the company, either. Your best bet here is to accrue as much power in the
company as you can so you can use your position for good and undo some of the
damage caused by The Denier's apathy.

There's no guarantee you will be the only black employee, so I hope these 18
descriptions help you orient yourself accordingly.

Understanding the Reading

1. **Summarizing** According to Thurston, how does The Chill One interact with The
   Black Employee (para. 12)?
2. **Analogy** Explain the connection between vampires, rich people, and black people.
   (para. 9).
3. **Thesis** Identify the thesis of the reading. Is it implied or stated?
4. **Vocabulary** Explain the meaning of each of the following words as it is used in the
   reading: *explicit* (para. 3), *inhabiting* (5), *alienate* (10), *subversion* (12), *brandishes* (15).

Analyzing the Writer's Technique

1. **Organization** How does Thurston order the steps in his process analysis essay? Is
   his organization effective? Why or why not?
2. **Level of Detail** Is there enough detail for the selection to be of practical use?
3. **Audience** Who is Thurston's audience? Does his advice apply to others outside
   this group?
4. **Patterns** What methods of development, in addition to process, does Thurston use
   in the essay?

Thinking Critically about Process Analysis

1. **Tone** How would you describe Thurston's tone? Use examples from the text to
   support your answer.
2. **Assumptions** In the first paragraph, what assumptions does Thurston make about
   his readers?

3. **Purpose** Why do you think the author wrote this essay?
4. **Credibility** Is Thurston qualified to offer advice on how to be The Black Employee? Why or why not?

Responding to the Reading

1. **Discussion** Discuss some awkward work experiences that you or a friend has had. What caused the awkwardness, and how was it resolved?
2. **Journal** Write a journal entry about a good relationship you have, or have had, with a coworker from a different racial or ethnic group, gender, or sexual orientation. What made this relationship work out so well? What social or cultural differences did you have to adjust to?
3. **Essay** Thurston describes three types of black employees and how to manage relationships with each of them. Think about your friends: Write an essay in which you classify them into three types and then offer advice on how to get along with each type. Before offering advice, be sure you describe the three categories in detail.

Working Together

Thurston presents three types of people who are on the Inter-Negro Spectrum of Hostility and how to deal with each of them. Working with a group of your peers, identify three types of students that can be found in a typical college classroom. Give each type of student a descriptive name and provide examples of their behavior and how to deal with it. You may use a humorous and sarcastic tone (like Thurston) or a more formal, academic one. Create a chart that displays the information and be prepared to share it with the class.

Apply Your Skills: Additional Essay Assignments

Write a process analysis essay on one of the following topics. Depending on the topic you choose, you may need to conduct research.

For more on locating and documenting sources, see Part 5.

To Express Your Ideas

1. How children manage their parents
2. How to relax and do nothing
3. How to find enough time for your children or girlfriend/boyfriend/spouse

To Inform Your Reader

4. How to avoid or speed up red-tape procedures
5. How a particular type of sports equipment protects an athlete
6. How to remain calm while giving a speech

To Persuade Your Reader

7. How important it is to vote in a presidential election
8. How important it is to select the right courses in order to graduate on time
9. How important it is to exercise every day

Cases Using Process Analysis

10. In your communication course, you are studying how friendships develop and the strategies that people use to meet others. Write an essay describing the strategies people use to make new friends.
11. You are employed by a toy manufacturer and have been asked to write a brochure that encourages children to use toys safely. Prepare a brochure that describes at least three steps children can follow to avoid injury.

SYNTHESIZING IDEAS   **INTERPERSONAL RELATIONSHIPS**

Both "How Not to Say the Wrong Thing" (pp. 332–34) and "Going Vegan: How to Have Your Eggless Cake and Eat It, Too!" (pp. 345–49) discuss, in part, how to deal with others. "Going Vegan" discusses how to handle potentially difficult family meals, and "How Not to Say the Wrong Thing" focuses on how to interact with other black people on the job.

Analyzing the Readings

1. Evaluate the level of detail in each essay. Which essay is more helpful?
2. Write a journal entry in which you discuss ways in which you or someone close to you could use the information from each of the essays to communicate with friends and family more effectively.

Essay Idea

Think of other situations in which interpersonal communication is important. Write a process essay explaining the steps in creating a positive interaction. For example, you might write about how to communicate with an instructor, the parents of your boyfriend or girlfriend, or an elderly neighbor or relative.

Chris A. Crumley/Alamy Stock Photo

15
Comparison and Contrast
Showing Similarities and Differences

WRITING QUICK START Study the photograph showing a nontraditional wedding. Then make two lists, one of ways an underwater wedding ceremony is similar to a traditional wedding and another of ways that it is different. You might include details about the attire of the bride and groom, the setting, the types of skills required, and so on. Then write a paragraph comparing this nontraditional wedding to more traditional ones.

Using **comparison and contrast** involves looking at similarities (**comparison**), differences (**contrast**), or both. You analyze similarities and differences when you make everyday decisions (when you shop for a pair of jeans or select a sandwich in the cafeteria) as well as when you make important decisions (deciding which college to attend or which person to date). Your paragraph about conventional and unconventional weddings is an example of comparison and contrast writing.

In this chapter you will learn to:

- **understand the purpose and function of comparison and contrast essays**
- **use graphic organizers to visualize comparison and contrast essays**
- **integrate comparison and contrast into an essay**
- **read and think critically about comparison and contrast**
- **plan, organize, draft, revise, and edit essays using comparison and contrast**

USING COMPARISON AND CONTRAST ▸ IN COLLEGE AND THE WORKPLACE

- For a course in *criminal justice,* your instructor asks you to participate in a panel discussion comparing organized crime in Italy, Japan, and Russia.
- For a *journalism course,* you are asked to interview two local television news reporters and write a paper contrasting their views on journalistic responsibility.
- As a *computer technician* for a pharmaceutical firm, you are asked to compare and contrast several models of tablet computers and recommend the one the company should purchase for its salespeople.

What Are the Characteristics of Comparison and Contrast Essays?

Whether used as the primary pattern of development or alongside other patterns, successful comparison and contrast writing generally meets several criteria.

Comparison and Contrast Has a Clear Purpose and Is Written for a Specific Audience

A comparison and contrast essay usually has one of three purposes.

- **To express ideas:** The purpose of an essay about an unconventional wedding could be to express the writer's love of the setting, his or her partner, or both. The audience for this essay might be the readers of an online discussion of wedding ceremony venues.
- **To inform:** The purpose of an essay about an unconventional wedding could be to inform readers about the variety of options couples have for their weddings. The audience for this essay might be wedding planners or engaged couples.
- **To persuade:** The purpose of an essay about the variety of wedding options could be to persuade couples and planners to consider other venues that would be more meaningful to them.

Comparison and Contrast Considers Shared Characteristics

You cannot compare or contrast two things unless they have something in common. When making a comparison, a writer needs to choose a **basis of comparison**—a fairly broad common characteristic on which to base the essay. The paragraph you wrote comparing conventional versus unconventional weddings may have focused on the similarities and differences in settings, skills needed, and so forth. For another essay comparing baseball and football, for example, a basis of comparison might be the athletic skills required or the rules and logistics of each sport.

To develop a comparison-contrast essay, the writer examines two subjects using **points of comparison**—characteristics relating to the basis of comparison. In an essay using athletic skills as a basis of comparison, for example, points of comparison might be height and weight requirements, running skills, and hand-eye coordination. In an essay based on rules and logistics, points of comparison might include scoring, equipment, and playing fields.

EXERCISE 15.1 ▸ **IDENTIFYING BASES OF COMPARISON**

For three items in the following list, identify two possible bases of comparison.

1. Two means of travel or transportation
2. Two means of communication (emails, telephone calls, letters, texts)
3. Two pieces of equipment
4. Two magazines or books
5. Two types of television programming

Comparison and Contrast Is Organized Point by Point or Subject by Subject

You probably organized your paragraph comparing conventional and unconventional weddings in one of two ways.

1. You wrote, first, about a conventional wedding and then about unconventional weddings (or vice versa)
2. You discussed each point of similarity or difference with examples from conventional and unconventional weddings

Most comparison and contrast essays use one of these two primary methods of organization:

- **Subject-by-subject organization.** The author describes the key points or characteristics of one subject before moving on to those aspects of a second subject.
- **Point-by-point organization.** The writer moves back and forth between two or more subjects, comparing them on the basis of several key points or characteristics.

Comparison and Contrast Fairly Examines Similarities, Differences, or Both

Depending on their purpose and audience, writers using comparison and contrast may focus on similarities, differences, or both. In an essay intended to *persuade* readers that performers Beyoncé Knowles and Taylor Swift have much in common in terms of talent and cultural influence, the writer would focus on similarities: hit records, millions of fans, and parts in movies. An essay intended to *inform* readers about the singers would probably cover both similarities and differences, discussing the singers' different childhoods or singing styles.

An essay focusing on similarities often mentions a few differences, usually in the introduction, to let readers know the writer is aware of the differences. Conversely, an essay that focuses on differences might mention a few similarities.

Whether you cover similarities, differences, or both in an essay, you should strive to treat your subjects fairly. Relevant information should not be purposely omitted to show one subject in a more favorable light. In an essay about Knowles and Swift, for instance, you should not leave out information about Swift's charitable contributions while mentioning Knowles's charitable causes in an effort to make Knowles appear to be the more charitable person.

Comparison and Contrast Makes a Point

A successful comparison and contrast essay has a main point that sparks readers' interest in the subjects rather than boring them with a mechanical listing of similarities or differences. This main point can serve as the **thesis** for the essay, or the thesis can be implied in the writer's choice of details.

An explicit thesis has three functions.

1. To identify the *subjects* being compared or contrasted
2. To suggest whether the focus is on *similarities, differences,* or *both*
3. To state the *main point* of the comparison or contrast

The following two sample theses meet all three criteria. Note, too, that each thesis suggests why the comparison or contrast is meaningful and worth reading about.

———— similarities ————   ———— subjects ————
Similar appeals in commercials for three popular breakfast cereals
———— main point ————
reveal America's obsession with fitness and health.

———— subjects ————
The two cities Niagara Falls, Ontario, and Niagara Falls, New York,
—— differences ——   —— main points ——
demonstrate two different approaches to appreciating nature and

preserving the environment.

EXERCISE 15.2 **WRITING AN EFFECTIVE THESIS STATEMENT**

For one of the topic pairs you chose in Exercise 15.1, select the basis of comparison that seems most promising. Then write a thesis statement that identifies the subjects, the focus (similarities, differences, or both), and the main point.

Comparison and Contrast Considers Significant and Relevant Shared Characteristics

A comparison and contrast essay considers characteristics that readers will find significant as well as relevant to the essay's purpose and thesis. In general, college writers should discuss at least three or four significant characteristics to support the thesis, describing or explaining each characteristic in detail so that readers can grasp the main point of the comparison or contrast. Writers often use sensory details, dialogue, examples, expert testimony, and other kinds of evidence to convince readers that the items being compared (or contrasted) are, in fact, similar (or dissimilar).

The following readings demonstrate the techniques discussed above for writing effective comparison and contrast essays. The first reading is annotated to show how Aaron Carroll uses these techniques to contrast alcohol with marijuana. As you read the second essay, try to identify how Sara Rashkin uses the techniques of comparison and contrast to demonstrate two different dating styles.

POINT-BY-POINT ORGANIZATION ◄ **READING**

Alcohol or Marijuana? A Pediatrician Faces the Question

Aaron E. Carroll

Dr. Aaron E. Carroll is a professor of pediatrics at Indiana University School of Medicine. His writing has appeared in national publications, such as *Bloomberg News* and *The Wall Street Journal*; he has also appeared on a variety of television news shows, including *Good Morning America* and *The Colbert Report*. His blog, *The Incidental Economist*, reports on health research and policy. This essay was published in *The Upshot*, an online blog for *The New York Times*.

Before Reading

1. **Preview:** Use the steps listed on page 28.
2. **Connect:** Consider marijuana and alcohol use on your own campus. What issues stemming from excessive drinking or drug use are you aware of on your college campus?

While Reading Study the annotations that accompany the reading to discover how the essay illustrates the characteristics of comparison and contrast.

As my children, and my friends' children, are getting older, a question that comes up again and again from friends is this: Which would I rather my children use—alcohol or marijuana?

Thesis: Indicates subjects being contrasted

The easy answer is to demonize marijuana. It's illegal, after all. Moreover, its potential downsides are well known. Scans show that marijuana use is associated with potential changes in the brain (Gilman et al.) It's associated with increases in the risk of psychosis (Di Forti et al.). It may be associated with changes in lung function or long-term cancer risk, even though a growing body of evidence says that seems unlikely (Pletcher et al.). It can harm memory (Schweinsburg et al.), it's associated with lower academic achievement (McLeod et al.), and its use is linked to less success later in life (Fergusson and Boden).

Purpose: To inform readers of the potential dangers associated with alcohol use and marijuana use and to decide which is likely to cause the least harm

Basis of comparison: Potential dangers alcohol versus marijuana use

But these are all associations, not known causal pathways. It may be, for instance, that people predisposed to psychosis are more likely to use pot. We don't know. Moreover, all of these potential dangers seem scary only when viewed in isolation. Put them next to alcohol, and everything looks different.   3

Point of comparison 1: Crime

Because marijuana is illegal, the first thing I think about before answering is crime. In many states, being caught with marijuana is much worse than being caught with alcohol while underage. But ignoring the relationship between alcohol and crime is a big mistake. The National Council on Alcoholism and Drug Dependence reports that alcohol use is a factor in 40 percent of all violent crimes in the United States, including 37 percent of rapes and 27 percent of aggravated assaults ("Alcohol").   4

No such association has been found among marijuana users. Although there are studies that can link marijuana to crime, it's almost all centered on its illegal distribution. People who are high are not committing violence.   5

Organization: Alternately contrasts alcohol use with marijuana use

People will argue that casual use isn't the issue; it's abuse that's worrisome for crime. They're right—but for alcohol. A recent study in *Pediatrics* investigated the factors associated with death in delinquent youth. Researchers found that about 19 percent of delinquent males and 11 percent of delinquent females had an alcohol use disorder (Teplin et al.). Further, they found that even five years after detention, those with an alcohol use disorder had a 4.7 times greater risk of death from external causes, like homicide, than those without an alcohol disorder.   6

Point of comparison 2: Health

When I'm debating my answer, I think about health as well. Once again, there's no comparison. Binge drinking accounted for about half of the more than 80,000 alcohol-related deaths in the United States in 2010, according to a 2012 report by the Centers for Disease Control and Prevention ("Vital Signs"). The economic costs associated with excessive alcohol consumption in the United States were estimated to be about $225 billion. Binge drinking, defined as four or more drinks for women and five or more drinks for men on a single occasion, isn't rare either. More than 17 percent of all people in the United States are binge drinkers, and more than 28 percent of people age 18 to 24. Binge drinking is more common among people with a household income of at least $75,000. This is a solid middle-class problem.   7

Transition: Indicates contrast

Marijuana, on the other hand, kills almost no one. The number of deaths attributed to marijuana use is pretty much zero. A study that tracked more than 45,000 Swedes for 15 years found no increase in mortality in those who used marijuana, after controlling for other factors (Andreasson and Allebeck). Another study published in the *American Journal of Public Health* followed more than 65,000 people in the United States and found that marijuana use had no effect at all on mortality in healthy men and women (Sidney et al.).   8

Point of comparison 3: Risk of being injured driving

Evidence: Provides detailed statistics to support danger of driving under the influence of alcohol versus marijuana

I think about which is more dangerous when driving. A 2013 case-control study found that marijuana use increased the odds of being in a fatal crash by 83 percent (Li et al.). But adding alcohol to drug use increased the odds of a fatal crash by more than 2,200 percent. A more recent study found that, after controlling for various factors, a detectable amount of THC, the active ingredient in pot, in the blood did not increase the risk of accidents at all (Compton and Berning).   9

Having a blood alcohol level of at least 0.05 percent, though, increased the odds of being in a crash by 575 percent.

I think about which substance might put young people at risk for being hurt by others. That's where things become even more stark. In 1995 alone, college students reported more than 460,000 alcohol-related incidents of violence in the United States ("Alcohol"). A 2010 prospective study found that mental and physical dating abuse were more common on drinking days among college students (Stappenbeck and Fromme). On the other hand, a 2014 study looking at marijuana use and intimate partner violence in the first nine years of marriage found that those who used marijuana had lower rates of such violence (Smith et al.). Indeed, the men who used marijuana the most were the least likely to commit violence against a partner.

Most people come out of college not dependent on the substances they experimented with there. But some do. So I also consider which of the two might lead to abuse. Even there, alcohol fares poorly compared with marijuana. While 9 percent of pot users eventually become dependent, more than 20 percent of alcohol users do (Lopez-Quintero et al.).

An often-quoted, although hotly debated, study in *The Lancet* ranked many drugs according to their harm score (Nutt et al.), both to users and to others. Alcohol was clearly in the lead. One could make a case, though, that heroin, crack cocaine, and methamphetamine would be worse if they were legal and more commonly used. But it's hard to see how pot could overtake alcohol even if it were universally legal. Use of marijuana is not rare, even now when it's widely illegal to buy and use. It's estimated that almost half of Americans age 18 to 20 have tried it at some point in their lives; more than a third of them have used it in the last year.

I also can't ignore what I've seen as a pediatrician. I've seen young people brought to the emergency room because they've consumed too much alcohol and become poisoned. That happens thousands of times a year ("College Drinking"). Some even die.

And when my oldest child heads off to college in the not-too-distant future, this is what I will think of: Every year more than 1,800 college students die from alcohol-related accidents ("College Drinking"). About 600,000 are injured while under alcohol's influence, almost 700,000 are assaulted, and almost 100,000 are sexually assaulted. About 400,000 have unprotected sex, and 100,000 are too drunk to know if they consented. The numbers for pot aren't even in the same league.

I'm a pediatrician, as well as a parent. I can, I suppose, demand that my children, and those I care for in a clinic, never engage in risky behavior. But that doesn't work. Many will still engage in sexual activity, for instance, no matter how much I preach about the risk of a sexually transmitted infection or pregnancy. Because of that, I have conversations about how to minimize risk by making informed choices. While no sex is preferable to unprotected sex, so is sex with a condom. Talking about the harm reduction from condom use doesn't mean I'm telling them to have sex.

10   **Point of comparison 4:** Risk for being hurt by others

11   **Point of comparison 5:** Risk of abuse

12

13   **Evidence:** Personal experience supports abuse

14

15

Similarly, none of these arguments I've presented are "pro pot" in the sense   16
that I'm saying that adolescents should go use marijuana without worrying about
consequences. There's little question that marijuana carries with it risks to people
who use it, as well as to the nation. The number of people who will be hurt from it,
will hurt others because of it, begin to abuse it, and suffer negative consequences
from it are certainly greater than zero. But looking only at those dangers, and
refusing to grapple with them in the context of our society's implicit consent for
alcohol use in young adults, is irrational.

Conclusion: States the thesis

When someone asks me whether I'd rather my children use pot or alcohol,   17
after sifting through all the studies and all the data, I still say "neither." Usually, I
say it more than once. But if I'm forced to make a choice, the answer is
"marijuana."

Links

"Alcohol, Drugs, and Crime." National Council on Alcoholism and Drug Dependence, 27 June 2014, 14:32, www.ncadd.org/about-addiction/addiction-update/alcohol-drugs-and-crime.

Andreasson, S., and P. Allebeck. "Cannabis and Mortality among Young Men: A Longitudinal Study of Swedish Conscripts." *Scandinavian Journal of Social Medicine*, vol. 18, no. 2 (1990), pp. 9–15, www.ncbi.nlm.nih.gov/pubmed/2320981.

"College Drinking." United States, National Institutes of Health, National Institute on Alcohol Abuse and Alcoholism, Dec. 2015, pubs.niaaa.nih.gov/publications/CollegeFactSheet/CollegeFact.htm.

Compton, Richard P., and Amy Berning. "Drug and Alcohol Crash Risk." *Traffic Safety Facts: Research Note*, United States Department of Transportation, National Highway Traffic Safety Administration, Feb. 2015, no. DOT HS 812 117.

Di Forti, Marta, et al. "Proportion of Patients in South London with First-Episode Psychosis Attributable to Use of High Potency Cannabis: A Case-Control Study." *The Lancet*, 18 Feb. 2015, doi:10.1016/S2215-0366(14)00117-5.

Fergusson, David M., and Joseph M. Boden. "Cannabis Use and Later Life Outcomes." *Addiction*, vol. 103, no. 6 (June 2008), pp. 969–76, doi:10.1111/j.1360-0443.2008.02221.x.

Gilman, Jodi M., et al. "Cannabis Use Is Quantitatively Associated with Nucleus Accumbens and Amygdala Abnormalities in Young Adult Recreational Users." *The Journal of Neuroscience*, vol. 34, no. 16 (16 Apr. 2014), pp. 5529-38, doi:10.1523/JNEUROSCI.4745-13.2014.

Li, Guohua, et al. "Drug Use and Fatal Motor Vehicle Crashes: A Case-Control Study." *Accident Analysis and Prevention*, vol. 60 (2013), pp. 205–10, www.cuinjuryresearch.org/wp-content/uploads/2013/10/Li-et-al-AAP-2013.pdf.

Lopez-Quintero, C., et al. "Probability and Predictors of Transition from First Use to Dependence on Nicotine, Alcohol, Cannabis, and Cocaine: Results of the National Epidemiologic Survey on Alcohol and Related Conditions (NESARC)." *Drug and Alcohol Dependence*, vol. 115, nos. 1–2 (1 May 2011), pp. 120–30, doi: 10.1016/j.drugalcdep.2010.11.004.

McLeod, John, et al. "Psychological and Social Sequelae of Cannabis and Other Illicit Drug Use by Young People: A Systematic Review of Longitudinal, General Population Studies." *The Lancet*, vol. 363, no. 9421 (15 May 2004), pp. 1579–88, www.sciencedirect.com/science/article/pii/S0140673604162004.

Nutt, David J., et al. "Drug Harms in the UK: A Multicriteria Decision and Analysis." *The Lancet*, vol. 376, no. 9752 (6 Nov. 2010), pp. 1558–65, doi:10.1016/S0140–6736(10)61462–6.

Pletcher, Mark J., et al. "Association between Marijuana Exposure and Pulmonary Function over Twenty Years." *Journal of the American Medical Association*, vol. 307, no. 2 (2012), pp. 173–81, doi:10.1001/jama.2011.1961.

Schweinsburg, A. D., et al. "The Influence of Marijuana Use on Neurocognitive Functioning in Adolescents." *Current Drug Abuse Review,* vol. 1, no. 1 (2008), pp. 99–111, www.ncbi.nlm.nih.gov/pubmed/19630709.

Sidney, S., et al. "Marijuana Use and Mortality." *American Journal of Public Health,* vol. 87, no. 4 (Apr. 1997), pp. 585–90, www.ncbi.nlm.nih.gov/pubmed/9146436.

Smith, P. H., et al. "Couples' Marijuana Use Is Inversely Related to Their Intimate Partner Violence over the First Nine Years of Marriage." *Psychology of Addictive Behavior,* vol. 28, no. 3 (Sept. 2014), pp. 734–42, doi:10.1037/a0037302.

Stappenbeck, Cynthia A., and Kim Fromme. "Longitudinal Investigation of Heavy Drinking and Physical Dating Violence in Men and Women." *Addictive Behaviors,* vol. 35, no. 5 (2010), pp. 479–85.

Teplin, Linda A., et al. "Firearm Homicide and Other Causes of Death in Delinquents: A Sixteen-Year Prospective Study." *Pediatrics,* vol. 134, no. 1 (June 2014), pp. 63–73, doi:10.1542/peds.2013-3966.

"Vital Signs: Binge Drinking Prevalence, Frequency, and Intensity among Adults—United States, 2010." *Morbidity and Mortality Weekly Report,* Centers for Disease Control and Prevention, vol. 61, no. 1 (13 Jan. 2012), pp. 14–19, www.cdc.gov/mmwr/preview/mmwrhtml/mm6101a4.htm?s_cid=mm6101a4_w.

Visualize a Comparison and Contrast Essay: Create Graphic Organizers

As noted earlier, you can organize a comparison and contrast essay in one of two ways: point by point or subject by subject. ("Alcohol or Marijuana? A Pediatrician Faces the Question" is organized point by point; "What Kind of H_2O Should You Drink?" which follows, is organized subject by subject.) Suppose you want to compare two houses (house A and house B) built by the same architect for the purpose of evaluating how the architect's style has changed over time. After brainstorming ideas, you decide to base your essay on these points of comparison:

For more on creating a graphic organizer, see pp. 35–37.

- layout
- size
- building materials
- landscaping

Point-by-Point Organization

Graphic Organizer 15.1 shows the basic structure of an essay using *point-by-point organization,* in which you go back and forth between the subjects (in this case, two houses), noting similarities and differences between them on each of the points of comparison.

GRAPHIC ORGANIZER 15.1 The Basic Structure of a Point-by-Point Comparison and Contrast Essay*

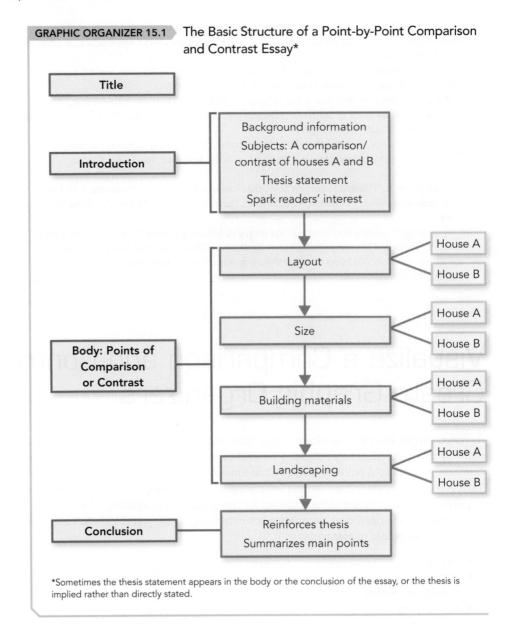

*Sometimes the thesis statement appears in the body or the conclusion of the essay, or the thesis is implied rather than directly stated.

Subject-by-Subject Organization

Graphic Organizer 15.2 shows the basic structure of an essay using *subject-by-subject organization*, in which you first discuss all the points of comparison—in this case, layout, size, building materials, and landscaping for the first subject (house A) before doing the same for the second subject (house B).

GRAPHIC ORGANIZER 15.2 The Basic Structure of a Subject-by-Subject Comparison and Contrast Essay*

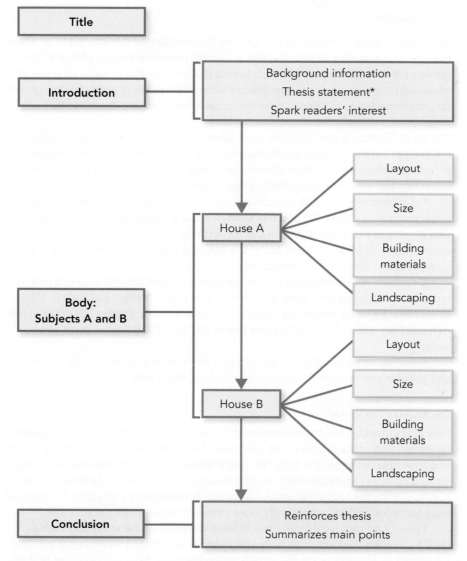

*Sometimes the thesis statement appears in the body or the conclusion of the essay, or the thesis is implied rather than directly stated.

What Kind of H$_2$O Should You Drink?

Sara Rashkin

Sara Rashkin is a writer based in Los Angeles. She contributed this article to *L.A. Weekly*, a free alternative-weekly tabloid that covers cultural events and topics of interest to local residents. **Before reading**, consider the brands (Dasani, Poland Springs) and types (flat, sparkling) of bottled water you are familiar with. **While reading**, highlight the subjects that Rashkin addresses. Then compare your notes with Graphic Organizer 15.3.

The act of drinking water seems to have become unnecessarily confusing. What is the average person to make of advertisements for "alkaline water" and discussions of "total dissolved solids"? How different can water taste? And what environmental impact do our decisions about bottled water have?   1

For guidance, we turned to water expert Martin Riese, who has been a certified water sommelier since 2010 and has studied water for more than a decade. He's also developed extensive water menus for restaurants, including fine-dining destination Patina and Ray's & Stark Bar at LACMA, and regularly teaches Water 101 classes for those who want to learn more.   2

Riese believes it's important to educate people about the differences in water types and to bring an increased sense of value to water. "People say 'only in L.A.' about having a water menu," he admits, "but we are wasting water like crazy in the city, and I say it's 'only in L.A.' that we live in the desert and no one cares about water."   3

From tap water to infused waters, here's the lowdown on source, taste, health and possible environmental implications of all kinds of H$_2$O.   4

Los Angeles Tap Water

Providing citywide safe drinking water requires disinfecting the water to kill harmful bacteria. Over the course of the past year, the Los Angeles Department of Water and Power made the switch from chlorine to chloramine (a combination of ammonia and chlorine) as its disinfectant. Chloramine is not a new treatment, but it is new to L.A. On the LADWP website, the switch is explained as an effort "to improve taste and odor, and to comply with more stringent water-quality regulations."   5

The city follows legal guidelines to keep the chloramine at an acceptable level for human consumption, although chloramine-treated water is not suitable for people on dialysis or for use in fish tanks. For those who are sensitive to it or don't like the taste, chloramine presents a challenge because it's notoriously difficult to filter out. Those who do like the taste are in luck, since this is the least expensive and most eco-friendly drinking water option, unless you have access to well water.   6

Riese says he does taste a difference in our tap water since the switch. "The chlorine is not as overpowering now," he says, "but I'm still not really a fan. You still can taste it, but at the same time I totally understand why they have to do it. They have to make sure it's safe."   7

Water sommelier Martin Riese with spring and mineral bottled waters.   REUTERS/Mario Anzuoni

Purified Water

Without access to glacier-fed tap water, many people in L.A. choose to use purified   8
water for drinking, showering and even brewing. Purified water is simply water
that has been processed to remove minerals and chemicals, resulting in a very low
TDS, or Total Dissolved Solids, in parts per million—a measurement of the mobile
charged ions in water including dissolved minerals, salts and metals. Magnesium,
calcium, sodium and potassium are some of the minerals commonly found naturally occurring in water, absorbed from the surroundings, along with trace elements like zinc and fluoride. Purified water that has had these minerals removed
can refer to both distilled water (where water is vaporized, which leaves the minerals behind, and then condensed into water again) and heavily filtered water.

Riese is among the many experts who believe purified water is not a healthy   9
drinking water choice. "People think it's just clean and sounds so good for you,"
Riese explains, "but it's actually very harmful water. This water is good for
machines. In Europe it's labeled 'do not drink.'" He adds: "The body runs on minerals, that's the reason we're eating and drinking." The UN's World Health Organization has published a report entitled "Health Risks of Drinking Demineralized
Water," which includes a warning that this water is "highly aggressive" and can
leach metals from pipes and minerals from food.

Many purified-water products have a few minerals added back in to improve   10
taste and to address health concerns about drinking "empty" water. At Intelligen-
tsia Coffee locations, you can try reverse osmosis–filtered tap water that has been
blended with water that retains some minerals—this is the water they currently
use for everything from brewing coffee to the dispenser of complimentary drinking

water. Many bottled water brands on the market are reverse osmosis–filtered tap water with minerals added. Coca-Cola and Pepsi long ago admitted that their water brands, Dasani and Aquafina, are filtered tap water. (Dasani bottles, for instance, are labeled "purified water enhanced with minerals" and the ingredients read: purified water, magnesium sulfate, potassium chloride, salt.) Nestlé Pure Life brand also uses municipal water and has a plant in Sacramento.

Spring and Mineral Waters

If taste is your priority in drinking water, it's easy to see why spring and mineral   11
waters are such big business. With a fascinating variety of water from all over the world, you can drink Iskilde one day, a still water with a rare mineral profile from an isolated aquifer in Denmark, and Vichy Catalan the next, a strong-tasting, naturally carbonated hot springs water from Spain that has been bottled since 1889.

It's the difference in the mineral amounts (the TDS measurement), as well as   12
the specific minerals present, that gives each water a unique taste. Consider that Iskilde has a TDS of 426 while Vichy has an astounding TDS of 3,052. (TDS levels for a single brand can vary from bottle to bottle.) Voss, a naturally low-mineral spring water from Norway, has a low TDS of about 22.

To be labeled mineral water, a water source must have a relatively constant   13
TDS level of 250 parts per million or higher. Spring water must come from an underground aquifer that either pushes to the surface naturally (referred to as an artesian spring) or is tapped so the water can be pumped up. The ground prevents contact with air and naturally filters many contaminants from the water while imparting minerals. Spring and mineral waters must be bottled at the source, and this water can be minimally processed to remove elements such as iron, but the bottled product must reflect the same composition as the original water.

Riese feels that many people no longer appreciate water varieties and their   14
health properties, and he points out that everything from mineral deficiencies to overeating to headaches can be linked to dehydration and poor water choices. He traces the history of bottled water to the early popularity of healing mineral springs—when people couldn't get to the springs, bottled water brought the springs to people. Roi, a Slovenian mineral water with the highest TDS Riese has ever encountered (7,500), is labeled the most magnesium-rich water in the world (you can even see the sediment on the glass), and it has been bottled since 1647.

As for bottles, Riese prefers glass ones, which are better than plastic at pro-   15
tecting water and do not affect taste the way plastic can. The shelf life of a glass bottle is three years, while it's just one year for a plastic bottle.

And therein lies the catch: To enjoy these waters anywhere but their place of   16
origin, you must buy bottles. If you want to avoid disposable bottles and pollution from bottling and shipping, tap water is the safer environmental choice (not to mention the economical one). But if you are choosing among all your bottled beverage options like juice and soda, bottled water has the least environmental cost. "Nobody is saying something about wine and beer, and those are much worse [in environmental impact]," Riese points out.

EXERCISE 15.3 ▶ DRAWING A GRAPHIC ORGANIZER

Using Graphic Organizer 15.1 as a basis, draw a graphic organizer for "Alcohol or Marijuana? A Pediatrician Faces the Question" (pp. 367–71).

GRAPHIC ORGANIZER 15.3 ▶ The Structure of "What Kind of H$_2$O Should You Drink?"

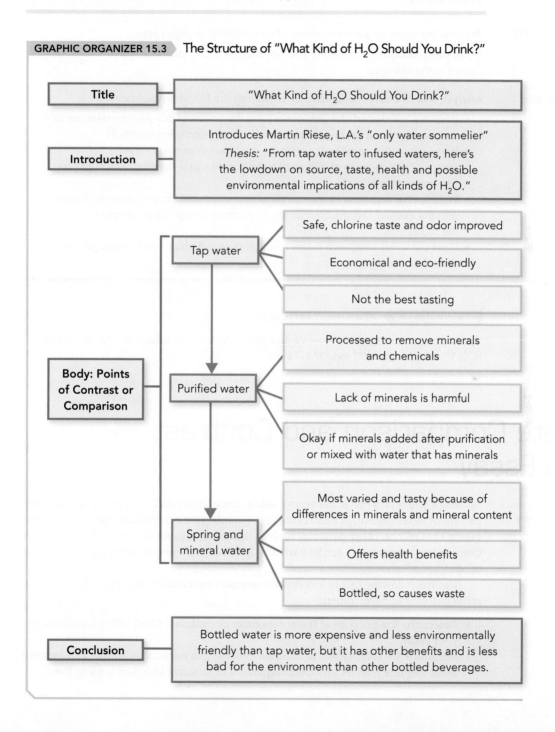

Title	"What Kind of H$_2$O Should You Drink?"
Introduction	Introduces Martin Riese, L.A.'s "only water sommelier" *Thesis:* "From tap water to infused waters, here's the lowdown on source, taste, health and possible environmental implications of all kinds of H$_2$O."

Body: Points of Contrast or Comparison

Tap water
- Safe, chlorine taste and odor improved
- Economical and eco-friendly
- Not the best tasting

Purified water
- Processed to remove minerals and chemicals
- Lack of minerals is harmful
- Okay if minerals added after purification or mixed with water that has minerals

Spring and mineral water
- Most varied and tasty because of differences in minerals and mineral content
- Offers health benefits
- Bottled, so causes waste

Conclusion
Bottled water is more expensive and less environmentally friendly than tap water, but it has other benefits and is less bad for the environment than other bottled beverages.

HOW WRITERS READ   **COMPARISON AND CONTRAST**

THE READING PROCESS	STRATEGIES
BEFORE READING	**Preview** the essay to get an overview of its content and organization.
	Make connections by comparing your knowledge and experience with the topic discussed in the selection.
AFTER READING	**Analyze and evaluate** the reading by answering the following questions.

- What are the **shared characteristics**? Are the points of comparison **relevant** to the thesis? Have any important points of comparison been **omitted**?
- How well do the **details** support these main points of the comparison or contrast? Would **more or different details** have made the comparison or contrast more convincing?
- What is your **response** to the comparison or contrast? Do you agree or disagree with the author? Did the comparison or contrast change your **perspective** on the topic?
- Does the writer treat each subject fairly and provide **balanced coverage**? Or does the coverage seem biased?

EXERCISE 15.4   **READING CRITICALLY**

Apply the questions in the "How Writers Read" box to the selection "What Kind of H$_2$O Should You Drink?" (pp. 374–76).

Integrate Comparison and Contrast into an Essay

For a reading that uses comparison and contrast as well as other patterns of development, see "On a Plate" (pp. 393–96).

Although you will write some essays using comparison and contrast as the primary pattern of development, in most cases you will integrate comparisons or contrasts into essays that rely on other patterns, such as description, process analysis, or argument. Comparisons or contrasts can be particularly effective in persuasive essays, as "Alcohol or Marijuana?" shows.

Use the following tips to incorporate comparison or contrast into essays based on other patterns of development.

1. **Determine the purpose of the comparison or contrast.** What will it contribute to your essay?
2. **Introduce the comparison or contrast clearly.** Use transitional words and expressions to guide readers into the comparison or contrast and then back to the

essay's primary pattern of development, and tell readers how the comparison or contrast supports your main point. Do not leave it to your audience to figure out why you have included the comparison.

3. **Keep the comparison or contrast short and to the point.** Avoid distracting readers from your main message.

4. **Organize the points of the comparison or contrast appropriately.** Use point-by-point or subject-by-subject organization, even though the comparison or contrast is part of a larger essay.

| PREWRITING | DRAFTING | REVISING | EDITING & PROOFREADING |

A Guided Writing Assignment[*]

COMPARISON AND CONTRAST

Your Essay Assignment

Write an essay comparing or contrasting a pair of subjects. Choose subjects to compare or contrast that your readers might find surprising or enlightening. Below are some options to help you get started.

- two or more forms of entertainment (movies, concerts, radio, music videos)
- two or more styles of communication, dress, or teaching
- two or more public figures
- the, right and wrong ways of doing something
- two or more different cultures' views on the roles that men and women should play

1 **Select an essay topic from the list above, or create one of your own.**

Consider your learning style when choosing subjects.

- Some topics are **concrete** (comparing public figures), while others are more **abstract** (comparing communication styles or cultural views). Consider your learning style and choose the option better suited to you.
- If you are a **social learner**, choose subjects with which your classmates are familiar so that you can discuss your subjects with them. Try group brainstorming about various subjects.
- **Social** and **creative learners** might prefer comparing artists' personalities or styles. **Verbal** and **rational learners** might prefer comparing opposing arguments.

[*] The writing process is *recursive*; that is, you may find yourself revising as you draft or prewriting as you revise. This is especially true when writing on a computer. Your writing process may also differ from project to project or from that of your classmates.

Consider your interests and experiences: Choose subjects that you **already know about**, **want to learn more about**, or **have experience with**.

Brainstorm, alone or in groups, a list of subjects you would like to write about. Since comparison and contrast can work with any two comparable subjects, you should be able to find a subject you and your reader will find engaging.

2 **Consider your purpose and audience, and choose a basis for comparison.**

Ask yourself these questions.

- Will my essay's **purpose** be to **express myself**, **inform**, or **persuade**? What **basis of comparison** will work best, given my purpose? To **inform** readers about two football positions, you could compare the height, weight, skills, and training of players at each position. To **persuade** readers that one quarterback was better than another, you could compare the number of interceptions, completions, and passing yards of each.

- Who is my **audience**? How much do my readers **already know** about the topic? What kind of **supporting details** will they find **convincing** and **engaging**? Readers who are football fans will need different information from those who do not watch the sport.

3 **Explore your subjects and develop points of comparison.**

Keeping your learning style in mind, **explore how your two subjects are similar**, **how they are different**, **or both**.

- Create a **two-column list** of similarities and differences. Jot down ideas in the appropriate column. (Rational, pragmatic, and verbal learners may prefer listing.)

- Ask a classmate to help you **brainstorm** by mentioning only similarities. For each similarity, generate a difference. (Creative and social learners may prefer brainstorming.)

- **Use visualization.** Draw a sketch of your subjects. (Concrete, spatial, and creative learners may prefer visualization.)

- **Create a scenario** in which your subjects interact. For example, if your topic is the cars of today and the cars of 1950, imagine asking your great-grandfather to drive a 2018 luxury car. How would he react? What would he say? (Emotional learners may prefer scenarios.)

4 **Draft your thesis statement.**

Your thesis statement **should**:
- identify the subjects,
- suggest whether you will focus on similarities, differences, or both
- state your main point

An effective thesis will also **engage your readers**, telling them why your comparison or contrast is important, surprising, or useful.

Example:

subjects

The mystery novels of <u>both</u> Robert B. Parker and Sue Grafton are popular because

main point — emphasis on similarities

readers are fascinated by the intrigues of witty, independent private detectives.

Team up with a classmate to review each other's thesis statement. Try to identify the subjects for comparison, the focus, and the main point. If these are unclear or ineffective, offer suggestions for improvement.

5 Choose a method of organization.

Decide whether you will use **point-by-point (Graphic Organizer 15.1)** or **subject-by-subject (Graphic Organizer 15.2)** organization.

- **Point-by-point** often works better for lengthy essays (because it keeps both subjects current in the reader's mind) and for complicated or technical subjects.
- **Subject-by-subject** organization tends to emphasize the larger picture.

If you are not sure which will be most effective, **create an outline or graphic organizer** for both patterns to see which works better.

6 Write a first draft of your comparison or contrast essay.

- The **introduction** should **spark your readers' interest**, **introduce your subjects**, provide any necessary **background information**, and include your **thesis**.
- The **body paragraphs** should include **topic sentences** that focus on **a point of comparison**.
  - For **point-by-point** organization, **discuss the subjects in the same order for each point**, and **arrange your points of comparison logically**, from simplest to the most complex, for example.
  - For **subject-by-subject** organization, **cover the same points** for both subjects **in the same order** in both halves of your essay, and use **transitions** such as *similarly*, *in contrast*, *on the one hand*, *on the other hand*, and *not only . . . but also* to alert readers as you **switch from one subject to the other**.
- The **conclusion** should remind readers of your **thesis** and offer a **final comment** on your comparison or contrast. If your essay is lengthy or complex, consider **summarizing** your main points in the conclusion.

7 Evaluate your draft, and revise as necessary.

Use **Figure 15.1, "Flowchart for Revising a Comparison or Contrast Essay,"** to evaluate and revise your draft.

FIGURE 15.1 ▶ Flowchart for Revising a Comparison or Contrast Essay

QUESTIONS   REVISION STRATEGIES

1. Highlight your thesis statement. Does it identify the subjects being compared; indicate whether you will compare, contrast, or both; and state your main point? Does it suggest why your comparison or contrast is meaningful?

NO ▶

- Consider your audience: What would make the comparison or contrast meaningful to your readers?
- Brainstorm reasons for making the comparison, or work backward from your reasons to revise your thesis.

YES
▼

(continued on next page) ▶

DRAFTING

REVISING

381

(Figure 15.1 continued)

QUESTIONS REVISION STRATEGIES

2. Write the basis of comparison at the top of the page. Is your basis of comparison clear? Does it clearly relate to your thesis?

 NO ▶

- Talk with a friend or classmate about your basis of comparison while he or she helps you think of a better basis for comparison.
- Review your points of similarity or difference and work backward to derive your basis of comparison.

 YES ▼

3. Place a ✔ next to the sentences that focus on similarities or mark an ✗ next to sentences that focus on differences. Have you included all significant points of comparison? Do you fairly examine similarities and differences? Is each similarity or difference significant, and does each support your thesis?

 NO ▶

- Delete insignificant or irrelevant similarities or differences.
- Review your prewriting to identify any significant points of comparison you overlooked.
- Conduct research or ask a classmate to suggest ideas.

 YES ▼

4. Reread your supporting paragraphs. Does each one have a clear topic sentence that relates to your point of comparison or contrast?

 NO ▶

- Add or revise the topic sentence to focus on the point of comparison.
- Consider splitting paragraphs that focus on more than one point or characteristic and combining paragraphs that focus on the same one.

 YES ▼

5. Draw a **wavy underline** under the concrete details in each paragraph. Do you include enough details to make your comparisons vivid and interesting? Have you provided roughly the same amount of detail for both subjects?

NO ▶

- Add or delete details as necessary.
- Review your prewriting to see if you overlooked any significant details.
- Brainstorm or research your subjects to come up with additional details.

 YES ▼

QUESTIONS	REVISION STRATEGIES
6. Draw a graphic organizer. Did you use either point-by-point or subject-by-subject organization consistently? Will your organization be clear to your reader? **NO** ▶	• Study your graphic organizer to find inconsistencies or gaps. • Reorganize your essay using one method of organization consistently. • Add transitions to make the shift to a new subject or point of comparison clearer.

YES ▼

QUESTIONS	REVISION STRATEGIES
7. Reread your introduction and conclusion. Does your introduction convey why your comparison is meaningful? Is your conclusion relevant and satisfying? **NO** ▶	• Revise your introduction to engage readers and emphasize the importance of your comparison. • Consider concluding with an action or way of thinking that is appropriate given your comparison.

8 Edit and proofread your essay.

Refer to Chapter 9 for help with:

• **editing sentences** to avoid wordiness, making your verb choices strong and active, and making your sentences clear, varied, and parallel

• **editing words** for tone and diction, connotation, and concrete and specific language

When proofreading, make sure:

• you use the **correct form of adjectives** and **adverbs** when **comparing two items** (comparative) or **three or more items** (superlative)

	Positive	Comparative	Superlative
Adjectives	sharp	sharper	sharpest
Adverbs	early	earlier	earliest

Example: Both *No Country for Old Men* and *True Grit* were suspenseful,

but I liked *True Grit* ~~best.~~ **better.**

Example: George, Casey, and Bob are all bad at basketball, but Bob's game

is ~~worse.~~ **worst.**

• items linked by **correlative conjunctions** (*either . . . or, neither . . . nor, not only . . . but also*) are in the **same grammatical form**

Example: The Grand Canyon is not only a spectacular tourist attraction but also

~~scientists consider it~~ a useful geological record **for scientists.**

383

Readings: Comparison and Contrast in Action

Border Bites

Heather Gianakos

Heather Gianakos was a first-year student when she wrote the following comparison-and-contrast essay for her composition course. Although she has always enjoyed both styles of cooking that she discusses, she needed to do some research to learn more about their history. As you read the essay, consider the writer's thesis and points of comparison.

Introduction: Indicates Gianakos will examine both similarities and differences but will focus on differences. Her thesis statement gives a basis of comparison of her two subjects, Mexican and southwestern cooking: the traditions and geographic locations of the people who developed them. It also makes a point: that these differences have led to the differences in the food.

Chili peppers, tortillas, tacos: All these foods belong to the styles of cooking known as Mexican, Tex-Mex, and southwestern. These internationally popular styles often overlap; sometimes it can be hard to tell which style a particular dish belongs to. Two particular traditions of cooking, however, play an especially important role in the kitchens of Mexico and the American Southwest — native-derived Mexican cooking ("Mexican"), and Anglo-influenced southwestern cooking, particularly from Texas ("southwestern"). The different traditions and geographic locations of the inhabitants of Mexico and of the Anglo American settlers in the Southwest have resulted in subtle, flavorful differences between the foods featured in Mexican and southwestern cuisine.   1

Subject A: southwestern

Subject B: Mexican

Point of comparison 1: The physical conditions in which the two styles developed. Notice that Gianakos uses point-by-point comparison, discussing both subjects in each paragraph and often using transitions between them. She also cites sources for her information.

Many of the traditions of southwestern cooking grew out of difficult situations — cowboys and ranchers cooking over open fires, for example. Chili, which can contain beans, beef, tomatoes, corn, and many other ingredients, was a good dish to cook over a campfire because everything could be combined in one pot. Dry foods, such as beef jerky, were a convenient way to solve food storage problems and could be easily tucked into saddlebags. In Mexico, by contrast, fresh fruits and vegetables such as avocados and tomatoes were widely available and did not need to be dried or stored. They could be made into spicy salsa and guacamole. Mexicans living in coastal areas could also enjoy fish and lobster dishes (Jamison and Jamison 5).   2

Corn has been a staple in the American Southwest and Mexico since the time of the Aztecs, who made tortillas (flat, unleavened bread, originally made from stone-ground corn and water) similar to the ones served in Mexico today (Jamison and Jamison 5). Southwesterners, often of European descent, adopted the tortilla but often prepared it with wheat flour, which was easily available to them. Wheat-flour tortillas can now be found in both Mexican and southwestern cooking, but corn is usually the primary grain in dishes with precolonial origins. Tamales (whose name derives from a word in Nahuatl, the Aztec group of languages) are a delicious example: A hunk of cornmeal dough, sometimes combined with ground meat, is wrapped in corn husks and steamed. In southwestern cooking, corn is often used for leavened corn bread, which is made with corn flour rather than cornmeal and can be flavored with jalapeños or back bacon.

Meat of various kinds is often the centerpiece of both Mexican and southwestern tables. However, although chicken, beef, and pork are staples in both traditions, they are often prepared quite differently. Fried chicken rolled in flour and dunked into sizzling oil or fat is a popular dish throughout the American southwest. In traditional Mexican cooking, however, chicken is often cooked more slowly, in stews or baked dishes, with a variety of seasonings, including ancho chiles, garlic, and onions.

Ever since cattle farming began in Texas with the early Spanish missions, beef has been eaten both north and south of the border. In southwestern cooking, steak—flank, rib eye, or sirloin—grilled quickly and served rare is often a chef's crowning glory. In Mexican cooking, beef may be combined with vegetables and spices and rolled into a fajita or served ground in a taco. For a Mexican food purist, in fact, the only true fajita is made from skirt steak, although Mexican food as it is served in the United States often features chicken fajitas.

In Texas and the Southwest United States, barbecued pork ribs are often prepared in barbecue cook-offs, similar to chili-cooking competitions. Such competitions have strict rules for the preparation and presentation of the food and for sanitation (Central Texas). However, while the

---

3 **Point of comparison 2:** The use of corn and wheat

4 **Point of comparison 3:** The use of chicken

Subject A: Southwestern

Subject B: Mexican

5 **Point of comparison 4:** The use of beef

Subject A: Southwestern

Subject B: Mexican

6 **Point of comparison 5:** The use of pork

Subject A: Southwestern

BBQ is seen as a southwestern specialty, barbecue ribs as they are served in southwestern-themed restaurants today actually come from a Hispanic and Southwest Mexican tradition dating from the days before refrigeration: Since pork fat, unlike beef fat, has a tendency to become rancid, pork ribs were often marinated in vinegar and spices and then hung to dry. Later the ribs were basted with the same sauce and grilled (Campa 278). The resulting dish has become a favorite both north

Subject B: Mexican

and south of the border, although in Mexican cooking, where beef is somewhat less important than in southwestern cooking, pork is equally popular in many other forms, such as chorizo sausage.

Conclusion: Gianakos returns to the idea of overlap mentioned in the introduction and makes clear her purpose—to inform readers about the differences between the two cuisines.

Cooks in San Antonio or Albuquerque would probably tell you that the food they cook is as much Mexican as it is southwestern. Regional cuisines in such areas of the Southwest as New Mexico, Southern California, and Arizona feature elements of both traditions; chimichangas—deep-fried burritos—actually originated in Arizona (Jamison and Jamison 11). Food lovers who sample regional specialties, however, will note—and savor—the contrast between the spicy, fried or grilled, beef-heavy style of southwestern food and the richly seasoned, corn- and tomato-heavy style of Mexican food.

7

Gianakos lists her sources at the end of her paper, following MLA style.

Works Cited

Campa, Arthur L. *Hispanic Culture in the Southwest*. U of Oklahoma P, 1979.

Central Texas Barbecue Association. 16 Aug. 2004, www.ctbabbq.com/rules/.

Jamison, Cheryl Alters, and Bill Jamison. *The Border Cookbook*. Harvard
　　Common, 1995.

Analyzing the Writer's Technique

1. **Background** Evaluate Gianakos's title and introduction. Do they provide the reader with enough background on her topic?
2. **Organization** Using a point-by-point organization, Gianakos presents her two subjects in the same order — first southwestern cuisine, then Mexican cuisine—for each point of comparison except in paragraph 3. Why do you think she discusses the two cuisines together in this paragraph?
3. **Sources** How does Gianakos's use of sources contribute to her essay?

Thinking Critically about Comparison and Contrast

1. **Response** Reread the first sentence of the essay. What type of cooking is mentioned here and never discussed again in the essay? How does this decision by Gianakos affect your response to the first paragraph and to the essay as a whole?
2. **Tone** Describe Gianakos's tone. Is it effective in this essay?
3. **Language** What do phrases such as "subtle, flavorful differences" (para. 1), "Food lovers" (7), and "richly seasoned" (7) contribute to the essay? If Gianakos had included more phrases like these, how would the essay be changed?
4. **Omissions** What comparisons did Gianakos not make that she could have made?

Responding to the Essay

1. **Discussion** In groups of two or three, discuss other regional cuisines that might make effective topics for a comparison and contrast essay. What traits do they share? What distinguishes them?
2. **Journal** Gianakos compares the cuisines of the American Southwest and Mexico using the traditions and geographic locations of the people who lived there as the basis of comparison. In your journal, explore several other possible bases of comparison that could be used to compare these cuisines.
3. **Essay** Write an essay comparing foods of two other regional cuisines.

▶ READING

His Marriage and Hers: Childhood Roots

Daniel Goleman

Daniel Goleman holds a PhD in behavioral and brain sciences and has published a number of books on psychology, including *The Brain and Emotional Intelligence: New Insights* (2011) and *Leadership: The Power of Emotional Intelligence* (2011). Goleman reported on the brain and behavioral sciences for *The New York Times* for many years and was elected a fellow of the American Association for the Advancement of Science for his efforts to bring psychology to the public. In his book *Emotional Intelligence* (1995), from which the following selection was taken, Goleman describes the emotional skills required for daily living and explains how to develop those skills. **Before reading**, preview the selection and make connections by thinking about the ways communication between men and women differ. **While reading**, notice how Goleman uses comparison and contrast to explore differences between the sexes and highlight his key points of comparison.

As I was entering a restaurant on a recent evening, a young man stalked out the door, his face set in an expression both stony and sullen. Close on his heels a young woman came running, her fists desperately pummeling his back while she yelled, "Goddamn you! Come back here and be nice to me!" That poignant, impossibly self-contradictory plea aimed at a retreating back epitomizes the pattern most commonly seen in couples whose relationship is distressed: She seeks to engage, he withdraws. Marital therapists have long noted that by the time a couple finds their way to the therapy office, they are in this pattern of engage-withdraw,

1

with his complaint about her "unreasonable" demands and outbursts, and her lamenting his indifference to what she is saying.

This marital endgame reflects the fact that there are, in effect, two emotional realities in a couple, his and hers. The roots of these emotional differences, while they may be partly biological, also can be traced back to childhood and to the separate emotional worlds boys and girls inhabit while growing up. There is a vast amount of research on these separate worlds, their barriers reinforced not just by the different games boys and girls prefer but by young children's fear of being teased for having a "girlfriend" or "boyfriend" (Maccoby and Jacklin). One study of children's friendships found that three-year-olds say about half their friends are of the opposite sex; for five-year-olds it's about 20 percent, and by age seven almost no boys or girls say they have a best friend of the opposite sex (Gottman). These separate social universes intersect little until teenagers start dating.

Meanwhile, boys and girls are taught very different lessons about handling emotions. Parents, in general, discuss emotions—with the exception of anger—more with their daughters than their sons (Brody and Hall). Girls are exposed to more information about emotions than are boys: when parents make up stories to tell their preschool children, they use more emotion words when talking to daughters than to sons; when mothers play with their infants, they display a wider range of emotions to daughters than to sons; when mothers talk to daughters about feelings, they discuss in more detail the emotional state itself than they do with their sons—though with the sons they go into more detail about the causes and consequences of emotions like anger (probably as a cautionary tale).

Leslie Brody and Judith Hall, who have summarized the research on differences in emotions between the sexes, propose that because girls develop facility with language more quickly than do boys, this leads them to be more experienced at articulating their feelings and more skilled than boys at using words to explore and substitute for emotional reactions such as physical fights; in contrast, they note, "boys, for whom the verbalization of affects is de-emphasized, may become largely unconscious of their emotional states, both in themselves and others" (p. 454).

At age ten, roughly the same percent of girls as boys are overtly aggressive, given to open confrontation when angered. But by age thirteen, a telling difference between the sexes emerges: Girls become more adept than boys at artful aggressive tactics like ostracism, vicious gossip, and indirect vendettas. Boys, by and large, simply continue being confrontational when angered, oblivious to these more covert strategies (Cairns and Cairns). This is just one of many ways that boys—and later, men—are less sophisticated than the opposite sex in the byways of emotional life.

When girls play together, they do so in small, intimate groups, with an emphasis on minimizing hostility and maximizing cooperation, while boys' games are in larger groups, with an emphasis on competition. One key difference can be seen in what happens when games boys or girls are playing get disrupted by someone getting hurt. If a boy who has gotten hurt gets upset, he is expected to get out of the way and stop crying so the game can go on. If the same happens among a group of girls who are playing, the game stops while everyone gathers around to help the girl who is crying. This difference between boys and girls at play epitomizes what Harvard's Carol Gilligan points to as a key disparity between the sexes: boys take pride in a lone, tough-minded independence and autonomy, while girls see themselves as part of a web of connectedness. Thus boys are threatened by anything that might challenge their independence, while girls are more threatened by a rupture in their relationships. And, as Deborah Tannen has pointed out in her book *You Just Don't Understand,* these differing perspectives mean that men and women want and expect very different things out of a conversation, with men content to talk about "things," while women seek emotional connection.

© Sally and Richard Greenhill/Alamy

Hera foto/Alamy

In short, these contrasts in schooling in the emotions foster very different   7
skills, with girls becoming "adept at reading both verbal and nonverbal emotional
signals, at expressing and communicating their feelings," and boys becoming
adept at "minimizing emotions having to do with vulnerability, guilt, fear, and
hurt" (Brody and Hall 454). Evidence for these different stances is very strong in the
scientific literature. Hundreds of studies have found, for example, that on average
women are more empathic than men, at least as measured by the ability to read
someone else's unstated feelings from facial expression, tone of voice, and other
nonverbal cues. Likewise, it is generally easier to read feelings from a woman's
face than a man's; while there is no difference in facial expressiveness among
very young boys and girls, as they go through the elementary-school grades boys
become less expressive, girls more so. This may partly reflect another key difference:
women, on average, experience the entire range of emotions with greater intensity
and more volatility than men—in this sense, women are more "emotional" than
men (Brody and Hall).

All of this means that, in general, women come into a marriage groomed for   8
the role of emotional manager, while men arrive with much less appreciation of
the importance of this task for helping a relationship survive. Indeed, the most
important element for women—but not for men—in satisfaction with their
relationship reported in a study of 264 couples was the sense that the couple
has "good communication" (Davis and Oathout). Ted Huston, a psychologist at
the University of Texas who has studied couples in depth, observes, "For the
wives, intimacy means talking things over, especially talking about the relationship
itself. The men, by and large, don't understand what the wives want from
them. They say, 'I want to do things with her, and all she wants to do is talk.' "
During courtship, Huston found, men were much more willing to spend time
talking in ways that suited the wish for intimacy of their wives-to-be. But once
married, as time went on the men—especially in more traditional couples—
spent less and less time talking in this way with their wives, finding a sense of
closeness simply in doing things like gardening together rather than talking
things over.

This growing silence on the part of husbands may be partly due to the fact   9
that, if anything, men are a bit Pollyannaish about the state of their marriage,
while their wives are attuned to the trouble spots: in one study of marriages, men
had a rosier view than their wives of just about everything in their relationship—
lovemaking, finances, ties with in-laws, how well they listened to each other,
how much their flaws mattered (Sternberg). Wives, in general, are more vocal
about their complaints than are their husbands, particularly among unhappy
couples. Combine men's rosy view of marriage with their aversion to emotional
confrontations, and it is clear why wives so often complain that their husbands
try to wiggle out of discussing the troubling things about their relationship. (Of
course this gender difference is a generalization and is not true in every case;
a psychiatrist friend complained that in his marriage his wife is reluctant to
discuss emotional matters between them and he is the one who is left to bring
them up.)

The slowness of men to bring up problems in a relationship is no doubt   10
compounded by their relative lack of skill when it comes to reading facial
expressions of emotions. Women, for example, are more sensitive to a sad
expression on a man's face than are men in detecting sadness from a woman's
expression.[1] Thus a woman has to be all the sadder for a man to notice her feelings
in the first place, let alone for him to raise the question of what is making her
so sad.

Consider the implications of this emotional gender gap for how couples   11
handle the grievances and disagreements that any intimate relationship
inevitably spawns. In fact, specific issues such as how often a couple has sex,
how to discipline the children, or how much debt and savings a couple feels
comfortable with are not what make or break a marriage. Rather, it is how a
couple discusses such sore points that matters more for the fate of their
marriage. Simply having reached an agreement about how to disagree is key
to marital survival; men and women have to overcome the innate gender
differences in approaching rocky emotions. Failing this, couples are vulnerable
to emotional rifts that eventually can tear their relationship apart. . . . [T]hese
rifts are far more likely to develop if one or both partners have certain deficits
in emotional intelligence.

Note

1. The research is by Dr. Ruben C. Gur at the University of Pennsylvania School of
   Medicine.

Works Cited

Brody, Leslie R., and Judith A. Hall. "Gender and Emotion." *Handbook of Emotions,* edited by Michael
    Lewis and Jeannette Haviland, Guilford Press, 1993.

Cairns, Robert B., and Beverley D. Cairns. *Lifelines and Risks.* Cambridge UP, 1994.

Davis, Mark H., and H. Alan Oathout. "Maintenance of Satisfaction in Romantic Relationships:
    Empathy and Relational Competence." *Journal of Personality and Social Psychology,* vol. 53, no. 2
    (1987), pp. 397–410.

Gottman, John. "Same- and Cross-Sex Friendship in Young Children." *Conversation of Friends,* edited
    by J. Gottman and J. Parker, Cambridge UP, 1986.

Maccoby, Eleanor, and C. N. Jacklin. "Gender Segregation in Childhood." *Advances in Child
    Development and Behavior,* edited by H. Reese, Academic Press, 1987.

Sternberg, Robert J. "Triangulating Love." *The Psychology of Love,* edited by Robert Sternberg and
    Michael Barnes, Yale UP, 1988.

Understanding the Reading

1. **Summarizing** In one or two sentences, explain the differences that Goleman
   claims exist between men's and women's ways of expressing emotion.
2. **Causes** According to Goleman, what are the root causes of the differences between
   how men and women express emotion?
3. **Details** How can the emotional differences between spouses cause marital difficulties, according to the writer?

4. **Differences** Explain how boys and girls play differently, according to Goleman.
5. **Vocabulary** Explain the meaning of each of the following words as it is used in the reading: *epitomizes* (para. 1), *articulating* (4), *ostracism* (5), *vendettas* (5), *disparity* (6), and *empathic* (7).

Analyzing the Writer's Technique

1. **Thesis** What is Goleman's thesis?
2. **Audience and Purpose** Identify the purpose of and intended audience for the essay.
3. **Points of Comparison** List the points of comparison, and for each, evaluate the evidence Goleman offers to substantiate his findings. Do you find the evidence sufficient and convincing? Why or why not? What other information might the writer have included?
4. **Objectivity** Do you think Goleman maintains an objective stance on the issue, despite his gender? Explain your answer.

Thinking Critically about Text and Visuals

1. **Organization** Discuss the type of organization the author used (point by point, subject by subject, or mixed). Does the organization seem to affect the author's fairness? Do you detect any bias? If so, explain.
2. **Language** How does the use of quotation marks around the word *unreasonable* (para. 1) affect its connotation?
3. **Tone** How does the real-life example in paragraph 1 affect the essay, especially its tone?
4. **Fact/Opinion** Do you consider the essay to be primarily fact, opinion, or informed opinion? Justify your answer.
5. **Visual** What key ideas from the essay do the photographs on page 389 illustrate?

Responding to the Reading

1. **Discussion** In groups of two or three, discuss Goleman's generalizations about men and women. Do any seem inaccurate and, if so, which one(s)? Discuss the evidence, if any, that would prove Goleman wrong.
2. **Journal** In your journal, describe a situation from your experience that either confirms or contradicts one of Goleman's generalizations.
3. **Essay** Make a list of the emotional differences and resulting behavioral conflicts between men and women that you have observed. Decide which differences Goleman explains. Write an essay reporting your findings.

Working Together

In small groups of three or four students, brainstorm a list of emotional differences between the sexes. Using that list as a springboard, work independently to compose a one-paragraph letter to an advice columnist describing a conflict that has arisen between a man and a woman. Trade letters with a member of your group. Then, taking on the role of the columnist, respond to your group member's letter, explaining the root of the problem—emotional differences—and offering a solution. Be creative with the name of the letter writer and the advice columnist. If your class has a blog or a discussion board, you may post these letters so that all members of the class can read them.

On a Plate

Toby Morris

Toby Morris is an illustrator and a comic artist from Auckland, New Zealand, who created the popular comic series *The Pencilsword*. In addition, he has published a graphic memoir entitled *Don't Puke on Your Dad: A Year in the Life of a New Father* (2013). The comic strip below appeared in *The Pencilsword*. **Before reading**, preview the selection and make connections by thinking of the different ways one might define success. **While reading**, notice how the author uses both words and visuals to explore differences in the life experiences of the two characters.

"On a Plate," by Toby Morris; published in *The Wireless*, 2015

"On a Plate," by Toby Morris; published in *The Wireless*, 2015

"On a Plate," by Toby Morris; published in *The Wireless*, 2015

"On a Plate," by Toby Morris; published in *The Wireless*, 2015

Understanding the Reading

1. **Topic** What groups in society do Richard and Paula represent?
2. **Thesis** What is the thesis of "On a Plate"? Is the thesis stated or implied?
3. **Details** Contrast Paula's living conditions with Richard's (frames 3–4).
4. **Differences** Compare Richard and Paula's approach to homework (frames 5–6, 11–12).

Analyzing the Writer's Technique

1. **Points of Comparison** Identify the points of comparison on which the visual story is based.
2. **Title** What is the meaning of the title?
3. **Organization** Evaluate the effectiveness of the point-by-point organization in the essay. How would the essay differ if it had been written using a subject-by-subject organization?
4. **Conclusion** Evaluate the story's conclusion. How does it reflect the thesis and organization of the visual story?

Thinking Critically about Text and Visuals

1. **Assumptions** What assumptions does the author make?
2. **Visual Details** What differences do you notice in the way that the author depicts the two fathers? What details in frame 11 of Richard's dorm room catch your eye?
3. **Graphics** What information and feelings are presented visually that would be difficult to express if only words were used?
4. **Bias** Do you think Toby Morris appears to favor one side of the comparison? What details make you think so?

Responding to the Reading

1. **Discussion** In small groups, discuss which values each member of the group holds dear. Be prepared to share your lists with the class and to defend your positions.
2. **Journal** Translate one pair of frames from "On a Plate" into writing. Try to convey all the details included in the frames, as well as the implied meaning of the frames. Then compare your "translation" with the frames themselves. What advantages and disadvantages does each method of communication have?
3. **Essay** Choose one life stage (infancy, childhood, teen years, young adulthood, old age) and write an essay exploring fully the advantages and disadvantages of the privileged and underprivileged in that life stage.

Working Together

In small groups, brainstorm an alternate ending to the story. Then add a final frame for both Richard and Paula. Sketch out the frames and include a caption for each. Be prepared to share your sketches and captions with the class.

Apply Your Skills: Additional Essay Assignments

For more on locating and documenting sources, see Part 5.

Using what you have learned in this chapter, write a comparison or contrast essay on one of the topics below. Depending on the topic you choose, you may need to conduct research.

To Express Your Ideas

1. Compare two families that you know or are part of. Include points of comparison that reveal what is valuable and important in family life.
2. Compare your values and priorities today with those you held when you were in high school.
3. Compare your lifestyle today with the lifestyle you intend to follow after you graduate from college.

To Inform Your Reader

4. Compare resources available through your college library with those available on the open Web.
5. Compare two types of social media, such as Snapchat and Instagram or Pinterest.

To Persuade Your Reader

6. Choose a technological change that has occurred in recent years, and argue either that it is beneficial or that its drawbacks outweigh its usefulness.
7. Compare two views on a controversial issue, arguing in favor of one of them.
8. Compare two methods of doing something (such as disciplining a child or training a pet), arguing that one method is more effective than the other.

Cases Using Comparison and Contrast

9. Imagine that you are taking a course in photography. Write a paper comparing and contrasting the advantages of black-and-white versus color images. Your instructor is your audience.
10. Imagine that you are working in the advertising department of a company that manufactures skateboards. Write a memo evaluating two periodicals and recommending which one the company should use to run its advertisements. Your manager is your audience.

Working Together

Form a small group of three or four students. Choose two restaurants that are familiar to all of you, and brainstorm a list of similarities and differences in the two restaurants. Then decide which restaurant you will recommend. Using this information, write a creative and entertaining thirty-second radio advertisement that will persuade listeners to choose Restaurant A over Restaurant B. Choose a member of your group to present the ad to the class.

> ### SYNTHESIZING IDEAS ▸ ATTITUDES TOWARD CLASS
>
> Both "Underground Lair: Inside a Chicken Processing Plant" (Chapter 12, pp. 289–93) and "On a Plate" (pp. 393–96) explore attitudes toward class.
>
> #### Analyzing the Readings
>
> 1. What attitudes toward class do the readings present?
> 2. Watch a television program, and then write a journal entry analyzing the attitudes toward class that the characters exhibit. How closely do the characters' attitudes match the attitudes presented in either reading?
>
> #### Essay Idea
> Write an essay explaining your attitude toward class and comparing or contrasting it to the attitude presented in either of the readings.

16

Classification and Division

Explaining Categories and Parts

Images Etc Ltd./Alamy

WRITING QUICK START The photograph on this page shows fruits and vegetables on display at a farmers' market. Notice that they are arranged by produce type. Can you imagine how difficult it would be to find what you need if all produce were randomly piled onto a table or shelf, with broccoli, pears, peppers, and bananas all mixed together? Most stores and markets group their products for the convenience of their customers.

Take a few minutes to brainstorm other ways a favorite store or Web site could group its products for customer convenience. You may propose a serious method or a humorous one. Then write a paragraph describing your system. List the characteristics of each product group, describe the products that belong in each group, and give each group a title.

Classification is a process of sorting people, things, or ideas into groups or categories to make them more understandable. You use classification daily, the same way you did in the Writing Quick Start. Your dresser drawers are probably organized by categories, with socks and sweaters in different drawers. Grocery stores, shopping Web sites, libraries, and even restaurant menus arrange items in groups according to similar characteristics.

Division breaks *one* item down into parts. For example, the humanities department at your college may be divided into English, modern languages, and philosophy, and the modern language courses might be divided into Spanish, French, Chinese, Italian, and Russian.

- In a *human physiology course*, you study the structure and parts of the human ear by identifying the function of each part.
- In preparing a *business management report*, you consider how debt liability differs for three types of businesses: a sole proprietorship, a partnership, and a corporation.
- While working as a *facilities planner*, your supervisor asks you to conduct a feasibility study of several new sites. You begin by sorting the sites into three categories: in-state, out-of-state, and international.

What Are the Characteristics of Classification and Division Essays?

A successful classification or division essay uses one principle of classification or division to create meaningful categories or parts that are broad enough to include all of the members of the group.

Classification Groups and Division Divides Ideas According to One Principle

Developing an effective set of categories or parts requires you to do two things.

- Choose **one principle of classification or division** and use it. An essay classifying fish could choose size or diet as a classification principle, not both. An essay about an aquarium could divide the topic according to either the type of fish displayed or the quality of the exhibits.
- Identify **a manageable number of categories or parts**. An essay classifying birds according to diet, for example, might use five or six types of diet, not twenty.

EXERCISE 16.1 **IDENTIFYING PRINCIPLES OF CLASSIFICATION OR DIVISION**

Brainstorm three different principles of classification or division for each of the following topics.

1. Sports teams
2. Fast-food restaurants
3. Television shows
4. Academic subjects
5. Novels

Purpose and Audience Drive the Writer's Choice of a Principle

Several different principles can be used to categorize groups or divide an item into parts, so writers should choose a principle of classification or division that is appropriate to their purpose and audience. For instance, to inform parents about the types of day-care facilities on or near campus, you might classify day-care centers according to the services they offer because your readers would likely be looking for that information. If you were writing to persuade readers to take their children to a new museum, you might divide the exhibits according to their suitability for children of different ages.

Categories and Parts Are Exclusive and Comprehensive

Choose categories (for classification) or parts (for division) that do not overlap. In other words, each item that you discuss should fit in no more than one category. A familiar example is age: The categories 25 to 30 and 30 to 35 are not mutually exclusive because someone who is 30 years old would fit into both. In an essay about the nutritional value of pizza, you could divide your topic into the nutritional attributes of carbohydrates, proteins, and fats, but you should not add a separate category for saturated fat because it is already contained in the fats category.

The categories or parts you choose should also be comprehensive. In a division essay, all the major parts of an item should be included. In a classification essay, each member of the group should fit into one category or another. For example, an essay categorizing fast-food restaurants according to the type of food they serve would have to include categories for pizza, hamburgers, hot dogs, tacos, and fried chicken.

EXERCISE 16.2 **CLASSIFYING AND DIVIDING BY CATEGORY**

Choose a principle of classification or division for two of the topics listed in Exercise 16.1. Then make a list of categories in which each item could be included or parts into which each item could be divided.

Classification or Division Fully Explains Each Category or Part

A classification or division essay should contain enough detail for readers to understand each category or part easily. Use facts, descriptions, quotations, comparisons, or examples to help readers to "see" your categories or parts.

Classification or Division Includes a Thesis

The thesis statement of a classification or division essay should identify the topic. It may also reveal the principle used to classify or divide the topic. In most cases it also should suggest why the classification or division is relevant or important.

Here are two examples of effective thesis statements.

Most people consider videos a form of entertainment; however, videos can also serve educational, commercial, and political functions.

Importance (implied)
Topic
Principle
Categories

The Grand Canyon is divided into two distinct geographical areas—the North Rim and the South Rim—each offering different views, activities, and climatic conditions.

The following readings demonstrate the techniques for writing effective classification or division essays discussed above. The first reading is annotated to point out how Jerry Newman classifies fast-food managers. As you read the second essay, try to identify for yourself how Michael Moss uses the techniques of division to show what makes potato chips nearly irresistible.

CLASSIFICATION ‹ **READING**

My Secret Life on the McJob: Fast Food Managers

Jerry Newman

Jerry Newman is Distinguished Teaching Professor Emeritus of Organization and Human Resources at the University at Buffalo (State University of New York) and coauthor of the textbook *Compensation,* Tenth Edition (2010). He has also worked as a business consultant at AT&T, Hewlett-Packard, RJR Nabisco, and McDonald's. This selection is from *My Secret Life on the McJob: Lessons in Leadership Guaranteed to Supersize Any Management Style* (2007), which Newman wrote after working at various fast-food restaurants to learn about their operation and management.

Before Reading

1. **Preview:** Use the steps on page 28.
2. **Connect:** How have the managers or bosses you have known treated their customers and employees?

While Reading Study the annotations and highlight the facts, descriptions, and examples that are especially effective in helping you understand how the author classifies the managers by type.

I thought all my fast food stores would be pretty similar. They weren't. Some stores made employees wear name tags, going as far as sending people home if they repeatedly didn't wear their name tags, while other stores didn't seem to care. In some stores crews socialized after work, but in others they barely talked to each other, even during work. Even though every chain had

1

Relevance: Relevance hinted at by writer's surprise at how varied stores were despite "edicts from headquarters"; for an audience reading about management styles, this topic would be important strict rules about every facet of food production and customer interaction, how employees were treated was part of an individual store culture, and this varied from store to store. These differences could often be traced to the managers' values and practices and how consistently they were applied both by the managers and by their *sensei*,[1] much more so than any edicts from headquarters. The best-run store I worked at was [a] Burger King; the worst-run store was also a Burger King. If corporate rules had a controlling impact, shouldn't stores have been much more similar? At one McDonald's the employees were extremely friendly; at another the tension between groups was palpable. The differences, I think, can be traced to the managers. The following is a sampler of the types of managers I encountered. Only the last group, performance managers, was good at finding a *sensei* and developing consistent people practices.

Thesis: Identifies topic and principle of classification

Organization: Categories indicated by section headings

Full explanation: Uses contrast, examples, and an anecdote to explain first category fully

The Toxic Manager

Most new employees learn through feedback. When you're first learning a job, there's relatively little ego involvement in feedback; good managers seem to know this and in early days of employment are quick to point out better ways of doing a task. [Toxic] managers, though, use sarcasm or disrespectful comments to indicate when they are unhappy with your work. One of the worst offenders I ran into was the store manager at Arby's, who admitted that the main reason he was hiring me was to change the store culture. He said he was tired of employees who were vulgar and disrespectful, but it didn't take long for me to realize that the role model for their behavior was actually the manager himself—Don. His attitude and style set the tone for everyone else in his store. Almost as bad, the key individual with the necessary attributes to be a *sensei* shared Don's disregard for the feelings of others. Don, in particular, didn't confine his wrath to "bad" employees. Bill, a diligent long-timer, messed up a coupon order. A customer had an entertainment book coupon for one Value Meal free with the purchase of another. There was a labyrinth of steps to complete some of the discounts correctly. When Bill made the error, it was right before the end of Don's shift, and Don tore into him, saying loudly enough for everyone to hear, "Well, I'm leaving before Bill can make my life any more miserable." It didn't take long to infect others with this lack of respect for employees.

2

The Mechanical Manager

The most common type of manager I encountered was the Mechanical Manager, who was for the most part either an assistant manager or a shift

3

---

[1]*Sensei:* A Japanese word for *teacher* or *master.* Newman uses it to mean an employee who is not a manager but is both highly skilled at his or her job and socially influential among fellow employees.

manager, not a full store manager. You could spot the Mechanical Managers from across the room—they did their jobs, day after day, as if fast food was slow death. They didn't want to be there, and they were just going through the motions. They typically had gotten their jobs because they were reliable crew members and had put in enough time that some reward was needed to keep them working. A promotion has a certain finality, though—it makes you confront reality: Is this what I want out of life? Most say "No," and that's probably why I didn't see very many store managers who were mechanical. Before most store managers had reached that level (one store manager told me it was a ten-year journey), those who weren't interested in fast food as a lifetime career had moved on to other career pursuits. While looking for other opportunities, though, they did what was necessary to get by. Luis at McDonald's was the perfect example.

In my first McDonald's experience I made myself a grid showing all of the sandwiches and their ingredients. After a day of having instructions blasted at me, I needed a visual training aid to finally put things together. I shared this grid with Luis on my third day, expecting he might already have training materials like this (as was the case at Wendy's) or that he could use it to train other visual learners. As I handed Luis the Excel spreadsheet, I watched his face and saw no reaction. None. He told me he'd leave it for Kris, the store manager. Clearly he saw the value in it—he didn't toss it, after all—but a reinforcing response for my initiative required a level of involvement he didn't or couldn't muster.

4

Full explanation: Uses definition, cause-effect, extended example (Luis), anecdote to explain second category fully

The Relationship Manager

The Relationship Manager was a relatively rare breed in my experience. James was the prototype. He led by building relationships and demonstrating that he cared about our destinies—hard to do when it seemed like every week someone was leaving and another person was coming on board. From the first day, James was very different from what I was used to. When I first met him for my job interview, he was fifteen minutes late because he was out picking up an employee whose car had broken down. I never saw any other manager pick up or take home a crew member who had transportation problems. In fact, at one store I watched Mary, an older worker teetering on the edge of poverty, sit in a booth out front for two hours waiting for her husband to pick her up after his shift at a Sam's Club. As I came to learn, this kindness wasn't unusual for James. And in being kind, James created a culture that was much more friendly and supportive than that in many of the other fast food places I had experienced. Even the way James responded to my quitting was refreshing. With my back problems becoming increasingly worse, I called James to tell him that I was quitting and dreaded leaving him in the lurch. But he was amazingly kind, telling me to take care of myself and forcefully telling me to pick up my check.

5

Full explanation: Uses extended example (James), anecdote, contrast to explain third category fully

The Performance Manager

Purpose and audience: Section returns to thesis—purpose is to explain traits of best ("performance") manager; audience is other business managers or readers interested in management

Organization: Moves from worst (toxic managers) to best (performance managers)

It's easy to spot the Performance Manager. Here relationships are still important, but now they serve as a means to ensure performance. Through word or deed she very quickly lets you know what is expected. I like this. No ambiguity, no doubt about what it takes to make the grade. The best at this was Kris, who, it seemed to me, watched for slackers much more closely than did the managers at other fast food places. She told me during the interview that I would be watching DVDs my first day. She also mentioned that one of the new people had taken three to four bathroom breaks while watching the videos, which was an excessive number, she thought. She also commented that she might be losing some people because she thought they were slower than they should be. I got the message: She would be watching my work and looking to see if I was going to goof off. My experience in other places was that you got fired for only two things: not showing up and insubordinate behavior. Clearly she was adding a third reason—poor performance. Good for her!   6

Full explanation: Uses definition, examples, extended example (Kris) to explain fourth category fully

Kris's watchful eye extended beyond bathroom breaks. I found out the hard way that taking breaks, even unpaid ones, wasn't allowed unless legally required. Apparently in New York State, you're not entitled to a break until after five hours of work. So when I asked Kris for a break before the appointed time, she answered with an emphatic "No." Kris's message was clearly that we do our jobs by the book, no exceptions.   7

Over time at this Burger King I began to notice that Kris wasn't a taskmaster all the time. Sure, during busy times she was prone to exhort the staff to work faster. And she didn't tolerate leaning (remember, "If you've got time to lean, you've got time to clean"). But this attitude relaxed a bit during slower times, and it especially relaxed for the better workers like Daniel, Eric, and Craig, three of the fastest guns on the sandwich assembly board.   8

Visualize a Classification or Division Essay: Create a Graphic Organizer

For more on creating a graphic organizer, see pp. 35–37.

Graphic Organizer 16.1 outlines the basic organization of a classification or division essay.

- The **introduction** announces the topic, gives background information, and states the thesis.
- The **body paragraphs** explain the categories or parts and their characteristics.
- The **conclusion** brings the essay to a satisfying close by reinforcing the thesis and offering a new insight on the topic.

GRAPHIC ORGANIZER 16.1 The Basic Structure of a Classification or Division Essay

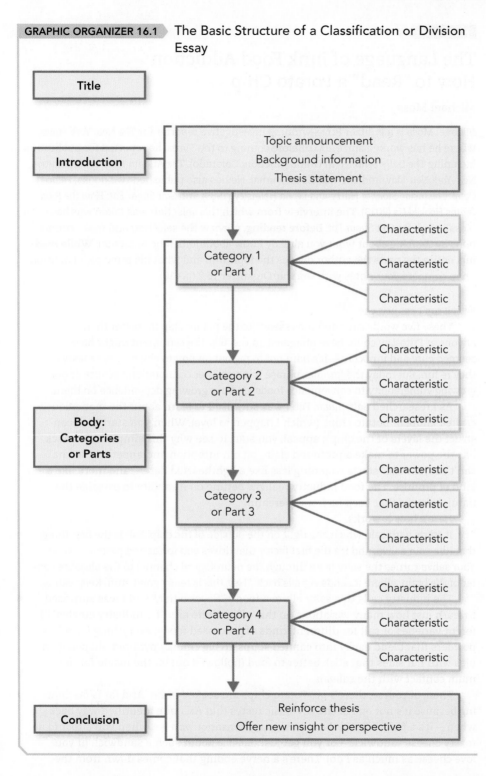

Title

Introduction — Topic announcement / Background information / Thesis statement

Category 1 or Part 1 — Characteristic / Characteristic / Characteristic

Category 2 or Part 2 — Characteristic / Characteristic / Characteristic

Body: Categories or Parts

Category 3 or Part 3 — Characteristic / Characteristic / Characteristic

Category 4 or Part 4 — Characteristic / Characteristic / Characteristic

Conclusion — Reinforce thesis / Offer new insight or perspective

The Language of Junk Food Addiction: How to "Read" a Potato Chip

Michael Moss

Michael Moss is a Pulitzer Prize–winning investigative reporter for *The New York Times*, where he has worked since 2000. Before coming to the *Times*, he reported for publications including *The Daily Sentinel* (in Grand Junction, Colorado), *The Atlanta Journal-Constitution*, *New York Newsday*, and *The Wall Street Journal*. He has also published two books, *Palace Coup: The Inside Story of Harry and Leona Helmsley* (1989) and *Salt Sugar Fat: How the Food Giants Hooked Us* (2013). The interview from which this selection was taken was based on Moss's work for *Salt Sugar Fat*. **Before reading**, preview the selection and make connections by thinking about what you already know about junk food addiction. **While reading**, notice the parts the author divides the topic into and what his principle of division is. Then compare your notes with Graphic Organizer 16.2 (p. 410).

Betcha can't eat just one.   1

These five words captured the essence of the potato chip far better than   2
anyone at Frito-Lay could have imagined. In the '60s, the sentiment might have
seemed cute and innocent—it's hard not to pig out on potato chips, they're tasty,
they're fun. But today the familiar phrase has a sinister connotation because of our
growing vulnerability to convenience foods, and our growing dependence on them.

As I researched *Salt, Sugar, Fat*, I was surprised to learn about the meticulously   3
crafted allure of potato chips (which I happen to love). When you start to decon-
struct the layers of the chip's appeal, you start to see why this simple little snack
has the power to make a profound claim on our attention and appetite. "Betcha
can't eat just one" starts sounding less like a lighthearted dare—and more like a
kind of promise. The food industry really is betting on its ability to override the
natural checks that keep us from overeating.

Here's how it works.   4

It starts with salt, which sits right on the outside of the chip. Salt is the first thing   5
that hits your saliva, and it's the first factor that drives you to eat and perhaps overeat.
Your saliva carries the salty taste through the neurological channel to the pleasure center of the brain, where it sends signals back: "Hey, this is really great stuff. Keep eating."

The industry calls this salty allure a food's "flavor burst," and I was surprised   6
to learn just how many variations on this effect there are. The industry creates different varieties of salt for different kinds of processed foods: everything from fine
powders that blend easily into canned soups, to big chunky pyramid-shaped gran-
ules with flat sides that stick better to food (hollowed out on the inside for maxi-
mum contact with the saliva).

Then, of course, there's fat. Potato chips are soaked in fat. And fat is fascinat-   7
ing because it's not one of the five basic tastes that Aristotle identified way back
when—it's a *feeling*. Fat is the warm, gooey sensation you get when you bite into a
toasty cheese sandwich—or you get just *thinking* about such a sandwich (if you
love cheese as much as I do). There's a nerve ending that comes down from the

brain almost to the roof of the mouth that picks up the feel of fat, and the industry thus calls the allure of fat "mouthfeel."

The presence of fat, too, gets picked up by nerve endings and races along the neu- 8 rological channel to the pleasure center of the brain. Which lights up, as strongly as it lights up for sugar. There are different kinds of fats—some good—but it's the saturated fats, which are common in processed foods, that are of most concern to doctors. They're linked to heart disease if over-consumed. And since fats have twice as many calories as sugar, they can be problematic from an obesity standpoint.

But potato chips actually have the entire holy trinity: They're also loaded with 9 sugar. Not added sugar—although some varieties do—but the sugar in most chips is in the potato starch itself, which gets converted to sugar in the moment the chip hits the tongue. Unlike fat, which studies show can exist in unlimited quantities in food without repulsing us, we do back off when a food is too sweet. The challenge is to achieve just the right depth of sweetness without crossing over into the extreme. The industry term for this optimal amount of sugar is called the "bliss point."

So you've got all three of the big elements in this one product. But salt, sugar, 10 and fat are just the beginning of the potato chip's allure. British researchers, for instance, have found that the more noise a chip makes when you eat it, the better you'll like it and the more apt you are to eat more. So chip companies spend a lot of effort creating a perfectly noisy, crunchy chip.

The chip has an amazing textural allure, too, a kind of meltiness on the tongue. 11 The ultraprocessed food product most admired by food company scientists in this regard is the Cheeto, which rapidly dissolves in your mouth. When that happens, it creates a phenomenon that food scientists call "vanishing caloric density." Which refers to the phenomenon that as the Cheeto melts, your brain interprets that melting to mean that the calories in the Cheeto have disappeared as well. So they tend to uncouple your brain from the breaks that keep your body from overeating. And the message coming back from the brain is: "Hey, you might as well be eating celery for all I care about all the calories in those disappearing Cheetos. Go for it."

Then there's the whole act of handling the chip—the fact that we move it 12 with our hand directly to the mouth. When you move a food directly to your mouth with your hand there are fewer barriers to overeating. You don't need to wait until you have a fork, or a spoon, or a plate to eat. You can eat with one hand while doing something else. These handheld products lead to what nutrition scientists call "mindless eating"—where we're not really paying attention to what we're putting in our mouths. This has been shown to be hugely conducive to overeating. One recent example is the Go-Gurt yogurt that comes in a collapsible tube. Once you open it, you can just squeeze out the yogurt with one hand while you're playing a computer game with the other.

The bottom line, which everyone in the food industry will tell you, is taste. 13 They're convinced that a good number of us will talk a good game on nutrition and health, but when we walk through the grocery store, we'll look for and buy the products that taste the best. And that's the cynical view: They will do nothing to improve the health profile of their products that will jeopardize taste. They're as hooked on profits as they are on salt, sugar, fat.

GRAPHIC ORGANIZER 16.2 The Structure of "The Language of Junk Food Addiction"

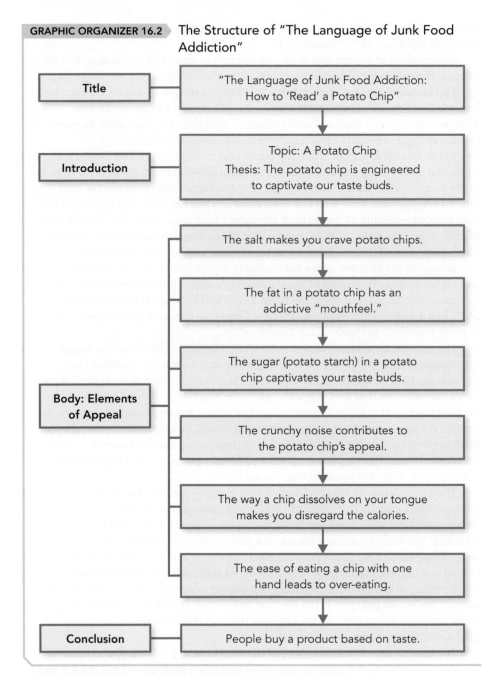

| Title | "The Language of Junk Food Addiction: How to 'Read' a Potato Chip" |

| Introduction | Topic: A Potato Chip
Thesis: The potato chip is engineered to captivate our taste buds. |

Body: Elements of Appeal

The salt makes you crave potato chips.

The fat in a potato chip has an addictive "mouthfeel."

The sugar (potato starch) in a potato chip captivates your taste buds.

The crunchy noise contributes to the potato chip's appeal.

The way a chip dissolves on your tongue makes you disregard the calories.

The ease of eating a chip with one hand leads to over-eating.

| Conclusion | People buy a product based on taste. |

EXERCISE 16.3 ▶ **DRAWING A GRAPHIC ORGANIZER**

Using Graphic Organizer 16.1 as a basis, draw a graphic organizer for "My Secret Life on the McJob: Fast Food Managers" (pp. 403–6). Note that because "My Secret Life on the McJob" is an excerpt from a book, it does not include a conclusion.

HOW WRITERS READ	CLASSIFICATION AND DIVISION
THE READING PROCESS	**STRATEGIES**
BEFORE READING	**Preview** the essay to get an overview of its content and organization.
	Make connections by thinking about the categories or parts into which the topic could be grouped or divided.
AFTER READING	**Analyze and evaluate** the reading by answering the following questions.
	• What is the **principle of classification or division**? Is it appropriate given the writer's **purpose**? Does it reflect the writer's **biases**? How?
	• Does the classification or division omit any **significant categories or parts**?
	• Has the writer provided **sufficient detail** about each category?
	• How is the essay **relevant** to your own experience? Would you have divided or classified the subject differently?

EXERCISE 16.4   READING CRITICALLY

Apply the questions in the "How Writers Read" box to the selection "The Language of Junk Food Addiction: How to 'Read' a Potato Chip" (pp. 408–9).

Integrate Classification or Division into an Essay

Classification and division are often used along with one or more other patterns of development.

- An essay that argues for stricter gun control may categorize guns in terms of their firepower, purpose, or availability.
- A narrative about a writer's frustrating experiences in a crowded international airport terminal may describe the different parts or areas of the airport.

When incorporating classification or division into an essay based on another pattern of development, keep the following tips in mind.

1. **Avoid focusing on why the classification or division is meaningful.** When used as a secondary pattern, the significance of the classification or division should be clear from the context in which it is presented.
2. **State the principle of classification briefly and clearly.**
3. **Name the categories or parts.** In the sentence that introduces the classification or division, name the categories or parts to focus your readers' attention on the explanation that follows.

For a reading that uses classification as well as other patterns of development, see "Empower Pupils to Beat the Bullies" (pp. 421–22).

A Guided Writing Assignment*

CLASSIFICATION AND DIVISION

Your Essay Assignment

Write a classification or division essay on a topic that you believe would interest other students at your college or readers who share an interest or experience of yours. Below are some options for general topics.

Classification
- types of pets
- types of sports fans
- types of movies

Division
- your family
- a sports team or extracurricular club
- a public place (building, stadium, park)

1 Select a topic, devise a principle of classification or division, and list the categories of which it is made up or the parts into which it breaks down.

Choose a topic idea, and then try one of the following suggestions to generate ideas for categories or parts.

- **Start from the categories or parts:** Brainstorm, freewrite, or use another idea-generating strategy to generate details describing your topic. Then categorize the details into logical groups. Look for three or four groups or parts that share a common thread.

- **Start from a principle of classification or division:** Think about a trait or principle (like degrees of enthusiasm for sports fans or types of horror films) and then freewrite, brainstorm with a friend or classmate, or use another strategy to come up with the specific types or parts.

In small groups, **test your categories (classification)** or **parts (division)** to make sure that:

1. **all members** of a category **fit** *or* **no essential parts** have been **omitted**
2. **all categories are exclusive** (each group member fits in one category only) or **no parts overlap**
3. categories or parts will **engage your readers**
4. **names** of categories or parts describe them **accurately**, emphasizing their **distinguishing features**

* The writing process is *recursive*; that is, you may find yourself revising as you draft or prewriting as you revise. This is especially true when writing on a computer. Your writing process may also differ from project to project and from that of your classmates.

PREWRITING

2 Consider your purpose, audience, and point of view.

Ask yourself these questions.

- What is my **purpose**, and who is my **audience**? How do they affect my **topic**, my **principle of classification** or **division**, and my **categories** or **parts**?

  Example: To *inform* novice Skype users about the software, your parts and details must be straightforward and nontechnical.

- How might **additional patterns of development** help readers understand and appreciate my topic?

  Example: A classification essay might also compare and contrast types of sports fans.

- What **point of view** best suits my purpose and audience? **First person** (*I, we*) or **second person** (*you*) may be appropriate in **informal writing** if your audience has **personal knowledge** of or **experience** with the topic. **Third person** (*he, she, it, they*) is appropriate in more **formal writing** or for topics **less familiar** to your audience.

3 Generate supporting details.

Try one of the following suggestions for generating supporting details that will engage your readers and reinforce your purpose.

1. Alone or in pairs, visit a place where you can **observe your topic or the people associated with it**. For example, to generate details about pets, visit a pet store or an animal shelter. Make notes on what you see and hear. Record conversations, physical characteristics, behaviors, and so forth. (Concrete and creative learners may prefer observing; social learners may prefer observing in pairs.)

2. **Conduct research** to discover facts, examples, and other details about your topic. (All learners, but especially pragmatic and independent learners, may prefer conducting research.)

3. **Use the patterns of development** to generate details. Ask yourself how the categories or parts are **similar or different (comparison and contrast)**, what **examples** you can use to illustrate the categories or parts **(illustration)**, what **stories or anecdotes** would help you distinguish categories or parts **(narration)**, or how you would **describe parts or group members** using **language that appeals to the senses (description)**. (All learners may benefit from using the patterns of development.)

4 Draft your thesis statement.

Your thesis statement should **identify your topic** and **reveal your principle of division or classification**. It should also suggest why your classification or division is **useful or important**. Notice how the following weak theses are strengthened by showing both what the categories are and why they are important.

Weak	**Revised**
There are four types of insurance that most people can purchase.	Understanding the four common types of insurance will help you protect yourself, your family, and your property against disaster.

Working Together. In groups of two or three students, take turns reading your thesis aloud. As group members listen, have them:

1. list your categories/parts
2. write down why they matter

Finally, as a group, discuss how writers could make their categories or parts more distinctive and how they could show readers why these categories or parts are useful or important.

5 Choose a method of organization.

- **Least-to-most** and **most-to-least** work well in classification essays. You might arrange categories in increasing order of importance or from most to least common, difficult, or frequent.

  Example: In writing about the parts of a hospital, you might describe the most important areas first (operating rooms, emergency department) and then move to less important areas (waiting rooms, cafeterias).

- **Chronological order** works well when one category occurs or is observable before another.
- **Spatial order** works well in division essays when describing a place.

  Example: In describing the parts of a baseball stadium, you might move from stands to playing field.

  Reviewing Chapter 7 may help you understand the methods of organization.

6 Draft your classification or division essay.

Use the following guidelines to keep your essay on track.

- The **introduction** should provide any **background** readers will need, include your **thesis statement**, and suggest why the classification or division is **useful** or **important**; it might also state your **principle of classification or division**.
- The **body paragraphs** should **name** and **elaborate on** your categories or parts, **explain the traits** they share, and **provide the details** readers need to understand and accept them. Be sure you devote roughly the **same amount of detail** to each category or part. **Headings** can help identify categories or parts discussed in multiple paragraphs; a **list** can help identify a large number of categories or parts; a **diagram** or **flowchart** may help make your system of classification or division clearer to readers. Include **transitions** such as *first, next, in contrast,* and *on the one/other hand* to keep readers on track as your essay moves from one category or part to another.
- The **conclusion** should bring your essay to a satisfying close, returning to your **thesis** and elaborating on why the classification or division is **useful** and **important** or **offering a new insight** or **perspective** on the topic.

7 Evaluate your draft and revise as necessary.

Use **Figure 16.1, "Flowchart for Revising a Classification and Division Essay,"** to evaluate and revise your draft.

FIGURE 16.1 Flowchart for Revising a Classification and Division Essay

QUESTIONS		REVISION STRATEGIES

1. Highlight your thesis statement. Do it and the rest of your introduction reveal your principle of classification or division and suggest why it is important?

 NO ▶

- Revise your thesis to make your justification stronger or more apparent.
- Add explanatory information to your introduction.

YES ▼

2. *Write* the principle of classification you used at the top of your paper. Do you use this principle consistently throughout the essay? Does it fit your audience and purpose? Does it clearly relate to your thesis?

 NO ▶

- Brainstorm other possible principles of classification or division, and decide if one better fits your audience and purpose.
- Revise your categories and parts to fit either your existing principle or a new one, or rewrite your thesis to reflect your principle of classification/division.

YES ▼

3. Underline the names of categories or parts. Do they cover all members of the group or all major parts of the topic? Are your categories or parts exclusive (not overlapping)?

 NO ▶

- Brainstorm or conduct research to add categories or parts.
- Revise your categories or parts so that each item fits into one group only.

YES ▼

4. Place a ✔ beside the details that explain each category or part. Does your essay fully explain each one? (If it reads like a list, answer "No.")

 NO ▶

- Brainstorm or do research to generate more details.
- Add examples, definitions, facts, and expert testimony to improve your explanations.

YES ▼

5. *Write* the method of organization you used at the top of your essay. Is the organization clear? Does this method suit your audience and purpose? Have you followed it consistently?

 NO ▶

- Refer to Chapter 7 to discover a more appropriate organizing plan.
- Revise the order of your categories or parts.
- Add transitions to make your organization clear.

YES ▼

(continued on next page) ▶

(Figure 16.1 continued)

6. <u>Underline</u> the topic sentence of each paragraph. Is each paragraph focused on a single category or part?

 NO ▶

- Consider splitting paragraphs that cover more than one category or part.
- Consider using headings to group paragraphs on a single category or part.

YES
▼

7. Reread your conclusion. Does it offer a new insight or perspective on the topic or explain why your classification or division is useful or important?

NO ▶

- Ask yourself: "So what? What is the point I'm trying to make?" Build your answers into the conclusion.

 Edit and proofread your essay.

Refer to Chapter 9 for help with:

- **editing sentences** to avoid wordiness, make your verb choices strong and active, and make your sentences clear, varied, and parallel
- **editing words** for tone and diction, connotation, and concrete and specific language

Pay particular attention to the following:

1. Avoid **short, choppy sentences,** which can make a classification or division essay sound dull and mechanical. Try combining a series of short sentences and varying sentence patterns and lengths.

Example: Working dogs ˄ , such as German shepherds and sheepherding dogs, are another one of the American Kennel Club's breed categories. ~~These include German shepherds and sheepherding dogs.~~

Example: ˄ The fountain pen, one ~~One~~ standard type of writing instrument ˄ ~~is the fountain pen.~~ ~~It~~ is sometimes messy and inconvenient to use.

2. Add a comma after **opening phrases or clauses longer than four words**.

Example: When describing types of college students ˄ , be sure to consider variations in age.

Example: Although there are many types of cameras ˄ , most are easy to operate.

Readings: Classification and Division in Action

The Use and Abuse of Facebook

Allison Cava

Allison Cava wrote the following essay in response to an assignment for her writing course, in which she was asked to write an essay about a type of social media, explaining its uses or users. As you read the essay, consider how effectively Cava explains her groupings. Does her principle of classification make sense? Does she provide enough detail to convince you that the groupings exist and that her topic is useful or important?

Since its introduction in February 2004 by then Harvard University sophomore Mark Zuckerberg (along with Dustin Moskovitz, Chris Hughes, and Eduardo Saverin), Facebook has become one of the most popular social-networking websites on the Internet. At first only available to college students, the website opened to high school students in 2005, and then to everyone—including organizations, such as colleges, businesses, news outlets, political campaigns, and nonprofit organizations—shortly thereafter, and by 2012 Facebook was up to about a billion users (*Evolution*). Now teens are using the site to post photos of themselves (when they're not using Instagram), parents are "friending" their children, grandparents are reconnecting with lost loves, and businesses and organizations ask patrons to "like" them on Facebook.

The site's initial purpose—and the reason it grew from just a handful of users on one campus to a huge number of users across the world—was to provide an easy way for users ("friends") to keep in touch by sharing status updates, interesting links, and photos with distant friends. These constructive uses have expanded to include companies posting their mission statements and advertising their products and

Title: Identifies Cava's subject

1   **Introduction:** First 2 paras. present history, original purpose, and current expanded purpose of Facebook for readers who may only know current version of software.

Support: Cava cites sources (throughout) to support her claims.

2

services; news outlets posting breaking news; colleges posting emergency alerts, closings, and course offerings; and politicians connecting with voters. In 2007, Barack Obama seemed innovative when he posted the announcement of his presidential aspirations on Facebook; now candidates are expected to have a Facebook page, and Facebook even offers tips for making the most of a post ("Less"). Sadly, these constructive uses have been tainted by annoying and even abusive practices. An awareness of these practices is the key to the responsible and enjoyable use of Facebook.

Thesis: Thesis identifies principle of classification and demonstrates usefulness/importance of recognizing categories of annoying and abusive practices

Among annoying Facebook practices is over-enthusiastic posting. Some users post frequent status updates about the most mundane events in their lives, continually post "cute" photos of their pets, or disproportionately message others, leading to timelines clogged with posts that just aren't that interesting. No wonder that 10 percent of adults who take a "Facebook vacation" say that they "just [weren't] interested"; 9 percent say that they stopped looking at Facebook because they were tired of the "drama" from their "friends"; and 7 percent say that they got "bored with [Facebook]" (Rainie et al.).   3

Organization: Topic sentence: Introduces first (least offensive) category of annoying practices: over-enthusiastic posting

Support: Cava offers examples to support claim that over-enthusiastic posting is boring and evidence to show boring posts drive users away

Another annoying use of Facebook is the gathering of huge quantities of "friends" in an effort to make users appear (and feel) more popular than they really are. The threshold limit of 5,000 Facebook "friends" one can acquire is far in excess of the number of friends one could possibly have in real life, but this huge number is considered normal in cyber-world (Ball), even though having a vast group of Facebook "friends" may not even be healthy: Psychotherapist Kim Schneiderman cites a study conducted at Edinburgh Napier University in which researchers saw a correlation between stress and the number of Facebook friends a person had. More annoying than simply *having* a vast number of "friends" is the process of *acquiring* a vast number of friends. To achieve this number, the Facebook friender must message others continually in hopes of being friended, reaching out to increasingly distant connections, like the friends of "friends" and the friends of friends of "friends."   4

Organization: Topic sentence: Provides transition to alert readers to second category

Support: Cava summarizes research and offers reason to support claim that over-"friending" is harmful and annoying

More serious are the users who post obnoxious comments or tag "friends" in embarrassing photos. Although a "friend" may untag her- or   5

Organization: Topic sentence: Introduces next topic; transition indicates the method of organization (from least to most annoying)

himself or report an offensive photo or message to try and have it removed from the Internet, the effort is almost always futile (Cheng): If someone has a direct link to the photograph, he or she can simply repost it to the detriment of others. Facebook "friends" may also cause trouble by responding nastily to another's posts. Schneiderman has noticed in her practice that Facebook has "wreaked mischief" in some of her clients' lives. For example, one client had to block her conservative brother from commenting on her statuses, as he started an argument with her politically liberal friends (Schneiderman 18).

More serious still are those who use Facebook to discredit or harm others. In one court case in Arkansas, Denise New was found guilty of harassing her own son on Facebook by posting messages to his profile using his name (Lesnick). Italian teen Carolina Picchio was also a victim, receiving "a steady barrage of abusive, offensive messages" from an ex-boyfriend and his pals that ended only when the girl jumped to her death from her bedroom window (Wedeman). Her sister and friends say they asked Facebook to remove the harassing posts, but according to them, nothing happened. Similarly, business rivals can post negative comments to undermine or even ruin a competitor. In fact, Facebook may provide a forum for the spread of abuse that otherwise would not have seen the light of day, information that we may be better off never being privy to (Schneiderman). For instance, people's comments about their bad experiences with college professors, doctors, or companies can help to widely publicize a skewed, discriminatory, or otherwise unfair view that could very well live on the Internet forever.

For all its faults, Facebook is still the most popular social networking site online. While it could do more to enforce its policies and suppress harassing behavior by trolls, many users keep coming back because they enjoy the benefits it affords them: the easy exchange of ideas, information and photographs instantly with anyone in the world, and the opportunity to keep friendships alive across vast distances and many years. In fact, its very popularity is part of its appeal: If all their friends and relatives weren't on Facebook, users would not have as many reasons to use it.

6

Support: Transition introduces an example to support Cava's claim about seriousness of abuse

Organization: Topic sentence: introduces last category; transition indicates that this is most abusive

Support: Cava uses examples to support claim that this category of abuse is most serious

7

Conclusion: Explains popularity of site despite abuses

Works Cited

Ball, Aimee Lee. "Are 5,001 Facebook Friends One Too Many?" *The New York Times*, 28 May 2010, www.nytimes.com/2010/05/30/fashion/30FACEBOOK.html.

Cheng, Jacquie. "Over 3 Years Later, 'Deleted' Facebook Photos Are Still Online." *Ars Technica*, 5 Feb. 2012, arstechnica.com/business/2012/02/nearly-3-years-later-deleted-facebook-photos-are-still-online/.

"The Evolution of Facebook." *The New York Times*, 24 July 2013, www.nytimes.com/interactive/technology/facebook-timeline.html?_r=0.

Lesnick, Gavin. "Mom Found Guilty in Facebook Harassment Case." *Arkansas Democrat-Gazette*, 27 May 2010, www.arkansasonline.com/news/2010/may/27/mom-found-guilty-facebook-harassment-case/.

"Less Than 100 Days until Election, Facebook Offers Tips for Campaigns." Facebook, 1 Aug. 2012, www.facebook.com/notes/government-and-politics-on-facebook/less-than-100-days-until-election-facebook-offers-tips-for-campaigns/10150937198965882/.

Rainie, Lee, et al. "Coming and Going on Facebook." Pew Research Center, 5 Feb. 2013, www.pewinternet.org/2013/02/05/coming-and-going-on-facebook/.

Schneiderman, Kim. "When Online Battles Become Offline Stresses." *Metro*, 18 July 2013, Boston ed., p. 18.

Wedeman, Benn. "Facebook May Face Prosecution over Bullied Teenager's Suicide in Italy." CNN, 31 July 2013, www.cnn.com/2013/07/31/world/europe/italy-facebook-suicide/.

Analyzing the Writer's Technique

1. **Purpose** According to Cava, why is it important to understand the types of annoying and abusive practices on Facebook?
2. **Support** How does Cava explain her categories of abuse and convince readers of the relative seriousness of the abuses she cites? What types of evidence does she use?
3. **Introduction and Conclusion** Evaluate Cava's introduction and conclusion. How successful are they at engaging readers' interest? Does she convey to readers a sense of her topic's importance or a new insight or perspective? Why or why not?

Thinking Critically about Classification and Division

1. **Connotation** What is the connotation of the word *troll* (para. 7)?
2. **Fact or Opinion** Reread the second sentence of paragraph 1. Is this fact or opinion? How can you tell?
3. **Sources** Evaluate Cava's use of sources. Are her sources convincing? What additional types of sources might have made her claims more convincing? Why?
4. **Tone** Consider Cava's tone. What kind of audience does she seem to be addressing?

Responding to the Essay

1. **Reaction** Cava clearly describes Internet abuses but offers few solutions to overcome them. What are possible solutions? Would the inclusion of these have improved her essay?
2. **Discussion** Discuss other principles of classification that might be used to classify types of posts or users of Facebook.
3. **Journal** Write a journal entry describing the ideal Facebook user.
4. **Essay** Cava's essay describes abusive uses of Facebook. Write an essay classifying positive uses of Facebook or another social media site.

CLASSIFICATION COMBINED WITH OTHER PATTERNS ◄ **READING**

Empower Pupils to Beat the Bullies

Ian Rivers

Ian Rivers is professor of human development in the School of Sport and Education at Brunel University. This essay is based on his inaugural lecture, entitled "A Land of Mythical Monsters and 'Wee Timorous Beasties': Reflections on Two Decades of Research on Bullying." **Before reading**, preview and make connections by thinking about situations in which you have observed or experienced bullying. What role, if any, did the bystanders play? **While reading**, notice how Rivers's classification essay also uses cause and effect to fully explain each category.

What are bystanders? Social psychology tells us that they are people who bear   1
witness to an event and who, by their action or inaction, can change the outcome of that event. Much of the research conducted on bystanders' behavior has cast them as passive, almost anaesthetized, observers whose behavior is very much secondary to the "event" taking place. While there has been much more interest in the role of bystanders in workplace bullying, it is only recently that school-based research has moved away from looking at their behavior—or the lack of it—and focused more on their own emotional well-being, in an attempt to understand why they do not intervene.

Together with colleagues from Boston College in the United States (V. Paul   2
Poteat) and York St. John University in the United Kingdom (Nathalie Noret), I have attempted to better understand the "mindset" of the bystander, in the hope that it will provide me with further clues as to why bullying continues, despite forty years

of research and intervention. In essence, this research has resulted in a recasting of the role of the bystander into three very distinct types of pupil: the confederate, the co-victim, and the isolate. These three types are very different from the pupil who does not engage; these are pupils who are desperate to avoid the torment being meted out on their classmate. This is not rocket science, but it does highlight a flaw in much of the research that has gone before: Without taking into account the experiences of bystanders, we may have underplayed the lasting impact that bullying can have on individuals and the school community.

So what do we learn if we recast the bystander in these three roles? We learn that the confederates of the bully may not be the mythical monsters we have demonized, but pupils who experience a great deal of emotional turmoil, such as feelings of self-loathing. This can lead to a series of harmful outcomes for all involved, such as an escalation in violence perpetrated against the victim (ironically to maintain a positive self-image), substance use, or truancy.

For the co-victim, clinical studies of community violence tell us that the potential for long-term psychological harm is just as real, as if the bystander had been the target of abuse. One systematic review of twenty-six studies of the implications of exposure to community violence among urban adolescents found a relationship between witnessing violence and poor mental health, post-traumatic stress, and, surprisingly, aggression. In fact, there is increasing anecdotal evidence to suggest that some of the most heinous acts of violence perpetrated in schools have been carried out by young people who were themselves victims of bullying.

For the isolate—those who try to distance themselves—the story is less clear. Very little is known about this group. Sometimes these pupils appear as reference groups or control groups in studies because they report little or no involvement in bullying. But if the fear of being humiliated or abused by others actively encourages these pupils to hide away, this protective defense mechanism (albeit effective in the short-term) may also have lasting detrimental effects. Isolating oneself may reduce feelings of personal failure, but it can also result in internalized hostility and self-loathing, which have been linked to depression and self-harm. Furthermore, isolation itself may not be a useful long-term strategy: It has been linked to unpopularity, especially among adolescents, and identifies isolates as potential bullying "targets" without friends to support or protect them.

So what can we do? As part of an expert panel convened in the United States, I reported on the findings from our study exploring correlations between being a bystander and contemplating suicide. One finding stood out from the others: Bystanders feel powerless. We need to empower pupils to stop bullying. But what does this mean? It means instilling in perpetrators a sense of disloyalty when they break the pupil code and victimize others. It means that every bully should know she or he has broken the code they have developed with their peers, that they have let themselves down and, more importantly, let everyone else down.

We do not need gimmicks, DVDs, complex strategies, or the myriad of for-profit resources that are out there. If we do need training in our schools, it is social skills training. As adults, we know how difficult it is to talk to strangers, and yet we presume that this comes naturally to children. Bullying is most prevalent in the first year of secondary school, we are told, so that may be a good place to reboot our efforts.

Understanding the Reading

1. **Categories** List the categories of bystanders that Rivers identifies.
2. **Effects** According to the author, how are bystanders affected by bullying?
3. **Details** Why does the author say isolation may not be a useful long-term strategy for coping with bullies?
4. **Vocabulary** Explain the meaning of each of the following words as it is used in the reading: *anaesthetized* (para. 1), *confederate* (2), *heinous* (4), *detrimental* (5), and *myriad* (7). Refer to your dictionary as needed.

Visualizing the Reading

What types of supporting information does Rivers supply to make his categories seem real and believable? Review the reading and complete the chart by filling in at least one effect people in each category may suffer. The first one has been done for you.

Category	Types of Support
1. The Confederate	Self-loathing, escalation in violence, substance use, truancy
2. The Co-victim	
3. The Isolate	

Analyzing the Writer's Technique

1. **Introduction** Is it helpful or unnecessary for Rivers to give his reasons for conducting research into the mindset of bystanders?
2. **Title** What is the function of the essay's title?
3. **Audience and Purpose** What is Rivers's purpose in writing this essay? Who is his audience?
4. **Patterns** What other patterns of development does Rivers use in the essay?

Thinking Critically about the Text

1. **Connotation** What is the connotation of "bystander"?
2. **Support** What types of evidence does Rivers use to support his ideas? Does he provide sufficient detail in each category? What other kinds of details might be helpful or persuasive?
3. **Meaning** What does the author mean when he refers to confederates as "the mythical monsters we have demonized" (para. 3)?
4. **Tone** Describe the tone of the essay. What does it reveal about Rivers's attitude toward his subject?

Responding to the Reading

1. **Discussion** Have you observed students acting as bullies or as bystanders? What information in the essay reflects your own experience? What, if anything, conflicts with your experience?

2. **Journal** Write a journal entry exploring how you think schools should address bullying. Explain whether you agree with the author that the answer lies in empowering students in the way he describes.

3. **Essay** Consider what the author means by "the pupil code" (para. 6). In your opinion, what are the essential elements of a pupil code? Write an essay defining the term and dividing your code into its key components. (Hint: You might use the author's ideas as a starting point and include loyalty to peers and/or respect for others.)

Apply Your Skills: Additional Essay Assignments

Write a classification or division essay on one of the following topics, using what you learned about classification and division in this chapter. Depending on the topic you choose, you may need to conduct research.

To Express Your Ideas

1. Explain whether you are proud of or frustrated with your ability to budget money. For example, you might classify budget categories that are easy to master versus those that cause problems.

2. Explain why you chose your career or major. Categorize the job opportunities or benefits of your chosen field, and explain why they are important to you.

For more on locating and documenting sources, see Part 5.

3. Divide a store—such as a computer store, clothing store, or grocery store—into departments. Describe where you are most and least tempted to overspend.

To Inform Your Reader

4. Write an essay for the readers of your college newspaper classifying college instructors' teaching styles.

5. Explain the parts of a ceremony or an event you have attended or participated in.

6. Divide a familiar substance (like toothpaste) or object (like a Web page or a basketball team) into its component parts.

To Persuade Your Reader

7. Categorize types of television violence to develop the argument that violence on television is either harmful to children or not harmful to children.

8. In an essay that categorizes types of parenting skills and demonstrates how they are learned, develop the argument that effective parenting skills can be acquired through practice, training, or observation.

Cases Using Classification or Division

9. Write an essay for an introductory education class identifying a problem you have experienced or observed in the public education system. Divide public education into parts to better explain your problem.

10. You oversee the development of the annual catalog for a large community college, including the section describing the services offered to students. Decide how that section of the catalog should be organized, and then list the categories it should include. Finally, write a description of the services in one category.

SYNTHESIZING IDEAS   **THE WORKPLACE**

Both "The Underground Lair: Inside a Chicken Processing Plant" (pp. 289–93) and "My Secret Life on the McJob: Fast Food Managers" (pp. 403–6) deal with employment in low-level service jobs. As you answer the following questions, keep in mind that both authors are professionals who were working under the guise of learning the habits, characteristics, and problems that everyday workers face in such jobs.

Analyzing the Readings

1. What workplace problems did both Thompson and Newman observe?
2. Write a journal entry exploring the differences and/or similarities that exist between working at a chicken processing plant and working at fast-food restaurants.

Essay Idea

Write an essay in which you explore attitudes toward and expectations about work. You might consider its value, besides a weekly paycheck, or you might examine what type of work is rewarding.

17

Definition

Explaining What You Mean

Pawel Wewiorski/Moment Select/Getty Images

WRITING QUICK START   Suppose your psychology instructor showed this photograph to the class and asked, "What type of human behavior is being exhibited here?" What would be your response? You might say the people in the photograph are demonstrating cooperation and compassion, for example.

Write a paragraph defining the motivation of the two people shown in the photograph. First choose a term that describes their motivation or behavior. Then write a brief definition of the term you chose and explain the qualities or characteristics of the motivation or behavior.

A **definition** explains the meaning of a term (or which meaning is intended when a word has several different meanings). Often a definition is intended for those who are unfamiliar with the thing or idea being defined. For example, you might define *slicing* to someone unfamiliar with golf or explain the term *koi* to a person unfamiliar with tropical fish.

You use definitions every day in a variety of situations. If you call a friend a *non-conformist*, for example, she might ask you what you mean. If you and a friend disagree over whether you are feminists, you might need to define the term in order to resolve your dispute. In the Writing Quick Start, you named and defined a motivation or behavior.

USING DEFINITION ▶ **IN COLLEGE AND THE WORKPLACE**

- On an exam for a *health and fitness course*, the following short-answer question appears: "Define the term *wellness*."

- Your *psychology instructor* asks you to write a paper exploring classical conditioning. As part of the essay, you need to define the concept and provide examples from everyday life.

- As a *chemical engineer* responsible for your department's compliance with the company's standards for *safety* and *work efficiency*, you write a brief memo to your staff defining each term.

What Are the Characteristics of Extended Definitions?

If you wanted to define the term *happiness*, you would probably have trouble coming up with a brief definition because the emotion is experienced in a wide variety of situations, and the term may mean different things to different people. However, you could explore the term in an essay and explain what it means to you. Such a lengthy, detailed definition is called an **extended definition**.

Extended definitions are particularly useful in exploring a topic's various meanings and applications. Some extended definitions begin with a brief standard definition that anchors the essay's thesis statement. Other extended definitions begin by introducing a new way of thinking about the term. Whatever approach is used, the remainder of the extended definition then clarifies the term by using one or more other patterns of development.

An Extended Definition Is Focused and Detailed

An extended definition focuses on a specific term and discusses it in detail. In the first reading (pp. 431–34), for example, the author defines *freeganism*. To explain the concept, she explores the origin of the word *freegan*, describes the freegan philosophy, explains how and where freegans forage for their food, and discusses safety measures.

An Extended Definition Often Includes a Standard Definition of the Term

A **standard definition**, such as the kind found in a dictionary, consists of three parts:

- the *term* itself
- the *class* to which the term belongs
- the *characteristics or details* that distinguish the term from all others in its class

Here are two examples.

┌── term ──┐ ┌class┐┌─────── distinguishing characteristics ───────┐
A wedding band is a ring, often made of gold, that brides and grooms exchange during a marriage ceremony.

┌── term ──┐   ┌── class ──┐   ┌── distinguishing characteristics ──┐
Dalmatian is a breed of dog that originated in Dalmatia; it has a short, smooth coat with black or dark brown spots.

To write an effective standard definition, use the following guidelines.

1. **Describe the class as specifically as possible.** This will make it easier for your reader to understand the term you define. Notice, for example, that for *Dalmatian*, the class is not *animal* or *mammal* but rather a *breed of dog*.
2. **Do not use the term (or forms of the term) as part of your definition.** Do not write, "*Mastery* means that one has *mastered* a skill." In place of *mastered*, you could use *learned*, for example.
3. **Include enough distinguishing characteristics so that your readers will not mistake the term for something similar within the class.** If you define *a food processor* as "an appliance that purees food," your definition would be incomplete because a blender also purees food. A more complete definition would be "an appliance with interchangeable blades that shreds, dices, chops, or purees food."
4. **Do not limit the definition so much that it becomes inaccurate.** Defining *bacon* as "a smoked, salted meat from the side of a pig that is served at breakfast" would be too limited because bacon is also served at other meals. To make the definition accurate, you could either delete "that is served at breakfast" or add a qualifying expression like "usually" or "most often" before "served."

Look at the following definition of the term *bully*, taken from a magazine article on the topic. As you read it, study the highlighting and marginal notes.

Term

Three characteristics

Example of power difference

Distinguishes *bullying* from similar terms

The term <u>bully</u> does not have a standard definition, but Dan Olweus, professor of psychology at the University of Bergen, has honed the definition to three core elements—bullying involves a pattern of *repeated aggressive behavior* with *negative intent* directed from one child to another where there is a *power difference*. Either a larger child or several children pick on one child, or one child is clearly more dominant than the others. Bullying is not the same as garden-variety aggression; although aggression may involve similar acts, it happens between two people of equal status. By definition, the bully's target has difficulty defending him- or herself, and the bully's aggressive behavior is intended to cause distress.

—Hara Estroff Marano, "Big. Bad. Bully."

EXERCISE 17.1 **WRITING STANDARD DEFINITIONS AND LISTING DISTINGUISHING CHARACTERISTICS**

Write a standard definition for two of the following terms, listing the distinguishing characteristics that you might use in building an extended definition.

1. Hero
2. Giraffe
3. Science fiction
4. Social media
5. Friendship

An Extended Definition Makes a Point

The thesis of an extended definition essay conveys why the term is worth reading about. The following thesis statements include a brief definition and make a point about the term:

┌─ term ─┐   ┌───── point ─────┐
Produced by the body, hormones are chemicals that are important to physical as well as emotional development.

Informative thesis: Makes a point about hormones that most would find relevant

┌─ term ─┐
Euthanasia, the act of ending the life of someone suffering from a terminal illness, is an issue that should not be legislated; rather, it should be a matter of personal choice.
└────────────── point ──────────────┘

Persuasive thesis: Makes a judgment regarding an important issue about which readers are likely to care

An Extended Definition Uses Other Patterns of Development

To explain the meaning of a term in an extended definition, you generally must integrate one or more other patterns of development into your essay. Suppose you want to define the term *lurking* as it is used in the context of the Internet, where it usually means reading postings or comments on an online forum without directly participating in the discussion. You could use:

- **narration** (Chapter 11) to relate a story about learning something by lurking
- **description** (Chapter 12) to describe the experience of lurking
- **illustration** (Chapter 13) to give examples of typical situations involving lurking

- **process analysis** (Chapter 14) to explain how to lurk in an Internet chat room
- **comparison and contrast** (Chapter 15) to compare and contrast lurking to other forms of observation
- **classification and division** (Chapter 16) to classify the reasons people lurk—for information, entertainment, and so on
- **cause and effect** (Chapter 18) to explain the benefits or outcomes of lurking
- **argument** (Chapters 19 and 20) to argue that lurking is an ethical or unethical practice

---

EXERCISE 17.2 ▸ **USING ADDITIONAL PATTERNS OF DEVELOPMENT**

For one of the terms listed in Exercise 17.1 (p. 429), describe how you might use two or three patterns of development in an extended definition of the term.

An Extended Definition May Use Negation and Address Misconceptions

Your extended definition essay may use **negation**—explaining what a term is *not*—to show how the term is different from the other terms in the same class. For example, in an essay defining rollerblading (in-line skating), you might clarify how it is unlike roller skating, which uses a different type of wheeled boot that allows different kinds of motions.

You can also use negation to clarify personal meanings. In defining what you mean by *relaxing vacation*, you might include examples of what is *not* relaxing for you: the pressure to see something new every day, long lines, crowded scenic areas, and many hours in a car each day.

In addition, your extended definition may address popular misconceptions about the term being defined. In an essay defining *plagiarism*, for instance, you might correct the mistaken idea that plagiarism only means passing off an entire paper written by someone else as your own, explaining that plagiarism also includes using excerpts from other writers' work without giving them credit.

EXERCISE 17.3 ▸ **USING NEGATION AND ADDRESSING MISCONCEPTIONS**

For two of the following broad topics, select a narrowed term and develop a standard definition of it. Then, for each term, consider how you could address misconceptions and use negation in an extended definition of the term.

1. A type of dance
2. A play, call, or player position in a sport
3. A piece of clothing (hat, jacket, jeans)
4. A term related to a course you are taking
5. A type of business

The following readings demonstrate the techniques for writing effective extended definition essays discussed above. The first reading is annotated to point out how Jan Goodwin defines *freegan*. As you read the second essay, try to identify for yourself how Mike Crissey uses the techniques of extended definition to explain what *dude* means.

> **READING**

Freegans: They Live Off What We Throw Away

Jan Goodwin

Jan Goodwin is a senior fellow at Brandeis University's Schuster Center for Investigative Journalism and a Soros Foundation Media Fellow. The winner of three Amnesty International UK Media Awards and a World Hunger Award, Goodwin has long been an activist for human rights and social justice. She wrote about the threat of extremism in the Muslim world in her books *Point of Honor* (1994) and *Caught in the Crossfire* (1987) and was a reporter for Lifetime Television's documentary *Defending Our Daughters* (1998). This reading was published in 2009 in the magazine *Marie-Claire*, for which Goodwin was senior international editor.

Before Reading

1. **Preview:** Use the steps listed on page 28.
2. **Connect:** What do you know about how and why some people scavenge for food or free merchandise?

While Reading Study the annotations to identify the characteristics of definition.

It's nearly closing time on a crisp Monday night at a Midtown Manhattan supermarket, when a burly crew begins tossing bulging black bags filled with the day's trash—crusty breads, salad-bar fixings, last week's fruits and vegetables—to the curb. Just then, a cadre of 15 jeans-and-sneakers-clad men and women turn the corner and quietly descend upon the heaps, gingerly opening and dissecting their contents. As they forage through the small mountains of discarded food, a 30-something woman sporting a green rain slicker calls out, "Over here, expensive Greek yogurt." Seconds later, a ponytailed guy wearing a backpack hollers, "Here's bacon and chicken for anyone who eats meat—and a perfect eggplant." Someone shouts a reminder not to tear the bags or leave litter on the ground, lest the store get fined. After less than 30 minutes, they excitedly depart the scene, each shouldering at least one tote bag filled with booty.

These urban foragers are neither homeless nor destitute. They are committed freegans, radical environmentalists (typically vegan) who reject our wasteful consumer culture by living almost entirely on what others throw away. Freegans rarely go hungry thanks to the colossal amount of food Americans dump every day—38 million tons annually, according to the Environmental Protection Agency. Here's another way to look at it: The United Nations says our leftovers could satisfy every single empty stomach in Africa. Those castoffs are composed, in part, of the less-than-perfect products consumers instinctively reject: bruised apples, wilted lettuce, dented cans. Who hasn't passed on an entire carton of eggs after

[margin annotations]

1 **Focus:** Activities and motivations of freegans

Narration: Anecdote demonstrates freegan foraging

2 **Negation:** Uses negation to address misconceptions

Definition: Thesis identifies class, distinguishing characteristics

One man's trash is another man's treasure. A "freegan" climbs into a dumpster behind a West Palm Beach supermarket in search of edible food. ZUMA Press, Inc./Alamy

discovering a single slight fracture among the dozen? Supermarkets can't unload the quarts of milk tagged with yesterday's use-by date—which many of us interpret as a product's expiration but in fact refers to its period of peak flavor. Meaning, there's still plenty of life left in those quarts.

Illustration: Examples explain motivation of freegans

Narration, description: Tells story of one freegan; describes Mon-Dragon so readers can visualize her

Freegans, like 24-year-old Leia MonDragon, a buxom Latina with a taste for   3
heavy eye makeup, feast on those castoffs. "It's amazing what you can find and the good condition it's in," she exclaims, holding aloft a week's worth of produce, including watermelon, summer squash, kale, tomatoes, onions, and bananas. Though technically past their prime, they look pristine. MonDragon also scored half gallons of soy milk and lemonade, both unopened and still chilled, and bagels that only an hour earlier were for sale. "I once found 200 one-pound bags of organic fair-trade coffee beans just dumped outside a store with the trash," she brags, like a woman combing the racks at a Gucci clearance sale.

Aside from the $1600 a month in rent MonDragon pays for her two-bedroom   4
Brooklyn apartment, which she shares with her boyfriend, Tate, their 1-year-old daughter, Uma, and her retired grandfather, just about everything she owns has been salvaged or handmade. She found her ivory faux-leather couch, dishes, and flatware on the street; many of Uma's clothes and toys were recovered from boxes abandoned on sidewalks and stoops, a common sight in New York, where apartment detritus—from halogen lamps to bed frames—is blithely left on the streets. MonDragon used to get around on a bicycle she and Tate cobbled together from discarded parts, but not long ago it was stolen. "So now I'm building another one," she says.

Though official figures are hard to come by, freegan ranks are believed to be   5
in the thousands, with an estimated 500 practitioners living in New York City

alone. Born of the extreme environmentalist and anti-globalization movements of the '90s, freeganism is a wholly modern crusade whose followers live off the grid while simultaneously exploiting it. Freegans gravitate toward cities—and their relentless mounds of garbage; Web sites keep devotees in close contact with each other so they can plan group foraging outings, recruit new members, and spread word of upcoming events, like move-out day at a college dorm, a veritable freegan Christmas. Using a discarded computer they restored, Mon-Dragon and her boyfriend routinely scour Craigslist for freebies. (The Web connection comes from a cable package her grandfather pays for.) "The only thing I don't have yet is a skillet. But I'll find one," MonDragon declares confidently, as she ladles dinner—tofu-and-veggie stir-fry with lime zest—from a large stockpot.

Background: Explains history of freeganism

MonDragon first embraced freeganism five years ago as a student at a Minnesota community college, where she met Tate. "We were broke, trying to find the money for even a simple meal like rice and beans," she explains. "We saw a freegan flyer and hooked up with some people who showed us how to do it. And just like that, we had a source of free food. It was amazing." The more time the pair spent with entrenched freegans, the more exposure they got to the movement's renegade rhetoric. Since relocating to New York two years ago, they have become ardent practitioners, positioning their lifestyle as a boycott of "corporate greed" and an alternative to capitalism. "It's so wrong when people are losing their jobs, struggling to survive, that stores are throwing out such vast quantities of good food," MonDragon sighs, as Papo, her wiry gray mutt, nips the hem of her long black skirt. She tosses him a roasted chicken leg, retrieved from her last supermarket trash run.

6

Narration: Continues MonDragon's story

MonDragon admits she was initially skeeved out by the prospect of eating garbage—Dumpsters are a frequent freegan haunt—but says she was reassured by the movement's common-sense safety measures. Some freegans show up for Dumpster dives armed with rubber gloves and antibacterial lotion. Produce is washed thoroughly, withered leaves discarded; baked goods bearing even a hint of mold are tossed. Everything undergoes a basic smell test. (Tate says he once scarfed down day-old sushi, despite its funky aroma, and ended up with food poisoning.) And since stores generally separate discarded food from, say, bathroom trash bins, the ickiest finds are usually just putrid meats and dairy. MonDragon decontaminates all salvaged housewares with a mixture of vinegar, baking soda, and hydrogen peroxide and launders all of Uma's secondhand stuffed animals and clothes. Though she draws the line at pre-owned underwear, instead buying new pairs from discount stores, MonDragon makes her own reusable sanitary napkins from cloth in much the same way women did a century ago. (Think that's hard-core? Some freegans squat in abandoned buildings and jerry-rig toilets that compost their own waste matter.) "People in this country are a lot more freaked out about dirt than they need to be. We need a little dirt in our lives for our immune systems to be strong," MonDragon says.

7

"Freegans have been living this way for years and are very healthy," says Dr. Ruth Kava, director of nutrition at the American Council on Science and Health.

8

Background: Explains risks of freeganism

"In fact, a freegan's biggest risk may be falling headfirst into a Dumpster." That, or being slapped with a fine—or worse—for trespassing on private property to scavenge. It's not uncommon for store owners, mistaking freegans for homeless people or burglars, to call the police. Two years ago, a pair of freegans in Steamboat Springs, CO, were sentenced to six months in jail after jumping a fence and taking a couple of handfuls of fruit and vegetables from a grocery store's trash.

Cause-effect: Explains why MonDragon restricts her searches to the street

For that reason, MonDragon confines her searches to whatever she finds on the street. She and Tate get by on less than $20,000 a year—he drives a taxi, and she clerks at a nonprofit during the summer. Their meager income is earmarked for inescapable expenses, like their tuition at a community college and rent. The couple qualifies for food stamps, which pay only for Uma's formula (MonDragon stopped breast-feeding once she started working).

Conclusion: Ends with quotation that demonstrates lack of want (negation from para. 2)

Though she lives hand to mouth, MonDragon insists she wants for nothing.   9 Her family eats three hearty meals a day; their closets are crammed with wool coats, shoes, shirts with tags still dangling from their sleeves. She's got an active social life, towing Uma to playdates with other freegan moms and fielding invitations to watch DVDs with freegan friends. A week earlier, she and Tate uncovered a hoard of unopened Chinese food inside a streetside trash can, still warm in its gleaming white containers. They took it to a friend's house for an impromptu dinner party. "We usually never take more than we need," she explains, unzipping her black Patagonia shell and tossing it onto her bed—everything from the taupe sheets to the queen-size mattress were recovered from the streets of Manhattan. "We don't need to. There will be more trash out there tomorrow."

Visualize an Extended Definition Essay: Create a Graphic Organizer

For more on creating a graphic organizer, see pp. 35–37.

Graphic Organizer 17.1 (p. 435) shows the basic organization of an extended definition essay.

- The **introduction** announces the term, provides background information, and usually includes the thesis statement (which briefly defines the term and indicates its significance to readers).
- The **body paragraphs**, which use one or more patterns of development, present the term's distinguishing characteristics along with supporting details.
- The **conclusion** refers back to the thesis and brings the essay to a satisfying close.

GRAPHIC ORGANIZER 17.1   The Basic Structure of an Extended Definition Essay

Title

Introduction
- Introduces the term
- Provides background information
- Thesis statement: gives standard definition and reveals the importance or significance of the term

Distinguishing characteristic(s)
Supporting details

Distinguishing characteristic(s)
Supporting details

Body (uses one or more patterns of development)

Distinguishing characteristic(s)
Supporting details

Distinguishing characteristic(s)
Supporting details

Conclusion
- Refers back to thesis
- Draws essay to a satisfying close

READING

Dude, Do You Know What You Just Said?

Mike Crissey

Mike Crissey is a staff writer for the Associated Press. The following article, which appeared in the *Pittsburgh Post-Gazette* on December 8, 2004, is based on research done by Scott Kiesling, a professor of linguistics at the University of Pittsburgh. Kiesling's work focuses on the relationship between language and identity, particularly in the contexts of gender, ethnicity, and class. **Before reading**, preview the selection and make connections by thinking about how you or others you know use the term *dude*. **While reading**, notice how the writer uses a combination of expert testimony, anecdotal evidence, and personal observations to support his main point.

Dude, you've got to read this. A University of Pittsburgh linguist has published a scholarly paper deconstructing and deciphering *dude,* the bane of parents and teachers, which has become as universal as *like* and another vulgar four-letter favorite. In his paper in the fall edition of the journal *American Speech,* Scott Kiesling says *dude* is much more than a greeting or catchall for lazy, inarticulate, and inexpressive (and mostly male) surfers, skaters, slackers, druggies, or teenagers. "Without context there is no single meaning that *dude* encodes and it can be used, it seems, in almost any kind of situation. But we should not confuse flexibility with meaninglessness," Kiesling said.

Originally meaning "old rags," a "dudesman" was a scarecrow. In the late 1800s, a "dude" was akin to a dandy, a meticulously dressed man, especially in the western United States. *Dude* became a slang term in the 1930s and 1940s among black zoot suiters and Mexican American pachucos. The term began its rise in the teenage lexicon with the 1982 movie *Fast Times at Ridgemont High.* Around the same time, it became an exclamation as well as a noun. Pronunciation purists say it should sound like "duhd"; "dood" is an alternative, but it is considered "uncool" or old.

To decode *dude,* Kiesling listened to conversations with fraternity members he taped in 1993 and had undergraduate students in sociolinguistics classes in 2001 and 2002 write down the first twenty times they heard *dude* and who said it during a three-day period. He's also a lapsed *dude*-user who during his college years tried to talk like Jeff Spicoli, the slacker surfer "dude" from *Fast Times at Ridgemont High.*

According to Kiesling, *dude* has many uses: an exclamation ("Dude!" and "Whoa, Dude!"); to one-up someone ("That's so lame, dude"); to disarm confrontation ("Dude, this is so boring"), or simply to agree ("Dude"). It's inclusive or exclusive, ironic or sincere.

Kiesling says *dude* derives its power from something he calls cool solidarity: an effortless or seemingly lazy kinship that's not too intimate; close, dude, but not that close. *Dude* "carries . . . both solidarity (camaraderie) and distance (non-intimacy) and can be deployed to create both of these kinds of stance, separately or together," Kiesling wrote. Kiesling, whose research focuses on language and masculinity, said that cool solidarity is especially important to young men—anecdotally the predominant *dude*-users—who are under social pressure to be close with other young men but not enough to be suspected as gay. "It's like *man* or *buddy.* There is often this male-male addressed term that says, 'I'm your friend but not much more than your friend,'" Kiesling said. Aside from its duality, *dude* also taps into nonconformity, despite everyone using it, and a new American image of leisurely success, he said.

The nonchalant attitude of *dude* also means that women sometimes call each other *dudes.* And less frequently, men will call women *dudes* and vice versa, Kiesling said. But that comes with some rules, according to self-reporting from students in a 2002 language and gender class at the University of Pittsburgh included in his paper. "Men report that they use *dude* with women with whom they are close friends, but not with women with whom they are intimate," according to his study.

His students also reported that they were least likely to use the word with parents, bosses, and professors. "It is not who they are but what your relationship is with them. With your parents, you likely have a close relationship, but unless you're Bart Simpson, you're not going to call your parent *dude,*" Kiesling said. "There are a couple of young professors here in their thirties and every once in a while we use *dude.* Professors are dudes, but most of the time they are not."

And *dude* shows no signs of disappearing. "More and more our culture is   8
becoming youth centered. In southern California, youth is valued to the point that
even active seniors are dressing young and talking youth," said Mary Bucholtz, an
associate professor of linguistics at the University of California, Santa Barbara. "I
have seen middle-aged men using *dude* with each other."

So what's the point, dude? Kiesling and linguists argue that language and how   9
we use it is important. "These things that seem frivolous are serious because we
are always doing it. We need to understand language because it is what makes us
human. That's my defense of studying *dude*," Kiesling said.

EXERCISE 17.4   **DRAWING A GRAPHIC ORGANIZER**

Using Graphic Organizer 17.1 or 17.2 as a basis, draw a graphic organizer for
"Freegans: They Live Off What We Throw Away" (pp. 431–34).

GRAPHIC ORGANIZER 17.2   The Structure of "Dude, Do You Know What
You Just Said?"

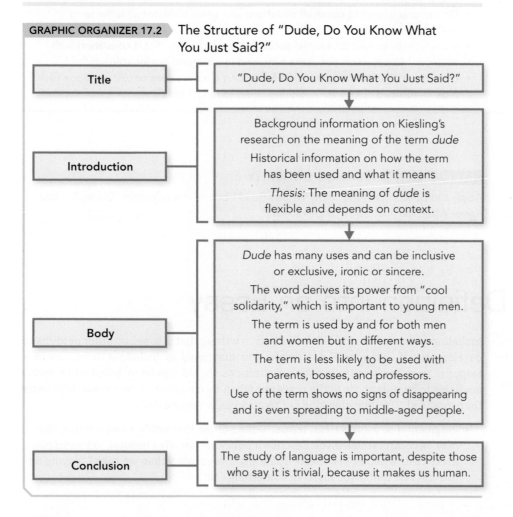

| Title | "Dude, Do You Know What You Just Said?" |

Introduction
- Background information on Kiesling's research on the meaning of the term *dude*
- Historical information on how the term has been used and what it means
- *Thesis:* The meaning of *dude* is flexible and depends on context.

Body
- *Dude* has many uses and can be inclusive or exclusive, ironic or sincere.
- The word derives its power from "cool solidarity," which is important to young men.
- The term is used by and for both men and women but in different ways.
- The term is less likely to be used with parents, bosses, and professors.
- Use of the term shows no signs of disappearing and is even spreading to middle-aged people.

Conclusion
- The study of language is important, despite those who say it is trivial, because it makes us human.

HOW WRITERS READ	DEFINITION
THE READING PROCESS	**STRATEGIES**
BEFORE READING	**Preview** the essay to get an overview of its content and organization. **Make connections** by thinking about what the term being defined means and how you would use it.
AFTER READING	**Analyze and evaluate** the reading by answering the following questions: • Does the writer effectively **distinguish the term** from other similar terms? (Give specific examples.) • Is each characteristic **understandable** and **distinct** (no overlap with other characteristics)? • Do the characteristics **cover all situations** and **uses** of the term? Is the term defined completely? • Is each characteristic **presented accurately** and in a way that is **consistent** with what you already know about the term and in a **fair** and **reasonable** way? • Does the author use language that has strong **connotations** or use language to **hide or mislead**? Does the definition seem to reflect **bias**?

EXERCISE 17.5   READING CRITICALLY

Apply the questions in the "How Writers Read" box to the selection "Dude, Do You Know What You Just Said?" (pp. 435–37).

Integrate Definition into an Essay

For a reading that uses definition as well as other patterns of development, see "Dating on the Autism Spectrum" (pp. 449–52).

Including standard or extended definitions in writing that is based on other patterns of development is common. For example, you may need to include a definition in a response to an essay exam question. Definitions should also be included when terms are likely to be unfamiliar to the reader or when terms may be understood differently than intended. The following kinds of terms usually require definition.

- **Judgmental or controversial terms.** Define terms that imply a judgment or that may be controversial. If you describe a policy as "fiscally unsound," for example, make clear whether you mean "spending more money than we earn," "paying an interest rate that is too high," or something else.

- **Technical terms.** When writing for a general audience, define specialized terms that readers may find unfamiliar. In law, for example, you may need to define terms like *writ, deposition, hearing,* and *plea* for a general audience.
- **Abstract terms.** Terms that refer to ideas or concepts, such as *loyalty, heroism,* and *conformity,* may need to be defined because they can seem vague or mean different things to different people.

In general, if you are not sure whether a term needs a definition, include one.

You may choose to provide your definition in a separate sentence or section, or you can incorporate a brief definition or synonym into a sentence, using commas, dashes, or parentheses to set off the definition, as in the following examples.

⌐───── term ─────⌐ ⌐───────── definition ──────────
Implicit memory, or the nonconscious retention of information about prior
⌐────────⌐
experiences, is important in eyewitness accounts of crimes.

⌐─ term ─⌐ ⌐─────────── definition ───────────
Empathy—a shared feeling of joy for people who are happy or distress for
⌐──────────⌐
people who are in pain—explains the success of many popular films.

| PREWRITING | DRAFTING | REVISING | EDITING & PROOFREADING |

A Guided Writing Assignment*

EXTENDED DEFINITION

The following guide will lead you through the process of writing an extended definition essay. Although the assignment focuses on definition, you will need to integrate one or more other patterns of development in order to develop your essay.

Your Essay Assignment

Write an extended definition essay on a term, activity, phenomenon, or object. You may choose something you are learning about, something you know well already, or something you or your fellow students are likely to be interested in. Below are some options.

---

* The writing process is *recursive*; that is, you may find yourself revising as you draft or prewriting as you revise. This is especially true when writing on a computer. Your writing process may also differ from project to project and from that of your classmates.

- a key concept from an introductory psychology, sociology, or economics course, such as ethnocentrism, diaspora, or monopoly capitalism
- a type of music, such as indie rock, free jazz, or hip hop
- an inappropriate behavior, such as distracted driving or stalking
- a type of television show, such as a situation comedy, game show, or reality TV show
- an unusual sport or leisure activity, such as curling or spelunking

1 Select a topic from the list above, or create one of your own.

Ask yourself these questions when choosing a topic.

- What do I **already know** about the topic? How much **research** will I have **time** to do?
- How much do **my readers** (other students at my college or university) **already know** about the topic?
- Will my readers be **interested** in the topic **already**, or will I need to **create interest**?

Collaborate: In small groups, take turns having other students tell you what they think your term means.

2 Narrow your topic to a more specific term to explore in your essay.

Use the following guidelines to narrow your general topic.

1. Start general. Use **branching** or **clustering** to come up with specific types of your general topic.

> Example: *Celebrity* is probably too broad a topic for a brief essay, but the topic could be narrowed to a particular type of celebrity, such as *a sports celebrity, a Hollywood celebrity, a local celebrity,* or *a political celebrity.*

2. Start specific. Think of a specific example of your topic and use that example as the focus of your definition essay.

> Example: You might choose Tom Brady or Kobe Bryant and use him to identify the characteristics that define "sports celebrity."

3 Consider your purpose, audience, and point of view.

- If you were writing an essay that defines "search engines," your **purpose** might be to **express** your frustration or success with using them to locate information, **inform** readers about the alternatives to Google, or **persuade** readers that Bing or Dogpile is superior to all others.
- What does my **audience already know**? What does the audience **need to know** to understand/accept my definition?
- What **point of view** best suits my purpose and audience? Most definition essays are written in the **third person** (*he, she, it, they*). **First person** (*I, we*) or **second person** (*you*) may be appropriate in **informal contexts** if you or your readers have **personal knowledge** of or **experience** with the topic.

4 Identify distinguishing characteristics and supporting details.

Try one or more of the following.

1. **Discuss** the term with a classmate, making notes as you talk. (All learners, but especially social learners, will benefit from discussing the term.)

2. **Brainstorm** a list of (a) words that describe your term, (b) people and things that might serve as examples of the term, and (c) everything a person would need to know to understand the term. (Verbal, pragmatic, and rational learners may prefer brainstorming.)

3. **Observe** a person who is associated with the term or who performs some aspect of it. Take notes on your observations. (Emotional and spatial learners may prefer observing.)

4. **Look up** the term's *etymology*, or origin, in the *Oxford English Dictionary, A Dictionary of American English,* or *A Dictionary of Americanisms*, all of which are available in the reference section of your library. Take notes; the word's etymology will give you some of its characteristics and details, and it might give you ideas on how to organize your essay. (Abstract and independent learners may prefer looking up the etymology.)

5. **Think of incidents or situations** that reveal the meaning of the term. (Concrete learners may prefer thinking of incidents or situations.)

6. **Think of similar and different terms** with which your reader is likely to be more familiar. (Abstract learners may prefer thinking of synonyms or antonyms.)

7. **Do a Google search** on your term. Visit three or four Web sites and take notes on what you discover. Keep track of your sources, so you can cite them later. (All learners, but especially creative learners, may benefit from performing a Google search.)

5 Generate supporting details.

Use the other patterns of development—for example:

1. **Narration:** Think of incidents or situations that reveal the meaning of the term.

2. **Description:** Observe a person who is associated with the term and take notes on what that person looks like, sounds like, and so forth.

3. **Illustration:** Brainstorm a list of examples.

4. **Comparison and contrast:** Think of similar and different terms with which you can contrast it.

6 Draft your thesis statement.

Your thesis should:

1. include a **brief definition** (including the class to which the term belongs and its key distinguishing characteristics)

2. convey why your extended definition might be **useful**, **interesting**, or **important** to readers

Notice how a weak thesis (in this case, a barebones definition) can be revised to reveal the writer's main point.

Example: The future of Wireless cable, ~~is~~ a means of transmitting television signals through the air by microwave, is uncertain

Collaboration. In small groups, take turns reading your thesis aloud. Have classmates try to identify the following:

- the term, the class to which it belongs, and its distinguishing characteristics
- the writer's main point

Consider revising if:

- the class is overly general
- the distinguishing characteristics lack specificity or are too limited
- group members cannot identify the main point

7 Choose a method of organization.

If you use **one main supporting pattern**, use the graphic organizers in the **related chapter** to organize your essay. If you use **several patterns of development**, use graphic organizers to **try out several organizations**, and then pick the most logical order.

8 Draft your extended definition essay.

Use the following guidelines to draft your essay.

- The **introduction** should **introduce the term**, provide any **background information** readers will need, and include your **thesis**. When introducing your term, it may be helpful to explain what the term is *not* as well as what it is or include a brief history of how your term has been used. But whatever you include, be sure you convey why your term is **worth reading about**.
- Each **body paragraph** should use one or more **patterns of development** (narration, description, or comparison and contrast, for example) to explain one of the term's distinguishing features. Be sure to include **enough details** for readers to understand each characteristic. Use **transitions** (such as *another, also,* or *in addition*) to guide readers as you move from characteristic to characteristic.

The **conclusion** should bring your essay to a satisfying close, revisiting your thesis and elaborating on **why understanding the term is useful, interesting,** or **important.**

9 Evaluate your draft and revise as necessary.

Use **Figure 17.1, "Flowchart for Revising an Extended Definition Essay,"** to guide your evaluation and revision.

1. Avoid the **awkward expressions *is when or is where*** in defining your term. Instead, name the class to which the term belongs.

    Example: Early bird specials ~~is when~~ restaurants ~~offer reduced price dinners~~ late in the afternoon and early in the evening.

    are reduced-priced dinners offered in

2. Make sure **subjects and verbs agree in number**. When two subjects are joined by *and*, the verb should be plural.

    Example: Taken together, the military and Medicare ~~costs~~ U.S. taxpayers an enormous amount of money.

    cost

FIGURE 17.1 Flowchart for Revising an Extended Definition Essay

QUESTIONS

REVISION STRATEGIES

1. Highlight your thesis statement. Does it include a brief definition of the term? Does it indicate why your extended definition is useful, interesting, or important?

 NO ▶

- Identify the class and distinguishing characteristics of your term, and incorporate a standard definition into your thesis.
- Ask yourself, Why is this definition worth reading about? Add your answer to your thesis

 YES
▼

2. Place ✔s beside the distinguishing characteristics of your definition. Do they make your term distinct from similar terms? Is each characteristic true in all cases?

 NO ▶

- Do additional research or prewriting to discover more characteristics and details you can add to the definition.
- Eliminate characteristics and details that limit the definition too much.

 YES
▼

3. Write the name of the pattern(s) of development you used in your essay. Does each clearly connect your details and help explain the distinguishing characteristics of your term?

 NO ▶

- Review the list of patterns on pages 429–30 and consider substituting or adding one or more of them to clarify your definition.

 YES
▼

4. [Bracket] the sections where you use negation or address misconceptions. Does each section eliminate possible misunderstandings? Are other misunderstandings possible?

 NO ▶

- Revise your explanation of what your term is not.
- Add facts or expert opinion to correct readers' mistaken notions about the term.

YES
▼

REVISING

(continued on next page) ▶ **443**

(Figure 17.1 continued)

QUESTIONS		REVISION STRATEGIES

5. Reread your supporting paragraphs. Does each one have a clear topic sentence that focuses on a particular characteristic? Is each paragraph well developed?

 NO ▶

- Consider combining paragraphs that cover the same characteristic or splitting paragraphs that cover more than one.
- Add or revise topic sentences and supporting details that focus on the characteristic.

 YES
▼

6. Reread your introduction and conclusion. Does the introduction provide necessary background information and hint at the point that will make your definition worth reading? Does your conclusion bring the essay to a satisfying close?

NO ▶

- Add background information that sets a context for the term you are defining and suggests the point you are making about the term.
- Revise your conclusion so that it lends closure, possibly by returning to the point you are making about the term.

10 Edit and proofread your essay.

Refer to Chapter 9 for help with:

- **editing sentences** to avoid wordiness, making your verb choices strong and active, and making your sentences clear, varied, and parallel
- **editing words** for tone and diction, connotation, and concrete and specific language

Pay particular attention to the following:

- When two nouns are joined by *or*, the verb should agree with the noun closest to it.

  Example: For most birds, the markings or wing span ~~are~~ ^{is} easily observed with a pair of good binoculars.

- When the subject and verb are separated by a prepositional phrase, the verb should agree with the subject of the sentence, not with the noun in the phrase.

  Example: The features of a hot-air balloon ~~is~~ ^{are} best learned by studying the attached diagram.

Readings: Extended Definition in Action

Guerrilla Street Art: A New Use of Public Space

Kate Atkinson

Kate Atkinson wrote the following essay for an assignment to write an extended definition of a specialized term related to one of her interests. Atkinson decided to write about guerrilla street art. As you read, note how Atkinson uses other patterns of development—such as description and illustration—to define guerrilla street art as a nontraditional art form growing in popularity.

Guerrilla street art is everywhere, if you look for it. There are countless examples in the small college town where I grew up, where the dense population of college students and artists breeds creativity. Just around the corner from my school, stickers litter sign posts, colorful graffiti is scrawled on exposed brick walls, homemade posters advertise local bands at the bus stop, and a cheerful Dr. Seuss character is stenciled on the sidewalk. These small works of art can easily go unnoticed, but they bring an unexpected vibrancy to the city and raise the controversial question of what constitutes art. By taking art out of its traditional context, guerrilla street artists use public space to create controversy and intrigue while at the same time making art free and accessible to a broad audience.

Common forms used by street artists today include graffiti, stenciling, poster art, sticker art, scratchiti, and yarn bombing. Graffiti, the most prevalent form of guerrilla street art, is unauthorized writing or drawing on a public surface. It dates back centuries (see Fig. 1), and artists have been known to use chalk, markers, paint, and even carving tools to inscribe their messages on public property. Graffiti is so common that it is difficult to travel far in most urban settings without coming across a word or image scrawled in spray paint on a public surface. Stenciling is simply a form of graffiti in which artists use precut stencils to guide their work. Posters and stickers are popular because they can be easily

1

Title: Atkinson identifies her subject and creates interest.

Introduction: Atkinson provides background information on guerrilla street art and explains by example what it is.

Distinguishing characteristics: Her thesis statement offers a brief definition and suggests the value and importance of guerrilla street art.

2 **Distinguishing characteristics:** Atkinson presents the first distinguishing characteristic and lists five examples. Notice that the first sentence in this paragraph is the topic sentence, which is supported by the rest of the paragraph—a pattern followed in each of the next three paragraphs.

Fig. 1. A graffiti-covered wall from Pompei, Italy. The explosion of the volcano Vesuvius preserved the ancient graffiti.

mass-produced and quickly applied. Posters are usually applied with a technique called "wheat pasting"—using a vegetable-based adhesive to attach posters to walls. Artists apply the clear paste with a roller in a thin layer to both sides of the poster, making it weather-proof and durable. Scratchiti is found almost everywhere there is glass. It became popular in the 1990s after New York City's Metropolitan Transportation Authority installed easily scratched, shatter-resistant glass in all its subway cars and clamped down on traditional aerosol graffiti. Scratchiti is popular because it is so easy to produce—all it requires is a knife, fingernail file, or even a key. But it is looked down upon as an art form, since doing more than scratching your initials or street name into the glass is difficult in this medium ("Scratchiti"). A less common street-art technique is "yarn bombing," in which craft artists knit colorful sheaths of wool and acrylic and wrap them around telephone poles and park benches. The finished pieces are eye-catching and unusual but not permanent or damaging to public property.

The various motives behind guerrilla street art are as diverse as the artwork itself and range from social and political activism to self-promotion of the artist. Artists embellish telephone poles with colorful yarn and train carriages with ornate murals as a way to reclaim and beautify public space. Others use public space as a billboard to advocate for a cause. An example of street art as political activism is artist Shepard Fairey's iconic

3

Distinguishing characteristic:
Atkinson discusses the motives of the artists and offers examples of the various motives.

image of Barack Obama (Wortham). The simple design combines a striking red, white, and blue portrait of Obama with the word "Hope." With the approval of Obama's 2008 campaign team, Fairey and his team dispersed and pasted, stenciled, or tacked the image onto countless public surfaces across the United States until it became an important facet of the campaign. The picture itself is powerful, but what made it even more effective as a campaign tool was the distribution of the image by supporters and the youth appeal that it garnered as a result.

Street art has many appeals. It is an easy way for new artists to gain notoriety, and anyone with a spray can and a flair for creativity can partake. A tag, which is an artist's signature or symbol, is the most common type of graffiti. Before the Obama campaign, Shepard Fairey gained international acclaim for a sticker depicting wrestler Andre the Giant and the word "Obey." The image soon became his tag and can be found in almost all of his work, making it instantly recognizable. The anonymity of street art also gives artists the freedom to express themselves without fearing the judgment of their peers. At worst, this freedom can result in crude or offensive inscriptions on public property; but at best, it can produce bold, striking statements. Guerrilla street art is contemporary and can be enjoyed without a visit to a museum. It is free and encourages the belief that art should be accessible and available to everyone. It is also a movement that anyone can take part in and that challenges traditional standards of art.

Due to the illicit nature of their art, the street artist community is shrouded in secrecy. In the film *Exit through the Gift Shop*, a documentary by notorious British street artist Banksy, hooded figures in ski masks are shown scaling buildings and perched precariously on ledges, armed with spray cans and buckets of industrial paste and always on the lookout for the police. Despite his celebrity, Banksy has managed to keep his identity anonymous, and his face is never shown in the film. It is common for street artists to be arrested for trespassing and vandalism, and the risk and intentional disobedience involved in street art adds to its appeal, especially among young people.

Guerrilla street art has blossomed from an underground movement to a cultural phenomenon. At the very least, it brings up the question of what constitutes art and whether public space is an appropriate place

Support: Atkinson uses sources to document an example of political activism, one of the motives.

4   **Distinguishing characteristic:** Atkinson discusses the appeal of street art and gives examples.

5

Distinguishing characteristic: Atkinson discusses the secrecy of the artists and uses Banksy as an example.

6

Conclusion: Atkinson comments on the street art movement as a cultural experience, explains its value.

for it. Although it does not adhere to all traditional standards of art, guerrilla street art provokes thought, brings beauty and intrigue to urban spaces that would otherwise go unnoticed, and is a tool for artists to exercise freedom of speech and expression.

Works Cited

Exit through the Gift Shop. Directed by Banksy, performances by Banksy and Thierry Guetta, Paranoid Pictures, 2010.

"Scratchiti." *The Cyber Bench—Documenting New York City Graffiti,* @149st, 2003, www.at149st.com/scratch.html.

Wortham, Jenna. "'Obey' Street Artist Churns Out 'Hope' for Obama." *Wired,* 21 Sept. 2010, www.wired.com/2008/09/poster-boy-shep/.

Analyzing the Writer's Technique

1. **Definition** How does Atkinson define *guerrilla art*?
2. **Effectiveness** Evaluate the effectiveness of the title, introduction, and conclusion.
3. **Terms** Locate one of each of these in the essay—a judgment term, a technical term, an abstract term, and a controversial term.

Thinking Critically about Definition

1. **Bias** Atkinson is not neutral on the subject of this essay. Explain her bias. How does this affect the essay?
2. **Sources** What other types of sources could Atkinson have included to make her essay more comprehensive? What do her two sources reveal about her attitude about the topic?
3. **Connotation** Atkinson uses words such as *vibrancy* (para. 1) and *blossomed* (6) to describe guerrilla street art. What kind of connotation do these words have, and how do the connotations play into the overall tone of the essay?
4. **Euphemism** Is "guerrilla street art" a euphemism? Why or why not? If so, how would the same idea be expressed in more direct language?
5. **Evaluation** Atkinson limits her definition of guerrilla street art to items that have no commercial or financial purpose. She does not mention posters promoting businesses or paid entertainment, signs and banners used for fund-raising by organizations, and advertising flyers, even though these items also are often displayed in the same places as those she does discuss and with the same lack of legal permission. How are these items similar to and different from the kinds of items she includes in her definition?

Responding to the Reading

1. **Reaction** Have you ever created any graffiti? Discuss how doing it made you feel. If you have ever created any, discuss how doing so might make you feel.
2. **Discussion** Discuss the value of work like Shepard Fairey's, which takes political messages and conveys them in street art. Why is this strategy effective? How does it reach a broader audience than other methods of communication?
3. **Journal** Write a journal entry discussing whether guerrilla art adds value to public space or devalues the space. How should the answer to this question be determined?

DEFINITION COMBINED WITH OTHER PATTERNS   **READING**

Dating on the Autism Spectrum

Emily Shire

Emily Shire is a writer for *The Week* and has also published articles in a number of other publications, including *Slate* and *The Forward*. This essay appeared in *The Atlantic* in 2013. **Before reading**, preview the selection and make connections by thinking about what you already know about autism. **While reading**, notice how Shire uses examples and quotations from personal interviews to make her extended definition vivid and convincing. Also, identify the patterns, other than definition, that she uses to develop her thesis.

---

1   The way to Paulette Penzvalto's heart is through her Outlook calendar. "Honestly, if you want to be romantic with me, send an email through Outlook and give me all the possible dates, locations, and times, so that I can prepare," she said.

2   The former Miss America contestant and Juilliard-trained opera singer knew she had a different conception of romance than her previous boyfriends had and, for that matter, everyone else. "People tend to think of romance as spur of the moment and exciting," she told me. "I think of romance as things that make sense and are logical." However, she didn't know why until this year when, at the age of 31, she was diagnosed with autism.

3   The aspects of autism that can make everyday life challenging—reading social cues, understanding another's perspectives, making small talk and exchanging niceties—can be seriously magnified when it comes to dating. The American Psychiatric Association defines autism as a spectrum disorder: Some people do not speak at all and have disabilities that make traditional relationships (let alone romantic ones) largely unfeasible, but there are also many who are on the "high-functioning" end and do have a clear desire for dating and romance.

4   Autism diagnosis rates have increased dramatically over the last two decades (the latest CDC reports show one in 50 children are diagnosed), and while much attention has been paid to early-intervention programs for toddlers and younger children, teens and adults with autism have largely been overlooked—especially when it comes to building romantic relationships.

5   Certain characteristics associated with the autism spectrum inherently go against typical dating norms. For example, while a "neuro-typical" person might

think a bar is a great place for a first date, it could be one of the worst spots for some-one on the spectrum. Dorsey Massey, a social worker who helps run dating and social programs for adults with various intellectual disabilities, explained, "If it's a loud, crowded place, an individual on the spectrum may be uncomfortable or distracted." Sensory issues may also make certain lights and noises especially unpleasant.

Seemingly basic, non-sexual touching may be an issue, as well. "It may give them discomfort for someone to kiss them lightly or hold their hand," Massey said. "They need pressure, and that's not typically what you think of with tender, romantic love."   6

Perhaps because so much of their behavior runs counter to mainstream con-ceptions of how to express affection and love, people with autism are rarely con-sidered in romantic contexts. A constant complaint among the individuals interviewed for this piece is the misconception that people with autism can't express love or care for others. "I think a lot of times someone will go out on a date with someone on the spectrum and think they're a robot," said Alex Plank, founder of WrongPlanet.net, a popular online autism community. "It's hard to read us if we don't explicitly say what we're feeling, but all the feelings are there."   7

In fact, people with autism may have greater emotional capacities. "Studies have shown that people with autism can have feelings that are stronger and deeper than those without autism," said John Elder Robison, bestselling author of *Look Me in the Eyes* and autism advocate. "Yet those feelings may be invisible to out-siders because we don't show them. Because we don't show them or the expected response, people make the wrong assumption about our depth of feeling about other people."   8

It's not that individuals on the spectrum do not have the same desire for love; they just may not know how to find it. Dr. Elizabeth Laugeson, an Assistant Clinical Professor at UCLA said, "If you asked a person with autism if they wanted a roman-tic relationship, they would probably say yes, but they would probably also say they don't know how to."   9

Partially from the emphasis on early intervention treatments, there's a dearth of dating skills programs, or, rather, effective ones for people on the spectrum. "Early intervention can significantly improve the outcome, but kids grow up, and we don't have the proper services," said Laugeson, who serves as director of UCLA PEERS, a program that teaches social, including romantic, interaction skills to teens and young adults on the spectrum.   10

Central to PEERS is the promotion of "ecologically valid" social skills, traits humans have been shown to exhibit in reality, rather than what we think we're "supposed" to do. "We know people with autism think very concretely," said Laug-eson. "Social skills can be abstract behavior that's difficult to describe, but we try to break it into concrete steps."   11

For example, PEERS will take the seemingly mundane, but actually complex act of flirting and translate it into a step-by-step lesson. "First, a couple notices each other across the room. They make eye contact and look away, and they look again and they look away," said Laugeson. "The look away makes it known you're safe, but the common error someone with autism can make is to stare, which can seem predatory and scare a person." People with autism are also specifically   12 instructed how to smile and for how long, since "another common mistake is to smile really big rather than giving a slight smile," said Laugeson. "A big smile can also be frightening."

Neuro-typical people often take flirting for granted as a fairly organic, coy, and   13
even fun back-and-forth, but for someone with autism, it is really a complex, nonsensical interaction. "Flirting still doesn't make sense to me. It seems like a waste of time," said Plank, who worked on a video with Laugeson to teach his WrongPlanet community members how to flirt. "If you think about it logically, you say things you wouldn't normally say, so it's harder. There are a whole other set of things you have to deal with."

While he didn't have PEERS to guide him, in college, Plank studied guys who   14
were always successful at picking up girls and started mimicking their behaviors. He quickly realized acting confident was the key to dating success, especially if you're a man.

However, maintaining that confidence may be the hardest part of dating for   15
someone on the spectrum, because of their difficulty processing social cues from others. "We will constantly not be able to read whether someone is interested, so you can have an insecurity about whether the person you're dating likes you," said Plank.

In heterosexual courtships where men are still often expected to pursue   16
women, males with autism are at a distinct disadvantage to their female counterpart. "For guys on the spectrum it's a one-way thing," said Robison. "We can be interested, but have no way to tell if they're interested in us."

Some women with autism may ultimately have an edge in the dating world. A   17
common trait of people on the spectrum is being extremely logical and straightforward. A blunt man may repulse women or get a slap in the face; think of how a woman would react if a date told her yes, she did look fat in that dress, or consider the famous 1989 study where a female researcher received positive responses to her request for sex from men on the street 69 to 75 percent of the time compared to her male counterpart who received not a single yes. Women who are forward are prized for it. "Especially if they're really attractive, neuro-typical guys appreciate when women are blunt," said Plank.

While Penzvalto doesn't necessarily think women with autism have it easier   18
than men, she has noticed that her neuro-typical dates have particularly valued many of her autistic traits. "I've found that people who are neuro-typical really appreciate the qualities that people on the spectrum possess: complete honesty and almost an inability to lie," she said.

However, both sexes on the spectrum struggle equally with the fear of rejec-   19
tion. Since so much of dating for adults with autism is trial by error, the risk of mistakes, and often embarrassing ones, is high. Jeremy Hamburgh, a dating specialist for people with special needs, including those on the autism spectrum, has noticed how hard his clients take initial failure with dating. "The risk and rewards are very different for people who are neuro-typical," he said. "The average neuro-typical person can go out and meet ten people, and do well with one, and feel success, but for those with special needs, who have been rejected all their lives, that can really hurt their self-esteem."

Plank has witnessed friends on the spectrum too quickly walk away from   20
dating for fear of rejection. "It's a numbers game in many ways and because people

on the spectrum use black-and-white thinking, they think they're doing something
wrong," he said. "I wish more people on the spectrum knew you need to practice,
you need to go out on more dates."

Worse, is that people on the spectrum may turn the blame on themselves for not   21
exhibiting neuro-typical norms for dating and romance. While interviewing subjects
on the spectrum for his documentary *Autism in Love*, filmmaker Matt Fuller noticed
how, "When something is perceived as inappropriate, and it gets addressed, they will
get embarrassed leading to a rabbit hole of self-deprecating thoughts." And Penzvalto,
too, remembers feeling self-conscious and abnormal for her views of dating and
romance. "I have struggled in the past with people telling me 'this is how it should be'
and having sort of a crisis of maybe I just don't get it, maybe I'm wrong," she said.

In fact, it was during one of those types of fights in a relationship earlier this   22
year that Penzvalto decided to be evaluated for autism. She realized past boyfriends' frustrations over her "rigid thinking" and "boundary issue" could be
explained by autism, and a subsequent psychological evaluation confirmed it.
However, rather than alarmed, she felt relief.

Perhaps because she had spent so much of her life trying to "act" normal and   23
conform to others' expectations for romance, knowing she had autism has helped
her become more comfortable with dating. It's a feeling not necessarily shared by all
members on the spectrum, but realizing why she saw love and romance the way she
does freed her from the pressure of neuro-typical standards. Now, she is following
her own heart. "The number one freedom I found in the diagnosis is I don't need to
really give into a partner's idea of what a relationship should or needs to look like,"
she said. "It's really liberating to know I've been living my life a certain way, and it
turns out that that's okay."

Understanding the Reading

1. **Explanation** How do the needs of people on the autism spectrum differ from
   those of "neuro-typical" people (those not on the autism spectrum)?
2. **Cause** Why do uninformed people believe that an autistic person is incapable of
   having a romantic relationship?
3. **Characteristics** What characteristic(s) do autistic women possess that may give them
   an advantage in dating? How might this (these) characteristic(s) be advantageous?
4. **Vocabulary** Explain the meaning of each of the following words as it is used in the
   reading: *inherently* (para. 5), *dearth* (10), *mundane* (12), and *predatory* (12).

Analyzing the Writer's Technique

1. **Source** How does the author's decision to include a quotation from a former Miss
   America contestant affect the reader's response to the article?
2. **Thesis** Restate Shire's thesis in your own words. How effective is it as the thesis of
   an extended definition essay? If you were revising her thesis, how might you
   change it?

3. **Introduction** Does the introduction provide all the background information you need to understand the essay? If not, what else should the author have included?
4. **Conclusion** Is the essay's conclusion satisfying? Why or why not?

Visualizing the Reading

Identify the other patterns of development Shire uses in the essay. Complete the following chart by listing the pattern and providing an example of how each pattern is used.

Pattern of Development	Examples
Comparison and contrast	Dating for neuro-typical people vs. people on the autism spectrum (first date in a bar, para. 5; perceptions of flirting, 12; fear of rejection, 19), men on the autism spectrum versus women on the autism spectrum (17–19)
Illustration	
Definition	
Process analysis	
Illustration	

FIGURE 17.2 Percentage of Children (Aged 6–17) Whose Parent(s) Report a Diagnosis of Autism Spectrum Disorder. *Source: CDC/NCHS, National Survey of Children's Health, 2007 and 2001–2012.*

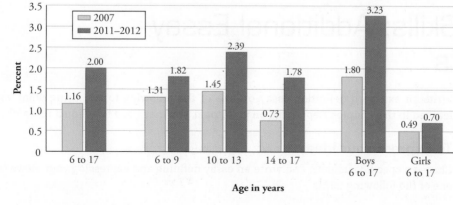

Thinking Critically about Text and Images

1. **Connotation** What connotation does the word *act* (para. 23) have? How does the use of quotation marks around the word affect your understanding of its meaning?
2. **Tone** Describe the tone of the essay. What does it reveal about Shire's attitude toward people on the autism spectrum?
3. **Sources** What types of sources does Shire use to support her thesis? What other types of sources might she have used to make her essay more convincing?
4. **Objectivity** How objective a view of people on the autism spectrum does Shire present? Identify any words, phrases, or examples that seem intended to influence the reader's emotional response to the article. Does her definition seem euphemistic or incomplete? Support your answers with evidence from the text.
5. **Visual** Examine Figure 17.2. Do you see any trends? How significant is the increase? What reasons, besides an actual increase in the number of children with autism spectrum disorder, may account for it?

Responding to the Reading

1. **Discussion** Discuss the challenges flirting, asking someone out, or even joining a conversation present. What "'ecologically valid' social skills" (para. 11) have you observed or practiced in these contexts? How would you instruct a younger friend or family member in the fine art of asking someone out on a date or joining a conversation among people you don't know well?
2. **Journal** Write a journal entry describing a time you (or someone you know) were totally misjudged or your motives were misunderstood.
3. **Essay** Write an essay defining a perfect date for your classmates.

Working Together

With a small group of fellow students, write a thirty-second public service announcement (PSA) promoting a class in responsible dating to share with the class. Start by naming the class, then brainstorm ideas, and write the PSA.

Apply Your Skills: Additional Essay Assignments

For more on locating and documenting sources, see Part 5.

Write an extended definition essay on one of the following topics, using what you learned in this chapter. Depending on your topic, you may need to conduct research.

To Express Your Ideas

Choose a specific audience and write an essay defining and expressing your views on one of the following terms.

1. Parenting
2. Assertiveness
3. Sexual harassment

To Inform Your Reader

4. Write an essay defining a term from a sport, hobby, or form of entertainment for a classmate who is unfamiliar with the term.

5. Write an essay for your instructor defining the characteristics of the "perfect job" you hope to hold after graduation.

6. Write an essay defining an important concept in a field of study, perhaps from one of your other courses. Your audience consists of students not enrolled in the course.

To Persuade Your Reader

"Freegans: They Live Off What We Throw Away" (pp. 431–34) addresses the issue of consumer waste and excess. Write an essay for readers of your local newspaper in which you define one of the terms listed below and demonstrate that the problem is either increasing or decreasing in your community.

7. Racism or ethnic stereotyping

8. Sexual discrimination

9. Age discrimination

Cases Using Definition

10. You are a fifth-grade teacher working on a lesson plan entitled "What Is American Democracy?" How will you limit the term *American democracy* to define it for your audience? What characteristics and details will you include?

11. Write a press release for a new menu item as part of your job as public relations manager for a restaurant chain. First, choose the new menu item, and then define the item and describe its characteristics using sensory details.

SYNTHESIZING IDEAS   **CULTURE**

Both "Freegans: They Live Off What We Throw Away" (pp. 431–34) and "Guerrilla Street Art" (pp. 445–48) discuss the activities of a subculture: Dumpster divers and graffiti artists.

Analyzing the Readings

1. In what ways does each self subgroup set itself apart from the larger society?
2. Write a journal entry exploring how some subgroups set themselves apart—for example, through dress, behavior, or language.

Essay Idea

Write an essay in which you explore a subgroup of college students, such as student democrats or vegans. Give examples of ways in which certain groups on campus set themselves apart through their language, their activities, or in some other way.

18
Cause and Effect

Using Reasons and Results to Explain

David Traiforos/Dembinsky Photo Associates/Alamy Stock Photo

In this chapter you will learn to:

- understand the purpose and function of cause-and-effect essays

- use graphic organizers to visualize cause-and-effect essays

- integrate cause and effect into an essay

- read and think critically about cause and effect

- plan, organize, draft, revise, and edit essays using cause and effect

WRITING QUICK START   Assume you are a journalist for your local newspaper reporting on a natural disaster that has occurred in a nearby town. Your task is to write a plausible account of the event to accompany the photograph shown here. In your paragraph, be sure to tell readers why the disaster occurred and what happened as a result of it.

The paragraph you wrote in the Writing Quick Start is an example of **cause-and-effect** (or causal) **analysis** because it considered *causes* (why the disaster occurred), *effects* (what happened because of the disaster), or both. You probably use causal analysis every day. If you decide to get a good night's sleep rather than pull an all-nighter because you know you do better on exams when you're well rested, that's cause-effect analysis. Causal analysis is frequently required in college classes too, where you might be asked to analyze and write about the causes of the Civil War or the effects of oxygen deprivation on the central nervous system.

USING CAUSE AND EFFECT   IN COLLEGE AND THE WORKPLACE

- For an essay exam in your *twentieth-century history course,* you are required to discuss the causes of U.S. involvement in the Korean War.

- For a *health and nutrition course,* you decide to write a paper on the relationship between diet and heart disease.

- For your job as an *investment analyst,* you need to explain why a certain company is likely to be profitable in the next year.

What Are the Characteristics of Cause-and-Effect Essays?

A successful causal analysis essay fully explains the causes or effects that are the focus of the essay's thesis and presents those causes or effects in a logical order.

Causal Analysis May Focus on Causes, Effects, or Both

Remember that *causes* are the reasons that something happened and *effects* are the results of the thing that happened. Some causes and effects are relatively easy to separate out.

Cause	Effect
You get a flat tire. ⟶	You are late for work.
You forget to mail a loan payment. ⟶	You receive a past-due notice.

EXERCISE 18.1 ▶ IDENTIFYING CAUSES

Alone or with a classmate, list one or more possible causes for each of the following events or phenomena.

1. You observe a peacock strutting down a city street.
2. The airline notifies you that the flight you had planned to take tonight has been canceled.
3. Your phone frequently rings once and then stops ringing.
4. Your town decides to fund a new public park.
5. A good friend keeps saying to you, "I'm too busy to get together with you."

EXERCISE 18.2 ▶ IDENTIFYING EFFECTS

Alone or with a classmate, list one or more possible effects for each of the following events.

1. You leave your backpack containing your wallet on the bus.
2. You decide to change your major.
3. Your spouse is offered a job in a city five hundred miles away from where you live now.
4. You volunteer as a Big Brother or Big Sister.
5. A close relative becomes very ill.

But causal analysis can be complex when it deals with an event or phenomenon that has multiple causes, multiple effects, or both. For example, you probably chose the college you attend (*one effect*) for a number of reasons (*multiple causes*).

Multiple Causes   **One Effect**

Courses available
Cost
Reputation   → College attended
Distance

One cause may also have several effects. For instance, the decision to quit your part-time job (*one cause*) will have several results (*multiple effects*).

One Cause   **Multiple Effects**

→ More study time
Quit job ──────────→ Less pressure
→ Less spending money

Related events or phenomena may have multiple causes and multiple effects. For instance, in urban areas, an increase in the number of police patrolling the street along with the formation of citizen watch groups (*multiple causes*) will result in less street crime and more small businesses moving into the neighborhood (*multiple effects*).

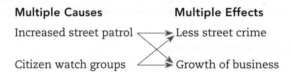

Multiple Causes   **Multiple Effects**

Increased street patrol ──→ Less street crime

Citizen watch groups ──→ Growth of business

In some cases, a series of events forms a **chain of consequences**.

Cause	**Effect**	**Effect**	**Effect**
You cannot find your car keys. →	You are late for class. →	You miss a surprise quiz. →	Your A quiz average is lowered to a B average.
	Cause	**Cause**	

Once you clearly identify causes and effects, you can decide whether to focus on causes, effects, or both.

Causal Analysis Includes a Clear Thesis Statement

An effective thesis statement for a cause-and-effect essay does the following.

- It identifies the topic.
- It makes an assertion about that topic.
- It suggests whether the essay focuses on causes, effects, or both.

Causes	causes topic The root causes of unsportsmanlike behavior lie in how society assertion elevates athletes to positions of fame and heroism, making them unaccountable for their behavior.
Effects	topic effects Unsportsmanlike behavior produces negative effects on fans, assertion other players, and the institutions they represent.
Causes and Effects	topic causes Unsportsmanlike behavior has deep roots in society's inflated assertion effects regard for athletes, producing negative effects on fans, other players, and the institutions they represent.

Causal Analysis Is Logically Organized

A good cause-and-effect essay is organized logically and systematically. You may present causes or effects in any logical order, but these are the most commonly used.

- *Chronological order*, the order in which causes or effects happened

   Example: An essay about causes of rising college tuition costs might begin with reasons for tuition increases in the late 1990s and move chronologically to current increases.

- *Most-to-least* or *least-to-most* order

   Example: An essay about increased immigration to the United States might begin with the most important causes and progress to less important causes.

Causal Analysis Explains Each Cause or Effect Fully

A causal analysis essay should present each cause or effect in a detailed and understandable way. For most cause-and-effect essays, you will need to research your topic to find evidence that supports your thesis. For instance, in an essay about the effects on children of viewing violence on television, you might conduct research to locate facts or statistics that document changes in children's behavior after watching violent programs or expert opinion supporting this claim.

You might use another pattern of development (such as illustrations, descriptions, or comparisons) to explain causes or effects. For example, an essay about why dishonesty and lying are common in social media may include reasons, but also give examples or narrate incidents of dishonesty, categorize the characteristics of the social media environment that make lying easy, or contrast face-to-face communication with online communication.

Causal Analysis May Challenge Readers' Assumptions or Offer Surprising Reasons

Cause-and-effect essays that merely repeat commonplace causes or effects will discourage the audience from reading on. Engaging causal analyses, in contrast, surprise readers by challenging popular assumptions, offering surprising reasons, or including interesting evidence. For example, an essay on the effects of capital punishment might attempt to dispel the notion that it deters crime, or it might surprise readers by contending that criminals are in fact deterred, but not for the reasons readers would be likely to assume.

Dealing with the causes or effects that readers assume to be primary is an effective strategy because it creates the impression that you have recognized other viewpoints and not overlooked important information. So essays that challenge readers' assumptions may first explain why the most popular explanation is false or inadequate before moving on to the writer's preferred cause or effect.

The following readings demonstrate the techniques for writing effective cause-and-effect essays. The first reading is annotated to point out how Alex Vitale explains the connection between police misconduct and the likelihood of indictment. As you read the second essay, try to identify for yourself how Adam Alter uses the techniques of causal analysis to support his claim that labels shape identity.

> **READING**

Why the Police Are Rarely Indicted for Misconduct

Alex S. Vitale

Alex Vitale is an associate professor of sociology at Brooklyn College and the author of *City of Disorder: How the Quality of Life Campaign Transformed U.S. Politics.* Vitale has also published numerous articles for publications such as *The Nation, The Abolitionist,* and *Gotham Gazette.* The essay that appears below was originally published online by *Al Jazeera America,* a news and current events media outlet.

Before Reading

1. **Preview:** Use the steps listed on page 28.
2. **Connect:** What incidences of perceived police misconduct have you read about in print or seen on television?

While Reading Study the annotations that accompany the reading to discover how the essay illustrates the characteristics of effective cause-and-effect writing.

Introduction: Grabs readers' attention with anecdote drawn from the headlines

On Monday evening, St. Louis County Prosecuting Attorney Robert P. McCulloch announced that a grand jury decided not to indict Ferguson, Missouri, police officer Darren Wilson for the August 9, 2015, shooting death of unarmed teenager Michael Brown. The announcement concluded a tumultuous summer of mass protests against police violence and racial discrimination. Although the decision will be a disappointment to many, those who follow prosecutions of police for use of excessive or unwarranted force say a decision not to indict Wilson is unsurprising.

1

There are major legal, institutional, and social impediments to prosecuting police. Thousands of officers are involved in shootings every year, resulting in about 400 deaths annually. However, successful criminal prosecution of a police officer for killing someone in the line of duty, if no corruption is alleged, is extremely rare. Even when officers are convicted, the charges are often minimal. For example, Coleman Brackney, a Bella Vista, Oklahoma, police officer who was convicted of misdemeanor negligent homicide in 2010 after shooting an unarmed teen to death while in custody in his cruiser, went on to rejoin the police and was recently appointed chief of police in Sulphur Springs, Oklahoma.

2

Thesis: Thesis forecasts multiple causes to explain a controversial effect

Effect

Structural Barriers

Heading: Signals Cause 1

There are significant structural barriers to successful police indictment or prosecution. For one, investigations are usually conducted by a combination of police detectives and investigators from the prosecutors' office. Prosecutors tend to take a greater role when there is a reason to believe that the shooting might not be justified. However, they must rely on the cooperation of the police to gather necessary evidence, including witness statements from the officer involved and other officers at the scene. In some cases they are the only living witnesses to the event.

3

Topic sentence for section 1

Cause 1a

Transition

Explanation offers support

The close collaboration between police and prosecutors, which is an asset in homicide investigations, becomes a hindrance in police shooting cases. In most cases, the prosecutors' reliance on the cooperation of police creates a fundamental conflict of interest. As a result, prosecutors are often reluctant to aggressively pursue these cases.

4

Cause 1b

Reasons offer support

Effect

Moreover, the local elected district attorneys often want to avoid being seen as inhibiting police power. Even in communities where distrust of police is common, no prosecutor ever got thrown out of office for defending the police. At its core, the public sees the DA's office as a defender of law and order and expects these officials to uphold them.

5

Cause 1c

Reasons offer support

The way prosecutors handled the Wilson case illustrates this conflict of interest. It took prosecutors months to collect and present evidence to the grand jury. While this has the appearance of thoroughness, it also has the effect of creating a public cooling-off period as short-term demands for prosecution become muted. The radically different approach of the St. Louis County DA is telling. Typically, prosecutors make a short presentation to the grand jury in which they call for specific charges to be considered and then put on their best show of the evidence to see if it passes muster. Indictments occur in more than 90 percent of cases, owing to the low threshold of probable cause and the one-sided nature of the proceedings. In Wilson's case, however, the DA said he planned to provide the grand jury with all the evidence and allow them to decide, without any prompting, whether an indictment was justified and for what offense.

6

Example offers support

The DA hoped to accomplish two things. First, this approach allowed him to absolve himself of any responsibility for the outcome. Second, it served to confuse and undermine the confidence of the grand jury. Normally, the jury is given clear guidance and overrules prosecutors only in extreme cases. By giving the jurors a

7

wide variety of conflicting evidence and little framework in which to evaluate it, the DA is opening the door to a he said/he said dynamic in which they may err on the side of caution and avoid an indictment.

Legal Hurdles

There are also huge legal hurdles to overcome. State laws that authorize police use of force, which are backed up by Supreme Court precedent, give police significant latitude in using deadly force. In the 1989 case *Graham v. Connor*, the Supreme Court ruled that officers may use force to effect a lawful arrest or if they reasonably believe that the person represents a serious physical threat to the officer or others. This means that police may use force over any resistance to arrest and that if the resistance escalates, officers may escalate their force. The court also said that the totality of circumstances must be judged with an understanding of the split-second nature of police decision-making.

Furthermore, in Missouri and many other states, even a perceived effort to take an officer's gun justifies the use of deadly force. Therefore, in judging the reasonableness of the officer's actions, the jury may consider factors such as the alleged perpetrator's size and previous actions as well as the officer's training and guidance. All this creates numerous avenues for justifying police action based on the officer's reasonable understanding of the situation rather than a more objective post hoc assessment.

Juror mindset creates yet another challenge to successful indictments and prosecutions. Grand juries and criminal court juries consist of local residents. Even in periods of heightened concern about police misconduct, most citizens retain a strong bias in favor of police. Popular culture and political discourse are suffused with commentaries about both the central importance of police in maintaining the basic structural integrity of society and the dangerous nature of their work. In addition, the legal standard for judging police misconduct calls on jurors to put themselves in the officers' shoes, further strengthening the tendency to identify with the police.

Race Relations

Another important dynamic in police prosecutions is the state of race relations in the United States. Despite the rhetoric about being a post-racial society, racial divisions and bias remain omnipresent in American society and nowhere more than in the realm of criminal justice. There is abundant evidence of jury bias in a variety of racially disparate criminal justice outcomes, including false convictions, application of the death penalty, and drug convictions. Research shows that whites have a generally more positive view of the police than blacks do. The sad reality is that white jurors are much more likely to side with police, regardless of the race of the officer and the person killed. This was seen in the Rodney King prosecutions in California, in which a mostly white suburban state court jury did not convict four Los Angeles Police Department officers in the severe beating of King after a high-speed car chase, despite the incident's being videotaped. (The jury acquitted

Margin annotations:

Heading: Signals Cause 2

Topic sentence for section 2

Cause 2a

Example offers support

Transition
Cause 2b

Effect

Cause 2c

Reasons offer support

Heading: Signals Cause 3

Topic sentence for section 3

Example offers support

Paragraph numbers: 8, 9, 10, 11

three of the four officers and deadlocked on a charge of excessive force against one officer.) A more diverse federal jury later found two of the officers guilty of violating King's civil rights.

Regardless of what happens in Brown's case, there are no simple fixes for these problems. Advocates such as the Rev. Al Sharpton have called for a federal prosecution. Even if federal officials get involved, they must bring a different kind of charge, related to civil rights violations. While this legal twist of logic has been an important check on failed state legal processes going back to the civil rights fights of the 1950s and 1960s, it is not a substitute for local criminal prosecution, especially in an era of heightened resistance to federal legitimacy.

Internal administrative accountability is sorely lacking. In "Jammed Up: Bad Cops, Police Misconduct, and the New York City Police Department," Robert Kane and Michael White show that police rarely face internal disciplinary charges for use of force. Recent reports from Philadelphia and Seattle show that even when officers are subject to discipline, the majority of such cases end up being overturned by arbitrators or courts as a result of extensive due process protections for police officers.

Instead, states should create a police prosecutor's office, or blue desk, that is more removed from local politics. While relying on state attorneys general has its own challenges, the outcomes are likely to be viewed as more legitimate. These blue desks could become repositories of expertise on police prosecutions. Even if tied to state politics, they might be better able to insulate themselves from accusations of overly aggressive prosecutions as well as charges of not supporting the police.

Laws on the use of force need reform. Police shootings were much more common in the 1970s when regulations about the use of force were even looser. In response to public outcries and rioting in the 1960s and '70s, local police began to tighten up regulations and offer training to officers, resulting in significant reductions in shootings. The 1984 Supreme Court case *Tennessee v. Garner* institutionalized some of these changes nationally, including making it unlawful for police to shoot a fleeing suspect. Since then, however, the courts have mostly expanded police authorization to use force.

Finally, the U.S. needs to dial back the dramatic expansion of police power over the last forty years. For example, the growing prevalence of paramilitary SWAT teams and the ongoing war on drugs have significantly contributed to excessive use of force. In part this happened through the combined direct enforcement practices of these two types of policing. But they also contributed indirectly to a larger ethos of militarized patrolling that equates policing with the use of force and a war footing. The public and its representatives need to realize that there are better ways to prevent crime and serve the community than licensing excessive police force.

12   **Conclusion:** Refers back to example in introduction; reviews possible solutions before offering a solution of his own

13

14   Transitions signal proposed solutions

15

16

Visualize Cause-and-Effect Essays: Create Graphic Organizers

For more on creating a graphic organizer, see pp. 35–37.

Graphic Organizers 18.1, 18.2, and 18.3 show the basic organization of three types of causal-analysis essays.

- Graphic Organizer 18.1 shows the organization of an essay that examines either causes *or* effects.
- Graphic Organizer 18.2 shows the organization of an essay that examines a chain of causes and effects.
- Graphic Organizer 18.3 shows two possible arrangements for an essay that focuses on multiple causes and effects.

All three types of causal analyses include an introduction (which identifies the event, provides background information, and states a thesis) as well as a conclusion. Notice in Graphic Organizers 18.2 and 18.3 that causes are presented before effects. Although this is the typical arrangement, writers sometimes use the reverse organization, discussing effects first and then causes to create a sense of drama or surprise.

GRAPHIC ORGANIZER 18.1   The Basic Structure of an Essay on Causes or Effects

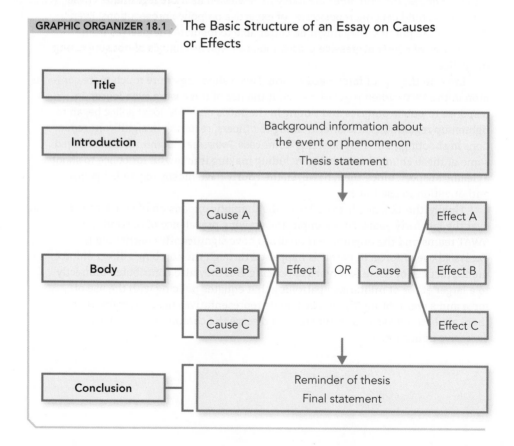

GRAPHIC ORGANIZER 18.2 The Basic Structure of an Essay on a Chain of Causes and Effects

GRAPHIC ORGANIZER 18.3 The Basic Structure of an Essay on Multiple Causes and Effects

How Labels Like *Black* and *Working Class* Shape Your Identity

Adam Alter

Adam Alter is an assistant professor of marketing and psychology at New York University. His research focuses on decision making, and he has published numerous articles in academic journals in psychology. He has also published a number of articles for general readers in publications such as *The New York Times, The Wall Street Journal,* and *Psychology Today.* This reading is from Alter's 2013 book *Drunk Tank Pink and Other Unexpected Forces That Shape How We Think, Feel, and Behave.* **Before reading**, preview the selection and make connections by thinking about the way labels affect how people are treated. Think of instances that illustrate or disprove this idea. **While reading**, highlight the effects Alter names as resulting from racial bias or social labeling. Then compare your notes with Graphic Organizer 18.4 on page 469.

Long ago, humans began labeling and cataloguing each other. Eventually, lighter-skinned humans became "whites," darker-skinned humans became "blacks," and people with intermediate skin tones became "yellow-," "red-," and "brown-skinned." These labels don't reflect reality faithfully, and if you lined up 1,000 randomly selected people from across the earth, none of them would share exactly the same skin tone. Of course, the continuity of skin tone hasn't stopped humans from assigning each other to discrete categories like "black" and "white"—categories that have no basis in biology but nonetheless go on to determine the social, political, and economic well-being of their members. 1

Social labels aren't born dangerous. There's nothing inherently problematic about labeling a person "right-handed" or "black" or "working class," but those labels are harmful to the extent that they become associated with meaningful character traits. At one end of the spectrum, the label "right-handed" is relatively free of meaning. We don't have strong stereotypes about right-handed people, and calling someone right-handed isn't tantamount to calling them unfriendly or unintelligent. 2

In contrast, the terms "black" and "working class" are laden with the baggage of associations, perhaps some of them positive, but many of them negative. During the height of the civil-rights struggle, one teacher showed just how willingly children adopt new labels. On April 4, 1968, Martin Luther King Jr. was murdered, and the next day thousands of American children went to school with a combination of misinformation and confusion. In Riceville, Iowa, Stephen Armstrong asked his teacher, Jane Elliott, why "they shot that king." Elliott explained that the "king" was a man named King who was fighting against the discrimination of "Negroes." The class of white students was confused, so Elliott offered to show them what it might be like to experience discrimination themselves. 3

Elliott began by claiming that the blue-eyed children were better than the   4
brown-eyed children. The children resisted at first. The brown-eyed majority was
forced to confront the possibility that they were inferior, and the blue-eyed minority faced a crisis when they realized that some of their closest friendships were
now forbidden. Elliott explained that the brown-eyed children had too much melanin, a substance that darkens the eyes and makes people less intelligent. Melanin
caused the "brownies," as Elliott labeled them, to be clumsy and lazy. Elliott asked
the brownies to wear paper armbands—a deliberate reference to the yellow armbands that Jews were forced to wear during the Holocaust. Elliott reinforced the
distinction by telling the brown-eyed children not to drink directly from the water
fountain, as they might contaminate the blue-eyed children. Instead, the brownies
were forced to drink from paper cups. Elliott also praised the blue-eyed children
and offered them privileges, like a longer lunch break, while she criticized the
brown-eyed children and forced them to end lunch early. By the end of the day, the
blue-eyed children had become rude and unpleasant toward their classmates,
while even the gregarious brown-eyed children were noticeably timid and
subservient.

News of Elliott's demonstration traveled quickly, and she was interviewed by   5
Johnny Carson. The interview lasted a few brief minutes, but its effects persist
today. Elliott was pilloried by angry white viewers across the country. One angry
white viewer scolded Elliott for exposing white children to the discrimination
that black children face every day. Black children were accustomed to the experience, the viewer argued, but white children were fragile and might be scarred
long after the demonstration ended. Elliott responded sharply by asking why
we're so concerned about white children who experience this sort of treatment
for a single day, while ignoring the pain of black children who experience the
same treatment across their entire lives. Years later, Elliott's technique has been
used in hundreds of classrooms and in workplace-discrimination training
courses, where adults experience similar epiphanies. Elliott's approach shows
how profoundly labels shape our treatment of other people and how even arbi-
trary damaging labels have the power to turn the brightest people into meek
shadows of their potential selves.

Four years before Jane Elliott's classroom demonstration, two psychologists   6
began a remarkable experiment at a school in San Francisco. Robert Rosenthal
and Lenore Jacobson set out to show that the recipe for academic achievement
contains more than raw intellect and a dozen years of schooling. Rosenthal and
Jacobson kept the details of the experiment hidden from the teachers, students,
and parents; instead, they told the teachers that their test was designed to identify which students would improve academically over the coming year—students
they labeled "academic bloomers." In truth, the test was an IQ measure with separate versions for each school grade, and it had nothing to do with academic
blooming. As with any IQ test, some of the students scored quite well, some
scored poorly, and many performed at the level expected from students of their
age group.

The next phase of the experiment was both brilliant and controversial. Rosenthal and Jacobson recorded the students' scores on the test, and then labeled a randomly chosen sample of the students as "academic bloomers." The bloomers performed no differently from the other students—both groups had the same average IQ score—but their teachers were told to expect the bloomers to experience a rapid period of intellectual development during the following year.

7

When the new school year arrived, each teacher watched as a new crop of children filled the classroom. The teachers knew very little about each student, except whether they had been described as bloomers three months earlier. As they were chosen arbitrarily, the bloomers should have fared no differently from the remaining students. The students completed another year of school and, just before the year ended, Rosenthal and Jacobson administered the IQ test again. The results were remarkable.

8

The first and second graders who were labeled bloomers outperformed their peers by 10–15 IQ points. Four of every five bloomers experienced at least a 10-point improvement, but only half the non-bloomers improved their score by 10 points or more. Rosenthal and Jacobson had intervened to elevate a randomly chosen group of students above their relatively unlucky peers. Their intervention was limited to labeling the chosen students "bloomers," and remaining silent on the academic prospects of the overlooked majority.

9

Observers were stunned by these results, wondering how a simple label could elevate a child's IQ score a year later. When the teachers interacted with the "bloomers," they were primed to see academic progress. Each time a bloomer answered a question correctly, her answer seemed to be an early sign of academic achievement. Each time she answered a question incorrectly, her error was seen as an anomaly, swamped by the general sense that she was in the process of blooming.

10

During the year, then, the teachers praised these students for their successes, overlooked their failures, and devoted plenty of time and energy to the task of ensuring that they would grow to justify their promising academic labels. The label "bloomer" did not just resolve ambiguity, in other words—it changed the outcome for those students.

11

EXERCISE 18.3   **DRAWING A GRAPHIC ORGANIZER**

Using Graphic Organizer 18.3 (p. 465), draw a graphic organizer for "Why the Police Are Rarely Indicted for Misconduct" (pp. 460–63).

GRAPHIC ORGANIZER 18.4 The Structure of "How Labels Like *Black* and *Working Class* Shape Your Identity"

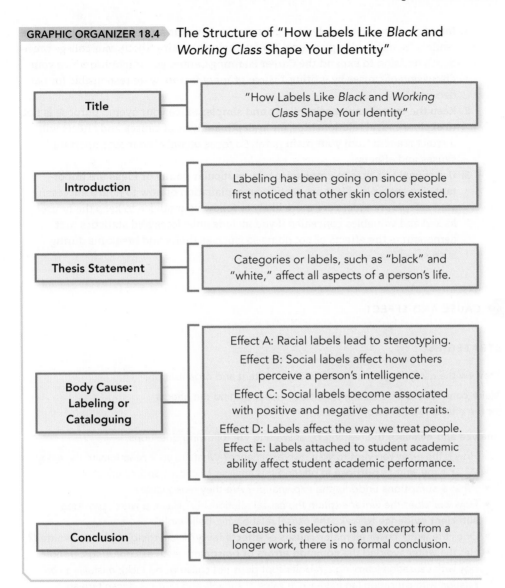

Title — "How Labels Like *Black* and *Working Class* Shape Your Identity"

Introduction — Labeling has been going on since people first noticed that other skin colors existed.

Thesis Statement — Categories or labels, such as "black" and "white," affect all aspects of a person's life.

Body Cause: Labeling or Cataloguing —
Effect A: Racial labels lead to stereotyping.
Effect B: Social labels affect how others perceive a person's intelligence.
Effect C: Social labels become associated with positive and negative character traits.
Effect D: Labels affect the way we treat people.
Effect E: Labels attached to student academic ability affect student academic performance.

Conclusion — Because this selection is an excerpt from a longer work, there is no formal conclusion.

Integrate Cause and Effect into an Essay

Although some of your essays will focus solely on causal analysis, other essays will combine cause and effect with other patterns. For example, in an essay comparing two popular magazines that have different journalistic styles, you might explain the effects of each style on the reading experience. Use the following tips to integrate causal analyses into essays that rely on other patterns of development.

For a reading that uses causal analysis as well as other patterns of development, see "Why Summer Makes Us Lazy" (pp. 481–83).

1. **Introduce the causal analysis.** Use transitional words and expressions to prepare readers for a causal explanation. For example, in writing about your college president's decision to expand the Career Planning Center, you might introduce your discussion of causes by writing, "Three primary factors were responsible for her decision."

2. **Keep the causal explanation direct and simple.** Since your overall purpose is not to explore causal relationships, an in-depth analysis of causes and effects will distract readers from your main point. So focus on only the most important causes and effects.

3. **Use causal analysis to emphasize why particular points or ideas are important.** For example, if you are writing an explanation of how to hold a successful yard sale, your readers are more likely to follow your advice to keep the house locked and valuables concealed if you include anecdotes and statistics that demonstrate the effects of not doing so (such as thefts and break-ins during such sales).

HOW WRITERS READ ⟩ CAUSE AND EFFECT

THE READING PROCESS	STRATEGIES
BEFORE READING	**Preview** the essay to get an overview of its content and organization.
	Make connections by thinking about the causes behind the effects (or the effects resulting from causes).
AFTER READING	**Analyze and evaluate** the reading by answering the following questions.

- How is the essay **relevant** to your own experience? What are your **reactions** to the essay?
- What is the writer's **purpose** in offering this analysis of causes and/or effects?
- What **assumptions** underlie the explanation? Are they reasonable?
- How well does the writer **explain** the causal relationship? Has the writer provided **sufficient evidence** to make the causal relationship believable?
- Does the writer cover **all major causes** or **effects fairly**? Is anything important omitted?
- Has the writer avoided the **common errors of reasoning**, such as *confusing chronology with causation* (carrying a rabbit's foot does not cause good luck); *mistaking correlation with causation* (an increase in sales of shovels and mittens doesn't mean shoveling causes people to buy mittens); and/or *misidentifying causal relationships* (does failure in school cause personal problems or vice versa? Maybe both are caused by some third factor)?

EXERCISE 18.4 ⟩

Apply the questions in the "How Writers Read" box to the selection "How Labels Like *Black* and *Working Class* Shape Your Identity" (pp. 466–68).

A Guided Writing Assignment*

CAUSE AND EFFECT

Your Essay Assignment

Write a causal analysis essay on a topic that you believe would interest readers of your college newspaper. You may consider causes, effects, or both. Below are some options.

- the popularity (or lack of popularity) of a public figure
- cheating on college exams
- a current trend or fad
- a major change or decision in your life
- a problem or event on campus or in the community

1 **Select a topic from the list above, or create one of your own.**

Consider the **length** of your essay as you choose your **topic** and decide whether to write about **causes**, **effects**, or **both**.

Example: You couldn't explore fully both causes and effects of child abuse in a five-page paper.

2 **Consider your purpose and audience, and choose a point of view.**

Ask yourself these questions.

- What is my **purpose**? A cause-and-effect essay for a college course may be both **informative** and **persuasive**.

  Example: An essay on academic cheating could examine the causes (informative) and propose policies to help alleviate the problem (persuasive).

- Who is my **audience**? How much do my readers **already know** about the topic? If your readers are **unfamiliar** with the topic you are writing about (or if the topic is complex), limit your focus to **the most important**, **obvious**, and **easily understood** causes or effects. If your audience is **generally familiar** with your topic, then you can deal with **less obvious** or **more complex causes or effects**. Take into consideration what your readers will think are the most likely causes or effects.

* The writing process is *recursive*; that is, you may find yourself revising as you draft or prewriting as you revise. This is especially true when writing on a computer. Your writing process may also differ from project to project and from that of your classmates.

- What **point of view** is most appropriate given my purpose and audience? Although academic writing usually uses the **third person** (*he, she, they*), you might use the **first person** (*I*) to relate relevant personal experiences.

3 Discover causes and effects.

Try one or more of the following idea-generating strategies.

- Write your topic in the middle of a page. Then alone or with a classmate, **brainstorm** possible causes and effects, listing causes on the left and effects on the right. (Creative and abstract learners may prefer brainstorming; social learners may prefer brainstorming in pairs.)
- **Replay the event in your mind.** Ask yourself, "Why did the event happen?" "What happened as a result of it?" Make notes on the answers. (Abstract learners may prefer replaying the event.)
- **Ask questions** (or have a friend ask the questions) about the problem or phenomenon and then write down answers. Did a chain of events cause the phenomenon? Try to identify causes and effects that are not obvious. (Rational and pragmatic learners may prefer asking questions.)
- **Research your topic.** Try Googling a keyword and making notes on possible causes and effects. (All learners can benefit from conducting research.)

4 Identify primary causes and effects.

Review your prewriting, and highlight what you see as the **primary**, or most important, **causes and effects**. Ask yourself:

- What causes or effects are the most **obvious** and **immediate**?
- What cause(s) or effects are the **most serious**? **For whom**?
- What causes or effects will my readers **expect me to address**?

Example:

Topic	*Effects of television violence on young viewers*
Primary Effects	An increase in aggressive behavior
	A willingness to accept violence as normal
Secondary Effects	Learning inappropriate or offensive words

Work Together
In groups of two or three, test your causes or effects.

1. Take turns presenting your primary causes or effects to the group. First, state your cause(s) or effect(s), and then explain why you think they are important:

    Example: I think _____ caused/is an effect of _____ because _____.

2. Have each member of the group rank each cause or effect as:
    (a) sufficient (enough) on its own
    (b) a contributing cause or minor effect
    (c) an unlikely cause or effect

3. Then compare notes and discuss what might be the most interesting or persuasive causes or effects to focus on.

Hint: Do not assume that the most obvious or simplest explanation is the only one. If a child often reports to the nurse's office complaining of a stomachache, a parent may reason that the child has digestive problems, but a closer study of the symptoms may reveal that the stomachaches are the result of stress.

5 Gather evidence to support your thesis.

Compile evidence—**facts and statistics, expert opinion, personal observation**—to support each cause or effect you will include. (Conduct research as needed.) Alone or with another student, consider whether one or more of the other **patterns of development** would help you support your thesis effectively. (Chapters 21 and 22 can help you find and select sources.)

Examples
- A **story** (narration) could demonstrate the effects a fad diet had on an individual.
- A **comparison** with a fad diet from an earlier era could show likely effects.
- **Examples** of earlier fads that have come and gone could show likely causes.

6 Draft your thesis statement.

An effective thesis statement should:

- **State the cause-and-effect relationship.** Do not leave it to your reader to figure out.

    Example: Breathing paint fumes in a closed environment can be dangerous ̭ for people People suffering from

    asthma and emphysema ̭ because their lungs are especially sensitive to irritants. are particularly vulnerable.

    The word *because* makes the cause-and-effect connection explicit. Adding *their lungs are especially sensitive to irritants* makes the cause more specific and focused.

- **Avoid overly broad or absolute assertions.**

    Example: Drugs are ̭ a major the root cause of inner-city crime.

    Example: Overemphasizing competitive sports ̭ may be is harmful to the psychological development of

    young children.

- **Avoid an overly assertive or dogmatic tone.**

  Example: ~~There is no question~~ that American youths have changed in response to the culture in

  _{Substantial evidence suggests}

  which they live.

Working together. In groups of two or three students, take turns reading your thesis statements aloud. While they listen, have group members write down the **cause-effect relationship** and identify any **qualifications**. Then, as a group, discuss how writers could make the cause-effect relationship more **plausible** and **specific**.

7 Choose a method of organization.

- **Chronological order** works well when a clear sequence of events is apparent.
- **Most-to-least order** works well to highlight one or two particularly important causes.
- **Least-to-most order** works well to create suspense.

Review Graphic Organizers 18.1, 18.2, and 18.3 (pp. 464–65) to find the graphic organizer that is closest to your essay's basic structure, or use the outline function in your word-processing program to create an outline for your essay.

8 Draft your cause-and-effect essay.

Use the following guidelines to keep your essay on track.

- Your **introduction** should **identify the topic** and **causal relationship** as well as draw your reader into the essay. Unless you want to give readers the sense of discovering the cause-effect relationship for themselves, you will likely include the **thesis statement** as well.
- Your **body paragraphs** should include a clear **topic sentence** and provide **sufficient evidence** (examples, statistics, expert opinion, comparisons, and so on). Use **transitional words** and **phrases** (such as *in addition, furthermore, more important,* or *finally*) as you move from one cause or effect to another, and use **transitional sentences** to alert readers that you are moving from discussing causes to discussing effects (or vice versa) or shifting to a different pattern of development. Use **qualifying words** and **phrases**, such as *perhaps, possible, it is likely,* and *most likely,* to limit your claims and avoid a dogmatic tone.
- Your **conclusion** should remind readers of your **thesis** and draw your essay to a **satisfying close**.

9 Evaluate your draft and revise as necessary.

Use **Figure 18.1, "Flowchart for Revising a Cause-and-Effect Essay,"** to evaluate and revise your draft.

FIGURE 18.1 Flowchart for Revising a Cause-and-Effect Essay

QUESTIONS | REVISION STRATEGIES

1. Highlight your thesis. Does it express a qualified, manageable assertion? (Can you prove your thesis?)

NO ▶
- Use a branching diagram to narrow your topic (see Chapter 4, pp. 100–101).
- Focus on only primary causes or effects.
- Add qualifying words or phrases to your thesis.

YES ▼

2. Place a ✔ by each cause. Mark an ✘ by each effect. Does your essay clearly focus on causes, effects, or both?

NO ▶
- Reconsider whether you want to explain causes, effects, or both. Will the essay be skimpy if you focus on only one? Will it be too long or too complicated if you discuss both?

YES ▼

3. [Bracket] the explanation for each cause or effect. Is each explained fully?

NO ▶
- Add anecdotes, observations, or other details and examples.
- Do research to locate facts, research studies, statistics, and expert opinions.

YES ▼

4. Write the method of organization (chronological, least-to-most, or most-to-least) you used at the top of your essay. Is it clear and effective? Do your ideas progress logically?

NO ▶
- Choose a different order if necessary.
- Rearrange your causes, effects, or both.

YES ▼

5. Circle any sections where you have recognized readers' assumptions and either supported or challenged them. Have you identified all likely preconceptions?

NO ▶
- Brainstorm popular ideas readers might assume about your topic and either support or challenge them.

YES ▼

(continued on next page) ▶

(Figure 18.1 continued)

REVISING

QUESTIONS		REVISION STRATEGIES

6. <u>Underline</u> each topic sentence. Is each paragraph focused on a separate cause or effect?

 NO ▶

- Combine closely related paragraphs.
- Split paragraphs that cover more than one cause or effect.

 YES ▼

7. Reread your introduction and conclusion. Do they provoke thought, engage readers, and provide a sense of completeness?

 NO ▶

- Revise your introduction so that it sets the tone of the essay, provides necessary background, and engages readers.
- Revise the conclusion so that it reaffirms your thesis and brings the essay to a satisfying close.

EDITING & PROOFREADING

10 Edit and proofread your essay.

Refer to Chapter 9 for help with:

- **editing sentences** to avoid wordiness, make your verb choices strong and active, and make your sentences clear, varied, and parallel
- **editing words** for tone and diction, connotation, and concrete and specific language

Watch out particularly for **wordy sentences** and **mixed constructions**.

1. **Revise wordy sentences.** Writers often use complex and compound-complex sentences to explain causal relationships. These sentences can sometimes become wordy and confusing, so look for ways to eliminate empty phrases and simplify your wording.

   Example: ~~As you are already well aware,~~ viruses ~~of certain types in a computer file~~ often create
   (Certain types of computer)

   errors that you cannot explain ~~in documents~~ and may eventually result in lost data.

2. **Revise to eliminate mixed constructions.** A mixed construction occurs when a writer connects phrases or clauses that do not fit together in a sentence.

   Example: ~~Samantha, although~~ she was late for work, ~~but~~ was not reprimanded by her boss.
   (Although)   (Samantha)

   Using both *although* and *but* makes this a mixed sentence. To avoid mixed constructions, check words that join your phrases and clauses. Pay attention to prepositions and conjunctions. Also, check to be sure that the subjects of your sentences can perform the actions described by the verbs. If not, revise the sentence to supply the appropriate verb.

   Example: The college ~~hopes~~ all students ~~will~~ take a freshman seminar.
   (encourages)   (to)

476

Readings: Cause and Effect in Action

Is Sharing Files Online Killing Music?

Title: Identifies cause and effect

Jonathan Adamczak

Jonathan Adamczak was asked to write a cause-and-effect essay that identified the causes, effects, or both causes and effects related to a phenomenon that interested him. He decided to examine how file sharing had affected the music business in the United States. As you read the essay, notice how he carefully presents both positive and negative effects. Highlight the effects he cites and indicate which effects are negative and which are positive.

1

The ways that humans have created and shared music have evolved throughout history in drastic ways. From prehistoric instruments and folk songs to vinyl records, international concert tours, and mp3 devices, music and musical performance have gone through many forms in order to adapt to human innovations. Perhaps the innovation with the strongest impact on music has been the advent of the Internet. The Digital Age has made certain aspects of pursuing a musical career much more difficult, while simultaneously presenting the music industry with unique opportunities to popularize new artists in ways that weren't possible before.

Introduction: Provides background, chronicling past innovations. Concludes with thesis statement, which identifies a single cause and multiple effects, and suggests organization

2

The most noticeable effect of the digitized music has been piracy, or the illegal downloading of music files and the subsequent decline in CD sales. At its peak in 2001, music industry revenue was $38 billion, but between 1999 and 2012, it lost almost half of that as CD sales plummeted (Pfanner, "Music Industry Sales"). Once pirating songs and albums from the Internet became an easy alternative for music consumers all over the world, CDs and other physical forms of recorded music started to become obsolete. A trade organization called the International Federation of the Phonographic Industry has claimed that digital piracy can account for

Effect 1 (negative): Identified in topic sentence. Suggests that effects will be presented in most-to-least order

Transition: Transition emphasizes cause-effect relationship

Support: Uses evidence from sources as support

the worldwide decline in music sales over the past decade (Pfanner, "Music Industry Counts"). While it's difficult to measure the financial effect on artists, the *New York Times* estimates that the music industry has lost hundreds of billions of dollars (Internet Piracy). The digitization of music has enabled millions of Internet users to access music at no cost without leaving their homes, reducing sales for record companies worldwide.

Effect 2 (negative): Announced in topic sentence

3

The rise of legal methods of listening to digital music, a product of a rapidly evolving music industry, has also become a financial burden on musicians and their labels. As the digital piracy problem has grown, Internet companies have begun seeking ways to offer music for free, while earning money from advertising. Music streaming services such as Pandora and Spotify are available for free in certain countries to those with Internet access. However, the money they receive for playing advertisements to listeners doesn't add up to what musicians and record companies used to earn from CD sales. Music labels earn somewhere between 0.4 and 0.7 cents per stream on Spotify, which adds up to $4,000 to $7,000 per million streams. The executive of BMG Rights Management noted that with that level of payment, almost no artists could make it professionally (Sisario). The shift from a CD economy to a digital music economy has decreased the profitability of music recording and distribution.

Effect 3 (negative): Announced in topic sentence

4

Furthermore, as the digitalization of music presents record labels with serious revenue loss, the effect is twofold. The problem of declining sales is compounded by the fact that record labels often use surplus funds to invest in new talent (Pfanner, "Music Industry Counts"). If labels are suffering shortages, there is less of a chance that young or up-and-coming musicians will find the means to gain new listeners. In this way, the rise of digital music exchange is actually helping to stifle new work.

Effect 4 (positive): Announced in topic sentence

Support: Uses example as evidence

5

Another consequence of computers and Internet access becoming more widely available is that new or aspiring artists find it easier to record and circulate their own music. Tyler Ward, a 24-year-old amateur singer and songwriter featured on NPR's *The Record*, tried out recording and posting cover songs on YouTube and ended up performing on the Ellen DeGeneres Show and touring the U.S., Canada, and Europe (Nelson). Whereas before the digital era, artists had to fight hard to publicize their albums, now anyone with an Internet signal and recording capability has a shot at being discovered. Big names like Justin Bieber and Soulja Boy were all made famous by the video-sharing website YouTube (Greene). While musicians used to pay to put their songs on vinyl, budding artists can now upload their music to the Internet for free and even sell their tracks from online platforms. With Bandcamp.com, musicians can upload their music and charge whatever download fee they choose. The Internet has equipped musicians with tools to help them get started.

Though the music industry has lost money because of digital piracy and declining CD sales, this very shift to a digitized economy has also produced the concept of online crowdfunding, a new way for musicians to raise money. Fundraising, too, has gone digital, and musicians can take advantage of a digitally engaged fan base and raise money electronically. Amanda Palmer, a singer and composer, raised over one million dollars through crowdfunding in the summer of 2012 and used the money to produce an album (Kelley). Not only can artists reach out more directly to their fans to ask for money, but also more of those earnings go straight to the artist, rather than to record labels. Although Bandcamp takes a 15% share of its users' profits, the rest of the money goes directly to artists (Shotwell). What profits the Internet has cut from the music industry by enabling piracy and low-paying streaming services, it has begun to return in the form of independent funding opportunities for new and amateur musicians.

Yet another consequence of the Digital Age that boosts promising new musicians is the far-reaching effects of social media and social networks. While the charts used to be topped by big-name labels and radio hits, recent hits, such as Carly Rae Jepsen's "Call Me Maybe," have made it to the mainstream with help from YouTube and Twitter (Sisario). Since these marketing channels are free, artists have an easier time than ever before disseminating their songs or albums to a large audience.

Since the beginning of the Digital Age, the evolution of music production has been momentous and complex, with both serious financial repercussions and more positive effects for new musicians looking to share their art. Rather than trying to halt these changes, artists would do well to embrace the creative challenges posed by the digital music industry.

6   **Effect 5 (positive):** Announced in topic sentence; transition highlights contrast with predigital era

7   **Effect 6 (positive):** Announced in topic sentence; transitions highlight shift to new effect uses contrast and examples as support

8   **Conclusion:** Revisits thesis and lends closure by emphasizing opportunities

While the negative effects of music's digitalization on industry profit may cloud our vision, our increasing capability to tap into a whole world's worth of musicians, and not just those signed to big labels, is exhilarating.

Works Cited

Greene, Amanda. "Ten YouTube Success Stories." *Woman's Day*, 8 July 2010, www.womansday.com/life/entertainment/a1731/10-youtube -success-stories-108958/.

"Internet Piracy and How to Stop It." *The New York Times*, 8 June 2011, www.nytimes.com/2011/06/09/opinion/09thu1.html. Editorial.

Kelley, Frannie. "Crowd Funding for Musicians Isn't the Future; It's the Present." *The Record*, National Public Radio, 25 Sept. 2012, www.npr .org/sections/therecord/2012/09/25/161702900/crowd-funding-for -musicians-isnt-the-future-its-the-present.

Nelson, Noah. "Covering Pop Hits on YouTube Is Starting to Pay." *The Record,* National Public Radio, 13 May 2013, www.npr.org/sections/ therecord/2013/05/13/182880665/covering-pop-hits-on-youtube-is -starting-to-pay.

Pfanner, Eric. "Music Industry Counts the Cost of Piracy." *The New York Times*, 21 Jan. 2010, www.nytimes.com/2010/01/22/business/ global/22music.html.

Pfanner, Eric. "Music Industry Sales Rise, and Digital Revenue Gets Credit." *The New York Times*, 26 Feb. 2013, www.nytimes .com/2013/02/27/technology/music-industry-records-first-revenue -increase-since-1999.html.

Shotwell, James. "Bandcamp.com Changes Business Model." *Alternative Press*, 20 July 2010, www.altpress.com/news/entry/bandcamp .com_changes_business_model/.

Sisario, Ben. "The New Rise of a Summer Hit: Tweet It Maybe." *The New York Times*, 21 Aug. 2012, www.nytimes.com/2012/08/22/business/ media/how-call-me-maybe-and-social-media-are-upending-music.html.

Analyzing the Writer's Technique

1. **Purpose** Describe Adamczak's purpose.
2. **Patterns** What other patterns of development does Adamczak use to support his thesis and maintain readers' interest?
3. **Introduction and Conclusion** Evaluate Adamczak's introduction and conclusion. How effectively do they stimulate the reader's interest and lend closure to the essay?

Thinking Critically about Cause and Effect

1. **Tone** Describe the tone of Adamczak's essay. What words and phrases suggest his attitude toward the changes in the music industry? Given his tone, who do you think was his audience?
2. **Additional Viewpoints** In paragraph 3, Adamczak paraphrases a comment from a BMG Rights Management executive. How might Adamczak's essay have changed if he had included the viewpoints of veteran and aspiring musicians?
3. **Objectivity** How objective does Adamczak seem in his evaluation of the changes in the music industry? Use evidence from the essay to support your claim.

Responding to the Essay

1. **Discussion** Do you regularly download music from the Internet? Do you use a streaming service? If so, consider how your Internet practices have contributed to the decreased profitability of the music business. Should you support musicians by buying their music from a service like Bandcamp or by contributing to crowd-sourcing efforts? Why or why not?
2. **Reaction** Adamczak mentions several effects of the digitization of the music business. What other effects may he have overlooked? For example, he did not explicitly focus on the effects digitization have had on those who enjoy listening to music.
3. **Journal** Adamczak focused on both the negative and the positive effects of the Internet on the music industry. Write a journal entry describing both the negative and positive effects that some other aspect of the Internet (such as social networking or online shopping) has had on your life.

> **READING**

Why Summer Makes Us Lazy

Maria Konnikova

Maria Konnikova is the author of *The New York Times* best-seller *Mastermind: How to Think Like Sherlock Holmes* (2013). She has published numerous articles for publications such as *Scientific American, The Atlantic, Slate,* and *The Wall Street Journal*. In addition, she blogs for *Big Think* and *The New Yorker* magazine. The essay that appears here was originally published in the *New Yorker*'s Elements blog in 2013. **Before reading**, preview and make connections by thinking about how seasons of the year affect your mood and performance. **While reading**, highlight the results of each scientific study that Konnikova uses to support the cause-and-effect relationship she proposes.

In his meticulous diaries, written from 1846 to 1882, the Harvard librarian John Langdon Sibley complains often about the withering summer heat: "The heat wilts & enervates me & makes me sick," he wrote in 1852. Sibley lived before the age of air-conditioning, but recent research suggests that his observation is still accurate: summer really does tend to be a time of reduced productivity. Our brains do, figuratively, wilt.

One of the key issues is motivation: when the weather is unpleasant, no one wants to go outside, but when the sun is shining, the air is warm, and the sky is blue, leisure calls. A 2008 study using data from the American Time Use Survey found that, on rainy days, men spent, on average, thirty more minutes at work than they did on comparatively sunny days. In 2012, a group of researchers from Harvard University and the University of North Carolina at Chapel Hill conducted a field study of Japanese bank workers and found a similar pattern: bad weather made workers more productive, as measured by the time it took them to complete assigned tasks in a loan-application process.

When the weather improved, in contrast, productivity fell. To determine why this was the case, the researchers assigned Harvard students data entry on either sunny or rainy days. The students were randomly assigned to one of two conditions: before starting to work, they were either shown six photographs of outdoor activities in nice weather, such as sailing or eating outdoors, or were asked to describe their daily routines. The researchers found that participants were less productive when they'd viewed pleasant outdoor photographs. Instead of focusing on their work, they focused on what they'd rather be doing—whether or not it was actually sunny or rainy outside (though the effect was stronger on sunny days). The mere thought of pleasant alternatives made people concentrate less.

But each season has its share of attractive days—and a skier's mind would likely have many opportunities to wander in the dead of winter. There's evidence, however, that in summer, our thinking itself may simply become lazier. In 1994, Gerald Clore, a pioneer in researching how ambient mood-altering phenomena affect cognition and judgment, found that pleasant weather can often lead to a disconcerting lapse in thoughtfulness. Clore's team approached a hundred and twenty-two undergraduates on days with either good or bad weather and asked them to participate in a survey on higher education. The better the weather, the easier it was to get the students to buy into a less-than-solid argument: on days that were sunny, clear, and warm, people were equally persuaded by both strong and weak arguments in favor of end-of-year comprehensive exams. When the weather was rainy, cloudy, and cold, their critical faculties improved: in that condition, only the strong argument was persuasive. Clore and his colleagues concluded that pleasant weather led people to embrace more heuristic-based thinking—that is, they relied heavily on mental shortcuts at the expense of actual analysis.

Summer weather—especially the muggy kind—may also reduce both our   5
attention and our energy levels. In one study, high humidity lowered concentration
and increased sleepiness among participants. The weather also hurt their ability to
think critically: the hotter it got, the less likely they were to question what they
were told.

The shift toward mindlessness may be rooted in our emotions. One common   6
finding is a link between relative sunshine and happiness: although people who live
in sunnier places, like Southern California, are no happier than those who live in the
harsher conditions of the Midwest, day-to-day variations in sunshine make a difference. People get happier as days get longer and warmer in the approach to the summer solstice, and less happy as days get colder and shorter. They also report higher
life satisfaction on relatively pleasant days. The happiest season, then, is summer.

A good mood, generally speaking, has in turn been linked to the same type   7
of heuristic, relatively mindless thinking that Clore observed in his pleasant-
weather participants. On the flip side, a bad mood tends to stimulate more rigorous analytical thought. Weather-related mood effects can thus play out in our
real-life decisions—even weighty ones. In one recent project, the psychologist Uri
Simonsohn found that students were more likely to enroll in a university that was
famous for its academic rigor if they visited on days that were cloudy. When the
weather turned sour, he concluded, the value they placed on academics increased.

There's a limit, however, to heat's ability to boost our mood: when tempera-   8
tures reach the kind of summer highs that mark heat waves all over the world, the
effect rapidly deteriorates. In a 2013 study of perceived well-being, the economist
Marie Connolly found that on days when the temperature rose above ninety
degrees, the negative impact on happiness levels was greater than the consequences of being widowed or divorced.

Conversely, the effects of heat on our brains aren't entirely negative. Many of   9
the behaviors that psychologists study follow a so-called inverted-U pattern: as
one factor steadily increases, a related behavior improves, plateaus, and then
starts to deteriorate. A famous example of this is the Yerkes-Dodson curve, which
charts the effect of stress on how well someone performs a given task. If we experience too little stress, or too much, our performance suffers. Like Goldilocks, we
want to get it just right. Similarly, our cognitive abilities seem to improve up to a
certain temperature, and then, as the temperature continues to rise, quickly
diminish. An early study suggested that the optimal temperature hovered around
seventy-two degrees Fahrenheit. A more recent review of the literature shows a
target of twenty-seven degrees Celsius, or roughly eighty-one degrees Fahrenheit.
(An important caveat, however, is that neither of these studies take humidity or
sunshine into account, two major factors when it comes to assessing the influence
of summer weather on behavior.)

Maybe best of all, blistering heat does give us a perfectly good reason to eat ice   10
cream: studies have shown again and again that blood glucose levels are tied to
cognitive performance and willpower. A bite of something frozen and sweet, boosting depleted glucose stores, might be just what a brain needs as the temperature
spikes.

Understanding the Reading

1. **Summarizing** List the changes in behavior Konnikova contends are affected by summer weather.
2. **Details** On what segment of the population did Uri Simonsohn conduct his research? Why did he choose to use this particular group of people as his research subjects?
3. **Recommendations** According to Konnikova, what type of food might help to raise glucose level and boost brain function in the summertime?

Analyzing the Writer's Technique

1. **Thesis** Identify Konnikova's thesis statement.
2. **Evidence** The author includes evidence consisting of data from the American Time Use Survey and the results of a research study by Harvard and the University of North Carolina at Chapel Hill. Why do you think she includes both sources of information?
3. **Vocabulary** Explain the meaning of each of the following words as it is used in the reading: *meticulous* (para. 1), *enervates* (1), *ambient* (4), *cognition* (4), and *heuristic* (4).

Thinking Critically about Cause and Effect

1. **Evaluation** Konnikova cites research conducted in the United States and Japan but none conducted in Europe. She also includes studies that were conducted on very specific segments of the population. How might broadening her research help strengthen the essay?
2. **Tone** How would you describe the tone of the essay? Use examples from the text to support your answer.
3. **Fact or Opinion** In paragraph 10, Konnikova states that "A bite of something frozen and sweet, boosting depleted glucose stores, might be just what a brain needs as the temperature spikes." Is Konnikova's statement fact or opinion? How do you know?
4. **Purpose** What does Konnikova hope to accomplish by writing this essay?

Responding to the Reading

1. **Discussion** The results of research study by Harvard and the University of North Carolina suggest that bad weather makes workers more productive. As a student, have you found this to be true? Why or why not? What about workers in general? Are there certain factors, for example type of work or type of worker, that might affect the veracity of this statement? What might those factors be?
2. **Journal** What is your favorite season of the year? Write a journal entry in which you explain why you favor this season over the other three.
3. **Essay** Write an essay in which you identify one or more surprising ways in which a person could improve his or her mental health.

Working Together

Using the information in Konnikova's essay, work with a partner to write an advertisement for ice cream as being the "magic bullet" for cognitive performance. Your ad must include both words and images. Try to capture the attention of your readers and leave them with a message they will remember. Be prepared to share your advertisement with the class.

CAUSE AND EFFECT COMBINED WITH OTHER PATTERNS   READING

The Mental Strain of Making Do with Less

Sendhil Mullainathan

Sendhil Mullainathan is a professor of economics at Harvard University. His areas of expertise include behavioral economics, development economics, and corporate finance. In addition to writing for professional journals and other media outlets, he, along with Eldar Shafir, coauthored a book titled *Scarcity: The New Science of Having Less and How It Defines Our Lives*. This essay originally appeared in *The New York Times*. **Before reading**, preview and make connections by thinking about how having too little (or too much) money affects you. **After reading**, highlight the reasons that doing without causes mental strain.

1   Diets don't just reduce weight, they can reduce mental capacity. In other words, dieting can make you dumber. Understanding why this is the case can illuminate a range of experiences, including something as far removed from voluntary calorie restriction as the ordeal of outright poverty.

2   Imagine that you are attending a late-afternoon meeting. Someone brings in a plate of cookies and places them on the other side of the conference table. Ten minutes later you realize you've processed only half of what has been said. Why? Only half of your mind was in the meeting. The other half was with the cookies: "Should I have one? I worked out yesterday. I deserve it. No, I should be good." That cookie threatened to strain your waistline. It succeeded in straining your mind.

3   This can happen even with no cookie in sight. Dieters conjure their own cookies: Psychologists find that dieters have spontaneous self-generated cravings at a much higher rate than nondieters (Hill). And these cravings are not the dieters' only distraction. Diets force tradeoffs: If you eat the cookie, should you skip the appetizer at dinner? But that restaurant looked so good!

4   Many diets also require constant calculations to determine calorie counts. All this clogs up the brain. Psychologists measure the impact of this clogging on various tasks: logical and spatial reasoning, self-control, problem solving, and absorption and retention of new information. Together these tasks measure "bandwidth," the resource that underlies all higher-order mental activity. Inevitably, dieters do worse than nondieters on all these tasks; they have less bandwidth.

One particularly clever study went further (Polivy et al.). It tested how dieters 5 and nondieters reacted to eating a chocolate bar. Even though the bar provided calories, eating it widened the bandwidth gap between dieters and nondieters. Nondieters ate and moved on, but dieters started wondering how to make up for the calories they had just ingested or, even more fundamentally, pondered, "Why did I eat the bar?"

In other words, diets do not just strain bandwidth because they leave us hun- 6 gry. They have psychological, not just physiological, effects. The basic insight extends well beyond the experience of calorie counting. Something similar happens whenever we make do with less, as when we feel that we have too little time, or too little money. Just as the cookie tugs at the dieter, a looming deadline preoccupies a busy person, and the prospect of a painful rent payment shatters the peace of the poor. Just as dieters constantly track food, the hyperbusy track each minute and the poor track each dollar.

As Professor Eldar Shafir at Princeton University and I argue in our new book, 7 *Scarcity: Why Having Too Little Means So Much*, a similar psychology of scarcity operates across these examples but with varying degrees of force. If a cookie can tax our mental resources, imagine how much more psychological impact other forms of scarcity can have. Take the case of poverty. In a paper published last month in *Science*, with Professors Anandi Mani at the University of Warwick and Jiaying Zhao at the University of British Columbia, Professor Shafir and I waded into politically charged territory. Some people argue that the poor make terrible choices and do so because they are inherently less capable. But our analysis of scarcity suggests a different perspective: Perhaps the poor are just as capable as everyone else. Perhaps the problem is not poor people but the mental strain that poverty imposes on anyone who must endure it.

One of our studies focused on Indian sugar cane farmers, who typically 8 feel themselves to be both poor and rich, depending on the season. They are paid once a year at harvest time. When the crop is sold, they are flush with cash. But the money runs out quickly, and by the time the next harvest arrives they are stretched thin: They are, for example, twenty times as likely to pawn an item before harvest as after it. Rather than compare poor and rich farmers, we compare each farmer to himself, when he is rich against when he is poor. This kind of comparison is important because it addresses valid concerns that differences in psychological tests merely reflect differences in culture or test familiarity.

We measured farmers' mental function—on what psychologists call fluid 9 intelligence and executive control—one month before and one month after harvest. And the effects were large: Preharvest I.Q., for example, was lower by about nine to ten points, which in a common descriptive classification is the distance between "average" and "superior" intelligence. To put that in perspective, a full night without sleep has a similar effect on I.Q.

Bandwidth scarcity has far-reaching consequences, whether we are talking 10 about poor farmers or affluent dieters. We all use bandwidth to make decisions at work, to resist the urge to yell at our children when they annoy us, or even to focus on a conversation during dinner or in a meeting. The diversity of these behaviors—combined with the size of the measurable effects—suggests a very different way to interpret the choices and behaviors of the poor. Just picture how distracting that cookie was, and multiply that experience by a factor of ten.

11   For dieters, bandwidth scarcity has one particularly important consequence, illustrated in one study that gave people a choice between fruit salad and cake (Shiv and Fedorikhin). Before choosing, half of the subjects had their bandwidth taxed: They were asked to remember a seven-digit number. The other half had a mentally less-demanding task: They were asked to remember a two-digit number. Those with less available bandwidth ate more cake: They were 50 percent more likely to choose cake than the others. There is a paradox here: Diets create mental conditions that make it hard to diet.

12   This may sound defeatist. But there are positive lessons for how to manage the different kinds of scarcity. The United States government, laudably, offers financial aid for low-income students to attend college. Qualifying for it, though, requires completing a densely packed ten-page booklet, mentally taxing for anyone. A one-page version would not only be simpler, but it would also recognize that the poor are short on bandwidth as well as cash. The same tactic—economizing on bandwidth—can be used in dieting. Take the Atkins diet, which effectively bans many foods, including bread and a lot of desserts. A ban is less complex than the tradeoffs and calorie accounting required by many other diets. While all diets require self-control, Atkins requires less thinking. This might explain its popularity, and even its effectiveness: A recent study shows that people persist longer with diets that require less thought (Mata et al.).

13   The same study had another interesting finding: It was the perceived complexity of a diet—not its actual complexity—that determined persistence. So keep this in mind the next time you're picking a diet to shed a few pounds. Try one that won't also shed a few I.Q. points.

Links

Hill, Andrew J. "The Psychology of Food Craving: Symposium on 'Molecular Mechanisms and Psychology of Food Intake.'" *Proceedings of the Nutrition Society*, vol. 66, no. 2, May 2007, pp. 277–85, doi:10.1017/S0029665107005502.

Mani, Anandi, et al. "Poverty Impedes Cognitive Function." *Science*, vol. 341, no. 6149, Aug. 2013, pp. 976–80, doi:10.1126/science.1238041.

Mata, Jutta, et al. "When Weight Management Lasts: Lower Perceived Rule Complexity Increases Adherence." *Appetite*, vol. 54, no. 1, Feb. 2010, pp. 37–43, doi:10.1016/j.appet.2009.09.004.

Mullainathan, Sendhil, and Eldar Shafir. *Scarcity: The New Science of Having Less and How It Defines Our Lives*. Picador Press, 2014.

Polivy, Janet, et al. "The Effect of Deprivation on Food Cravings and Eating Behavior in Restrained and Unrestrained Eaters." *International Journal of Eating Disorders*, vol. 38, no. 4, Dec. 2005, pp. 301–9, doi:10.1002/eat.20195.

Shiv, Baba, and Alexander Fedorikhin. "Heart and Mind in Conflict: The Interplay of Affect and Cognition in Consumer Decision Making." *Journal of Consumer Research*, vol. 26, no. 3, Dec. 1999, pp. 278–92, doi:10.1086/209563.

Understanding the Reading

1. **Definition** According to Sendhil Mullainathan, what is *bandwidth scarcity?*
2. **Comparison** What similarity does the author see in an Indian sugar cane farmer who has too little money and a person who has too little time?
3. **Conclusion** What does the author conclude about persistence in dieting?

Analyzing the Writer's Technique

1. **Thesis** Identify Mullainathan's thesis statement. Is it stated or implied?
2. **Sources** The author includes several references to scientific studies. How do these references affect your reaction to his analysis? How do they affect the overall tone of the selection?
3. **Vocabulary** Explain the meaning of each of the following words as it is used in the reading: *illuminate* (para. 1), *conjure* (3), *affluent* (10), *paradox* (11), and *laudably* (12).

Visualizing the Reading

Mullainathan identifies one overall effect that scarcity has on one's mental capacity: It decreases mental bandwidth. This decrease in bandwidth also has effects, both psychological and physiological. Use the chart below to summarize the effect of decreased bandwidth on dieters (scarcity of food). The first one is done for you.

Cause	Effects
Decreased bandwidth	It diminishes logical reasoning.

Thinking Critically about Cause and Effect

1. **Fact or Opinion** In paragraph 7, Mullainathan speaks for himself and a group of researchers when he says, "Perhaps the problem is not poor people but the mental strain that poverty imposes on anyone who must endure it." Is Mullainathan's statement fact or opinion? How do you know?
2. **Evidence** Mullainathan cites a number of sources that he regards as authorities on the topic. Based on the information in the references list, explain how you could determine whether the authors of those sources were in fact authorities. Going beyond the reference list, what other information could you use to determine whether a source was authoritative?
3. **Purpose and Audience** Why do you think the author wrote this essay? Who do you think he expected to read this selection, and how might his intended audience have influenced the decisions he made as a writer?

To learn more about evaluating sources, see Chapter 21.

4. **Tone** How would you describe the tone of the essay? Use examples from the text to support your answer.

Responding to the Reading

1. **Discussion** Do you agree with Mullainathan's thesis that having less of something affects the way you think and behave? Why or why not?
2. **Journal** What do you have too little of in your life? Write a journal entry in which you explain the scarcity that exists in your life and the effect(s) that this scarcity has on your behavior and your thinking.
3. **Letter** Using Mullainathan's research as your source, write a clever letter to your English professor explaining the reasons (at least three of them) why you have not turned in a major assignment that was due a week ago. Your letter should have a greeting, an introductory paragraph, at least three body paragraphs, a concluding paragraph, a closing, and a signature.

Working Together

In the final paragraph of "The Mental Strain of Making Do with Less," Mullainathan urges prospective dieters to choose a diet that will help them shed pounds, not I.Q. points. Working with a small group of your peers, research at least three popular diets and evaluate them according to Mullainathan's recommendations for a good diet plan. Once you have found the one that you think Mullainathan would most favorably endorse, create a thirty-second television infomercial for it. Be sure to focus on the psychological as well as the physiological effects of the plan. Be prepared to explain to the class the reason(s) Mullainathan would recommend the diet.

Apply Your Skills: Additional Essay Assignments

Write a cause-and-effect essay on one of the following topics, using what you learned about causal analysis in this chapter. Depending on your topic, you may need to conduct research.

For more on locating and documenting sources, see Chapters 22 and 23.

To Express Your Ideas

1. Write an essay explaining the causes of a "bad day" you recently experienced.
2. Suppose you or a friend or relative won a large cash prize in a national contest. Write an essay about the effects of winning the prize.

To Inform Your Reader

3. Young children frequently ask "*Why?*" Choose a *why* question you have been asked by a child or think of a *why* question you have always wondered about (Examples: Why is the sky blue? Why are sunsets red? Why do parrots learn to talk?). Write an essay answering your question. Your audience is young children.
4. Write an essay explaining how you coped with a stressful situation.
5. Write a memo to your supervisor at work explaining the effects of requiring employees to work overtime.

To Persuade Your Reader

6. Write a letter to the dean of academic affairs about a problem at your school. Discuss causes, effects, or both and propose a solution to the problem.

7. Write a letter to the editor of your local newspaper explaining the possible effects of a proposed change in your community and urging citizens to take action for or against it.

8. Write a letter to the sports editor of your city's newspaper. You are a fan of a professional sports team, and you just learned that the team has been sold to new owners who may move the team to a different city. In your letter, explain the effects on the city and the fans if the team moves away.

Cases Using Cause and Effect

9. Your psychology professor invites you to participate in a panel discussion on the psychology of humor. You are required to research this question: What makes a joke funny? Conduct research on the topic and write a paper summarizing your findings for the panel discussion.

10. A controversy has arisen concerning the use of campus computer networks. Students use the college computer system to send personal email as well as to complete course-related tasks, and some students have complained that the campus network is being used to post messages on social networking sites that defame the character of other students. In a letter to the student newspaper, either defend the students' right to use the campus computer network to post such messages or call for a policy that limits such use. Give reasons in support of your position.

SYNTHESIZING IDEAS   **DISCRIMINATION**

Both "Right Place, Wrong Face" (pp. 235–37) and "How Labels Like *Black* and *Working Class* Shape Your Identity" (pp. 466–68) deal with the effects of discrimination.

Analyzing the Readings

1. While both authors address discrimination, they use two very different approaches: One focuses on a single personal experience; the other describes two experiments in detail. They also use two different points of view. Explain the advantages and disadvantages of each approach and point of view. To what type(s) of audience does each appeal?

2. Write a journal entry exploring whether you feel the incidents of discrimination in these two essays are typical and representative of discrimination in U.S. society.

Essay Idea

Write an essay in which you describe the effects of discrimination on a particular person or group with which you are familiar. Define what discrimination the group faces and propose solutions. (You need not limit yourself to racial discrimination; you might discuss age, sex, weight, or workplace discrimination, for example.)

© Stuart Jenner/Shutterstock.com

19
Reading Arguments

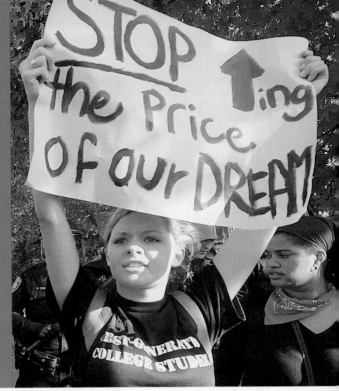

Mark Ralson/Getty

In this chapter you will learn to:

- recognize the basic parts of an argument

- identify three types of claims

- understand the key elements of support in an argument: reasons, evidence, emotional appeals, and refutations

- identify the structure of an argument

- read, analyze, and think critically about arguments

WRITING QUICK START The photograph on this page was taken on a state university campus in California where students were demonstrating against tuition increases. Although this sign is too small to list their reasons for opposing the increases, the students might say they cannot afford to pay more for tuition, that increased tuition is being used to build an expensive and unnecessary new sports stadium, and so forth.

Choose another issue that concerns many college students on your campus, statewide, or nationally. Write a paragraph that identifies the issue, takes a position on it, and offers reasons that others should accept your position.

The paragraph you just wrote in the Writing Quick Start is an example of a brief argument. An **argument** makes a claim and offers reasons and evidence in support of the claim. You make and evaluate arguments at home, work, and school every day. A friend may try to convince you to share an apartment, or your parents may urge you to save more money. In your college courses and in the workplace, you often need to judge claims and weigh the evidence presented in favor of arguments.

This chapter will show you how to read, analyze, and evaluate arguments, and you will learn strategies for writing effective argument essays.

- To prepare for a class discussion in a *sociology course,* you read and evaluate an essay proposing a solution to the gentrification of cities.

- In a *mass communication class,* your instructor assigns three articles that take different positions on the issue of whether journalists should provide graphic coverage of accidents and other human tragedies. Your instructor asks you to articulate your opinion on this issue.

- While working as a *purchasing agent* for a carpet manufacturer, you are listening to a sales pitch by a sales representative trying to convince you to purchase a new type of plastic wrapping used for shipping carpets.

What Are the Basic Parts of an Argument?

In everyday conversation, an argument can be a heated exchange of ideas between two people. College roommates might argue over who should clean the sink or who left the door unlocked the previous night. Colleagues in a company might argue over policies or procedures. However, there is a difference between an emotional, irrational argument and a rational, effective argument.

An effective argument is a logical, well-thought-out presentation of ideas that makes a claim about an issue and supports that claim with evidence. This does not mean that emotion has no place in an argument. In fact, many sound arguments combine emotion with logic.

Even a casual conversation can make a reasoned argument, as in the following.

Damon: I've been called for jury duty. I don't want to go. They treat jurors so badly!
Maria: Why? Everybody is supposed to do it.
Damon: Have you ever done it? I have. First of all, they force us to serve, whether we want to or not. And then they treat us like criminals. Two years ago I had to sit all day in a hot, crowded room with other jurors while the TV was blaring. I couldn't read, study, or even think! No wonder people will do anything to get out of it.

Damon is arguing that jurors are treated badly. He offers two reasons to support his claim and uses personal experience to support the second reason (that jurors are treated "like criminals"), which also serves as an emotional appeal.

An effective argument must clearly state an *issue,* make a *claim,* and offer *support.* In many cases an argument also recognizes or refutes (argues against) opposing viewpoints.

Graphic Organizer 19.1 shows the basic components of an argument. Note that unlike the graphic organizers in Part 3, the model graphic organizer that follows does not necessarily reflect the order in which the ideas are presented. Rather, it provides a visual representation of the components of an argument. The arguments you read may address opposing views before presenting reasons and evidence in support of the writer's claim, for example.

GRAPHIC ORGANIZER 19.1 The Basic Parts of an Argument Essay

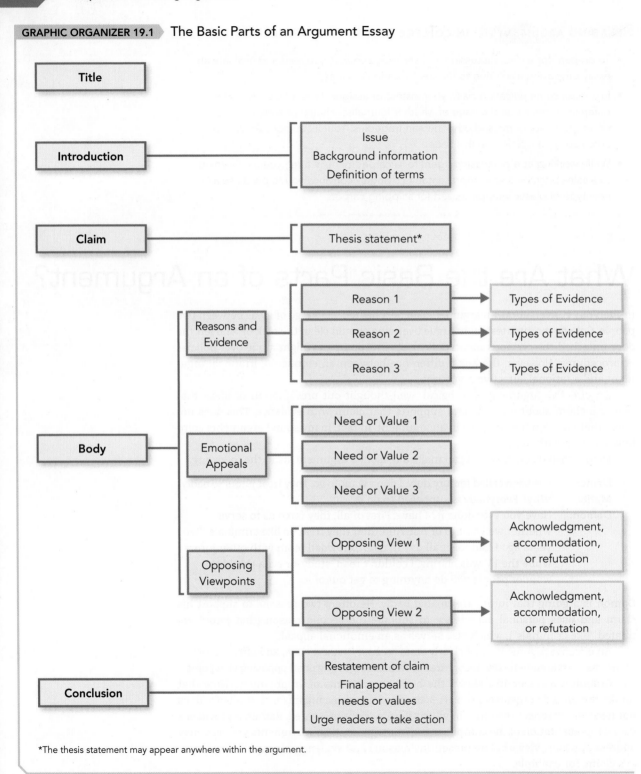

*The thesis statement may appear anywhere within the argument.

The Issue Is a Controversial Topic

An argument is concerned with an **issue**—a controversy, a problem, or an idea about which people hold different points of view. In the exchange between Damon and Maria, the issue is "fairness of jury duty."

The Claim Is the Writer's Point

The claim is the point the writer tries to prove, usually the writer's view on the issue. In Damon and Maria's conversation, the claim is that "jury duty is unfair." The claim often appears as part of the thesis statement in an argument essay. In some essays, however, it is implied rather than stated directly.

There are three types of claims.

1. **Claims of fact** are statements that can be proved or verified. Of course, readers are not likely to be interested in arguments about long-established claims of fact, such as how far the moon is from the earth; instead, claims of fact in argument essays focus on facts that are in dispute or not yet well established.

   Example   Excessive use of the Internet has shortened college students' attention spans.

2. **Claims of value** are statements that express an opinion or judgment about whether one thing or idea is better or more desirable than other things or ideas. Issues involving questions of right or wrong, acceptable or unacceptable, often lead to claims of value. Since claims of value are subjective, they cannot be proved definitively.

   Example   Doctor-assisted suicide is a violation of the Hippocratic oath and therefore should not be legalized.

3. **Claims of policy** are statements offering one or more solutions to a problem. Often the verbs *should, must,* or *ought* appear in the claim. Like claims of value, claims of policy cannot be proved definitively.

   Example   The motion picture industry must accept greater responsibility for the consequences of violent films.

EXERCISE 19.1   PREDICTING ISSUES AND CLAIMS

For each of the following titles, predict the issue and the claim the essay would make.

1. "The Drugs I Take Are None of Your Business"
2. "Watch That Leer and Stifle That Joke at the Water Cooler"
3. "Crazy in the Streets: A Call for Treatment of Street People"
4. "Penalize the Unwed Dad? Fat Chance"
5. "A Former Smoker Applauds New Laws"

EXERCISE 19.2 WRITING CLAIMS

On your own or with one or two classmates, choose two of the following issues and write two different types of claims for each. For example, if one statement is a claim of value, the other should be a claim of policy or a claim of fact.

1. Legalization or decriminalization of marijuana
2. Stem cell research
3. Music piracy and the Internet
4. Protection for endangered species
5. College course requirements

The Support Includes Reasons, Evidence, and Appeals

The support in an argument consists of the ideas and information intended to convince readers that the claim is sound or believable. In Damon and Maria's conversation, Damon provides two key pieces of support.

1. People are forced to serve.
2. Potential jurors are treated like criminals.

Three common types of support are *reasons*, *evidence*, and *emotional appeals*.

Reasons. A **reason** is a general statement that backs up a claim. It explains why the writer's view on an issue is reasonable or correct. However, reasons alone are not sufficient support for an argument. Each reason must be supported by evidence and is sometimes accompanied by emotional appeals.

Evidence. The **evidence** provided in an argument usually consists of facts, statistics, examples, expert opinion, and observations from personal experience.

Claim	Reading aloud to preschool and kindergarten children improves their chances of success in school.
Facts	First-grade children who were read to as preschoolers learned to read earlier than children who were not read to.
Statistics	A 1998 study by Robbins and Ehri demonstrated that reading aloud to children produced a 16 percent improvement in the children's ability to recognize words used in a story.
Expert Opinion	Pam Allyn, author of over sixty educational publications and well-known childhood literacy advocate urges parents to read aloud to their preschool children frequently.
Examples	Stories about unfamiliar places or activities increase a child's vocabulary. For example, reading a story about a farm to a child who lives in a city apartment will acquaint the child with such new terms as *barn*, *silo*, and *tractor*.
Personal Experience	When I read to my three-year-old son, I notice that he points to and tries to repeat words.

Emotional appeals. Emotional appeals evoke the **needs** or **values** that readers are likely to share.

- **Appealing to needs:** People have both physiological **needs** (food and drink, health, shelter, safety, sex) and psychological needs (a sense of belonging or accomplishment, self-esteem, recognition by others, self-fulfillment). Your friends and family, people who write letters to the editor, personnel directors who write job listings, and advertisers all appeal to needs, directly or indirectly.
- **Appealing to values:** A **value** is a principle or quality that is considered important, worthwhile, or desirable, such as freedom, justice, loyalty, friendship, patriotism, duty, and equality. Arguments often appeal to values that the writer assumes most readers will share.

The public service announcement below appeals to both viewers' needs and values. The picture of the cute dog appeals to viewers' needs by evoking the emotional attachment

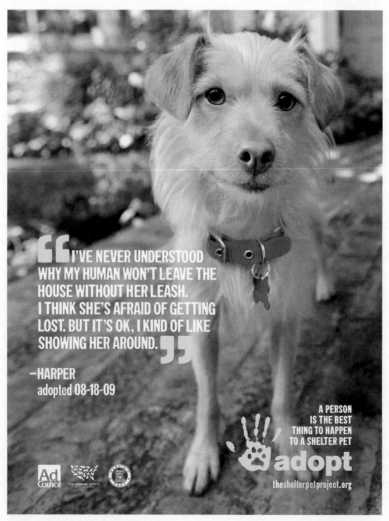

Ad Council/theshelterpetproject.org

to companion animals (either our own or other people's pets) that many of us share. The text, "a person is the best thing to happen to a shelter pet," also appeals to viewers' need to be needed. The ad appeals to values as well by evoking the principle that caring for others, including animals, is important.

EXERCISE 19.3 ▶ **PROVIDING REASONS AND EVIDENCE**

Imagine you are the director of a day care center justifying expenditures to the board of directors. Choose two of the following items, and write a paragraph providing reasons for the purchases and offering evidence to show how each item would benefit the children.

1. Tropical fish tank
2. Microwave
3. Read-along books with audio recordings
4. Set of Dr. Seuss books
5. One or more tablet computers

The Refutation Responds to Alternative Viewpoints

A **refutation**, also called a *rebuttal*, recognizes and argues against opposing viewpoints. Refutation involves finding a weakness in the opponent's argument by casting doubt on the opponent's reasons or by questioning the accuracy, relevance, and sufficiency of the opponent's evidence.

Suppose you want to argue that you deserve a raise at work (your claim). To support your claim, you will remind your supervisor of the contributions and improvements you have made, your length of employment, your conscientiousness, and your promptness. But you suspect that your supervisor may still turn you down, not because you don't deserve the raise but because other employees might demand a similar raise. By anticipating this potential objection, you can build into your argument the reasons that the objection is not valid. You may have more time invested with the company and have taken on more responsibilities than the other employees, for example.

If an opponent's argument is too strong to refute, most writers will acknowledge or accommodate the opposing viewpoint in some way. They **acknowledge** an opposing view simply by stating it. They **accommodate** an opposing view by noting that it has merit and modifying their position or finding a way of addressing it. In an argument opposing hunting, for example, a writer might simply *acknowledge* the view that hunting bans would cause a population explosion among deer. The writer might *accommodate* this opposing view by stating that if a population explosion were to occur, the problem could be solved by reintroducing natural predators into the area.

The following readings illustrate the components of effective argument essays. The first reading is annotated to point out those components. As you read the second essay, try to identify for yourself the claim and the supporting reasons, evidence, and emotional appeals Brian Palmer includes. Look, too, for places where Palmer refutes, accommodates, or acknowledges opposing views on tipping.

Are Zoos the Best Answer for Animals?

Suzanne Nguyen

Suzanne Nguyen was a first-year student when she wrote the following essay for her composition course.

Title: Identifies issue, suggests claim, and engages readers with a rhetorical question

Zoo-goers gather in the African mammals corner of the park to admire three new lionesses. These lionesses, the guide explains, were recently rescued from an illegal animal trading ring and efforts are underway to rehabilitate them for release back into the wild. A visitor raises his hand, asks the guide for more details on their rehabilitation program, and is told that staff members implement enrichment activities that promote the animals' natural behaviors. There is no evidence of enrichment activity in the lionesses' exhibit and the guide does not offer specific examples. The other visitors look impressed, nonetheless, and filter out. A little girl runs back to the glass in front of the lionesses and bangs against it repeatedly, trying to elicit a response from the animals. Instead of stopping her, her mother smiles and snaps a few photos of her daughter next to the glass. One of the lionesses ignores the girl and tries to sleep; one licks its nearly hairless, chapped paws continuously; the other paces anxiously within its small enclosure and swipes at the glass in front of the girl. Many people have witnessed similar scenes at zoos and have become aware of the animals' sometimes subpar living conditions and the lackluster rehabilitation programs these institutions devise. While they seemingly offer a fun, family-friendly way to view and learn more about animals and their habitats, zoos too often prioritize entertainment over animal care and rehabilitation and, thus, should be abolished in favor of true wildlife preservation organizations.

1

Introduction: Engages readers with an anecdote and appeals to readers' concerns for animals

Claim: Thesis statement makes claims of value and policy

As the example of the lionesses suggests, captivity in zoos can take a severe toll on the emotional well-being of animals. The more time that animals spend in captivity, the more they demonstrate abnormal, repetitive behaviors, such as excessive licking, de-feathering, pacing, head bobbing, and so on. These abnormal behaviors stem from depression, anxiety, and distress (Mason et al. 164). A captive animal must depend

2

Reason 1: Topic sentence states first reason. Transition links para. to anecdote in introduction. Information from two sources provides supporting evidence.

on its keepers to provide its mental, physical, and social needs. While many zoos try to design enrichment programs that discourage the adoption of abnormal repetitive behaviors, often entertainment is incorporated into these activities, and frequently, purposeful enrichment is replaced by gimmicks and animal shows that will attract more people to the institution. These ulterior motives often lead to animals' loss of sanity and do not accomplish their most important goal: preparing an animal for a life outside of captivity (Smith).

Frequently, zoos advertise their rehabilitation programs and supposed success stories as reasons for their existence, but many do not adequately support reintegration of rescued animals into the wild. A 2008 reintegration study conducted by researchers at the University of Exeter showed that only 30 percent of animals released from zoos into the wild survived. Why? One reason is that zoo animals are not taught to fear and avoid humans, but instead learn to tolerate their presence, making the animals easy targets of poachers and fearful residents (Jule et al. 356). Another reason is that animals who live most of their lives in captivity for the purpose of viewing pleasure, especially animals that do not spend enough time with members of their own species, do not have the opportunity to develop the learned behaviors that will help them survive in their natural habitats (Jule et al., 357). As a result, many of the animals not killed by humans die of starvation or become prey themselves. Essentially, the majority of animals released from zoos perish because they are left without survival tools in an unfamiliar place.

3

Perhaps the most important reason that zoos fail their animal inhabitants is that zoos prioritize their entertainment value to paying customers over their animals' welfare. Such institutions are more concerned with profits gained from tourist attractions (such as guided tours, food stands, souvenir shops, and other amusement park perks) than they are with pursuing the path to reintegration. The Columbus Zoo and Aquarium offers one such example. In an interview with the Columbus Zoo and Aquarium's director emeritus, Jack Hanna claims that conservation awareness is at the core of his work (McConnell). However, he spends most of the interview boasting about the zoo's revenue and monetary growth, rather than about wildlife conservation work. In photographs

4

Reason 2: Topic sentence states second reason. Statistics from a source provides evidence. Rhetorical question ("Why?") engages readers.

Reason 3: Topic sentence states third reason. Transition suggests organization from least to most important reason. Analysis of interview provides support.

published with the interview, Hanna is shown posing with a variety of wild animals at photo shoots—a practice condemned by many wildlife activists as animal exploitation. (See fig. 1.) In the past decade, this zoo has purchased a water park and golf course, and established additional food stands to accommodate the resulting influx of guests. While these changes have boosted park visitation and revenue, they do little to inspire confidence in their institutions' dedication to animal conservation.

Photo provides support

Fig. 1. Jack Hanna poses with actress and singer Debbie Gibson and a lemur at the 2012 Daytime Emmy Awards.

Many zoo enthusiasts and supporters praise the improvements and successes zoos have achieved since their early days and choose to focus on an optimistic future for their animals instead of dwelling on the shortcomings they have yet to correct. Without zoos, they argue, how will the general public be exposed to wildlife, learn to value wild animals, and become supporters of conservation efforts? The answer is easy: through organizations such as sanctuaries and wildlife reservations. Reserves, such as the Chincoteague National Wildlife Refuge in Virginia, and sanctuaries, such as Big Cat Rescue in Florida, use a variety of resources to educate the public and promote conservation awareness. The proliferation of social media makes these organizations highly

5

Conclusion: Acknowledges and rebuts opposing view, and offers alternative to zoos

Photo: AP Images, Todd Williamson/Invision/AP

accessible, and donations benefit their animals directly instead of being funneled into snack bars and bathrooms. Living conditions for animals in reserves and sanctuaries are spacious and resemble more closely their natural environments. Enrichment activities are for the animals' benefit only, and do not take the form of cheap tricks designed to attract an audience. True wildlife preservation organizations have proven that it is possible to educate the public while providing safe, spacious, clean living environments for endangered animals, all without the need for mass attraction gimmicks, so who needs zoos?

Concludes with another rhetorical question

Works Cited

Jule, Kristen R., et al. "The Effects of Captive Experience on Reintroduction Survival in Carnivores: A Review and Analysis." *Biological Conservation*, vol. 141, no. 2, Feb. 2008, pp. 355–63. *Science Direct*, www.sciencedirect.com/science/article/pii/S0006320707004417.

Mason, G., et al. "Why and How Should We Use Environmental Enrichment to Tackle Stereotypic Behaviour?" *Applied Animal Behaviour Science*, vol. 102, no. 3–4, Feb. 2007, pp. 163–88. *Science Direct*, www.sciencedirect.com/science/article/pii/S0168159106001900.

McConnell, Kitty. "Q&A: The Columbus Zoo's Jack Hanna." *Columbus CEO*, Feb. 2014, www.columbusceo.com/content/roundup/2014/02/jack-hanna.html?page=all.

Smith, Laura. "Zoos Drive Animals Crazy." *Slate*, 20 June 2014, www.slate.com/blogs/wild_things/2014/06/20/animal_madness_zoochosis_stereotypic_behavior_and_problems_with_zoos.html.

EXERCISE 19.4 **WRITING A SUMMARY**

Check your understanding of the argument by writing a summary of "Are Zoos the Best Answer for Animals?" (pp. 499–502).

EXERCISE 19.5 **DRAWING A GRAPHIC ORGANIZER**

Using Graphic Organizers 19.1 (p. 494) or 19.2 (p. 506) as a basis, draw a graphic organizer for "Are Zoos the Best Answer for Animals?"

READING

Tipping Is an Abomination

Brian Palmer

Brian Palmer is a journalist and regular columnist for the online magazine *Slate*, where he writes a column, "Explainer: Answers to Your Questions about the News," and for *The Washington Post*, where he writes a "How and Why" column. The following essay appeared in *Slate* in 2013.

Before Reading

1. **Preview:** Use the steps listed on page 28.
2. **Connect:** How much do you tip? If you ever worked in a restaurant, how did that affect your tipping?

While Reading Identify the reasons and evidence Palmer uses to support his claim. Check the reasons and evidence you identify against those listed in Graphic Organizer 19.2 (p. 506).

When wealthy Americans brought home the practice of tipping from their European vacations in the late 19th century, their countrymen considered it bribery. State legislatures quickly banned the practice. But restaurateurs, giddy at the prospect of passing labor costs directly to customers, eventually convinced Americans to accept tipping. 1

We had it right the first time. Tipping is a repugnant custom. It's bad for consumers and terrible for workers. It perpetuates racism. Tipping isn't even good for restaurants, because the legal morass surrounding gratuities results in scores of expensive lawsuits. 2

Tipping does not incentivize hard work. The factors that correlate most strongly to tip size have virtually nothing to do with the quality of service. Credit card tips are larger than cash tips. Large parties with sizable bills leave disproportionately small tips. We tip servers more if they tell us their names, touch us on the arm, or draw smiley faces on our checks. Quality of service has a laughably small impact on tip size. According to a 2000 study, a customer's assessment of the server's work only accounts for between 1 and 5 percent of the variation in tips at a restaurant. 3

Tipping also creates a racially charged feedback loop, based around the widely   4
held assumption—explored in an episode of *Louie*, in the Oscar-winning film *Crash*,
and elsewhere—that African-Americans tend to be subpar tippers. There seems to
be some truth to this stereotype: African-Americans, on average, tip 3 percentage
points less than white customers. The tipping gap between Hispanics and whites
is smaller, but still discernible in studies. This creates an excuse for restaurant
servers to prioritize the needs of certain ethnic groups over others.

Irrelevant or insidious factors will dominate the tipping equation until quality   5
of work becomes the main driver of tip size, but that's unlikely to happen. And tip
size isn't the real problem anyway. The real problem is that restaurants don't pay
their employees a living wage. The federal "tip credit" allows restaurants to pay
their tipped employees as little as $2.13 per hour, as long as tips make up the
shortfall—which turns a customer into a co-employer. Although federal and state
law requires restaurants to ensure that tips bring employees up to minimum wage,
few diners know that. (Hosts/hostesses, bussers, and food runners, who receive a
small fraction of the servers' tips, often fall short of minimum wage on some
nights.) The tip credit has turned the gratuity into a moral obligation, and we
ought to cut it from our statute books with a steak knife.

The only real beneficiary of the preposterously complicated tip credit is law-   6
yers. Imagine what it's like for a company running restaurants in multiple states.
There's no tip credit in some states, like California and Washington, where tipped
employees must be paid the full minimum wage. Hawaii allows the tip credit only
if the combined tip and cash wage surpass the statewide minimum hourly wage
by 50 cents. New York and Connecticut have different minimum wages for servers,
hotel employees, and bartenders.

Then you have to consider time that employees spend on activities not likely   7
to yield tips. Applebee's, for example, has suffered a series of legal setbacks in lawsuits brought by tipped employees seeking back pay for time spent cleaning toilets
and washing glassware.

The laws regarding tip sharing and tip pooling, which occur in virtually every   8
restaurant, are even more complicated. Federal law allows mandatory tip sharing,
but only among employees who customarily receive either direct or indirect tips.
That means servers, bussers, food runners, and hosts and hostesses can be
required to pool their tips with each other, but not with managers. Unfortunately,
the line between service and management is fuzzy in many restaurants, and differences between state laws further complicate matters. A California judge ordered
Starbucks to pay $105 million in 2008 for forcing 100,000 baristas to share tips with
supervisors. Last week, the New York Court of Appeals reached the opposite conclusion, ruling that New York law allows the arrangement. Chili's has also lost a
multimillion dollar judgment over tip sharing.

The entire mess is begging for some certainty and predictability. Restaurants   9
need a clear set of rules to follow. Servers should have a steadier income stream.
Hosts and bussers, who have relatively little interaction with customers, ought not
to be involved in tipping at all. Customers need more clarity as well, instead of
worrying at the end of a meal if the waiter, or your guests, approve of your 17 percent tip.

I'd like to propose a solution. First, ask your state and federal representatives to 10 abolish the tip credit, which would turn tips back into actual gratuities: something given free of obligation. Second, announce your tipping practice to your server as soon as you sit down. Virtually every other employee in America knows how much they'll be paid up front, and somehow the man who sells me shoes and the woman who does my dry cleaning still manage to provide adequate service. I have no doubt waiters and waitresses are the same. Finally, tip a flat, but reasonably generous, dollar amount per person in your party. Around 20 percent of Americans, mostly older people, tip a flat amount already, so it's not exactly revolutionary. A server's pay shouldn't be linked to whether or not you have room for dessert.

Analyze the Basic Components of an Argument

As you read an argument, consider the basic aspects of all persuasive writing: the author's credibility, purpose, and audience, and the reasons and evidence he or she provides as support.

For more on evaluation, see Chapters 3, 5, and 21.

Analyze the Writer's Credibility, Purpose, and Audience

Ask yourself: Why does the writer want to convince me of this? What does he or she stand to gain, if anything? Be particularly skeptical if a writer stands to profit personally from your acceptance of an argument.

Use the tone and the formality or informality of the author's language to figure out the type of audience—receptive, hostile, interested but skeptical—the author is expecting to address. How receptive the intended audience is expected to be might help you understand and evaluate the writer's argument. For example, writers addressing a receptive audience may not argue as carefully for their claims as would writers addressing a skeptical or hostile audience.

Consider also the writer's knowledge and trustworthiness. Ask yourself whether the writer has a thorough understanding of the issue, acknowledges opposing views and represents them fairly, and establishes common ground with readers by acknowledging their needs and values.

Assess the Writer's Reasons and Evidence

To assess the reasons and evidence, ask yourself questions like these: Does the writer offer enough reasons, do those reasons make sense, and are they relevant? Does the author supply enough evidence, and is that evidence accurate, complete, representative, up-to-date, and taken from reputable sources? Are the authorities cited experts in their field? Are sources cited formally or informally?

GRAPHIC ORGANIZER 19.2 The Structure of "Tipping Is an Abomination"

Title — "Tipping Is an Abomination"

Introduction — *Issue:* Tipping

Background information:
- Tipping was a European custom imported to the U.S. in the nineteenth century.
- It was initially seen as bribery and banned by state legislatures.
- It was embraced by restaurateurs to pass labor costs on to customer.

Claim — Tipping is objectionable.

Body

Reason: Tipping does not incentivize hard work because tip size and quality of service are almost unrelated.

Evidence:
- Service quality accounts for only 1%–5% of tip.
- Other nonrelevant factors influence tip size: payment type (credit card payers tip better), group size (small groups tip better), and intimacy gestures (wait staff who introduce themselves, touch patrons, draw smiley faces on checks get bigger tips).

Reason: The perceived tipping gap between ethnic groups creates stereotypical thinking that results in inequitable levels of service.

Evidence:
- Blacks tend to tip 3% less than whites.
- Hispanics tip more than blacks but less than whites.

Reason: "Tip credit" allows restaurants to underpay staff and turns tipping into a "moral obligation."

Evidence:
- Restaurants may pay as little as $2.13/hr.
- Nonwaitstaff may sometimes make less than minimum wage.

Opposing viewpoint: Lawyers benefit from variability in laws.

Evidence:
- Tip credit and minimum wage laws vary state by state.
- Tip sharing/pooling laws vary state by state.

Conclusion — Solution
- Restaurants: Make rules clear; abolish tipping credits.
- Employers: Give a steady income.
- Customers: Announce tipping policy in advance, tip a flat rate per person.

TABLE 19.1 ▶ Common Unfair Emotional Appeals

Unfair Emotional Appeal	Example
Name-calling: Using an emotionally loaded term to create a negative response	"That reporter is an *egotistical bully.*"
Ad hominem: Attacking the opponent rather than his or her position on the issue	"How could anyone who didn't fight in a war criticize the president's foreign policy?"
False authority: Quoting the opinions of celebrities or public figures about topics on which they are not experts	"According to singer Jennifer Hope, entitlement reform is America's most urgent economic problem."
Plain folks: Urging readers to accept an idea or take an action because it is suggested by someone who is just like they are	"Vote for me. I'm just a regular guy."
Appeal to pity: Arousing sympathy by telling hard-luck or excessively sentimental stories	"Latchkey children come home to an empty house or apartment, a can of soup, and a note on the refrigerator."
Bandwagon: Appealing to readers' desire to conform ("Everyone's doing it, so it must be right")	"It must be okay to exceed the speed limit, since so many people speed."

Assess the Emotional Appeals

Emotional appeals are a legitimate part of an argument. However, writers should not attempt to manipulate readers' emotions to distract them from the issue and the evidence. Table 19.1 presents some common unfair emotional appeals.

When assessing appeals to values, pay attention to the language the author uses and how he or she defines terms. Underline any terms that can have more than one meaning. Then read through the essay to see if the author defines these terms clearly and uses them consistently. Pay particular attention to words that appeal to values, and remember that not everyone considers the same principles or qualities important or agrees on their definition.

Evaluate Opposing Viewpoints

If an argument essay takes into account opposing viewpoints, you must evaluate how the writer presents them. Ask yourself the following questions.

- **Does the author state the opposing viewpoint clearly?**
- **Does the author present the opposing viewpoint fairly and completely?** That is, does the author treat the opposing viewpoint with respect or attempt to discredit or demean those holding the opposing view? Does the author present all the major parts of the opposing viewpoint or only those parts that he or she is able to refute?
- **Does the author clearly show why he or she considers the opposing viewpoint wrong or inappropriate?** Does the author apply sound logic? Does the author provide reasons and evidence?
- **Does the author acknowledge or accommodate points that cannot be refuted?**

Detect Faulty Reasoning

For more on reasoning, see Chapter 20, pp. 524–26.

In some arguments, a writer may commit **fallacies**, errors in reasoning or thinking. Fallacies can weaken an argument, undermine a writer's claim, and call into question the relevancy, believability, or consistency of supporting evidence. Table 19.2 provides a brief review of the most common types of faulty reasoning.

EXERCISE 19.6   **EVALUATING AN ARGUMENT**

Working in a group of two or three students, analyze one of the reading selections in this or the next chapter using the preceding guidelines.

TABLE 19.2   Common Fallacies

Fallacy	Example
Circular reasoning (begging the question): Using the claim (or part of it) as evidence by simply repeating the claim in different words	"*Cruel* and unusual experimentation on helpless animals is *inhumane.*"
Hasty generalization: Drawing a conclusion based on insufficient evidence or isolated examples.	"Based on the three chocolate cakes I just tasted, I can tell you that chocolate cake is overly sweet."
Sweeping generalization: Claiming that something applies to all situations or instances without exception	"All TV remotes are easy to use."
False analogy: Comparing two situations that are not sufficiently similar; just because two items or events are alike in some ways does not mean they are alike in all ways.	"A human body needs rest after strenuous work, and a car needs rest after a long trip."
Non sequitur ("It does not follow" in Latin): Joining two or more ideas when no logical relationship exists between them	"Because my sister is financially independent, she will make a good parent."
Red herring: Distracting readers from the main issue by raising an irrelevant point.	In an argument about banning advertisements for alcohol on TV, mentioning that some parents give their children sips of alcohol could distract readers from the main issue.
Post hoc fallacy ("after this, therefore because of this" in Latin): Assuming that event A caused event B simply because B followed A.	"Student enrollment fell dramatically this semester because of the recent appointment of the new college president." (Other factors may have contributed to the decline in enrollment.)
Either-or fallacy (false dilemma): Arguing that there are only two sides to an issue and that only one of them is correct.	"Marijuana must be *either* legalized *or* banned." (A third alternative is to legalize marijuana for medical use, such as to reduce nausea for those undergoing chemotherapy.)

HOW WRITERS READ	ARGUMENT
THE READING PROCESS	**STRATEGIES**
BEFORE READING	**Preview** the essay to get an overview of its content and organization. **Make connections** by thinking about what claim the author is likely to make, given the title, and how you feel about the issue.
WHILE READING	**Analyze and evaluate** the reading by answering the following questions. • What **issue** is the writer tackling? What is his or her **claim**, or position, on the issue? • What are the author's main **reasons**, and what **evidence** does the author offer? • What **needs** or **values** does the author seem to be appealing to? • Does the author present and respond to **opposing views** fairly?
AFTER READING	**Analyze and evaluate** the reading by answering the following questions. • What are the author's **credentials**? Many books and magazine articles will include a headnote or minibiography, or you can Google the author's name. (Be sure you're selecting the correct person, especially if the writer has a common name.) Is the writer an **authority** on the topic? • Does the author provide **compelling and relevant reasons** to support his or her claim? Is the evidence **accurate**, **complete**, **representative**, **up-to-date**, and **sufficient** to make the claim convincing? • Does the author use **emotional appeals fairly**? • Has the writer avoided the **common errors of reasoning**, such as *circular reasoning, sweeping generalizations*, or the *either-or fallacy*?

EXERCISE 19.7   **READING CRITICALLY**

Apply the questions in the "How Writers Read" box to the selection "Tipping Is an Abomination" (pp. 503–5).

Readings: Arguments in Action

READING

Trigger Happy

Jenny Jarvie

Jenny Jarvie is a freelance writer living in Atlanta. She has worked as a staff reporter for both the *Los Angeles Times* and the London *Sunday Telegraph*, and her work has also appeared in *Poetry* magazine. **Before reading**, preview and make connections by thinking about any course materials you may have found disturbing or offensive. Did your instructor warn you that the material might be controversial or upsetting? **While reading**, notice the many examples the author provides. What is the cumulative effect of all these examples?

The "trigger warning" has spread from blogs to college classes. Can it be stopped?   1

The headline above would, if some readers had their way, include a "trigger   2 warning"—a disclaimer to alert you that this article contains potentially traumatic subject matter. Such warnings, which are most commonly applied to discussions about rape, sexual abuse, and mental illness, have appeared on message boards since the early days of the Web. Some consider them an irksome tic of the blogosphere's most hypersensitive fringes, and yet they've spread from feminist forums and social media to sites as large as *The Huffington Post*. Now, the trigger warning is gaining momentum beyond the Internet—at some of the nation's most prestigious universities.

Last week, student leaders at the University of California, Santa Barbara,   3 passed a resolution urging officials to institute mandatory trigger warnings on class syllabi. Professors who present "content that may trigger the onset of symptoms of Post-Traumatic Stress Disorder" would be required to issue advance alerts and allow students to skip those classes. According to UCSB newspaper the *Daily Nexus*, Bailey Loverin, the student who sponsored the proposal, decided to push the issue after attending a class in which she "felt forced" to sit through a film that featured an "insinuation" of sexual assault and a graphic depiction of rape (Miller-Leonard). A victim of sexual abuse, she did not want to remain in the room, but she feared she would only draw attention to herself by walking out.

On college campuses across the country, a growing number of students are   4 demanding trigger warnings on class content. Many instructors are obliging with alerts in handouts and before presentations, even emailing notes of caution ahead of class. At Scripps College, lecturers give warnings before presenting a core curriculum class, the "Histories of the Present: Violence," although some have questioned the value of such alerts when students are still required to attend class. Oberlin College has published an official document on triggers,[1] advising faculty members to "be aware of racism, classism, sexism, heterosexism, cissexism,[2] ableism,[3] and other issues of privilege and oppression," to remove triggering material when it doesn't "directly" contribute to learning goals and "strongly consider" developing a policy to make "triggering material" optional. Chinua Achebe's *Things Fall Apart*, it states, is a novel that may "trigger readers who have experienced racism, colonialism, religious persecution, violence, suicide, and more." Warnings

---

[1]This document appears to have been removed from Oberlin's website.

[2]*Cissexism:* Prejudice against transgender people

[3]*Ableism:* Prejudice against the able bodied

have been proposed even for books long considered suitable material for high-schoolers: Last month, a Rutgers University sophomore suggested that an alert for F. Scott Fitzgerald's *The Great Gatsby* say, "TW: suicide, domestic abuse, and graphic violence" (Wythe).

What began as a way of moderating Internet forums for the vulnerable and mentally ill now threatens to define public discussion both online and off. The trigger warning signals not only the growing precautionary approach to words and ideas in the university, but a wider cultural hypersensitivity to harm and a paranoia about giving offense. And yet, for all the debate about the warnings on campuses and on the Internet, few are grappling with the ramifications for society as a whole.

Not everyone seems to agree on what the trigger warning is, let alone how it should be applied. Initially, trigger warnings were used in self-help and feminist forums to help readers who might have post-traumatic stress disorder to avoid graphic content that might cause painful memories, flashbacks, or panic attacks. Some Web sites, like Bodies Under Siege, a self-injury support message board, developed systems of adding abbreviated topic tags—from SI (self injury) to ED (eating disorders)—to particularly explicit posts. As the Internet grew, warnings became more popular, and critics began to question their use. In 2010, Susannah Breslin wrote in *True/Slant* that feminists were applying the term "like a Southern cook applies Pam cooking spray to an overused nonstick frying pan"—prompting *Feministing* to call her a "certifiable asshole" (Vanessa), and *Jezebel* to lament that the debate has "been totally clouded by ridiculous inflammatory rhetoric" (North).

The term only spread with the advent of social media. In 2012, *The Awl's* Choire Sicha argued that it had "lost all its meaning." Since then, alerts have been applied to topics as diverse as sex, pregnancy, addiction, bullying, suicide, sizeism, ableism, homophobia, transphobia, slut shaming, victim blaming, alcohol, blood, insects, small holes, and animals in wigs. Certain people, from rapper Chris Brown to sex columnist Dan Savage, have been dubbed "triggering." Some have called for trigger warnings for television shows such as *Scandal* and *Downton Abbey*. Even the *New Republic* has suggested the satirical news site *The Onion* carry trigger warnings.

At the end of last year, *Slate* declared 2013 the "Year of the Trigger Warning," noting that such alerts had become the target of humor. *Jezebel*, which does not issue trigger warnings, raised hackles in August by using the term as a headline joke: "It's Time To Talk About Bug Infestations [TRIGGER WARNING]." Such usage, one critic argued, amounted to "trivializing" such alerts and "trolling people who believe in them" (McUncool). And in Britain, Suzanne Moore, a feminist columnist for *The Guardian*, was taken to task when she put a trigger warning on her Twitter bio line, mocking those who followed her feeds only to claim offense. Some critics have ridiculed her in turn: "Trigger warning, @Suzanne_moore is talking again."

The backlash has not stopped the growth of trigger warnings, and now that they've entered university classrooms, it's only a matter of time before warnings are demanded for other grade levels. As students introduce them in college newspapers, promotional material for plays, even poetry slams, it's not inconceivable that they'll appear at the beginning of film screenings and at the entrance to art exhibits. Will newspapers start applying warnings to articles about rape, murder, and war? Could they even become a regular feature of speech? "I was walking down Main Street last night when—trigger warning—I saw an elderly woman get mugged."

The *Geek Feminism Wiki* states that trigger warnings should be used for   10
"graphic descriptions or extensive discussion" of abuse, torture, self-harm, suicide, eating disorders, body shaming, and even "psychologically realistic" depictions of *the mental state* of people suffering from those; it notes that some have gone further, arguing for warnings before the "depiction or discussion of any consensual sexual activity [and] of discriminatory attitudes or actions, such as sexism or racism" ("Trigger Warning"). The definition on the *Queer Dictionary Tumblr* is similar, but expands warnings even to discussion of *statistics* on hate crimes and self-harming.

As the list of trigger warning–worthy topics continues to grow, there's scant   11
research demonstrating how words "trigger" or how warnings might help. Most psychological research on PTSD suggests that, for those who have experienced trauma, "triggers" can be complex and unpredictable, appearing in many forms, from sounds to smells to weather conditions and times of the year. In this sense, anything can be a trigger—a musky cologne, a ditsy pop song, a footprint in the snow.

As a means of navigating the Internet, or setting the tone for academic   12
discussion, the trigger warning is unhelpful. Once we start imposing alerts on the basis of potential trauma, where do we stop? One of the problems with the concept of triggering—understanding words as devices that activate a mechanism or cause a situation—is it promotes a rigid, overly deterministic approach to language. There is no rational basis for applying warnings because there is no objective measure of words' potential harm. Of course, words can inspire intense reactions, but they have no intrinsic danger. Two people who have endured similarly painful experiences, from rape to war, can read the same material and respond in wholly different ways.

Issuing caution on the basis of potential harm or insult doesn't help us negoti-   13
ate our reactions; it makes our dealings with others more fraught. As Breslin pointed out, trigger warnings can have the opposite of their intended effect, luring in sensitive people (and perhaps connoisseurs of graphic content, too). More importantly, they reinforce the fear of words by depicting an ever-expanding number of articles and books as dangerous and requiring of regulation. By framing more public spaces, from the Internet to the college classroom, as full of infinite yet ill-defined hazards, trigger warnings encourage us to think of ourselves as more weak and fragile than we really are.

What's more, the fear of triggers risks narrowing what we're exposed to.   14
Raechel Tiffe, an assistant professor in Communication Arts and Sciences at Merrimack College, Massachusetts, described a lesson in which she thought everything had gone well, until a student approached her about a clip from the

television musical comedy *Glee* in which a student commits suicide. For Tiffe, who uses trigger warnings for sexual assault and rape, the incident was a "teaching moment"—not for the students, but for her to be more aware of the breadth of students' sensitivities.

As academics become more preoccupied with students' feelings of harm, they risk opening the door to a never-ending litany of requests. Last month [February 2014], students at Wellesley College protested a sculpture of a man in his underwear because, according to the Change.org petition, it was a source of "triggering thoughts regarding sexual assault" (Sethi). While the petition acknowledged the sculpture may not disturb everyone on campus, it insisted we share a "responsibility to pay attention to and attempt to answer the needs of all of our community members." Even after the artist explained that the figure was supposed to be sleepwalking, students continued to insist it be moved indoors.   15

Trigger warnings are presented as a gesture of empathy, but the irony is they lead only to more solipsism, an over-preoccupation with one's own feelings—much to the detriment of society as a whole. Structuring public life around the most fragile personal sensitivities will only restrict all of our horizons. Engaging with ideas involves risk, and slapping warnings on them only undermines the principle of intellectual exploration. We cannot anticipate every potential trigger—the world, like the Internet, is too large and unwieldy. But even if we could, why would we want to? Bending the world to accommodate our personal frailties does not help us overcome them.   16

Links

Breslin, Susannah. "Trigger Warnings Don't Work. Here's Why." *True/Slant*, 14 Aug. 2010, trueslant.com/susannahbreslin/2010/04/14/trigger-warnings-dont-work-hereswhy/.

McUncool (Joshua D.). "So . . . Is Jez Just Making Fun of Trigger Warnings Now?" *GroupThink*, 2 Aug. 2013, groupthink.kinja.com/so-is-jez-just-making-fun-of-trigger-warnings-now-1003465242.

Miller-Leonard, Tiana. "A.S. Senate Passes Proposal to Label Trauma-Provoking Academic Content." *Daily Nexus*, University of California, Santa Barbara, 27 Feb. 2014, dailynexus.com/2014-02-27/a-s-senate-passes-proposal-to-label-trauma-provoking-academic-content/.

North, Anna. "Trigger-Angry: The Politics of Internet Trigger Warnings." *Jezebel*, 14 Apr. 2010, jezebel.com/5516969/trigger-angry-the-politics-of-internet-trigger-warnings.

Sethi, Mira. "Mostly-Naked Man Appears on College Campus. Mostly-Idiotic Controversy Ensues." *New Republic*, 5 Feb. 2014, newrepublic.com/article/116493/tony-matellis-naked-man-statue-shouldnt-shock-wellesley-students.

Sicha, Choire. "When 'Trigger Warning' Lost All Its Meaning." *The Awl*, 30 May 2012, theawl.com/when-trigger-warning-lost-all-its-meaning-31acf9a2012d#.9sqc4fqed.

"Trigger Warning." *Geek Feminism Wiki*, geekfeminism.wikia.com/wiki/Trigger_warning. Accessed 1 Feb. 2017.

Vanessa. "Susannah Breslin: Certifiable Asshole." *Feministing*, 13, Apr. 2010, feministing.com/2010/04/13/susannah-breslin-certifiable-asshole/.

Wythe, Philip. "Trigger Warnings Needed in the Classroom." *The Daily Targum*, 18 Feb. 2014, www.dailytargum.com/article/2014/02/trigger-warnings-needed-in-classroom.

Understanding the Reading

1. **Summary** Summarize Jarvie's opinion regarding trigger warnings and quote one or more sentences from the essay that concisely express her opinion.
2. **Evidence** What type of evidence does Jarvie rely on primarily?
3. **Reasons** List at least four reasons that Jarvie provides to support the idea that trigger warnings may have many negative unintended consequences.
4. **Vocabulary** Explain the meaning of each of the following words as it is used in the reading: *irksome* (para. 2), *ramifications* (5), *inflammatory* (6), *deterministic* (12), *solipsism* (16), *unwieldy* (16).

Analyzing the Writer's Technique

1. **Issue and Claim** What specific issue does Jarvie discuss? What type(s) of claim does she make?
2. **Audience** Who is Jarvie's intended audience?
3. **Examples** What is *The Onion* (para. 7)? Why would the author argue that the mere idea that *The Onion* should carry trigger warnings is ridiculous?
4. **Appeals** To which values does Jarvie appeal in "Trigger Happy"?
5. **Unfair Appeals** In paragraph 6, Jarvie notes that the Web site *Feministing* has labeled Susannah Breslin a "certifiable asshole." What type of unfair emotional appeal has *Feministing* resorted to?

Visualizing the Reading

Create a graphic organizer for the argument in this essay.

Thinking Critically about Argument

1. **Tone** Describe Jarvie's tone. Highlight key words or phrases that reveal this tone.
2. **Sources** Discuss the author's use of sources. Has she consulted a reasonable number of sources? How does her engagement (or lack of engagement) with sources reflect on her credibility?
3. **Connotation** What connotation does the phrase "trigger warning" have in Jarvie's article?
4. **Refutation and Opposing Viewpoints** Does Jarvie present opposing viewpoints? If so, how does she present them and what is her response to them?

Responding to the Reading

1. **Reaction** What is your response to Jarvie's examples and her argument? Do you find yourself basically agreeing with her or basically disagreeing with her about trigger warnings?
2. **Rebuttal** Imagine that you must respond to (rebut) Jarvie's article. List at least three reasons why trigger warnings may be valuable in the college classroom.

3. **Journal** In your journal, compile a list (either brief or extensive) of the topics that you find disturbing. Would you be sufficiently disturbed by any of these topics to ask your instructors to warn you about assignments that discuss these topics?

4. **Essay** Write an essay in which you examine a controversial movement, such as Occupy Wall Street or Black Lives Matter. How does this movement make society aware of important information? Are the movement's goals clear, and how do its members go about achieving these goals? How effective is the movement in terms of getting its message across? How might the movement become more successful in terms of opening people's minds and bringing about social change?

READING

The Trigger Warning Myth

Aaron R. Hanlon

Aaron R. Hanlon teaches English at Colby College in Waterville, Maine. He is also an advisor for Georgetown University's Modern Language Association/Mellon Foundation "Connected Academics" project. He is particularly interested in science writing and how people organize knowledge. He has contributed articles to *The Atlantic*, *Salon*, *The Chronicle of Higher Education*, and *New Republic*, from which the following article is taken. It was written in response to an article that had appeared previously in *New Republic*. **Before reading**, preview the reading and make connections by thinking about whether students should be warned about classes that may contain objectionable content. **While reading**, notice how the author recognizes and responds to alternative views.

I never imagined becoming a defender of trigger warnings. This is the first time 1 I've written (or spoken) the word "microaggressions" in recent memory. I have been and continue to be a proponent of the idea that the best way to handle wrong-headedness and hate speech is to address these with corrective speech, to present ideas, rationales, and evidence that overwhelm ignorance and bigotry with a blistering light. Accordingly, when vulgar or emotionally challenging material is part of the subject matter I'm responsible for teaching, or serves an otherwise specific pedagogical purpose, I'm not shy about it.

Here's a brief and by no means exhaustive list of things I've carefully selected 2 for college syllabi and deliberately taught in college courses: a pair of poems about impotence and premature ejaculation; a satire about slaughtering human infants and feeding them to "persons of quality and fortune"; a poem that uses the c-word twice in a mere 33 lines, and describes King Charles II in coitus with his mistress with the phrase "his dull, graceless bollocks hang an arse"; a novel in which a wealthy man gets his maid to marry him by kidnapping her and continually cornering her with unwanted sexual advances; a graphic history of the torture methods and other cruelties done to African slaves leading up to the Haitian Revolution;

a poem written in the voice of a male domestic servant and attempted rapist contacting his victim from prison.

The items on this list, and many others on my syllabi, could be censored by those on the left, since many of them could be triggering for students suffering from post-traumatic stress. In another context, however, they could be censored from the right, by people who tell the sexual assault survivor balking at a literary rape scene to "grow up," then turn around and oppose the teaching of sexually explicit material because it's "trash."   3

In both cases, censoring this material is a bad idea, and providing context is the best avenue for explaining why. If you read the list above and wonder how or why any serious person would teach such material at a prestigious (and expensive) college, consider the authors behind the list. It includes works by major, canonical authors from antiquity to the eighteenth century, such as Ovid, Aphra Behn, Jonathan Swift, John Wilmot, Samuel Richardson, and Lady Mary Wortley Montagu. It also includes the historian C. L. R. James's *The Black Jacobins*, one of the definitive histories of the Haitian Revolution. Simply put, leaving this stuff off the syllabus because it might be triggering is not an option.   4

As I've explained elsewhere (Hanlon) however, I use trigger warnings in the classroom as a way of preparing students who may be suffering from post-traumatic stress disorder while also easing the entire class into a discussion of the material. The thinking behind the idea that trigger warnings are a form of censorship is fundamentally illogical: Those who offer warnings, at our professional discretion, about potentially triggering material are doing so precisely because we're about to teach it! If we used trigger warnings to say, effectively, "don't read this, it's scary," then there'd be no need to warn in the first place; we'd just leave the material off the syllabus.   5

It's true that giving a warning runs the risk of students avoiding or disengaging with the material out of fear of being triggered (in my three years of teaching, students have come to office hours to discuss sensitive material, but not one has left class or failed to turn in an assignment because of a trigger warning). If a student disengages, however, a professor still can (and should) follow up in a couple of ways. One is to have a private conversation with the student about the material, away from the pressures of the classroom; another is to take the student's response as an occasion to check in with the student and make sure they have access to campus mental health resources. Few of the media voices catastrophizing trigger warnings seem to understand that professors' interactions with students in the classroom and during office hours are some of the most important ways of catching mental health (or time management, or substance abuse) issues in our students that may need further attention. While the purpose of trigger warnings is not to screen for mental health problems, being attuned to how students are reacting to material, and prompting them to react to the hard stuff, can help us catch problems before they become real catastrophes.   6

For those of you who are imagining scores of students using professors' trigger warnings disingenuously, as a way to get out of class or a reading assignment, this isn't (for most of us) our first rodeo. Students use deception all the time, but an   7 office hours summons is really all we need to determine whether the student might need help from a mental health professional or was just trying to game the system. In most cases, however, when you warn students that something might be emotionally challenging or explicit, most of them do exactly what we do when someone tells us to watch out for something lurid: They become even more curious.

While a miniscule number of colleges and universities have gone so far as 8 to codify trigger warnings for professors, most trigger warnings exist as a pedagogical choice that professors make in situations over which we exercise considerable control. (And have existed as such for much longer than the present debate suggests: While "trigger warning" was not part of my vocabulary as an undergraduate, introductory comments like "we're going to spend some time today on lynching images, so prepare yourselves for graphic and difficult material" were indeed.)

Professors give warnings of all sorts that, when not explicitly entangled in the 9 national politics of political correctness, amount less to coddling than to minimizing chances of disengagement with material. "Block off more time this weekend than you usually do, since the reading for Monday is a particularly long one," for instance, is a reasonable way of reducing the number of students who show up unprepared by issuing a warning. "Today we're discussing a poem about rape, so be prepared for some graphic discussion, and come to office hours if you have things to say about the poem that you're not comfortable expressing in class," meanwhile, is a similarly reasonable way of relieving the immediate pressure to perform in class, which stresses out so many students.

Those of us who occasionally use trigger warnings are not as naïve as we're 10 made out to be; we understand that there is no magical warning that will assuage all anxieties and protect students from all traumas, nor is there a boilerplate trigger warning or trigger warning policy that professors can be reasonably expected to follow formulaically. Rather, trigger warnings are, in practice, just one of a set of tools that professors use with varying degrees of formality to negotiate the give-and-take of classroom interactions. If you take away the media hysteria surrounding trigger warnings, you're left with a mode of conversational priming that we all use: "You might want to sit down for this"; "I'm not sure how to say this, but. . . ." It's hardly anti-intellectual or emotionally damaging to anticipate that other people may react to traumatic material with negative emotions, particularly if they suffer from PTSD; it's human to engage others with empathy. It's also human to have emotional responses to life and literature, responses that may come before, but in no way preclude, a dispassionate analysis of a text or situation.

I'm not blind to the problems with trigger warnings and hyperbolic political cor- 11 rectness. The examples Lukianoff and Haidt cite [in their article in *The Atlantic*, "The Coddling of the American Mind" (September 2015)] are alarming: Harvard law students asking professors not to use the word "violate"; Brandeis students calling even critical acknowledgment of racial stereotypes of Asian-Americans "microaggressions"; Northwestern professor Laura Kipnis being accused of Title IX violations for an article she wrote for *The Chronicle of Higher Education*. But I'm not convinced that we can lay these problems—and by extension, adverse developments in the mental health of college students—at the feet of trigger warnings.

The backlash against trigger warnings is part of a larger iteration of back-   12
lash against political correctness, which tells us something important about
where the public thinks the power lies. People on the margins may get press for
tweeting things like "kill all white men" (Soave) and the occasional professor
may be undeservedly shamed or ousted for running afoul of students with certain P.C. language expectations. In both scenarios, however, the heart of the
matter is who holds the authority to choose the best (or worst) course of action.
The P.C. backlash and the trigger warning backlash hold a common fallacy:
They see pushback from the margins and mistake it for threats to the most
institutionally powerful.

"Kill all white people" is a despicable sentiment, but in practice it's not white   13
people who face the gravest threats of being gunned down by those who wield the
authority to do so. Similarly, students can demand trigger warnings or sensitivity
trainings, but students remain more vulnerable to institutional power than the
professors who assign their grades or the administrators who adjudicate their mis-
steps. And if there exist situations in which professors really are "terrified" by our
students, and students are actually lapsing into mental distress because we're too
afraid to cross them, then the problem is much bigger than trigger warnings. The
problem is mistrusting the experience and authority of professors in our roles as
teachers and intellectual caregivers. If we can lose our jobs either for teaching
traumatic material or for failing to warn students adequately about it, what's really
happening here isn't that we're ruining students by coddling them; we're losing
the authority we rely on to be sensitive to students' anxieties without giving in to
them, to use techniques like trigger warnings judiciously without being forced to
use them in some generalized and codified way.

The trigger warning problem isn't actually a trigger warning problem; it's what   14
happens when the messy business of teaching and learning, and the complex
challenges to students' mental well-being, become flashpoints in the culture wars.
The effect of this entanglement is an exaggerated impression of trigger warnings
that draws on the most extreme examples, a tactic that mirrors and plays into . . .
partisan politics. Of course, some may consider trigger warnings to be "bad for
American democracy" and call on universities to "officially and strongly discourage" them. Instead of seeking new sources of outrage around trigger warnings,
though, we should understand more thoroughly why this particular pedagogical
choice, one of so many, has become a national wedge issue. That trigger warnings
are rare, and may be of occasional benefit to professors like me who employ them,
is too inconvenient a reality for those who are busy waging war on political
correctness.

Links

Hanlon, Aaron R. "My Students Need Trigger Warnings, and Professors Do, Too." *New Republic*,
    17 May 2015, newrepublic.com/article/121820/my-students-need-trigger-warnings-and
    -professors-do-too.
Soave, Robby. "Diversity Officer Who Tweeted 'Kill All White Men' Deserves Ridicule, Not
    Arrest." *Reason.com*, "Hit & Run," 19 May 2015, 11:06 a.m., reason.com/blog/2015/05/19/
    diversity-officer-who-tweeted-kill-all-w.

Understanding the Reading

1. **Definitions** According to Hanlon, what is a "trigger warning"? What is a "micro-aggression"?
2. **Reasons** What is the key reason that Hanlon believes trigger warnings are useful and necessary?
3. **Key Point** Ultimately, what does the author see as the main, underlying reason that instructors should offer trigger warnings?
4. **Vocabulary** Explain the meaning of each of the following words as it is used in the reading: *proponent* (para. 1), *canonical* (4), *catastrophizing* (6), *disingenuous* (7), *preclude* (10), *hyperbolic* (11).

Analyzing the Writer's Technique

1. **Claim** What is Hanlon's claim? Is it a claim of fact, value, or policy? Explain how you know.
2. **Appeals** What types of emotional appeals does Hanlon make? Identify the needs and values to which he appeals.
3. **Evidence** What types of evidence does Hanlon use to support his claim?
4. **Reasoning** Are there any errors in reasoning? If so, explain.

Visualizing the Reading

Create a graphic organizer for the argument in this essay.

Thinking Critically about Argument

1. **Opposing Viewpoints** Does the author discuss, acknowledge, or rebut opposing viewpoints? If so, how? Are these opposing viewpoints representative of the arguments against trigger warnings?
2. **The Larger Issue** According to "The Trigger Warning Myth," why is the "trigger warning problem" much larger than the debate over whether students should be warned when they are about to encounter potentially sensitive or offensive material?
3. **Tone** Describe Hanlon's tone. Highlight several words or phrases that reveal this tone.
4. **Denotation and Connotation** What are the denotation and connotation of "political correctness" (para. 12)?

Responding to the Reading

1. **Reaction** What is your reaction to Hanlon's article? How, if at all, did Hanlon's article affect your thinking or change your opinion?
2. **Discussion** The author blames "partisan politics" (para. 14) for the controversy that has erupted over trigger warnings. Bring to class several examples of issues that are politically divisive. What are the various sides of each issue, what types of claims (fact, value, policy) are made for each? What criteria would you use to judge which side of the argument you favor?

3. **Journal** What is the most disturbing thing you have read or viewed in recent weeks or months? What was the subject matter, and why did it disturb you? What benefit (if any) did you receive from reading or viewing that material?

4. **Essay** Write an essay in which you argue for or against one of the following (all of which may be subject to trigger warnings): sex education in high schools, dissection of animals in biology courses, corporal punishment in schools, laws that require people to use a bathroom on the basis of their birth gender.

SYNTHESIZING IDEAS   TRIGGER WARNINGS

"Trigger Happy" (pp. 509–13) and "The Trigger Warning Myth" (pp. 515–18) take opposing viewpoints on the topic of trigger warnings.

Analyzing the Readings

1. Having read these two essays, which do you think more effectively acknowledges and accommodates opposing viewpoints, and how does this affect whether you accept the writer's position?

2. One of the essays is heavily researched, while the other relies heavily on the author's own experience as a college professor. Which makes a more compelling case? Which do you think would provide a better model for your own writing, and why?

Essay Idea

Write an essay in which you refute either Jarvie's or Hanlon's main claim. Use evidence from the essays in this chapter to support your position, and conduct research as needed.

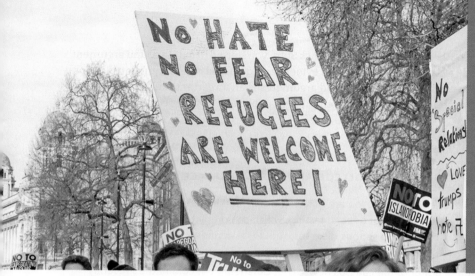

Jane Campbell/Alamy Stock Photo

WRITING QUICK START   The poster shown here makes an implicit argument based on a widely shared opinion that America is (and should continue to be) a "melting pot." Write a brief argument (one to three paragraphs) that either agrees or disagrees with this opinion about the acceptance of new immigrants. Assume that you are writing to an audience that shares your view.

Be sure to:

- identify the issue
- state your position on the issue (your claim)
- offer at least one reason why your position is reasonable and should be accepted

Then, alone or with one or two classmates, revise your argument to appeal to an audience that disagrees with your position. How would your original argument have to change? What needs or values could you use to appeal to this new group? What ideas and attitudes would you need to acknowledge, accommodate, or refute?

In this chapter you will learn to:

- understand the purpose and function of argument essays
- use graphic organizers to visualize argument essays
- integrate argument into an essay
- plan, organize, draft, revise, and edit essays using argument

521

By following the steps in the Writing Quick Start, you started to build a **sound argument**: you made a claim, supported it with evidence, and refuted or accommodated opposing views. The ability to construct sound arguments is an important skill. Many political, social, and economic issues are resolved through public and private debate that involves argument.

USING ARGUMENT   **IN COLLEGE AND THE WORKPLACE**

- In a *health science course*, you are part of a group working on an argument essay claiming that the results of genetic testing, which can predict a person's likelihood of contracting serious diseases, should be confidential.

- As a student member of the *affirmative action committee* on campus, you write a letter to the editor of the campus newspaper defending the committee's recently drafted affirmative action plan for minorities and women.

- As a *lawyer* representing a client whose hand was seriously injured on the job, you argue to a jury that your client deserves compensation for the work-related injury.

What Are the Characteristics of Argument Essays?

In developing an argument essay, you need to select a controversial issue, make a clear and specific claim that takes a position on the issue, and give reasons and evidence to support the claim that will appeal to your audience. In addition, you should follow a logical line of reasoning; use emotional appeals appropriately; and acknowledge, accommodate, or refute opposing views.

Arguments Focus on Arguable, Narrowly Defined Issues

An **issue** is a controversy, problem, or idea about which people disagree. When writing an argument, be sure your issue is controversial. For example, *free public education* is an important topic, but it is not particularly controversial. (Most people would be in favor of at least some forms of free public education.) Instead, you might choose the issue *free public college education* or *universal, free prekindergarten education*.

Depending on the issue you choose and the audience you write for, a clear definition of the issue may be required. In addition, your readers may need background information. For example, in an argument about awarding organ transplants, you may need to give general readers information about the scarcity of organ donors versus the number of people who need transplants.

The issue you choose should be narrow enough to deal with adequately in an essay-length argument. For a brief (three- to five-page) essay on organ transplants, for instance, you could narrow your focus to transplants of a particular organ or to one aspect of the issue, such as who should and should not receive them. A narrow focus will allow you to offer more detailed reasons and evidence and respond to opposing viewpoints more effectively.

EXERCISE 20.1	LIMITING A TOPIC AND PROVIDING BACKGROUND INFORMATION

Working alone or with a partner, choose two of the following issues. For each issue, use two or more strategies from Chapter 4 to limit the topic. Then list the background information readers might need to understand the issue.

1. Moral implications of state-operated lotteries
2. Computer networks and the right to privacy
3. Speech codes on campus
4. Religious symbols on public property
5. Mandatory drug testing

An Argumentative Thesis Makes a Specific Claim and May Call for Action

To build a convincing argument, you need to make a clear and specific **claim**, one that states your position on the issue clearly. To keep your essay on track, state your claim in a strong thesis in the introduction or early in the essay. As you gain experience in writing arguments, you can experiment with placing your thesis later in the essay.

For more on types of claims, see Chapter 19, p. 495.

Here are a few examples of how general claims can be narrowed to create clear and specific thesis statements.

Statewide   regulate the child-to-caregiver ratio and the qualifications of workers
More standards are needed to ~~protect children~~ in day care centers.

                   testing of cosmetics and skin-care products on
The ~~use of~~ animals ~~in testing~~ should be prohibited.

While all arguments make and support a claim, some, like claims of policy, also call for a specific action to be taken. An essay opposing human cloning might urge readers to voice their opposition in letters to congressional representatives, for example.

Be careful about the way you state your claim. In most cases, avoid an absolute statement that applies to all cases; your claim will be more convincing if you qualify, or limit, it by using words and phrases like *probably, often,* and *for the most part.* For example, the claim, "Single-sex educational institutions are *always* more beneficial to girls than coeducational schools are," could easily be undermined by a critic by citing a single exception. If you qualify your claim—"Single-sex educational institutions are *often* more beneficial to girls than are coeducational schools"—then an exception would not necessarily weaken the argument.

Choose two of the following issues. For each issue, write two thesis statements—one that makes a claim and contains a qualifying term and another that makes a claim and calls for action.

1. Controlling pornography on the Internet
2. Limiting immigration
3. Limiting political campaign spending
4. Restricting testing of beauty products on animals
5. Promoting competitive sports for young children

Effective Arguments Are Logical

The reasons and evidence in an argument should follow a logical line of reasoning. The most common types of reasoning are induction and deduction (see Figure 20.1). **Inductive reasoning** begins with evidence and moves to a conclusion; **deductive reasoning** begins with a commonly accepted statement, or *premise*, and shows how a conclusion follows from it. You can use one or both types of reasoning to keep your argument on a logical path.

FIGURE 20.1   Inductive and Deductive Reasoning

Inductive reasoning.   Think of inductive reasoning as a process of coming to a conclusion after observing a number of examples. For example, suppose you go shopping for a new pair of sneakers. You try on one style of Nikes. The sneakers don't fit, so you try a different style. That style doesn't fit either. You try two more styles, neither of which fits. Finally, because of your experience, you draw the conclusion that either you need to remeasure your feet or Nike does not make a sneaker that fits your feet.

When you use inductive reasoning, you make an *inference,* or guess, about the cases that you have not experienced. In doing so, you run the risk of being wrong. When building an inductive argument, be aware of some potential pitfalls.

- Consider as many possible explanations for the cases you observe as you can. In the sneaker example, perhaps the salesperson brought you the wrong size.
- Be sure that you have *sufficient* and *typical* evidence on which to base your conclusion. Suppose you learn that one professional athlete was involved in a driving-while-intoxicated incident and that another left the scene of an auto accident. If, from these limited observations, you conclude that professional athletes are irresponsible, your reasoning is faulty because these two cases are not typical of all professional athletes and not sufficient for drawing a conclusion. (If you draw a conclusion based on insufficient evidence or isolated examples, you have committed the fallacy of **hasty generalization**. You may also have committed a **sweeping generalization**—drawing a conclusion that applies to all cases without exception.)

For more on common fallacies, see Chapter 19, Table 19.2, p. 508.

When you use inductive reasoning in an argument essay, the conclusion becomes the claim, and the specific pieces of evidence support your reasons for making the claim. For example, suppose you make a claim that Pat's Used Cars is an unethical business from which you should not buy a car. As support you might offer the following reasons and evidence.

Reason	Pat's Used Cars does not provide accurate information about its products.
Evidence	My sister's car had its odometer reading tampered with. My best friend bought a car whose chassis had been damaged, yet the salesperson claimed the car had never been in an accident.

Reason	Pat's Used Cars doesn't honor its commitments to customers.
Evidence	The dealership refused to honor the ninety-day guarantee for a car I purchased there. A local newspaper recently featured Pat's in a report on businesses that fail to honor guarantees.

Deductive reasoning.   Deductive reasoning begins with **premises**—statements that are generally accepted as true. Once the premises are accepted as true, the conclusion must also be true. The most common deductive argument is a **syllogism**, which consists of two premises and a conclusion.

When you use deductive reasoning, putting your argument in the form of a syllogism will help you write your claim, then organize and evaluate your reasons and

Syllogism	Definition	Example
Major Premise	A general statement about a group	Food containing dairy products makes you ill.
Minor Premise	A statement about an individual belonging to that group	Frozen yogurt contains dairy products.
Conclusion	Logically necessary result	Frozen yogurt will make you ill.

evidence. Suppose you want to support the claim that state funding for Kids First, an early childhood program, should remain intact. You might use the following syllogism to build your argument.

Major Premise	State-funded early childhood programs have increased the readiness of at-risk children to attend school.
Minor Premise	Kids First is a popular early childhood program in our state, where it has had many positive effects.
Conclusion	Kids First is likely to increase the readiness of at-risk children to attend school.

Your thesis statement would be, "Because early childhood programs are likely to increase the readiness of at-risk children to attend school, state funding for Kids First should be continued." Your evidence would be information demonstrating the effectiveness of Kids First, such as the school performance of at-risk students who attended Kids First versus the school performance of at-risk students who did not and the cost of remedial education in later years versus the cost of Kids First.

Effective Arguments Depend on Careful Audience Analysis

For more on audience analysis, see Chapter 4, pp. 103–5.

To build a convincing argument, you need to know your audience. Analyze your audience to determine their education, background, and experience. Then also consider the following:

1. How familiar your audience is with the issue
2. Whether your audience is likely to agree, be neutral or wavering, or disagree with your claim

This knowledge will help you select reasons and evidence and choose appeals that your readers will find compelling.

Agreeing audiences. Agreeing audiences are the easiest to write for because they already accept your claim. When you write for an audience that is likely to agree with your claim, the focus is usually on urging readers to take a specific action. Instead of having to offer large amounts of facts and statistics as evidence, you can concentrate on reinforcing your shared viewpoint and building emotional ties with your audience. By doing so, you encourage readers to act on their beliefs.

Neutral or wavering audiences.   Although they may be somewhat familiar with the issue, neutral or wavering audiences may have questions about, misunderstandings about, or no interest in the issue. When writing for this type of audience, emphasize the importance of the issue or shared values, and clear up misunderstandings readers may have. Your goals are to make readers care about the issue, establish yourself as a knowledgeable and trustworthy writer, and present solid evidence in support of your claim.

Disagreeing audiences.   The most challenging audience is one that holds viewpoints in opposition to yours. The people in such an audience may have strong feelings about the issue and may distrust you because you don't share their views. In writing for a disagreeing audience, your goal is not necessarily to persuade readers to adopt your position but rather to convince them to consider your views. To be persuasive, you must follow a logical line of reasoning. Rather than stating your claim early in the essay, it may be more effective to build slowly to your thesis, first establishing **common ground**, a basis of trust and goodwill, by mentioning shared values, interests, concerns, and experiences.

EXERCISE 20.3   DEVELOPING AN ARGUMENT FOR A SPECIFIC AUDIENCE

Choose one of the following claims and discuss how you would argue in support of it for (a) an agreeing audience, (b) a neutral or wavering audience, and (c) a disagreeing audience.

1. Public school sex education classes should be mandatory because they help students make important decisions about their lives.
2. Portraying the effects of violent crime realistically on television may help reduce the crime rate.
3. Children who spend too much time interacting with a computer may fail to learn how to interact with people.

Effective Arguments Present Reasons and Evidence Readers Will Find Compelling

In developing an argument, you need to provide reasons for making a claim. A **reason** is a general statement that backs up a claim; it answers the question, "Why do I have this opinion about this issue?" You also need to support each reason with evidence.

Suppose you want to argue that high school uniforms should be mandatory. You might give three reasons.

1. Uniforms reduce clothing costs for parents.
2. They help eliminate distractions in the classroom.
3. They reduce peer pressure.

You would need to support each of your reasons with some combination of evidence, such as facts, statistics, examples, personal experience, or expert testimony. Carefully linking your evidence to reasons helps your readers see how the evidence supports your claim.

Choose reasons and evidence that will appeal to your audience. In the argument about mandatory school uniforms, high school students would probably not be impressed by your first reason, but they might be persuaded by your second and third reasons if you cite evidence that appeals to them, such as personal anecdotes from other students. For an audience of parents, facts and statistics about reduced clothing costs and improved academic performance would be appealing types of evidence.

Effective Arguments Appeal to Readers' Needs and Values

For more on emotional appeals, see Chapter 19, p. 497.

Although an effective argument relies mainly on credible evidence and logical reasoning, **emotional appeals** to readers' needs and values can help support and strengthen a sound argument. **Needs** can be biological or psychological (food and drink, sex, a sense of belonging, self-esteem). **Values** are principles or qualities that readers consider important, worthwhile, or desirable. Examples include honesty, loyalty, privacy, and patriotism.

Effective Arguments Recognize Alternative Views

Recognizing and countering alternative perspectives on an issue forces you to think hard about your claims. When you anticipate readers' objections, you may find reasons to adjust your reasoning and develop a stronger argument. Readers will also be more willing to consider your claim if you take their point of view into account.

You can recognize alternative views in an argument by acknowledging, accommodating, or refuting them.

1. **Acknowledge** an alternative viewpoint by admitting that it exists and showing that you have considered it.

   Example Readers opposed to mandatory high school uniforms may argue that a uniform requirement will not eliminate peer pressure because students will use other objects to gain status, such as backpacks, iPads, and smartphones. You could acknowledge this viewpoint by admitting that there is no way to stop teenagers from finding ways to compete for status.

2. **Accommodate** an alternative viewpoint by acknowledging readers' concerns, accepting some of them, and incorporating them into your argument.

   Example In arguing for mandatory high school uniforms, you might accommodate readers' view that uniforms will not eliminate peer pressure by arguing only that uniforms will eliminate one major and expensive means of competing for status.

3. **Refute** an opposing viewpoint by demonstrating the weakness of the opponent's argument.

Example   To refute the viewpoint that uniforms force students to give up their personal style, you can argue that the majority of students' lives are spent outside school, where uniforms are not necessary and where each student is free to express his or her individuality.

EXERCISE 20.4 ▶ IDENTIFYING OPPOSING VIEWPOINTS

For the three claims listed in Exercise 20.3, identify opposing viewpoints and consider how you could acknowledge, accommodate, or refute them.

The following readings demonstrate the techniques for writing effective argument essays discussed above. The first reading is annotated to point out how Tyler Huckabee makes an arguable claim, provides reasons and evidence in support of his claim, and responds to alternative views. As you read the second essay, pay particular attention to the logic of the argument and the strategies William Safire uses to appeal to his audience.

READING

The Problem with Saying "All Lives Matter"

Tyler Huckabee

Title: Clearly identifies the issue

Tyler Huckabee is currently the managing editor of *Relevant* magazine, where this essay originally appeared. Previously, he has run a homeless shelter in Chicago and taught literature to high school students.

Before Reading

1. **Preview:** Use the steps listed on page 28.
2. **Connect:** What have you heard about the Black Lives Matter movement?

While Reading Study the annotations that accompany the reading to discover how the essay illustrates the characteristics of effective cause-and-effect writing.

Imagine that you wake up late one night to the sound of your home being burglarized. Through the crack in your bedroom door, you see several figures hauling out your television, computers, and nice china to their getaway car parked outside.   1

Thinking quickly, you dial 911 on your iPhone.   2

"911, what's your emergency?"   3

"Help!" you whisper. "My home is being robbed!"   4

"Stay where you are, Miss," the other voice assures you. "We'll look into it."   5

"Thank you," you whisper. "My address is—"   6

"Woah, ma'am," the voice on the other end says. "Why are you bringing addresses into this?"   7

Introduction: Begins with a hypothetical case that makes an appeal to shared values.

"What?" you say. "My home is being robbed! Aren't you going to come and stop   8
them?"

"Well, I don't know why you need to make this about *your home*, ma'am," the   9
operator says. "All houses matter."

There is a difference between something being true and something being rele-   10
vant. In the above conversation with an imaginary 911 operator, what he was saying
was very true. All houses do matter. But at the moment, it wasn't relevant. It wasn't
even helpful. All things considered, it was downright dangerous. You had an actual
crisis going on at your house—that's why your house mattered. While the operator
was lecturing you on how important all houses are, bandits were trying to figure out
whether they could get all your stuff in one load or if they'd have to make two trips.

It's the same error people who respond to "Black Lives Matter" with "All Lives   11
Matter" are making. It's not that what they're saying isn't true. It's just that it's
unhelpful. It's an attempt to erase an actual crisis under the guise of being fair.
And by continuing to use "All Lives Matter" to drown out the cry of "Black Lives
Matter," the real problems the movement is trying to address are being ignored.
"All Lives Matter" is useless. It is destructive. It is hurtful. We need to stop saying it.

Black Lives Matter

Following the death of Trayvon Martin, three women named Alicia Garza, Patrisse   12
Cullors, and Opal Tometi began tweeting #blacklivesmatter. What started as a
hashtag became an ethos, and has transcended Twitter to become a true movement, one of the most forceful and ubiquitous of this young century. It has no official leaders or spokespeople. There's no agreed-upon charter. The only thing being
insisted upon is the value of black lives. As the Web site has it, it's "a call to action
and a response to the virulent anti-black racism that permeates our society."

The idea that racism remains a very real reality in America is contentious, but   13
it shouldn't be. The studies proving anti-black racism remains a common, if not
foundational, reality of everyday American life are too numerous to cite in one article, so we'll go with just a few.

We might as well begin with preschool: Black children make up 18 percent of   14
America's preschool population, but represent nearly half of all out-of-school sus-
pensions ("Data Snapshot"). This treatment continues into the court system,
where black children are eighteen times more likely to be tried as adults than
their white peers (Goff et al. 526). It also extends to the job market, in which white
college graduates are twice as likely to land a job as black college graduates (Jones
and Schmitt 2). We haven't even gotten to the justice system yet, in which black
people are given 20 percent longer sentences than white people are for the same
crimes ("Report " 12). (For more on institutional racism, go read every word of
Ta-Nehisi Coates's "The Black Family in the Age of Mass Incarceration," *The Atlantic*,
Oct. 2015.)

Context Matters

These numbers could go on and on, but even if they didn't, it should be clear that   15
the people who say racism remains a real, frequent reality in America have their
heads on straight. They are not making this up. Those who suggest that black

Transition: Shows how opening anecdote relates to claim that saying "all lives matter" is irrelevant and unhelpful

Thesis: Makes a claim of fact in dispute or not yet proven, value (that saying "all lives matter" is unacceptable), and policy (offers a solution)

Topic sentence: Provides background about Black Lives Matter campaign

Topic sentence: Is supported by facts and statistics in paras. 14–15 (note that in a more academic style, the evidence would appear in same para. as topic sentence)

Author provides multiple sources to support assertion (these were provided as links; in-text citations have been added)

Topic sentence: Reason 1, refers back to statistics in para. 14

people are imagining racism aren't just devaluing someone else's experience—they're ignoring the plain facts. It was in the face of these facts that #blacklivesmatter sprung, but now anywhere that cry is heard, you can be sure that someone else will come along with the rebuttal: "All Lives Matter."

It certainly *sounds* reasonable enough, and in most contexts, it would be. But the thing is, when people say "Black Lives Matter," they are acknowledging an important context that involves several centuries of slavery, civil rights, mass incarceration, and brutality. It's specifically highlighting the value of black lives because, historically, this country has often ignored that value.

> 16   **Topic sentence:** Acknowledges and refutes alternative view; the transition highlights coming refutation

The problem with "All Lives Matter" is that it *ignores context*. It's like the 911 operator who doesn't understand why you're worried about your own house or, as *The Daily Beast*'s Arthur Chu says, like someone who "runs through a cancer fundraiser screaming 'THERE ARE OTHER DISEASES TOO'" (@arthur_affect). The context of "Black Lives Matter" is not that other lives don't. The context of "Black Lives Matter" is that the value of black lives remains under assault in the United States.

> 17   **Topic sentence:** Reason 2, continues refutation
>
> Uses analogy from 1st section and analogy from a source as support

Love Matters

When a parent says, "I love my son," you don't say, "What about your daughter? Don't you love *all* your children?" When the president says "God bless America," we don't say, "Shouldn't God bless *all* countries?" And when a person says "Black Lives Matter," we should not say "All Lives Matter." It is an attempt to diminish the ongoing reality of white supremacy in America. It's effectively a way of demeaning other people's stories, like Job's friends who kept trying to point to the bigger picture of God's ultimate plan instead of truly listening to Job and mourning his grief. It is rude. It is hurtful. It is dismissive. And it has to stop.

> 18
>
> **Topic sentence:** Reason 3

And yes, some people who associate themselves with #blacklivesmatter have called for police deaths. Some Christians have called for abortion clinics to be bombed. The cries of a few fringe groups do not invalidate an entire movement, thank God.

> 19   Acknowledges opposing view
>
> Offers refutation

So when you hear the words "Black Lives Matter," don't be so quick to assume it's a judgment about white lives. Instead, see "Black Lives Matter" for what it is: a rallying cry to make a difference and take down the unjust status quo that holds racial equality at bay in America. You can join the movement and commit yourself to the social and economic liberation of black people, or you can choose to stand on the sidelines. But don't silence the cry with the words "All Lives Matter." This is an emergency.

> 20   **Conclusion:** Summarizes key points and calls readers to action

Links

@arthur_affect (Arthur Chu). "Do people who change #*BlackLivesMatter* to #*AllLivesMatter* run thru a cancer fundraiser going 'THERE ARE OTHER DISEASES TOO.'" *Twitter*, 27 Nov. 2014, 9:03 a.m., twitter.com/arthur_affect/status/538015166634680320.

"Data Snapshot: School Discipline." *Civil Rights Data Collection*, U.S. Department of Education, Office for Civil Rights, March 2014, ocrdata.ed.gov/Downloads/CRDC-School-Discipline-Snapshot.pdf.

Goff, Phillip Atiba, et al. "The Essence of Innocence: Consequences of Dehumanizing Black Children." *Journal of Personality and Social Psychology*, vol. 106, no. 4, 2014, pp. 526-45.

Jones, Janelle, and John Schmitt. "A College Degree Is No Guarantee." Center for Economic and Policy Research, May 2014, cepr.net/documents/black-coll-grads-2014-05.pdf.

"Report of The Sentencing Project to the United Nations Human Rights Committee." The Sentencing Project, Aug. 2013, sentencingproject.org/wp-content/uploads/2015/12/Race-and-Justice-Shadow-Report-ICCPR.pdf.

Visualize an Argument Essay: Create a Graphic Organizer

For more on creating a graphic organizer, see pp. 35–37.

Graphic Organizer 20.1 (p. 534) will help you analyze arguments as well as plan those that you write. Unlike the graphic organizers in Part 3, this organizer does not necessarily show the order in which an argument is presented. Some arguments, for example, may begin with a claim, whereas others may start with evidence or opposing viewpoints. In addition, not every element will appear in every argument. Thus you will likely need to adapt this organizer to fit the essays you analyze and write.

READING ▶

Abolish the Penny

William Safire

William Safire (1929–2009), a former speechwriter for President Richard Nixon and Vice President Spiro Agnew, was a longtime political columnist for *The New York Times*. He was also well known for "On Language," his column on grammar, usage, and etymology in the weekly *New York Times Magazine*, and he published many books, including novels, collections of his columns, and *Before the Fall: An Inside View of the Pre-Watergate White House* (2005). He won the Pulitzer Prize for commentary in 1978. **Before reading**, preview and make connections by thinking about how useful pennies are to you: Do you use them when you pay for something in cash or just toss them into a penny jar? **While reading**, notice how Safire gives his own reasons for abolishing the penny and anticipates possible counterarguments.

1   Because my staunch support of the war in Iraq has generated such overwhelming reader enthusiasm, it's time to reestablish my contrarian credentials. (Besides, I need a break.) Here's a crusade sure to infuriate the vast majority of penny-pinching traditionalists: The time has come to abolish the outdated, almost worthless, bothersome, and wasteful penny. Even President Lincoln, who distrusted the notion of paper money because he thought he would have to sign each greenback, would be ashamed to have his face on this specious specie.

2   That's because you can't buy anything with a penny any more. Penny candy? Not for sale at the five-and-dime (which is now a "dollar store"). Penny-ante poker? Pass the buck. Any vending machine? Put a penny in and it will sound an alarm. There is no escaping economic history: it takes nearly a dime today to buy what a penny bought back in 1950. Despite this, the U.S. Mint keeps churning out a billion pennies a month.

3   Where do they go? Two-thirds of them immediately drop out of circulation, into piggy banks or—as the *Times*'s John Tierney noted five years ago—behind chair cushions or at the back of sock drawers next to your old tin-foil ball. Quarters and dimes circulate; pennies disappear because they are literally more trouble than they are worth. The

remaining 300 million or so—that's 10 million shiny new useless items punched out every day by government workers who could be more usefully employed tracking counterfeiters—go toward driving retailers crazy. They cost more in employee-hours—to wait for buyers to fish them out, then to count, pack up, and take them to the bank—than it would cost to toss them out. That's why you see "penny cups" next to every cash register; they save the seller time and the buyer the inconvenience of lugging around loose change that tears holes in pockets and now sets off alarms at every frisking place.

Why is the U.S. among the last of the industrialized nations to abolish the peskiest little bits of coinage? At the G-8 summit next week, the Brits and the French—even the French!—who dumped their low-denomination coins thirty years ago, will be laughing at our senseless jingling. The penny-pinching horde argues: those $9.98 price tags save the consumer 2 cents because if the penny was abolished, merchants would "round up" to the nearest dollar. That's pound-foolish: the idea behind the 98-cent (and I can't even find a cent symbol on my keyboard any more) price is to fool you into thinking that "it's less than 10 bucks." In truth, merchants would round down to $9.95, saving the consumer billions of paper dollars over the next century.   4

What's really behind America's clinging to the pesky penny? Nostalgia cannot be the answer; if we can give up the barbershop shave with its steam towels, we can give up anything. The answer, I think, has to do with zinc, which is what pennies are mostly made of; light copper plating turns them into red cents. The powerful, outsourcing zinc lobby—financed by Canadian mines as well as Alaskan—entices front groups to whip up a frenzy of save-the-penny mail to Congress when coin reform is proposed.   5

But when the penny is abolished, the nickel will boom. And what is a nickel made of? No, not the metallic element nickel; our 5-cent coin is mainly composed of copper. And where is most of America's copper mined? Arizona. If Senator John McCain would get off President Bush's back long enough to serve the economic interests of his Arizona constituents, we'd get some long-overdue coin reform.   6

What about Lincoln, who has had a century-long run on the penny? He's still honored on the $5 bill, and will be as long as the dollar sign remains above the 4 on keyboards. If this threatens coin reformers with the loss of Illinois votes, put Abe on the dime and bump F.D.R.[1]   7

What frazzled pollsters, surly op-ed[2] pages, snarling cable talkfests, and issue-starved candidates for office need is a fresh source of hot-eyed national polarization. Coin reform can close the controversy gap and fill the vitriol void. Get out those bumper stickers: Abolish the penny!   8

---

[1] F.D.R.: Franklin Delano Roosevelt, U.S. president from 1933 to 1945.
[2] op-ed: the opinion section of the newspaper that is opposite the editorial page.

EXERCISE 20.5   CREATING A GRAPHIC ORGANIZER

Using Graphic Organizer 20.1 or 20.2 as a basis, draw a graphic organizer for "The Problem with Saying 'All Lives Matter'" (pp. 529–31).

GRAPHIC ORGANIZER 20.1   The Basic Structure of an Argument Essay

Title

Introduction	Issue Background Definition of terms

Claim	Thesis statement*

Body

Reasons and Evidence
- Reason 1 → Types of Evidence
- Reason 2 → Types of Evidence
- Reason 3 → Types of Evidence

Emotional Appeals
- Need or Value 1
- Need or Value 2
- Need or Value 3

Opposing Viewpoints
- Opposing View 1 → Acknowledgment, accommodation, or refutation
- Opposing View 2 → Acknowledgment, accommodation, or refutation

Conclusion	Restatement of claim Final appeal to needs or values Urging readers to take action

*The thesis statement may appear anywhere within the argument.

GRAPHIC ORGANIZER 20.2 The Structure of "Abolish the Penny"

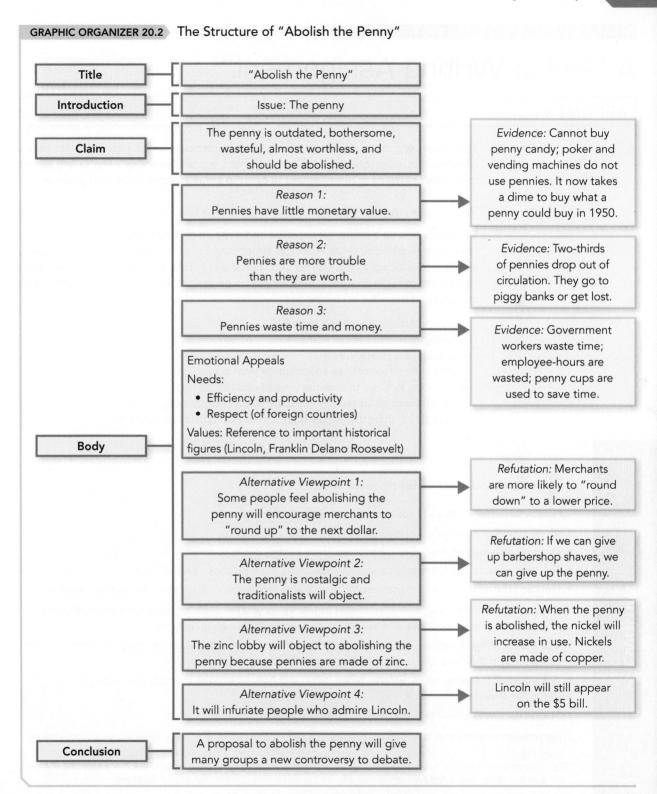

Title — "Abolish the Penny"

Introduction — Issue: The penny

Claim — The penny is outdated, bothersome, wasteful, almost worthless, and should be abolished.

Evidence: Cannot buy penny candy; poker and vending machines do not use pennies. It now takes a dime to buy what a penny could buy in 1950.

Reason 1: Pennies have little monetary value.

Reason 2: Pennies are more trouble than they are worth.

Evidence: Two-thirds of pennies drop out of circulation. They go to piggy banks or get lost.

Reason 3: Pennies waste time and money.

Evidence: Government workers waste time; employee-hours are wasted; penny cups are used to save time.

Emotional Appeals
Needs:
- Efficiency and productivity
- Respect (of foreign countries)

Values: Reference to important historical figures (Lincoln, Franklin Delano Roosevelt)

Body

Alternative Viewpoint 1: Some people feel abolishing the penny will encourage merchants to "round up" to the next dollar.

Refutation: Merchants are more likely to "round down" to a lower price.

Alternative Viewpoint 2: The penny is nostalgic and traditionalists will object.

Refutation: If we can give up barbershop shaves, we can give up the penny.

Alternative Viewpoint 3: The zinc lobby will object to abolishing the penny because pennies are made of zinc.

Refutation: When the penny is abolished, the nickel will increase in use. Nickels are made of copper.

Alternative Viewpoint 4: It will infuriate people who admire Lincoln.

Lincoln will still appear on the $5 bill.

Conclusion — A proposal to abolish the penny will give many groups a new controversy to debate.

PREWRITING   DRAFTING   **REVISING**   EDITING & PROOFREADING

A Guided Writing Assignment*

ARGUMENT

The following guide will lead you through the process of writing an argument essay. Although the assignment focuses on argument, you will probably need to use one or more other patterns of development in order to argue effectively for your position.

Your Essay Assignment

Take a position on a controversial issue and write an argument that makes a narrowly focused arguable claim, offers logical supporting reasons and evidence that readers will find convincing, appeals to readers' needs and values, and takes alternative viewpoints into consideration. You may choose an issue that interests you or your readers or select one from the list below.

- buying American-made products
- racial quotas in college admissions policies
- paying college athletes
- providing a free college education to prisoners
- donating kidneys to save the lives of others
- an environmental problem or issue in your community
- mandatory drug testing for high school extracurricular activities

1 Choose and narrow a controversial issue.

To check whether an issue is controversial, try the following.

- Alone or with a classmate, brainstorm different sides of the issue.
- Draw an idea map of the issue, connecting ideas as they come to mind.
- Talk with experts; ask them to give you a sense of the main positions on the issue.
- Google your issue plus *discussion forum*. Then scan a forum to get a sense of the posters' positions.

The issues listed in the assignment, and most of the issues you are likely to come up with initially, are very broad. Try one or more of these strategies to **narrow** the issue you have chosen.

- **Use a branching diagram.** Type your issue at the left, and then subdivide the topic into three or more categories on the right. Choose a subcategory and repeat the process.
- **Ask yourself** the *who*, *what*, *where*, *when*, *why*, and *how* **questions** to focus your attention on particular aspects of the issue.
- **Freewrite** about your topic, and then read what you've written.

Then consider whether you can explore your topic fully in a brief essay. If not, try another narrowing strategy.

*The writing process is *recursive*; that is, you may find yourself revising as you draft or prewriting as you revise. This is especially true when writing on a computer. Your writing process may also differ from project to project or from that of your classmates.

2 Consider your purpose, audience, and point of view.

Use **idea-generating strategies** appropriate to your learning style to generate evidence and appeals that will be most effective given your readers. For example, verbal learners may wish to freewrite, pragmatic learners may wish to create lists or columns, and social learners may wish to discuss these issues with classmates.

Purpose: What do you want to **happen as a result** of your argument?
. . . change readers' minds?
. . . make readers more certain of their beliefs?
. . . inspire readers to take a specific action?

Audience: Who are your **readers**, and how best can you **tailor your argument** to them? **Ask yourself questions like these:**

- What do my readers **already know** about the issue?
- Is my audience likely to **agree, be neutral/wavering**, or **disagree** with my position?
- What **needs** are likely to affect my readers' position on the issue? What **values** do my readers hold that are likely to affect their views? What shared needs or values can I use to establish **common ground** with my readers?

Point of view: What point of view is most appropriate to **your position** and **purpose** and to your **relationship with your readers**?

- The **first person** will help your readers feel close to you and accept you or your experiences as part of your argument.
- The **second person** may help you establish a familiarity with your audience.
- The **third person** works well when you want to establish an objective, impersonal tone.

3 Explore your issue.

To come to a more nuanced understanding, explore your issue thoroughly before taking a position.

1. Make a **tentative claim** and list reasons that support it. Then **switch sides**, and brainstorm reasons and evidence to support an alternative view.
2. Create a table with three columns. In the center column, type your issue; in the first column **list pros** and in the third, **cons**.
3. Conduct a **mock argument** with a classmate. Choose opposing views on the issue and defend your positions.

Use the ideas you come up with when drafting your argument.

4 Research your issue.

- Find **books** from reliable publishers on your issue.
- Find **articles** in academic journals and well-respected magazines and newspapers on your issue.
- Search **YouTube** to find news programs and documentaries on your issue.
- Search your issue on **Google Scholar** and examine the first few pages of results.

Then take notes on the most relevant sources to use when drafting your argument. (**Hint:** Sources can not only provide evidence to support your position; they can also provide background information and deepen your insight into a range of viewpoints.)

Note: To avoid **accidental plagiarism**, be sure to enclose quotations in quotation marks and use your own words and sentences when summarizing and paraphrasing information from sources. Also record all publication details you will need to cite your sources (author, title, publisher and site, publication date, page numbers, and so on).

5 Consider alternative viewpoints.

Drawing on your research, brainstorm reasons those holding **alternative positions** would be likely to offer. Choose the reasons your readers are likely to find most persuasive, and then decide whether you should **acknowledge, accommodate,** or **refute** those reasons.

- **Acknowledge** an opposing viewpoint by mentioning it in your claim.

  Example: ⎡———— acknowledges alternative view ————⎤ Although speed-limit laws are intended to save lives, the conditions that apply to specific highways should be taken into account when enforcing them.

  Doing so shows that you take the view seriously but that you think your claim outweighs it.

- **Accommodate** an alternative viewpoint by finding a portion of the opposing argument that you can build into your argument.

  Example: ⎡———— accommodates alternative view ————⎤ Clearly, poor instruction in high school must take some of the blame for so many high school graduates being unprepared for college. But with class sizes in many high schools in our district now exceeding thirty-five, even the most conscientious teachers struggle to educate all of their students.

- **Refute** an alternative viewpoint by pointing out problems or flaws in your opponent's reasoning or evidence. You could:
  give a counterexample (an exception to the opposing view),
  question the opponent's facts by presenting alternative facts or statistics or an alternative interpretation,
  question the credibility of "experts,"
  question outdated examples, facts, or statistics,
  present the full context of statistics or quotations, and
  point to any examples of faulty or fallacious reasoning, such as examples that are not representative (sweeping generalization) or conclusions based on too little evidence (hasty generalization). (For more on fallacious reasoning, see p. 508.)

Collaboration. In small groups, take turns offering examples that show how each member plans to acknowledge, accommodate, or refute opposing views; critique those strategies; and suggest more effective approaches. Then work independently to list opposing viewpoints for your own argument and develop strategies for dealing with the opposition.

6 **Draft your thesis statement.**

Be sure your **thesis . . .**

makes an **arguable claim,**

Unarguable Fact In recent years, U.S. consumers have experienced an increase in credit card fraud.

is **specific** enough to explore fully, and

Too General Many problems that U.S. consumers complain about are mostly their own fault.

avoids **absolutes.**

Too Absolute U.S. consumers have no one but themselves to blame for the recent increase in credit card fraud.

Here is an example of a thesis that is **arguable, specific,** and appropriately **limited:**

Example: Although the carelessness of merchants and electronic tampering contribute to the problem, U.S. consumers are largely to blame for the recent increase in credit card fraud.

7 **Choose a line of reasoning and a method of organization.**

Choose a line of reasoning that best suits your audience.

- **Inductive reasoning** allows readers to draw their own conclusions based on the evidence you present and so **may work best with readers who disagree with your position.**
- **Deductive reasoning** may work best with readers who agree or are neutral or wavering; readers who disagree with your position may feel railroaded by this approach.

Here are four common ways to organize an argument.

Method 1 (deductive)	Claim/ thesis	Reasons/ evidence	Alternative viewpoints
Method 2 (deductive)	Claim/ thesis	Alternative viewpoints	Reasons/ evidence
Method 3 (inductive)	Reasons/ evidence	Alternative viewpoints	Claim/ thesis
Method 4 (inductive)	Alternative viewpoints	Reasons/ evidence	Claim/ thesis

Method 1 works best with agreeing audiences, methods 2 and 3 with neutral or wavering audiences, and method 4 with disagreeing audiences.

Also decide how to **arrange your reasons and evidence** as well as the **alternative views** you canvass: From strongest to weakest? Most to least obvious? Most to least familiar? Draw graphic organizers or make outlines to try out each alternative. (Outlines may work best for verbal and rational learners, and graphic organizers for spatial learners, but using techniques that challenge you can be helpful, too.)

8 Draft your argument essay.

Use the following guidelines to keep your essay on track.

- Your **introduction** should identify the **issue**, offer needed **background**, define **terms** that may be misunderstood, engage **readers**, and create **goodwill**. (Try opening with an attention-getting fact, statistic, or quotation; an engaging anecdote or story; or counterarguments your readers are likely to accept.) Most argument essays also include a thesis statement in which the writer states her or his **claim.**

- Your **body paragraphs** should state your **reasons** (one per paragraph) and provide appropriate **supporting evidence**. Body paragraphs should also **acknowledge**, **accommodate**, or **refute** compelling alternatives.

- Use **transitions** such as *also* and *in addition* to move clearly from reason to reason; use **transitional sentences** such as, "Those opposed to the death penalty claim . . .," to introduce an opposing viewpoint and, "Contrary to what those in favor of the death penalty maintain . . .," to signal a refutation.

  Cite sources of all **quotations**, **summaries**, or **paraphrases** of ideas or information, using an appropriate citation style. (See Chapter 23, MLA style, pp. 603–28; APA style, pp. 628–44.)

  Finally, establish an appropriate **tone**: For a serious issue, use a serious, even somber, tone; for a call to action, use an energetic, enthusiastic tone; with a disagreeing audience, use a friendly, nonthreatening tone. Avoid statements that allow no room for alternative viewpoints ("It is obvious that . . .") and language that may insult or alienate your reader ("Anybody who thinks differently just does not understand the issue").

- Your **conclusion** should remind readers of your **thesis**. Depending on your readers, you might also make a final appeal to **values**, urge readers to take **a specific action**, project what **might happen in the future**, or call for **further research**.

9 Evaluate your draft and revise as necessary.

Use **Figure 20.2, "Flowchart for Revising an Argument Essay,"** to evaluate and revise your draft.

FIGURE 20.2 Flowchart for Revising an Argument Essay

QUESTIONS   REVISION STRATEGIES

1. Circle the section of your essay where you introduce the issue. Do you define the issue clearly and limit it sufficiently? Do you provide enough background information?

 NO ▶

- Use a branching diagram or questioning to limit your issue. (See Chapter 4, pp. 100–102.)
- Ask a friend unfamiliar with the issue to read this section and tell you what else he or she needs to know.

 YES ▼

2. Highlight your thesis. Does is make a clear, specific claim? Does it take a stand on a controversial issue?

 NO ▶

- Replace vague or overly broad words with more specific ones.
- Limit the claim to a more specific issue.
- Add a qualifying word or phrase (such as *may, possibly*) to limit your claim.

 YES ▼

QUESTIONS		REVISION STRATEGIES

3. Describe briefly your intended audience. Do you take into account readers' knowledge of and attitude toward the issue? Do you appeal to readers' needs and values?

 NO ▶
- Add background information.
- Brainstorm to discover needs, values, and experiences you share with your readers.
- Add reasons and evidence based on those needs, values, and experiences.

 YES ▼

4. Place a ✔ by each supporting reason and an ✘ by each piece of evidence that supports a reason. Do you have enough reasons and evidence?

 NO ▶
- Brainstorm to discover compelling reasons.
- Conduct research to find solid evidence.

 YES ▼

5. Label the parts of your argument. Does each step follow logically from the one before and lead logically to the one after? Is your reasoning free of errors? Does the order make sense given your audience?

 NO ▶
- Create an outline or graphic organizer using inductive or deductive reasoning.
- Adjust your organization to appeal to your readers—agreeing, neutral, or disagreeing. (See Step 7 of the Guided Writing Assignment, p. 539.)
- Check for and correct faulty reasoning and fallacies. (See Chapter 19, p. 508.)

 YES ▼

6. [Bracket] sections where you present opposing viewpoints. Do you effectively acknowledge, accommodate, or refute the most important opposing viewpoints?

 NO ▶
- Conduct research to get a clearer understanding of opposing viewpoints.
- Modify your claim to accommodate an alternative viewpoint.
- Identify and refute weaknesses in opposing viewpoints.
- Point out unfair uses of appeals or faulty reasoning.

 YES ▼

7. Review your introduction and conclusion: Does the introduction identify the issue, define terms, provide background, and engage readers? Does your conclusion appeal to values or inspire action?

 NO ▶
- Revise your introduction to start with a compelling anecdote, fact, or commonly held misconception.
- Revise your conclusion to refer back to the introduction, make a strong emotional appeal, or urge readers to take a specific action.

REVISING

10 Edit and proofread your essay.

Refer to Chapter 9 for help with:

- **editing sentences** to avoid wordiness, make your verb choices strong and active, and make your sentences clear, varied, and parallel
- **editing words** for tone and diction, connotation, and concrete and specific language

Watch out particularly for **ambiguous pronouns** and **problems with the subjunctive mood**.

1. **Look for and correct ambiguous pronouns.** A pronoun must refer to another noun or pronoun, called its *antecedent*. The pronoun's antecedent should be clearly named, not just implied.

   Example: Children of divorced parents are often shuttled between two homes, and ~~that~~ can be
   _{this lack of stability}
   ^
   confusing and disturbing to them.

2. **Use the subjunctive mood correctly.** In an argument, you often write about what would or might happen in the future. When you use the verb *be* to speculate about future conditions, use *were* in place of *was*.

   Example: If all animal research _{were} ~~was~~ outlawed, progress in the control of human diseases would be
   ^
   slowed dramatically.

Reading: Argument in Action

> STUDENTS WRITE

Pull the Plug on Explicit Lyrics

James Sturm

James Sturm wrote this essay when he was a student at Kalamazoo College, where he graduated with a degree in international and area studies. As you read, notice how Sturm uses comparison and contrast as well as illustration to strengthen his argument.

Title: The title indicates Sturm's position on the issue of explicit lyrics.

Introduction: Sturm captures readers' interest by talking about youthful rebellion. In his thesis statement, he clearly states his claim of policy.

Many kids pass through a rebellious phase in middle school. If the teacher asks them to stop throwing pencils, they toss one more. If the sign reads "No Trespassing," they cross the line. If they hear their

1

father listening to classical music, they tune in to rap and punk rock. Unfortunately, the lyrics in rap and punk rock can be quite explicit and may have a negative effect on impressionable youngsters. For this reason, music with explicit lyrics should be off-limits until the age of sixteen.

Currently, the government takes a rather laissez-faire attitude with regard to the music industry. Thousands of albums are readily available to young people regardless of explicit content. In fact, the main control mechanism for protecting youthful consumers from harmful content comes from the recording companies themselves. Under the Parental Advisory campaign of the Recording Industry Association of America (RIAA), it is the responsibility of artists and record labels themselves to decide if their albums should receive the infamous "Parental Advisory: Explicit Content" label. Children are allowed to purchase the albums regardless ("Parental Advisory").

This lack of regulation would not be a problem if the music did not produce negative effects on its listeners. Although it is difficult to prove statistically that music full of hateful content fuels similar attitudes in its listeners, it requires only common sense to understand why. That is, people are influenced by what they think about. If a child thinks, for example, that he is unimportant or unloved, then he will act out in various ways to gain attention from his peers. Problem thinking is a result of a variety of influences, including friends, parents, and the media. Negative music, if listened to frequently enough, naturally implants negative thoughts in the minds of its listeners.

Furthermore, consider the unique influence of music as opposed to other forms of media. Unlike movies, video games, and magazines, music has a way of saturating one's mind. Everyone knows the feeling of having a song "stuck" in their head, repeating itself throughout the day. Unlike a movie, which is seen once, discussed among friends, and then forgotten, a song can remain lodged in one's mind for weeks on end. And if the songs are steeped in content such as violence against women, happiness found in harmful drugs, and hatred of the police, these themes will continue reverberating in the minds of the listener, slowly desensitizing them

2

Background: Sturm offers background information about government regulation and record labeling, providing a source citation.

3 **Reason 1:** After providing a transition and accommodating an opposing viewpoint, Sturm presents his first reason and supports it with an example.

4 **Reason 2:** Sturm presents his second reason and supports it by establishing common ground with his audience. Here and in the next paragraph, he includes transitions between his reasons.

to otherwise repulsive ideas. Becoming numb to such ideas is the first step toward passively agreeing with them or even personally acting upon them.

Reason 3: Sturm presents his third reason and accommodates two opposing viewpoints; he refers back to the previous paragraph to create coherence.

Whereas adults can usually listen to such music with no behavioral ramifications, children are far more susceptible to its subtle influence. With less experience of life, a lower level of maturity, and a lack of long-term thinking, young people are prone to make impulsive decisions. Providing them with access to music that fuels negative and harmful thoughts is a dangerous decision. We live in an age where violent tragedies such as school shootings are increasingly commonplace. Although various factors contribute to such acts of violence, hatred-themed music is likely a part of the equation. Therefore, given the influential power of music and the heightened effect it can have on those still in the developmental stage of their lives, young people should have limited access to music with explicit lyrics.

5

Sturm offers an explanation for choosing sixteen as an age cutoff.

Sixteen years of age would be a reasonable cut-off. Until children reach that age, they should not be allowed to purchase music with a Parental Advisory label. At sixteen, they are becoming young adults and making more and more of their own decisions. Before sixteen, they are weathering the turbulent transition from middle school to high school. This transition should not be accompanied by music that promotes rebellion as a means of coping with stress and difficulty. After reaching age sixteen, however, most young people will have obtained a driver's license, and the freedom that it allows eliminates the possibility of protecting youth from certain music. That is, those with a driver's license can seek out their own venues to hear explicit content, whether concerts or elsewhere.

6

Opposing viewpoints: In this paragraph and the next two, Sturm recognizes three opposing viewpoints and accommodates each of them. Notice that he cites a source for the first viewpoint and includes transitions between them.

The main critique of efforts to curtail young teens' access to explicit music is not new. Many say that it's pointless to censor music's explicit content because, as the RIAA's Web site contends, "music is a reflection, not a cause; it doesn't create the problems our society faces, it forces us to confront them" ("Freedom of Speech"). It is true that music reflects our culture. But it is also true that music fuels the perpetuation of that culture, for better or for worse. Guarding youth from explicit music does not equate to ignoring the issues raised in the music. It merely delegates that task to adults rather than to children.

7

Another critique says that limiting youth access to explicit music would take a financial toll on the music industry. This is true, but it would

8

also force the music industry to adapt. We can either allow the youth of our nation to adapt to the music industry, or we can force the industry to adapt to an impressionable generation of kids.

A third critique is that even if explicit music were restricted to those of a certain age, younger kids would find access to it anyway. This is a legitimate concern, especially given the explosion of music-downloading software. But if not only music outlet stores but also online companies such as Amazon.com and iTunes were included in the regulations, progress would surely come.

9

Hip-hop artist Ja Rule has spoken in favor of the current Parental Advisory system, saying, "That's what we can do as musicians to try to deter the kids from getting that lyrical content." But he added, "I don't think it deters the kids—it's just another sticker on the tape right now" (Bowes). Even some hip-hop artists agree that protecting the minds of our youth is a necessity. But until laws are passed to restrict access to this music, the "Parental Advisory" label will just be another logo on the CD cover.

10

Conclusion: Sturm quotes a hip-hop artist (and cites the source) to offer final support for his claim.

Works Cited

Bowes, Peter. "Spotlight on Explicit Lyrics Warning." *BBC News World Edition*, 27 May 2002, news.bbc.co.uk/2/hi/entertainment/2010641.stm.

"Freedom of Speech." *Recording Industry Association of America*, riaasalestool.shoshkey.com/aboutus.php?content_selector=Freedom-Of-Speech. Accessed 18 Sept. 2015.

"Parental Advisory." *Recording Industry Association of America*, 2016, www.riaa.com/resources-learning/parental-advisory-label/.

Analyzing the Writer's Technique

1. **Thesis** Analyze Sturm's thesis statement. What does it suggest about the organization of the essay? What aspect of the essay does it give no hint about?
2. **Evidence** What additional types of evidence could Sturm have used to support his reasons?
3. **Definition** How precisely does Sturm define the term *explicit lyrics*? Does his definition need to be more precise? Why or why not?

Thinking Critically about Argument

1. **Author's Attitude** What is Sturm's attitude toward explicit lyrics? Highlight words and phrases that reveal it.
2. **Fact or Opinion** Is Sturm relying on fact, opinion, or both to support his argument? Identify passages that support your answer.
3. **Audience** Who is Sturm's main audience? How do you know?
4. **Euphemism** What is "explicit music" a euphemism for?
5. **Needs and Values** To what needs and values does Sturm appeal?

Responding to the Reading

1. **Discussion** Discuss Sturm's proposal to ban the sale of "explicit music" to children. How are other media, such as books, movies, magazines, and TV shows, treated similarly or differently when it comes to children?
2. **Journal** What is the benefit, if any, of having explicit lyrics in music? Why are they needed, or why should they be allowed at all?
3. **Essay** Write an essay discussing the following dilemma: A middle school student wants to listen to explicit music, but it is not legally available to her age group. Her parents do not want her to have access to such music. Is there a compromise position? What advice would you offer to each side?

Apply Your Skills: Additional Essay Assignments

To Persuade Your Reader

Write an argument essay on one of the following issues.

1. Professional sports
2. E-waste (electronic waste)
3. Alternative energy options
4. Genetic testing
5. Presidential campaigns

Narrow the issue to one that is arguable, such as a problem that could be solved by reforms or legislation. Narrow the issue to one that can be addressed in a brief paper (3–5 pages). Depending on the issue you choose, you may need to conduct research. Your audience is your classmates and instructor.

Cases Using Argument

1. Write an essay for a sociology course, arguing your position on the following statement: The race of a child and that of the prospective parents should be taken into consideration in making adoption decisions.
2. You have a job as a copyeditor at a city newspaper. Write a proposal that explains and justifies your request to work at home one day per week. Incorporate into your argument the fact that you could use your home computer, which is connected to the newspaper's computer network.

Joelle Sedlmeyer/Getty Images

PART FIVE

Writing with Sources

21

Planning a Research Project and Evaluating Sources

fatihhoca/Getty Images

In this chapter you will learn to:

- identify the kinds of information you need to make your ideas convincing

- distinguish among types of sources, and choose those that are most reliable and relevant to your research

- devise a working thesis and research questions

- analyze and think critically about resources

WRITING QUICK START   Suppose you are enrolled in a public speaking class. Your instructor has chosen the topic of preschool and will divide the class into two teams. One team will argue for free, public preschool, and the other team will argue against it. At this point, you don't know which team you'll be on. Write a brief statement summarizing what you think the pros and cons of free public preschool are. Then indicate what further information you would need in order to defend either position.

Before planning a speech or writing in detail about the pros or cons of public preschool, you would probably need to consult several sources to learn more about it. What information would you need to support your ideas? What types of sources would be useful? How would you be sure the information contained in your sources is relevant and reliable? How would you detect whether a source exhibits bias?

This chapter will answer these and other questions about choosing and evaluating useful sources. It will also lead you through the process of planning a project with sources. Graphic Organizer 21.1 lists the research skills covered in this chapter, placing them within the context of the process of writing a research project as a whole.

GRAPHIC ORGANIZER 21.1 Writing a Paper with Sources

Planning a Research Project and Evaluating Sources

- Define the assignment.
- Choose an interesting and workable topic.
- Narrow and discover ideas about your topic.
- Write a working thesis and list research questions.
- Choose appropriate source types (primary/secondary, scholarly/popular/reference, books/articles/media).
- Evaluate and think critically about your sources.

Finding Sources, Taking Notes, and Synthesizing

- See Chapter 22

Drafting, Revising, and Formatting a Research Project

- See Chapter 23

Documenting Your Sources

- See Chapter 23

USING RESEARCH ▸ **IN COLLEGE AND THE WORKPLACE**

- *For an astronomy course,* you are asked to write a two-page report on black holes. Your textbook contains basic information on the subject, but you need to consult other sources to complete the assignment.

- *For a political science class,* you need to write a five-page research project on a current issue (such as homeland security or the electoral college), explaining the issue and reporting on current developments.

- *You are a journalist* and will interview your state governor. You need background information on the governor's position on several issues of local concern. You also need to interview politicians or local groups who may disagree with the governor's positions.

Write from Sources: Use Sources to Make Your Own Ideas Convincing

To learn more about documenting sources in MLA and APA style, see Chapter 23, pp. 603–28, 628–44.

The papers you write in college are intended to be serious works of scholarship. This means that instructors will expect you to support your own ideas with convincing evidence from reliable sources and to document those sources. When you write a research project, you don't simply glue together the facts, statistics, information, and quotations you find in sources. Like any other essay-length writing, a research project must have a thesis that your body paragraphs support with reasons and evidence. Although the information from outside sources is not your own, the interpretation you give it should be.

When you are writing a research project, instructors will expect you to use information from sources whenever your topic demands more factual information than you can provide from your personal knowledge and experience. For example, use information from sources to:

- **Make general comments more specific.** For example, instead of writing that "the crime rate in Boston has decreased over the past few years," specify the years over which the decrease has occurred, and use official police statistics to show the exact percentage of the decrease in each year.
- **Provide specific examples to illustrate your main points.** For example, if you are writing about why some online companies charge a restocking fee for returns made after thirty days, locate a business with such a policy and find out its rationale.
- **Use sources to supply technical information.** For example, if you are writing about a drug that lowers high blood pressure, gather information about its manufacturer, ingredients, effectiveness, cost, and side effects so that you can make informed, accurate comments.
- **Support opinions with concrete evidence.** To support the claim that more federal assistance is needed for public education, you might provide facts and statistics showing how much less federal assistance is provided now than was provided in earlier decades, or you could quote education experts to support your position.
- **Provide historical information or context.** If you are writing about space stations, for example, find out when the first one was established, what country launched it, and what it has been used for. These details add useful background information to your research project.
- **Compare information about similar events or ideas with those you are discussing.** For example, if you are writing about a president's intervention in a labor strike, find out if other presidents have intervened in similar strikes. You can then point out similarities and differences.

For more on synthesizing, see pp. 580–83.

Instructors will also expect you to **synthesize**, or make connections, among sources. When you synthesize information and ideas, you engage in a kind of conversation with your sources, making connections among ideas and information that reinforce or challenge each other to create new meaning of your own. Synthesis allows you to:

- **Explore different points of view.** For example, in a paper about the consequences of divorce on children, you might use some sources that discuss the negative consequences and others that discuss the benefits.
- **Review key ideas on a topic.** For example, in a paper for an economics class explaining the reasons for increased income disparity in the past ten years, you might begin by reviewing the main reasons others have offered and respond to ideas you agree or disagree with.
- **Understand your topic in depth.** For example, synthesizing information and ideas from a variety of sources on global warming will help you see the issue from a variety of perspectives, leading you to think more deeply about the issue.

Plan Your Research Project

The best place to start a research project is at your desk. There you can think about the assignment and devise a plan for completing it. This section describes several tasks that you should accomplish *before* you begin your research. (See Graphic Organizer 21.1, p. 549.)

Define the Assignment

Before you begin researching an assigned topic, be sure you understand your instructor's expectations. Often the assignment will be written on the syllabus. Read the assignment carefully, noting all the requirements, which may include the following:

- the length of the final paper (number of pages, exclusive of the works-cited page)
- the number and types of sources you must use (for example, an assignment may specify that your works cited list must include at least three books and at least ten articles)
- the purpose of the assignment—**informative** projects ask you to *explain* a topic (for example, "Explain the treatment options for breast cancer") or *explore* an issue (for example, "Examine the pros and cons of legalizing casino gambling"); **persuasive** projects ask you to *defend* or *argue for* a position (for example, "Argue for or against your college's proposal to eliminate athletic scholarships")
- the genre of the assignment and the format you must follow (for example, are you writing a case study? a lab report? an evaluation?)
- any limitations placed on the research (for example, "No citations from Wikipedia," "No sources published before 2012," "No citations from for-profit organizations")
- the due date and any penalties for lateness
- the documentation style you are required to follow (see Chapter 23)

If your instructor announces the assignment in class, write down what he or she says, including as many details as possible. Sometimes instructors make "model papers" available for students to consult. Don't miss any opportunity to learn from, and be inspired by, these models.

Often major research projects are announced the first week of class. Because a large research project is a major undertaking, your professor is trying to give you as much time as possible to think about, plan, write, and revise your paper. As you proceed through the course, create a schedule for deciding on a topic, conducting the research, writing your first draft, revising your paper, ensuring your citations follow the required format exactly, and polishing your paper. You might build time into your schedule to discuss your ideas or share your drafts with friends or classmates or to get feedback from a writing center tutor.

Do not wait until the last minute to begin a research project! Writing a research project is a multistep process; it is likely to be a large part of your final grade, so put your best foot forward and devote the time necessary to making it the best it can be.

Choose an Interesting and Workable Topic

Most instructors allow you to choose your own topic for a research project. You will save time in the long run if you spend enough time at the outset choosing a topic that is both interesting and workable. Too many students waste hours researching a topic that they finally realize is too difficult, broad, or ordinary. The following tips will help you avoid such pitfalls.

1. **Choose a topic that interests you.** You will be able to write more enthusiastically if you work with a topic that captures your interest. If you have trouble choosing a topic, brainstorm with a classmate or friend.
2. **Choose a manageable topic.** Make sure you can adequately cover the topic within the assigned length of your paper. For example, don't try to write about all kinds of family counseling programs in a five- to ten-page paper. Instead, limit your topic to one type, such as programs for troubled adolescents.
3. **Avoid ordinary topics.** Familiar subjects that have been thoroughly explained in many sources seldom make good topics. For example, the subjects of "childhood obesity" and "reality TV" have been thoroughly discussed in many newspapers and magazines and *ad nauseam* on Web sites. If you choose such a topic, be sure to come up with a different slant on it. A conversation will often help you discover new angles on ordinary topics.
4. **Choose a practical topic.** Topics that are in the news or for which a new breakthrough has just been reported do not typically make good choices because often little reliable information is available. Topics that require extensive technical knowledge that you lack do not typically make good choices because they may require more research than you can do in the time allowed.

Narrow and Discover Ideas about Your Topic

For more on narrowing a topic and discovering ideas, see Chapter 4.

To write effectively, you must narrow your topic enough that you can explore it thoroughly in the space allowed. The following techniques will help you narrow your topic as well as discover ideas about it.

Do some preliminary reading.   To get a sense of the scope, depth, and breadth of your topic, as well as to identify more manageable subtopics, you might skim an article on your topic in a general encyclopedia, such as *Encyclopaedia Britannica*, or in a specialized encyclopedia, such as *The McGraw-Hill Encyclopedia of Science and Technology*. Searching for your topic in your library's holdings, in a specialized database such as the weekly *CQ Researcher* (which contains thousands of articles on current topics) or even Google can also help you identify the subtopics into which a topic can be broken. You can also ask a reference librarian for assistance.

Try prewriting.   To uncover an interesting angle on your topic or to narrow a broad topic, use one or more prewriting techniques. A branching diagram may be particularly helpful in narrowing a topic. The questioning technique, which challenges you to see your topic from different perspectives—psychological, sociological, scientific or technical, historical, political, and economic—can help you find an interesting subtopic or get an interesting angle. Here is how one student used questioning to analyze different perspectives on television advertising.

Topic: Television Advertising

Perspective	Questions
Psychological	• How does advertising affect people? • Does it affect everyone the same way? • What emotional appeals are used, and how do they work?
Sociological	• Do different age groups respond differently to ads? • Is advertising targeted toward specific racial and ethnic groups?
Scientific or technical	• How are ads produced? • Who writes them? • Are the ads tested before they are broadcast?
Historical	• What is the history of advertising? • When and where did it begin?
Political	• What legislation affects the content of advertising? • Why are negative political advertisements effective?
Economic	• How much does a television ad cost? • Is the cost of advertising added to the price of the product?

This list of questions yielded a wide range of interesting subtopics about advertising, including emotional appeals, targeting ads to specific racial or ethnic groups, and negative political advertising. You might work with a friend or classmate to devise and answer questions.

EXERCISE 21.1 ▶ NARROWING A TOPIC FOR A RESEARCH PROJECT

Working with one or two classmates, narrow each of the following topics until you reach a topic that would be manageable for a five- to ten-page research project.

1. Taxes
2. U.S. prison system
3. Health care reform
4. Drones
5. Alternative energy sources

Choose a broad topic for your research project. Come up with one on your own, or choose one of the broad topics below. Your audience consists of your classmates. Begin by using one or more prewriting techniques to generate ideas and narrow your focus. Then reread your work and highlight useful ideas.

1. Extreme sports
2. Adopting children from foreign countries
3. Employer-employee relations
4. Internet or identity fraud
5. Piracy of intellectual property (books, music, etc.)

Feel free to consult with your instructor about your topic. Your instructor may suggest a way to narrow your topic, recommend a useful source, or offer to review your outline.

Write a Working Thesis and List Research Questions

For more on drafting and revising a thesis statement, see Chapter 5, pp. 119–24.

Once you have chosen and narrowed a topic, try to determine, as specifically as possible, the kinds of information you need to know about it. Begin by writing a working thesis for your paper and listing the research questions you need to answer.

For example, one student working on the general topic of child abuse used prewriting and preliminary reading to narrow his focus to physical abuse and its causes. Since he already had a few ideas about possible causes, he used those ideas to write a working thesis. He then used his thesis to generate a list of research questions. Notice how the student's questions follow from his working thesis.

Working Thesis	The physical abuse of children often stems from parents' emotional instability and a family history of child abuse.
Research Questions	If a person was physically abused as a child, how likely is that person to become an abusive parent?
	What kinds of emotional problems seem to trigger the physical abuse of children?
	Which cause is more significant—a family history of abuse or emotional problems?
	Is there more physical abuse of children now than there was in the past, or is more abuse being reported?

A working thesis and a list of research questions will help you approach your research in a focused way. Instead of running helter-skelter from one aspect of your topic to another, you will be able to identify the specific information you need from sources.

EXERCISE 21.2 ▶ WRITING A WORKING THESIS AND RESEARCH QUESTIONS

For one of the following topics, write a working thesis and four or more research questions.

1. Methods of controlling pornography online
2. The possibility that some form of life has existed (or currently exists) on other planets
3. The rise of celebrity worship in the United States (or in any other country)
4. Benefits of tracing your family's genealogy (family tree)
5. Ways that elderly family members affect family life

RESEARCH PROJECT IN PROGRESS 2 ▶

Review the list of ideas you generated in Research Project in Progress 1. Underline the ideas for which you need further details or supporting evidence, and list the information you need. Then, using the preceding guidelines, write a working thesis and a list of research questions.

Consider Source Types

Once you have a working thesis and a list of research questions, stop for a moment. Think about which kinds of sources will be most useful, appropriate, relevant, and reliable. Keep in mind that you are unlikely to find all the sources you need online. Researchers must be equally skilled at locating sources in print and in electronic formats.

The types of sources that you will be expected to use will vary from discipline to discipline and assignment to assignment. The sources that are most appropriate will depend on your writing situation:

To learn more about the writing situation, see Chapter 4, pp. 102–6.

- the assignment
- your purpose for writing
- your audience
- the genre (or type) of writing you are expected to produce

For example, if you were writing an article for a local PTA newsletter (genre) to inform (purpose) parents (audience) about the school board's decision to provide more nutritious lunches for children, you might interview the school's nutritionist and gather data comparing the nutritional value of the typical new lunch (mini carrots, pita, hummus, and roasted chicken) to the nutritional value of the typical previous lunch (pizza, french fries, and Jell-o). You might also talk with the parents in the school district who were instrumental in getting the lunch menu improved and perhaps even ask some of the children their opinions regarding the new menu.

In contrast, if you were writing a research project (genre) for a history class (audience: your instructor) in which you argued (purpose) that skilled military commanders enabled the South to prolong the American Civil War, you might consult diaries or let-ters written by Union and Confederate generals, scholarly books and journal articles on Civil War battles and strategy, and maps showing troop movements.

Use Primary and Secondary Sources

The examples above mention primary (or firsthand) sources, such as interviews, let-ters, and diary entries, as well as secondary sources, such as books and articles. **Primary sources** include the following:

- historical documents (letters, diaries, speeches),
- literary works, autobiographies,
- original research reports,
- eyewitness accounts, and
- your own interviews, observations, or correspondence.

For example, a report on a study of heart disease written by the researcher who con-ducted the study is a primary source, as is a novel by William Faulkner. In addition, what *you* say or write can be a primary source. Your own interview with a heart attack survivor for a paper on heart disease is a primary source.

Secondary sources, in contrast, report or comment on primary sources. A journal article that reviews several previously published research reports on heart disease is a secondary source. A book written about William Faulkner by a literary critic or biogra-pher is a secondary source.

Depending on your topic, you may use primary sources, secondary sources, or both. For a research project comparing the speeches of Abraham Lincoln with those of Franklin D. Roosevelt, you would probably read and analyze the speeches and listen to recordings of Roosevelt delivering his speeches (primary sources). But to learn about Lincoln's and Roosevelt's domestic policies, you would probably rely on several histo-ries or biographies (secondary sources).

Use Scholarly, Popular, and Reference Sources

For more on using a database to narrow sources by type, see Chapter 22, pp. 568, 570 (Figure 22.2).

In addition to primary and secondary, sources can also be classified as scholarly, popu-lar, or reference sources. **Scholarly sources** are written by professional academics and scientific researchers and include both books by university presses or professional publishing companies and articles in discipline-specific academic journals that are edited by experts in the field. University presses include Oxford University Press, Prince-ton University Press, and the University of Nebraska Press (among many others).

There are thousands of highly regarded academic journals, ranging from *Nature* (a key journal in biology and the life sciences) to *The Lancet* (an important medical journal) to *American Economic Review* (a key journal for economists). Articles in academic jour-nals often fall into two main categories.

1. Reports on original research conducted by the writer.
2. Surveys of previous research on a topic to identify key areas of agreement, which then become part of the accepted body of knowledge in the discipline.

Many scholarly sources are **peer reviewed**, which means the articles and books undergo a rigorous process of review by other scholars in the same discipline before they are accepted for publication. For these reasons, scholarly resources are accepted as accurate and reliable, and they usually form the basis of most research in academic papers.

Reference works are well-organized compendiums of facts, data, and information. They are intended to be consulted to answer specific questions rather than to be read from beginning to end. Dictionaries, encyclopedias, and thesauruses are common reference works. Reference works are increasingly available through the databases your library subscribes to, but you may also be able to consult them in print.

Students and researchers frequently use discipline-specific reference works. For example, students of literature might consult *Gale Artemis Literary Sources* or *The Oxford Companion to English Literature*. Like scholarly resources, reference works are checked closely for accuracy, which makes them reliable sources of information. Many reference works also include suggestions for further reading, which can help researchers in their quest for additional resources. While reference works are a handy place to look up background information, they are not appropriate sources on which to base a research project.

Popular sources (newspapers, magazines, and general-interest nonfiction books) typically discuss what is going on in the "real world." For example, they publish stories about what happened and to whom—effects of a piece of legislation on a community, one woman's story of overcoming adversity to become successful in college or business. The subject matter is treated in a way that makes it accessible to most readers. Difficult topics are explained simply. One type of popular source, known as a **trade journal**, is aimed at people in specific professions. Trade journals provide the latest information on new ideas, products, personnel, events, and trends in an industry.

"Popular" does not necessarily mean unreliable. For example, a newspaper like *The Wall Street Journal* and a magazine like *Time* are good sources of information. The articles they publish are written by journalists who are trained in methods of research. Some popular magazines such as *Scientific American* and *The Economist* are quite serious indeed. At the other end of the spectrum are mass-circulation magazines, like *People* and *Sports Illustrated*, that are concerned primarily with celebrities and showmanship. Sources at the "celebrity" end of the spectrum may be useful for finding examples, but these publications will often have little or no academic credibility.

For more on evaluating sources, see pp. 559–63.

Table 21.1 summarizes some of the differences between scholarly and popular sources. For most college research projects, consulting and citing more serious popular sources is acceptable, but academic research projects generally do not rely solely on popular sources. Distinguishing among scholarly, popular, and reference sources when they are accessed through a database can be tricky, since visual cues, like the glossy paper and splashy photographs, that distinguish popular sources from scholarly ones are missing. Instead, you can use database tools or consult a reference librarian to help you determine source type.

TABLE 21.1 A Comparison of Scholarly Journals and Popular Sources

	Scholarly Journals	Popular Sources
Who reads it?	Researchers, professionals, students	General public
Who writes it?	Researchers, professionals	Reporters, journalists, freelance writers
Who decides what to publish in it?	Other researchers (peer reviewers)	Editors, publishers
What kind of information does it contain?	Results of research studies and experiments, statistics and analysis, in-depth evaluations of specialized topics, overviews of all the research on a subject (literature review), technical vocabulary, bibliographies and references	Articles of general interest, easy-to-understand language, news items, interviews, opinion pieces, no bibliographies (sources cited informally within the article)
How often is it published?	Mostly quarterly (every three months)	Daily (newspapers), weekly or monthly (magazines)
What are some examples?	*Journal of Bioethics, American Journal of Family Law, Film Quarterly*	*Popular Science, Psychology Today, The Week*

Use Books, Articles, and Media Sources

A useful way to choose appropriate source types is to consider your needs in terms of the depth and type of content the source provides. **Books** often take years of study to produce and are often written by authorities on the subject, so they are likely to offer the most in-depth, comprehensive discussions of topics. Most scholarly books also provide pages and pages of research citations to help you dig further into any topic you find interesting or useful. Printed books provide an index to help you locate specific topics; e-books allow you to conduct keyword searches.

Articles are much briefer than books. In fact, most articles are under twenty pages, and some are as short as two or three pages. They tend to be more focused than books, exploring just one or two key points. They may also be more up-to-date, since they can be written and produced more rapidly than books can.

Most of the articles you access through your library's databases begin with an **abstract**, or brief summary. Reading the abstract can help you determine whether the article will be useful to your research. Keyword searches in electronic articles can help you locate the topics you are researching, and many academic databases use keywords to link you to other articles that may be useful in your research.

For more on keyword searching, see Chapter 22, pp. 566–68.

Media sources, such as photographs and information graphics, documentaries, podcasts, or works of fine art, can be useful sources of ideas and information. While in popular sources, media items may be used to illustrate a text simply to attract readers, in academic texts, media must play a more substantial role. Use images in printed texts, or video and sound files in online texts, to illustrate a concept or to provide an example, but do not include illustrations merely for window dressing. Finally, keep in mind that documentaries may include fictional elements. Evaluate media sources carefully before including them as sources.

As you seek answers to your research questions, you will likely need to consult various types of sources. Let's suppose you are writing a research project about narcissistic personality disorder (NPD), a recognized psychological disorder in which a person is obsessively concerned with ideas of his or her own personal superiority, power, and prestige. Through the process of narrowing your topic, you have decided to focus your paper on the behaviors associated with the disorder. What types of sources might you use?

- To help your readers understand exactly what NPD is, you might look to a reference book, such as the *Diagnostic and Statistical Manual of Mental Disorders,* 5th edition (DSM-V), a key reference work in psychology. The DSM is published by the American Psychological Association, which makes it a reliable resource.
- To research the real-world behaviors of people with NPD, you might consult several types of books. Scholarly books written by psychologists and published by university presses might offer case studies of people with NPD. You will likely also find books written by people who have NPD, in which they talk about their experiences and feelings. By using both types of sources, you can explore two sides of the issue: not only the clinical, diagnostic side of NPD but also the human side of it.
- To get your audience interested in your topic, you might begin by talking about celebrity behaviors that may reveal NPD. If you can find videos of celebrity interviews in which the celebrity exhibits behaviors associated with NPD, you will have found a good, reliable source to cite.

Evaluate Sources

Evaluating sources is an essential part of writing a paper using research. Unless you locate solid, relevant, and reliable sources and think critically about the ideas presented in each, your essay will lack academic rigor and credibility.

Choose Relevant Sources

A *relevant* source contains information that helps you answer one or more of your research questions. Ask yourself the following questions to determine whether a source is relevant.

1. **Is the source appropriate for your intended audience, or is it too general or too specialized?**

2. **Is the source up-to-date or recent enough for your purposes?** In rapidly chang- ing fields of study, outdated sources are not useful unless you need to give a his- torical perspective.

Choose Reliable Sources

A *reliable* source is honest, accurate, and credible. Ask the following questions to help you determine whether a source is reliable.

1. **Is the source scholarly?** Although scholars often disagree with one another, they make a serious attempt to present accurate information.

2. **Does the source have a solid reputation?** Some news sources — magazines such as *Time* or *The Economist* and newspapers such as *The Washington Post* and *The New York Times* — are known for responsible reporting, whereas other newspapers and magazines have a reputation for sensationalism or bias. Such sources may be useful when you are exploring multiple perspectives on an issue, but be careful about interpreting articles in these publications as "the truth."

3. **What is the publication's purpose?** Why was the source published? In the case of general-interest magazines like *The Week*, which summarizes many articles from magazines and newspapers around the world, the purpose is clear: to provide readers with a wide variety of perspectives on issues of local and global impor- tance. The purpose of a flyer left in your mailbox may be to introduce a new business in your neighborhood or to get you to convert to a new religion. To determine purpose, look for a link on the publication's Web site labeled "About Us" or "Mission Statement."

4. **Is the source professionally edited and presented?** Professionally published, reli- able sources are generally free of typographical errors. Materials with obvious mistakes, as well as amateur typesetting or design, are often unreliable. Blogs may be good sources of viewpoint pieces, but a blog may just be one person's online diary. Such blogs may be subject to heavy bias as well as possible factual errors.

5. **Is the author an expert in the field?** Check the author's credentials. Information about authors may be given in a headnote, in a link to the author's biography, in the preface, or elsewhere. You might also check a reference work such as *Contem- porary Authors* or Google the author to verify credentials.

6. **Does the author approach the topic fairly and objectively?** A writer who states a strong opinion is not necessarily biased. However, a writer who ignores opposing views, distorts facts, or ignores information that does not fit his or her opinion is presenting a biased and incomplete view of a topic.

7. **Can the content be verified?** The content in reliable sources can be verified in other reliable sources. Be cautious about using a piece of information you can find in only one source. Also be skeptical of any source that purports to sum- marize research or cite facts but does not provide a list of works cited (or, in the case of popular sources, attribution within the article or in footnotes or links).

For more on evaluating sources, see Chapter 3, pp. 56–71.

EXERCISE 21.3   **EVALUATING THE RELEVANCE AND RELIABILITY OF SOURCES**

Working in a small group, discuss the context in which the sources listed for each topic below would or would not be considered appropriate sources.

1. Topic: Caring for family members with Alzheimer's disease
   a. Introductory health and nutrition textbook
   b. Article in *Woman's Day* titled "Mother, Where Are You?"
   c. Article from a gerontology journal on caring for aging family members
2. Topic: Analyzing the effects of heroin use on teenagers
   a. Newspaper article written by a former heroin user
   b. Article from *the Journal of Neurology* on the biochemical effects of heroin on the brain
   c. Web page on teenage drug use published by the National Institutes of Health
3. Topic: Implementing training programs to reduce sexual harassment in the workplace
   a. Article from *The Christian Science Monitor* titled "Removing Barriers for Working Women"
   b. Personal Web site or blog relating an incident of harassment on the job
   c. Training manual for employees of General Motors

Evaluate Resources in the Digital Landscape

Use special care in evaluating the quality of the electronic materials you consult. In addition to the guidelines listed above, also consider the following.

- If you accessed the source through a library database or found the source through your college library's catalog, it is most likely reliable.
- If the source is an electronic version of a respected print publication (such as *The New York Times* or *The Boston Globe*), the source is likely reliable. Be careful, however, about distinguishing between content that is edited and checked by the publication (and is therefore reliable) and links to other sources or any comments posted by readers.
- If the source does not specify its authorship or does not provide any information about the author's qualifications, proceed with caution.
- If the source contains factual errors, poor layout or design, too many photos and not enough words, or highly charged or emotional language, these are all signs that the source may be biased and lack credibility.

Think Critically about Sources

As you select sources for possible use in your paper, it is important to think critically about each. The following list of questions will help you analyze and evaluate sources.

- **Analyze the author's ideas.** Does the author make reasonable inferences, use reliable evidence, and make it clear when he or she is expressing an opinion?
- **Analyze the author's language.** Does the author's use of connotation and figurative language reveal bias? What does the author's tone indicate about his

For more on identifying bias by examining the writer's use of language, assumptions, generalizations, or omissions, see Chapter 3, pp. 56–71.

or her attitude? Does the author use euphemisms to hide something or to spare feelings?

- **Analyze the author's assumptions, generalizations, and omissions.** Are the author's assumptions and generalizations fair and reasonable? Are they supported by evidence? Do they reinforce or challenge social standards? Does any information seem to be omitted or treated in a less than thorough or complete way?

The way an author presents ideas, the language an author uses, and the assumptions, generalizations, and omissions that he or she makes may all help you detect bias. **Bias** refers to a publisher's or writer's own views or particular interest in a topic. A biased source is not necessarily unreliable, but you need to recognize bias when you see it and find additional sources that present other points of view. Pay particular attention to the writer's tone.

Many relevant and reliable sources demonstrate bias. Some provide only a portion of the information you need for your paper. For example, if you are writing an essay on problems in the nursing profession, *The American Journal of Nursing* might be a reliable source, but it would probably not contain articles that are critical of nurses.

Other sources may have a strong opinion and present information from that point of view. For example, suppose you are writing an essay on home schooling for an introductory education class, and you find a book titled *The Home Schooling Movement: What Children Are Missing*. The author taught at a public high school for thirty years. This book may offer valuable information, but you need to recognize that its author supports classroom instruction and so may emphasize the shortcomings of home schooling or downplay its advantages. To use a biased source effectively, take the author's point of view into consideration as you evaluate the evidence the source provides.

EXERCISE 21.4   **EXAMINING SOURCES FOR BIAS**

Examine each of the following sources and their annotations. Discuss whether the source is likely to be objective (O), somewhat biased (SB), or heavily biased (HB).

1. Roleff, Tamara L., editor. *Gun Control: Opposing Viewpoints.* Greenhaven Press, 2007.

   This book contains several articles that present the pros and cons of different issues relating to gun control. The articles are written by experts and give bibliographic references.

2. Malcolm X. *The Autobiography of Malcolm X.* Ballantine Books, 1965.

   Malcolm X tells his life story in this autobiography, which was published just before his death.

3. Green, Amy. "Missions Boot Camp." *Christianity Today,* vol. 52, no. 2, Feb. 2008, www.christianitytoday.com/ct/2008/march/.

   This article describes a summer camp for young people heading off on mission trips.

4. Fink, George, editor. *Encyclopedia of Stress.* Academic Press, 2007.

   Four volumes of in-depth coverage related to the psychology and physiology of stress.

The following worksheet can help you evaluate the relevance and reliability of sources.

Worksheet: Evaluating Sources

Title: _____

Author: _____

Author's qualifications or experience: _____

Publication information (journal, volume, issue; publisher, URL):

_____

Month, date, and year of publication: _____

Is this source up-to-date? ☐ yes ☐ no

Type of source: ☐ primary ☐ secondary ☐ multimedia
                 ☐ book ☐ article (specify: _____)
                 ☐ scholarly work ☐ reference work ☐ popular source

Is the source appropriate for your audience? ☐ yes ☐ no

Does the source have a good reputation? ☐ yes ☐ no

   Does the source exhibit bias? ☐ yes ☐ no

What evidence do you have that the source is biased?

_____

_____

   Are opinions clearly stated as such? ☐ yes ☐ no

What is the purpose of the source? _____

   Who publishes the source? _____

   What are the publisher's goals? _____

Are the visual aids included with the source useful and credible? ☐ yes ☐ no

Is the source professionally presented and edited? ☐ yes ☐ no

Does the source contain any factual errors? ☐ yes ☐ no

Does the source provide documentation for all of its cited sources, either within the text or in a Works Cited/References section (or both)? ☐ yes ☐ no

Are there any hints that information has been omitted? ☐ yes ☐ no

If yes, describe: _____

22
Finding Sources, Taking Notes, and Synthesizing Ideas

© Peter Essick/Aurora Photos

In this chapter you will learn to:

- use keywords effectively to find sources using your library's catalog and databases and Internet search engines

- conduct field research: interviews, surveys, and observations

- take effective notes: annotating and highlighting, summarizing, and paraphrasing information

- evaluate your research

- synthesize information and ideas from sources

- create an annotated bibliography

WRITING QUICK START   Suppose you are enrolled in a seminar on the environment. Your instructor gives the class a number of photographs and directs students to choose one and write a paper about the environmental issues it portrays. You've chosen the photograph shown here, which appeared in a *National Geographic* article titled "High-Tech Trash: Will Your Discarded TV End Up in a Ditch in Ghana?" Write a brief statement describing the environmental issue the photograph illustrates. Consider where you might go to learn more about this issue, and make a list of the sources you would consult.

What issue did you write about? What sources of information did you list? This chapter will show you how to find and evaluate a variety of sources; how to conduct field research; and how to record, connect, and make sense of what you learn from sources. To do all this effectively, you must approach the research process in a systematic way. Graphic Organizer 22.1 lists the research skills you will need to develop, placing the skills covered in this chapter within the context of the process of writing a research project as a whole.

GRAPHIC ORGANIZER 22.1 Writing a Research Project Using Sources

Planning a Research Project and Evaluating Sources — • See Chapter 21

Finding, Taking Notes on, and Evaluating Sources —
- Conduct keyword searches.
- Find sources using your library search options.
- Conduct field research.
- Take notes that summarize and paraphrase.
- Synthesize ideas and information from sources with your own ideas.

Drafting, Revising, and Formatting a Research Project — • See Chapter 23

Documenting Your Sources — • See Chapter 23

USING RESEARCH IN COLLEGE AND THE WORKPLACE

- For an *anthropology course*, you are asked to write a research project in which you analyze the differences between the religious practices of two cultures.

- For an *art history course*, you must write a biography of a famous Renaissance artist as a final research project.

- As *supervisor* of a health care facility, you decide to conduct a survey of the staff to determine employees' interest in flexible working hours.

Get an Overview of Library Sources

Your college library is an immense collection of print, media, and online sources. Learning your way around the library is the first step in locating sources effectively.

Learn Your Way around the Library

It is a good idea to become familiar with your college library *before* you need to use it. Following are a few ways to do so.

1. **Take a tour of the library.** Many colleges offer formal library tours during the first few weeks of the term, or your instructor may arrange one. On a tour, you'll learn where everything is located and discover how to use important services, such as interlibrary loan (borrowing materials from other libraries), and how to find reliable sources using your library's search tools. Check the library, too, for places to study, such as a library carrel or cubicle or a room where you can collaborate with classmates.

2. **Take a tour of your library's Web site.** Most college libraries provide access to rich resources through the library's Web site (see Figure 22.1). Often students can search for books, articles, multimedia sources, and more; access citation (or reference) managers (to help you manage sources and create lists of works cited or references); request sources through interlibrary loan; find a list of library hours or extended hours during midterms and finals; or ask a reference librarian for help. Visit your library's Web site to find out what services are available online as well as face-to-face.

Make Use of Reference Librarians

Reference librarians can help you at any stage in the research process, advising you about what sources to use and where to locate them. For example, reference librarians can help you do all of the following.

- Use library resources to make a topic broader, narrower, or more relevant.
- Get you started by steering you toward reference resources or basic books and articles that provide background information on your topic.
- Identify other libraries or special collections that might be relevant to your research, then help you request those materials through interlibrary loan.
- Help you decide which search terms to use, identify appropriate specialized databases, and learn how to search those databases most efficiently.
- Obtain the full text of articles for which you have only summary information (abstracts).
- Show you how to use various citation management systems such as EndNote, Zotero, and RefWorks. (Citation management systems allow you to store and format bibliographic material from your sources in a number of popular citation styles.)

In short, reference librarians can often save you time, so don't hesitate to ask them for help.

Use Keywords Effectively

Whether you use your library's search options or Google, you will use **keywords**, words or phrases that describe your topic, to search for information. You type your keywords into a search box and hit "Enter," and the search engine scans all the items in its index

FIGURE 22.1   Sample Library Home Page

The Montgomery College Library home page allows students to search for books, articles, and other resources all through a single portal. The home page also provides access to a wealth of other useful information.

for those that include your keywords. In other words, to search effectively, you must figure out which words your sources are likely to use and use those as your keywords. The tips below can help improve your search results.

- **More specific terms yield more relevant results.** For example, if you were writing about alternative political parties in the United States, using keywords like *politics* or even *political parties* would be too broad. Searching on phrases like *third parties in the United States* would reduce the number of hits and make those hits more relevant. If you are having difficulty coming up with keywords, use a reference resource, like a specialized encyclopedia, to find the terms those writing about a topic would be likely to use.
- **Include synonyms.** To make sure your search yields the best results, brainstorm a list of synonyms for your keywords and search for those terms as well. For example, if you are searching for information on *welfare reform*, you might also search for *entitlement programs*, *government benefits*, and *welfare spending*.
- **Use full names and titles.** Search for people using full names, including middle initials when available. If the name is common, add other pieces of information, such as the college or university where the person teaches. When searching for books or articles, use complete titles.
- **Use the advanced search functions.** For example, Google's advanced search feature allows you to search for an exact phrase and to exclude words that should not appear in your search results (among other options). Google also allows you to filter your results by language, reading level, date, region, and several other criteria. Library catalogs and databases also allow you to narrow your results, for example, to scholarly articles or to books published within a specific timeframe, in a specific language, or on a specific subject.
- **Use subject headings.** Most libraries and database vendors (such as EBSCO or LexisNexis) use standard subject headings to index their contents. To generate more relevant search results, make sure your keywords match the Library of Congress subject headings, or use the Thesaurus or Subject Terms link on the search page to check and refine your list of keywords. For instance, checking the thesaurus for a medical database may reveal that the ideal search term is not *heart attack* but *myocardial infarction*.

If your keyword searches are returning too many results or too many irrelevant results, try the following.

- Combine keywords to make your search terms more specific, or remove search terms to broaden your results.
- Once you find a relevant source, look at the subject terms associated with it, and use those for subsequent searches.
- Conduct a new search using a specialized database.
- Read the tool's search tips or FAQs for specific advice on how to improve your results.

Keep in mind that effective research requires ingenuity and persistence, so don't give up too easily.

Use Appropriate Search Tools

As you analyze your writing assignment, you will likely find yourself wondering where to begin. The key entry portal for research is your library's homepage. Student researchers may also benefit from using **research**, or **subject**, **guides**, discipline- and course-specific lists of useful resources. Each research guide has been created by a librarian and is tailored to the kinds of assignments that college students get regularly.

Search for Books and Other Library Holdings

Libraries own a variety of source types: books and e-books, magazines and newspapers (in print), some printed government documents, special collections, and multimedia items such as video and audio recordings. Researchers identify relevant items in the library's collection by accessing a computerized catalog, which allows users to search online for sources by keyword, title, author, or subject from terminals in the library as well as from computers at home or in a campus computer lab. Some systems, like the one shown in Figure 22.2, allow users to narrow a search by subject, author, and publication date. Often the catalog will indicate not only where an item is shelved, but also whether it has been checked out and when it is due back.

Once you have a specific call number, use a library floor plan and the call number guides posted on shelves to locate the appropriate section of the library and the book you need. While looking for your book, be sure to scan the surrounding books, which are usually on related topics. You may discover other useful sources that you overlooked in the catalog.

Search for Articles in Your Library's Databases

College libraries subscribe to databases that list articles in **periodicals**, publications that are issued at regular intervals (daily, weekly, monthly, or quarterly), such as scholarly journals, magazines, and newspapers. Database entries usually include an **abstract**, or brief summary of the article, as well as information about the article itself (title, author, publishing information, and keywords used in the article). As with library catalogs, databases allow users to refine their searches by limiting results by date or publication type, for example. They also may allow you to email, print, or save relevant articles.

Many articles will be available through the database in full text. They may appear in PDF format, which usually shows the article just as it appeared in the periodical, or in HTML format, which is usually text only. For articles that are not available in full text, a librarian can help you request them via interlibrary loan.

Your library probably subscribes to general databases and specialized ones. **General databases** list articles on a wide range of subjects in both popular magazines and scholarly journals. Academic Search Complete (Figure 22.3, p. 571), for example, provides abstracts (or summaries) for articles in over 16,000 periodicals and offers the full text of articles in over 8,500 of those periodicals.

Specialized databases index either articles within specific academic disciplines, or fields, or particular types of articles, such as book reviews, abstracts of doctoral

FIGURE 22.2 Library Catalog Search Results

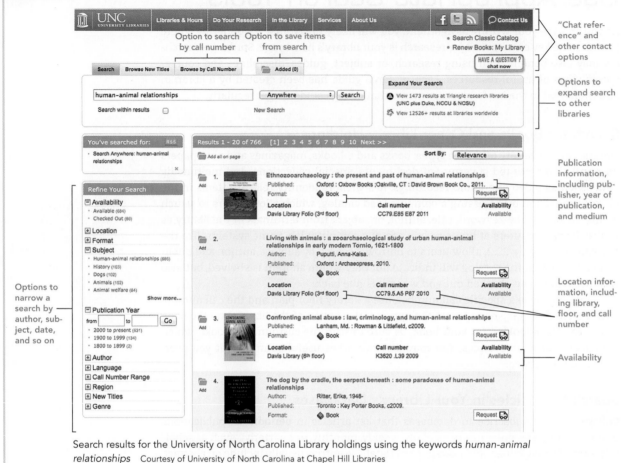

Search results for the University of North Carolina Library holdings using the keywords *human-animal relationships*   Courtesy of University of North Carolina at Chapel Hill Libraries

dissertations, and articles and essays published in books. Some examples of specialized databases are *Book Review Digest Plus, Dissertation and Theses, PsycArticles, Web of Science,* and *Sociological Abstracts.*

Note: Names of databases may change, the number of sources a database indexes or includes full text for may change, and database vendors may make different packages of databases available at different times, so consult a reference librarian if you are not sure which database to use.

Use the Internet for Research, with Caution

The Internet provides access to millions of Web sites, but you need to use a search engine to find them. **Search engines** allow you to find information by typing a keyword or phrase into a search box. Google is such a popular search engine that you might never have used anything else, but other excellent search engines exist, and some of them are listed below.

Search Engine	Why try it?
Bing.com	Bing provides a list of results in the main column but also includes a list of "Related searches," which may help you refine your search strategy.
Dogpile.com	Dogpile is a metasearch engine; in other words, it draws its results from a variety of other search engines.
DuckDuckGo.com	DuckDuckGo allows users to search anonymously and lists all results on a single page, making less clicking necessary.

Because different search engines may generate different results, it is a good idea to try your search on more than one search engine.

While the Internet is an amazing resource for researchers, the quality of the content you will find varies wildly. As a result, researchers must evaluate content very carefully before relying on it.

For more on evaluating sources, see Chapter 3, pp. 60–70, and Chapter 21, pp. 559–63.

FIGURE 22.3 Academic Search Complete: Sample Search Results

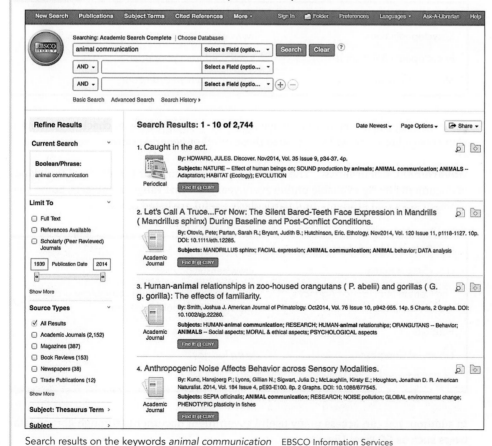

Search results on the keywords *animal communication*   EBSCO Information Services

News sites. Newspapers, television and radio networks, and magazines have companion Web sites that provide current information and late-breaking news stories. Some of the most useful are listed below.

BBC	www.bbc.co.uk
CNN	www.cnn.com
The Wall Street Journal	www.wsj.com
The New York Times	www.nytimes.com
National Public Radio	NPR.org
The Washington Post	www.washingtonpost.com

General reference sites.   Reference works are available online, through the Web or through the databases your library subscribes to. Some of the most useful general reference sites are listed below.

Britannica Online	www.eb.com
Encyclopedia.com	www.encyclopedia.com
Encyclopedia Smithsonian	www.si.edu/encyclopedia
Merriam-Webster Online	www.merriam-webster.com

Some of these sites may not be available for free through Google; check to find out if your college library provides access to these or other general reference sources.

Government documents. The federal government makes hundreds of thousands of documents freely available online every year on a vast range of subjects. Some government sites that students find particularly useful are listed below.

U.S. Bureau of Labor Statistics	www.bls.gov
U.S. Census Bureau	www.census.gov
The Central Intelligence Agency's World Fact Book	www.cia.gov/library/publications/resources/the-world-factbook/index.html
FedStats	fedstats.sites.usa.gov
Library of Congress	www.loc.gov
National Institutes of Health	www.nih.gov

In addition, you can access many useful government documents through library databases such as *CQ Press Library*.

Conduct Field Research

Depending on your research topic, you may need—or want—to conduct field research to collect original information. This section discusses three common types of field research.

1. Interviews
2. Surveys
3. Observation

All of these methods generate primary source material.

Conduct Interviews

An **interview** allows you to obtain firsthand information from a person who is knowledgeable about your topic. For example, if the topic of your research project is *treatment of teenage alcoholism*, it might be a good idea to interview an experienced substance abuse counselor who works with teenagers. Use the following suggestions to conduct effective interviews.

1. **Choose interviewees carefully.** Be sure your interviewees work in the field you are researching or are experts on your topic.
2. **Arrange your interview by phone or email well in advance.** Describe your project and purpose, explaining that you are a student working on an assignment, and indicate the amount of time you think you'll need.
3. **Plan the interview.** Do some research to make sure the information you need is not already available through more traditional sources. Then devise a list of questions you want to ask. Try to ask *open questions*, which generate discussion, rather than *closed questions*, which can be answered in a word or two. For example, "Do you think your company has a promising future?" could be answered yes or no, whereas, "How do you account for your company's turnaround last year?" might spark a detailed response. Open questions usually encourage people to open up and reveal attitudes as well as facts.
4. **Take notes during the interview.** Write the interviewee's responses in note form and ask whether you may quote him or her directly. If you want to record the interview, be sure to ask the interviewee's permission.
5. **Evaluate the interview.** As soon as possible after the interview, reread your notes and fill in information you did not have time to record. Also write down your reactions while they are still fresh in your mind.

Conduct Surveys

A **survey** is a set of questions designed to elicit information quickly from a large number of people. Surveys are often used to assess people's attitudes or intentions. They can be conducted face-to-face, by phone, or online.

Use the following suggestions to prepare effective surveys.

1. **Clarify the purpose of the survey.** Prepare a detailed list of what you want to learn from the survey.

2. **Design your questions.** A survey can include closed or open questions or both, but most surveys use mostly closed questions (either multiple-choice or ranking), so responses can be tabulated easily.
3. **Test your survey questions.** Try out your questions on a few classmates, family members, or friends to be sure they are clear, unambiguous, and easily understood.
4. **Select your respondents.** Your respondents—the people who provide answers to your survey—must be *representative* of the group you are studying and must be *chosen at random*. One way to draw a random sample is to give the survey to every fifth or tenth name on a list or to every fifteenth person who walks by.
5. **Summarize and report your results.** Tally the results and look for patterns in the data. In your project, discuss your overall findings, and explain the purpose of the survey as well as how you designed it. Include a copy of the survey and tabulations in an appendix.

Conduct Observations

An **observation** (of an event, a scene, or an activity) can be an important primary source in a research project. For instance, you might observe children at play to analyze differences in play between boys and girls. Firsthand observation can yield valuable insights on the job as well. You might, for example, need to observe and report on the condition of hospital patients or the job performance of your employees.

Use the following tips to conduct observations effectively.

1. **Arrange your visit in advance.** Unless you are conducting an observation in a public place, obtain permission from the company or organization in advance. Make the purpose of your visit clear when arranging your appointment.
2. **Take detailed notes on what you observe.** Write down the details you will need to describe the scene vividly in your paper. Observe the scene from different angles or perspectives. You might sketch the scene, especially if you are a spatial learner, or record a video if you have permission to do so.

For more on creating a dominant impression, see Chapter 12, p. 264.

3. **Create a dominant impression.** As soon as possible after your visit, evaluate your observations. Think about what you saw and heard. Then describe your dominant impression of what you observed and the details that support it.

Work with Sources: Take Notes, Summarize, and Paraphrase

For more on previewing, see Chapter 2, pp. 27–30.

Reading sources involves some special skills. Unlike textbook reading, in which your purpose is to learn and recall the material, you usually read sources to extract the information you need about a topic. Therefore, you can often read sources selectively, previewing the source to identify relevant sections and reading just those sections.

Take Effective Notes

Your purpose in conducting research is to explore your topic, consider multiple perspectives, and gradually arrive at your own main point—your thesis. As you conduct research, your ideas will develop, and you will generate topic sentences based on a synthesis of sources that you've read. In fact, the development of these integrated or synthesized ideas is a key goal of writing a research project.

Because you must give credit to those who informed your thinking, be particularly cautious when cutting and pasting source materials into your notes. Always place quotation marks around anything you have cut and pasted. Be sure to clearly separate your ideas from the ideas you found in sources. If you copy an author's exact words, place the information in quotation marks, and write the term *direct quotation* as well as the page number(s) in parentheses after the quotation. If you write a summary note (see pp. 576–77) or paraphrase (see pp. 577–79), write *paraphrase* or *summary* and the page number(s) of the source. Be sure to include page numbers; you'll need them to double-check your notes against the source and to create an in-text citation. Be sure to record all the information you will need to create a complete works-cited or reference entry.

For more on creating entries in a works-cited or references list, see Chapter 23, pp. 607–28, 631–44.

Note-taking tools.   Many students use a series of computer folders or a notebook for their research. In a notebook, you might use section dividers for different components of your research; in a computer folder, you might use various subfolders. A notebook or computer file is a good place to store copies of research materials that you have copied or downloaded.

While many students prefer to take notes in computer files or notebooks, some researchers still like to use index cards for note-taking. (There are also programs available that allow you to create computerized note cards.) Note cards allow you to arrange and rearrange the material to experiment with different ways of organizing your project. If you decide to use note cards, put information from only one source or about only one subtopic on each card. At the top of the card, indicate the author of the source and the page numbers on which the information appears, and note the subtopic that the note covers. Figure 22.4 shows a sample note card. Use a separate set of note cards or a

FIGURE 22.4   Sample Note Card

Schmoke & Roques 17–25

Medicalization

Medicalization is a system in which the government would control the release of narcotics to drug addicts.

— would work like a prescription does now — only gov't official would write prescription

— addicts would be required to get counseling and health services

— would take drug control out of hands of drug traffickers (paraphrase, 18)

separate section of your notebook or computer file to list the bibliographic information you will need to cite the source. (See Figure 22.5 on p. 580 for a worksheet to help you record the information you will need.)

Citation (or reference) managers, programs like Mendeley, RefWorks, and Zotero, can be useful tools throughout the research process because they allow you to save sources, take notes, and incorporate those notes into your research project as you write. They may also help you format your works cited or reference list entries.

For more on annotating and highlighting, see Chapter 2, pp. 34–45.

Annotating and highlighting source materials. Annotating and highlighting (or underlining) can be a useful system of engaging closely with source materials. You may annotate and highlight using a pencil and a highlighting marker or using the annotation and highlighting features available with some electronic documents. You can then store these annotated documents in a notebook pocket, a computer file, or a citation manager. Remember to be selective about what you mark or comment on as you annotate, keeping the purpose of your research in mind.

Take Notes That Summarize, Paraphrase, or Quote

Much of your note-taking should summarize, or condense, information from sources, since you will mostly not need the exact wording or the kinds of details you would include in a paraphrase.

After summarizing, paraphrasing is probably the second-most common form your notes should take. Paraphrase when recording the supporting details is important, but paraphrase only the ideas or details you intend to use. Both summarizing and paraphrasing force you to understand the source.

Including **direct quotations**—writers' exact words—is probably the least common form your notes should take, but including quotations in your notes can still be advisable, even necessary. Use quotations to record wording that is unusual or striking, capture technical details you might get wrong, or report the exact words of an expert on your topic.

Summarize

As you write summary notes, keep the following in mind.

- Everything you put in summary notes must be *in your own words and sentences*.
- Your summary notes should accurately reflect the relevant main points of the source.

For more on writing summaries, see Chapter 2, pp. 42–43.

Use the guidelines below to write effective summary notes.

1. **Record only information that relates to your topic and purpose.**
2. **Write notes that condense the author's ideas into your own words.** Include key terms and concepts or principles, but omit specific examples, quotations, your opinion, or anything else that is not essential to the author's main point. (You can write comments in a separate note.)
3. **Record the ideas in the order in which they appear in the original source.** Reordering ideas might affect the meaning.
4. **Reread your summary to determine whether it contains enough information.** Consider whether it would it be understandable to someone who has not read the original source.

5. Record the complete publication information for the sources you summarize.
Unless you summarize an entire book or poem, you will need to include page
references when you write your paper and prepare a works-cited list.

A sample summary of the first four paragraphs of the essay "Dude, Do You Know
What You Just Said?" (p. 436) appears below. Read or reread paragraphs 1–4, and then
study the summary.

Sample Summary

"Dude, Do You Know What You Just Said?" reports on the findings of Scott Kiesling, a linguist who has studied the uses and meanings of the popularly used word
dude. Historically, *dude* was first used to refer to a dandy and then became a slang
term used by various social groups. For his study, Kiesling listened to tapes of fraternity members and asked undergraduate students to record uses of the term. He
determined that it is used for a variety of purposes, including to show enthusiasm
or excitement, one-up someone, avoid confrontation, and demonstrate agreement.

Paraphrase

When you paraphrase, you restate the author's ideas *in your own words and sentences*.
You do not condense ideas or eliminate details as you do in a summary; instead, you
keep the author's intended meaning but express that meaning in different sentence
patterns and vocabulary. In most cases, a paraphrase is approximately the same length
as the original material.

When paraphrasing, be careful not to *plagiarize*—that is, do not use an author's
words or sentences as if they were your own. Merely replacing some words with synonyms is not enough; you must also use your own sentence structures and may want to
reorganize the presentation of ideas. Reading the excerpt from a source below and comparing it, first, with the acceptable paraphrase that follows and then with the example
that includes plagiarism will help you see what an acceptable paraphrase looks like.

For more on avoiding plagiarism, see Chapter 23,
pp. 589–91.

Excerpt from Original

Learning some items may interfere with retrieving others, especially when
the items are similar. If someone gives you a phone number to remember, you
may be able to recall it later. But if two more people give you their numbers, each
successive number will be more difficult to recall. Such proactive interference
occurs when something you learned earlier disrupts recall of something you
experienced later. As you collect more and more information, your mental attic
never fills, but it certainly gets cluttered.

David G. Myers, *Psychology*

Acceptable Paraphrase

According to David Myers, when proactive interference happens, things you
have already learned prevent you from remembering things you learn later. In
other words, details you learn first may make it harder to recall closely related
details you learn subsequently. You can think of your memory as an attic. You can
always add more junk to it. However, it will become messy and disorganized. For
example, you can remember one new phone number, but if you have two or more
new numbers to remember, the task becomes harder.

Unacceptable Paraphrase—Includes Plagiarism

Replaces terms with synonyms

Copied terms and phrases

When you learn some things, it may interfere with your ability to remember others. This happens when the things are similar. Suppose a person gives you a phone number to remember. You probably will be able to remember it later. Now, suppose two persons give you their numbers. Each successive number will be harder to remember. Proactive interference happens when something you already learned prevents you from recalling something you experience later. As you learn more and more information, your mental attic never gets full, but it will get cluttered.

The unacceptable paraphrase does substitute some synonyms—*remember* for *retrieving*, for example—but it is still an example of plagiarism. Not only are some words copied directly from the original, but also the structure of the sentences is nearly identical to the original.

Paraphrasing can be tricky, because letting an author's language creep in is easy. These guidelines will help you paraphrase without plagiarizing.

1. **Read first; then write.** Read material more than once before you try paraphrasing. To avoid copying an author's words, cover up the passage you are paraphrasing (or switch to a new window on your computer), and then write.

2. **Use synonyms that do not change the author's meaning or intent, and if you must use distinctive wording of the author's, enclose it in quotation marks.** Consult a dictionary or thesaurus if necessary. Note that for some specialized terms and even for some commonplace ones, substitutes may not be easy to come by. In the acceptable paraphrase above, the writer uses the key term *proactive interference*, as well as the everyday word *attic*, without quotation marks. However, if the writer paraphrasing the original were to borrow a distinctive turn of phrase, this would need to be in quotation marks. Of course, deciding when quotation marks are or are not needed requires judgment, and if you are not sure, using quotation marks is never wrong.

For more on varying sentence structure, see Chapter 9, pp. 195–205.

3. **Use your own sentence structure.** Using an author's sentence structure can be considered plagiarism. If the original uses lengthy sentences, for example, your paraphrase may use shorter sentences. If the original phrases something in a compound sentence, try recasting the information in a complex one.

4. **Rearrange the ideas if possible.** If you can do so without changing the sense of the passage, rearrange the ideas. In addition to using your own words and sentences, rearranging the ideas can make the paraphrase more your own. Notice that in the acceptable paraphrase above, the writer starts by introducing the term *proactive interference*, whereas in the original source, this term is not used until the fourth sentence.

Be sure to record the publication information (including page numbers) for the sources you paraphrase. You will need this information to document the sources in your paper.

EXERCISE 22.1   WRITING A PARAPHRASE

Write a paraphrase of the following excerpt from a source on animal communication.

> Another vigorously debated issue is whether language is uniquely human. Animals obviously communicate. Bees, for example, communicate the location of food through an intricate dance. And several teams of psychologists have taught various species of apes, including a number of chimpanzees, to communicate with humans by signing or by pushing buttons wired to a computer. Apes have developed considerable vocabularies. They string words together to express meaning and to make and follow requests. Skeptics point out important differences between apes' and humans' facilities with language, especially in their respective abilities to order words using proper syntax. Nevertheless, these studies reveal that apes have considerable cognitive ability.
>
> David G. Myers, *Psychology*

EXERCISE 22.2   EVALUATING A PARAPHRASE FOR PLAGIARISM

The piece of student writing below is a paraphrase of a source on the history of advertising. Working with another student, evaluate the paraphrase and discuss whether it would be considered an example of plagiarism. If you decide the paraphrase is plagiarized, rewrite it so that it is not.

Original Source

> Everyone knows that advertising lies. That has been an article of faith since the Middle Ages—and a legal doctrine, too. Sixteenth-century English courts began the Age of Caveat Emptor by ruling that commercial claims—fraudulent or not—should be sorted out by the buyer, not the legal system. ("If he be tame and have ben rydden upon, then caveat emptor.") In a 1615 case, a certain Baily agreed to transport Merrell's load of wood, which Merrell claimed weighed 800 pounds. When Baily's two horses collapsed and died, he discovered that Merrell's wood actually weighed 2,000 pounds. The court ruled the problem was Baily's for not checking the weight himself; Merrell bore no blame.
>
> Cynthia Crossen, *Tainted Truth*

Paraphrase

> It is a well-known fact that advertising lies. This has been known ever since the Middle Ages. It is an article of faith as well as a legal doctrine. English courts in the sixteenth century started the Age of Caveat Emptor by finding that claims by businesses, whether legitimate or not, were the responsibility of the consumer, not the courts. For example, there was a case in which one person (Baily) used his horses to haul wood for a person named Merrell. Merrell told Baily that the wood weighed 800 pounds, but it actually weighed 2,000 pounds. Baily discovered this after his horses died. The court did not hold Merrell responsible; it stated that Baily should have weighed the wood himself instead of accepting Merrell's word.

FIGURE 22.5   Bibliographic Information Worksheet

Author(s) _____

Title and subtitle of source _____

Title of work source appears in (if any): Journal/anthology/Web site _____

Other contributors: Editor/translator/director _____

Version: Edition/director's cut _____

Volume/issue _____

Publisher/sponsor _____

Publication date _____

Location: Pages/URL/DOI (Digital Object Identifier) _____

Record Quotations

For more on how to adjust a quotation to fit your sentence, see Chapter 23, pp. 595–99.

When writing your paper, you may adjust a quotation to fit your sentence, so long as you do not change the meaning of the quotation, but when taking notes, be sure to record the quotation precisely as it appears in the source. Also provide the page number(s) on which the material being quoted appears in the original source. In your notes, be sure to indicate that you are copying a direct quotation by including quotation marks, the term *direct quotation*, and the page number(s) in parentheses.

Keep Track of Sources

For more on citing sources, see Chapter 23, pp. 593–99.

In addition to gathering information from sources, you must carefully record the information you will need to cite each source. Using a form like the one shown in Figure 22.5 can help you make sure you record all the information you will need. Using a citation manager (p. 594) can also help.

Work with Sources: Evaluate Your Notes and Synthesize

Before you begin drafting, you'll need to make sense of the information you've gathered by synthesizing information and ideas. **Synthesis** means "a pulling together of information to form a new idea or point." You synthesize information every day. For example, after you watch a preview of a movie, talk with friends who have seen the film, and read a review of it, you then pull together the information you have acquired and come up with your own idea—that the movie is your cup of tea, or that you will probably not like it.

You often synthesize information for your college courses. In a biology course, for instance, you might evaluate your own lab results, those of your classmates, and the data in your textbook or another reference source to reach a conclusion about a particular experiment.

Synthesis involves putting ideas together to see how they agree, disagree, or otherwise relate to one another. When working with sources, ask yourself the following questions.

- Do my sources reinforce or contradict one another?
- How do their claims and lines of reasoning compare?
- Do they make similar or dissimilar assumptions and generalizations?
- Is their evidence alike in any way?

Before you begin the synthesis process, however, you must evaluate the sources you've consulted in terms of how well they suit your purposes and audience.

Evaluate Your Research

Before you began researching your topic, you most likely wrote a *working thesis*—a preliminary statement of your main point about the topic—and a list of research questions you hoped to answer. Then, as you researched your topic, you may have discovered facts, statistics, or experts' ideas about the topic that surprised you.

As you evaluate your research notes, keep the following questions in mind.

1. What research questions did I begin with?
2. What answers did I find to those questions?
3. What other information did I discover about my topic?
4. What conclusions can I draw from what I've learned?
5. How does my research affect my working thesis?

For more on evaluating the reliability of sources, see Chapter 21, p. 560.

In many cases, the answers to these questions will influence your thinking on the topic, requiring you to modify your working thesis. If you can't answer these questions in a way that you find satisfactory, you will need to conduct more research to clarify or refine your thinking. In some cases, you may even need to rethink the direction of your research project.

The process of evaluating your research will often result in decisions not to use specific sources in your final paper. Perhaps the source does not provide any new or relevant information; perhaps it comes from a source that you decide is unreliable; perhaps you have too much information to fit in the length of your assignment, and you need to narrow your focus. View this research as information that has contributed to your understanding of the topic, and then set aside the note cards or move the information to a separate notebook section or file where it will not get in your way.

Use Categories to Synthesize Information from Sources

In order to make sense of what you've learned, you will need to find patterns in the information you have gathered. One way to find patterns is to categorize information according to your research questions. For example, one student found numerous sources on and answers to his research question "What causes some parents to abuse their children physically?" After rereading his research notes, he realized the information could be divided into three categories:

Category	Sources
1. Lack of parenting skills	Lopez, Wexler, Thomas
2. Emotional instability	Wexler, Harris, Thompson, Wong
3. Family history of child abuse	Thompson, Harris, Lopez, Strickler, Thomas

Evaluating his research in this way made him see that he needed to revise both his working thesis and the scope of his paper to include lack of parenting skills as a major cause of child abuse. Notice how he modified his working thesis accordingly:

- ~~The main reasons that~~ Some children are physically abused ~~are~~ because of their parents' emotional instability, ~~and~~ family history of child abuse, and lack of parenting skills.

For controversial topics, you may want to categorize the information you've gathered in terms of each position on the issue (pro, con, or somewhere in between). Alternatively, you could categorize information in terms of the reasons sources offer to support their positions. On the issue of gun control legislation, for example, some sources may favor it for national security reasons: Gun control makes it harder for terrorists to acquire guns. Others may favor it for statistical reason: Statistics prove that owning a gun does not prevent crime. Still others may favor it for emotional reasons: A loved one was injured or killed by a firearm.

If your research project focuses on comparing or contrasting two things (for example, communism and capitalism), you could categorize the information you found on each subtopic separately, and then use that organized information to prepare an outline or graphic organizer of your paper.

Draw a Graphic Organizer to Synthesize Sources

Using a graphic organizer is another way to make sense of the information you gather from sources. Simply the process of creating a graphic organizer may reveal patterns, as well as show you how main ideas and supporting details connect.

Suppose, for example, that you are arguing in favor of adopting voluntary simplicity—the minimizing of personal possessions and commitments to create a happier, more manageable life. You have located three reliable and relevant sources on voluntary simplicity, but each develops the idea somewhat differently.

1. Source 1 (Walker) is a practical how-to article that includes some personal examples.
2. Source 2 (Parachin) offers a theoretical look at statistics about workloads and complicated lifestyles and the reasons that voluntary simplicity is appealing.
3. Source 3 (Remy) presents some strategies for simplifying but emphasizes the values of a simplified life.

Graphic Organizer 22.2 presents a sample organizer that synthesizes information from these three sources.

Depending on the types of information you uncover, you can use a variety of organizer formats: If all your sources compare and contrast the same things, such as the policies and effectiveness of two U.S. presidents, you could adapt one of the graphic organizers for comparison and contrast shown in Chapter 15. If most of your sources focus on effects, such as the effects of a recession on retail sales and employment, you

GRAPHIC ORGANIZER 22.2 Synthesizing Sources

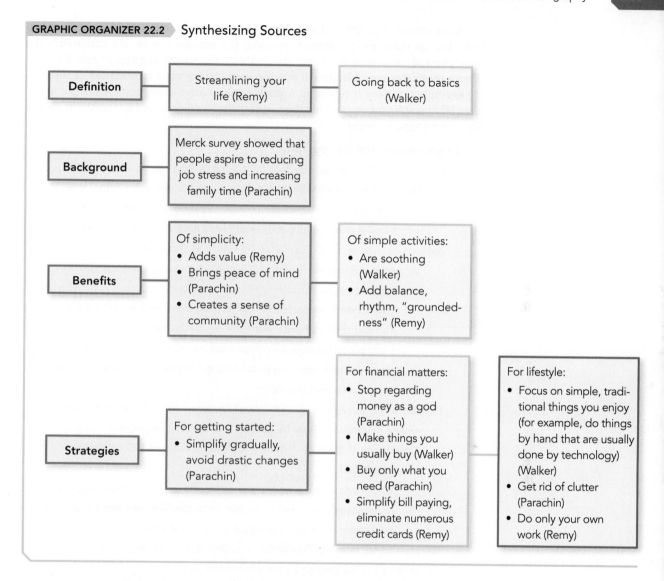

Definition — Streamlining your life (Remy) — Going back to basics (Walker)

Background — Merck survey showed that people aspire to reducing job stress and increasing family time (Parachin)

Benefits —
Of simplicity:
- Adds value (Remy)
- Brings peace of mind (Parachin)
- Creates a sense of community (Parachin)

Of simple activities:
- Are soothing (Walker)
- Add balance, rhythm, "grounded-ness" (Remy)

Strategies —
For getting started:
- Simplify gradually, avoid drastic changes (Parachin)

For financial matters:
- Stop regarding money as a god (Parachin)
- Make things you usually buy (Walker)
- Buy only what you need (Parachin)
- Simplify bill paying, eliminate numerous credit cards (Remy)

For lifestyle:
- Focus on simple, tradi-tional things you enjoy (for example, do things by hand that are usually done by technology) (Walker)
- Get rid of clutter (Parachin)
- Do only your own work (Remy)

could adapt one of the cause-and-effect graphic organizers shown in Chapter 18. What-ever style of organizer you use, be sure to keep track of the sources for each idea and to include them in your organizer.

Create an Annotated Bibliography

As part of the process of writing a research project, some instructors may require you to create an **annotated bibliography,** a list of sources that includes both publication information and a brief summary for each source. Annotated bibliographies are useful ways to document your research process, so they include all the sources you consulted in researching your topic.

Your writing situation will influence the information you include in your annotations, but for most college research projects, the annotations should summarize the main point of the source. They may also evaluate the source in terms of how it relates to your thesis. For example, does it provide useful background information or supporting examples, or does it represent a popular alternative viewpoint? A sample annotated bibliography for researching the use of digital textbooks and e-learning in college classrooms appears below.

Sample Annotated Bibliography

Bajarin, Ben. "Reinventing the Book for the Digital Age." *Time*, 12 Nov. 2013, techland.time.com/2013/11/12/reinventing-the-book-for-the-digital-age/.

> This article from a general-interest magazine describes the features that e-books provide while suggesting even more ideas for future e-books.

deNoyelles, Aimee, et al. "Exploring Students' E-Textbook Practices in Higher Education." *Educause Review*, 2015, er.educause.edu/articles/2015/7/exploring-students-etextbook-practices-in-higher-education.

> This scholarly article reports results from a two-year study by the authors. The authors found that e-textbook use has grown over the course of the study period because e-textbooks are cheaper and more convenient than print textbooks, but instructors are not keeping pace with students' appetites for e-textbooks.

Falc, Emilie O. "An Assessment of College Students' Attitudes towards Using an Online E-Textbook." *Interdisciplinary Journal of E-Learning and Learning Objects,* vol. 9, 2013, pp. 1–12, www.ijello.org/Volume9/IJELLOv9p001-012Falc831.pdf.

> This article from a scholarly journal reports on research studying student experiences with e-textbooks. Recommendations are given for faculty to guide their students on effective use of e-textbooks.

Keengwe, Jared. *Research Perspectives and Best Practices in Educational Technology Integration*. Information Science Reference, 2013.

> This book provides research-based information on how e-learning can be integrated into the college classroom in ways that make technological, practical, and educational sense.

Tichi, Cecelia. "What the E-Book Should Be." *The Chronicle of Higher Education*, 15 Apr. 2016, chronicle.texterity.com/chronicle/20160415b?folio=B25.

> This article from a periodical aimed at college faculty discusses the way e-books should change in relation to students' study habits.

RESEARCH PROJECT IN PROGRESS 3

For the topic you worked on in Research Projects in Progress 1 and 2, locate a minimum of six sources that answer one or more of your research questions. Your sources should include at least one book, one magazine article, one scholarly journal article, one Internet source, and two other sources of any type. On a scale of 1 to 5 (where 1 is low, 5 is high), rank the relevance and reliability of each source you located using the guidelines provided in Chapter 21 (pp. 559–63). Use the following chart to structure your responses.

Source	Relevancy Rating	Reliability Rating
1. _____	_____	_____
2. _____	_____	_____
3. _____	_____	_____
4. _____	_____	_____
5. _____	_____	_____
6. _____	_____	_____

RESEARCH PROJECT IN PROGRESS 4

For the three most relevant and reliable sources you identified in Research Project in Progress 3, use the suggestions on pages 574–80 to take notes on your sources. Your goal is to provide information and support for the ideas you developed earlier. Choose a system of note-taking, writing summary notes and paraphrases, annotating and underlining, and recording quotations as needed. As you work, try to answer your research questions and keep your working thesis in mind.

RESEARCH PROJECT IN PROGRESS 5

For the three sources you worked with in Research Project in Progress 4, use the suggestions on pages 581–83 to synthesize your notes using categories or a graphic organizer. As you work, keep your research questions and working thesis in mind. After synthesizing, consider whether you need to alter your working thesis or conduct additional research.

23

Drafting, Revising, and Formatting a Research Project

© Barry Lewis/Alamy

In this chapter you will learn to:

- organize and draft your research project

- avoid plagiarism by understanding what to document and giving credit to all your sources

- integrate sources into your research project effectively with signal phrases (attributions) and in-text citations

- follow the proper guidelines for integrating quotations into your research project

- revise and prepare a final draft of your research project

- document your sources in MLA or APA format

WRITING QUICK START Suppose you were assigned to write a research project for a mass communication course on a topic related to human communication involving two or more people. You decided to write about issue-oriented art, examining how artists make political or social statements through their art. After reviewing numerous sources, you decided to focus on one artist—Banksy. You drafted a working thesis, examined Banksy's works, and synthesized commentaries on and evaluations of Banksy's art. Now you are ready to revise your thesis, organize your ideas, and begin drafting your essay.

Based on what you have learned about drafting and revising from earlier chapters and from your instructor, write a paragraph describing how you will follow through on the process of drafting and revising your research project. Also consider how writing and revising a research project might differ from writing a paper that does not rely on outside sources.

In Chapter 21 you learned how to plan a project using sources and how to choose and evaluate useful information. Chapter 22 gave you advice on finding sources, taking notes, making sense of information from sources, and synthesizing sources as you prepare to compose your research project. This chapter continues the research process by showing you how to organize, draft, revise, and document a research project using sources. Graphic Organizer 23.1 presents an overview of the process.

GRAPHIC ORGANIZER 23.1   Writing a Paper Using Sources

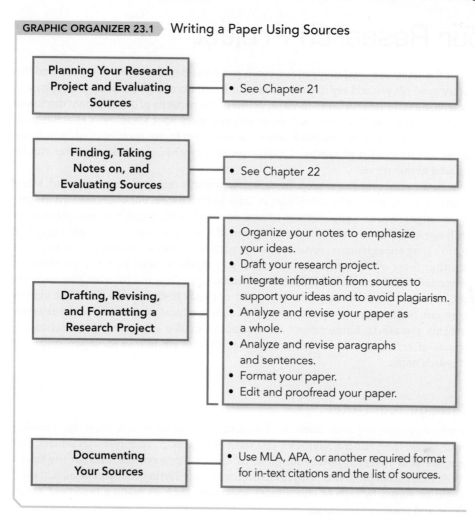

| Planning Your Research Project and Evaluating Sources | • See Chapter 21 |

| Finding, Taking Notes on, and Evaluating Sources | • See Chapter 22 |

| Drafting, Revising, and Formatting a Research Project | • Organize your notes to emphasize your ideas.
• Draft your research project.
• Integrate information from sources to support your ideas and to avoid plagiarism.
• Analyze and revise your paper as a whole.
• Analyze and revise paragraphs and sentences.
• Format your paper.
• Edit and proofread your paper. |

| Documenting Your Sources | • Use MLA, APA, or another required format for in-text citations and the list of sources. |

USING RESEARCH   IN COLLEGE AND THE WORKPLACE

- For a *business management course*, you are required to research a Fortune 500 company and write a report on its history and current profitability. At least two of your sources must be from the Internet.

- For a *social problems course*, you are asked to identify a social problem in your area, research the causes of the problem, and report your findings in a research paper.

- As *human resources director* of a publishing company, you are asked to research editorial salaries in the publishing industry and submit a report that your company will use to decide whether to change salary levels for editors.

Organize Your Research Project

For more on using categories or a graphic organizer to synthesize ideas, see Chapter 22, pp. 582–83.

Your first step in organizing your research project is deciding what you'll say and the order in which you will say it. Think about which pattern of organization—chronological, spatial, most-to-least or least-to-most, or one of the patterns of development discussed in Parts 3 and 4 of this text—will allow you to convey your ideas most effectively. As you plan your organization, think about the best ways to use sources to support those ideas. Creating a list of synthesis categories or a synthesis graphic organizer can be helpful in this regard.

In the planning stage, keep the research project's required length in mind. Many essay assignments can be completed in three or four pages, but your research assignment might require a paper of ten, fifteen, or even twenty pages. Can you get enough mileage out of your topic and organization? If you think your current plan may not yield a long enough paper, consider using another pattern of development to explore another facet of the topic. For example, you might be able to write an effective extended definition essay on the topic of home-schooling, but for a lengthy research project on home-schooling you may need not only to define the term but also to compare or contrast home-schooling with public education, to explore the reasons parents choose to home-school their children or the effects of home-schooling (cause-effect), and so on. Below are some additional guidelines for organizing your research paper.

Arrange Your Notes

Start by considering your thesis or the categories you identified while synthesizing your notes. Then list the subtopics you want to explore in your research project, and arrange your research notes into these categories. For example, files for the thesis "Prekindergarten programs provide children with long-lasting educational advantages" might be sorted by type of educational advantage, such as reading readiness, social skills, and positive self-image.

If you used . . .	then . . .
note cards	sort them into piles by subtopic or category.
a research notebook	pull out pages and keep the notes on each subtopic in a separate manila folder.
photocopies of sources	attach sticky notes to indicate the subtopic and place copies in separate manila folders for each subtopic.
computer files	copy and paste notes into folders by subtopic.
a citation (or reference) manager	save notes and sources in separate subfolders for each subtopic.

Regardless of the medium in which you worked, be careful to keep track of which material belongs to which source as you rearrange your notes. Once your notes are organized by subtopic, you are ready to develop your outline or graphic organizer.

Develop an Outline or Graphic Organizer

Use an outline or a graphic organizer to show how you plan to arrange the divisions and subdivisions you intend to use. Preparing such a plan is especially important for a research project because you are working with a substantial amount of information. Without something to follow, it is easy to get lost and write an unfocused paper.

For more on creating outlines and graphic organizers, see Chapter 7, pp. 161–64.

LEARNING STYLE OPTIONS

Pragmatic learners tend to prefer organizing in detail before they begin to write. If this is your tendency, make sure that you are open to change and new ideas as you draft. Creative learners, in contrast, may prefer to start writing and try to structure the paper as they work. Most students should not take this approach, however; those who do should allow extra time for reorganizing and making extensive revisions.

Whatever your learning style, writing an outline or sketching a graphic organizer can help you test several different organizations. Be sure to save your original outline or graphic organizer and any revised versions as separate files in case you need to return to earlier versions.

> **RESEARCH PROJECT IN PROGRESS 6**
>
> Using the synthesis categories or graphic organizer that you developed for Research Project in Progress 5 (p. 585), sort your notes into categories and evaluate your working thesis. Then prepare an outline or a graphic organizer for your research project.

Avoid Plagiarism

After you have decided what source information to use, you will need to build that information into your essay. Three common methods for extracting information—summarizing, paraphrasing, and quoting—are discussed in Chapter 22 (pp. 576–80). In general, it is best to paraphrase or summarize information rather than quote it directly unless the wording is unusual, beautiful, or unique or if you want to provide the exact statement of an expert on the topic. Quotations are also appropriate when discussing works of literature and historical (primary) sources. (More information on integrating quotations into your paper appears on pp. 593–99.)

Regardless of how you integrate sources, be sure to acknowledge and document all ideas or information you have borrowed from sources that is not common knowledge (p. 591). Remember that you must cite your sources regardless of whether you are using direct quotations, paraphrases, or summaries and regardless of whether the information or ideas came to you from a book, an article, a Web site, or even a conversation. Failing to cite a source, even by mistake, may be considered plagiarism.

What Is Plagiarism?

Plagiarism is the use of someone else's ideas, wording, organization, or sentence structure without acknowledging the source. At most schools, both intentional (deliberate) plagiarism and unintentional (accidental) plagiarism are considered serious forms of cheating and carry the same academic penalties — generally a failing grade or even permanent expulsion. Buying a paper and submitting it as your own work is plagiarism, but so is copying text from a source into your notes and then incorporating it into your essay as if it were your own idea, because you no longer realize that it is another writer's work.

Instructors may use Internet tracking resources like Turnitin.com, or they may paste a student's paper into a Google search box to check for plagiarism, so managing the information you have borrowed from sources is crucial. The quick reference guide below can help you determine if you have plagiarized.

Quick Reference Guide to Plagiarism

You have plagiarized if you:

- copied information word for word without using quotation marks, whether or not you acknowledge the source
- paraphrased information (put it in your own words and sentences) without acknowledging the source
- borrowed someone else's organization, sentence structure, or sequence of ideas without acknowledging the source
- reused someone else's visual material (graphs, tables, charts, maps, diagrams, and so on) without acknowledging the source
- submitted another writer's paper as your own

How Can You Avoid Plagiarism?

Plagiarism is a serious matter, but it can be avoided if you follow these tips.

- **Take careful notes.** Place anything you copy directly in quotation marks and record the source. Record the source for any information you quote, paraphrase, summarize, or even comment on.
- **Be sure to separate your own ideas from ideas expressed in the sources you are using.** Use different colors, different font sizes, different sections of a notebook, or different computer files to distinguish your ideas from those of others. Or take notes in two columns, with ideas and information from sources in one column and your own comments in another.
- **Never copy and paste directly from an online source into your paper.** Instead, cut and paste information you want to save into a separate file. Enclose the material you pasted in quotation marks to remind yourself that it is someone else's wording, and record the source information.

- **Paraphrase information from sources carefully.** Paraphrasing is a great way to test your understanding of sources and to avoid overquoting, but be careful that when you paraphrase, you restate the author's ideas in your own words and sentences.
- **Record all the information you will need to access and cite the source.** Include the name of the site, the URL, your date of access, and so on.

What Sources Do You Need to Document?

You must document all information and ideas you get from a source unless that information is common knowledge. But what is common knowledge, and how can you tell? **Common knowledge** is information that is widely available and undisputed. The fact that George Washington was the United States' first president is common knowledge; so is the fact that the earth revolves around the sun. A good rule of thumb is that if a piece of information is available in a minimum of three reliable sources, then it is considered common knowledge. Of course, you will never be wrong if you cite the source, and you can always ask your instructor or a reference librarian if you are unsure about whether to document something. Table 23.1 also summarizes the types of material that *do* and *do not* require documentation.

Draft Your Research Project

When drafting your research project, keep the following guidelines in mind.

1. **Remember your audience.** Academic audiences will expect you to take a serious, academic tone, and may expect you to use the third person (*he, she, it*). The third

For detailed instructions on how to paraphrase without plagiarizing, see Chapter 22, pp. 577–80. See also the bibliographic worksheet in Figure 22.6, p. 580, which can help you record all the information you need to cite your sources fully.

For more on tone, see Chapter 3, pp. 64–66; for more on audience, see Chapter 4, pp. 103–5.

TABLE 23.1 What Does and Does Not Require Documentation

Documentation Required	Documentation Not Required
• Summaries, paraphrases, and quotations from sources • Obscure or recently discovered facts (such as a little-known fact about Mark Twain or a recent discovery about Mars) • Others' opinions • Others' field research (results of opinion polls, case studies, statistics) • Quotations or paraphrases from interviews you conduct • Others' visuals (photographs, charts, maps, Web images) • Information from others that you use to create visuals (data you use to construct a table, graph, or other visual)	• Common knowledge (George Washington was the first U.S. president, the earth revolves around the sun) • Facts that can be found in numerous sources (winners of Olympic competitions, names of Supreme Court justices) • Standard definitions of academic terms • Your own ideas or conclusions • Your own field research (surveys or observations) • Your own visuals (such as photographs you take)

person is more impersonal, sounds less biased, and may lend credibility to your ideas. Although your instructor may know a great deal about your topic, he or she may want you to demonstrate that you understand key terms and concepts, so definitions and explanations may be required.

For more about placing the thesis statement, see Chapter 5, p. 124.

2. **Follow the introduction, body, and conclusion format, and for most research projects, place your thesis in the introduction.** A straightforward organization, with your thesis in the introduction, is usually the best choice for a research project, since it allows readers to see from the outset how your supporting reasons relate to your main point. However, for projects analyzing a problem or proposing a solution, placing your thesis near the end may be more effective. For example, if you were writing an essay proposing stricter traffic laws on campus, you might begin by documenting the problem—describing accidents that have occurred and detailing their frequency. You might conclude your essay by suggesting that your college lower the speed limit on campus and install two new stop signs.

3. **Follow your outline or graphic organizer, but feel free to make changes as you work.** You may discover a better organization, think of new ideas about your topic, or realize that a subtopic belongs in a different section. Don't feel compelled to follow your outline or organizer to the letter, but be sure to address the topics you list.

4. **Refer to your source notes frequently as you write.** If you do so, you will be less likely to overlook an important piece of evidence. If you suspect that a note is inaccurate in some way, check the original source.

For more on writing and placing topic sentences, see Chapter 6, pp. 141–44; for more on supporting your ideas with evidence, see Chapter 5, pp. 125–31.

5. **State and support the main point of each paragraph.** Use your sources to substantiate, explain, or provide detail to support your main points. Make clear for your readers how your paragraph's main point supports your thesis as well as how the evidence you supply supports your paragraph's main point. Support your major points with evidence from a variety of sources. Doing so will strengthen your position. Relying on only one or two sources may make readers think you did insufficient research. But remember that your research project should not be just a series of facts, quotations, and statistics taken from sources. The basis of the paper should be *your* ideas.

For more on using transitions, see Chapter 6, pp. 149–50.

6. **Use strong transitions.** Because a research project may be lengthy or complex, readers need strong transitions to guide them from paragraph to paragraph and section to section. Make sure your transitions help readers understand how you have divided the topic and how one point relates to another.

7. **Use source information in a way that does not mislead your readers.** Although you are presenting only a portion of someone else's ideas, make sure you are not using information in a way that is contrary to the writer's original intentions.

8. **Include source material only for a specific purpose.** Just because you discovered an interesting statistic or a fascinating quote, don't feel that you must use it. Information that doesn't support your thesis will distract your reader and weaken your paper. Images may add visual interest, but in most academic disciplines, illustrations should be used only when they serve a useful purpose (such as when they provide evidence or are the subject of your analysis, as for an art history project).

GRAPHIC ORGANIZER 23.2 The Structure of a Paragraph in a Research Project

Topic Sentence
- Identifies what the paragraph is about (should be the writer's idea)
- Offers a reason to believe that the writer's thesis statement is true
- Connects to the previous paragraph

Supporting Evidence
- Supports the topic sentence with evidence, such as examples, facts, statistics, or definitions
- Supports the topic sentence by summarizing, paraphrasing, or quoting information or ideas from sources
- Includes in-text citations to identify evidence that comes from sources

Analysis
- Explains how the evidence supports the paragraph's main point
- Provides a transition to the next paragraph

9. **Incorporate in-text citations for your sources as you draft.** Whenever you paraphrase, summarize, or quote a source, be sure to include an in-text citation. The sections "Use In-Text Citations to Integrate Source Information" (pp. 593–96), "MLA Style for In-Text Citations" (pp. 603–7), and "APA Style for In-Text Citations" (pp. 628–31) can help you incorporate in-text citations effectively.

Use Research to Support Your Ideas

Supporting paragraphs in research projects have three parts, as shown in Graphic Organizer 23.2. Each of these three parts is crucial: Without a topic sentence, readers are left to wonder what the main point is. Without the evidence, readers are left to wonder whether the main point is supported. Without the analysis, readers are left to make sense of the evidence and figure out how the evidence supports the topic on their own. Of course, writers must also connect the parts within the paragraph and connect the paragraph to the rest of the essay. The paragraph in Figure 23.1 shows this three-part structure at work. (The essay from which it was taken appears on pp. 621–28.)

Use In-Text Citations to Integrate Source Information

When writing a research project, the goal is to support your own ideas with information from sources and to integrate that information so that you achieve an easy-to-read flow. Along with transitions and strategic repetition, **in-text citations** (brief references

FIGURE 23.1 Sample Paragraph from a Research Project

Transitions

Topic sentence

In-text citation

Supporting evidence

Writer's analysis

One of the major reasons that research into animal emotions was traditionally avoided is that scientists fear being accused of *anthropomorphism*—the act of attributing human qualities to animals. To do so is perceived as unscientific and has been cause for much debate in the scientific community (Bekoff, *Emotional Lives* 124–25). However, Frans de Waal, of the Yerkes Regional Primate Research Center in Atlanta, argues that if people are not open to the possibility of animals having emotions, they may be overlooking important information about both animals and humans. He defends his position in his book, *Primates and Philosophers*. The term *anthropodenial*, which he coined, "denotes willful blindness to the human-like characteristics of animals, or the animal-like characteristics of ourselves" (65). De Waal proposes that because humans and animals are so closely related, it would be impossible for one not to have some characteristics of the other. He contends, "While it is true that animals are not humans, it is equally true that humans are animals. Resistance to this simple yet undeniable truth is what underlies the resistance to anthropomorphism" (65). If de Waal is correct, then we should see animal emotions as on a continuum with humans' and can infer the existence of animal emotions through their behavior, just as we infer the emotions of fellow humans.

to sources in the body of your paper) make this seamless flow possible. These in-text citations direct readers to the list of works cited (or references) at the end of the research project, where they can find all the information they need to locate the sources for themselves. When used effectively, in-text citations also mark where the writer's ideas end and information from sources begins.

Many academic disciplines have a preferred format, or style, for in-text citations and lists of works cited (or references). In English and the humanities, the preferred documentation format is usually that of the Modern Language Association (MLA) and is known as **MLA style**. In the social sciences, the guidelines of the American Psychological Association (APA) are often used; these guidelines are called **APA style**. These are the two most widely used formats and are discussed in detail later in this chapter. A third popular style, which many scientists follow, was created by the Council of Science Editors (CSE); you can find a book detailing CSE style in your college library; citation managers, like RefWorks or EndNote, can also help you format citations in CSE style.

In MLA style, an in-text citation usually includes the author's last name and the page number(s) on which the information appeared in the source. (Use just the author's name for one-page sources and online sources, like Web pages, that do not have page numbers.) This information can be incorporated in two ways:

1. In a signal, or attribution, phrase
2. In a parenthetical citation

Using a signal phrase. When using a **signal phrase**, include the author's name with an appropriate verb before the borrowed material, and put the page number(s) in parentheses at the end of the sentence.

signal phrase   page number

As Jo-Ellan Dimitrius observes, big spenders often suffer from low self-esteem (143).

Using a signal phrase before and a page number after borrowed material also helps readers clearly distinguish *your* ideas from those of your sources. Notice how the writer in Figure 23.1 uses in-text citations to make clear where information from sources begins and ends.

Often, providing some background information about the author the first time you mention a source is useful to readers, especially if the author is not widely known.

relevant background information

Jo-Ellan Dimitrius, a jury-selection consultant whose book *Reading People* discusses methods of predicting behavior, observes that big spenders often suffer from low self-esteem (143).

Such information helps readers understand that the source is relevant and credible.

Using a signal phrase will help you integrate information from sources smoothly into your paper. Most summaries and paraphrases and *all* quotations need such an introduction. Compare the paragraphs below.

Quotation Not Integrated

Anecdotes indicate that animals experience emotions, but anecdotes are not considered scientifically valid. "Experimental evidence is given almost exclusive credibility over personal experience to a degree that seems almost religious" (Masson and McCarthy 3).

Quotation Integrated

Anecdotes indicate that animals experience emotions, but anecdotes are not considered scientifically valid. Masson and McCarthy, who have done extensive field observation, comment, "Experimental evidence is given almost exclusive credibility over personal experience to a degree that seems almost religious" (3).

In the first example paragraph, the quotation is merely dropped in. In the second, the signal phrase, including background of the source authors, smooths the connection.

When writing signal phrases, vary the verbs you use and where you place the signal phrase. The following verbs are useful for introducing many kinds of source material:

advocates	contends	insists	proposes
argues	demonstrates	maintains	shows
asserts	denies	mentions	speculates
believes	emphasizes	notes	states
claims	explains	points out	suggests

In most cases, a neutral verb such as *states, explains,* or *maintains* will be most appropriate. Sometimes, however, a verb such as *denies* or *speculates* may more accurately reflect the source author's attitude.

Using a parenthetical citation.   When you are merely citing facts or have already identified a source author, a **parenthetical citation** that includes the author's last name and the page number may be sufficient.

> Some behavioral experts claim that big spenders often suffer from low
>
> parenthetical citation
> self-esteem (Dimitrius 143).

Integrate Quotations into Your Research Project

Although quotations can lend interest to your research project and provide support for your ideas, they must be used appropriately. The following sections answer some common questions about the use of quotations. (The in-text citations below follow MLA style. See pp. 628–31 for creating in-text citations in APA style.)

Using quotations.   Do not use quotations to reveal ordinary facts and opinions. Rather, quote only when:

- The author's wording is unusual, noteworthy, or striking. The quotation "Injustice anywhere is a threat to justice everywhere" from Martin Luther King Jr.'s "Letter from Birmingham Jail" is probably more effective than any paraphrase.
- The original words express the exact point you want to make, and a paraphrase might alter or distort the statement's meaning.
- The statement is a strong, opinionated, exaggerated, or disputed idea that you want to make clear is not your own.

Formatting long quotations.   Both MLA and APA style require indenting lengthy quotations as a block by half an inch, but the two styles differ in terms of what is considered lengthy. In MLA style, quotations of more than three lines of poetry or more than four lines of prose get indented as a block; in APA style, quotations of more than forty words get indented as a block. Like a shorter quotation in the main text, always introduce a block quotation with a signal phrase. Use a colon at the end of the signal phrase if it is a complete sentence, as in the following example:

> . . . In her book *Through a Window,* which elaborates on her thirty years of experience studying and living among the chimps in Gombe, Tanzania, Jane Goodall gives the following account of Flint's experience with grief:
>
> > Flint became increasingly lethargic, refused most food and, with his immune system thus weakened, fell sick. The last time I saw him alive, he was hollow-eyed, gaunt and utterly depressed, huddled in the vegetation close to where Flo had died. . . . The last short journey he made, pausing to rest every few feet, was to the very place where Flo's body had lain. There he stayed for several hours, sometimes

staring and staring into the water. He struggled on a little further, then curled up—and never moved again. (196–97)

Unlike a shorter quotation in the main text, the page numbers in parentheses appear *after* the final sentence period. (For a short quotation within the text, the page numbers within parentheses *precede* the period.)

Punctuating quotations.   There are specific rules and conventions for punctuating quotations. The most important rules are listed below.

1. **Use single quotation marks to enclose a quotation within a quotation.**

   Coleman and Cressey argue that "concern for the 'decaying family' is nothing new" (147).

2. **Use a comma after a verb that introduces a quotation.** Begin the first word of the quotation with a capital letter (enclosed in brackets if it is not capitalized in the source).

   As Thompson and Hickey report, "There are three major kinds of 'taste cultures' in complex industrial societies: high culture, folk culture, and popular culture" (76).

3. **When a quotation is not introduced by a verb, it is not necessary to use a comma or capitalize the first word.**

   Buck reports that "pets play a significant part in both physical and psychological therapy" (4).

4. **Use a colon to introduce a quotation preceded by a complete sentence.**

   The definition is clear: "Countercultures reject the conventional wisdom and standards of the dominant culture and provide alternatives to mainstream culture" (Thompson and Hickey 76).

5. **For a paraphrase or quotation integrated into the text, punctuation *follows* the parenthetical citation; for a block quotation, the punctuation *precedes* the parenthetical citation.**

   Integrated

   Scientists who favor a related scientific theory called *mutual altruism* believe that animals help each other because, when they themselves need help, they would like to be able to count on reciprocal assistance (Hemelrijk 480).

   Block

   Franklin observed the following scene:

   > Her unhappy spouse moved around her incessantly, his attention and tender cares redoubled. . . . At length his companion breathed her last; from that moment he pined away, and died in the course of a few weeks. (qtd. in Barber 116)

6. **Place periods and commas inside quotation marks.**

> "The most valuable old cars," notes antique car collector Michael Patterson, "are the rarest ones."

7. **Place colons and semicolons outside quotation marks.**

> As Buck demonstrates, "Petting a dog increases mobility of a limb or hand" (4); petting a dog, then, can be a form of physical therapy.

8. **Place question marks and exclamation points inside quotation marks when they are part of the original quotation; place them outside when they belong to your own sentence.**

> The instructor asked, "Does the text's description of alternative lifestyles agree with your experience?"

> Is the following definition accurate: "Sociolinguistics is the study of the relationship between language and society"?

Adapting quotations.   Use the following guidelines when adapting quotations to fit in your own sentences.

1. **You must copy the spelling, punctuation, and capitalization exactly as they appear in the original source, even if they are in error.** (See the last item on this list, item 5, for the only exception.) If a source contains an error, copy it with the error and add the word *sic* (Latin for "thus") in brackets immediately following the error.

> According to Bernstein, "The family has undergone rapid decentralization since Word [sic] War II" (39).

2. **You can emphasize words in a quotation by italicizing them.** However, you must add the notation *emphasis added* in parentheses at the end of the sentence to indicate the change.

> "In *unprecedented* and *increasing* numbers, patients are consulting practitioners of every type of complementary medicine" (Buckman and Sabbagh 73; emphasis added).

3. **You can omit part of a quotation, but you must add an ellipsis—three spaced periods (. . .)—to indicate that material has been deleted.** You may delete words, sentences, paragraphs, or entire pages as long as you do not distort the author's meaning by doing so.

> According to Buckman and Sabbagh, "Acupuncture . . . has been rigorously tested and proven to be effective and valid" (188).

When an omission falls at the end of a quoted sentence, use the three spaced periods after the sentence period.

> Thompson maintains that "marketers need to establish ethical standards for personal selling. . . . They must stress fairness and honesty in dealing with customers" (298).

If you are quoting only a word or phrase from a source, do not use an ellipsis before or after it because it will be obvious that you have omitted part of the original sentence. If you omit the beginning of a quoted sentence, you need not use an ellipsis unless what you are quoting begins with a capitalized word and appears to be a complete sentence.

4. **You can add words or phrases in brackets to make a quotation clearer or to make it fit grammatically into your sentence.** Be sure that in doing so you do not change the original sense.

> Masson and McCarthy note that the well-known animal researcher Jane Goodall finds that "the scientific reluctance to accept anecdotal evidence [of emotional experience is] a serious problem, one that colors all of science" (3).

5. **You can change the first word of a quotation to a capital or lowercase letter to fit into your sentence.** If you change it, enclose it in brackets.

> As Aaron Smith said, "The . . ." (32).
>
> Aaron Smith said that "[t]he . . ." (32).

RESEARCH PROJECT IN PROGRESS 7 ▶

Using your research notes, your revised thesis, and the organizational plan you developed for your research project, write a first draft. Be sure to integrate sources carefully and to include in-text citations. (See pp. 603–7 for MLA style guidelines for in-text citations; see pp. 628–31 for APA style.)

Revise Your Research Project

Revise a research project in two stages. First, focus on the project as a whole; then consider individual paragraphs and sentences for effectiveness and correctness. If time allows, wait at least a day before rereading your research project.

For more on revision, see Chapter 9.

Analyze and Revise Your Project as a Whole

Begin by evaluating your project as a unified piece of writing. Focus on general issues, overall organization, and the key points that support your thesis. Use the flowchart in Figure 23.2 (p. 600) to help you discover the strengths and weaknesses of your research project as a whole. You might also ask a classmate to review your draft by using the questions in the flowchart.

Analyze and Revise Paragraphs and Sentences

After evaluating your project as a whole, check each paragraph to be sure that it supports your thesis and integrates sources appropriately. Then check your sentences for correct structure, transitions, and in-text citation format. Use your earlier work with Figure 23.1 (p. 594) to guide your analysis.

RESEARCH PROJECT IN PROGRESS 8 ▶

Using the questions in Figure 23.2 (p. 600), revise the first draft of your research project.

FIGURE 23.2 ▶ **Flowchart for Revising a Research Project**

QUESTIONS	REVISION STRATEGIES

1. Highlight your thesis statement. Is it clear and specific? Is the assertion based on some of your own (and not just the sources') ideas about the subject?

 ▶

- Delete your thesis statement. Then have a peer read the paper and tell you what he or she believes the thesis is.
- Brainstorm about the main point you wish to make.
- Review the guidelines for writing a thesis in Chapter 5, pages 119–24.

2. Underline the topic sentence of each paragraph. Does each topic sentence make a point that supports your thesis? Does each topic sentence express your own ideas?

 ▶

- Revise any topic sentences that do not support the thesis.
- Revise any topic sentences that rely too heavily on ideas from sources.
- Eliminate any points that don't truly support the thesis.

3. [Bracket] the information and ideas that support each topic sentence. Do you analyze or explain how this information supports your point? Do you use a variety of sources? Do you avoid strings of quotations?

 ▶

- Rewrite to show how source material supports your point.
- Replace some quotations with summaries or paraphrases, so more of your research project is in your own words.

4. Draw a circle around terms that are essential to your thesis or that your audience might not know. Is each defined?

NO ▶

- Add definitions where necessary.
- Read the circled terms and definitions to a classmate and ask if he or she understands them.
- Ask the classmate to read your project and circle any terms he or she doesn't understand.

QUESTIONS	REVISION STRATEGIES

5. Place a checkmark ✔ next to each idea that came from an outside source. Do you give credit to each source in an in-text citation? Is it clear where source material begins and ends?

NO ▶
- Add in-text citations wherever you need them for all paraphrases, summaries, and quotations. Include a signal phrase (*Dr. X argues, Professor Y claims*) and follow the source material with a page reference (pp. 595–96).
- Vary the verbs you use and the placement of signal phrases to avoid ineffective repetition (pp. 595–96).

YES
▼

6. Draw a box around your introduction and conclusion. Does the introduction provide a context for your research? Is the conclusion satisfying and relevant?

NO ▶
- Revise your introduction to provide background or to capture your readers' attention with a dramatic anecdote or quotation.
- Revise your conclusion to propose action or a way of thinking that is appropriate in light of the research.
- Review the strategies for introductions and conclusions in Chapter 7 (pp. 164–67).

Prepare Your Final Draft

After you have revised your project and compiled a list of references or works cited, you are ready to prepare the final draft. Following are some guidelines to help you format, edit, and proofread your final paper. For an example of an essay in MLA style, see "Do Animals Have Emotions?" by Nicholas Destino (pp. 621–28). For an example of an essay in APA style, see "Schizophrenia: Definition and Treatment" by Sonia Gomez (pp. 638–44).

Format Your Research Project

Academic papers should follow a standard format that meets the expectations of the genre in which you are writing. For example, if you are writing a research report for a psychology class, you will probably be expected to include a title page, an abstract, and headings for each of your main sections. If you are writing a research paper for a literature class, in contrast, no title page or abstract is typically required, and headings are considered necessary only in lengthy essays.

The following guidelines are common for writing projects in the humanities. If your instructor suggests or requires a different format, be sure to follow it. If your instructor does not recommend a format, these guidelines would likely be acceptable.

1. **Paper.** Use 8½- by 11-inch white paper. Use a paper clip; do not staple or use a binder.

2. **Your name and course information.** Position your name at the left margin one inch from the top of the page. Underneath it, on separate lines, list your instructor's name, your course name and number, and the date. (If you are following APA style, include this information and your title on a title page. See p. 639 for an example.)

3. **Title.** Place the title one double-spaced line below the date, and center it. Capitalize the first and last words and all other important words (all except articles, coordinating conjunctions, and prepositions). Do not underline or italicize your title or put quotation marks around it. Start your paper one double-spaced line below the title.

4. **Margins, spacing, and indentation.** Use one-inch margins. Double-space your paper (including your name and course information, your title, block quotations, and works-cited entries). Indent block quotations and the first line of each paragraph half an inch, and use a **hanging indent** (first line flush left, subsequent lines indented half an inch) in the list of works cited.

5. **Numbering of pages.** Number all pages using arabic numerals (1, 2, 3) in the upper-right corner. Place the numbers half an inch below the top of the paper. (If you include a title page, do not number it and do not count it in your numbering.) Precede each page number with your last name, leaving a space between your name and the number. (If you are following APA style, include a shortened form of your title instead of your last name.)

6. **Headings.** The system recommended by the American Psychological Association (APA) should work for most research projects. Main headings should be centered; subheadings should begin at the left margin. Capitalize first, last, and other important words.

7. **Visuals.** If you include tables and figures (graphs, charts, maps, photographs, and drawings) in your paper, label each table or figure with an arabic numeral (*Table 1, Table 2; Fig. 1, Fig. 2*) and give it a title. Place the table number and title on separate lines above the table. Give each figure a number and title and place the figure number and title below the figure. Capitalize figure and table titles as you would any other title.

Edit and Proofread Your Research Project

For more on editing and proofreading, see Chapter 9.

As a final step, edit and proofread your revised paper for errors in grammar, spelling, punctuation, mechanics, and documentation style. As you edit and proofread, check for the types of errors you commonly make, and watch for these ten common problems.

1. **Long, cumbersome sentences.** Try splitting them into separate sentences.

2. **Incomplete sentences.** Correct sentence fragments (a group of words that cannot stand alone as a sentence because it is missing a subject, a complete verb, or both), comma splices (two or more independent clauses linked by a comma but without a coordinating conjunction), and run-on (or fused) sentences (two or more independent clauses joined without a punctuation mark or coordinating conjunction).

3. **Verb problems.** Avoid tense shifts (shifting from present to past or future tense) throughout your paper unless there is a good reason to do so. Also, make sure the subjects and verbs in all your sentences agree in person (*first:* I, we; *second:* you; *third:* he/she/it/they) and number (singular/plural). Be particularly careful when words come between the subject and verb.

4. **Wordiness.** Avoid wordy expressions (*at this particular point in time* rather than simply *now*), redundancy (*dashing quickly*), intensifiers (such as *very* or *really*), and weak verb-noun combinations (*wrote a draft* rather than *drafted*).

5. **Inappropriate tone/level of diction.** Avoid slang, abbreviations, and emoticons (☺). Aim for a clear and direct tone, and use words with appropriate connotations.

6. **Incorrect in-text citations.** Make sure you punctuate and format them to conform to MLA style, APA style, or that of another system of documentation.

7. **Inaccurate direct quotations.** Check quotations carefully against the original source for accuracy, and double-check your use of quotation marks, capital letters, commas, and ellipses.

8. **Plagiarism.** Avoid plagiarism by carefully quoting, paraphrasing, and summarizing the ideas of others, and citing your sources for all ideas and opinions and all facts except those that are common knowledge.

9. **Incorrect formatting.** Check that you have formatted your paper consistently, following these or your instructor's formatting instructions. Check the citations in your list of works cited carefully using the models provided later in the chapter (pp. 607–21, 631–38).

10. **Incomplete list of works cited/references.** Make sure all sources cited in your paper are included in the list in alphabetical order.

RESEARCH PROJECT IN PROGRESS 9 ▶

Edit and proofread your research project, paying particular attention to the questions in the preceding list.

Document Your Sources: MLA Style

The system described in this section is recommended by the Modern Language Association (MLA) and is described in detail in the *MLA Handbook*, Eighth Edition (available from most libraries). MLA style uses in-text citations within the text of a research project and a list of works cited at the end to document the sources used. If you are unsure whether to use MLA style, check with your instructor.

The first student paper at the end of this section ("Do Animals Have Emotions?" pp. 621–28) models the use of MLA style.

Use MLA Style for In-Text Citations

Your paper must include in-text citations—either signal phrases (attributions) or parenthetical citations—for all material you paraphrase, summarize, or quote from sources. Many instructors prefer that you use signal phrases rather than only parenthetical citations in most places because signal phrases allow you to put sources in context.

For more about using signal phrases and parenthetical citations, see pp. 593–96.

For either type of citation, use the following rules.

- Omit the word *page(s)* or the abbreviation *p.* or *pp.*
- Place the sentence period after the closing parenthesis unless the citation follows a block quotation. (See p. 597.)
- If a quotation ends the sentence, insert the closing quotation mark before the parentheses enclosing the page reference.

Examples showing in-text citations in MLA style follow.

Directory of MLA In-Text Citation Models

1. One author

In his classic analysis of post-war advertising techniques, Vance Packard claims that . . . (58).

. . . (Packard 58).

2. Two authors. Include both authors' names, in either a signal phrase or a parenthetical citation.

Marquez and Allison assert . . . (74).

. . . (Marquez and Allison 74).

3. Three or more authors. Include the first author's last name followed by *et al.*, which means "and others" in Latin.

Hong et al. maintain . . . (198).

. . . (Hong et al. 198).

4. Two or more works by the same author(s). When citing two or more sources by the same author or group of authors, include the full title in a signal phrase, or a brief version of the title in a parenthetical citation.

In *For God, Country, and Coca-Cola*, Pendergrast describes . . . (96).

. . . (Pendergrast, *For God* 96).

5. **Corporate or organizational author.** Use the group's full name in the signal phrase; you may abbreviate common words when providing a parenthetical citation.

> The American Diabetes Association estimates that the cost of diagnosed diabetes in the United States in 2012 was $245 billion.

> The cost of diagnosed diabetes in the United States in 2012 was estimated at $245 billion (Amer. Diabetes Assn.).

(There is no page number in these in-text citations because the information comes from an unpaginated digital source. See pp. 606–7.)

6. **No author named.** If the author is unknown, use the full title in a signal phrase or a shortened form in parentheses.

> According to the article "Medical Mysteries and Surgical Surprises," . . . (79).

> . . . ("Medical Mysteries" 79).

7. **Authors with the same last name.** Include the first initial of these authors in all parenthetical citations. Use the complete first name if both authors have the same first initial.

> John Dillon proposes . . . (974).

> . . . (J. Dillon 974).

8. **Two or more sources in the same citation.** When citing two or more sources of one idea in parentheses, list the authors (or titles) in alphabetical order, and separate the citations with a semicolon.

> . . . (Breakwater 33; Holden 198).

9. **Entire work.** When referring to an entire work, name the author in a signal phrase or parentheses.

> In *For God, Country, and Coca-Cola*, Pendergrast presents an unauthorized history of Coca-Cola, the soft drink and the company that produces it.

10. **Chapter in an edited book or work in an anthology.** An *anthology* is a collection of writings (articles, stories, poems) by different authors. In the in-text citation, name the author who wrote the work (not the editor of the anthology) and include the page number(s) from the anthology. The corresponding entry in the list of works cited begins with the author's last name; it also names the editor of the anthology.

In-Text Citation

> According to Ina Ferris . . . (239).

> . . . (Ferris 239).

Works-Cited Entry

> Ferris, Ina. "The Irish Novel 1800–1829." *Cambridge Companion to Fiction in the Romantic Period*, edited by Richard Maxwell and Katie Trumpener, Cambridge UP, 2008, pp. 235–49.

11. **Multivolume work.** When citing two or more volumes of a multivolume work, indicate the volume number, followed by a colon and the page number.

> Terman indicates . . . (2: 261).
>
> . . . (Terman 2: 261).

When you cite only one volume in your research project, create an in-text citation as you would for any other single-volume work.

12. **Indirect source.** Use the abbreviation *qtd. in* to indicate that you are using a source that is cited in another source.

> As Arthur Miller says, "When somebody is destroyed everybody finally contributes to it, but in Willy's case, the end product would be virtually the same" (qtd. in Martin and Meyer 375).

13. **Personal communication (interview, letter, email, conversation).** Name of the person in your text, and mention the type of communication (interview, letter, and so on).

> In an interview with Professor Emilio Lopez, . . .

14. **Literary work.** Readers may find it helpful if you include information that will help them locate the material in any edition. For novels, cite the page and chapter number: (109; *ch.* 5). For plays, cite the act and/or scene number: (35; *sc.* 1). For poetry, cite the book or part number and line numbers: (6.129-30). If you are citing lines of poetry only, use the word *line* or *lines* in the first reference and then just the line numbers in subsequent references:

> **First reference**   (lines 12–15)
>
> **Later references**   (16–18).

15. **Encyclopedia or dictionary entry.** Mention the word or entry in your text in italics. If more than one definition is given in the dictionary, include the definition number in your in-text citation.

> The term *prion* was coined by Stanley B. Prusiner from the words *proteinaceous* and *infectious* plus *-on* ("Prion," def. 2).

16. **Digital source.** In general, a digital source is cited like its printed counterpart. Give enough information in the citation so that readers can locate the source in your list of works cited. If the digital source provides page numbers, you should provide them too. If the source uses another ordering system, such as paragraph (*par.* or *pars.*), section (*sec.*), or screen (*screen*) numbers, provide those instead.

> Brian Beckman argues that "centrifugal force is a fiction" (par. 6).
>
> . . . (Beckman, par. 6).

If the source does not have paragraph or page numbers, which is often the case, do not add them. Instead, just cite the work by author, title, or whatever begins your entry in the list of works cited.

Author

> Teresa Schmidt discusses . . .
>
> . . . (Schmidt).

Title

> The "Band of Brothers" section of the History Channel site . . .
>
> . . . ("Band").

Use MLA Style for the List of Works Cited

Follow these general guidelines when preparing your list of works cited.

1. Include only the sources that you paraphrase, summarize, or quote in your research project. If you consulted a work but did not cite it, do not include it in the list of works cited.
2. Put the list on a separate page at the end of your paper. Type *Works Cited*, centered, at the top of the page; do not use quotation marks, italics, or boldface for the heading.
3. Alphabetize the list by the first important word in each citation, usually the author's last name. (Ignore articles: *A, An,* or *The*.)
4. Capitalize the first and last word of each title and all words except for articles (*a, an, the*), coordinating conjunctions (*and, but, for, nor, so, yet*), and prepositions (*in, of, on, off, up,* and so on).
5. Format the list with a hanging indent (usually a setting on the ruler or on the paragraph tab), so the first line is flush with the left margin and subsequent lines are indented by half an inch.
6. Double-space the whole list.

GENERAL GUIDELINES FOR CREATING ENTRIES IN THE WORKS CITED LIST

An MLA-style citation includes the following:

1. *The author (if named) + period.* Authors' names appear last name first, with a comma between first and last names.

2. *The title + period.* Titles of self-contained works, such as books, websites, and television series, are italicized; titles of works contained within other works, such as articles from magazines or journals, are enclosed in quotation marks.

3. *"Container" information.* The MLA calls any work a "container" that is made up of other works, so a journal is a container because it "contains" articles; a television series is a container because it is made up of episodes. Follow the container title and all but the last item of information about the container with a comma. End the container section with a period. If a source appears in multiple containers—for example, you cite an article that appears in a journal (container 1) via a database (container 2)—include information about the second container after the first.

   - **The title of the "container" + comma.** Titles of containers (books, periodicals, databases, and so on) are typically italicized.
   - **Other contributors + comma.** Other contributors may include the editor, translator, producer, actor, illustrator, and so on.

- **Version + comma.** The version may be the edition number or name (seventh edition, revised edition), abridged edition, director's cut, and so on.
- **Number + comma.** The number may be the volume number of a multivolume work, volume and issue number of a journal, or disk number of a set of DVDs.
- **Publication information + comma.** Publication information may include the name of the publisher, government agency, or site sponsor. The MLA does not require the place of publication.
- **Publication date + comma.** The publication date will be a year for movies and books; a month, year, and season for most journals; a month and year for monthly magazines; and a day, month, and year for weekly magazines and daily newspapers.
- **Source location + period.** The source location may be page numbers for a printed text, a URL or DOI (digital object identifier, a permanent code) for an online text; or a time stamp for an online video or audio file.

4. *Additional information + period.* You may decide to include original publication information for a reprinted book (if relevant to your readers), an access date for an undated online source, or a label for an unusual source type or a source type readers will not be able to identify based solely on the citation (such as a letter to the editor, a typescript, or a lecture.)

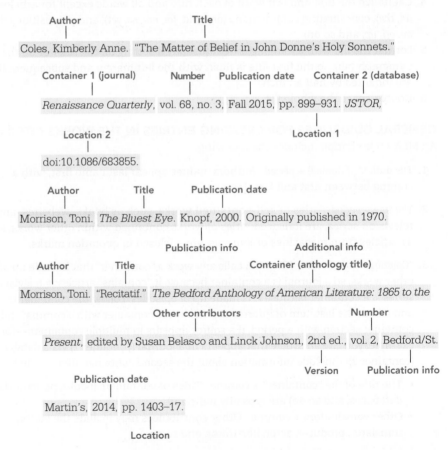

Author | Title

Coles, Kimberly Anne. "The Matter of Belief in John Donne's Holy Sonnets."

Container 1 (journal) | Number | Publication date | Container 2 (database)

Renaissance Quarterly, vol. 68, no. 3, Fall 2015, pp. 899–931. *JSTOR,*

Location 2 | Location 1

doi:10.1086/683855.

Author | Title | Publication date

Morrison, Toni. *The Bluest Eye.* Knopf, 2000. Originally published in 1970.

Publication info | Additional info

Author | Title | Container (anthology title)

Morrison, Toni. "Recitatif." *The Bedford Anthology of American Literature: 1865 to the*

Other contributors | Number

Present, edited by Susan Belasco and Linck Johnson, 2nd ed., vol. 2, Bedford/St.

Version | Publication info

Publication date

Martin's, 2014, pp. 1403–17.

Location

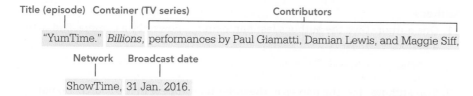

Title (episode) Container (TV series)   Contributors

"YumTime." *Billions*, performances by Paul Giamatti, Damian Lewis, and Maggie Siff,

Network   Broadcast date

ShowTime, 31 Jan. 2016.

A variety of models for different types of sources follow. However, you may need to combine information from one or more models to create a citation for a work you are using. (Some models included here are created by applying the MLA's rules to create citation models they do not supply.)

For instance, to cite a reading from this textbook, you would need to treat it as a work in an anthology (p. 618) in an edition other than the first (p. 612):

> Goleman, Daniel. "His Marriage and Hers: Childhood Roots." *Successful College Writing: Skills, Strategies, Learning Styles*, by Kathleen T. McWhorter, 7th ed., Bedford/St. Martin's, 2017, pp. 387–91.

Directory of MLA Works-Cited Models

Authors

Books and Other Self-Contained Works

Articles in Periodicals and Other Works Contained in Longer Works

Authors

1. **One author.** Give the author's last name first, followed by a comma. End with a period.

   Rybszynski, Witold.

2. **Two authors.** List the names in the order they appear in the source. Do not reverse the order of the second author's names.

   Botkin, Daniel B., and Diana Pérez.

3. **Three or more authors.** List the first author, last name first, followed by *et al.* (which means "and others" in Latin).

   Lewin, Benjamin, et al.

4. **Corporation or organization as author.** List the organization or corporation as the author, omitting any initial article (*A*, *An*, or *The*). If author and publisher are the same, omit the author and include the publisher following the title.

   National Kidney Foundation.

   United States, Government Accountability Office.

5. **No author named.** Begin with the title. If the source is self-contained work, such as a book, italicize the title; if the source is part of another, larger work (for example, if the work is an article in a newspaper or magazine), set it in quotation marks.

   Go Ask Alice.

   "California Sues EPA over Emissions."

6. **Author using a pseudonym.** Use the name as it appears in the source; if you know the author's real name, insert it following the pseudonym, in parentheses.

   Atrios (Duncan Black).

7. **Two or more works by the same author(s).** Alphabetize the works by title, ignoring the article (*A*, *An*, or *The*). For entries after the first, replace the author's name with three hyphens followed by a period.

   Coates, Ta-Nehisi. *The Beautiful Struggle: A Father, Two Sons, and an Unlikely Road to Manhood.* Spiegel and Grau, 2008.

   ---. *Between the World and Me.* Spiegel and Grau, 2015.

Books and Other Self-Contained Works. Most of the information you will need to cite a book appears on the book's title page and copyright page (see Figure 23.3). In printed books, these two pages appear toward the beginning of the text; in e-books, they may appear elsewhere.

FIGURE 23.3 Where to Find Documentation Information for a Book

CITING A BOOK

1. *Author.* Begin with the author's name, last name first.

2. *Title.* Provide the full title and subtitle in italics.

3. *Publisher.* Use the full name of the publisher (*Houghton Mifflin* or *Basic Books*). Omit business words or abbreviations, such as *Company*, *Ltd.*, or *Inc.* Standardize punctuation, using the word *and* in place of & (ampersand). For university presses, use the abbreviations *U* (for *University*) and *P* (for *Press*).

4. *Date.* Use the most recent publication year listed on the book's copyright page.

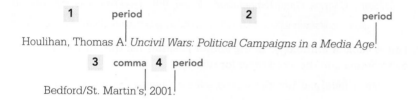

| **1** | period | | **2** | | period |

Houlihan, Thomas A. *Uncivil Wars: Political Campaigns in a Media Age.*

| **3** | comma | **4** | period |

Bedford/St. Martin's, 2001.

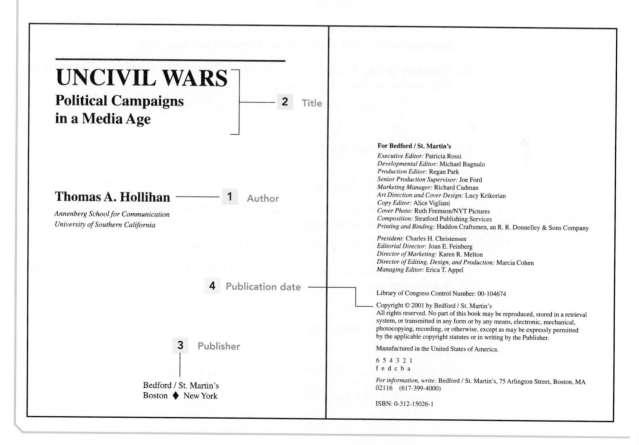

8. **Basic format for a book.** Include the author (last name first), title, publisher, and publication date. If you are citing an e-book, add information about the e-reader used. If you're citing an online book, add information about the second, digital "container," including the name of the Web site on which the online book appears and the permalink URL.

Print

Crystal, David. *Language Play*. U of Chicago P, 1998.

E-Book

Larson, Steig. *The Girl with the Dragon Tattoo*. Alfred A. Knopf, 2008. Kindle.

Online

Dickens, Charles. *Great Expectations*. Estes, 1881. *Google Books*, play.google.com/
store/books/details?id=fhUXAAAAYAAJ&rdid=book-fhUXAAAAYAAJ&rdot=1.

9. **Edited book or anthology.** In the author position, list the editor's name followed by a comma and the word *editor* (or *editors*).

Szeman, Imre, and Timothy Kaposy, editors. *Cultural Theory: An Anthology*.
Wiley-Blackwell, 2011.

For a model for a chapter from an edited book, a work in an anthology, or an introduction, preface, foreword, or afterword, see page 618.

10. **Translated book.** After the title, include the phrase *Translated by*, followed by the first and last names of the translator.

Kawakami, Hiromi. *Manazuru*. Translated by Michael Emmerich, Counterpoint
Press, 2010.

11. **Edition other than the first.** Indicate the number of the edition following the title.

Barker, Ellen M. *Neuroscience Nursing*. 3rd ed., Mosby-Elsevier, 2008.

12. **Multivolume work.** If the reference is to all the volumes in a multivolume work, give the number of volumes at the end of the citation.

Stark, Freya. *Letters*. Edited by Lucy Moorehead, Compton Press, 1974-82. 8 vols.

If the reference is to one volume in a multivolume work, give the number of the volume you used before the publisher.

Stark, Freya. *Letters*. Edited by Lucy Moorehead, vol. 5, Compton Press, 1978.

13. **Encyclopedia or dictionary entry**

Print

Robinson, Lisa Clayton. "Harlem Writers Guild." *Africana: The Encyclopedia
of the African and African American Experience*, 2nd ed., Oxford UP, 2005,
p. 163.

Online

> "House Music." *Wikipedia*, 16 Nov. 2015, en.wikipedia.org/wiki/House_music.

14. **Entire Web site or blog.** You may not be able to find all the information for a Web site or blog that you would typically include for a book. If you cannot find all the information you need to create a complete citation, include as much as you can. If the Web site lacks an update or publication date, include an access date at the end of your citation. If the title of the Web site is very similar to the name of the organization that publishes the Web site, you may omit the name of the publisher.

> LaMoreaux, Andrew M., editor. *The Huntington Archive of Buddhist and Related Art.* The Ohio State U, 2017, www.huntingtonarchive.osu.edu/.

> Railton, Stephen. *Mark Twain in His Times.* U of Virginia Library, 2012, twain.lib .virginia.edu/.

> *Transparency International: The Global Coalition against Corruption.* 2016, www .transparency.org/.

> *The Newton Project.* U of Sussex, 2016, www.newtonproject.sussex.ac.uk/prism .php?id=1.

> Bae, Rebecca. Home page. Iowa State U, 2015, www.engl.iastate.edu/rebecca -bae-directory-page/.

> Kiuchi, Tatsuro. *Tatsuro Kiuchi: News & Blog*, tatsurokiuchi.com/. Accessed 3 Mar. 2016.

15. **Government document.** If a specific author is listed, include the information about the government, department, and agency that produced the document following the title, in the publisher position. If no author is listed, begin with the government, department, and agency. If the author and publisher are the same, begin the citation with the title.

> Buchalter, Alice R., and Patrick M. Miller. *The National Advisory Committee for Aeronautics: An Annotated Bibliography.* NASA, 9 Mar. 2015, www.nasa.gov/ connect/ebooks/hubble_25_detail.html.

> *Federal Student Loans: Repaying Your Loans.* United States, Department of Education, Federal Student Aid, 2015, studentaid.ed.gov/sa/sites/default/files/repaying -your-loans.pdf.

> United States, Department of Agriculture, Food and Nutrition Service, Child Nutrition Programs. *Eligibility Manual for School Meals: Determining and Verifying Eligibility.* National School Lunch Program, July 2015, www.fns.usda.gov/sites/ default/files/cn/SP40_CACFP18_SFSP20-2015a1.pdf.

16. **Film, DVD, or streamed video.** Begin with the title, unless you are focusing on the work of the director or another contributor, in which case list that person in the author position. Include the name of the production company in the publisher position and the release date in the publication date position. For supplementary material on a DVD, include the title of that information, along with the information for the movie; at the end of the citation include the disc number if there was more than one disc. If you watched the video online, include the URL.

Film

La La Land. Directed by Damien Chazelle, performances by Ryan Gosling and Emma Stone, Summit Entertainment, 2016.

Scott, Ridley, director. *The Martian*. Performances by Matt Damon, Jessica Chastain, Kristen Wiig, and Kate Mara, Twentieth Century Fox, 2015.

DVD

"Sweeney's London." *Sweeney Todd: The Demon Barber of Fleet Street*, directed by Tim Burton, produced by Eric Young, DreamWorks, 2007, disc 2.

Streamed

Lewis, Paul. "Citizen Journalism." *YouTube*, 14 May 2011, www.youtube.com/watch?v=9APO9_yNbcg.

17. **Music recording.** Begin with a contributor or title of the work, depending on the focus of your research project. Include the composer or performer and the title of the recording or composition as well as the production company, and the date. Titles of recordings should be italicized, but titles of compositions identified by form (for example, Symphony No. 5) should not.

Blige, Mary J. "Don't Mind." *Life II: The Journey Continues (Act 1)*, Geffen, 2011.

Bizet, Georges. *Carmen*. Performances by Jennifer Larmore, Thomas Moser, Angela Gheorghiu, and Samuel Ramey, Bavarian State Orchestra and Chorus, conducted by Giuseppe Sinopoli, Warner, 1996.

18. **Pamphlet**

Rainie, Lee, and Maeve Duggan. *Privacy and Information Sharing*. Pew Research Center, 14 Jan. 2016, www.pewinternet.org/files/2016/01/PI_2016.01.14_Privacy -and-Info-Sharing_FINAL.pdf.

19. **Lecture or public address.** Begin with the person who delivered the address, the title of the speech (if any) in quotation marks, the lecture's sponsor, the date, and the place where the lecture occurred.

Eugenides, Jeffrey. Portland Arts and Lectures, 30 Sept. 2003, Arlene Schnitzer Concert Hall, Portland, OR.

Burden, Amanda. "How Public Spaces Make Cities Work." *TED.com*, Mar. 2014, www.ted.com/talks/amanda_burden_how_public_spaces_make_cities_work.

If the fact that the source is a lecture is unclear from the information provided, you may want to include the label *Lecture* or *Speech* at the end of the citation.

20. **Personal interview.** Begin with the name of the person interviewed, the words *Personal interview*, and the date on which the interview took place.

> Freedman, Sasha. Personal interview. 10 Nov. 2014.

21. **Live performance.** Include the title of the work performed and the names of the writer, composer, or performers; the theater or location of the performance; and the date of the performance.

> Piano Concerto no. 3. By Ludwig van Beethoven, conducted by Andris Nelsons,
>
> performances by Paul Lewis and Boston Symphony Orchestra, Symphony Hall,
>
> Boston, 9 Oct. 2015.

Articles in Periodicals and Other Works Contained in Longer Works. A periodical is a publication that appears at regular intervals: Newspapers generally appear daily, magazines weekly or monthly, and scholarly journals quarterly. In periodicals, the information you will need to cite may appear on the first page of the article (see Figure 23.4), or you may need to look at a combination of places (the first page of the article, the cover of the periodical, the Web page or Web site on which the article appears, and so on).

FIGURE 23.4 **Where to Find Documentation Information for a Periodical**

CITING AN ARTICLE IN A PERIODICAL

1. *Author.* Begin with the author's name, last name first.

2. *Title.* Provide the full title of the article, including the subtitle, in quotation marks.

3. *Periodical title.* Give the full title of the magazine, journal, or newspaper that "contains" the article, including any initial *A*, *An*, or *The*. Italicize the periodical title.

4. *Number and/or publication date.* For scholarly journals, give the volume and issue numbers and date of publication (often a season and year or just a year): *vol. 54, no. 1, Autumn 2012.* For newspapers and magazines, give the date: day, month, year (or month, year, for monthly magazines); abbreviate the names of months except for *May, June,* and *July.*

5. *Location.* For a print publication, include page numbers; for an online publication, include the DOI (digital object identifier, a permanent code) or URL (permalink preferred). If pages are not consecutive, include the first page number and a plus sign (+).

| **1** | period | **2** | period | **3** | comma | **4** | comma | **5** | period |

Remnick, David. "Patriot Games." *The New Yorker,* 3 Mar. 2014, pp. 30–35.

(continued)

LETTER FROM SOCHI

2 ———— PATRIOT GAMES

Vladimir Putin lives his Olympic dream.

1 ———————— BY DAVID REMNICK

A quarter century ago, as jubilant citizens took sledgehammers to the Berlin Wall, Vladimir Vladimirovich Putin, an officer in the Dresden station of the K.G.B., fed a raging furnace with the documentary evidence of Soviet espionage activities in East Germany. Putin was grateful for his Dresden posting. He had grown up in a pretty wife and two young daughters, and enough leisure to play Ping-Pong, fish in the rivers outside town, and drink beer in the city's pubs and breweries. He drank so much beer that he gained twenty-five pounds. Now the happy days were ending. The Wall had been breached, and Putin was shovelling top-secret files into the fire so few months, Putin slipped back home to Leningrad and took a position as "vice-rector"—the residential spy—at the local university.

As the Soviet Union began to unravel, there was a pervasive mood of desperation in its most repressive offices. Occasionally, that desperation took on comic dimensions. One fall morning in 1990, when I was working as a Moscow correspondent, I was reading a stack of newspapers—a requirement of the job—and came across an article of tangy interest in *Komsomolskaya Pravda*. The headline read "MISS K.G.B."; below was a photograph of a woman in her twenties, named Katya Mayorova, provocatively adjusting the strap of her bulletproof vest. She had, it seemed, won a beauty

Putin's aim was to put on a display of renewed national confidence and modernity. "Russia is back," officials kept insisting.

Leningrad, an uneven student with early dreams of serving the state. One of his grandfathers was a cook for Lenin and Stalin. His father was an undercover operative during the war. Putin's parents barely survived the Nazi siege; an older brother did not. After a rough upbringing, Putin had enjoyed a halcyon four years in Dresden. He had quickly, he recalled in a book-length interview, that "the furnace burst." This was early in November, 1989. Later, angry Germans threatened to break into the K.G.B. compound. Putin's superiors called Moscow for reinforcements, but, he says, "Moscow was silent." The state was failing even its most resolute foot soldiers. Within a contest at Lubyanka, the K.G.B. headquarters. This was new. I took a sip of coffee. The article described how Comrade Mayorova wore her vest with "exquisite softness, like a Pierre Cardin model." Beyond "mere beauty," her talents included the ability to deliver a karate kick "to her enemies' head." I called Lubyanka, which, by now, had a press

30   THE NEW YORKER, MARCH 3, 2014

5   **3**   **4**

22. **Article in a magazine.** Provide the complete publication date of the magazine—day, month, and year for weekly magazines and month and year for monthly magazines. For an online version of a magazine, replace the page numbers with the URL. If you accessed the article through a database, add information about the database (the second "container") to the end of the citation.

Print

> Butler, Kiera. "Works Well with Others." *Mother Jones*, Jan./Feb. 2008, pp. 66–69.

Online

> Seabrook, John. "Behind the Cellar Door." *The New Yorker*, 23 Jan. 2017, www
> .newyorker.com/magazine/2017/01/23/behind-the-cellar-door.

Database

> Sharp, Kathleen. "The Rescue Mission." *Smithsonian*, Nov. 2015, pp. 40–49. *OmniFile*
> *Full Text Select*, web.b.ebscohost.com.ezproxy.bpl.org/.

23. **Article in a newspaper.** Include the full title of the newspaper, including any initial *A*, *An*, or *The*. If the newspaper article does not appear on consecutive pages, give the first page number followed by a plus sign. If an edition name (*National ed.*) appears on the newspaper's first page, include it after the date. If you read a newspaper article online, replace page numbers with a permalink URL.

Print

> Sherry, Allison. "Volunteers' Personal Touch Turns High-Tech Data into Votes." *The*
> *Denver Post*, 30 Oct. 2012, pp. 1A+.

> Urbina, Ian. "Gas Wells Recycle Water, but Toxic Risks Persist." *The New York Times*,
> 2 Mar. 2011, late ed., pp. A1+.

Online

> Wolfers, Justin, et al. "1.5 Million Missing Black Men." *The New York Times*, 20 Apr.
> 2015, nyti.ms/1P5Gpa7.

24. **Article in a scholarly journal.** Give the volume and issue number and the month or season (if provided). If you accessed the article online, replace page numbers with the permalink URL or DOI (digital object identifier, a permanent code). If you accessed the journal through a database your school's library subscribes to, add the information about that database at the end of the citation.

Print

> Matchie, Thomas. "Law versus Love in *The Round House*." *Midwest Quarterly*,
> vol. 56, no. 4, Summer 2015, pp. 353–64.

Online

> Bryson, Devin. "The Rise of a New Senegalese Cultural Philosophy?" *African Studies*
> *Quarterly*, vol. 14, no. 3, Mar. 2014, pp. 33–56, asq.africa.ufl.edu/files/Volume
> -14-Issue-3-Bryson.pdf.

Database

> Coles, Kimberly Anne. "The Matter of Belief in John Donne's Holy Sonnets." *Renaissance*
> *Quarterly*, vol. 68, no. 3, Fall 2015, pp. 899–931. *JSTOR*, doi:10.1086/683855.

25. **Editorial or letter to the editor.** Cite the article or letter beginning with the author's name (if provided), and add the word *Editorial* or *Letter* followed by a

period at the end of the citation. Often editorials are unsigned, and letters to the editor omit titles.

Editorial

"Hurricane Sandy and the Poor." *The New York Times*, 19 Sept. 2013, p. A30. Editorial.

Letter to the Editor

Ginn, Lee. *Wired*, Dec. 2008, p. 19. Letter.

26. **Chapter in an edited book or work in an anthology.** List the author and title of the work, followed by the title and editor of the anthology. (Include the words *edited by* before the editor's name.) Publisher, date, and the pages on which the work appears follow.

Riss, Jacob. "How the Other Half Lives." *The Affordable Housing Reader*, edited by J. R. Tighe, Routledge, 2013, pp. 6–13.

27. **Introduction, preface, foreword, or afterword**

Aaron, Hank. Foreword. *We Are the Ship: The Story of Negro League Baseball*, by Kadir Nelson, Disney Publishing, 2008, p. vi.

28. **Book or film review.** List the reviewer's name and title of the review. After the title, add *Review of* and give the title and author of the book. For a film review, replace *by* with *directed by*. Include publication information for the review itself, not for the material reviewed.

Peters, Justin. "Original Sin." Review of *Spam: A Shadow History of the Internet*, by Finn Brunton, *Columbia Journalism Review*, vol. 52, no. 3, 2013, pp. 58–59.

29. **Published interview.** Start with the person interviewed; include the title of the interview (if any), followed by the person conducting the interview. End with the publication information for the source in which the interview appeared.

Blume, Judy. "Judy Blume in Conversation with Lena Dunham." Interview by Lena Dunham. *The Believer*, vol. 12, no. 1, Jan. 2014, pp. 39+.

FIGURE 23.5 **Where to Find Documentation Information for a Source on a Web Site**

CITING A DOCUMENT ON A WEB SITE

1. *Author.* Include the name of the author, if provided. If the author is an organization, include the name only if it is substantially different from the name of the Web site. Otherwise, begin with the title of the source.

2. *Title.* Enclose the titles of Web pages in quotation marks; italicize the titles of Web sites and other self-contained works.

3. *Web site title.* Include the title of the Web site (if any), in italics. Include the publisher of a Web site only if the name of the publisher is substantially different from the name of the Web site.

4. *Date of publication.* Give the most recent date of publication. It may appear on the home page or at the bottom of the Web page.

5. *Location.* Give the permalink URL, if available; if a permalink URL isn't available, give the site's URL.

1 period **2** period **3**

Sirhindi, Marcella. "Jamini Roy: Bengali Artist of Modern India." The Huntington Archive

of Buddhist and Asian Art, 2017, huntingtonarchive.org/Exhibitions/JaminiRoy.php.

comma **4** comma **5** period

5

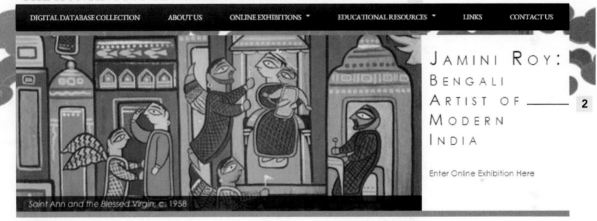

5

huntingtonarchive.org/Exhibitions/JaminiRoy.php

THE HUNTINGTON ARCHIVE of Buddhist and Asian Art — **3**

DIGITAL DATABASE COLLECTION   ABOUT US   ONLINE EXHIBITIONS ▾   EDUCATIONAL RESOURCES ▾   LINKS   CONTACT US

JAMINI ROY: **2**
BENGALI
ARTIST OF
MODERN
INDIA

Enter Online Exhibition Here

Saint Ann and the Blessed Virgin, c. 1958

December 14, 1997 - May 17, 1998
Samuel P. Harn Museum of Art
University of Florida | P.O. Box 112700
Gainesville, FL 32611-2700

1 — Curated by Marcella Sirhindi | © Text by Marcella Sirhindi | © Photographs provided by Samuel P. Harn Museum of Art

RELATED SITES

SAMUEL P. HARN MUSEUM OF ART
AT THE UNIVERSITY OF FLORIDA

**PLEASE NOTE: NOT ALL OF THE IMAGES
CONTAINED WITHIN OUR ONLINE
EXHIBITION SECTIONS ARE COPYRIGHTED
PROPERTY OF THE HUNTINGTON
ARCHIVE. WE MAY BE UNABLE TO
GRANT PERMISSION TO USE ALL
REQUESTED IMAGES.*

BIOGRAPHY OF THE ARTIST
Jamini Roy (1887-1972) is among the most significant and influential Indian artists of the 20th century. He enjoyed a great deal of respect and fame during his lifetime. His work is still held in high esteem in India and is achieving growing international renown. Roy received formal training at the Calcutta College of Art (also known as Government School of Art) where he learned academic methods then in vogue in the West, and achieved his early fame as a portrait painter in the European tradition. Eventually, however, the artist rejected these conventions to cultivate a personal painting style inspired largely by traditional Indian folk and village arts, particularly those of his native Bengal. Jamini Roy utilized his considerable skill and intelligence to create a body of work that resonates with the history of modern India. Thus, an exhibition and catalogue of works by Jamini Roy is a particularly appropriate way to acknowledge the 50th anniversary of Indian independence as a colony of the British Empire.

4 — © 2017 The Huntington Archive | Columbus, Ohio 43210 | huntingtonarchive@gmail.com
Home | Digital Database Collection | About Us | Online Exhibitions | Educational Resources | Links | Contact Us

Courtesy The John C. and Susan L. Huntington Photographic Archive of Buddhist and Asian Art

30. **Document on a Web site.** Include an access date if no date of publication is provided.

> Gallagher, Sean. "The Last Nomads of the Tibetan Plateau." *Pulitzer Center on Crisis*
>> *Reporting*, 25 Oct. 2012, pulitzercenter.org/reporting/china-glaciers-global
>> -warming-climate-change-ecosystem-tibetan-plateau-grasslands-nomads.

> "Social and Historical Context: Vitality." *Arapesh Grammar and Digital Language*
>> *Archive Project*, Institute for Advanced Technology in the Humanities, www
>> .arapesh.org/socio_historical_context_vitality.php. Accessed 22 Mar. 2016.

31. **Posting to an online discussion list or newsgroup.** For a discussion group, include the author's name or handle (if both are available, include the handle with the name in parentheses), the title or subject line enclosed in quotation marks, the name of the Web site on which the group is found, the site sponsor (if substantially different from the name of the Web site), the date of posting, and the URL. If possible, cite an archived version. If the posting has no title, label it *Online posting*.

> Yen, Jessica. "Quotations within Parentheses (Study Measures)." *Copyediting-L*, 18
>> Mar. 2016, list.indiana.edu/sympa/arc/copyediting-l/2016-03/msg00492.html.

32. **Twitter post (tweet).** Include the name or handle (if you know both, include the name in parentheses after the handle); the whole post; any hashtags; the site name, date, and time; and URL.

> @grammarphobia (Patricia T. O'Conner and Steward Kellerman). "Is 'if you will,' like, a
>> verbal tic? http://goo.gl/oYrTYP #English #language #grammar #etymology #usage
>> #linguistics #WOTD." *Twitter*, 14 Mar. 2016, 9:12 a.m., twitter.com/grammarphobia.

33. **Episode of a television or radio program.** Include the episode title, the program title (in italics), key contributors (writer, director, performers), the network, and the date of the broadcast. If you streamed the broadcast, include the URL.

Broadcast

> "Free Speech on College Campuses." *Washington Journal*, narrated by Peter Slen,
>> C-SPAN, 27 Nov. 2015.

Streamed

> "Obama's Failures Have Made Millennials Give Up Hope." *The Rush Limbaugh*
>> *Show*, narrated by Rush Limbaugh, Premiere Radio Networks, 14 Apr. 2014,
>> www.rushlimbaugh.com/daily/2014/04/14/obama_s_failures_have_made
>> _millennials_give_up_hope.

34. **Interview on a television or radio program.** Begin with the name of the person interviewed, the words *Interview by*, and the interviewer's name, if relevant. End with information about the program (as in an episode of a television or radio program).

> Russell, David O. Interview by Terry Gross. *Fresh Air*, WNYC, 20 Feb. 2014.

35. **Episode on a podcast.** Cite an episode of a podcast as you would a short work from a Web site.

McDougall, Christopher. "How Did Endurance Help Early Humans Survive?" *TED*

    Radio Hour, National Public Radio, 20 Nov. 2015, www.npr.org/2015/11/20/

    455904655/how-did-endurance-help-early-humans-survive.

36. **Short online audio or video segment.** Cite a short online audio segment or video
as you would a short work from a Web site.

Nayar, Vineet. "Employees First, Customers Second." *YouTube*, 9 June 2015,

    www.youtube.com/watch?v=cCdu67s_C5E.

Fletcher, Antoine. "The Ancient Art of the Atlatl." *Russell Cave National Monument*,

    narrated by Brenton Bellomy, National Park Service, 12 Feb. 2014, www

    .nps.gov/media/video/view.htm?id=C92C0D0A-1DD8-B71C-07CBC6E8970CD73F.

RESEARCH PROJECT IN PROGRESS 10

For the final paper you prepared in Research Project in Progress 9, prepare a list of
works cited in MLA style.

STUDENTS WRITE

The following research project was written by Nicholas Destino for his first-year writing course while he was a student at Niagara County Community College. Destino used
MLA style for documenting his sources and formatted his research project using the
instructions in this chapter (pp. 601–2). Notice how he uses in-text citations and quotations to provide evidence that supports his thesis.

1 inch ½ inch Destino 1 1 inch

Nicholas Destino

Professor Thomas

English 101

18 Nov. 2018

Do Animals Have Emotions?

½ inch — Somewhere in the savannas of Africa a mother elephant is dying in the

company of many others of her kind. Some of them are part of her family;

some are fellow members of her herd. The dying elephant tips from side to

side and seems to be balancing on a thin thread in order to sustain her life.

Many of the other elephants surround her as she struggles to regain her

balance. They also try to help her by feeding and caressing her. After many

attempts by the herd to save her life, they seem to realize that there is simply

nothing more that can be done. She finally collapses to the ground in the

presence of her companions. Most of the other elephants move away from

Header: Student's name and
page number

Double-spaced identification:
Writer's name, instructor's name,
course title, and date

Title: Centered and
double-spaced

Destino 2

the scene. There are, however, two elephants who remain behind with the dead elephant—another mother and her calf. The mother turns her back to the body and taps it with one foot. Soon the other elephants call for them to follow and eventually they do (Masson and McCarthy 95). These movements, which are slow and ritualistic, suggest that elephants may be capable of interpreting and responding to the notion of death.

The topic of animal emotions is one that, until recently, has rarely been discussed or studied by scientists. However, since the now-famous comprehensive field studies of chimpanzees by the internationally renowned primatologist Jane Goodall, those who study animal behavior have begun to look more closely at whether animals feel emotions. As a result of their observations of various species of animals, a number of these researchers have come to the conclusion that animals do exhibit a wide range of emotions, such as grief, sympathy, and joy.

One of the major reasons that research into animal emotions was traditionally avoided is that scientists fear being accused of *anthropomorphism*—the act of attributing human qualities to animals. To do so is perceived as unscientific and has been cause for much debate in the scientific community (Bekoff, *Emotional Lives* 124–25). However, Frans de Waal, of the Yerkes Regional Primate Research Center in Atlanta, argues that if people are not open to the possibility of animals having emotions, they may be overlooking important information about both animals and humans. He defends his position in his book, *Primates and Philosophers*. The term *anthropodenial*, which he coined, "denotes willful blindness to the human-like characteristics of animals, or the animal-like characteristics of ourselves" (65). De Waal proposes that because humans and animals are so closely related, it would be impossible for one not to have some characteristics of the other. He contends, "While it is true that animals are not humans, it is equally true that humans are animals. Resistance to this simple yet undeniable truth is what underlies the resistance to anthropomorphism" (65). If de Waal is correct, then we should see animal emotions as on a continuum with humans' and can infer the existence of animal emotions through their behavior, just as we infer the emotions of fellow humans.

In many instances, their behaviors (and presumably, therefore, their emotions) are uncannily similar to the behaviors of humans. Consider grief: In "Animal Emotions: Exploring Passionate Natures," Marc Bekoff provides several examples of animals who exhibit behaviors that can

---

Citation: Parenthetical in-text citation of a work with 2 authors

Sources: Abbreviated title included because another work by this author cited earlier

Sources: Signal phrase, with author background, establishes author credentials and introduces paraphrase and quotation; page number follows quotation

Sources: Titles included because 2 works by this author are cited

Destino 3

only reflect their grief. He notes that sea lions wail at the loss of their young, dolphins struggle to save their babies, and orphaned elephants who have witnessed their mothers' deaths have been observed to wake up screaming (866). In his book *The Emotional Lives of Animals*, he includes a description from Cynthia Moss's *Elephant Memories* about elephants suffering the loss of one of their group:

½ inch ← They stood around Tina's carcass, touching it gently. . . . Because it was rocky and the ground was wet, there was no loose dirt; but they tried to dig into it . . . and when they managed to get a little earth up they sprinkled it over the body. Trista, Tia, and some of the others went off and broke branches from the surrounding low brushes and brought them back and placed them on the carcass. . . . By nightfall they had nearly buried her with branches and earth. Then they stood vigil over her for most of the night and only as dawn was approaching did they reluctantly begin to walk away. (qtd. in Bekoff, *Emotional Lives* 66–67)

Diane Ackerman, a columnist for *The New York Times* who writes regularly about the intersection of human and animal worlds, notes that "[b]iologists tell of sea lions wailing when their babies have been mutilated by killer whales, of grief-stricken monkey mothers carrying dead infants around for days, of geese singing both halves of a duet when their partners have died."

Perhaps the most extreme case of grief experienced by an animal is exemplified by the story of Flint, a chimp, when Flo, his mother, died. In her book, *Through a Window*, which elaborates on her thirty years of experience studying and living among the chimps in Gombe, Tanzania, Jane Goodall gives the following account of Flint's experience with grief.

Flint became increasingly lethargic, refused most food and, with his immune system thus weakened, fell sick. The last time I saw him alive, he was hollow-eyed, gaunt and utterly depressed, huddled in the vegetation close to where Flo had died. . . . The last short journey he made, pausing to rest every few feet, was to the very place where Flo's body had lain. There he stayed for several hours, sometimes staring and staring into the water. He struggled on a little further, then curled up—and never moved again. (196–97)

Quotation: Quote longer than four lines indented half an inch and not enclosed in quotation marks; period precedes citation

Sources: Citation for indirect source

Quotation: First letter of a quotation changed to lowercase to fit into sentence

Sources: Author's credentials included within the text

Sources: Page number follows quotation

Destino 4

Of course, animal emotions are not limited to sadness and grief. Indeed, evidence indicates that animals also experience happier emotions, such as sympathy and joy. Many scientists who study animal behavior have found that several species demonstrate sympathy for one another. In other words, they act as if they care about one another. It is probably safe to assume that no animal displays behaviors more closely associated with sympathy than chimpanzees. Those who have studied apes in the wild, including de Waal, have observed that animals who had been fighting make up with one another by kissing and hugging. Chimps have also been found to console the loser of a fight or try to restore peace (Wilford).

Sympathy and caring have been noted in non-primate species as well. Researchers have found that young barn owls are "impressively generous" towards each other, saving portions of their food for smaller and hungrier owls (Angier). Likewise, the *Nature* episode "Animal Odd Couples" documents a number of instances in which animals of one species have cared for animals of another. In one example (00:25:26-00:31:41), Jack, a goat, led Charlie, a blind horse, around the ranch where they lived *every day for sixteen years,* until Jack's death (fig. 1). The animals' caretaker even compared Jack to the television

Fig. 1.   Seeing is believing: Jack leading Charlie (a blind horse). Film still from "Animal Odd Couples" (00:27:23).

Sources: Information at beginning of this paragraph can be found in many sources, so does not need to be documented

Sources: Information from a source paraphrased, no page number because source is an online newspaper

Title of television program and episode used in signal phrase

Information from source is summarized

Figure number included in text and caption

Destino 5

character Lassie, describing how Jack got human help to rescue Charlie after he became trapped in a grove of trees following a microburst of wind.

What makes this example particularly noteworthy is that the animals were of different species. Had the goat been helping another goat, it would be easy to assume that the act of caring was the result of what scientists call *genetic altruism,* animals helping others of their own species because there is something in it for them — namely, the assurance that their kin (and, therefore, their genes) will continue. This theory certainly provides an adequate, unbiased scientific explanation for why animals might care for others. However, if animals really help each other out only when doing so will perpetuate their species, then Jack would have had no genetic reason to help Charlie.

There is another popular explanation for why an animal would help another from a different species. Scientists who favor a related scientific theory called *mutual altruism* believe that animals will help each other because, when they themselves need help, they would like to be able to count on reciprocal assistance (Hemelrijk 480). This theory is a plausible, nonanthropomorphic explanation for why animals show sympathy, regardless of whether they actually feel sympathy. This point is crucial because, after all, humans can't actually observe how an animal feels; we can only observe how it behaves. It is then up to the observer to draw some logical conclusions about why animals behave in the ways they do.

The mutual altruism theory, however, can also be disputed. In many cases, animals have helped others even when the receiver of the help would probably never be in a position to return the favor. For example, there are many accounts of dolphins helping drowning or otherwise endangered swimmers. Phil Mercer, on the BBC Web site, reported that dolphins stopped a shark from attacking swimmers off the coast of New Zealand. The animals surrounded the swimmers for about forty minutes while the great white shark circled. When the swimmers reached the shore, they remarked that they were sure that the dolphins acted deliberately to save them. Marathon swimmer Matril Strel also believes that he was deliberately helped by pink dolphins during his 2007

Citation of a Web page includes only author's name and site's sponsor; no page numbers available swim of the entire Amazon River, even believing that he heard them communicating (Butler).

Not only do animals show sympathy, but they are also clearly able to express joy. For example, Takahisa Matsusaka, a primatologist, has found that when chimpanzees demonstrate "panting" while tickling or chasing each other, the chance of such play becoming aggressive is reduced (222). Dog laughter has been observed to soothe other dogs, even when the other dogs are not playing (Bekoff, *Emotional Lives* 56). According to Jaak Panksepp, an author at J. P. Scott Center for Neuroscience, Mind, and Behavior, "Research on rough-housing play in mammals, both sapient and otherwise, clearly indicates that the sources of play and laughter in the brain are both instinctual and subcortical," meaning that many animals, and not just humans, are evolutionarily hardwired to laugh. Panksepp reports that rats who are tickled emit high-frequency chirps, and the process socially bonds them so that they want to spend time with other rats who chirp (62).

The actions of animals who are not able to laugh uproariously also indicate that they feel joy. John Webster, a professor of animal husbandry at the University of Bristol, said the following about joy:

> Sentient animals have the capacity to experience pleasure and are motivated to seek it. . . . You only have to watch how cows and lambs both seek and enjoy pleasure when they lie with their heads raised to the sun on a perfect English summer's day. (qtd. in Bekoff, *Emotional Lives* 55)

In short, animals exhibit a large number of behaviors that indicate that they possess not only the capacity to feel but the capacity to express their feelings in some overt way, sometimes through vocalizations, but most often through body language. If these are not proof enough that animals have emotions, people need look no further than their own beloved cat or dog. Pets are so frequently the cause of joy, humor, love, sympathy, empathy, and even grief that it is difficult to imagine that animals could elicit such emotions in humans without actually having these emotions themselves. The question, then, is not, *do* animals have emotions? but *which* emotions do animals have and *to what degree* do they feel them?

Destino 7

Works Cited

Ackerman, Diane. "The Lonely Polar Bear." *The New York Times*, 2 July
2011, www.nytimes.com/2011/07/03/opinion/sunday/03gus.html?_r=0.

Angier, Natalie. "The Owl Comes into Its Own." *The New York Times*, 25
Feb. 2013, www.nytimes.com/2013/02/26/science/long-cloaked-in
-mystery-owls-start-coming-into-full-view.html?.

"Animal Odd Couples." *Nature*, PBS, 7 Nov. 2012, www.pbs.org/wnet/
nature/animal-odd-couples-full-episode/8009/.

Bekoff, Marc. "Animal Emotions: Exploring Passionate Natures." *Bioscience*,
vol. 50, no. 10, Oct. 2000, pp. 861–70, bioscience.oxfordjournals.org/
content/50/10/861.full.

---. *The Emotional Lives of Animals*. New World Library, 2007.

Butler, Rhett A. "Marathon Swimmer: An Interview with the First Man to
Swim the Length of the Amazon." *Mongabay.com*, 23 Jan. 2011, news
.mongabay.com/2011/01/marathon-swimmer-an-interview-with-the-first
-man-to-swim-the-length-of-the-amazon/.

de Waal, Frans. *Primates and Philosophers*. Princeton UP, 2006.

Goodall, Jane. *Through a Window: My Thirty Years with the Chimpanzees of
Gombe*. Houghton Mifflin, 1990.

Hemelrijk, Charlotte K. "Support for Being Groomed in Long-Tailed
Macaques, *Macaca Fasciularis.*" *Animal Behaviour*, vol. 48, no. 2,
Aug. 1994, pp. 479–81.

Masson, Jeffrey Moussaieff, and Susan McCarthy. *When Elephants Weep:
The Emotional Lives of Animals*. Dell Publishing, 1995.

Matsusaka, Takahisa. "When Does Play Panting Occur during Social Play in
Wild Chimpanzees?" *Primates*, vol. 45, no. 4, Oct. 2004, pp. 221–29.
SpringerLink, doi:10.1007/s10329-004-0090-z.

Mercer, Phil. "Dolphins Prevent NZ Shark Attack." *BBC News*, 23 Nov. 2004,
news.bbc.co.uk/2/hi/asia-pacific/4034383.stm.

Panksepp, Jaak. "Beyond a Joke: From Animal Laughter to Human Joy?"
Science, vol. 308, no. 5718, 1 Apr. 2005, pp. 62–63. *JSTOR*, doi:10.1126/
science.1112066.

Works-cited list appears on a new page; heading is centered; entries are double spaced

Entries alphabetized by author's last name

First line of each entry is flush left with margin; subsequent lines indented half an inch

Destino 8

Wilford, John Noble. "Almost Human, and Sometimes Smarter." *The New York Times*, 17 Apr. 2007, www.nytimes.com/2007/04/17/science/17chimp.html?_r=0.

Document Your Sources: APA Style

The system described in this section is recommended by the American Psychological Association (APA) and is described in detail in *The Publication Manual of the American Psychological Association*, Sixth Edition (available from most libraries). APA style uses in-text citations within the text of a research project and a list of references at the end to document the sources used. If you are unsure whether to use APA style, check with your instructor. The student paper that appears at the end of this section ("Schizophrenia: Definition and Treatment," pp. 638–44) uses APA style.

Use APA Style for In-Text Citations

Your paper must include in-text citations for all material you summarize, paraphrase, or quote from sources. There are two basic ways to write an in-text citation:

1. **Use a signal phrase (attribution) and publication date (in parentheses).** Mention the author's name in a phrase or sentence introducing the material, include the year of publication in parentheses immediately following the author's name, and at least for quotations, include the page number on which the borrowed material appears, in parentheses.
2. **Use a parenthetical citation.** In parentheses, include the author's last name, the year of publication, and (at least for quotations) the page number (separated by commas).

APA style requires only that you include page numbers for quotations, but your instructor may want you to include a page number for paraphrases and summaries as well, so make sure you ask. Signal phrases allow you to put your sources in context, so use a signal phrase for most citations. For either type of citation, follow these rules.

- Place the sentence period after the closing parenthesis. When a quotation ends the sentence, insert the closing quotation mark before the opening parenthesis. Block quotations are an exception to these rules; see page 597.

- For direct quotations, include the page number after the year, separating it from the year with a comma. Use the abbreviation *p.* or *pp.* followed by a space and the page number.

Signal Phrase

Avery and Ehrlich (2008) said "nasal sounds are made with air passing through the nose" (p. 21).

Parenthetical Citation

Snorts, snores, and other such sounds are created "with air passing through the nose" (Avery & Ehrlich, 2008, p. 21).

The following section provides guidelines for formatting in-text citations in APA style.

Directory of APA In-Text Citation Models

1. **One author**

   According to Adams (2009), . . .

   . . . (Adams, 2009).

2. **Two authors.** Include both authors' last names and the year in a signal phrase or parenthetical citation. In parenthetical citations, replace the word *and* with an ampersand (&).

   Avery and Ehrlich (2008) have asserted . . .

   . . . (Avery & Ehrlich, 2008).

3. **Three to five authors.** Include all authors' last names the first time the source is mentioned. In subsequent references to the same source, use the first author's last name followed by *et al.* (Latin for "and others").

   ### First Reference

   Lewin, Krebs, Kilpatrick, and Goldstein (2011) have found . . .

   . . . (Lewin, Krebs, Kilpatrick, & Goldstein, 2011).

Later References

> Lewin et al. (2011) discovered . . .
>
> . . . (Lewin et al., 2011).

4. **Six or more authors.** Use the first author's last name followed by *et al.* in all in-text citations.

5. **Two or more works by the same author(s).** Cite the works chronologically, in order of publication.

> Gaerlan (2001, 2011) believed that . . .
>
> . . . (Gaerlan, 2001, 2011).

6. **Two or more works by the same author in the same year.** Add the lowercase letter *a* after the publication year for the first source as it appears alphabetically by title in your reference list. Add the letter *b* to the publication year for the source that appears next, and so forth. Include the years with the corresponding lowercase letters in your in-text citations. (See p. 633 for the corresponding reference entries.)

> Adams (2009a) believed that . . .
>
> . . . (Adams, 2009a).

7. **Authors with the same last name.** Use the first author's initials with his or her name.

> Research by V. M. Hoselton (2001) exemplified . . .
>
> . . . (V. M. Hoselton, 2001).

8. **No author named.** Use the first few words of the title and the year in the signal phrase or parenthetical citation. Italicize a book title; put the title of a journal article in quotation marks. Unlike the entry in the list of references, use standard capitalization in the in-text citation. (See p. 633.)

> As noted in "Gluten Free Recipes" (2009), . . .
>
> . . . ("Gluten Free Recipes," 2009).

9. **Two or more sources in the same citation.** When citing two or more sources in parentheses, put a semicolon between them and list them in alphabetical order.

> . . . (Hoffman, 2011; Murphy, 2009)

10. **Specific part of a work.** When quoting, paraphrasing, or summarizing a passage, include the page number on which the passage appears. If the work does not have page numbers, use paragraph numbers, if provided (with the abbreviation *para.*), or the heading of the section in which the material appears.

> Pinker (2007) offered an explanation for why swearing occurs across cultures:
>
> > Obscenities "may tap into deep and ancient parts of the emotional brain" (p. 331).
>
> If obscenities "tap into deep and ancient parts of the emotional brain" (Pinker, 2007, p. 331), then it makes sense that swearing occurs across cultures.

11. **Chapter in an edited book or work in an anthology.** An *anthology* is a collection of writings by different authors. In the in-text citation, name the author who wrote the work (*not* the editor of the anthology) and give the year the anthology was published. The corresponding entry in the list of references begins with the author's last name; it also names the editor of the anthology.

In-Text Citation

> As Pedelty (2010) noted . . .
>
> . . . (Pedelty, 2010).

References Entry

> Pedelty, M. (2010). Musical news: Popular music in political movements. In S. E. Bird (Ed.), *The anthropology of news and journalism: Global perspectives* (pp. 215–240). Bloomington: Indiana University Press.

12. **Multivolume work.** When you cite one volume of a multivolume work, include the year of publication for that volume.

> Terman (2008) indicated . . .
>
> . . . (Terman, 2008).

When you cite two or more volumes of a multivolume work, give inclusive years for the volumes.

> Terman (2008–2011) indicated . . .

13. **Indirect sources.** When you quote a source indirectly (rather than from the original source), include the words *cited in* along with the information for the source in which you found the quote.

> According to Ephron, . . . (as cited in Thomas, 2009, p. 33).

14. **Personal interviews, letters, emails, and conversations.** Give the last name and initial of the person, the source of the communication, and the exact date. Do not include these sources in the list of references.

> . . . (J. Lopez, personal communication, October 30, 2011).

15. **Internet sources.** For direct quotations, give the author, year, and page (if available) in the signal phrase or parenthetical citation. If paragraph numbers are available, cite them with the abbreviation *para.*

> Stevens (2011) has maintained . . .
>
> . . . (Stevens, 2011).

Use APA Style for the List of References

Follow these general guidelines for preparing the list of references.

1. List only the sources you cite in your paper. If you consulted a source but did not cite it in your paper, do not include it in the list of references.

2. Put the list on a separate page at the end of your paper. The heading *References* should be centered an inch below the top of the page. Do not use quotation marks, italics, or bold type for the heading.

3. Alphabetize the list by the entry's first important word (author's last name or, if no author is named, first key word of the title). Give the author's last name, followed by a comma and his or her initial or initials (not the full first name) and a space between initials: *Myers, D. G.* For works with multiple authors, list all authors' names in inverted order.

> Avery, P., & Ehrlich, S. (2008). *Teaching American English pronunciation.* New York, NY: Oxford University Press.

4. Put the publication date in parentheses after the author's name.

5. For titles of books and articles capitalize the first word, the first word following a colon, and any proper nouns (names). For titles of periodicals, capitalize all important words.

6. Include the word *A*, *An*, or *The* at the beginning of titles.

7. Italicize titles of books and names of journals, newspapers, and magazines. Do not italicize, underline, or use quotation marks with article titles.

8. For magazine and journal articles, italicize the volume number.

9. Indent the second and all subsequent lines half an inch—hanging indent style.

10. Double-space the entire list.

A variety of models for different types of sources follow. However, you may need to combine information from one or more models to create a citation for a work you are using. For instance, to cite a reading from this textbook, you would need to treat it as a work in an anthology (p. 634) in an edition other than the first (p. 635):

> Goleman, D. (2017). His marriage and hers: Childhood roots. In K. T. McWhorter, *Successful college writing: Skills, strategies, learning styles* (7th ed.), pp. 387–91. Boston, MA: Bedford/St. Martin's.

Directory of APA Reference Models

Authors

1. **One author.** Put the author's last name first, followed by her or his initials. If the author has more than one initial, include a space in between.

   Myers, W. D.

2. **More than one author.** Use inverted order (last name, initial) for all authors' names. Separate names with commas and use an ampersand (&) before the last author's name.

   Myers, W. D., & Myers, C.

   For citations with more than seven authors, list the first six (in the order they appear on the title page), an ellipsis (. . .), and then the last author's name.

   Frank, H., Smithson, D., Roberts, C., Johnson, F. T., Ng, N., Washington, F. D., . . .
   Doyle, A. C.

3. **Two or more works by the same author(s).** Begin each entry with the author's name. Arrange the entries in chronological order of publication.

   Pollan, M. (2006).
   Pollan, M. (2008).

4. **Two or more works by the same author in the same year.** Arrange the works alphabetically by title; then assign a lowercase letter (*a*, *b*, *c*) to the year of publication for each source. (See p. 630 for the corresponding in-text citation.)

   Folger, T. (2014a). Beyond the Higgs Boson. . .
   Folger, T. (2014b). Melting away. . . .

5. **Work with no author named.** Start the entry with the title; alphabetize it by the first important word (ignore *A*, *An*, or *The*).

   Go ask Alice. (1971). New York, NY: Avon Books.

6. **Agency or corporation as author.** List the agency as the author. If the publisher is the same as the author, write *Author* for the name of the publisher.

   Bill and Melinda Gates Foundation. (2013). *Feedback for better teaching: Nine principles for using measures of effective teaching*. Seattle, WA: Author.

Books. Most of the information you will need to cite a book appears on the book's title page and copyright page. (See Figure 23.3, p. 611.) In printed books, these two pages appear toward the beginning of the text; in e-books, they may appear elsewhere.

CITING A BOOK

1. *Author.* Begin with the author's surname and initial(s): *Myers, D. G.*

2. *Year.* Include the year of publication, in parentheses. Use the most recent copyright year if more than one appears on the copyright page: *(2016).*

3. *Title.* Italicize the title of the book. Capitalize only the first word of the title and subtitle (if any) and any proper nouns (*Juan*) or adjectives (*French*).

4. *Place of publication.* Give the city of publication followed by the postal abbreviation for the state and a colon (*Hillsdale, NJ:*). For cities outside the United States, add the country after the city.

5. *Publisher.* Include the name of the publisher, followed by a period. Use a shortened form of the name: *Alfred A. Knopf* would be listed as *Knopf.* Omit words such as *Publishers* and abbreviations such as *Inc.,* but do not omit the word *Books* or *Press* if it is part of the publisher's name: *Academic Press, Basic Books.*

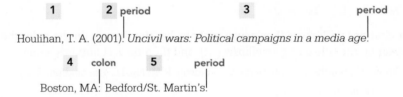

Houlihan, T. A. (2001). *Uncivil wars: Political campaigns in a media age.*

Boston, MA: Bedford/St. Martin's.

Books and Other Long Works

7. **Edited book or anthology.** List the editor's or editors' names, followed by the abbreviation *Ed.* or *Eds.* in parentheses and a period.

> Bradley, B., Feldman, F., & Johansson, J. (Eds.). (2013). *The Oxford handbook of the*
>
> *philosophy of death.* New York: Oxford University Press.

8. **Chapter in an edited book or work in an anthology.** List the author of the work first and then the date the anthology was published. The title of the work follows. Then name the editor of the anthology (not in inverted order), give the title of the anthology (italicized), and insert the inclusive page numbers in parentheses for the work (preceded by *pp.*). The publication information follows in normal order.

> Dachyshyn, D. (2006). Refugee families with preschool children: Adjustment to life in
>
> Canada. In L. Adams (Ed.), *Global migration and education: Schools, children*
>
> *and families* (pp. 251–262). London, England: Erlbaum.

9. **Translated book.** After the title, include the initial(s) and last name of the translator followed by a comma and *Trans*.

> Kawakami, H. (2010). *Manazuru* (M. Emmerich, Trans.). Berkeley, CA: Counterpoint.

10. **Edition other than the first**

> Myers, D. G. (2014). *Exploring psychology* (9th ed.). New York, NY: Worth.

11. **Article from an encyclopedia or dictionary**

Print

> Robinson, L. C. (2005). Harlem Writers Guild. *Africana: The encyclopedia of the African and African American experience*. (2nd ed.). Oxford, England: Oxford University Press.

Online

> Calef, S. (2008). Dualism and mind. In J. Fieser & B. Dowden (Eds.), *The Internet encyclopedia of philosophy*. Retrieved from http://www.iep.utm.edu

12. **Multivolume work.** Give the volume numbers in parentheses after the title. If all volumes were not published in the same year, the publication date should include the range of years.

> McAuliffe, J. D. (Ed.). (2001–2006). *Encyclopedia of the Qur'an* (Vols. 1–5). Leiden, The Netherlands: Brill.

13. **Article in a multivolume work.** Include the author and title of the article, as well as the title, volume number, and publication information for the work.

> Meerdink, J. E. (2006). Sleep. In *Encyclopedia of human development* (Vol. 3, pp. 1180–1181). Thousand Oaks, CA: Sage.

14. **Government publication.** List the agency as the author, followed by the date. Include the document or publication number if available. If you access the government publication online, include the retrieval information.

> U.S. Office of Management and Budget. (2009). *A new era of responsibility: Renewing America's promise*. Washington, DC: Government Printing Office.

> U.S. Justice Department, Federal Bureau of Investigation. (2011, August 2). *Byte out of history: Communist agent tells all*. Retrieved from http://www.fbi.gov/news /stories/august/communist_080211/communist_080211

Articles in Periodicals. A periodical is a publication that appears at regular intervals: Newspapers generally appear daily, magazines weekly or monthly, and scholarly journals quarterly. In periodicals, the information you will need to cite may appear on the first page of the article (see Figure 23.4, p. 615), or you may need to look at a combination of places (the first page of the article, the cover of the periodical, the Web page or Web site on which the article appears, and so on).

CITING AN ARTICLE IN A PERIODICAL

1. *Author.* Follow the basic format for listing authors' names (see p. 633). If no author is listed, begin with the article title and alphabetize the entry by its title (ignoring the words *A*, *An*, or *The*).

2. *Date.* For articles in journals, the year of publication appears in parentheses following the author's name. For articles in newspapers and magazines, the month and day, if relevant, follow the year.

3. *Article title.* Do not enclose article titles in quotation marks. Capitalize only the first word of the article title, along with any proper nouns or proper adjectives (*American*) and the first word following a colon.

4. *Periodical title.* Italicize the name of the periodical. Use standard capitalization.

5. *Volume/issue.* For scholarly journals and magazines, give the volume number in italics; if each issue is paginated separately, starting with page 1, give the issue number in parentheses and roman type.

6. *Pages.* The abbreviation *p.* or *pp.* is used only in entries for newspaper articles.

7. *DOI/URL.* If you accessed the work online, end the citation with the digital object identifier (DOI), a permanent code. If there is no DOI, insert the URL of the homepage for the journal. If the source will be difficult to find from the home page, include the words *Retrieved from* followed by the source's specific URL. If necessary, break URLs before punctuation marks, such as dots (.), slashes (/), and question marks (?). DOIs and URLs are not followed by periods.

1   2 period   3   period
Kar, R. B. (2017). The evolutionary game-theoretic foundations of law.

4   comma 5 6 period   7
Law & Social Inquiry, 42(1), 38–48. doi:10.1111/lsi.12277

comma

15. **Article in a scholarly journal.** If issues in each volume are numbered continuously (issue 1 ends on page 159 and issue 2 begins on page 160, for example), omit the issue number. If the journal article has been assigned a DOI (digital object identifier), add it at the end of the citation. If you access the source online, but it has not been assigned a DOI, include the URL for the homepage of the journal. If the article would be difficult to find from the homepage, include the words *Retrieved from* and the URL.

> Carter, M. (2013, April 6). The moral identity and group affiliation. *Current Research in Social Psychology, 21*(1). *Retrieved from* http://www.uiowa.edu/grpproc /crisp/crisp21_1.pdf

16. **Article in a weekly magazine.** Include the day, month, and year of publication. If you accessed the magazine online, omit the page numbers and include the URL of the homepage.

Print

> Levy, S. (2005, April 18). In the new game of tag, all of us are it. *Newsweek, 145*(16), 14.

Online

> Friend, T. (2017, January 9). Mike Mill's anti-Hollywood family films. *The New Yorker, 92*(44), 116. Retrieved from www.newyorker.com

17. **Article in a monthly magazine.** Include the month of publication after the year.

> Purple, M. (2013, October). Road ragin'. *American Spectator, 46*(8), 64–65.

18. **Article in a newspaper.** Include the year, month, and day in parentheses following the author's name. Page numbers for newspaper articles should be preceded by a *p.* or *pp.* If you accessed the newspaper article online, omit the page numbers and include the URL of the homepage.

Print

> Gugliotta, G. (2012, November 27). Looking to cities, in search of global warming's silver lining. *The New York Times*, p. D3.

Online

> Sullivan, P. (2008, May 6). Quiet Va. wife ended interracial marriage ban. *The Washington Post*. Retrieved from http://www.washingtonpost.com

19. **Editorial or letter to the editor.** Cite the editorial or letter beginning with the author's name (if available). Include *Editorial* or *Letter to the editor* in brackets following the title (if any). If the author's name is not available, begin with the title.

> Exposing the pay gap [Editorial]. (2013, September 25). *The New York Times*, p. A28. Retrieved from http://www.nytimes.com

> Ginn, L. (2008, December). [Letter to the editor]. *Wired, 16*(12), 19.

20. **Book or film review.** List the reviewer's name, the date, and the title of the review. In brackets, give a description of the work reviewed, including the medium (*book* or *motion picture*), title, and the author for a book or the year for a film.

> Gottlieb, R. (2017, June 8). "Make 'em cry, make 'em laugh, make 'em wait." [Review of the books *The king of inventors: A life of Wilkie Collins*, by Catherine Peters, and *Wilkie Collins*, by Peter Ackroyd.] *The New York Review of Books, 64*(10), 25–28.

Other Sources

21. **Document posted on an organization's Web site.** Treat the author of a document on a Web site as you would the author of a book or article, and treat the title of a work on a Web site as you would an article in a periodical. If you access the source online, include "Retrieved from" and the publisher's name;

omit this if the publisher is listed as the author and insert "Retrieved from" before the URL. (Note: APA spells *website* all lowercase.) If the document is not dated or the content could change, include a retrieval date.

> Amnesty International. (2005). *Afghanistan: Addressing the past to secure the future*. Retrieved from http://web.amnesty.org/library/Index/ENGASA110032005
>
> National Safety Council. (2010). *Distracted driving*. Retrieved from http://www.nsc.org/safety_road/Distracted_Driving/Pages/distracted_driving.aspx
>
> Gallagher, S. (2012, October 25). *The last nomads of the Tibetan Plateau*. Retrieved from Pulitzer Center on Crisis Reporting website: pulitzercenter.org/reporting/china-glaciers-globalwarming-climate-change-ecosystem-tibetan-plateau-grasslands-nomads

22. Film, video, or DVD

> Greenfield, L. (Director). (2006). *Thin* [Motion picture]. New York, NY: Home Box Office.

23. Television program

> Murphy, R. (Writer), & Buecker, B. (Director). (2011). Comeback [Television series episode]. In I. Brennan, R. Murphy, & B. Falchuk (Creators), *Glee*. New York, NY: Fox Broadcasting.

24. Computer software

> Rosenbloom, C., & American Dietetic Association. (2006). Sports nutrition: Client education [Computer software]. Chicago, IL: American Dietetic Association.

RESEARCH PROJECT IN PROGRESS 11

For the final paper you prepared in Research Project in Progress 10, prepare a list of references in APA style.

STUDENTS WRITE

The following research project was written by Sonia Gomez for her introductory psychology course. She used APA style for formatting her paper and documenting her sources. Notice her use of in-text citations and paraphrases and summaries of sources to provide evidence in support of her thesis.

SCHIZOPHRENIA: DEFINITION AND TREATMENT 1

Schizophrenia: Definition and Treatment

Sonia Gomez

Psychology 101

Professor McCombs

Identification: Double-space and include on title page: writer's name, course title, and instructor's name.

Information on title page should be centered vertically and horizontally. (Vertical centering not shown here.)

SCHIZOPHRENIA: DEFINITION AND TREATMENT 2

Abstract

Schizophrenia is a mental/brain disorder that affects about 1% of the population. The five types of schizophrenia include paranoid, disorganized, catatonic, undifferentiated, and residual. There are three categories of symptoms—positive, disorganized or cognitive, and negative. The causes of schizophrenia are not well known, but there is likely a genetic component and an environmental component. The structure of the brain of schizophrenics is also unusual. Treatments include drug therapy with typical and atypical anti-psychotics and psychosocial and cognitive-behavioral therapies.

Abstract: Include an abstract, a brief summary of the report; heading centered, not bold

Formatting: Double-space essay, leave one-inch margins on all sides

Title: Repeat full title just before text of paper begins; title centered, not bold

Schizophrenia: Definition and Treatment

The disorder schizophrenia comes with an ugly cultural stigma. There is a common belief that all schizophrenics are violent. In fact, they are more a danger to themselves than to others because they often commit suicide. Many of the movies, books, and TV shows in our culture do not help to diminish this stigma. The movie *A Beautiful Mind*, for example, features a paranoid schizophrenic who comes close to harming his family and others around him because of his hallucinations and delusions. He believes that the government is out to get him (Grazer & Howard, 2001). Many people are afraid of schizophrenics and believe their permanent home should be in a mental hospital or psychiatric ward. This paper helps to dispel misperceptions of the disorder by providing facts about and treatments of the disorder.

Introduction: Presentation of the topic researched by Gomez

Sources: Authors named in parenthetical citation; ampersand (&), not the word *and*, between names

What Is Schizophrenia?

Heading: First-level heading is centered, bold

Schizophrenia is a mental/brain disorder that affects about 1% of the population or 2.2 million Americans (National Institutes of Mental Health, 2016). This disease can be very disruptive in people's lives. It causes problems with communication and maintaining jobs. It is a widely misunderstood disease; many people believe schizophrenics to be dangerous. There is no cure for schizophrenia, but it can often be successfully treated (National Institutes of Mental Health, 2016). Schizophrenia does not seem to favor a specific gender or ethnic group. The disease rarely occurs in children. Hallucinations and delusions usually begin between ages sixteen and thirty (National Alliance on Mental Illness, 2017).

Sources: No individual author named, so Web site sponsor listed as author

Types of Schizophrenia

Heading: Second-level heading at left margin, bold

There are five types of schizophrenia—paranoid, disorganized, catatonic, undifferentiated, and residual. People with paranoid schizophrenia are illogically paranoid about the world around them. They often hold false beliefs about being persecuted. People with disorganized schizophrenia are confused and incoherent and jumble their speech. People with disorganized schizophrenia often show symptoms of schizophasia—creating their own words and using them in a word salad, a jumbling of coherent and noncoherent words.

SCHIZOPHRENIA: DEFINITION AND TREATMENT 4

People with catatonic schizophrenia are usually immobile and unresponsive to everything around them. Undifferentiated schizophrenia is diagnosed when the patient does not fit into the other three categories. Residual schizophrenia occurs when schizophrenic symptoms have decreased but still exist (WebMD, 2017).

Symptoms of Schizophrenia

The symptoms of schizophrenia are separated into three categories— positive, disorganized or cognitive, and negative. Positive symptoms include hallucinations and delusions (WebMD, 2017). According to Barch (2003), disorganized or cognitive symptoms cause the person to be unable to think clearly. Disorganized or cognitive symptoms include difficulty communicating, use of nonsense words, inability to focus on one thought, slow movement, inability to make decisions, forgetfulness and losing of things, repetitive movements, inability to make sense of everyday senses, and problems with memory. Negative symptoms are an absence of normal behavior (WebMD, 2017). They include a lack of emotion or inappropriate emotions, isolation, lack of energy and motivation, loss of interest or pleasure in life, problems functioning in everyday life (such as bad hygiene), rapid mood changes, and catatonia (remaining in the same position for a long time) (WebMD, 2017).

The diagnosis of schizophrenia is often difficult because it can be confused with a number of other mental disorders including bipolar disorder. The process of diagnosis begins with an interview by a psychiatrist. The patient is usually tested for other physical illnesses using various blood tests. If the symptoms last for at least six months and there is seemingly no other cause of the problem, the person is considered to have schizophrenia (National Alliance on Mental Illness, 2017).

Causes of Schizophrenia

No one is completely sure of the causes of schizophrenia. Most scientists believe that genetics are involved, and it seems that there is either a genetic mutation in DNA or a gene that can be activated by a number of situations. Scientists are coming very close to determining the exact chromosome where

Sources: Author named in text; date follows in parentheses

SCHIZOPHRENIA: DEFINITION AND TREATMENT   5

the gene for schizophrenia might be located (Conklin & Iacono, 2002). The

circumstances surrounding birth may have a great effect on whether the child's

schizophrenic gene becomes activated or not. For example, if a fetus is exposed

to viruses or malnourished before birth or if there are complications during birth,

the gene may be activated. Conklin and Iacono (2002) reported a link between

schizophrenia and complications during birth that result in lack of oxygen

(hypoxia). Also, Bower (2008) observed that poor children or children who deal

with highly stressful situations may be more likely to develop the disorder.

Besides all of these factors, the brains of schizophrenics seem to be

different from other people's. People with schizophrenia have an imbalance

of dopamine and glutamate in their brains. The ventricles at the center of

the brain seem to be larger, and there appears to be a loss of brain tissue in

comparison with a normal brain (Figure 1).

Figure 1. Brain-tissue loss. The image shows a loss of brain tissue (the

areas in red) for the teens with schizophrenia. (Internet Mental Health

Initiative, 2001; image by Thompson, Vidal, Rapoport, & Toga, *UCLA*

Laboratory of Neuro Imaging)

Sources: Authors named in text, so *and,* not ampersand (&), used between names

Illustration: The figure is referred to in the text; the word *Figure* and a figure number appears in the caption. Professional publications in psychology require authors to place figures on a separate page at the end of the paper, but your instructor may prefer that you integrate your figures.

Also, some areas of the brain seem to have more or less activity than normal brains do. According to Conklin and Iacono (2002), these abnormalities in the brain appear to be preexisting rather than caused by the disease. Schizophrenia tends to appear during puberty because of hormonal interactions occurring in the brain (WebMD, 2017).

Treatment

There is a wide variety of treatments for schizophrenia. Typical antipsychotic drugs, such as chlorpromazine and perphenazine, are an obvious choice, especially for people with hallucinations and delusions. They can help to clear up thinking problems. However, many of these drugs cause unpleasant side effects such as nausea and anxiety. Because of this, schizophrenics may stop taking or refuse to take their medication. Many of these antipsychotic drugs have not changed since the 1950s. In the 1990s, a new set of drugs—atypical antipsychotics—was developed. Clozapine was one of these drugs, and it was deemed very effective. However, it can cause agranulocytosis, a loss of white blood cells. Between the constant testing for agranulocytosis and the cost of clozapine, many schizophrenics did not particularly like the drug (National Institutes of Mental Health, 2017).

Other treatments do not rely on medication. Psychosocial and cognitive-behavioral therapies are often used. People with schizophrenia can learn illness-management skills. They can go to rehabilitation, and their families can be educated about how to care for them. Self-help groups are also common. However, if the disease becomes unmanageable, the person with schizophrenia may end up in the hospital. Electroconvulsive therapy, in which seizures are induced, is one of the more extreme treatments for schizophrenia. It is often used to treat catatonia. If the schizophrenia is still unmanageable, a lobotomy may be performed. A lobotomy is surgery in which the connections to and from the prefrontal cortex are cut. Lobotomies cause severe personality changes; they were used much more often in the 1950s than they are today (National Alliance on Mental Illness, 2017).

People with schizophrenia are very susceptible to substance abuse. Many schizophrenics have severe drinking problems, and tobacco addiction is also

SCHIZOPHRENIA: DEFINITION AND TREATMENT 7

common. It is harder for them than most people to break this addiction. If they combine substance abuse treatment with the other treatments for their disease, they get much more beneficial results (WebMD, 2017).

Conclusion

As scientists begin to understand schizophrenia, better treatments are becoming available. There is starting to be a better outlook for schizophrenics, and because of this, the public might develop a more sympathetic view of schizophrenics.

Conclusion: Conclusion is indicated by heading (bold and centered). Gomez references her introduction in her conclusion.

SCHIZOPHRENIA: DEFINITION AND TREATMENT 8

References

Barch, D. (2003). Cognition in schizophrenia: Does working memory work? *Current Directions in Psychological Science, 12*(4), 146–150. doi:10.1111/1467-8721.01251

Bower, B. (2008). Rare mutations tied to schizophrenia. *Science News, 173*(14), 222.

Conklin, H., & Iacono, W. (2002). Schizophrenia: A neurodevelopmental perspective. *Current Directions in Psychological Science, 11*(1), 33–37.

Grazer, B. (Producer), & Howard, R. (Director). (2001). *A beautiful mind* [Motion Picture]. Los Angeles, CA: Universal Pictures.

Internet Mental Health Initiative. (2001, September 24). UCLA maps how schizophrenia engulfs teen brains. Retrieved from http://newsroom.ucla .edu/releases/UCLA-Researchers-Map-How-Schizophrenia-2701

National Alliance on Mental Illness. (2017). Schizophrenia. In *Mental health conditions.* Retrieved from https://www.nami.org/Learn-More/Mental -Health-Conditions/Schizophrenia

National Institutes of Mental Health. (2016, February). Schizophrenia. In *Health topics.* Retrieved from http://www.nimh.nih.gov/health/topics /schizophrenia/index.shtml

WebMD. (2017). Schizophrenia guide. In *Mental health center.* Retrieved from http://www.webmd.com/schizophrenia/guide/default.htm

References: Heading centered, not bold; list appears on a new page.

DOI: The DOI is provided when available for printed and online works.

Formatting: Double-spaced throughout

Entries: Alphabetize entries by first important word (author's last name, name of sponsor, or first key word of title if no author named). Only the first word and proper nouns/adjectives are capitalized in titles of shorter works (such as articles in a periodical, or Web pages on a Web site). First, last, and all key words are capitalized in titles of longer, stand-alone works (such as books, periodicals, films, Web sites).

URLs: The URL is provided for Web sites and Web pages.

Academic and Business Applications

24

Reading and Writing about Literature

Mirrorpix/Contributor/Getty Images

In this chapter you will learn to:

- develop a general approach to reading literature
- understand the language of literature
- analyze short stories
- analyze poetry
- write a literary analysis

WRITING QUICK START   Suppose your American literature instructor asks you to read carefully "The Bean Eaters," a poem by Gwendolyn Brooks (1917–2000). Brooks was a major American writer of poetry as well as fiction and nonfiction prose. She was the first African American woman to win a Pulitzer Prize for poetry (for *Annie Allen*, 1949). "The Bean Eaters" was originally published in 1960, in a collection of poems of the same title.

After reading "The Bean Eaters," how would you describe the life of the elderly couple shown in the photo on this page? (Note that the couple in the photo is not the couple described in the poem.) Using information about the life of the elderly couple presented in "The Bean Eaters," as well as your own experience with elderly people, write a paragraph describing what you think the couple's relationship might be like. How does Brooks's description of one elderly couple help you understand other elderly people like the man and woman in the photo?

The Bean Eaters

Gwendolyn Brooks

> They eat beans mostly, this old yellow pair.
> Dinner is a casual affair.
> Plain chipware on a plain and creaking wood,
> Tin flatware.
> Two who are Mostly Good.   5
> Two who have lived their day,
> But keep on putting on their clothes
> And putting things away.
> And remembering . . .
> Remembering, with twinklings and twinges,   10
> As they lean over the beans in their rented back room that
> is full of beads and receipts and dolls and cloths,
> tobacco crumbs, vases and fringes.

Both "The Bean Eaters" and the paragraph you wrote in the Writing Quick Start paint a picture of an elderly couple. Through carefully selected details, the poem describes the couple's daily activities, memories of the past, and current economic situation ("They eat beans mostly," "Plain chipware," and "rented back room" reveal that the couple is poor). The poem also suggests that routine is important to the couple ("But keep on putting on their clothes / And putting things away") and that their memories of the past are both good ("twinklings") and bad ("twinges").

"The Bean Eaters" suggests an answer to a question many students ask: "Why should I read or write about literature?" This poem, like all other literature, is about the experiences people share. Literature often deals with large issues: What is worthwhile? What is moral? What is beautiful? When you read and write about literature, you gain insights into many aspects of human experience and thereby enrich your own life.

The first half of this chapter offers a general approach to reading and understanding literature. The second half focuses on the characteristics of literary analysis and provides a Guided Writing Assignment. Although literature can take many forms—including poetry, short stories, biography, autobiography, drama, essays, and novels—this chapter concentrates on two literary genres: short stories and poetry.

LITERATURE IN COLLEGE AND THE WORKPLACE

- Your *art history professor* asks you to read Ernest Hemingway's *For Whom the Bell Tolls* (a novel set during the Spanish Civil War) and to write a paper discussing its meaning in conjunction with Picasso's *Guernica,* a painting that vividly portrays a scene from that war.

- In a *film class,* you watch *Romeo and Juliet,* directed by Franco Zeffirelli. Your instructor asks you to read excerpts from Shakespeare's *Romeo and Juliet* and write a paper evaluating how successfully the film portrays Juliet.

- You work for a *children's book store.* Your supervisor has asked you to read several children's books that she is considering featuring during story hour and to write an evaluation of each.

A General Approach to Reading Literature

Textbooks focus primarily on presenting factual information, but works of literature are concerned with interpreting ideas, experiences, and events. Literature uses facts, description, and details to convey larger meanings.

The following general guidelines will help you read literary works effectively.

For more on previewing, see Chapter 2, pp. 27–31.

1. **Preview the work before reading it.** Be ready to respond to the work; don't make up your mind about it before you study the work in earnest. Read background information about the author and the work and study the title. Read the first few and last few paragraphs of a short story, and quickly skim the pages in between to notice the setting, the names of the characters, and the amount of dialogue. Read poems through once to get an initial impression.

2. **Read to establish the literal meaning first.** During the first reading of a work, establish its literal meaning. Who is doing what, when, and where? Identify the general subject, specific topic, and main character. What is happening? Describe the basic plot, action, or sequence of events. Establish where and during what time period the action occurs.

3. **Then reread slowly and carefully to study the language.** Works of literature use language in unique and creative ways, requiring you to read them slowly. Interact with the work by jotting down your reactions as you read. Include hunches, insights, feelings, and questions. Highlight or underline key words, phrases, or actions that seem important or that you want to reconsider later. Mark interesting uses of language, such as striking phrases or descriptions, as well as sections that hint at the deeper meaning of the work. Note that literature often bends the rules of grammar and usage. Writers of literature may use sentence fragments, ungrammatical dialogue, or unusual punctuation to create a particular effect. When you encounter such instances, remember that most writers bend the rules for a purpose. Ask yourself what that purpose is.

4. **Reread once again to identify themes and patterns and piece together your interpretation.** Study your annotations to identify the conflict and discover how the

ideas in the work link together to suggest a theme. **Themes** are large or universal topics that are important to nearly everyone. For example, the theme of a poem or short story might be that independence is a crucial component of true happiness or that growing up involves a loss of innocence. Think of the theme as the main point a poem or short story makes. To understand the work's theme, consider why the writer wrote the work and what message, view, or lesson about human experience the writer is trying to communicate. (For more about themes, see pp. 655–56.)

5. **Write one or more paragraphs identifying the conflict and how it gets resolved, and stating what you think is the main theme.** Concluding your study of a work of literature with your own statement will help you move from comprehension of the work to your own interpretation and analysis of its significance.

Literary works are complex; you should not expect to understand a poem or short story immediately. You will need to reread parts or the entire work several times; its meanings will often come clear only gradually.

Understand the Language of Literature

Many writers, especially writers of literary works, use figures of speech to describe people, places, or objects and to communicate ideas. Figurative language is language used in a nonliteral way; it makes sense imaginatively or creatively but not literally. Three common figures of speech—*similes, metaphors,* and *personification*—make comparisons. Writers often use another literary device, *symbols,* to suggest larger themes. In addition, some writers use *irony* to convey the incongruities of life.

For more on figures of speech, see Chapter 9 (pp. 210–11) and Chapter 12 (p. 265).

Similes, Metaphors, and Personification

Similes and metaphors are comparisons between two unlike things that have at least one common trait. A **simile** uses the word *like* or *as* to make a comparison, whereas a **metaphor** states or implies that one thing is another thing. If you say, "My father's mustache is a house painter's brush," your metaphor compares two dissimilar things—a mustache and a paintbrush—that share a common trait: straight bristles. If you say, "Martha's hair looks like she just walked through a wind tunnel," your simile creates a more vivid image of Martha's hair than if you simply stated, "Martha's hair is messy." Here are some additional examples from literary works.

Simile

My soul has grown deep like the rivers.

Langston Hughes, "The Negro Speaks of Rivers"

Metaphor

Time is but the stream I go a-fishing in.

Henry David Thoreau, *Walden*

When writers use **personification**, they attribute human characteristics to objects or ideas. A well-known example of personification is found in an Emily Dickinson poem in which the poet likens death and immortality to passengers in a carriage: "Because I could not stop for Death—/ He kindly stopped for me—/ The carriage held but just Ourselves—/ and Immortality." Like similes and metaphors, personification often creates a strong visual image.

Symbols

A **symbol** suggests more than its literal meaning. The sun breaking through the clouds, for instance, might suggest hope; the color white often suggests innocence and purity. Because the writer does not directly state the abstract idea that a symbol represents, a symbol may suggest more than one meaning. A white handkerchief, for example, might symbolize retreat in one context but good manners in another. Some literary critics believe the white whale in Herman Melville's novel *Moby-Dick* symbolizes evil, whereas others see the whale as representing the forces of nature.

To recognize symbols in a literary work, look for objects that are given a particular or unusual emphasis. The object may be mentioned often, may be suggested in the title, or may appear at the beginning or end of the work. Also be on the lookout for familiar symbols, such as flowers, doves, and colors.

Irony

Irony is literary language or a literary style in which actions, events, or words are contrary to what readers expect. For example, a prizefighter cowering at the sight of a spider is ironic because you expect prizefighters to be brave, a fire station burning down is ironic because you expect that a firehouse would be protected against fires, and a student saying that she is glad she failed an important exam is ironic because you expect the student to be upset that she failed the exam.

EXERCISE 24.1 ▶ **FIGURES OF SPEECH IN EVERYDAY LANGUAGE**

Working with another student, make a list of common metaphors and similes; examples of personification; and symbols you have heard or seen in everyday life, in films or television programs, or in works of literature.

Analyze Short Stories

A **short story** is a brief fictional narrative. Short stories are shorter than novels, and their scope is much more limited. For example, a short story may focus on one event in a person's life, whereas a novel may chronicle the events in the lives of an entire family. Like a novel, a short story makes a point about some aspect of the human experience.

When analyzing short stories, pay particular attention to five key elements.

1. Setting
2. Characters
3. Point of View
4. Plot
5. Theme

A worksheet on pages 656–57 will help you analyze short stories in terms of these five elements.

Read "The Story of an Hour" before continuing with this section of the chapter. The sections that follow will explain these five key elements and how each of them works in this short story.

SHORT STORY ‹ READING

The Story of an Hour

Kate Chopin

Kate Chopin (1851–1904), a nineteenth-century American writer, is best known for her novel *The Awakening* (1899), which outraged early literary critics with its portrayal of a woman in search of sexual and professional independence. As you read the following short story, originally published in *Vogue* magazine in 1894, look for, highlight, and annotate the five primary elements of short stories discussed in this chapter.

Knowing that Mrs. Mallard was afflicted with a heart trouble, great care was taken to break to her as gently as possible the news of her husband's death. 1

It was her sister Josephine who told her, in broken sentences, veiled hints that revealed in half concealing. Her husband's friend Richards was there, too, near her. It was he who had been in the newspaper office when intelligence of the railroad disaster was received, with Brently Mallard's name leading the list of "killed." He had only taken the time to assure himself of its truth by a second telegram, and had hastened to forestall any less careful, less tender friend in bearing the sad message. 2

She did not hear the story as many women have heard the same, with a paralyzed inability to accept its significance. She wept at once, with sudden, wild abandonment, in her sister's arms. When the storm of grief had spent itself she went away to her room alone. She would have no one follow her. 3

There stood, facing the open window, a comfortable, roomy armchair. Into this she sank, pressed down by a physical exhaustion that haunted her body and seemed to reach into her soul. 4

She could see in the open square before her house the tops of trees that were all aquiver with the new spring life. The delicious breath of rain was in the air. In the street below a peddler was crying his wares. The notes of a distant song which someone was singing reached her faintly, and countless sparrows were twittering in the eaves. 5

There were patches of blue sky showing here and there through the clouds that had met and piled one above the other in the west facing her window. 6

She sat with her head thrown back upon the cushion of the chair, quite motionless, except when a sob came up into her throat and shook her, as a child who has cried itself to sleep continues to sob in its dreams. 7

She was young, with a fair, calm face, whose lines bespoke repression and   8
even a certain strength. But now there was a dull stare in her eyes, whose gaze was
fixed away off yonder on one of those patches of blue sky. It was not a glance of
reflection, but rather indicated a suspension of intelligent thought.

There was something coming to her and she was waiting for it, fearfully. What   9
was it? She did not know, it was too subtle and elusive to name. But she felt it, creep-
ing out of the sky, reaching toward her through the sounds, the scents, the color that
filled the air.

Now her bosom rose and fell tumultuously. She was beginning to recognize   10
this thing that was approaching to possess her, and she was striving to beat it back
with her will—as powerless as her two white slender hands would have been.

When she abandoned herself a little whispered word escaped her slightly   11
parted lips. She said it over and over under her breath: "Free, free, free!" The vacant
stare and the look of terror that had followed it went from her eyes. They stayed
keen and bright. Her pulses beat fast, and the coursing blood warmed and relaxed
every inch of her body.

She did not stop to ask if it were not a monstrous joy that held her. A clear   12
and exalted perception enabled her to dismiss the suggestion as trivial.

She knew that she would weep again when she saw the kind, tender hands   13
folded in death; the face that had never looked save with love upon her, fixed and
gray and dead. But she saw beyond that bitter moment a long procession of years to
come that would belong to her absolutely. And she opened and spread her arms out
to them in welcome.

There would be no one to live for during those coming years; she would live   14
for herself. There would be no powerful will bending her in that blind persistence
with which men and women believe they have a right to impose a private will
upon a fellow creature. A kind intention or a cruel intention made the act seem no
less a crime as she looked upon it in that brief moment of illumination.

And yet she had loved him—sometimes. Often she had not. What did it mat-   15
ter! What could love, the unsolved mystery, count for in face of this possession of
self-assertion which she suddenly recognized as the strongest impulse of her being.

"Free! Body and soul free!" she kept whispering.   16

Josephine was kneeling before the closed door with her lips to the keyhole,   17
imploring for admission. "Louise, open the door! I beg; open the door—you will
make yourself ill. What are you doing, Louise? For heaven's sake open the door."

"Go away. I am not making myself ill." No; she was drinking in a very elixir of   18
life through that open window.

Her fancy was running riot along those days ahead of her. Spring days, and   19
summer days, and all sorts of days that would be her own. She breathed a quick
prayer that life might be long. It was only yesterday she had thought with a shudder
that life might be long.

She arose at length and opened the door to her sister's importunities. There   20
was a feverish triumph in her eyes, and she carried herself unwittingly like a
goddess of Victory. She clasped her sister's waist, and together they descended the
stairs. Richards stood waiting for them at the bottom.

Some one was opening the front door with a latchkey. It was Brently Mallard who 21 entered, a little travel-stained, composedly carrying his gripsack and umbrella. He had been far from the scene of accident, and did not even know there had been one. He stood amazed at Josephine's piercing cry; at Richards' quick motion to screen him from the view of his wife.

But Richards was too late. 22

When the doctors came they said she had died of heart disease—of joy 23 that kills.

Setting

The **setting** of a short story is the time, place, and circumstance in which the story occurs. The setting provides the framework and atmosphere in which the plot develops and characters interact. For example, Charles Dickens's "A Christmas Carol" is set in nineteenth-century London in December. When analyzing setting, consider other events that might have occurred in that place and time and how those events might affect the story.

The setting of "The Story of an Hour" is the Mallards' home, and the events take place during the course of one hour. The place and time are unclear, but the events seem to be taking place in the past, before women commonly worked outside the home or could divorce easily.

Characters

The **characters** are the actors in the story. They reveal themselves through dialogue, actions, appearance, thoughts, and feelings. Drawing a character map (Figure 24.1) can help you understand the relationships among characters. On a blank piece of paper, write the main character's name inside a circle. Then add other characters'

FIGURE 24.1 Sample Character Map for "The Story of an Hour"

names, connecting them with lines to the main character. On the connecting lines, briefly describe the relationships between characters and the events or other factors (such as emotions) that affect their relationship.

The **narrator**, the person who tells the story, may also comment on or reveal information about the characters. The narrator is not necessarily the author of the story. The narrator can be one of the characters in the story or an onlooker who observes but does not participate in the action. Think critically about what the narrator reveals about the personalities, needs, and motives of the characters and whether the narrator's opinions may be colored by his or her perceptions and biases.

"The Story of an Hour" is centered on one principal character, Louise Mallard; Brently Mallard, a secondary character, is her husband, whose reported death and reappearance are the focus of Mrs. Mallard's thoughts, feelings, and actions. The narrator describes but does not participate in the action.

Point of View

The **point of view** is the perspective from which the story is told. There are two common points of view: first person and third person.

- In the **first-person** (*I, we*) point of view, the narrator tells the story as he or she sees or experiences it ("I saw the crowd gather at the cemetery"). A first-person narrator may be one of the characters or someone observing but not participating in the story.
- In the **third-person** (*he, she, they*) point of view, the narrator tells the story as if someone else is experiencing it ("*Laura* saw the crowd gather at the cemetery"). Third-person narrators fall into three categories.
  1. The narrator reports only the actions that can be observed from the outside but does not know or report the characters' thoughts.
  2. The narrator enters the minds of one or more (but not all) characters and writes about their thoughts and motives.
  3. The *omniscient*, or all-knowing, third-person narrator is aware of and reports on the thoughts and actions of all characters in the story.

To identify the point of view, consider who is narrating the story and what the narrator knows about the characters' actions, thoughts, and motives. "The Story of an Hour" is told by an omniscient narrator who is not directly involved in the story. The narrator is knowledgeable about Mrs. Mallard's actions and feelings, and seems to report them sympathetically. Rather than present her as an uncaring or even cruel woman actively planning her life after her husband's death, the narrator establishes her as helpless and acted upon. Mrs. Mallard perceives that something "was approaching to possess her," powerless to "beat it back with her will" (para. 10).

Plot

The **plot** is the basic story line—that is, the sequence of events and actions through which the story's meaning is expressed. (See Figure 24.2.) The plot often centers on a

FIGURE 24.2 The Plot Structure of a Story

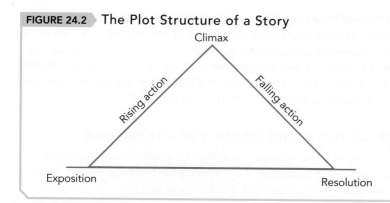

conflict—a problem or clash between opposing forces—and the resolution of the conflict. Once the scene is set and the characters are introduced (the **exposition**), a problem or conflict arises. Suspense and tension build as the conflict unfolds (**rising action**) and the characters wrestle with the problem. The events come to a **climax**, or turning point. Finally, the conflict is resolved and the story concludes (**falling action** and **resolution**). For stories with complicated plots that flash backward and forward in time, creating a time line, a chronological listing of events, may be helpful.

The plot of "The Story of an Hour" is straightforward: Mrs. Mallard is told that her husband was killed in a railroad accident and then discovers that he is still alive. The important part of the story occurs in Mrs. Mallard's mind and bodily responses, as she grasps the meaning of her husband's death and looks ahead to life without him.

Theme

The **theme** of a story is its central or dominant idea—the main point the author makes about the human experience. (Recall that themes are large or universal topics that are important to nearly everyone.) Readers do not always agree about a story's theme. Therefore, in analyzing a short story, you must give evidence to support your interpretation of the theme. The following suggestions will help you uncover clues.

1. **Study the title.** What meanings does it suggest?
2. **Analyze the main characters.** Do the characters change? If so, how, and in response to what?
3. **Look for broad statements about the conflict.** What do the characters and narrator say about the conflict or their lives?
4. **Look for symbols, figures of speech, and meaningful names** (Young *Goodman* Brown, for example).

Once you uncover a theme, try expressing it in a sentence rather than as a single word or brief phrase. For example, saying that a story's theme is "dishonesty" or "parent-child relationships" does not reveal the story's full meaning. When expressed as a sentence, however, a story's theme becomes clear: "Dishonesty sometimes *pays*" or "Parent-child relationships are often struggles for power and control."

One possible theme of "The Story of an Hour" is that independence is key to human happiness: When Mrs. Mallard learns that she is free of her husband, she becomes elated and looks forward to the years of freedom ahead of her. She dies when she realizes that her newfound freedom was illusory; her husband is alive. Another possible theme is that things are not always as they seem: Mrs. Mallard foresees an independent life ahead of her but is forced to realize that she is not free after all.

EXERCISE 24.2 ▶ **IDENTIFYING THE ELEMENTS OF A TV PROGRAM**

Working in groups of two or three, choose a television situation comedy and watch one episode, either together or separately. After viewing the program, identify each of the following elements: setting, characters, point of view, and plot. Then consider whether you think the episode has a theme.

Use the worksheet below to guide your analysis of short stories.

Worksheet for Analyzing Short Stories

Author:

Title:

Year of Publication:

Publisher:

Medium:

Setting: Time

1. In what time period (century or decade) does the story take place?
2. What major events (wars, revolutions, famines, political or cultural movements) occurred during that time, and what bearing might they have on the story?

Setting: Place

1. In what geographic area does the story take place? (Try to identify the country and the city or town, as well as whether the area is an urban or rural one.)
2. Where does the action occur? (For example, does it occur on a battlefield, in a living room, or on a city street?)
3. Why is the place important? (Why couldn't the story occur elsewhere?)

Characters

1. Who are the main characters in the story?
2. What are the distinguishing qualities and characteristics of each character?
3. Why do you like or dislike each character?
4. How and why do characters change (or not change) as the story progresses?

Point of View

1. Is the narrator a character in the story or strictly an observer?
2. Is the narrator knowledgeable about the motives, feelings, and behavior of any or all of the characters?
3. Does the narrator affect what happens in the story? If so, how? What role does the narrator play?

Plot

1. What series of events occurs? Summarize the action.
2. What is the conflict? Why does it occur? How does it build to a climax?
3. How is the conflict resolved?
4. Is the *resolution,* or outcome, satisfying? Why or why not?

Theme

1. What is the theme? What broad statement about life or the human experience does the story suggest?
2. What evidence from the story supports your interpretation of the theme?

Love in L.A.

Dagoberto Gilb

Dagoberto Gilb (b. 1950) was born in Los Angeles to a Mexican mother and an American father. After high school, Gilb worked full time while attending community college. Later, he attended the University of California, Santa Barbara, where he earned a BA and MA. He worked in construction until 1992. His first book of stories, *The Magic of Blood* (from which "Love in L.A." is taken), was published in 1993. Gilb has won several literary awards, including the prestigious PEN/Faulkner Award, for his fiction, which focuses on the Latino experience in America. He is currently the director of CentroVictoria, a center for Mexican American literature and culture in Houston.

Jake slouched in a clot of near-motionless traffic, in the peculiar gray of concrete, smog, and early morning beneath the overpass of the Hollywood Freeway on Alvarado Street. He didn't really mind because he knew how much worse it could be trying to make a left onto the onramp. He certainly didn't do that every day of his life, and he'd assure anyone who'd ask that he never would either. A steady occupation had its advantages and he couldn't deny thinking about that too. He needed an FM radio in something better than this '58 Buick he drove. It would have crushed velvet interior with electric controls for the L.A. summer, a nice warm heater and defroster for the winter drives at the beach, a cruise control for those longer trips, mellow speakers front and rear of course, windows that hum closed, snuffing out that nasty exterior noise of freeways. The fact was that he'd probably

1

have to change his whole style. Exotic colognes, plush, dark nightclubs, maitais and daiquiris, necklaced ladies in satin gowns, misty and sexy like in a tequila ad. Jake could imagine lots of possibilities when he let himself, but none that ended up with him pressed onto a stalled freeway.

Jake was thinking about this freedom of his so much that when he glimpsed its green light he just went ahead and stared bye bye to the steadily employed. When he turned his head the same direction his windshield faced, it was maybe one second too late. He pounced the brake pedal and steered the front wheels away from the tiny brakelights but the smack was unavoidable. Just one second sooner and it would only have been close. One second more and he'd be crawling up the Toyota's trunk. As it was, it seemed like only a harmless smack, much less solid than the one against his back bumper. 2

Jake considered driving past the Toyota but was afraid the traffic ahead would make it too difficult. As he pulled up against the curb a few carlengths ahead, it occurred to him that the traffic might have helped him get away, too. He slammed the car door twice to make sure it was closed fully and to give himself another second more, then toured front and rear of his Buick for damage on or near the bumpers. Not an impressionable scratch even in the chrome. He perked up. Though the car's beauty was secondary to its ability to start and move, the body and paint were clean except for a few minor dings. This stood out as one of his few clearcut accomplishments over the years. 3

Before he spoke to the driver of the Toyota, whose looks he could see might present him with an added complication, he signaled to the driver of the car that hit him, still in his car and stopped behind the Toyota, and waved his hands and shook his head to let the man know there was no problem as far as he was concerned. The driver waved back and started his engine. 4

"It didn't even scratch my paint," Jake told her in that way of his. "So how you doin'? Any damage to the car? I'm kinda hoping so, just so it takes a little more time and we can talk some. Or else you can give me your phone number now and I won't have to lay my regular b.s. on you to get it later." 5

He took her smile as a good sign and relaxed. He inhaled her scent like it was clean air and straightened out his less-than-new but not unhip clothes. 6

"You've got Florida plates. You look like you must be Cuban." 7

"My parents are from Venezuela." 8

"My name's Jake." He held out his hand. 9

"Mariana." 10

They shook hands like she'd never done it before in her life. 11

"I really am sorry about hitting you like that." He sounded genuine. He fondled the wide dimple near the cracked taillight. "It's amazing how easy it is to put a dent in these new cars. They're so soft they might replace waterbeds soon." Jake was confused about how to proceed with this. So much seemed so unlikely, but there was always possibility. "So maybe we should go out to breakfast somewhere and talk it over." 12

"I don't eat breakfast." 13

"Some coffee then."   14

"Thanks, but I really can't."   15

"You're not married, are you? Not that that would matter that much to me.   16
I'm an openminded kinda guy."

She was smiling. "I have to get to work."   17

"That sounds boring."   18

"I better get your driver's license," she said.   19

Jake nodded, disappointed. "One little problem," he said. "I didn't bring it. I just   20
forgot it this morning. I'm a musician," he exaggerated greatly, "and, well, I dunno, I
left my wallet in the pants I was wearing last night. If you have some paper and a
pen I'll give you my address and all that."

He followed her to the glove compartment side of her car.   21

"What if we don't report it to the insurance companies? I'll just get it fixed   22
for you."

"I don't think my dad would let me do that."   23

"Your dad? It's not your car?"   24

"He bought it for me. And I live at home."   25

"Right." She was slipping away from him. He went back around to the back of   26
her new Toyota and looked over the damage again. There was the trunk lid, the
bumper, a rear panel, a taillight.

"You do have insurance?" she asked, suspicious, as she came around the back   27
of the car.

"Oh yeah," he lied.   28

"I guess you better write the name of that down too."   29

He made up a last name and address and wrote down the name of an insur-   30
ance company an old girlfriend once belonged to. He considered giving a real
phone number but went against that idea and made one up.

"I act too," he lied to enhance the effect more. "Been in a couple of movies."   31

She smiled like a fan.   32

"So how about your phone number?" He was rebounding maturely.   33

She gave it to him.   34

"Mariana, you are beautiful," he said in his most sincere voice.   35

"Call me," she said timidly.   36

Jake beamed. "We'll see you, Mariana," he said holding out his hand. Her hand   37
felt so warm and soft he felt like he'd been kissed.

Back in his car he took a moment or two to feel both proud and sad about his   38
performance. Then he watched the rear view mirror as Mariana pulled up behind
him. She was writing down the license plate numbers on his Buick, ones that he'd
taken off a junk because the ones that belonged to his had expired so long ago. He
turned the ignition key and revved the big engine and clicked into drive. His sense
of freedom swelled as he drove into the now moving street traffic, though he
couldn't stop the thought about that FM stereo radio and crushed velvet interior
and the new car smell that would even make it better.

Analyze Poetry

Poetry is written in lines and stanzas instead of in sentences and paragraphs. Because of the genre's unique format, poets often express ideas in compact and concise language, and reading and analyzing a short poem may take as much time and effort as analyzing an essay or a short story. To grasp the meaning of a poem, pay attention to the sound and meaning of individual words and consider how the words work together to convey meaning. The worksheet on pages 661–62 can serve as a guide as you analyze poetry.

Use the following general guidelines to read and analyze poetry effectively.

1. **Read the poem through once, using the poem's punctuation as a guide.** Try to get a general sense of what the poem is about. If you come across an unfamiliar word or a confusing reference, keep reading. Although poetry is written in lines, each line may not make sense by itself. Meaning often flows from line to line, and a single sentence can be composed of several lines. Use the poem's punctuation to guide you. If there is no punctuation at the end of a line, read the line with a slight pause at the end and with an emphasis on the last word. Think about how the poet breaks lines to achieve a certain effect.

LEARNING STYLE OPTIONS

2. **Read the poem several more times, annotating as you read.** The meaning of the poem will become clearer with each successive reading. At first you may understand some parts but not others. If you are a spatial or an abstract learner, try to visualize, or see, what the poem is about. If you are a pragmatic or rational learner, you will probably want to work through the poem line by line, from beginning to end. With poetry, however, this approach does not always work. Instead, you may need to use later stanzas to help you understand earlier ones. If you find certain sections of the poem difficult or confusing, read these sections aloud several times. You might try copying them, word for word. Look up the meanings of any unfamiliar words in a dictionary.

   As you read, highlight striking elements (figures of speech, symbols, revealing character descriptions, striking dialogue, and the like) and record your reactions. (A sample annotated passage appears in Figure 24.3, p. 663.) Pay particular attention to the following.

   • **The speaker and tone.** Try to understand the speaker's viewpoint or feelings to figure out who he or she is. Also consider the speaker's tone: Is it serious, challenging, sad, frustrated, joyful? To determine the tone, read the poem aloud. Your emphasis on certain words or the rise and fall of your voice may provide clues to the tone; you may "hear" the poet's anger, despondency, or elation.
   • **To whom the poem is addressed.** Is it written to a person, the reader, an object? Consider the possibility that the poet may be writing to work out a personal problem or express strong emotions.
   • **Allusions.** Look up unfamiliar **allusions**, or references, to people, objects, or events outside the poem. If you see Oedipus mentioned in a poem, for example, you may need to use a dictionary or encyclopedia to learn that he was a figure in Greek mythology who unwittingly killed his father and married his mother. Your knowledge of Oedipus would then help you interpret the poem.

- **The language of the poem.** Consider the *connotations*, or shades of meaning, of words in the poem. Study the poem's use of descriptive language, similes, metaphors, personification, and symbols.
- **The poem's theme.** What does the title of the poem mean? What can it tell you about the poem's theme? Does the poem's overall meaning involve a feeling, a person, a memory, or an argument? Paraphrase the poem; express it in your own words and connect it to your own experience. Then link your ideas together to discover the poem's overall meaning. Ask yourself: What is the poet trying to tell me? What is the theme?

For more on connotations, see Chapters 3 and 9, pp. 61–62, 209; for more on descriptive language, see Chapter 12, pp. 261–65.

3. **Write a response.** Copying passages from the poem and responding to those passages in writing can help you explore your reaction to the poem and grasp its meaning. Choose quotations from the poem that convey a main point or opinion, reveal a character's motives, or say something important about the plot or theme. Describe your reaction to each quotation, interpreting, disagreeing with, or questioning it. Comment on the language of the quotation and relate it to other quotations or elements in the work. Here is a sample response to Frost's "Two Look at Two."

"With thoughts of the path back, how rough it was" (line 5)	The couple's past has been difficult; returning to daily life may be difficult, too. Nature is rough and challenging.
. . . "This is all," they sighed, "Good-night to woods.". . . (lines 13–14)	The couple will soon come to the end— of their relationship or their lives.

Worksheet for Analyzing Poetry

Poet:

Poem:

Year of Publication:

Source:

Medium:

Speaker, Tone, and Addressee

1. Who is the speaker? What do you know about him or her? What tone does the speaker use? To whom is he or she speaking?
2. What emotional atmosphere or mood does the poet create? Do you sense, for example, a mood of foreboding, excitement, or contentment?
3. Does the poem express emotion? If so, for what purpose?
4. How does the poem make you feel—shocked, saddened, angered, annoyed, happy? Write a sentence or two describing your reaction.

Allusions

5. Does the poem make references to people, events, or other works of art or literature?
6. How do these allusions affect the tone or meaning of the poem?

Language

7. How does the poet use language to create an effect? Does the poet use similes, metaphors, personification, or symbols?
8. Does the poem rhyme? If so, does the rhyme affect the meaning? (For example, does the poet use rhyme to emphasize key words or phrases?)

Theme

9. What is the meaning of the poem's title?
10. What is the theme of the poem?

READING ▶ POEM

Two Look at Two

Robert Frost

Robert Frost (1874–1963) is a major American poet whose work often focuses on familiar objects, natural scenes, and the character of New England. In his early life Frost was a farmer and teacher; later he became a poet in residence at Amherst College and taught at Dartmouth, Yale, and Harvard. Frost was awarded Pulitzer Prizes for four collections of poems: *New Hampshire* (1923), from which "Two Look at Two" is taken; *Collected Poems* (1930); *A Further Range* (1936); and *A Witness Tree* (1942). As you read the selection, use the questions in the preceding worksheet to think critically about the poem.

Love and forgetting might have carried them
A little further up the mountain side
With night so near, but not much further up.
They must have halted soon in any case
With thoughts of the path back, how rough it was   5
With rock and washout, and unsafe in darkness;
When they were halted by a tumbled wall
With barbed-wire binding. They stood facing this,
Spending what onward impulse they still had
In one last look the way they must not go,   10
On up the failing path, where, if a stone
Or earthslide moved at night, it moved itself;
No footstep moved it. "This is all," they sighed,
"Good-night to woods." But not so; there was more.
A doe from round a spruce stood looking at them   15
Across the wall, as near the wall as they.
She saw them in their field, they her in hers.
The difficulty of seeing what stood still,
Like some up-ended boulder split in two,
Was in her clouded eyes: they saw no fear there.   20
She seemed to think that two thus they were safe.

Then, as if they were something that, though strange,
She could not trouble her mind with too long,
She sighed and passed unscared along the wall.
"*This*, then, is all. What more is there to ask?"   25
But no, not yet. A snort to bid them wait.
A buck from round the spruce stood looking at them
Across the wall, as near the wall as they.
This was an antlered buck of lusty nostril,
Not the same doe come back into her place.   30
He viewed them quizzically with jerks of head,
As if to ask, "Why don't you make some motion?
Or give some sign of life? Because you can't.
I doubt if you're as living as you look."
Thus till he had them almost feeling dared   35
To stretch a proffering hand—and a spell-breaking.
Then he too passed unscared along the wall.
Two had seen two, whichever side you spoke from.
"This *must* be all." It was all. Still they stood,
A great wave from it going over them,   40
As if the earth in one unlooked-for favor
Had made them certain earth returned their love.

The poem takes place on a mountainside path, near dusk. A couple walking along
the path finds a tumbled wall. Looking beyond the wall, the couple encounters first a
doe and then a buck. The doe and buck stare at the human couple and vice versa;
hence the title "Two Look at Two." Neither the animals nor the humans are frightened;

FIGURE 24.3   A Sample Annotated Passage from "Two Look at Two"

Love and forgetting might have carried them

A little further up the mountain side

With night so near, but not much further up. ← — limitations of humans

They must have halted soon in any case

With thoughts of the path back, how rough it was ← — road of life? difficulty of life

With rock and washout, and unsafe in darkness;

When they were halted by a tumbled wall ← — separates man and nature— Why is it tumbled?

With barbed-wire binding. They stood facing this, ← — sharp, penetrating

Spending what onward impulse they still had

In one last look the way they must not go, ← — prohibited from crossing both couples observe each other and continue with their lives. The action is described by a third-person narrator who can read the thoughts of the humans. The speaker creates an objective tone by reporting events as they occur.

In "Two Look at Two," Frost considers the relationship between humans and nature. The wall is symbolic of the separation between them. Beyond the wall the couple looks at "the way they must not go" (line 10). Although humans and nature are separate, they are also equal and in balance. These qualities are suggested by the title as well as by the actions of both couples as they observe each other in a nonthreatening way. The third-person point of view contributes to this balance in that the poem's narrator is an outside observer rather than a participant. One possible theme of the poem, therefore, is the balance and equality between humans and nature.

As you read the following poem, "How I Discovered Poetry," by Marilyn Nelson, use the guidelines for reading a poem (pp. 660–61) and the worksheet (pp. 661–62) to help you analyze its elements and discover its meaning

READING **POEM**

How I Discovered Poetry

Marilyn Nelson

Marilyn Nelson (b. 1946) is an American poet and translator and the author of books for young adults. She is the author of numerous collections of poetry, including *The Homeplace* (1990); *The Fields of Praise: New and Selected Poems* (1997), in which this poem appeared; and *The Cachoiera Tales and Other Poems* (2005), which won the L. E. Phillabaum Award and was a finalist for the Los Angeles Book Award for poetry. Her most recent work is *How I Discovered Poetry* (2014), a memoir in verse form. In 2012 Nelson was awarded the Frost Medal by the Poetry Society of America, and in 2013 she was elected to the board of chancellors of the Academy of American Poets. Respond to the poem as you read it by making notes in the margin.

It was like soul-kissing, the way the words
filled my mouth as Mrs. Purdy read from her desk.
All the other kids zoned an hour ahead to 3:15,
but Mrs. Purdy and I wandered lonely as clouds borne
by a breeze off Mount Parnassus. She must have seen   5
the darkest eyes in the room brim: The next day
she gave me a poem she'd chosen especially for me
to read to the all except for me white class.
She smiled when she told me to read it, smiled harder,
said oh yes I could. She smiled harder and harder   10
until I stood and opened my mouth to banjo playing
darkies, pickaninnies, disses and dats. When I finished
my classmates stared at the floor. We walked silent
to the buses, awed by the power of words.

PREWRITING > DRAFTING > REVISING > EDITING & PROOFREADING

A Guided Writing Assignment*

LITERARY ANALYSIS

A **literary analysis** essay, sometimes called *literary criticism* or a *critique*, analyzes and interprets one or more aspects of a literary work. As with other types of essays, writing a literary analysis involves generating ideas through prewriting, developing a thesis, collecting supporting evidence, organizing and drafting, analyzing and revising, and editing and proofreading.

Keep in mind that a literary analysis does not merely summarize the work, but rather analyzes and interprets it. In a literary analysis, you take a position on some aspect of the work and support your position with evidence. In other words, you assume the role of a literary critic, in the same way that a film critic argues for his or her judgment of a film rather than simply reporting its plot.

A literary analysis has the following characteristics.

- It makes a point about one or more elements of a literary work.
- It includes and accurately documents evidence from the work. (It may also include evidence from outside sources.)
- It assumes that the audience is somewhat familiar with the work but not as familiar as the writer of the analysis.
- It has a serious tone and is written in the present tense.

Your Essay Assignment

Write a literary analysis of a poem or short story, focusing on one element of the work. You may analyze a work of your own choosing, a work your instructor assigns, or one of the works reprinted in this chapter.

- Gwendolyn Brooks, "The Bean Eaters" (p. 647)
- Kate Chopin, "The Story of an Hour" (pp. 651–53)
- Dagoberto Gilb, "Love in L.A." (pp. 657–59)
- Robert Frost, "Two Look at Two" (pp. 662–63)
- Marilyn Nelson, "How I Discovered Poetry" (p. 664)

* The writing process is recursive; that is, you may find yourself revising as you draft or prewriting as you revise. This is especially true when writing on a computer. Your writing process may also differ from project to project and from that of your classmates.

1 Read and analyze your writing assignment carefully.

Ask yourself these questions about your **writing situation**.

- What is my **purpose** for writing? To explain one element of the work? To argue for my interpretation?
- What are my **instructor's expectations**? What will he or she be looking for?
- Given my and my instructor's goals for the assignment, how much should I assume that **my readers already know** about the author, genre, or literary work?
- Am I allowed to do **research** to find out what others have said about the work or to find background information about the author?
- How will I use **additional patterns of development** within my literary analysis? For example, you will likely use illustration to cite examples to support your analysis. In addition, you might compare or contrast two main characters or analyze a plot by discussing causes and effects.

2 Explore the work of literature and generate ideas.

Try one or more of the following suggestions to devise **a focus** and generate **ideas**.

- **Highlight** and **annotate** the work. Focus on striking details, such as figures of speech, symbolic images, actions and reactions of characters, repetition, and so on. (All, especially verbal and independent learners, can benefit from highlighting and annotating.)
- **Freewrite.** Explore your reaction to the work or use a word or image from the work as a jumping off point. (Creative, emotional, and verbal learners will benefit especially from freewriting.)
- **Discuss the literary work with classmates.** Move from general meaning to a more specific paragraph-by-paragraph or line-by-line examination. Then discuss your interpretation of the work's theme. (Social and emotional learners will especially benefit from discussing the work with classmates.)
- **Write a summary.** Doing so may lead you to raise and answer questions about the work. (Rational and pragmatic learners will benefit especially from summarizing.)
- **Draw a time line or a character map.** For stories with plots that flash back or forward in time, a time line can help you envision the sequence of events. A character map can help you understand characters' relationships. (Rational, pragmatic, and spatial learners will benefit especially from creating a time line or character map.)

3 Conduct background research.

If your instructor allows it, you may develop an interesting focus by putting the work into **context**.

- **Read about the author's background.** Look for connections between the work and the author's life. For example, writing an interpretation of Charles Dickens's "A Christmas Carol" might be easier if you understand the author's own impoverished childhood.
- **Explore the historical context.** Research the historical, social, economic, and political context of the work. Understanding conditions of the poor in nineteenth-century England might help you understand Dickens's portrayal of the Cratchit family.
- **Discover parallel works or situations.** Compare the work to a film or television show or to your own experience to develop insight. For example, comparing your own experience of school English with that of the narrator in "How I Discovered Poetry" may enhance your understanding.
- **Apply theories you have learned about in other classes.** Theories from your psychology class may help you understand Mrs. Mallard's reaction to the news of her husband's death in "The Story of an Hour."

Evaluate your ideas and choose an approach to your literary analysis.

Here are several **possible approaches** you might choose to take in a literary analysis.

- **Evaluate symbolism.** Discuss how the author's use of images and symbols creates a particular mood and contributes to the overall meaning of the work.
- **Analyze conflicts.** Focus on their causes, effects, or both.
- **Evaluate characterization and interpret relationships.** Discuss how characters are presented; analyze how their true nature is revealed or how they change in response to circumstances.
- **Explore themes.** Discover an important point or theme the work conveys, and back up your ideas with examples from the work.

5 **Draft your thesis statement.**

Your **thesis** should:

- include the **author's name** and the **work's title**
- indicate the **element** of the work you will analyze (its theme, characters, or use of symbols, for example)
- state the **main point** you will make about that element

Notice how the writers include all three elements in these two example thesis statements.

> **Example:** ┌── author ──┐ ┌────── title ──────┐
> Flannery O'Connor's short story "A Good Man Is Hard to Find"
> element (symbol)   main point
> uses color to depict various moods throughout the story.

> **Example:** ┌──author──┐ ┌title┐   main point
> In Susan Glaspell's play *Trifles*, the female characters are treated condescendingly
> ┌──element (symbol)──┐
> by the males, and yet the women's interest in so-called trivial matters leads them to
> interpret the "trivial" pieces of evidence that solve the murder mystery.

Working Together. In groups of two or three students, take turns presenting your thesis statements and main supporting evidence. As group members listen, have them note the element you will analyze and your main point. They should be able to restate your main point in their own words; if they can't, your main point may not be clear. Brainstorm as a group to:

- clarify your thesis
- add the missing element
- identify evidence or insights the writer may have overlooked

 Choose a method of organization.

One of these **methods of organization** may work well in a literary analysis.

- Use **least-to-most** order to highlight one or more important reasons or causes.
- Use **chronological order** to explore events as they occur in the work of literature or the process by which an author makes events or connections clear.
- Use **point-by-point** or **subject-by-subject** order to compare or contrast characters or works of literature.

7 Draft your literary analysis.

Use the following guidelines to keep your essay on track.

- The **introduction** should name the **author** and **title,** present your **thesis,** and suggest why your analysis is **useful** or **important.** Try to engage **readers' interest** by including a meaningful **quotation** or a comment on the **universality** of a **character** or **theme,** for example.

- Each **body paragraph** should include a **topic sentence** that states your main point, a point that supports your thesis, and enough **evidence** to support your main point. Include **quotations** or **paraphrases** from the work of literature as support, identified by **page numbers** (for a short story) or **line numbers** (for a poem). Include a **works-cited entry** at the end of your paper indicating the edition of the work you used. Use plot summary only where necessary to make the analysis clear. Write in the **"literary present" tense** (see step 9 below), except when discussing events that occur before the story or poem begins.

- The **conclusion** should **reaffirm your thesis** and give the essay a sense of **closure.** You may want to tie your conclusion to your introduction or offer a final word on your main point.

8 Evaluate your draft, and revise as necessary.

Use **Figure 24.4, "Flowchart for Revising a Literary Analysis Essay,"** to help you discover the strengths and weaknesses of your draft. You might also ask a classmate to review your draft using the questions in the flowchart.

FIGURE 24.4 Flowchart for Revising a Literary Analysis Essay

QUESTIONS

REVISION STRATEGIES

1. Highlight your thesis statement. Does it identify the work, the one aspect of it you are analyzing, and the main point of your analysis?

 NO ▶

- Revise your thesis so that all of these items are included.
- Ask a classmate to read your thesis and convey his or her understanding of your main point.

 YES ▼

2. Place a ✔ by the evidence from the literary work that supports your thesis. Is all of your evidence relevant to your thesis? Is there enough evidence?

 NO ▶

- Delete examples that do not support your thesis or that might be confusing to readers.
- Add relevant quotations, paraphrases, and summaries.
- Explain how the examples support your point.

 YES ▼

3. [Bracket] each quotation from the work. Do you cite each quotation so readers can locate it in the work of literature?

 NO ▶

- Include paragraph, page, or line numbers for each quotation.
- Include a works-cited entry for the edition of the work you used.

 YES ▼

4. Review your assignment. Does your essay achieve your and your instructor's goals?

 NO ▶

- Add information about the author, plot, characters, or other elements as needed.
- Make sure you go beyond summary to interpret and analyze the work of literature.

 YES ▼

5. Circle each verb. Have you used the present tense appropriately?

 NO ▶

- Use the present tense to discuss the writing of the story or events within it.
- Use the past tense to discuss events that occurred before the action of the story begins.

 YES ▼

6. Place an ✗ next to words that reveal your feelings or judgments about the work. Does your tone suggest a serious, objective view of the work?

 NO ▶

- Tone down or eliminate any overly critical or enthusiastic statements.
- Avoid slang or overly casual language.

 YES ▼

7. Review each body paragraph. Does each have a clear topic sentence? Does each focus on one main point or idea?

 NO ▶

- Be sure each paragraph has a clear topic sentence that supports your thesis statement.
- Combine closely related paragraphs or split paragraphs that cover two or more main points or ideas.

 YES ▼

(continued on next page) ▶

REVISING

(Figure 24.4 continued)

QUESTIONS   REVISION STRATEGIES

8. Reread your introduction and conclusion. Does the introduction suggest the importance of your thesis and engage your readers' interest? Does your conclusion lend closure?

- Ask yourself why your audience would be interested in your thesis, and incorporate the answer in your introduction.
- End by referring back to your introduction or showing why the work of literature is relevant or important.
- Use the guidelines in Chapter 7 (pp. 164–67).

9 Edit and proofread your essay.

Refer to Chapter 9 for help with:

- **editing sentences** to avoid wordiness, make your verb choices strong and active, and make your sentences clear, varied, and parallel
- **editing words** for tone and diction, connotation, and concrete and specific language

Pay particular attention to the following:

1. **Use the literary present tense.** Even though the poem or short story was written in the past, as a general rule write about the events in it and the author's writing of it as if they were happening in the present. An exception to this rule occurs when you are referring to a time earlier than that in which the narrator speaks, in which case a switch to the past tense is appropriate.

   Example: Keats in "Ode on a Grecian Urn" ~~referred~~ *refers* to the urn as a "silent form" (line 44).

   Example: In "Two Look at Two," it is not clear why the couple *decided* to walk up the mountainside path.
   The couple made the decision before the action in the poem began.

2. **Punctuate quotations correctly.** Direct quotations from a literary work, whether spoken or written, must be placed in quotation marks. Omitted material should be marked by an ellipsis (. . .). The lines of a poem when they are run together in an essay are separated by a slash (/).

   Example: In "Two Look at Two," Frost concludes that "the earth in one unlooked-for favor / Had made them certain earth returned their love" (lines 41–42).

   Periods and commas appear within quotation marks. Question marks and exclamation points precede or follow quotation marks, depending on the meaning of the sentence. In the example below, the question mark goes inside the closing quotation marks because it is part of Frost's poem (line 32). Notice, too, that double and single quotation marks are required for a quotation within a quotation. (See Chapter 23, pp. 596–99 for more on incorporating quotations into your writing.)

   Example: The buck seems "to ask, 'Why don't you make some motion'?" (line 32).

The Short, Happy Life of Louise Mallard

Irina Dudnik

Irina Dudnik wrote this literary analysis for her first-year writing class. As you read the essay, notice her thesis. How does she use quotations from the story to support her claim? How does she weave those quotations into her essay?

Title: Captures author's main point—that Louise Mallard's happiness only lasted for one hour

"There was something coming to her and she was waiting for it, fearfully. What was it? She did not know, it was too subtle and elusive to name" (652). So writes the narrator about Louise Mallard, the main character in Kate Chopin's short story "The Story of an Hour." Set toward the end of the nineteenth century, the story follows Mrs. Mallard's reaction to the news of her husband's death, which develops from grief to a state of suspended emotion to a sense of utter freedom. Chopin's tale delivers a powerful message about the repression that women like Mrs. Mallard suffered under the cultural institution of marriage built on male dominance. What makes this message so powerful is the fact that Louise Mallard's sense of freedom isn't immediate or simple, but once it develops, there's no going back.

When her sister breaks the news that her husband is dead, Mrs. Mallard bursts into "a storm of grief" (651), weeping in her sister's arms, and then retreats to her room. Ironically, it is here in her room, in an armchair facing an open window, that Mrs. Mallard develops her sense of freedom. It is first revealed in the contrast between the way she sits down, "pressed down by a physical exhaustion that haunted her body and seemed to reach into her soul" (651), and in the freshness she sees through the open window, in which "the tops of trees . . . were all aquiver with the new spring life" (651), the open window symbolizing a means of escape and a pathway to a fresh life. Chopin takes care that the first signals of Mrs. Mallard's repression come through her senses, so that readers can learn with Mrs. Mallard just how deeply she has internalized the effects of marriage.

Like Mrs. Mallard, readers only become aware of the character's newfound sense of freedom gradually. They share her experience as she

1 **Introduction:** Begins with a quotation that suggests main point, identifies page

Identifies setting and shows relevance

Thesis: Thesis focuses on Mrs. Mallard's developing sense of liberation

2 **Organization:** Uses chronological organization, following Mrs. Mallard's developing response

Support: Uses quotations to support claim about Mrs. Mallard's changing feelings

Interpretation: Explains meaning of quotations and symbolism

3 **Paragraph:** Topic sentence makes point of paragraph clear

Evidence: Quotations support point topic sentence makes

stares out the window with eyes that reflect "a suspension of intelligent thought" (652). This "subtle and elusive" feeling doesn't come in words or accusations. It comes through her senses, "the sounds, the scents, the color" (652) showing that her confinement is so penetrating that it has mapped itself onto the way she experiences the world around her.

The fact that readers can't name the feeling Louise Mallard has until she can name it herself effectively conveys how deep her sense of captivity has been. At last, Mrs. Mallard names how she feels— "[f]ree, free free!"—and she (and her readers) begin to see more than just an open window (652). She can envision the freedom that window represents, the "years to come that would belong to her absolutely" (652). And Chopin emphasizes Mrs. Mallard's bodily feeling of freedom just as much as her mental understanding: "Now her bosom rose and fell tumultuously . . . her pulses beat fast, and the coursing blood warmed and relaxed every inch of her body" (652). The fact that it takes a while to name her freedom, and to recognize the sensations in her body as relief and joy, shows that the kind of repression Mrs. Mallard felt in her marriage worked on a deep, psychological level.

4

Interpretation: Explains meaning of quotations, how they support thesis

Transitions: Uses transitional words and phrases to show that she is moving to another reason

But this is not the only reason that this kind of confinement is so difficult to identify. By showing readers how Mrs. Mallard grapples with her husband's death, Chopin shows them not only how much harm has been caused by lack of self-determination but also that the harm can coexist with affection, kindness, and even love. The story makes clear that Mr. Mallard was no monster: His "face . . . had never looked save with love upon her" (652). Here, Chopin challenges the notion that physical or verbal harm are the only kinds that can cause suffering or that oppression has to be inflicted on purpose. Mr. Mallard loved his wife, and she had at times even loved him, but here she is whispering, "Free! Body and soul free!" (652), and readers know that her happiness is not a matter of love (or the lack of it). Her happiness at the end of the story is about life's possibilities and how rich they can feel to a person who can now make decisions for herself: "What could love . . . count for in the face of this possession of self-assertion which she suddenly recognized as the strongest impulse of her being?" (652). By leading readers away from the picture of

5

her husband as a cruel tyrant, Chopin helps them understand that relationships not only need to be free of violence but also need to be built on mutual independence.

When Mrs. Mallard is given even an hour-long understanding of what living for herself feels like, she can't survive a return to dependency: Brently Mallard, whose death was misreported, walks in the front door, and his wife collapses, dead. After watching Mrs. Mallard come to understand just what her husband's absence means, readers can now understand what her husband's presence means. The power of this story is in the way it uncovers the complicated relationship between repression and love and the way this understanding is felt in the body. Chopin's brilliant story sheds light on the underbelly of marital bliss, but more importantly, it implores her readers to recognize and reject repression, in whatever form it takes, before it is too late.

6   **Conclusion:** Shows how dramatic ending relates to thesis, title of essay

Work Cited

Chopin, Kate. "The Story of an Hour." *Successful College Writing*, 7th ed., by Kathleen McWhorter, Bedford/St. Martin's, 2018, pp. 651-53.

Works cited: Cites edition of story used

Analyzing the Writer's Technique

1. **Thesis** Does Dudnik provide sufficient evidence to support her thesis? Choose one example Dudnik offers and evaluate its effectiveness.
2. **Introduction and Conclusion** Evaluate Dudnik's introduction and conclusion. In what ways could they be improved?
3. **Development** Which paragraphs are particularly well developed? Which, if any, need further development?

Responding to the Essay

1. **Discussion** How does Dudnik's interpretation of "The Story of an Hour" compare with yours?
2. **Journal** Dudnik discusses the issue of marriage and repression as it existed in the nineteenth century. Write a journal entry exploring whether and how this issue has changed in the time that has elapsed since then.

25
Essay Examinations and Portfolios

Oogy flunks his cave drawing final—

© www.Cartoonstock.com

In this chapter you will learn to:

- **prepare for and take essay examinations**

- **create a writing portfolio**

WRITING QUICK START   The cartoon on this page humorously comments on the process of taking tests. No doubt you've taken tests throughout your school years, and they are an important part of college classes as well. Assume you are taking a short, timed writing test. You have been asked to write about your experiences with taking tests. You might write about how you prepare for exams or share test-taking tips, for example. You have fifteen minutes to complete the writing test.

In completing the timed writing test in the Writing Quick Start, did you feel pressured by the fifteen-minute limit? How did you decide what to write about? Did you have as much time as you would have liked to organize, plan, develop, and revise your ideas? Probably not.

You may wonder why instructors give essay exams and other kinds of timed writing assignments. In many college courses, essay exams allow instructors to determine how well students have grasped important concepts and whether they can organize and integrate key concepts with other material. In addition, essay exams require students to use different and more advanced thinking skills than they use when taking a more objective type of exam, such as a multiple-choice test. For instance, an essay exam for a history course might require you to pull ideas together and focus on larger issues, perhaps analyzing historical trends or comparing two political figures.

This chapter will help you prepare for the timed essay exams you will encounter in college. Although the chapter focuses on essay exams, you can also apply the skills you learn here to other kinds of writing assignments you need to complete under time pressure. This chapter will also help you prepare a portfolio of your writing.

TIMED WRITING AND PORTFOLIOS **IN COLLEGE AND THE WORKPLACE**

- For the midterm exam in your *philosophy of religion course*, you have one hour to answer the following essay question: "Contrast the beliefs of Islam with those of either Judaism or Christianity."

- For a *business communication class*, you are asked to assemble a portfolio that illustrates your mastery of the six course objectives.

- As a *freelance artist*, you need to prepare a portfolio of your illustration styles to help art directors evaluate your work.

Prepare for and Take Essay Examinations

Doing well on essay examinations involves not only preparing for the exam, but also analyzing and answering the exam's questions clearly and fully.

Prepare for Essay Exams

Because essay exams require you to produce a written response, the best way to prepare for them is by organizing and writing.

Create study sheets to synthesize information. Most essay exams require you to *synthesize*, or pull together, information. To prepare for this task, try to identify the key topics in a course, and then create a **study sheet** for each main topic. Study sheets help you organize, consolidate, and study complex or detailed information.

For more on synthesizing sources, see Chapter 22, pp. 581–83.

To prepare a study sheet, draw on information from your textbook as well as from class notes, handouts, previous exams (look for emphasized topics), and assigned readings. You can organize a study sheet in a variety of ways. For example, you might:

- draw a graphic organizer to create a visual study sheet
- create a time line to connect historical events
- write an outline to organize information
- construct a comparison-and-contrast chart to see relationships among topics
- develop a list of categories and use them to organize information

Whatever method of organization you use for your study sheet, be sure to include key information about each topic: definitions, facts, principles, theories, events, research studies, and the like.

Here is part of one student's study sheet for a speech communication course on the topic *audience analysis*.

Sample Study Sheet

Topic: Audience Analysis

1. Demographic characteristics
   —Age and gender
   —Educational background (type and level of education)
   —Group membership (people who share similar interests or goals)
   —Social and religious activities
   —Hobbies and sports
2. Psychological characteristics
   —Beliefs (about what is true or false, right or wrong)
   —Attitudes (positive or negative)
   —Values (standards for judging worth of thoughts and actions)

EXERCISE 25.1 ▶ **PREPARING A STUDY SHEET**

Use the preceding guidelines to prepare a study sheet on a general topic that you expect will be covered on an upcoming exam in one of your courses.

Predict essay exam questions. Once you prepare study sheets for a particular course, the next step is to predict questions that might be asked on an essay exam. Although essay exam questions usually focus on general topics, themes, or patterns, these questions generally also require you to supply details in your response. For example, an essay question on a psychology exam might ask you to compare and contrast the James-Lange and Cannon-Bard theories of motivation. Your answer would focus on the similarities and differences between these key theories, incorporating relevant details where necessary.

Use the following strategies to help you predict the types of questions you might be asked on an essay exam.

1. **Group topics into categories.** Review your textbook, class notes, and study sheets to devise categories. For example, if you find a chapter on kinship in your anthropology textbook and several entries in your class notes on this topic, a question on kinship is likely to appear on an essay exam for the course.
2. **Study your syllabus and objectives.** These documents contain important clues about what your instructor expects you to learn during the course.
3. **Study previous exams.** Notice which key ideas are emphasized in previous exams. If you had to explain the historical significance of the Boston Tea Party on

your first American history exam, you can predict that future exams will ask you to explain the historical significance of other events.

4. **Listen to your instructor's comments.** When your instructor announces or reviews material for an upcoming essay exam, pay close attention to the key topics he or she reveals or to the areas he or she suggests that you study.

5. **Draft possible essay questions.** Use Table 25.1 (p. 680) to draft possible essay questions using key verbs that hint at how you must answer effectively.

EXERCISE 25.2 ▶ **PREDICTING ESSAY QUESTIONS FOR A COLLEGE COURSE**

For an upcoming essay exam in one of your courses, predict and write at least three possible questions your instructor might ask about the course material.

Draft answers in outline form.   After you predict several possible essay exam questions, the next step is to write a brief, rough outline of the information that answers each question. Be sure each outline responds to the *wording* of the question; that is, it should *explain*, *compare*, *describe*, or do whatever else the question asks (see Table 25.1, p. 680). Writing a rough outline will strengthen your recall of the material. It will also save you time during the actual exam because you will have already spent some time thinking about, organizing, and writing about the material.

Here is a sample essay question and an informal outline written in response to it.

Essay Question

Explain how material passes in and out of cells by crossing plasma membranes.

Informal Outline
Types of Transport

1. Passive—no use of cellular energy; random movement of molecules
   a. Diffusion—molecules move from areas of high to areas of low concentration (example: open bottle of perfume, aroma spreads)
   b. Facilitated diffusion—similar to simple diffusion; differs in that some kinds of molecules are moved more easily than others (helped by carrier proteins in cell membrane)
   c. Osmosis—diffusion of water across membranes from area of lower to area of higher solute concentration
2. Active—requires cellular energy; usually movement against the concentration gradient
   a. Facilitated active transport—carrier molecules move ions across a membrane
   b. Endocytosis—material is surrounded by a plasma membrane and pinched off into a vacuole
   c. Exocytosis—cells expel materials

EXERCISE 25.3   **PREPARING AN INFORMAL OUTLINE**

For one of the questions you predicted in Exercise 25.2, prepare a brief informal outline in response to the question.

Reduce informal outlines to key-word outlines.   To help you recall your outlined answer during the exam, reduce it to a brief key-word outline or list of key topics. Here is a sample key-word outline for the essay question about cells:

Key-Word Outline

Types of Transport

1. Passive
   —Diffusion
   —Facilitated diffusion
   —Osmosis
2. Active
   —Facilitated active transport
   —Endocytosis
   —Exocytosis

EXERCISE 25.4   **PREPARING A KEY-WORD OUTLINE**

Reduce the outline answer you wrote in Exercise 25.3 to a key-word outline.

Take Essay Exams

Once you have done some preparation, you should be more confident about taking an essay exam. The general guidelines below will help you when you confront the exam itself.

1. **Arrive at the room where the exam is to be given a few minutes early.** You can use this time to collect your thoughts and get organized.
2. **Sit in the front of the room.** You will be less distracted and better able to see and hear the instructor as last-minute directions or corrections are announced.
3. **Read the directions carefully.** Some exams may direct you to answer only one of three questions, whereas other exams may ask you to answer all questions.
4. **Consider your audience and purpose.** For most essay exams, your instructor is your audience. Since your instructor is already knowledgeable about the topic, your purpose is to demonstrate what you know about the topic. Therefore, you should write thorough and complete answers, pretending that your instructor knows only what you tell him or her.

5. **Preview the exam and plan your time carefully.** Read through the whole exam to get a complete picture of the task at hand and then plan how you will complete the exam within the allotted time. If you have fifty minutes, spend roughly ten minutes planning; thirty minutes writing; and ten minutes editing, proofreading, and making last-minute changes. Begin by writing a brief thesis statement. Then jot down the key supporting points and number them in the order you will present them. Leave space under each supporting point for your details. If the question is one you had predicted, write down your keyword outline. If an idea for an interesting introduction or an effective conclusion comes to mind, jot it down as well. At the end of your allotted time for writing, reread your essay and correct surface errors.

6. **Notice the point value of each question.** If your instructor assigns points to each question, use the point values to plan your time. For example, spend more time answering a 30-point question than a 10-point question.

7. **Choose topics or questions carefully.** Often you will have little or no choice of topic or question. If you do have a choice, choose the topics or answer the questions that you know the most about. If the question asks you to write about a broad topic, such as a current social issue, narrow the topic to one you can write about in the specified amount of time.

8. **Answer the easiest question first.** Answering the easiest question first will boost your confidence and allow you to spend the remaining time working on the more difficult questions. Generally if an exam contains both objective and essay questions, get the objective questions out of the way first.

9. **Remember that your first draft is your final draft.** Plan on writing your first draft carefully and correctly so that it can serve as your final copy. However, you can always make minor changes and additions as you write or edit and proofread.

Analyze Essay Exam Questions

Essay exam questions are often concise, but if you read them closely, you will find that they *do* specifically tell you what to write about. Consider the following sample essay question from a sociology exam.

> **Choose a particular institution, define it, and identify its primary characteristics.**

The question tells you exactly what to write about—*a particular institution* (you get to choose one). In addition, the key verbs *define* and *identify* tell you how to approach the subject. To get full credit for this essay question, then, you would have to give an accurate definition of the institution you chose and discuss its primary characteristics.

Table 25.1 lists key verbs commonly used in essay exam questions along with sample questions and tips for answering them. As you study the list, notice that many of the verbs suggest a particular pattern of development. For example, *trace* suggests using a narrative sequence, and *justify* suggests using argumentation. For key verbs such as *explain* or *discuss*, you might use a combination of patterns.

TABLE 25.1	Responding to Key Verbs in Essay Exam Questions	
Key Verbs	Sample Essay Questions	Tips for Answering Questions
Compare	Compare the poetry of Judith Ortiz Cofer with that of Julia Alvarez.	Show how the poems are similar as well as different; use details and examples.
Contrast	Contrast classical and operant conditioning.	Show how the two types of conditioning are different; use details and examples.
Define	Define *biofeedback* and describe its uses.	Give an accurate explanation of the term with enough detail to demonstrate that you understand it.
Discuss	Discuss the halo effect, and give examples of its use.	Consider important characteristics and main points; include examples.
Evaluate	Evaluate the accomplishments of the feminist movement over the past fifty years.	Assess merits, strengths, weaknesses, advantages, or limitations.
Explain	Explain the functions of amino acids.	Use facts and details to make the topic or concept clear and understandable.
Illustrate	Illustrate with examples from your experience how culture shapes human behavior.	Use examples that demonstrate a point or clarify the idea.
Justify	Justify laws outlawing smoking in federal buildings.	Give reasons and evidence that support the action, decision, or policy.
List	List the advantages and disadvantages of sales promotions.	List or discuss one by one; use most-to-least or least-to-most organization.
Summarize	Summarize Maslow's hierarchy of needs.	Briefly review all the major points.
Trace	Trace the life cycle of a typical household product.	Describe its development or progress in chronological order.

Write Essay Answers

Use the following guidelines to write the answers to essay questions.

1. **Since your first-draft essay exam is also your final draft, write in complete and grammatically correct sentences from the start.** Supply sufficient detail and follow a logical organization. It is acceptable to cross out words or sentences neatly and indicate corrections in spelling or grammar.

2. **Add ideas neatly.** If you think of an idea you would like to add to your answer, write the sentence at the top of the paper and draw an arrow to indicate where it should be inserted.

3. **Provide a brief introduction and, in some cases, a conclusion.** Depending on how much time you have, the introduction may consist of only your thesis statement, or it may also include necessary background information on the topic. Write a conclusion only if the question seems to require a final evaluative statement.

4. **If you run out of time, jot the unfinished portion of your outline at the end of the essay.** Your instructor may give you partial credit.

Write your thesis statement. Your thesis statement should be clear and direct. Identify your subject and suggest your approach to the topic. Often the thesis statement answers the essay exam question. Consider the following examples.

For more on writing a thesis, see Chapter 5, pp. 119–24.

Essay Exam Question	Thesis Statement
Explain how tides are produced in the Earth's oceans. Account for seasonal variations.	The Earth's gravitational forces are responsible for producing tides in the Earth's oceans.
Distinguish between bureaucratic agencies and other government decision-making bodies.	Bureaucratic agencies are distinct from other government decision-making bodies because of their hierarchical organization, character, culture, and professionalism.

Your thesis may also suggest the organization of your essay. For example, if the question asks you to explain the differences between primary and secondary groups, you might state your thesis as follows: "Primary groups differ from secondary groups in their membership, purpose, level of interaction, and level of intimacy." Your essay would then discuss membership first, purpose second, and so on.

EXERCISE 25.5 ▸ **WRITING THESIS STATEMENTS FOR ESSAY EXAM QUESTIONS**

Write thesis statements for two of the following essay exam questions.

1. Define and illustrate the meaning of the term *freedom of the press*.
2. Distinguish between the medical care provided by private physicians and that provided by medical clinics.
3. Choose a recent television advertisement and describe its rational and emotional appeals.
4. Evaluate a current news program in terms of its breadth and depth of coverage, objectivity, and political and social viewpoints.

Develop supporting details. Write a separate paragraph for each of your key points. For example, in an essay answer distinguishing primary from secondary groups, devote one paragraph to each distinguishing feature: membership, purpose, level of

For more on topic sentences, see Chapter 6, pp. 141–44.

interaction, and level of intimacy. The topic sentence for each paragraph should identify and briefly explain the key point. For example, a topic sentence for the first main point about groups might be: "Membership, or who belongs, is one factor that distinguishes primary from secondary groups." The rest of the paragraph would explain membership: what constitutes membership, what criteria are used to decide who belongs, and who decides.

Whenever possible, supply examples to make it clear that you can apply the information you have learned. Keep in mind that your goal is to demonstrate your knowledge and understanding of the material.

For more on editing and proofreading, see Chapter 9.

Reread and proofread your answer.   Leave enough time to reread and proofread your essay answer. First, reread to make sure you have answered all parts of the question. Then reread your answer, checking it for content. Add missing information, correct vague or unclear sentences, and add facts or details. Next, proofread for errors in spelling, punctuation, and grammar. A clear, nearly error-free essay makes a positive impression on your instructor and identifies you as a serious, conscientious student. An error-free essay may also improve your grade.

> **EXERCISE 25.6**   **WRITING A COMPLETE ESSAY EXAM ANSWER**
>
> For the essay question you worked on in Exercise 25.5, use the preceding guidelines to write a complete essay answer.

> **STUDENTS WRITE**
>
> ## Essay Exam Response
>
> ### Ronald Robinson
>
> The model essay exam response on the next page was written by Ronald Robinson for his sociology course. First read the exam question below and then read Robinson's essay exam. As you read, consider how effectively and fully Robinson has answered the exam question. The essay has been annotated to point out the essay's key features.

Essay Exam Question

Distinguish between fads and fashions, explaining the characteristics of each type of group behavior and describing the phases each usually goes through.

Essay Exam Answer

Fashions and fads, types of collective group behavior, are distinct from one another in terms of their duration, their predictability, and the number of people involved. Each type follows a five-stage process of development.

A fashion is a temporary trend in behavior or appearance that is followed by a relatively large number of people. Although the word *fashion* often refers to a style of dress, there are fashions in music, art, and literature as well. Trends in clothing fashions are often engineered by clothing designers, advertisers, and the media to create a particular "look." The hip-hop look is an example of a heavily promoted fashion. Fashions are more universally subscribed to than fads. Wearing athletic shoes as casual attire is a good example of a universal fashion.

A fad is a more temporary adoption of a particular behavior or look. Fads are in-group behaviors that often serve as identity markers for a group. Fads also tend to be adopted by smaller groups, often made up of people who want to appear different or unconventional. Unlike fashions, fads tend to be shorter-lived, less predictable, and less influenced by people outside the group. Examples of recent fads are bald heads, tattoos, and tongue piercings. Fads are usually harmless and have no long-range effects.

Fashions and fads each follow a five-phase process of development. In the first phase, latency, the trend exists in the minds of a few people but shows little evidence of spreading. In the second phase, the trend spreads rapidly and reaches its peak. After that, the trend begins a slow decline (phase three). In the fourth phase, its newness is over and many users drop or abandon the trend. In its final phase, quiescence, nearly everyone has dropped the trend, and it is followed by only a few people.

Introduction: Includes only the thesis statement

Body paragraph 1: Definition and characteristics of *fashion*

Body paragraph 2: Definition and characteristics of *fad*

Body paragraph 3: Description of 5-phase process

Create Portfolios

A **portfolio** is a collection of materials that represents a person's work. It may be a digital file or a print collection of materials. It often demonstrates or exemplifies skill, talent, or proficiency. Architects create portfolios that contain drawings and photographs of buildings they have designed. Sculptors' portfolios may include photographs of their sculptures, as well as copies of reviews, awards, or articles about their work. Similarly, your writing instructor may ask you to create a portfolio that represents your skill and proficiency as a writer. Think of your portfolio as a summary of your development as a writer over time.

Understand Your Purposes for Creating a Writing Portfolio

Instructors assign writing portfolios for two main reasons.

- **Grading and assessment.** Your instructor may use your collection of writing to evaluate your mastery of the objectives outlined in the course syllabus. That evaluation will become part of your final grade in the course.
- **Learning, reflection, and self-assessment.** Building a portfolio makes you think about yourself as a learner and as a writer. By building a writing portfolio, you learn a great deal about the writing process, assess your strengths and weaknesses as a writer, and observe your own progress as you build writing proficiency.

Think of your writing portfolio as an opportunity to present yourself in the best possible way—highlighting the work you are proud of and demonstrating the skills you have mastered. It is also an opportunity, as you track your progress, to realize that your hard work in the course has paid off.

Decide What to Include in Your Portfolio

Instructors often specify what their students' portfolios should include. If you are uncertain about what to include, ask your instructor. You might ask to see a sample of a portfolio that meets your instructor's expectations.

To get the best grade on your portfolio, be sure you can answer each of the following questions about the portfolio and its contents.

- How many writing projects should I include? Are there limits to what I can include?
- Should the portfolio include only writing done in the course, or can I include materials I wrote for other courses or outside school (work-related email or service-learning projects, for example)?
- What version(s) should be included—drafts, outlines, and revisions or just the final drafts?
- Should writing projects be based on personal experience, research, or some combination of these?
- Is the portfolio limited to essays, or can multimedia projects (such as time lines or presentation slides), research notes, or completed class exercises also be included?
- How should the portfolio be organized?
- What type of introductory letter or essay is required? What length and format are appropriate?
- How much does the portfolio count in my grade?
- What is the due date, or is the portfolio to be submitted at various intervals throughout the term?
- How will it be graded? That is, is the grade based on improvement or only on the quality of the work included?

Use Your Course Syllabus as a Guide

Your course syllabus is an important guide to deciding what to include in your portfolio. If it contains objectives, which outline what your instructor expects you to learn in the course, you can use several or all of these objectives to structure your portfolio. Suppose one objective states, "Students will develop prewriting strategies that accommodate their learning style." Then in your portfolio, you might include a copy of the results of the Learning Style Inventory (pp. 19–24) and then show examples of your use of two or more prewriting strategies. If another objective states, "Students will demonstrate control over errors in sentence structure, spelling, and punctuation," you would want to include examples of essays in which you identified and corrected these types of errors. You might also include a list of exercises you completed to develop mastery.

Organize and Prepare to Present Your Portfolio

Begin collecting materials for your portfolio as soon as your instructor assigns it. If you wait until the due date to assemble what you need, you may have already discarded or misplaced important prewriting, revision materials, or drafts.

Use physical or online folders divided into sections to hold any of your prewriting, outlines, or graphic organizers. If you are including research materials, include your notes and annotated sources. Also keep peer-review comments as well as papers with your instructor's comments. Save backup copies of your files on a thumb drive or to the cloud.

Use the following suggestions to present a well-organized portfolio.

- **Cover page.** Include a cover or title page that provides your name, course number, instructor's name, and date. (Ask your instructor if you're not sure a title page is required.)
- **Table of contents.** Include a table of contents that identifies the elements in the portfolio and the page number (or a link) on which each piece begins. Number the portfolio consecutively from beginning to end. Since your essays may already have page numbers, put the new page numbers in a different position or use a different color font. If your instructor has not indicated how the contents should be sequenced, choose a method of organization that presents your work and skill development in the best possible way. For example, if you are including two writing projects to demonstrate your effective use of narration, you might present the better one first, thereby making the strongest possible first impression. If you are trying to show growth in your ability to use narration, you might present the stronger writing project second. Use Table 25.2 (p. 686) to guide your selection and sequence.
- **Reflective letter or essay.** Most instructors will expect you to include an essay or a letter that reflects on your development as a writer. This essay is the key to the portfolio, since it reflects on and explains the portfolio's contents. It should explain how your portfolio is organized and give an overview of its contents and why you chose them. It should also include an appraisal of what you learned in the course and discuss your strengths, weaknesses, and development as a writer. Point out specific examples in the portfolio to support your claims.

TABLE 25.2 Guidelines for Building a Writing Portfolio

If you are asked to . . .	Include . . .
demonstrate your growth as a writer	• weak writing projects from early in the semester and your best writing projects from later in the semester. • an essay that demonstrates major changes from first to final draft.
demonstrate your ability to approach writing as a process	• work you did for topic selection, generating ideas, drafting, revising, and proofreading. • first and final drafts that show your writing project gradually developing and evolving as you worked.
feature your best work of the semester	• writing projects that solidly exemplify the method of organization you are using. • writing projects that demonstrate your ability to develop and support ideas. • writing projects that demonstrate thoughtfulness and creativity.
demonstrate your ability to write for a variety of audiences and purposes	• writing projects for courses in different areas of study. pieces that use widely different tones or levels of diction. • non-course-related, nonacademic, and multimedia compositions, if allowed.
demonstrate your ability to use library and Internet sources	• research projects that cite sources accurately in a list of works cited or references. • research projects that use both library and Internet sources rather than one or the other.

- **Drafts.** Attach earlier drafts to the final draft, or place all drafts in a single subfolder, clearly labeling each draft. Date and label each piece so that your instructor can identify its place within your growth process and so that he or she knows what it demonstrates. For example, if an essay demonstrates your ability to use narration, label it as such.

Your portfolio represents you. Be sure it is neat, complete, and carefully assembled.

What Should You Avoid?

Here are a few things to avoid when building your portfolio.

- **Avoid writing about writing in general.** Instead, write about what you learned about *your* writing. That is, do not repeat points from the textbook about the writing process. Instead, explain how you used that information to become a better writer.
- **Do not exaggerate your progress or say what you think the instructor wants to hear.** Instead, be honest and forthright in assessing your progress.
- **Avoid flattery or praise of the instructor or the course.** Most instructors will give you a separate opportunity to evaluate the course and their teaching methods.

Portfolio Contents and Reflective Letter

Bryan Scott

The portfolio assignment below was given to Bryan Scott, a nursing student and former Marine, for his first-year writing course.

Portfolio Assignment

For your final assignment you will submit a portfolio containing the following:

- A table of contents listing the titles and page numbers of all included writing pieces
- A reflective letter that introduces your portfolio
- One series of writing pieces (prewriting, outlines, drafts) that demonstrates your ability to move successfully through the steps in the writing process
- At least two pieces of writing that demonstrate your growth as a writer
- One piece of writing done this term for another class
- Essays that demonstrate your ability to use various methods of organization
- A limited number of materials of your own choice

In your reflective letter, include answers to the following questions.

1. What are your current strengths and weaknesses as a writer?
2. What specific writing skills have you developed?
3. How have you changed as a writer?
4. How has your awareness of learning style improved your ability to write?
5. What critical reading and thinking skills have you learned, *or* in what ways have you strengthened your critical reading and thinking skills?

Scott organizes his reflective letter using the principles of good writing he learned in the course: Within this organization, he is able to identify his strengths and weaknesses as a writer throughout the letter, discuss learning styles, and analyze his essays. Compare the assignment Scott received with his table of contents and reflective letter.

CONTENTS

Scott 1

Bryan Scott

May 16, 2017

Final Portfolio

English 109

From the Marines to the Writing Classroom

I enrolled in this course because it was a required course in my
nursing curriculum, but I can now say that I am glad that it was required.
As a former Marine, I had little experience with writing, other than
writing emails and texts to my wife and parents. Now, as I prepare for a
career as a nurse, I realize that writing is an important communication
skill. Writing reports about patients, such as "Nursing Care Plan: Patient
4," requires me to present clear, precise, and accurate information about
patients and their care. Through this course I have learned to do so.
Although I improved in almost every area of writing, my greatest
improvements were in approaching writing as a process, moving from
personal to informative writing, and developing an awareness of
audience.

Through this course I have learned to view writing as a process rather
than a "write-it-once-and-I-am-done" activity. As shown in the packet of
writing for "The Wall at Sunset," I have discovered the value of prewriting
as a way of coming up with ideas. Before I started writing this essay,

I knew that visiting the Vietnam Veterans Memorial had been an emotional experience for me, but I found that mapping helped me define and organize my feelings. Since I am a spatial learner, I could visualize the wall and map my responses to seeing the names of other soldiers. My first draft in the packet demonstrates my ability to begin with a thesis statement and build ideas around it. My second draft shows how I added detail and arranged my impressions into an organized essay. My final draft shows my ability to catch most errors in spelling, grammar, and punctuation.

Moving from personal writing to informative writing was a valuable learning experience that is essential for my career. My first essay, "The Wall at Sunset," was a very personal account of my visit to the Vietnam Veterans Memorial, as was the essay "How the Marines Changed My Life," a personal account of life in the U.S. Marine Corps. While I had a lot to say about my own experiences, I found it difficult to write about topics that did not directly involve me. I found that learning to use sources, especially online sources, helped me get started with informative writing. By visiting news Web sites, doing online and library research, and reading blogs, I learned to move outside of myself and begin to think about and become interested in what other people were saying and thinking. My essay "Miracle in the Operating Room" demonstrates my ability to use sources, both print and digital, to learn how kidney transplants are done.

As I moved from personal to informative writing, I found that the patterns of development provided a framework for developing and organizing informative writing. Process seemed to be an effective way to present information for the essay "Miracle in the Operating Room." My essay "Emotional Styles of Athletes" initially contained a lot of my own personal impressions (see the first draft that I have included), but by using classification, I was able to focus on characteristics of athletes rather than on my opinions of them.

Before I took this course, I had no idea that I should write differently for different audiences. My essay "How the Marines Changed My Life"

Scott 3

was written for my classmates, many of whom had no military experience. I found I had to explain things about chain of command, regimentation, and living conditions—all things that I and other Marines are familiar with. In my case report for my nursing class, "Nursing Care Plan: Patient 4," my audience was other nurses and medical staff, even doctors. Because I was writing for a specialized audience, I could mention medical terms, procedures, and medications freely without defining them. However, in "Miracle in the Operating Room," I was writing for a general, nonspecialized audience, so I realized it was necessary to explain terms such as *dialysis*, *laparoscopy*, and *nephrectomy*. This essay and my nursing case report demonstrate my ability to write in a clear, direct, and concise manner in my chosen field for different audiences.

While I developed many strengths as a writer, I am still aware of many weaknesses. I have difficulty with descriptive writing; I just cannot come up with words to paint a visual picture as effectively as I would like. Fortunately, nursing will not require much creative description. I also have difficulty choosing a topic. Although I found the suggestions in our textbook helpful, I still feel as if I am overlooking important or useful topics. Finally, I have not benefited from peer review as much as others have. I still find myself uncomfortable when accepting criticism and revision ideas from other students. Perhaps my military training to look to authority for direction is still getting in the way.

6

As I developed strengths as a writer, I also became a more critical reader and thinker. I am enclosing my annotations for the professional essay "Bad Conduct, by the Numbers." These annotations demonstrate my ability to ask questions and challenge the author. I also found enlightening discussions in the text on connotative language, bias, and fact and opinion. These are things I had never thought much about, and now I find myself being aware of these things as I read. Overall, by taking this course, I have become a more serious and aware writer and have come to regard writing as a rewarding challenge.

7

I'd like to push the envelope, go the extra mile, and think outside the box to try to facilitate a win-win solution to the over utilization of buzzwords...

Proactive
Synergy
Brain Dump
Incentivize

Cartoonstock

26

Multimedia Presentations and Business Writing

Develop and Deliver
Presentations

In this chapter you will learn to:

- **prepare and deliver multimedia presentations**
- **create a résumé and job application letter**
- **use electronic media for workplace communication**

WRITING QUICK START   The cartoon on this page illustrates a common issue for people making a presentation—speaking clearly to their audience. Imagine that you have to make a presentation on the topic of college costs. How might your presentation change depending on whether your audience was made up primarily of instructors, parents, or the state representatives making funding decisions?

Success in college and on the job depends on your ability to speak effectively to your audience and to communicate clearly, correctly, and concisely. Many college professors use oral presentations to give students practice with this vital workplace and life skill, as well as to assess their students' understanding of a topic or issue. One professor has said, "If they can talk about it, I know they understand it." At work, you may give a presentation to customers about a new product or to colleagues to help them understand a new process or business endeavor. Even in your personal life, you may be called on to give a speech to the Parent-Teacher Association or to give a toast at a wedding or anniversary party.

Clearly, learning to prepare and give an effective presentation is a valuable experience that will make you a more confident student and a more valued employee. Even more important is learning to communicate effectively in writing with potential employers, colleagues, clients, patients, supervisors, vendors, and so forth.

MULTIMEDIA PRESENTATIONS ▶ **IN COLLEGE AND THE WORKPLACE**

- For a *sociology class,* you conduct field research on college students' attitudes about a particular trend and report your findings.

- For a *public speaking class,* you make a presentation about learned helplessness, an important concept in your first-year psychology class.

- As a *sales representative* for a Web site design company, you create and give a presentation to a group of restaurant owners to demonstrate how a Web site can increase their visibility and profitability.

Develop and Deliver Multimedia Presentations

A **multimedia presentation** is a presentation to an audience—either face-to-face or online—using visual aids. The visual aids may be a simple prop or poster or presentation slides that may include graphics, video, sound files, animation, and other media. By learning to make a presentation to an audience, you will gain self-confidence and become a more effective communicator.

Plan Your Presentation

The more carefully you plan your presentation, the more comfortable you will be in delivering it. The sections that follow detail the steps to follow in planning a presentation.

For more on choosing and narrowing a topic, see Chapter 4, pp. 100–102.

Select your topic. First, make sure you understand the assignment and the type of presentation you are to give. Then consider your audience: What topics are important to your listeners and will sustain their interest? Here are a few suggestions for choosing a topic.

- **Choose a topic that you find interesting or know something about.** You will find it easier to exude and generate enthusiasm if you speak about a topic that is familiar and that you enjoy.
- **Choose a topic that is appropriate and of value to your audience.** Learning how to choose a day care center may be of value to young parents, but you may have difficulty sustaining the interest of average college students with such a topic. Trivial topics such as how to create a particular hairstyle or a report about characters on a soap opera are unlikely to have sufficient merit for college instructors.

- **Choose a topic you can explain fully in the time allotted.** If your topic is too broad, your presentation will go over time, or you may resort to generalities that lack supporting evidence.

Identify your purpose.   Determine whether your purpose is to express, inform, or persuade. Then define your purpose more specifically. For a persuasive presentation, for example, do you want to convince the audience that a change in policy is needed or simply to encourage them to consider the issue with an open mind?

For more information on determining your purpose, see Chapter 4, pp. 102–3.

Research your topic.   Unless your presentation is to be based on your personal knowledge or experience, you will need to research your topic.

For more on researching, see Chapters 21 and 22.

Consider what type of visual aids are appropriate.   Visual aids, from maps and photographs to Prezi or PowerPoint presentation slides with embedded sound and video files, add interest to your presentation and can be used to reinforce your message and make your ideas clear and concrete. Use flip charts or presentation slides to show your main points in outline form, which may make your presentation easier to follow. Presentation programs also allow you to integrate sound, photo, and video files into your presentation seamlessly. Ask your instructor what is permissible and what media are available for classroom use.

Some speakers find that using visual aids builds their confidence and lessens their apprehension. Such aids distract speakers from thinking about themselves and how they look, and lessen concerns that speakers will forget what they were planning to say to their audience. However, presentation slides must be used effectively to avoid "Death by PowerPoint."

To learn more about using presentation slides effectively, see pp. 694–95, 696.

Draft Your Presentation

Once you have made a plan, begin drafting your presentation.

Develop a thesis and generate supporting ideas.   Based on your research, create a working thesis. Use idea-generating strategies to develop a variety of supporting reasons, and consider which will be most effective, given your purpose and audience.

For idea-generating strategies, see Chapter 4; for more about developing and supporting a thesis, see Chapter 5.

Organize your presentation.   Using one of the patterns of organization from Parts 3 and 4 will make your presentation easier for your audience to follow and for you to remember the order of your main points. For example, you could use classification to organize a presentation on types of procrastinators, providing four main categories of procrastinators with descriptive details to explain each. When organizing, consider saving your most convincing evidence or examples for last, as audience members are likely to recall the end of your presentation more clearly than the beginning.

For more on organizing, see Chapter 7, pp. 156–61. Also see the chapters in Part 3 for planning presentations using one of the patterns of development.

Draft the body of your presentation.   When you write an essay, your readers can reread if they miss a point. When you give a presentation, your listeners do not have that option, so reiterate your thesis frequently to make your presentation easier to follow, and use plenty of transitions to ensure that your listeners don't get lost.

(Presentation slides showing your main points in the order you present them can also help your audience follow along.)

Select evidence that your audience would find convincing. Including different types of evidence that reinforce one another, such as statistics to support the examples you include, will help listeners recall your main points. Emotional appeals can be more memorable for an audience than statistics, but reinforce any emotional appeals you make with concrete evidence. Including meaningful evidence adds credibility to your presentation.

To learn more about emotional appeals, see Chapter 19, pp. 497–98, 507.

Work references to your sources into your presentation. Use signal phrases to incorporate references to authors or works (or both), and include background information about the author or work, to provide context. If you use quotations, avoid tedious expressions such as "I quote here" or "I want to quote an example." Instead, integrate your quotations into your speech as you would integrate quotations into an essay.

To learn more about using signal phrases and integrating quotations, see Chapter 23, pp. 593–99.

Draft your introduction and conclusion. Your introduction should grab your audience's attention, introduce your topic, and establish a relationship between you and your audience. To build a relationship with your audience, try to make connections with them. You might mention others who are present; refer to a shared situation (a previous class or another student's presentation); or establish common ground by referring to a well-known event, personality, or campus issue.

To learn more about writing introductions and conclusions, see Chapter 7, pp. 164–67.

Your conclusion is a crucial part of your presentation because it is your last opportunity to leave a strong impression on your audience. You should summarize your speech and let the audience know your presentation is ending. The conclusion should also remind listeners of the importance of your topic. Consider closing with a powerful quotation or anecdote that reinforces your main point.

Create Presentation Slides

Presentation software, like PowerPoint and Prezi, allows you to list or summarize your main points and to embed multimedia evidence—audio, video, and image files—in support of your claims. While PowerPoint allows a linear presentation of electronic slides, Prezi allows zooming in and out of specific parts of your presentation. (**Hint:** To create a presentation using Prezi, start by drawing an idea map and use that map to plan an easy-to-follow path through the presentation.)

- **Use presentation software to aid understanding.** Project key words or concepts you want to emphasize or provide an outline so your audience can follow your main points.
- **Use a design template that suits your audience and purpose.** A simple color scheme with a sharp contrast between text and background will be easiest to read. Avoid using reds and greens if differences between the two colors are significant, because color-blind members of the audience will not be able to differentiate between them. Use subdued color schemes and easily readable fonts (such as Arial or **Verdana**) for business or academic presentations. For PowerPoint slides, use just a few animation schemes (how text enters and leaves a slide) consistently.

- **Format your slides so they are easily readable.** Use a large point size (usually 24 points or greater) so everyone in the audience can read the text easily. Keep the number of words per slide low: Slides crammed with text are difficult to read, and if audience members are busy reading lengthy slides, they are not listening to what you are saying. A good rule of thumb is to use no more than six bullet points per slide, with no more than six words per bullet point. (If you can do so clearly, use just words and phrases rather than complete sentences.)
- **Use presentation software to display visuals and graphics.** Photos, cartoons, graphics, and embedded videos can convey your message in a memorable way. They also keep your audience interested and alert. But keep graphics simple, so the audience can take them in at a glance, and use visuals and graphics only when they are relevant to your point, not just as decoration.
- **Edit your slides carefully.** Check for errors in spelling, grammar, and formatting as well as other kinds of typos. Run the entire slide show for yourself several times before presenting it to correct any errors you find.

On the next page is a sample Prezi presentation designed by student Nicholas Destino, whose research project appears in Chapter 23 (pp. 621–28). He used his research to create this presentation for his first-year composition class. This introductory slide shows all the slides at once; as he navigates through his presentation, the Prezi zooms in on each circle, enlarging it, so audience members can easily read the text. Destino included a list of works cited at the end of his presentation to document the sources he used.

Rehearse Your Presentation

Practice is the key to comfortable and effective delivery. The following tips can help you rehearse effectively.

- **Practice giving the entire presentation, not just parts of it.** Rehearse at least three or four times, using your visual aids. Try to improve your presentation each rehearsal.
- **Time yourself.** If you are over or seriously under the time limit, make necessary cuts or additions, and edit your presentation slides accordingly.
- **If possible, rehearse the presentation in the room in which you will give it.** This will make you more comfortable on the day of the presentation and gives you an opportunity to find out in advance if the room can support the technology you plan to use.
- **Rehearse in front of an audience of a few friends or classmates.** Ask them for constructive criticism. Some students record their presentations on their smart phones to build their confidence and identify areas that need improvement.

Overcome Stage Fright

Many students are nervous about making presentations. Often called "stage fright," this apprehension is normal. You can often overcome presentation anxiety by following these suggestions.

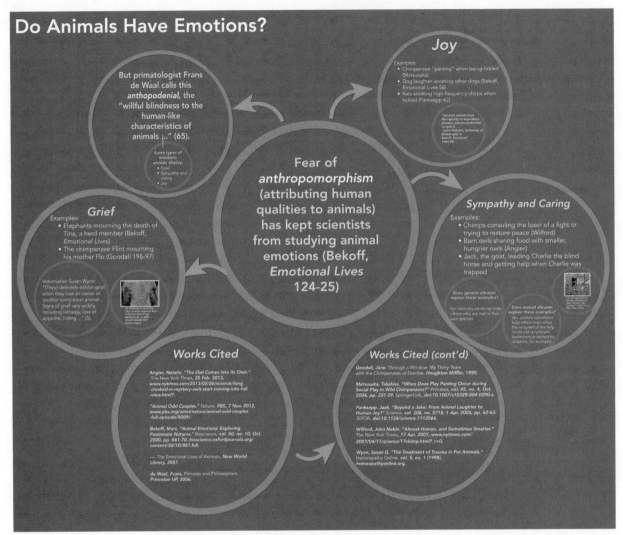

Elephant photo: OLAF KRAAK/Stringer/Getty Images

- **Prepare thoroughly.** Knowing you have put together a solid, interesting presentation can build your self-confidence.
- **Practice, practice, practice.** To reduce the newness of the task, practice your presentation several times. (See the previous section on rehearsal.)
- **Use desensitization.** If someone is afraid of snakes, a therapist might begin by showing the person a photograph, then a video, then a small snake at a distance, and so forth, gradually building up the person's tolerance. You can use the same technique to overcome your fear of oral presentations. Begin by asking or answering a question in class. Then try practicing your speech on a group of friends. Eventually you will become more comfortable with public speaking and ready to make a presentation to the class.

- **Use visualization.** Visualization involves imagining yourself successfully completing a task. For a presentation, create a mental recording that begins with your arrival at the classroom and takes you through each step: confidently walking to the front of the room, beginning your presentation, engaging your audience, handling your notes, and so on. Visualize the presentation positively, and avoid negative thoughts, to create the image of yourself as a successful speaker. Review your visualized performance often, especially on the day of your presentation. As you give your presentation, try to model the look and feel of your visualization.
- **Imagine a friend in the audience.** If you feel conspicuous, try to imagine that you are talking to one friend or one friendly and supportive classmate. Looking directly at one member of the audience at the beginning of your presentation can help.

Deliver an Effective Presentation

The delivery of your presentation ultimately determines its effectiveness. Use the suggestions below, as well as Table 26.1, to improve the delivery of your presentation.

- **Avoid using too many notes or a detailed outline.** Instead, construct a key-word outline that will remind you of major points in the order you wish to present them.

TABLE 26.1 Frequently Asked Questions for Making Presentations

Question	Suggested Solutions
What should I do if I go blank?	Refer to your notes or presentation slides.
	Ask if there are any questions. Even if no one asks any, the pause will give you time to regroup.
What should I do if classmates are restless, uninterested, or even rude?	Make eye contact with as many members of the class as possible as you speak.
	For a particularly troublesome person, you might lengthen your eye contact.
	Change the tone or pitch of your voice.
	Try to make your speech more engaging by asking questions or using personal examples.
What should I do if I accidentally omit an important part of the presentation?	Go back and add it in. Say something like, "I neglected to mention . . ." and present the portion you skipped.
What if I realize that my speech will be too short or too long?	If you realize it will be too short, try to add examples, anecdotes, or more detailed information.
	If you realize it will be too long, cut out examples or summarize instead of fully explaining sections that are less important.

- **Make eye contact with your audience.** Make the audience part of your presentation.
- **Move around a little rather than standing stiffly.** Use gestures to add an expressive quality to your presentation.
- **Speak slowly.** Speaking too fast is a common mistake, but try not to overcompensate by speaking so slowly that your audience loses interest.

Prepare and Deliver Online Presentations

At some point in your education or career, you may be asked to use an online meeting application, such as GoToMeeting or WebEx, which allows you to conduct virtual meetings with instructors, colleagues, clients, and vendors. These applications allow others to view what you have on your computer screen, so you can pull up documents, spreadsheets, presentation slides, and anything else for everyone to look at together in real time. You may communicate by phone, by Skype, or via Google Hangouts, or another online system. The following tips will help you give an effective Web-based presentation.

- **Become familiar with the technology in advance.** Your audience may become restless if you cannot resolve technical difficulties quickly.
- **Review all documents and materials prior to the meeting.** Be sure you know where to find the documents you need to display.
- **Prepare thoroughly, but be ready to adjust your presentation in response to questions from the audience.** You should know the content well enough to respond to a question or comment that draws you away from your prepared remarks.
- **Turn off all notifications and programs that are running on your computer.** You do not want an email from a friend popping up on your screen while you are delivering a presentation.

Create Effective Business Documents

Business writing will be an important part of your life after college. Good business writing is concise and correct. It is often more direct than some forms of academic or personal writing. Because you are judged on the business documents that you write, prepare materials that will present you and your accomplishments in the best light possible.

Prepare a Résumé and Job Application Letter

A **résumé** (Figure 26.1) is a complete listing of all of your education, training, and work experience in an easy-to-read format. A **job application (or cover) letter** (Figure 26.2, p. 700) highlights the qualifications that make you right for the job and convinces the employer that you are an excellent candidate for the opening. Because your application packet will determine whether a potential employer will interview you, tailor each one to the job for which you are applying.

FIGURE 26.1   Sample Résumé

Martin Simms

20600 Main Street • Silver Spring, MD 20906

301-555-5555 • martin.simms@gmail.com

Objective

A marine science internship at Phillips Wharf Environmental Center

Education

B.S., Biology (GPA 3.5)   Expected May 2018
    University of Maryland, College Park

A.S., Science (GPA 3.7)   May 2016
    Montgomery College, Rockville Campus

Volunteer Experience

Guide, Underground Railroad Experience Hike   2014–Present
    Woodlawn Manor Culture Park
    Montgomery County, MD

Coordinator, Green Club   2013–2014
    Oak View Elementary School
    Silver Spring, MD

Relevant Skills

Completed Science and Math Coursework

- Proficient at applying mathematics in a laboratory setting
- Completed calculus for life sciences, principles of genetics, principles of chemistry II (3.8 average)

Work Well in a Group

- Effectively collaborate with a diverse group of people
- Ensure work is split equally and fairly among teammates
- Maintain a constant pace when working with a group

Experience Interacting with the Public

- Succinctly convey a message to people, regardless of their background knowledge
- Ensure audience stays engaged by reading nonverbal cues from patrons
- Remain positive when faced with a difficult patron
- Tailor lessons to meet the needs of different audiences

Work Well with Children

- Vary content to suit a child's age and interest levels
- Devise fun activities suitable to children of different ages

References

Available on request

Contact information: Displayed at the top of the page

Headings: Boldfaced type used to make résumé easy to read

Organization: Reverse chronological order used for information under Education, and Volunteer Experience, so most recent item listed first

Student currently has little experience, so skills categorized by topic

Key words: Key words from job advertisement used so skills and experience match words in employer's electronic job database

Proofreading: Résumé proofread carefully to correct spelling, punctuation, and capitalization errors

Block style: Standard block style used (double line space between paragraphs, type aligned at left edge)

Formatting: Return address appears at top of page

Formatting: Inside address follows the date

Salutation: Letter begins with salutation ("Dear Ms. Cannon:")

Content: Opening paragraph identifies desired position; second, and third paragraphs describe relevant details of Martin Simms's volunteer experience, not everything in résumé

Content: Fourth paragraph provides contact information

Closing: The letter ends with standard closing: "Sincerely"; signature follows closing, and name typed below

> **FIGURE 26.2**   **Sample Job Application Letter**
>
> 20600 Main Street
> Silver Spring, MD 20906
>
> February 29, 2017
>
> Ms. Melissa Cannon, Administrator
> Phillips Wharf Environmental Center
> 6129 Tilghman Island Road
> Tilghman, MD 21671
>
> Dear Ms. Cannon:
>
> I am writing in response to your advertisement for a marine science intern. I believe that I am an ideal applicant: Not only am I a biology major, but I also have volunteer experience educating the public (both adults and children).
>
> As a volunteer on the Underground Railroad Experience Hike, I work closely with another guide to write and deliver a coordinated, professional presentation simulating the Underground Railroad experience. Our presentation explains how those seeking freedom found their way north and survived on the trail and is tailored to the audience. (We highlight different elements for an audience of Cub Scouts than we do for a group of seniors from Leisure World.)
>
> Interacting with children is a particular strength of mine: As coordinator of the Oak View Elementary School Green Club, I created entertaining activities for children in grades three through five that taught them about the importance of environmental preservation while also engaging their attention.
>
> I believe that my skills meet the needs of your internship, especially regarding my proven ability to work with children. I would welcome the opportunity to discuss at your convenience how my qualifications can meet your needs. I can be contacted at 301-944-2222 or at martin.simms@gmail.com.
>
> Thank you for considering my application. I look forward to hearing from you.
>
> Sincerely,
>
> *Martin Simms*
>
> Martin Simms

Most employers invite applicants to upload résumés and job application (or cover) letters to their Web sites or to send the application letter as an email message with the résumé attached. If you are sending a hard copy résumé and job application letter, print both documents on good-quality white paper.

Follow these tips when preparing your résumé.

- **Tailor your resume.** Don't create a one-size-fits-all résumé. Instead, tailor it to the specific job you are applying for. Use key words from the advertisement (such as *marine science intern*) and active verbs (*collaborate, devise*) to show what you can do.
- **Simple is best.** Prepare your résumé as a document with an unlined, white background, as if you were going to print it on 8½ x 11-inch paper. Leave 1-inch margins on all sides. Do not include graphics, colors, or elaborate underlining and formatting. If possible, save your résumé in PDF format. Be sure to check it carefully before sending.
- **Display your name, address, and contact information at the top of the page.** Check that your contact information is correct. (A computer's spell-check function will not identify such mistakes.)
- **Fit your résumé onto a single page whenever possible.** If providing a printed copy, use only one side of an 8½- x 11-inch sheet of paper. Write clearly and concisely, and use categories (such as "Education," "Experience," and "Skills") so that potential employers can scan your résumé quickly.
- **List education and experience, in reverse chronological order.** Include dates you attended school or received a degree, listing your most recent education and experience first. If your relevant experience is scant (as it is for many new college graduates), include a section highlighting your skills.
- **Specify how the employer can obtain your references.** This is usually done by stating, "References are available on request," but be prepared to supply references by asking instructors or previous employers whether they are willing to give you a good recommendation and whether you can share their contact information with prospective employers.
- **Proofread carefully.** Résumés must be clear, concise, and free of errors in grammar, punctuation, mechanics, and spelling.

For more about proofreading, see Chapter 9, pp. 211–13.

Follow these tips when writing a job application letter or email.

- **Use standard business formats.** Block-style business letters have one-inch margins on all sides and are single-spaced, with an extra line space between paragraphs. All type is aligned at the left edge of the page. (The sample job application letter in Figure 26.2 is in block style.) Use letterhead or list your address at the top of the page. The date should appear below your address, and the address of the person to whom you are writing should appear below the date. Job applications, like résumés, should be prepared with a white, unlined background.
- **Include a formal salutation and closing.** Begin with "Dear Ms.____:" or "Dear Mr. ____:" and call the company for a name if you are unsure to whom you should address your letter. Close with "Sincerely," or "Yours truly," followed by your signature. Formal salutations and closings are appropriate, even when sending a job application by email.
- **Include key information in the body.** If submitting your job application letter by email, use the subject line to identify the job you are applying for. In both job

application emails and letters, identify the job you are applying for in the opening paragraph. You may also indicate where you learned about the position or where it was posted or listed. The middle paragraphs should briefly state the skills and experiences that make you especially qualified. (Do not repeat everything you have listed in your résumé.) At the end of the letter, indicate that you are available for an interview at the employer's convenience or specify when you are available.

- **Proofread carefully.** If job application letters or emails are not clear, concise, and free of errors in grammar, punctuation, mechanics, and spelling, they are likely to wind up in the "reject" pile.
- **Follow instructions for uploading your documents.** If you are applying by email, be sure to double-check that you have attached your résumé before hitting "send."

Use Electronic Media for Business Writing

In your career, you will likely use digital media—email (Figure 26.3) but perhaps also Facebook, Twitter, text messages, and interoffice information management systems—as your main means of communication. Follow the tips below to communicate effectively with supervisors, colleagues, clients, and other business contacts.

FIGURE 26.3   Sample Business Email

Subject line: Accurately reflects memo's main point

Attachment: File mentioned in email message is attached

Proofreading: Writer uses correct grammar, spelling, and punctuation; writes formally, as is appropriate in business correspondence

Automatic signature: Includes sender's complete name, title, company, address, and telephone and fax numbers

Klenk File - Message

File   Edit   View   Insert   Format   Tools   Table   Window   Help

Send | Options... ▾ | HTML

To... Ryan Thompson

Cc...

Subject: Klein Construction: Corrected Billing

Attach... Klein billing corrected.doc (24 KB)   Attachment Options...

Calibri ▾ 10 ▾ A ▾ B *I* U

Dear Mr. Thompson:

Attached please find the corrected billing for Klein Construction. My research indicated that we overbilled the project for lumber. I have included the correct numbers. Let me know if you need anything else on this matter.

Kaitlyn Botano, Office Assistant
Thompson Supply
345 West End Avenue
Pittsburgh, PA 12231
Phone: 555-212-2121
Fax: 555-212-2122

- **Keep it brief and get right to the point.** Typically the most important information is in the first paragraph. Paragraphs are usually only one to three sentences long, and wordiness is frowned upon. Messages overall are usually brief (just a few paragraphs), so they can be scanned quickly for important information. If more detail is required, supporting documents may be attached.

For more about writing concisely, see Chapter 9, pp. 195–97.

- **Do not say anything you do not want shared.** Online communications can easily be forwarded to others. Remember at all times that you are representing your employer and serving as the voice of your company. Do not say anything in an email that you would not say to your entire company and all your clients.
- **Use a specific and relevant subject line.** Using a specific and relevant subject line is crucial, not only so recipients can know how to prioritize the communications they receive, but also to locate important messages later. Without a subject line that clearly references a client, case number, file name, or other specific identifier, a message can be impossible to retrieve. Be particularly careful when replying that you adjust the subject line as needed.
- **Write in complete words and sentences and with a moderately formal tone.** Avoid online slang (such as *LOL* and *OMG*) and emoticons (such as the smiley face), avoid writing in all capital or all lowercase letters, and always reread email messages to be sure the tone is cordial and professional. Abbreviations are acceptable, but only if your recipient will understand them.

For more about tone and level of diction, see Chapter 9, pp. 206–8.

- **Copy only people who need to be informed about the topic.** Do not automatically "carbon copy" (cc) your boss or everyone else in your company on every message. Avoid "Reply all" unless the content of your reply is truly relevant to "all."
- **Remember to attach relevant files.** It makes more work for everyone if you forget to include the attachment.
- **Use an automatic signature file.** An automatic signature should include your name, title, company address, and telephone and fax numbers so that people can contact you easily.
- **Proofread carefully.** You are a representative of your business, so take the time to communicate concisely and professionally, and proofread your messages carefully before sending.

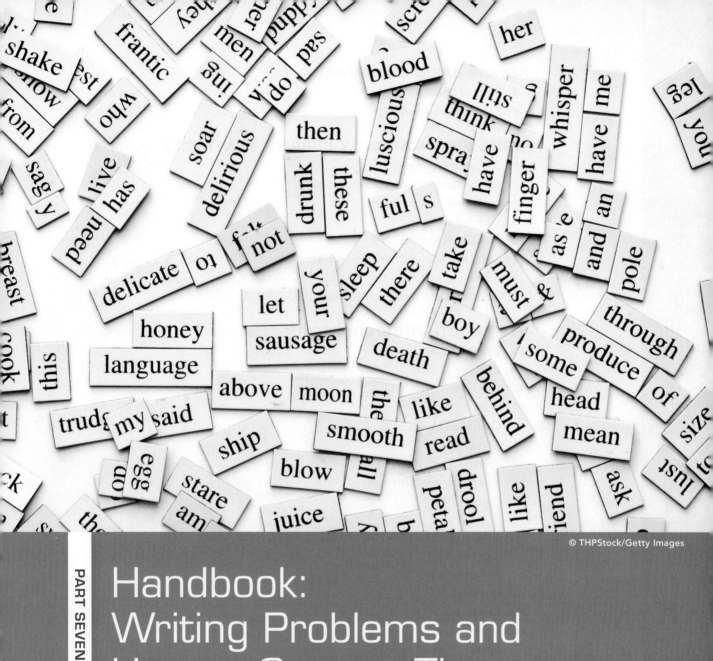

PART SEVEN

Handbook:
Writing Problems and
How to Correct Them

Review Basic Grammar

1   Parts of Speech

Each word in a sentence acts as one of eight parts of speech: *nouns, pronouns, verbs, adjectives, adverbs, conjunctions, prepositions,* and *interjections.* These are the building blocks of our language. Often, to revise your writing or to correct sentence errors, you need to understand how a word or phrase functions in a particular sentence.

1a   Nouns

A **noun** names a person (*waiter, girlfriend*), a place (*classroom, beach*), a thing (*textbook, computer*), or an idea (*excitement, beauty*). **Proper nouns** name specific people (*Professor Wainwright*), places (*Texas*), things (*Xbox*), or ideas (*Marxism*) and are always capitalized.

> ▶ *James* drove to *Williamsville* in a *Toyota* in *March.*

Common nouns name one or more of a general class or type of person, place, thing, or idea and are not capitalized.

> ▶ A *holiday* is a *celebration* of an *event.*

Collective nouns name groups: *class, jury, team.* **Concrete nouns** name tangible things that can be tasted, seen, touched, smelled, or heard: *instructor, exam, desk.* **Abstract nouns** name ideas, qualities, beliefs, and conditions: *love, faith, trust.*

Most nouns express **number** and can be singular or plural: *one test, two tests; one pen, five pens.* **Count nouns** name items that can be counted. Count nouns can be made plural, usually by adding *-s* or *-es: one telephone, three telephones; one speech, ten speeches.* Some count nouns form their plurals in an irregular way: *mouse, mice; goose, geese.* **Noncount nouns**—such as *water, anger, courage,* and *knowledge*—name ideas or entities that cannot be counted. Most noncount nouns do not have a plural form.

See Section 26 of this Handbook for more on count and noncount nouns.

1b   Pronouns

Pronouns are words that take the place of nouns. The noun or pronoun to which a pronoun refers is called the pronoun's **antecedent**.

> ▶ Because the *researcher* developed a new drug, *she* became famous.
>
> The noun *researcher* is the antecedent of the pronoun *she.*

Personal pronouns name specific people, places, or things. Personal pronouns come in three cases that describe a pronoun's function in a sentence. The **subjective case** indicates that a pronoun is a subject—a doer of an action (*I, you, he, she, it, we, they*).

> ▶ *She* asked questions about the job.

The **objective case** indicates that a pronoun is an object—a receiver of an action (*me, you, him, her, it, us, them*).

▶ The career counselor has been advising *her*.

The **possessive case** indicates ownership or belonging (*my, mine, your, yours, his, her, hers, its, our, ours, your, yours, their, theirs*).

▶ *His* enthusiasm for the company does not match *theirs*.

Personal pronouns also indicate **person**, to distinguish among the speaker (first person: *I, we*), the person spoken to (second person: *you*), and the person or thing spoken about (third person: *he, she, it, they*). The **gender** of personal pronouns identifies them as masculine (*he, him*), feminine (*she, her*), or neuter (*it*). Personal pronouns also show **number**: singular (one person or thing: *I, you, he, she, it*) or plural (more than one person or thing: *we, you, they*).

Demonstrative pronouns point out a particular person or thing: *this, that, these,* and *those*. A demonstrative pronoun can be used as an adjective to describe a noun.

▶ *These* research procedures are questionable.

Reflexive pronouns indicate that a subject performs actions to, for, or on itself. Reflexive pronouns end in *-self* or *-selves*.

	Singular	**Plural**
First person	myself	ourselves
Second person	yourself	yourselves
Third person	himself	themselves
	herself	
	itself	

▶ We allowed *ourselves* two hours to complete the experiment.

Intensive pronouns have the same forms as reflexive pronouns and are used to emphasize their antecedents.

▶ Not even the computer programmer *herself* could correct the error.

Reflexive and intensive pronouns cannot be used as the subject of a sentence, and their antecedents must appear in the same sentence as the pronoun.

Incorrect	*Myself* disagreed with the speaker's proposal, despite my sympathy with the movement.
Correct	I *myself* disagreed with the speaker's proposal, despite my sympathy with the movement.

Interrogative pronouns introduce or ask a question.

Refer to People	who, whoever, whom, whomever, whose
Refer to Things	what, which

▶ *Who* will pay the bill?

Relative pronouns introduce **dependent clauses** that function as adjectives. Relative pronouns refer back to a noun or pronoun that the clause modifies.

Refer to People	who, whoever, whom, whomever, whose
Refer to Things	that, what, whatever, which, whose

> A **dependent clause** contains a subject and a verb but does not express a complete thought.

▶ The research *that* caused the literacy-test controversy was outdated.

▶ Sylvia Plath was married to Ted Hughes, *who* later became poet laureate of England.

Indefinite pronouns do not refer to specific nouns; they refer to people, places, or things in general (*everyone, anywhere, everything*). Commonly used indefinite pronouns include the following:

Singular

another	either	nobody	somebody
anybody	enough	none	someone
anyone	everybody	no one	something
anything	everyone	nothing	
anywhere	everything	one	
each	neither	other	

Plural

both	many	several
few	others	

▶ Hardly *anyone* had heard of the Sapir-Wharf hypothesis.
▶ Although a number of psychologists have researched brain dominance, *few* have related it to learning style.

Several indefinite pronouns, such as *all, any, more, most, some,* and *none,* can be either singular or plural, depending on their antecedent (see 5e).

The **reciprocal pronouns** *each other* and *one another* indicate an interchange of information or physical objects between two or more parties.

▶ The debate semifinalists congratulated each other on their scores.

> See Section 7 of the Handbook for more on pronoun usage.

1c Verbs

Verbs show action (*read, study*), occurrence (*become, happen*), or a state of being (*be, feel*). There are three types of verbs: action verbs, linking verbs, and helping verbs (also called auxiliary verbs).

Action verbs express physical or mental activities.

▶ My hair *grew* longer and longer.

▶ Amelia *thought* her answer was correct.

Action verbs may be either transitive or intransitive. A **transitive verb** (TV) has a **direct object** (DO) that receives the action and completes the meaning of the sentence. (In the examples, S stands for *subject*.)

    S   TV   DO

▶ Juan *wrote* lyrics for songs.

An **intransitive verb** (IV) does not need a direct object to complete the meaning of the sentence.

    S   IV

▶ The lights *flickered*.

Some verbs can be either transitive or intransitive, depending on how they are used in a sentence.

Intransitive   The student *wrote* quickly.

Transitive   The student *wrote* a paper on hypnotism.

Linking verbs show existence, explaining what something is, was, or will become. A linking verb connects a word to words that describe it.

▶ Dr. Lopez *is* the new college president.

▶ Their answers *were* evasive.

The forms of the verb *be* (*am, is, are, was, were, be, being, been*) are linking verbs. Some action verbs can also function as linking verbs. These include *appear, become, feel, grow, look, prove, remain, seem, smell, sound, stay,* and *taste.*

▶ The sky *grew* dark.

▶ Something in the kitchen *smells* delicious.

Helping verbs, also called **auxiliary verbs**, are used along with action or linking verbs to indicate tense, mood, or voice or to add further information. A **verb phrase** is a combination of one or more helping verbs and a main verb.

Simple Verb   The newspaper *reports* the incident.

Simple Verb +   The newspaper *should report* the incident.
Helping Verb

Helping verbs include the different forms of *do, be,* and *have* (which can also serve as main verbs in a sentence) along with *can, could, may, might, must, shall, should, will,* and *would.*

Verb forms.   All verbs except *be* have five forms: the base form, the past tense, the past participle, the present participle, and the *-s* form for the present tense when the subject is singular and in the third person.

The first three forms are called the verb's principal parts. The base form is the form of the verb as it appears in the *dictionary: review, study, prepare.* For regular verbs, the past tense and past participle are formed by adding -*d* or -*ed* to the base form. For regular verbs ending in y, the y is changed to i: *rely, relied*. For one-syllable regular verbs ending in a vowel plus a consonant, the consonant is doubled: *plan, planned* (see 25c).

	Regular	**Irregular**
Base form	walk	run
Past tense	walked	ran
Past participle	walked	run
Present participle	walking	running
-s form	walks	runs

Irregular verbs follow no set pattern to form their past tense and past participle.

Forms of Common Irregular Verbs

Base Form	**Past Tense**	**Past Participle**
be	was/were	been
become	became	become
begin	began	begun
bite	bit	bitten, bit
blow	blew	blown
build	built	built
burst	burst	burst
catch	caught	caught
choose	chose	chosen
come	came	come
dive	dived, dove	dived
do	did	done
draw	drew	drawn
drive	drove	driven
eat	ate	eaten
fall	fell	fallen
feel	felt	felt
fight	fought	fought
find	found	found
fling	flung	flung
fly	flew	flown
get	got	gotten, got
give	gave	given
go	went	gone
grow	grew	grown
have	had	had
know	knew	known
lay	laid	laid
lead	led	led
leave	left	left
lie	lay	lain
lose	lost	lost

Base Form	Past Tense	Past Participle
make	made	made
prove	proved	proved, proven
ride	rode	ridden
ring	rang	rung
rise	rose	risen
run	ran	run
say	said	said
set	set	set
sit	sat	sat
speak	spoke	spoken
swear	swore	sworn
swim	swam	swum
take	took	taken
tear	tore	torn
tell	told	told
think	thought	thought
throw	threw	thrown
wear	wore	worn
win	won	won
write	wrote	written

See Section 6 of the Handbook for more about verb forms.

If you are unsure of a verb's principal parts, check your dictionary.

Verb tense. The **tenses** of a verb express time. They convey whether an action, a state of being, or an occurrence takes place in the present, past, or future. There are six basic tenses: present, past, future, present perfect, past perfect, and future perfect. There are also three groups of tenses: simple, perfect, and progressive.

Simple tenses indicate whether an action occurs in the present, past, or future.

▶ He *loves* Kabuki theater.
▶ I *downloaded* their new release immediately.
▶ Oprah's reputation *will grow*.

Perfect tenses indicate that the action was or will be finished by the time of some other action.

▶ By now, Rosa *has taken* the exam.
▶ Dave Matthews *had* already *performed* when they arrived.
▶ The centennial celebration *will have begun* before he completes the sculpture.

Progressive tenses indicate that the action does, did, or will continue.

▶ She *is going* to kindergarten.
▶ When the ambulance arrived, he *was sweating* profusely.
▶ During spring break, we *will be basking* on a sunny beach.

A Summary of Verb Tenses

Present Tense

Simple present: happening now or occurring regularly

- He *performs* his own stunts.

Present progressive: happening now; going on (in progress) now

- The governor *is considering* a Senate campaign.

Present perfect: began in the past and was completed in the past or is continuing now

- The children's benefactor *has followed* their progress closely.

Present perfect progressive: began in the past and is continuing now

- She *has been singing* in nightclubs for thirty years.

Past Tense

Simple past: began and ended in the past

- The doctor *treated* him with experimental drugs.

Past progressive: began and continued in the past

- They *were* not *expecting* any visitors.

Past perfect: occurred before a certain time in the past or was completed before another action was begun

- The birds *had eaten* all the berries before we knew they were ripe.

Past perfect progressive: was taking place until a second action occurred

- He *had been seeing* a psychiatrist before his collapse.

Future Tense

Simple future: will take place in the future

- The play *will begin* on time.

Future progressive: will both begin and end in the future

- After we get on the plane, *we will be sitting* for hours.

Future perfect: will be completed by a certain time in the future or before another action will begin

- By next month, the new apprentice *will have become* an expert.

Future perfect progressive: will continue until a certain time in the future

- By the time she earns her Ph.D., she *will have been studying* history for twelve years.

Most of the time you will not need to think about verb tense; you will use the correct tense automatically. There are, however, a few situations in which you need to pay special attention to verb tense.

- Use the present tense to make a generalization or to state a principle or fact.

▶ Thanksgiving *falls* on the fourth Thursday of November each year.
▶ Walking *is* excellent exercise.

- Use the present tense to indicate an action that occurs regularly or habitually.

  ▶ My sister *takes* frequent trips to Dallas.

- Use the present tense when referring to literary works and artwork, even though the work was written or created in the past.

  ▶ *Hamlet is* set in Denmark.

- Use the present tense to refer to authors no longer living when you are discussing their works.

  ▶ Borges frequently *employs* magical realism in his fiction.

Voice.   A verb is in the **active voice** when the subject of the clause or sentence performs the action of the verb.

▶ The diplomats *have arrived*.
▶ He *plays* soccer professionally.

A verb is in the **passive voice** when the subject of a clause or sentence is the receiver of the action that the verb describes. Passive verbs are formed using a form of *be* and the past participle of a verb.

▶ The child *was* badly *bitten* by mosquitoes.
▶ Her car *was stolen*.

Since the passive voice may make it difficult for your readers to understand who is performing the action of a sentence, in most writing situations, use the active voice. If you do not know who performed an action, however, or if you want to emphasize the receiver of the action, consider using the passive voice.

Passive Voice	The evidence had been carefully removed by the defendant.
Active Voice	The defendant had carefully removed the evidence.

Mood.   The **mood** of a verb indicates whether it states a fact or asks a question (**indicative**); gives a command or direction (**imperative**); or expresses a condition, wish, or suggestion (**subjunctive**). The subjunctive mood is also used for hypothetical situations or impossible or unlikely events.

Indicative	Redwood trees can pull moisture from the air.
Imperative	Read the play and write an analysis of it.
Subjunctive	It would be nice to win the lottery.

The subjunctive mood, often used in clauses that begin with *if* or *that*, expresses a wish, suggestion, or condition contrary to fact. Use the base form of the verb for the present subjunctive. For the verb *be*, the past tense subjunctive is *were*, not *was*.

▶ I suggested that she *walk* to the station.

▶ The new student in my morning class wished that he *were* more outgoing.

1d Adjectives

Adjectives modify a noun or pronoun by describing it, limiting it, or giving more information about it. They answer the following questions.

Which one?   The *cutest* puppy belongs to the neighbors.

What kind?   Use only *academic* sources for the paper.

How many?   *Several hundred* protesters gathered at City Hall.

There are three types of adjectives: descriptive, limiting, and proper. **Descriptive adjectives** name a quality of the person, place, thing, or idea that they describe.

   yellow backpack   *pretty* face   *disturbing* event

Limiting adjectives narrow the scope of the person, place, or thing they describe.

   my laptop   *second* building   *that* notebook

Proper adjectives are derived from proper nouns. They are always capitalized.

   Japanese culture   *Elizabethan* England   *Scandinavian* mythology

The articles *a, an,* and *the* appear immediately before nouns and are considered adjectives. *The* refers to a specific item, while *a* and *an* do not. *A* is used before words that begin with consonant sounds. *An* is used before words that begin with vowel sounds.

▶ *The* person behind us laughed.

   The refers to a specific person.

▶ *An* answer will be forthcoming.

   Some answer will be provided.

The can also be used to refer to a group or class of items.

▶ *The* cat is *a* playful animal.

For more on the use of adjectives, see Section 9 of the Handbook. For more on articles, see Section 26 of the Handbook.

1e Adverbs

Adverbs modify verbs, adjectives, other adverbs, entire sentences, or clauses by describing, qualifying, or limiting the meaning of the words they modify. They answer the following questions.

How?	Andrea Bocelli performed *brilliantly*.
When?	*Later*, they met to discuss the proposal.
Where?	The taxi driver headed *downtown*.
How often?	The bobcat is *rarely* seen in the wild.
To what extent?	He agreed to cooperate *fully* with the investigation.

Most adverbs end in -ly:

particularly   beautifully   secretly

Note that not all words ending in -ly are adverbs; some are adjectives (*scholarly*, *unfriendly*). Common adverbs that do not end in -ly include *almost*, *never*, *quite*, *soon*, *then*, *there*, *too*, and *very*. Some words can function as either adjectives or adverbs depending on their use in the sentence.

Adjective	The flu victims were finally *well*.
Adverb	His paper was *well* written.

Adverbs that modify adjectives or other adverbs appear next to the word they modify.

▶ Tired sloths move *especially* slowly.

▶ A pregnant woman may feel *extremely* tired.

Adverbs that modify verbs can appear in several different positions, however.

▶ He *carefully* put the toys together.
▶ He put the toys together *carefully*.

For more on the use of adverbs, see Section 9 of the Handbook.

1f Conjunctions

Conjunctions connect words, phrases, or clauses. **Coordinating conjunctions** connect words or word groups of equal importance. There are seven coordinating conjunctions: *and, but, for, nor, or, so,* and *yet.*

▶ He attended the inauguration *but* looked unhappy.

Coordinating conjunctions must connect words, phrases, or clauses of the same kind. For example, *and* may connect two nouns, but it cannot connect a noun and a clause.

Nouns	Books by *Russell Simmons* and *Glenn Beck* were on the recommended reading list.
Phrases	We searched *in the closets* and *under the beds*.
Clauses	*Custer graduated last in his West Point class*, but *he distinguished himself in the Civil War.*

Conjunctions that are used in pairs are called **correlative conjunctions**: *as . . . as, both . . . and, either . . . or, just as . . . so, neither . . . nor, not . . . but, not only . . . but also,* and *whether . . . or.*

▶ *Neither* the strikers *nor* the management was satisfied with the compromise.

Subordinating conjunctions connect **dependent clauses** to **independent clauses**. They connect ideas of unequal importance. Often used at the beginning of a dependent clause, subordinating conjunctions indicate how a less important idea (expressed in a dependent clause) relates to a more important idea (expressed in an independent clause). Here is a list of common subordinating conjunctions and the relationships they express.

> A **dependent clause** contains a subject and a verb but does not express a complete thought.
>
> An **independent clause** contains a subject and a verb and can stand alone as a sentence.

Subordinating Conjunctions

Time
after, before, until, when, while
▶ *While* the sky was still dark, the army prepared for battle.

Cause or effect
because, since, so that
▶ *Since* he doesn't like math, he should avoid calculus.

Condition
even if, if, unless, whether
▶ We don't do volunteer work *unless* it is for a good cause.

Circumstance
as, as far as, as if, as soon as, as though, even if, even though, in order to
▶ In-line skating is a popular sport, *even though* it is somewhat dangerous.

Conjunctive adverbs link sentence parts that are of equal importance; they also serve as modifiers. Conjunctive adverbs show the following relationships between the elements they connect.

Conjunctive Adverbs

Time
afterward, finally, later, meanwhile, next, subsequently, then
▶ The candidates campaigned for months; *finally*, a primary election was held.

Example
for example, for instance, to illustrate
▶ Some members of the party—*for example*, the governor—supported another candidate.

Continuation or addition
also, furthermore, in addition, in the first place, moreover
▶ He is poorly organized; *in addition*, his arguments are not logical.

Cause or effect
accordingly, as a result, consequently, hence, therefore, thus, unfortunately
▶ *As a result*, he may convince few voters.

Differences or contrast
however, nevertheless, on the contrary, on the other hand, otherwise
▶ *Nevertheless*, he has support from some groups.

Emphasis	in fact, in other words, that is, undoubtedly
	▶ *In fact*, some politicians are tired of constantly needing to raise money for campaigns.
Similarities or comparison	conversely, in contrast, likewise, similarly
	▶ *In contrast*, their opponents have received many large donations.

1g Prepositions

A **preposition** is a word or phrase that links and relates a noun or a pronoun (the object of the preposition) to the rest of the sentence. A **prepositional phrase** includes the preposition along with its object and modifiers. Prepositions often show relationships of time, place, direction, or manner.

▶ Steve Prefontaine could run *despite* excruciating pain.
▶ The continental shelf lies *beneath* the ocean.

Common Prepositions

about	below	except	outside	under
against	beneath	for	over	underneath
along	beside	from	past	unlike
among	between	in	since	until
around	beyond	near	through	up
as	by	off	throughout	upon
at	despite	on	till	with
before	down	onto	to	within
behind	during	out	toward	without

Compound prepositions consist of more than one word.

▶ *According to* historical records, the town is three hundred years old.
▶ The department gained its reputation *by means of* its diversity.

Common Compound Prepositions

according to	because of	in place of	out of
along with	by means of	in regard to	up to
aside from	except for	in spite of	with regard to
as of	in addition to	instead of	with respect to
as well as	in front of	on account of	

1h Interjections

Interjections are words that express surprise or some other strong feeling. An exclamation point or a period often follows an interjection; a comma may precede or follow an interjection if it is a mild one.

▶ *Oh,* it wasn't important.
▶ *Ouch!*
▶ There were no fires reported last month, *by the way.*

2 ▸ Sentence Structure

2a Sentence parts

A **sentence** is a group of words that expresses a complete thought about something or someone. Every sentence must contain two basic parts: a subject and a predicate.

Subjects.   The **subject** of a sentence names a person, place, or thing and tells whom or what the sentence is about. It identifies the performer or receiver of the action expressed in the predicate.

▶ *Lady Gaga,* the flamboyant performer, has made savvy decisions about her career.
▶ The *clock* on the mantel was given to her by her grandmother.

The noun or pronoun that names what the sentence is about is called the **simple subject**.

▶ *Mozart* began composing at the age of four.
▶ The postal *worker* was bitten by a dog.

The simple subject of an imperative sentence is understood as *you,* but *you* is not stated directly.

▶ Be quiet.

   The sentence is understood as *[You] be quiet.*

The **complete subject** is the simple subject plus its modifiers—words that describe, identify, qualify, or limit the meaning of a noun or pronoun.

  ┌── complete subject ──┐
▶ A series of very bad *decisions* doomed the project.
  ┌──── complete subject ────┐
▶ There are too many *books* to fit on the shelves.

A sentence with a **compound subject** contains two or more simple subjects joined by a coordinating conjunction (*and, but, for, nor, or, so,* or *yet*).

▶ *Joel* <u>and</u> *Ethan Coen* produce and direct their films.
▶ *A doctor* <u>or</u> *a physician's assistant* will explain the results.

Predicates.   The **predicate** of a sentence indicates what the subject does, what happens to the subject, or what is said about the subject. The predicate, then, can indicate an action or a state of being.

| **Action** | Plant respiration *produces* oxygen. |
| **State of Being** | Stonehenge *has existed* for many centuries. |

The **simple predicate** is the main verb along with its helping verbs.

A **helping verb** (also called an **auxiliary verb**) combines with a main verb to indicate tense, mood, or voice or to add further information.

- ▶ Reporters *should call* the subjects of their stories for comment.
- ▶ A snow bicycle for Antarctic workers *has been developed*.

The **complete predicate** consists of the simple predicate plus its modifiers and any objects or complements.

A **complement** is a word or group of words that describes or renames a subject or an object.

    ┌──────── complete predicate ────────┐
- ▶ The growth of Los Angeles *depended* to a large extent on finding a way to get

    ┌──────────┐
    water to the desert.

    ┌──────── complete predicate ────────┐
- ▶ Watching fishing boats *is a relaxing and pleasant way to spend an afternoon*.

A **compound predicate** contains two or more predicates that have the same subject and that are joined by *and*, *but*, *or*, *nor*, or another conjunction (see 1f).

- ▶ AIDS drugs *can save many lives* <u>but</u> *are seldom available in poor countries that need them desperately*.
- ▶ President Johnson <u>neither</u> *wanted to run for a second term* <u>nor</u> *planned to serve if elected*.

Objects.   A **direct object** is a noun or pronoun that receives the action of a verb. A direct object answers the question, What? or Whom?

- ▶ The Scottish fiddler played a lively *reel*.

    The noun *reel* answers the question, What did he play?

- ▶ The crowd in the stadium jeered the *quarterback*.

    The noun *quarterback* answers the question, Whom did they jeer?

An **indirect object** is a noun or pronoun that names the person or thing to whom or for whom something is done.

- ▶ Habitat for Humanity gave *him* an award for his work.
- ▶ A woman on a bench tossed the *pigeons* some crumbs.

Complements.   A **complement** is a word or group of words that describes a subject or object and completes the meaning of the sentence. There are two kinds of complements: subject complements and object complements.

    A **linking verb** (such as *be*, *become*, *feel*, *seem*, or *taste*) connects the subject of a sentence to a **subject complement**, a noun, a noun phrase, or an adjective that renames or describes the subject.

- ▶ Michael Jackson was a *much-loved performer*.

▶ She was *too disorganized to finish her science project.*

An **object complement** is a noun, a noun phrase, or an adjective that modifies or renames the **direct object**. Object complements appear with transitive verbs (such as *name, find, make, think, elect, appoint, choose,* and *consider*), which express action directed toward something or someone.

A **direct object** receives the action of the verb: *He drove me home.*

▶ The council appointed him *its new vice president.*
▶ The undercooked meat made several children *sick.*

2b Phrases

A **phrase** is a group of related words that lacks a subject, a predicate, or both. A phrase cannot stand alone as a sentence. Phrases can appear at the beginning, middle, or end of a sentence and can help make your writing more detailed and interesting.

Without Phrases	The burglars escaped.
	Bus travel is an inexpensive choice.
With Phrases	Startled by the alarm, the burglars escaped without getting any money.
	For adventurers on a budget, bus travel, while not luxurious, is an inexpensive choice.

There are four common types of phrases: prepositional phrases, verbal phrases, appositive phrases, and absolute phrases.

Prepositional phrases. A **prepositional phrase** consists of a preposition (*in, above, with, at, behind*), the object of the preposition (a noun or pronoun), and any modifiers of the object. Prepositional phrases usually function as adjectives or adverbs to tell more about people, places, objects, or actions. They can also function as nouns. A prepositional phrase generally adds information about time, place, direction, or manner.

Adjective Phrase	The plants *on the edge of the field* are weeds.
	On the edge and *of the field* tell *where.*
Adverb Phrase	New Orleans is very crowded *during Mardi Gras.*
	During Mardi Gras tells *when.*
Noun Phrase	*Down the hill* is the shortest way to town.
	Down the hill acts as the subject of the sentence.

Each of the following sentences has been edited to include a prepositional phrase or phrases that expand the meaning of the sentence by adding detail.

▶ He fell *on the icy sidewalk.*
▶ The ship suddenly appeared *through the mist near the shore.*

Verbal phrases. A **verbal** is a verb form used as a noun (the *barking* of the dog), an adjective (a *barking* dog), or an adverb (continued *to bark*). It cannot be used alone as the verb of a sentence, however. The three kinds of verbals are participles, gerunds, and infinitives. A **verbal phrase** consists of a verbal and its modifiers.

Participles and participial phrase.　All verbs have two participles: present and past. The **present participle** is the -ing form of a verb (*being, hoping, studying*). The **past participle** of most verbs ends in -d or -ed (*hoped, consisted*). The past participle of irregular verbs has no set pattern (*been, ridden*). Both the present participle and the past participle can function as adjectives modifying nouns and pronouns.

▶ The planes flew over the foggy airport in a *holding* pattern.

▶ The pot was made of *molded* clay.

A **participial phrase**, which consists of a participle and its modifiers, can also function as an adjective in a sentence.

▶ The suspect, *wanted for questioning* on robbery charges, had vanished.

Gerunds and gerund phrase.　A **gerund** is the present participle, or -ing form, of a verb that functions as a noun in a sentence.

▶ *Driving* can be a frustrating activity.
▶ The government has not done enough to build *housing*.

A **gerund phrase** consists of a gerund and its modifiers. Like a gerund, a gerund phrase is used as a noun and can therefore function in a sentence as a subject, a direct object, an indirect object, an object of a preposition, or a subject complement.

Subject	*Catching the flu* is unpleasant.
Direct Object	All the new recruits practiced *marching*.
Indirect Object	One director gave his *acting* a chance.
Object of a Preposition	An ambitious employee may rise by *impressing* her boss.
Subject Complement	The biggest thrill was the *skydiving*.

Infinitives and infinitive phrases.　An **infinitive** is the base form of a verb preceded by *to*: *to study, to sleep*. An **infinitive phrase** consists of the infinitive plus any modifiers or objects. An infinitive phrase can function as a noun, an adjective, or an adverb.

Subject	*To become* an actor is my greatest ambition.
Adjective	She had a job *to do*.
Adverb	The weary travelers were eager *to sleep*.

Sometimes the *to* in an infinitive phrase is understood but not written.

▶ Her demonstration helped me learn the software.

Note: Be sure to distinguish between infinitive phrases and prepositional phrases beginning with the preposition *to*. In an infinitive phrase, *to* is followed by a verb (*to paint*); in a prepositional phrase, *to* is followed by a noun or pronoun (*to a movie*).

Appositive phrases. An **appositive** is a word that explains, restates, or adds new information about a noun. An **appositive phrase** consists of an appositive and its modifiers.

▶ Ben Affleck, *a famous actor,* is very active in trying to improve conditions in the Congo.

The appositive phrase adds information about the noun *Ben Affleck.*

Absolute phrases. An **absolute phrase** consists of a noun or pronoun and any modifiers, usually followed by a participle. An absolute phrase modifies an entire sentence, not any particular word or words within the sentence. It can appear anywhere in a sentence and is set off from the rest of the sentence with commas.

▶ *Their shift completed,* the night workers walked out at sunrise.
▶ *An unsuspecting insect clamped in its mandible,* the praying mantis, *its legs folded piously,* appears serenely uninvolved.

2c Clauses

A **clause** is a group of words that contains a subject and a predicate. A clause is either independent (also called *main*) or dependent (also called *subordinate*). An **independent clause** can stand alone as a grammatically complete sentence.

▶ Einstein was a clerk at the Swiss Patent Office.
▶ Ethnic disputes followed the disintegration of Yugoslavia.

A **dependent clause** has a subject and a predicate, but it cannot stand alone as a grammatically complete sentence because it does not express a complete thought. A dependent clause usually begins with either a subordinating conjunction or a relative pronoun that connects it to an independent clause.

Common Subordinating Conjunctions

after	in as much as	that
although	in case that	though
as	in order that	unless
as far as	in so far as	until
as if	in that	when
as soon as	now that	whenever
as though	once	where
because	provided that	wherever
before	rather than	whether
even if	since	while
even though	so that	why
how	supposing that	
if	than	

Relative Pronouns

that	whatever	who (whose, whom)
what	which	whoever (whomever)

┌──── dependent clause ────┐
▶ *When the puppies were born*, the breeder examined them carefully.

            dependent
┌   clause ┐
▶ Van Gogh's paintings began to command high prices *after he died*.

┌──── dependent clause ────┐
▶ Isadora Duncan, *who personified modern dance*, died in a bizarre accident.

When joined to independent clauses, dependent clauses can function as adjectives, adverbs, or nouns and are known as **adjective clauses** (also called **relative clauses**), **adverb clauses**, or **noun clauses**. A noun clause can function as a subject, an object, or a complement.

┌──── adjective clause ────┐
▶ Graphic novels, *which were once considered "kid stuff,"* are now taken seriously.

┌──── adverb clause ────┐
▶ The whistle blew *as the train approached the crossing*.

┌── noun clause ──┐
▶ The starving artist ate *whatever he could get*.

Relative pronouns are generally the subject or object in their clauses. *Who* and *whoever* change to *whom* and *whomever* when they function as objects. Sometimes the relative pronoun or subordinating conjunction is implied or understood rather than stated.

▶ African rituals are among the subjects [that] the essay discusses.

    That is the understood relative pronoun in the subordinate clause.

A dependent clause may contain an implied predicate. When a dependent clause is missing an element that can be inferred from the context of the sentence, it is called an **elliptical clause**.

▶ The shooting of former Congresswoman Gabrielle Giffords disturbed
┌── elliptical clause ──┐
Americans *more than gang shootings*.

    The predicate *disturbed them* is implied.

2d Types of Sentences

A sentence can be classified as one of four basic types: simple, compound, complex, or compound-complex.

Simple sentences. A **simple sentence** has one main or **independent clause** and no subordinate or **dependent clauses**. A simple sentence contains at least one subject and one predicate. It may have a compound subject, a compound predicate, and various phrases, but it has only one clause.

An **independent clause** contains a subject and a verb and can stand alone as a sentence.

A **dependent clause** contains a subject and a verb but does not express a complete thought.

▶ She sprints.
▶ She and her teammates sprint.
▶ She and her teammates sprint and run laps.
▶ She and her teammates in the track-and-field events sprint and run laps to achieve their goal of winning medals.

Compound sentences. A **compound sentence** consists of two or more independent clauses and no dependent clauses. The two independent clauses are usually joined with a comma and a coordinating conjunction (*and, but, for, nor, or, so,* or *yet*).

▶ She runs laps, but her teammates practice throwing the javelin.

Sometimes two clauses are joined with a semicolon and no coordinating conjunction.

▶ She runs laps; her teammates practice throwing the javelin.

Or they may be joined with a semicolon and a conjunctive adverb (such as *nonetheless* or *still*), followed by a comma.

▶ She runs laps; however, her teammates practice throwing the javelin.

Complex sentences. A **complex sentence** has one independent clause and one or more dependent clauses. The dependent clauses usually begin with a subordinating conjunction or a relative pronoun (see 2c for a list).

▶ They are training *while he recovers from a sprained ankle.*
▶ Runners *who win their event at more than one local track meet* will be eligible for the district trials.

Compound-complex sentences. A **compound-complex sentence** contains two or more independent clauses and one or more dependent clauses.

▶ She and her teammates won the meet, and as they were celebrating, a reporter approached them for an interview.
▶ A reporter approached them while they were celebrating their victory, and after they doused him with champagne, they answered his questions.

Write Grammatically Correct Sentences

3 Sentence Fragments

A **sentence fragment** is a group of words that cannot stand alone as a complete sentence. A fragment is often missing a subject, a complete verb, or both.

Fragment Are hatched in sand.

This group of words does not tell *who* or *what* are hatched in sand. It lacks a subject.

A **sentence** is a group of words that must include at least one independent clause (a subject and a verb that express a complete thought).

Fragment   Especially his rebounding ability.

> This group of words has a subject, *his rebounding ability*, but lacks a verb.

Fragment   To notice a friendly smile.

> This group of words lacks both a subject and a verb. *To notice* is not a complete verb. It is an infinitive.

A group of words can have both a subject and a verb but still be a fragment because it does not express a complete thought.

subject   verb

Fragment   Because the *number* of voters *has* declined.

> This group of words does not tell what happened as a result of the voter decline. Its meaning is incomplete.

Notice that the preceding fragment begins with the subordinating conjunction *because*. A clause that begins with a subordinating conjunction cannot stand alone as a complete sentence.

For a list of common subordinating conjunctions, see 2c.

Word groups that begin with a relative pronoun (*that, which, who*) are also not complete sentences.

subject verb

Fragment   Which *scientists studied* for many years.

> The group of words does not tell *what* the scientists studied.

Finally, when a word group begins with a transitional word or phrase (*for example, also*), make sure that it includes both a subject and a verb.

subject

Fragment   For example, *the Gulf Coast of Florida.*

Use the flowchart on page 727 to help you decide whether a particular word group is a complete sentence or a sentence fragment. Also try reading your essays backward from the end to the beginning, sentence by sentence, to check for fragments. This method allows you to evaluate each sentence in isolation, without being distracted by the flow of ideas throughout the essay. You might also try turning each sentence into a *yes* or *no* question by adding a helping verb, such as *do, does,* or *did.* A complete sentence can be turned into a *yes* or *no* question, but a fragment cannot.

A **verbal** is a verb form used as a noun (*the barking of the dog*), an adjective (*a barking dog*), or an adverb (*continued to bark*).

An **independent clause** contains a subject and a verb and can stand alone as a sentence.

Sentence   Sociology has wide applications.

Yes/No Question   Does sociology have wide applications?

Fragment   While sociology has wide applications.

Yes/No Question   [Cannot be formed]

A sentence fragment can be revised in two general ways: (1) by attaching it to a nearby sentence or (2) by rewriting the fragment as a complete sentence. The method you choose depends on the element the fragment lacks as well as your intended meaning.

FIGURE 1   How to Identify a Fragment

QUESTIONS   REVISION STRATEGIES

1. Does the word group have a subject? (Note that the subject may be understood as *you*. Example: [*You*] *Close the door*.)   **NO** ▶   It is a fragment. Revise.

YES ▼

2. Does the word group have a complete verb? (Note that **verbals** are not complete verbs.)   **NO** ▶   It is a fragment. Revise.

YES ▼

3. Does the word group express a complete idea? If it begins with a subordinating word (*although, since, if*), a relative pronoun (*that, which, who*), or a transitional word or phrase (*for example, likewise, also*), does the word group contain an **independent clause**?   **NO** ▶   It is a fragment. Revise.

YES ▼

4. It is a sentence.

▶ ~~Are~~ hatched in sand.
    Certain turtle eggs are (above "Are")

▶ Jamal is a basketball player of many talents/, Especially his rebounding ability. (*e* above "E")

▶ ~~To~~ notice a friendly smile.
    Sam was too busy to (above "To")

▶ ~~Because the~~ number of voters has declined.
    The (above "Because the")

3a   Join a fragment lacking a subject to another sentence or rewrite it as a complete sentence.

Attach a fragment lacking a subject to a neighboring sentence if the two are about the same person, place, or thing.

▶ Jessica speaks Spanish fluently. ~~And~~ reads French well. (*and* above "And")

As an alternative, you can also add a subject to turn the fragment into a complete sentence.

▶ Jessica speaks Spanish fluently. ~~And~~ reads French well.
  (She also)

3b Add a helping verb to a fragment lacking a complete verb.

Make sure that every sentence you write contains a *complete* verb. For example, verb forms ending in -*ing* need helping verbs to make them complete. Helping verbs include forms of *do, be,* and *have* as well as such words as *will, can, could, shall, should, may, might,* and *must.* When you use an -*ing* verb form in a sentence without a helping verb, you create a fragment. To correct the fragment, add the helping verb.

▶ The college *is* installing a furnace to heat the library.

3c Join a fragment that lacks both a subject and a verb to another sentence, or add the missing subject and verb.

An **infinitive** is a verb form made up of *to* plus the base form (*to run, to see*).

Often, fragments lacking a subject and verb begin with an **infinitive** such as *to hope, to walk,* and *to play,* which are not complete verbs, or they begin with an -*ed* or -*ing* form of a verb. Revise a fragment that begins with an infinitive or an -*ed* or -*ing* verb form by combining it with a previous sentence.

▶ I plan to transfer next semester. ~~To~~ live closer to home.
  (to)

▶ Robert E. Lee and Ulysses S. Grant met on April 9, 1865. ~~Bringing~~ an end to the Civil War.
  (bringing)

You can also revise a fragment beginning with an infinitive or an -*ed* or -*ing* verb form by adding both a subject and a verb to make it a complete sentence.

▶ Linda was reluctant to go out alone at night. ~~To~~ walk across campus from the library.
  (She was unwilling to)

▶ Kyle was determined to do well on his math exam. ~~Studied~~ during every available hour.
  (He studied)

Watch out for fragments that begin with a transitional word or phrase. They can usually be corrected by joining them to a previous sentence.

▶ Annie has always wanted to become an orthopedist. ~~That~~ is, a bone specialist.
  (—that)

3d Join a fragment beginning with a subordinating word to another sentence, or drop the subordinating word.

You can correct a fragment beginning with a subordinating word by joining it to the sentence before or after it.

▶ The students stared spellbound. ~~While~~ the professor lectured.
  (while)

▶ Until Dr. Jonas Salk invented a vaccine, ~~Polio~~ was a serious threat to public health.
  (polio)

As an alternative, you can revise this type of fragment by dropping the subordinating word.

> The
> ~~Because the~~ 800 area code for toll-free dialing is overused. New codes—888
> and 877—have been added.

3e Join a fragment beginning with a relative pronoun such as *who* or *whom* to another sentence, or rewrite it as a complete sentence.

Another common type of sentence fragment begins with a relative pronoun. **Relative pronouns** include *who, whom, whose, whoever, whomever, what, whatever, which,* and *that.*

> whose
> My contemporary fiction instructor assigned a novel by Stephen King/~~Whose~~ work I admire.

> It
> The dodo is an extinct bird. ~~That~~ disappeared in the seventeenth century.

Professional writers sometimes use sentence fragments intentionally to achieve special effects, particularly in works of fiction or articles written for popular magazines. An *intentional* fragment may be used to emphasize a point, answer a question, recreate a conversation, or make an exclamation. However, you should avoid using intentional fragments in academic writing. Instructors and other readers may find the fragments distracting or too informal, or they may assume you used a fragment in error.

EXERCISE 3.1

Correct any fragments in the following sentences. Some groups of sentences may be correct as written.

> , especially
> More people are going to college every year. ~~Especially~~ young women.

1. In the past, higher education was only accessible to a small number of people. However, access to higher education has expanded over the last 200 years.
2. In the United States, for example. Colleges and universities provide education to Americans of all classes and backgrounds.
3. At first, state universities were publicly funded schools. That trained students in fields such as engineering, education, and agriculture.
4. During the nineteenth and early twentieth centuries. Graduates of state universities played a key role in America's development as an industrial and economic power.
5. The number of students in college. Increased greatly in the years after World War II.
6. Because federal funding from the 1944 GI Bill made it possible. Millions of returning veterans attended colleges.
7. Many people credit this program with helping to create a strong middle class. In the United States during the 1950s and 1960s.
8. Now, about two-thirds of high school graduates will attend college. Because, on average, those with bachelor's degrees earn over $20,000 more a year than people with only high school diplomas do.
9. Most people agree that America needs an educated workforce to compete globally.
10. However, as education costs continue to rise. Some wonder whether a traditional four-year college is always worth the expense.

> **EXERCISE 3.2**

Rewrite the following passage as needed to eliminate sentence fragments.

▶ How much and what kind of intervention should be undertaken/~~On~~ behalf of
  endangered species? ^{on}

    Gila trout are endangered in some stretches of water. That are managed as
designated wilderness. A hands-off policy would be their doom. Because exotic
trout species now swim in the same streams. Gila trout can survive the competition and the temptation to interbreed only if they swim in isolated tributaries. In
which a waterfall blocks the upstream movement of other fish. Two decades ago,
one such tributary was fortified. With a small concrete dam. In other words, a dam
deliberately built in the wilderness. It is often difficult to choose the right way. To
manage a wilderness area. A scientific grasp of the way the ecosystem works is
essential. Yet not always available.

4   Run-on Sentences and Comma Splices

A **run-on sentence** occurs when two or more independent clauses are joined without a
punctuation mark or a coordinating conjunction. Run-on sentences are also known as
fused sentences.

                          ━━━━━ independent clause ━━━━━   ━━━ independent

Run-on   A television addict is dependent on television I have suffered this

Sentence   clause ━━━━━

               addiction for years.

A **comma splice** occurs when two or more independent clauses are joined with a
comma but without a coordinating conjunction (such as *and, or,* or *but*).

                          ━━━━━ independent clause ━━━━━   ━━━ independent

Comma   A typical magic act includes tricks and illusions, both depend on

Splice   clause ━━━

               deception.

               Notice that only a comma separates the two independent clauses, caus-
               ing the comma splice.

Another type of comma splice occurs when a word other than a coordinating conjunction is used with a comma to join two or more independent clauses.

                          ━━━━━ independent clause ━━━━━

Comma   A typical magic act includes tricks and illusions, however, both

Splice   independent clause ━━━

               depend on deception.

    In the preceding sentence, *however* is a conjunctive adverb, not a coordinating con-
junction. There are only seven coordinating conjunctions: *and, but, for, nor, or, so,* and *yet*.

Recognizing Run-on Sentences and Comma Splices

Many students have difficulty spotting run-on sentences and comma splices in their own writing. Use the flowchart below to help you identify these types of errors in your sentences.

FIGURE 2   How to Identify a Run-on Sentence or Comma Splice

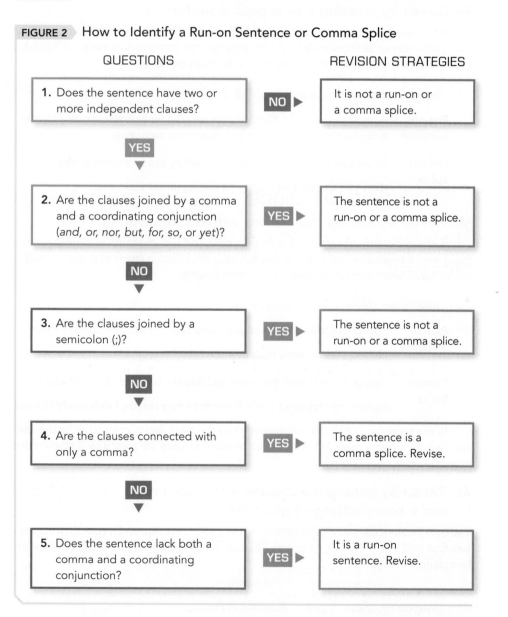

QUESTIONS   REVISION STRATEGIES

1. Does the sentence have two or more independent clauses? — **NO** ▶ It is not a run-on or a comma splice.

YES ▼

2. Are the clauses joined by a comma and a coordinating conjunction (*and, or, nor, but, for, so,* or *yet*)? — **YES** ▶ The sentence is not a run-on or a comma splice.

NO ▼

3. Are the clauses joined by a semicolon (;)? — **YES** ▶ The sentence is not a run-on or a comma splice.

NO ▼

4. Are the clauses connected with only a comma? — **YES** ▶ The sentence is a comma splice. Revise.

NO ▼

5. Does the sentence lack both a comma and a coordinating conjunction? — **YES** ▶ It is a run-on sentence. Revise.

Correcting Run-on Sentences and Comma Splices

There are four basic ways to correct a run-on sentence or comma splice. Choose the method that best fits your sentence or intended meaning.

4a Revise by creating two separate sentences.

Correct a run-on sentence or comma splice by creating two separate sentences. Make sure each independent clause has the appropriate end punctuation mark—a period, a question mark, or (on rare occasions) an exclamation mark.

period　　　　　　　　period
Independent clause ! *Independent clause* !

Run-on Sentence A résumé should be directed to a specific audience. ^It^ should emphasize the applicant's potential value to the company.

Comma Splice To evaluate a charity, you should start by examining its goals^./^ ^T^then you should investigate its management practices.

4b Revise by joining the clauses with a semicolon (;).

When the independent clauses are closely connected in meaning, consider joining them with a semicolon. Note that a coordinating conjunction (such as *and, or,* or *but*) is *not* included when you revise with a semicolon (see 4c).

semicolon
Independent clause **;** *Independent clause.*

Run-on Sentence Specialty products are unique items that consumers take time purchasing ^;^these items include cars, parachutes, and skis.

Comma Splice Studies have shown that male and female managers have different leadership styles ^;/^as a result, workers may respond differently to each.

In the second example, the semicolon joins the two clauses connected by the conjunctive adverb *as a result.* When two independent clauses are joined by a conjunctive adverb, a semicolon is needed.

4c Revise by joining the clauses with a comma and a coordinating conjunction.

Two independent clauses can be joined by using *both* a comma and a coordinating conjunction (*and, but, for, nor, or, so,* or *yet*). The coordinating conjunction indicates how the two clauses are related.

comma + coordinating conjunction
↓
Independent clause , *and* *independent clause.*

Run-on Sentence	Closed-minded people often refuse to recognize opposing views~$\land$~*and* they reject ideas without evaluating them.
Comma Splice	Some educators support home schooling,~$\land$~*but* others oppose it vehemently.

4d Revise by making one clause dependent or by turning one clause into a phrase.

A **dependent clause** contains a subject and a verb but does not express a complete thought. It must always be linked to an independent clause. You can correct a run-on sentence or a comma splice by adding a **subordinating conjunction** (such as *because* or *although*) to one of the independent clauses, thereby making it a dependent clause. The subordinating conjunction makes the thought incomplete and dependent on the independent clause.

subordinating conjunction
↓

Because   *dependent clause,*   *independent clause*.

or

subordinating conjunction
↓

Independent clause   *because*   *dependent clause*.

Run-on Sentence	Facial expressions are very revealing they are an important communication tool.
Independent Clause	Facial expressions are very revealing.
Dependent Clause	*Because* facial expressions are very revealing
Joined to Independent Clause	Because facial expressions are very revealing, they are an important communication tool.

You can also correct a run-on sentence or a comma splice by changing one of the independent clauses to a phrase.

Phrase,   *independent clause.*

or

Independent clause,   *phrase*.

or

Beginning of independent clause,   *phrase,*   *end of independent clause*.

Comma Splice	Medieval peasants in Europe ate a simple, hearty diet, they relied almost totally on agriculture.

Independent Clause	Medieval peasants in Europe ate a simple, hearty diet.
Clause Reduced to Phrase	having a simple, hearty diet
Embedded in Independent Clause	Medieval peasants in Europe—having a simple, hearty diet—relied almost totally on agriculture.

Note: A comma or commas may or may not be needed to separate a phrase from the rest of the sentence, depending on how the phrase affects the meaning of the sentence (see 12e). Here are two more examples that show how to revise run-on sentences and comma splices using subordination.

Run-on Sentence	Distributors open big-budget movies late in the week, ~~they hope~~ hoping moviegoers will flock to theaters over the weekend.
Comma Splice	Although the ~~The~~ remote fishing lodge has no heat or electricity, ~~nevertheless~~ it is a popular vacation spot.

EXERCISE 4.1

Correct any run-ons or comma splices in the following sentences.

▶ A deadly nerve poison is found on the skin of some Amazon tree frogs; native tribes use the poison on the tips of their arrows when they hunt.

1. Nearly every American child dreams of going to Disney World, it has become one of the most popular family vacation destinations.
2. Shopping through online bookstores is convenient, some people miss the atmosphere of a traditional bookstore.
3. Openness is one way to build trust in a relationship another is to demonstrate tolerance and patience.
4. In the 1960s some Americans treated Vietnam veterans disrespectfully this situation has changed dramatically since that time.
5. William Faulkner wrote classic novels about life in the U.S. South, Eudora Welty has also written vividly about southern life.
6. With large bodies and tiny wings, bumblebees have long been a puzzle, how do they fly?
7. The Taj Mahal is aptly called the Pearl Mosque it glows in the moonlight with unearthly beauty.
8. The Supreme Court often makes controversial decisions, the justices must decide how to interpret the Constitution.
9. Although the clouds were threatening, the storm had not yet struck, however, most boats turned toward shore.
10. Restoring a painting is, indeed, delicate work too much enthusiasm can be dangerous.

Correct any run-on sentences and comma splices in the following paragraph. Some sentences may be correct as written.

▶ Some people believe dreams are revealing, ^but^ others think the brain is simply unloading excess information.

Throughout recorded history, people have been fascinated by dreams, they have wondered what meaning dreams hold. Whether the dreams are ominous or beautiful, people have always wanted to understand them. There are many ancient stories about dream interpretation one of these is the biblical story of Daniel. Daniel is able to interpret a ruler's dream, this power to interpret convinces the ruler that Daniel is a prophet. Other early writers considered the topic of dream interpretation, to Latin writers, some dreams were meaningful and some were not. Meaningful dreams could reveal the future, these writers argued, but other dreams were simply the result of eating or drinking too much. Sigmund Freud, the founder of psychoanalysis, dramatically changed the field of dream interpretation he believed that dreams come from the subconscious. According to Freud, ideas too frightening for the waking mind often appear in dreams, patients in Freudian therapy often discuss dream images. Today, not everyone agrees with Freud, scientists trying to understand the brain still pay attention to dreams. They are certain that dreams reflect modern life more and more people today dream about computers.

5 Subject-Verb Agreement

Subjects and verbs must agree in person and number. **Person** refers to the forms I or *we* (first person), *you* (second person), and *he, she, it,* and *they* (third person). **Number** shows whether a word refers to one thing (singular) or more than one thing (plural). In a sentence, subjects and verbs need to be consistent in person and number: *I drive, you drive, she drives.*

Subject-verb agreement errors often occur in complicated sentences, in sentences with compound subjects, or in sentences where the subject and verb are separated by other words or phrases. The following sections will help you look for and revise common errors in subject-verb agreement.

5a Make sure the verb agrees with the subject, not with words that come between the subject and verb.

▶ The *number* of farm workers *has* remained constant over several decades.

The subject *number* is singular and requires a singular verb, even though the words *of farm workers* appear between the subject and verb.

5b Use a plural verb when two or more subjects are joined by *and*.

▸ A dot and a dash represents the letter A in Morse code.

▸ Basketball star Shaquille O'Neal, comedian D. L. Hughley, and actor Tom
Arnold ~~was~~ were all born on March 6.

5c Revise to make the verb agree with the subject closest to it when two or more subjects are joined by *or, either . . . or,* or *neither . . . nor*.

When two or more singular subjects are joined by *or, either…or,* or *neither…nor,* use a singular verb.

▸ *Math* or *accounting appears* to be a suitable major for you.
▸ Either the *waiter* or the *customer has* misplaced the bill.
▸ Neither the *doctor* nor the *patient is* pessimistic about the prognosis.

When one singular and one plural subject are joined by *or, either…or,* or *neither…nor,* the verb should agree in number with the subject nearest to it.

▸ Neither the *sailors* nor the *boat was* harmed by the storm.

▸ Neither the *boat* nor the *sailors were* harmed by the storm.

▸ Either my daughters or my wife waters that plant daily.

5d Use a singular verb with most collective nouns, such as *family, couple,* and *class*.

When a **collective noun** refers to a group as one unit acting together, use a singular verb. When the members of the group are acting as individuals, use a plural verb. To make their meaning clearer and avoid awkwardness, writers often add *members* or a similar noun.

▸ The school *committee has* voted to increase teachers' salaries.

   The committee is acting as a unit.

▸ The family ~~are~~ is living in a cramped apartment.

▸ The *team members are* traveling by train, bus, and bike.

   The team members are acting individually.

▸ The members of the jury ~~is~~ are divided and unable to reach consensus.

5e Use a singular verb with most indefinite pronouns, such as *anyone, everyone, each, every, no one,* and *something.*

Indefinite pronouns do not refer to a specific person, place, or object. They refer to people, places, or things in general. Singular indefinite pronouns include the following: *each, either, neither, anyone, anybody, anything, everyone, everybody, everything, one, no one, nobody, nothing, someone, somebody, something.*

▶ *Everyone* in this room is welcome to express an opinion.

▶ Neither of the candidates ~~have~~ has run for office before.

Other indefinite pronouns, such as *several, both, many,* and *few,* take a plural verb.

▶ Every year *many succeed* in starting new small businesses.

▶ Several of you jog*s* at least three miles a day.

Some indefinite pronouns, such as *all, any, more, most, some,* and *none,* take either a singular or a plural verb depending on the noun they refer to. To decide which verb to use, follow this rule: Treat the indefinite pronoun as singular if it refers to something that cannot be counted and as plural if it refers to more than one of something that can be counted.

▶ Most of the water go*es* into this kettle.

You cannot count water.

▶ Some of the children in the study choose*s* immediate rather than delayed rewards.

You can count children.

5f Revise to make verbs agree with the antecedents of *who, which,* and *that.*

When a **relative pronoun** (*who, which, that*) refers to a singular noun, use a singular verb. When it refers to a plural noun, use a plural verb.

▶ Toni Morrison, *who enjoys* unique success as both a popular and a literary author, won the Nobel Prize in literature in 1993.

Who refers to Toni Morrison, and because *Toni Morrison* is singular, the verb *enjoys* is singular.

▶ Look for *stores that display* this sign.

That refers to *stores,* a plural noun.

Using *one of the* often leads to errors in subject-verb agreement. The phrase *one of the* plus a noun is plural.

▶ A pigeon is *one of the two birds that drink* by suction.

That refers to *birds,* and since *birds* is plural, the verb *drink* is plural.

However, *only one of the* plus a noun is singular: *The cheetah is the only one of the big cats that has nonretractable claws.*

An **antecedent** is the noun or pronoun to which a pronoun refers.

A **relative pronoun** introduces a dependent clause that functions as an adjective: *the patient who injured her leg.*

5g Revise to make the verb agree with a subject that follows it.

When a sentence begins with either *here* or *there* (which cannot function as a subject) or with a **prepositional phrase**, the subject often follows the verb. Look for the subject after the verb and make sure the subject and verb agree.

▶ There is a false *panel* somewhere in this room.

▶ Under the stairs lurks a solitary *spider.*

5h Make sure a linking verb agrees with its subject, not a word or phrase that renames the subject.

Linking verbs, such as forms of *be* and *feel, look,* and *taste,* connect a subject with a word or phrase that renames or describes it. In sentences with linking verbs, the verb should agree with the subject.

▶ The *bluebell* is any of several plants in the lily family.

▶ The *issue* discussed at the meeting *was* the low wages earned by factory workers.

5i Use a singular verb when the subject is a title.

▶ *Gulliver's Travels* ~~are~~ ᶦˢ a satire by the eighteenth-century British writer Jonathan Swift.

5j Use singular verbs with singular nouns that end in -s, such as *physics* and *news.*

▶ *Linguistics deals* with the study of human speech.

EXERCISE 5.1

Correct any subject-verb agreement errors in the following sentences. Some sentences may be correct as written.

▶ Most of the people in the world believes that learning a second language is important.

1. Many members of the international business community communicates by speaking English, the international language of business.
2. A student in most non-English-speaking industrialized nations expect to spend six or more years studying English.
3. The United States are different.
4. Working for laws that requires all Americans to speak English is a fairly common U.S. political tactic.

5. In American schools, often neither a teaching staff nor enough money have been available for good foreign-language programs.
6. Some linguists joke that a person who speaks two languages are called bilingual, while a person who speaks one language is called American.
7. Some states around the country has begun to change this situation.
8. If a class is given lessons in a foreign language, the students feel that they will be better prepared for the new global economy.
9. In a Spanish or French class, children of immigrants for whom English was a second language learns a new language and perhaps gains a new appreciation of their parents' accomplishments.
10. Everyone who study a foreign language are likely to benefit.

EXERCISE 5.2

Correct any sentences with subject-verb agreement errors in the following paragraph. Some sentences may be correct as written.

Everyone in the colder climates want to know whether the next winter will be severe. The National Weather Service, however, usually predict the weather only a short time in advance. Another method of making weather predictions are popular with many Americans. According to folklore, there is a number of signs to alert people to a hard winter ahead. Among these signs are the brown stripe on a woolly bear caterpillar. If the brown stripe between the caterpillar's two black stripes are wide, some people believe the winter will be a short one. Another of the signs that indicate a hard winter is a large apple harvest. And, of course, almost everyone in the United States have seen news stories on February 2 about groundhogs predicting the end of winter. Folk beliefs, which are not based on science, seems silly to many people. Neither the National Weather Service nor folklore are always able to forecast the weather accurately, however.

6 ▶ Verb Forms

Except for *be*, all English verbs have five forms.

Base Form	Past Tense	Past Participle	Present Participle	-s Form
move	moved	moved	moving	moves

▶ Many designers *visit* Milan for fashion shows each year.
▶ Sarah *visited* her best friend in Thailand.
▶ Students have *visited* the state capital every spring for decades.
▶ His cousin from Iowa is *visiting* this week.
▶ Maria *visits* her grandmother in Puerto Rico as often as possible.

6a Use -s or -es endings for present tense verbs that have third-person singular subjects.

The -s form is made up of the verb's base form plus -s or -es.

▶ Mr. King *teaches* English.

A third-person singular subject can consist of a singular noun, a singular pronoun (*he, she,* and *it*), or a singular indefinite pronoun (such as *everyone*).

Singular Noun	The flower opens.
Singular Pronoun	He opens the door.
Singular Indefinite Pronoun	Everybody knows the truth.

▶ She ~~want~~ to be a veterinarian.
     wants

▶ None of the townspeople ~~understand~~ him.
                      understands

6b Do not omit -ed endings on verbs.

For more on verb tense, see 1c and 27a.

For regular verbs, both the past tense and the past participle are formed by adding -*ed* or -*d* to the base form of the verb.

▶ She *claimed* to be the czar's daughter, Anastasia.
▶ The defendant *faced* his accusers.

Some speakers do not fully pronounce the -*ed* endings of verbs (*asked, fixed, supposed to, used to*). As a result, they may unintentionally omit these endings in their writing.

▶ He ~~talk~~ to the safety inspectors about plant security.
     talked

▶ They ~~use~~ to order lattes every morning.
      used

6c Use the correct form of irregular verbs such as *lay* and *lie*.

The verb pairs *lay* and *lie* and *sit* and *set* have similar forms and are often confused. Each verb has its own meaning: *lie* means to recline or rest on a surface, and *lay* means to put or place something; *sit* means to be seated, as in a chair, and *set* means to place something on a surface.

▶ Our dog likes to ~~lay~~ on the couch all afternoon.
                  lie

▶ Let me ~~set~~ in this chair for a while.
        sit

6d Use the active and passive voice appropriately.

For more on irregular verbs, see 1c.

When a verb is in the **active voice**, the subject performs the action.

Active Voice   The Mississippi River flows into the Gulf of Mexico.

When a verb is in the **passive voice**, the subject receives the action.

Passive Voice   The computer file was deleted.

> Notice that the sentence in the passive voice does not tell *who* deleted the file.

The active voice expresses ideas more vividly and emphatically than does the passive voice. Whenever possible, use the active voice in your sentences.

    The colonists threw tea
▶ ~~Tea was thrown~~ into Boston Harbor ~~by the colonists.~~
     ^   ^

    No one is allowed to sell illegal
▶ ~~Illegal~~ drugs ~~are not allowed to be sold.~~
     ^   ^

Sentences in the passive voice may seem indirect, as if the writer is purposely withholding information. In general, use the passive voice sparingly. There are two situations in which it is the better choice, however.

1. When you do not know or do not want to reveal who performed the action of the verb:

   Passive   Several historic buildings had been torn down.

2. When you want to emphasize the object of the action rather than the person who causes the action:

   Passive   The poem "My Last Duchess" by Robert Browning was discussed in class.

> In this sentence, the title of the poem is more important than the people who discussed it.

6e Use the present tense when writing about literary works, even though they were written in the past.

                     depicts
▶ Chaucer's *Canterbury Tales* ~~depicted~~ a tremendously varied group of travelers.
                                ^

6f Be sure to distinguish between the immediate past and the less immediate past.

Use the past perfect form of the verb, formed by adding *had* to the past participle, to indicate an action that was completed before another action or a specified time.

   Unclear   Roberto finished three research papers when the semester ended.

> Roberto did not finish all three right at the end of the semester.

   Revised   Roberto had finished three research papers when the semester ended.

For more on verb tense, see 1c and 27a

EXERCISE 6.1

Correct the errors in verb form in the following sentences. Some sentences may be correct as written.

>   United States entered the
> ▶ The Spanish-American War ~~was entered by the United States~~ in 1898.

1. When the nineteenth century change into the twentieth, many people in the United States became eager to expel Spain from the Americas.
2. Cuba, an island that lays ninety miles off the Florida coast, provided them with an excuse to do so.
3. Cuban rebels were trying to free themselves from Spain, and many Americans wanted to help them.
4. In addition, many people in the United States wanted to take over Spain's territories for a long time.
5. The United States won the war very quickly and assume control of Cuba, the Philippines, Guam, and Puerto Rico.
6. Cuba was allow to take control of its own affairs right away.
7. Puerto Rico became a commonwealth in 1952, a position that place it between statehood and independence.
8. In a 1998 election, the people of Puerto Rico were offered the option of full statehood.
9. It was rejected by them.
10. Many Puerto Ricans are worried that statehood would destroy the native culture of their island, and none of them want that to happen.

EXERCISE 6.2

Correct the errors in verb form in the following paragraph. Some sentences may be correct as written.

>   contains
> ▶ Walt Whitman's *Leaves of Grass* ~~contain~~ long, informally structured poems.

    Walt Whitman was usually considered one of the greatest American poets. He spent almost his whole life in Brooklyn, New York, but he like to write about all of America. He was fired from several jobs for laziness and admitted that he liked to lay in bed until noon. But he had a vision: He wanted to create an entirely new kind of poetry. Rhyme was considered unimportant by him, and he did not think new American poetry needed formal structure. Unfortunately for Whitman, his great masterpiece, *Leaves of Grass,* was not an overnight success. Ralph Waldo Emerson admire it, but Whitman sold very few copies. He revise it continuously until his death. Today, people admires *Leaves of Grass* for its optimism, its beautiful language, its very modern appreciation of the diversity of America, and its astonishing openness about sexuality. Whitman's body of work still move and surprise readers.

7   Pronoun Problems

Pronouns are words used in place of nouns. They provide a quick, convenient way to refer to a word that has already been named. Common problems in using pronouns include problems with pronoun reference, agreement, and case.

Pronoun Reference

A pronoun should refer clearly to its **antecedent**, the noun or pronoun for which it substitutes.

    If an antecedent is missing or unclear, the meaning of the sentence is also unclear. Use the following guidelines to make certain your pronoun references are clear and correct.

7a   Make sure each pronoun refers clearly to one antecedent.

▶ The hip-hop radio station battled the alternative rock station for the highest ratings.

▶ Eventually, ~~it~~ won. *(the alternative rock station)*

The revised sentence makes it clear which station won: the alternative rock station.

7b   Be sure to check for vague uses of *they, it,* and *you.*

They, it, and *you* often refer vaguely to antecedents in preceding sentences or to no antecedent at all.

Omitted Antecedent   On the Internet, they claimed that an asteroid would collide with the earth.

     On the Internet does not explain what *they* refers to.

Clear   On the Internet, a blog claimed that an asteroid would collide with the earth.

     Adding the noun *a blog* clears up the mystery.

▶ When political scientists study early political cartoons, ~~it provides~~ *they gain* insight into historical events.

▶ In Florida, ~~you often hear~~ *people often talk* about hurricane threats of previous years.

7c   Make sure pronouns do not refer to adjectives or possessives.

Pronouns must refer to nouns or other pronouns. Adjectives and possessives cannot serve as antecedents, although they may seem to suggest a noun the pronoun *could* refer to.

▶ He became so depressed that ~~it made him~~ *he was* unable to get out of bed.

The pronoun *it* seems to refer to the adjective *depressed,* which suggests the noun *depression.* This noun is not in the sentence, however.

stocks

▶ The stock market's rapid rise made ~~it~~ appear to be an attractive investment.
                                        ^

The pronoun *it* seems to refer to *stock market's*, which is a possessive, not a noun.

7d Make sure the pronouns *who, whom, which,* and *that* refer to clear, specific nouns.

These storms make

▶ Lake-effect storms hit cities along the Great Lakes. ~~That makes~~ winter travel
                                                        ^
treacherous.

EXERCISE 7.1

Correct any errors in pronoun reference in the following sentences.

are

▶ Innovative codes are important because ~~it means that~~ they ~~will be~~ hard to
                                                             ^
break.

1. A country at war must be able to convey information to military personnel. That is always a challenge.
2. The information's importance often requires it to be transmitted secretly.
3. Military strategists use codes for these transmissions because they baffle the enemy.
4. They say that "invisible ink," which cannot be seen until the paper is heated, was once a popular way to communicate secretly.
5. Lemon juice and vinegar are good choices for invisible ink because you can't see them unless they are burned.
6. During World War II, U.S. government code specialists hired Navajo Indians because it is a difficult and little-studied language.
7. In early code writing, it involved substituting letters throughout the message.
8. These cryptograms are no longer used to transmit messages because they are too simple.
9. The Nazis' Enigma code was extremely difficult to crack. This was an enormous problem for the Allied forces.
10. Alan Turing's mathematical genius saved the day. He was a British civil servant who finally solved the Enigma code.

An **antecedent** is the noun or pronoun to which a pronoun refers.

Person indicates whether the subject is speaking (first person: *I, we*), is being spoken to (second person: *you*), or is being spoken about (third person: *he, she, it, they*).

Number is a term that classifies pronouns as singular (*I, you, he, she, it*) or plural (*we, you, they*).

Pronoun-Antecedent Agreement

Pronouns and **antecedents** must agree in **person, number,** and **gender.** The most common agreement error occurs when pronouns and antecedents do not agree in number. If the antecedent is singular, use a singular pronoun. If the antecedent is plural, use a plural pronoun.

In most situations you will instinctively choose the correct pronoun and antecedent. Here are a few guidelines to follow for those times when you are unsure of which pronoun or antecedent to use.

7e Use singular pronouns to refer to indefinite pronouns that are singular in meaning.

Singular indefinite pronouns include the following:

another	anywhere	everyone	none	other
anybody	each	everything	no one	somebody
anyone	either	neither	nothing	someone
anything	everybody	nobody	one	something

▶ *Each* of the experiments produced *its* desired result.

▶ If *anyone* wants me, give *him or her* my email address.

▶ *Everyone* in America should exercise *his or her* right to vote so *his or her* voice can be heard.

If the pronoun and antecedent do not agree, change either the pronoun or the indefinite pronoun to which it refers. If you need to use a singular pronoun, use *he or she* or *him or her* to avoid sexism.

▶ ~~Everyone~~ should check their credit card statements monthly.
     People ^

▶ Everyone should check ~~their~~ credit card statement monthly.
                         his or her ^

An alternative is to eliminate the pronoun or pronouns entirely.

▶ No one should lose ~~their~~ job because of family responsibilities.
                      a ^

Note: Overuse of *him or her* and *his or her* can create awkward sentences. To avoid this problem, you can revise your sentences in one of two ways: by using a plural antecedent and a plural pronoun or by omitting the pronouns altogether.

The indefinite pronouns *all, any, more, most,* and *some* can be either singular or plural, depending on how they are used in sentences. When an indefinite pronoun refers to something that can be counted, use a plural pronoun to refer to it. When an indefinite pronoun refers to something that cannot be counted, use a singular pronoun to refer to it.

▶ Of the tropical plants studied, *some* have proven *their* usefulness in fighting disease.

   Because the word *plants* is a plural, countable noun, the pronoun *some* is plural in this sentence.

▶ The water was warm, and *most* of it was murky.

   Water is not countable, so *most* is singular.

ref

Gender is a way of classifying pronouns as masculine (*he, him*), feminine (*she, her*), or neuter (*it, its*).

An **indefinite pronoun** does not refer to a specific person, place, or object. It refers to people, places, or things in general (*anywhere, everyone, everything*).

7f Use a plural pronoun to refer to a compound antecedent joined by *and*.

▶ The *walrus and the carpenter* ate *their* oysters greedily.

Exception: When the singular antecedents joined by *and* refer to the same person, place, or thing, use a singular pronoun.

▶ As *a father and a husband, he* is a success.

Exception: When *each* or *every* comes before the antecedent, use a singular pronoun.

▶ *Every* nut and bolt was in *its* place for the inspection.

When a compound antecedent is joined by *or* or *nor,* the pronoun should agree with the noun closer to the verb.

▶ Either the panda or the sea otters should have ~~its~~ new habitat soon.
　　　　　　　　　　　　　　　　　　　　　　their

7g Use a singular or plural pronoun to refer to a collective noun, depending on the meaning.

A **collective noun** names a group of people or things acting together or individually (*herd, class, team*) and may be referred to by a singular or plural pronoun depending on your intended meaning. When you refer to a group acting together as a unit, use a singular pronoun.

▶ The *wolf pack* surrounds *its* quarry.

The pack is acting as a unit.

When you refer to the members of the group as acting individually, use a plural pronoun.

▶ After the false alarm, *members* of the bomb squad returned to *their* homes.

The members of the squad acted individually.

EXERCISE 7.2

Correct any errors in pronoun-antecedent agreement in the following sentences. Some sentences may be correct as written.

▶ Every scientist has ~~their~~ own idea about the state of the environment.
　　　　　　　　　his or her

1. Neither the many species of dinosaurs nor the flightless dodo bird could prevent their own extinction.

2. A team of researchers might disagree on its conclusions about the disappearance of the dinosaur.
3. However, most believe that their findings indicate the dodo died out because of competition from other species.
4. In one way, animals resemble plants: Some are "weeds" because it has the ability to thrive under many conditions.
5. Any species that cannot withstand their competitors may be doomed to extinction.
6. When a "weed" and a delicate native species compete for its survival, the native species usually loses.
7. If the snail darter and the spotted owl lose their fight to survive, should humans care?
8. Everyone should be more concerned about the extinction of plants and animals than they seem to be.
9. Every extinction has their effect on other species.
10. The earth has experienced several mass extinctions in its history, but another would take their toll on the quality of human life.

Pronoun Case

Most of the time you will automatically know which form, or *case,* of a pronoun to use: the **subjective, objective,** or **possessive** case. A pronoun's case indicates its function in a sentence. When a pronoun functions as a subject in a sentence, the subjective case (*I*) is used. When a pronoun functions as a **direct object,** an **indirect object,** or an **object of a preposition,** the objective case (*me*) is used. When a pronoun indicates ownership, the possessive case (*mine*) is used.

Subjective Case	Objective Case	Possessive Case
I	me	my, mine
we	us	our, ours
you	you	your, yours
he, she, it	him, her, it	his, her, hers, its
they	them	their, theirs
who	whom	whose

Use the following guidelines to correct errors in pronoun case.

7h   Read the sentence aloud without the noun and the word *and* to decide which pronoun to use in a compound construction (*Yolanda and I, Yolanda and me*).

> **Incorrect**   Yolanda and me graduated from high school last year.
>
> > If you mentally delete *Yolanda and,* the sentence sounds wrong: *Me graduated from high school last year.*

A **direct object** receives the action of the verb: *He drove me home.*

An **indirect object** indicates to or for whom an action is performed: *I gave her the keys.*

An **object of a preposition** is a word or phrase that follows a preposition: *with him, above the table.*

Revised	Yolanda and I graduated from high school last year.
	If you mentally delete *Yolanda and*, the sentence sounds correct: *I graduated from high school last year.*
Incorrect	The mayor presented the citizenship award to Mrs. Alvarez and I.
	If you delete *Mrs. Alvarez and*, the sentence sounds wrong: *The mayor presented the citizenship award to I.*
Revised	The mayor presented the citizenship award to Mrs. Alvarez and me.
	If you delete *Mrs. Alvarez and*, the sentence sounds correct: *The mayor presented the citizenship award to me.*

7i   Read the sentence aloud with the pronoun as the subject when a pronoun follows a form of the verb *be* (*is, are, was, were*).

Incorrect	The leader is him.
	If you substitute *him* for *the leader*, the sentence sounds wrong: *Him is the leader.*
Revised	The leader is he.
	If you substitute *he* for *the leader*, the sentence sounds correct: *He is the leader.*

▶ The best singer in the group is ~~her~~ she.

7j   Read the sentence aloud without the noun to determine whether *we* or *us* should come before a noun.

▶ If we hikers frighten them, the bears may attack.

If you mentally delete *hikers*, the sentence sounds correct: *If we frighten them, the bears may attack.*

▶ The older children never paid attention to us kindergartners.

If you mentally delete *kindergartners*, the sentence sounds correct: *The older children never paid attention to us.*

7k   Choose the correct pronoun form for a comparison using *than* or *as* by mentally adding the verb that is implied.

▶ Diedre is a better athlete than I [am].
▶ The coach likes her better than [he likes] me.

7l   Use *who* or *whoever* when the pronoun functions as the subject of a sentence. Use *whom* or *whomever* when the pronoun functions as the object of a verb or preposition.

To decide whether to use *who* or *whom* in a particular question, answer the question yourself by using the words *he* or *him* or *she* or *her*. If you use *he* or *she* in the answer,

An **object** is the target or recipient of the action described by the verb: *I gave her the keys*.

An **object of a preposition** is a word or phrase that follows a preposition: *with him, above the table*.

you should use *who* in the question. If you use *him* or *her* in the answer, use *whom* in the question.

Question	(*Who, Whom*) photocopied the article?
Answer	*She* photocopied the article.
Correct Pronoun	*Who* photocopied the article?
Question	To (*who, whom*) is that question addressed?
Answer	It is addressed to *him*.
Correct Pronoun	To *whom* is that question addressed?

Similarly, to decide whether to use *who* or *whom* in a **dependent clause**, turn the dependent clause into a question. The pronoun you use to answer that question will tell you whether *who* or *whom* should appear in the clause.

A **dependent clause** contains a subject and a verb but does not express a complete thought.

▶ Aphra Behn's *Oronooko* dramatizes the life of a slave ~~whom~~ who came from African royalty.

> If you ask the question (*Who, whom*) *came from African royalty?*, the answer, *He came from African royalty*, indicates that the correct pronoun is *who*.

▶ The leader ~~who~~ whom we seek must unite the community.

> If you ask the question (*Who, whom*) *do we seek?*, the answer, *We seek him*, indicates that the correct pronoun is *whom*.

7m Use a possessive pronoun to modify a gerund.

▶ *His moralizing* has never been welcome.

> The possessive pronoun *his* modifies the gerund *moralizing*.

A **gerund** is an *-ing* form of a verb that functions as a noun (*complaining, jogging*).

Gerunds are often confused with **participles** because both end in *-ing*.

Participle	Teenagers across the United States watched *her singing* on *American Idol*.
	The teenagers watched her, not the singing.
Gerund	The professor discovered *their cheating* on the final exam.
	The cheating was discovered, not the students doing the cheating.

A **participle** is an *-ing* or *-ed* form of a verb that is used as an adjective (*the terrifying monster*) or with a helping verb to indicate tense (*he was running away*). Pronouns used with participles should be in the objective case; pronouns used with gerunds should be in the possessive case.

EXERCISE 7.3

Correct any errors in pronoun case in the following sentences. Some sentences may be correct as written.

▶ Cave explorers, ~~whom~~ who are called spelunkers, sometimes find underground rooms no one has seen before.

1. Whomever discovers a large cave is usually able to attract tourists.

2. Much of Kentucky's Mammoth Cave was explored in the 1830s by Stephen Bishop, a slave who worked as a cave guide.
3. Few spelunkers today are better known than he.
4. Following the success of Mammoth Cave, many Kentucky cavers hoped to make a fortune from them spelunking.
5. Floyd Collins was one Kentucky native whom searched his property for caves.
6. In January 1925, a falling rock trapped Collins, whom was spelunking in a narrow passage in Sand Cave.
7. When his brothers found him, Collins and them worked unsuccessfully to free his trapped leg.
8. For several days, the most famous man in Kentucky was him.
9. The plea to rescue Floyd Collins was answered by whoever could travel to rural Kentucky.
10. Them failing to save Collins was a terrible tragedy for his family and the rescuers.

EXERCISE 7.4

Correct any errors in pronoun reference, agreement, and case in the following paragraph. Some sentences may be correct as written.

> She
> ▶ ~~Her~~ and her husband married for love, which was unusual at the time.
>   ^

Lady Mary Wortley Montagu, whom was a wealthy aristocrat, was one of the eighteenth century's most interesting characters. Few women then were as well educated as her. Every parent wanted their daughter to be charming, not intellectual, so Lady Mary secretly taught herself Latin. When her husband was appointed ambassador to Turkey, she and he traveled there together. Her letters to friends in London, which were later published, were filled with detail. She described a Turkish bath's atmosphere so vividly that it became a popular setting for paintings and literature. She also learned that smallpox was rare in Turkey. Of the Turkish people she met, most had gotten his or her immunity to smallpox from a kind of inoculation. This had an effect on Lady Mary herself. Lady Mary's children were among the first British citizens who were inoculated against it.

8   Shifts and Mixed Constructions

A **shift** is a sudden, unexpected change in point of view, verb tense, voice, mood, or level of diction that may confuse your readers. Shifting from a direct to an indirect question or quotation can also confuse readers. A **mixed construction** is a sentence containing parts that do not sensibly fit together. This chapter will help you identify and correct shifts and mixed constructions in your sentences.

Shifts

8a Refer to yourself, your audience, and the people you are writing about in a consistent way.

Person shows the writer's point of view. Personal pronouns indicate whether the subject is the speaker (first person: *I, we*), the person spoken to (second person: *you*), or the person or thing spoken about (third person: *he, she, it, they, one*).

For more on person, see 1b and Chapter 4, p. 105.

Inconsistent	*I* discovered that *you* could touch some of the museum exhibits.
	Notice that the writer shifts from first-person *I* to the second-person *you*.
Consistent	*I* discovered that *I* could touch some of the museum exhibits.
	The writer uses the first-person *I* consistently within the sentence.

▶ When people study a foreign language, ~~you~~ ^{they} also learn about another culture.

8b Maintain consistency in verb tense throughout a paragraph or an essay unless the meaning requires you to change tenses.

Inconsistent	The virus *mutated* so quickly that it *develops* a resistance to most vaccines.
	The sentence shifts from past to present.
Revised	The virus *mutates* so quickly that it *develops* a resistance to most vaccines.

Shifts between the present and past tense are among the most common shifts writers make.

▶ The city's crime rate continues to drop, but experts disagree~~d~~ on the reasons.

8c Change verb tense when you want to indicate an actual time change.

Use the present tense for events that occur in the present; use the past tense for events that occurred in the past. When the time changes, be sure to change the tense. Notice the intentional shifts in the following passage (the verbs are in italics).

> Every spring migratory birds *return* to cooler climates to raise their young. This year a pair of bluejays *is occupying* a nest in my yard, and I *spy* on them. The hatchlings *are growing* larger and *developing* feathers. Last spring, robins *built* the nest that the jays now *call* home, and I *watched* them every morning until the young birds *left* home for the last time.

As the events switch from this year (present) to the previous year (past), the writer changes from the present tense (*is occupying*) to the past tense (*built*).

For more on verb tense, see 1c and 27a.

In the **active voice**, the subject of the sentence performs the action.

In the **passive voice**, the subject receives the action.

8d Use a consistent voice.

Needless shifts between the **active voice** and the **passive voice** can disorient readers and create wordy sentences.

▶ ~~One~~ <u>The researchers gave one</u> group of volunteers ~~was given~~ a placebo, and ~~the researchers~~ <u>they</u> treated another group with the new drug.

▶ Drought and windstorms made farming impossible, and <u>the specter of starvation forced</u> many families ~~were forced~~ to leave Oklahoma ~~by the specter of starvation.~~

To change a sentence from the passive voice to the active voice, make the performer of the action the subject of the sentence. The original subject of the sentence becomes the direct object. Delete the form of the verb *be*.

For more on voice, see 1c and 6d.

Passive   The restraining order was signed by the judge.

Active   The judge signed the restraining order.

8e Avoid sudden shifts from indirect to direct questions or quotations.

An indirect question tells what a question is or was.

Indirect Question   The defense attorney asked where I was on the evening of May 10.

Direct Question   "Where were you on the evening of May 10?"

Avoid shifting from direct to indirect questions.

▶ Sal asked what could ~~I~~ <u>he</u> do to solve the problem.

8f Use a consistent mood throughout a paragraph or an essay.

For more on mood, see 1c.

Mood indicates whether the sentence states a fact or asks a question (**indicative mood**); gives a command or direction (**imperative mood**); or expresses a condition contrary to fact, a wish, or a suggestion (**subjunctive mood**). The subjunctive mood is also used for hypothetical situations or impossible or unlikely events.

Inconsistent

You shouldn't expect to learn ballroom dancing immediately, and remember that even Fred Astaire had to start somewhere. First, find a qualified instructor. Then, you should not be embarrassed even if everyone else seems more graceful than you are. Finally, keep your goal in mind, and you need to practice, practice, practice.

This paragraph contains shifts between the indicative and imperative moods.

Consistent

Don't expect to learn ballroom dancing immediately, and remember that even Fred Astaire had to start somewhere. First, find a qualified instructor. Then, don't be embarrassed if everyone else seems more graceful than you are. Finally, keep your goal in mind, and practice, practice, practice.

This revised paragraph uses the imperative mood consistently.

8g Use a consistent level of diction.

Your level of diction can range from formal to informal. The level you choose should be appropriate for your audience, your subject matter, and your purpose for writing. As you revise your essays, look for inappropriate shifts in diction, such as from a formal to an informal tone or vice versa.

> William H. Whyte's studies of human behavior in public space yielded a number of surprises. Perhaps most unexpected was the revelation that people seem to be drawn toward, rather than driven from, crowded spaces. They tend to congregate near the entrances of stores or on street corners. Plazas and shopping districts crowded with pedestrians attract more pedestrians. For some reason, people seem
> enjoy gathering together in public spaces.
> to ~~get a charge out of hanging out where lots of other folks are hanging out, too.~~

For academic writing, including class assignments and research papers, use formal language.

For more on levels of diction, see Chapter 9, pp. 207–8.

EXERCISE 8.1

Correct the shifts in person, verb tense, voice, mood, and level of diction in the following sentences.

> many parents have studied
> ▶ Experts continue to break new ground in child psychology, and their research.
> ~~has been studied by many parents.~~

1. A new idea about the development of children's personalities had surprised many American psychologists because it challenges widely accepted theories.
2. We wondered whether our professor knew of the new theory and did she agree with it.
3. Personality is believed by some experts to be the result of parental care, but other specialists feel that biology influences personality more strongly.
4. Most parents think you have a major influence on your child's behavior.
5. The new theory suggests that children's peers are a heck of a lot more influential than parents.
6. Peer acceptance is strongly desired by children, and they want to be different from adults.
7. If adults were to think about their childhood experiences, they realize that this idea has merit.
8. Most adults recall that in childhood, your friends' opinions were extremely important to you.
9. The way people behave with family members is often different from the way we act with our friends.
10. Jittery moms and dads would be really, really relieved if this hypothesis were proven.

Correct the shifts in person, verb tense, voice, mood, and level of diction in the following paragraph.

▶ Some artists long ago used techniques that still ~~surprised~~ ^surprise^ modern students of their work.

Museum visitors can see paintings by the seventeenth-century Dutch artist Jan Vermeer, but you cannot see how he achieved his remarkable effects. Most of his paintings showed simply furnished household rooms. The people and objects in these rooms seem so real that the paintings resembled photographs. Vermeer's use of perspective and light would also contribute to the paintings' realism. Some art historians believe he used a gizmo called a *camera obscura*. This machine projected an image onto a flat surface so you could draw it. For most experts, Vermeer's possible use of technological aids does not make his totally fabulous results less impressive. It is agreed by art historians that the paintings are masterpieces. Vermeer's paintings are admired even more now than they are in his own lifetime.

Mixed Constructions

8h Make sure clauses and phrases fit together logically.

A **mixed construction** contains phrases or clauses that do not work together logically and that cause confusion in meaning.

Mixed   The fact that the marathon is twenty-six miles, a length that explains why I have never finished it.

The sentence starts with a subject (*The fact*) followed by a dependent clause (*that the marathon is twenty-six miles*). The sentence needs a predicate to complete the independent clause; instead it includes a noun (*a length*) and another dependent clause (*that explains why I have never finished it*). The independent clause that begins with *The fact* is never completed.

Revised   The marathon is twenty-six miles long, which is why I have never finished it.

In the revision, the parts of the sentence work together.

To avoid mixed constructions in your writing, it often helps to check the words that connect clauses and phrases, especially prepositions and conjunctions.

8i Make subjects and predicates consistent.

Faulty predication occurs when a subject does not work grammatically with its predicate.

Faulty   The most valued trait in an employee is a person who is loyal.

>   A person is not a trait.

Revised   The most valued trait in an employee is loyalty.

> ▶ Rising health-care costs decrease ~~the number of people who can afford~~ health insurance ~~for many people.~~

the number of people who can afford

>   Costs do not decrease health insurance.

8j   Avoid the constructions *is when*, *is where*, and *reason . . . is because*.

Faulty   Indigestion is when you cannot digest food.

Revised   Indigestion is the inability to digest food.

> ▶ Gravitation is ~~where~~ one body ~~is being attracted by~~ another.

the attraction of   for

> ▶ ~~The reason~~ I enjoy jogging ~~is~~ because it provides outdoor exercise.

Correct the mixed constructions in the following sentences.

> ▶ ~~The reason~~ internships are valuable ~~is~~ because they give students real-world experience.

1. Many interns earn college credit for their work, but they also gain practical experience and important contacts.
2. Surveys showing that college graduates who intern receive higher salary offers than their classmates who do not.
3. The fact that students must be careful, as all internships are not created equal.
4. The most important qualities are an intern with curiosity and a good work ethic.
5. A good internship is when the intern gains knowledge and skills in a professional environment.
6. Some companies provide little guidance that interns do not learn much from the experience.
7. Other companies may use unpaid interns that is free labor instead of hiring full-time employees.
8. The U.S. Department of Labor has strict guidelines that apply to unpaid internships.
9. Companies do not meet these federal requirements, because they must pay minimum wage or face lawsuits.
10. By having these strict federal standards, some worry that companies will eliminate internship programs rather than risk any legal problems.

9 Adjectives and Adverbs

Adjectives and adverbs are powerful. Used appropriately, they can add precision and force to your writing, as the following excerpt demonstrates.

> Seated cross-legged on a brocade pillow, wrapped in burgundy robes, was a short, rotund man with a shiny pate. He looked very old and very tired. Chhongba bowed reverently, spoke briefly to him in the Sherpa tongue, and indicated for us to come forward.
>
> Jon Krakauer, *Into Thin Air*

Adjectives modify nouns or pronouns and indicate which one, what kind, or how many. **Adverbs** modify verbs, adjectives, other adverbs, clauses, or entire sentences and indicate how, when, where, how often, or to what extent. (See also 1d and 1e.)

The two most common errors involving adjectives and adverbs occur when writers use (1) an adjective instead of an adverb (or vice versa) and (2) the wrong form of an adjective or adverb in a comparison. Use the following guidelines to identify and correct these and other common errors in your writing.

9a Use adverbs, not adjectives, to modify verbs, adjectives, or other adverbs.

Although in conversation you may often use adjectives in place of adverbs, you should be careful in your writing to use adverbs to modify verbs, adjectives, or other adverbs.

▶ Those pants are ~~awful~~ ^{awfully} expensive.

▶ The headlights shone ~~bright.~~ ^{brightly.}

9b Use adjectives, not adverbs, after linking verbs.

Linking verbs, often forms of *be* and other verbs such as *feel, look, make,* and *seem,* express a state of being. A linking verb takes a **subject complement**—a word group that completes or renames the subject of the sentence. Verbs such as *feel* and *look* can also be action verbs. When they function as action verbs in a sentence, they may be modified by an adverb.

If you are not sure whether a word should be an adjective or adverb, determine how it is used in the sentence. If the word modifies a noun, it should be an adjective.

Adjective Our *waiter* looked *slow.*

Slow modifies the word *waiter,* a noun. In this sentence, *looked* is a linking verb.

Adverb Our waiter looked *slowly* for some menus.

In this sentence, *looked* is expressing an action and is not a linking verb; *slowly* modifies *looked.*

9c Use *good* and *bad* as adjectives; use *well* and *badly* as adverbs.

▶ Einstein was not a *good student*.

The adjective *good* modifies the noun *student*.

▶ Einstein did not *perform well* in school.

The adverb *well* modifies the verb *perform*.

▶ He did ~~bad~~ badly in the leading role.

The adverb *badly* modifies the verb *did*.

When you are describing someone's health, *well* can also function as an adjective.

▶ The disease was in remission, but the *patients* were not yet *well*.

9d Be careful not to use adjectives such as *real* and *sure* to modify adverbs or other adjectives.

▶ The produce was crisp and ~~real~~ really fresh.

The adverb *really* modifies the adjective *fresh*.

9e Avoid double negatives.

A sentence with two negative words or phrases contains a **double negative**, which conveys a positive meaning. Do not use two negatives in a sentence unless you want to express a positive meaning (for example, *not uncommon* means "common").

▶ The company is not doing ~~nothing~~ anything to promote its incentive plan.

▶ No one under eighteen ~~can't~~ can vote in the presidential election.

Positive Meaning Intended

Athletic sportswear is not uncommon as casual attire.

9f Use the comparative form of adjectives and adverbs to compare two things; use the superlative form to compare three or more things.

Adjectives and adverbs can be used to compare two or more persons, objects, actions, or ideas. The **comparative** form of an adjective or adverb compares two items. The **superlative** form compares three or more items. Use the list on the next page to check the comparative and superlative forms of most regular adjectives and adverbs in your sentences.

	Comparatives	**Superlatives**
One-syllable adjectives and adverbs	Add -er: *colder, faster*	Add -est: *coldest, fastest*
Two-syllable adjectives	Add -er: *greasier**	Add -est: *greasiest**
Adjectives with three or more syllables or adverbs ending in -ly	Add *more* in front of the word: *more beautiful, more quickly*	Add *most* in front of the word: *most beautiful, most quickly*

Irregular adjectives and adverbs form their comparative and superlative forms in unpredictable ways, as the following list illustrates.

	Comparative	**Superlative**
Adjectives		
good	better	best
bad	worse	worst
little	less	least
Adverbs		
well	better	best
badly	worse	worst
Words That Function as Adjectives and Adverbs		
many	more	most
some	more	most
much	more	most

Do not use comparative or superlative forms with absolute concepts, such as *unique* and *perfect*. Something cannot be more or less unique, for example; it is either unique or not unique.

▶ This is ~~the most~~ $\overset{a}{\wedge}$ unique solution to the pollution problem.

9g Check your comparisons to be sure they are complete when using comparative and superlative forms.

An incomplete comparison can leave your reader confused about what is being compared.

Incomplete	The Internet works more efficiently.
Revised	For sending correspondence and documents, the Internet works more efficiently than the postal service.
Incomplete	The catcher sustained the most crippling knee injury.
Revised	The catcher sustained the most crippling knee injury of his career.

*To form the comparative and superlative forms of adjectives ending in -y, change the y to i and add -er or -est.

9h Do not use *more* or *most* with the *-er* or *-est* form of an adjective or adverb.

▶ The hypothesis must be ~~more~~ clearer.

Correct any errors involving adjectives and adverbs in the following sentences.

                       the most
▶ *Wikipedia* is probably ~~a more~~ popular reference source in the world.

1. The site is an open source, online encyclopedia where anyone can contribute, even if he or she writes bad or inaccurate.
2. *Wikipedia* has many advantages that reflect good upon it as a source.
3. There is not nothing more convenient for getting information real quick.
4. In a way, encyclopedias are more unique because Web sites can grow to include any subject that anyone finds interesting.
5. *Wikipedia* relies heavy on the knowledge and interests of millions of people, rather than on the choices of a small group of experts.
6. The site has some really downsides too.
7. Some of the information on *Wikipedia* can be awful inaccurate.
8. Many teachers and professors don't allow no students to use *Wikipedia* for research.
9. When students rely entire on the site, their papers usually don't get good grades.
10. If they choose to use the site, students should make it more clearer to their professors that they have researched their subjects thorough.

Correct any errors involving adjectives and adverbs in the following paragraph. Some sentences may be correct as written.

▶ Originating in China, *feng shui* is a traditional~~ly~~ art of balancing elements to achieve harmony.

    Feng shui is taken very serious in many Asian societies. Some Hong Kong business executives, for example, will not feel comfortably working in an office until it has been approved by a *feng shui* master. Other people are more interested in *feng shui* for its elegance. A room designed with this idea in mind looks tranquilly. The name *feng shui* means "wind and water," and balancing elements is the more important aspect of the art. Some people believe that this balance brings good luck. Others will admit only that surroundings can have a psychologically effect. It is easier to feel comfortable in a room designed according to *feng shui* principles. The placement of doors, windows, and furnishings contributes to the peaceful effect. Whether *feng shui* is magic or simple great interior design, something about it seems to work.

10 Misplaced and Dangling Modifiers

A **modifier** is a word or group of words that describes, changes, qualifies, or limits the meaning of another word or group of words in a sentence.

> ▶ The contestant *smiled delightedly.*

The adverb *delightedly* modifies the verb *smiled.*

> ▶ *Pretending to be surprised,* he greeted the guests.

The adjective phrase *Pretending to be surprised* modifies the pronoun *he.*

Modifiers that are carefully placed in sentences give your readers a clear picture of the details you want to convey. However, when a sentence contains a **misplaced modifier,** it is hard for the reader to tell which word or group of words the modifier is supposed to be describing.

10a Place modifiers close to the words they describe.

Misplaced	The mayor *chided* the pedestrians for jaywalking *angrily.*
	The adverb *angrily* should be closer to the verb it modifies, *chided.* Here, the adverb appears to be modifying *jaywalking,* so the sentence is confusing.
Revised	The mayor *angrily chided* the pedestrians for jaywalking.
Misplaced	The press *reacted* to the story leaked from the Pentagon *with horror.*
	The adverb phrase *with horror* should explain how the press reacted, not how the story was leaked, so the modifier should be closer to the verb *reacted.*
Revised	The press *reacted with horror* to the story leaked from the Pentagon.

10b Make sure each modifier clearly modifies only one word or phrase in a sentence.

When a modifier is placed near or next to the word or phrase it modifies, it may also be near another word it could conceivably modify. When a modifier's placement may cause such ambiguity, rewrite the sentence, placing the modifier so that it clearly refers to the word or phrase it is supposed to modify.

Unclear	The film's attempt to portray war accurately depicts a survivor's anguish.
	Does the film attempt to portray war accurately, or does it accurately depict a survivor's anguish? The following revisions eliminate the uncertainty.
Revised	In its The ~~film's~~ attempt to portray war accurately depicts a survivor's anguish. , the film
Revised	film The ~~film's attempt to portray war~~ accurately depicts a survivor's in its attempt to portray war realistically. anguish*!*

10c Revise a dangling modifier by rewriting the sentence.

A **dangling modifier** is a word or phrase that does not modify or refer to anything in a sentence. Instead, it seems to modify something that has been left out of the sentence. A dangling modifier can make the meaning of a sentence unclear, inaccurate, or even comical. Most dangling modifiers appear at the beginning or end of sentences.

Dangling   After singing a thrilling ballad, the crowd surged toward the stage.

This sentence suggests that the crowd sang the ballad.

Dangling   Laying an average of ten eggs a day, the neighboring farmer is proud of his henhouse.

This sentence suggests that the farmer lays eggs.

To revise a sentence with a dangling modifier, follow these steps.

1. Identify the word or words that the modifier is supposed to modify.
2. Revise the sentence to correct the confusion either by changing the modifier into a clause with its own subject and verb or by rewriting the sentence so that the word being modified becomes the subject.

▶ After ~~singing~~ a thrilling ballad, the crowd surged toward the stage.
   ^Kelly sang^

▶ Laying an average of ten eggs a day, the neighboring farmer ~~is~~ proud of his henhouse.
   his prize chickens give   reason to be

Correct any misplaced or dangling modifiers in the following sentences.

▶ Hoping to get a message from outer space, a huge telescope. ~~has been built.~~
   scientists have built

1. Solar systems exist throughout the galaxy like our own.
2. So far, no proof on other planets of the existence of life forms has been found.
3. A tremendously powerful telescope searches distant stars for signs of life in the Caribbean.
4. Astronomers monitor signals coming from other parts of the solar system carefully.
5. Wondering whether humans are alone in the universe, the telescope may provide answers.
6. Most of the signals have been caused by cell phone and satellite interference received so far.
7. While trying to intercept signals from other planets, a signal has also been sent from earth.
8. The message is on its way to other parts of our galaxy, containing information about earth.
9. The message will take twenty thousand years to reach its destination or more.
10. A signal sent to earth similarly would take a long time to reach us.

EXERCISE 10.2

Correct any misplaced or dangling modifiers in the following paragraph. Some sentences may be correct as written.

▶ The measurement is now based on atomic vibrations. ~~of one second.~~ *of one second*

Making sure standard weights and measures are the same all over the world is an important task. To trade internationally, a kilogram in Mexico must weigh the same as a kilogram in Japan. In the past, countries set standards for weighing and measuring individually. One English king declared a yard to be the distance from his nose to his thumb egotistically. Weight was once measured in barleycorns, so unethical merchants soaked barleycorns to make them heavier in water. Today, the metric system is the worldwide standard, and the weight of the U.S. pound is based even on the standard kilogram. In France, a cylinder is the world standard kilogram made of platinum. Securely, this official kilogram is kept in an airtight container. Nevertheless, losing a few billionths of a gram of weight each year, world standards might eventually be affected. Hoping to find a permanent solution, scientists want to base the kilogram measurement on an unchanging natural phenomenon.

Use Punctuation Correctly

11 ▶ End Punctuation

The end of a sentence can be marked with a period (.), a question mark (?), or an exclamation point (!).

11a Use a period to mark the end of a sentence that makes a statement, gives an instruction, or includes an indirect question; use periods with most abbreviations.

Writers seldom omit the period at the end of a sentence that makes a statement or gives directions.

Statement	Amnesty International investigates human-rights violations.
Instruction	Use as little water as possible during the drought.

Writers sometimes mistake an indirect question for a direct one, however.

An **indirect question** is a statement that reports what was asked or is being asked: *He asked where the classroom was.*

▶ Most visitors want to know where the dinosaur bones were found~~?~~.

This sentence states what question was asked; it does not ask the question directly.

Many abbreviations use periods (*Mass., Co., St.,*). If you are not sure whether an abbreviation should include periods, check a dictionary.

When an abbreviation that uses periods ends a sentence, an additional period is not needed.

> ▶ My brother works for Apple Computer, Inc.~~.~~

Note, however, that the Modern Language Association (MLA) recommends omitting periods in abbreviations that consist of capital letters (*IBM, USA, BC*) but including periods in abbreviations that consist of lowercase letters (*a.m.*).

11b Use a question mark to end a sentence that asks a direct question.

Direct Question   Why was the flight delayed?

When a question is also a quotation, the question mark is placed within the quotation marks (see also 15d).

> ▶ "What did she want?~~,~~" Marcia asked.

11c Use an exclamation point to end a sentence that expresses a strong emotion or a forceful command.

> ▶ Altering experimental results to make them conform to a hypothesis is never ethical!

Use exclamation points sparingly; they lose their impact when used too frequently.

> ▶ Government officials immediately suspected terrorism.~~!~~

EXERCISE 11.1

Correct any errors in the use of end punctuation marks in the following sentences. Some sentences may be correct as written.

> ▶ Is it possible that hemophilia in the Russian czar's family contributed to the Russian Revolution~~.~~?

1. When the daughters of Queen Victoria of England, who carried the gene for hemophilia, married royalty in Germany and Russia, those royal families inherited hemophilia as well?
2. The Russian czar's only son and heir to the throne suffered from hemophilia.
3. You might ask if internal bleeding can occur when a hemophiliac receives a bruise?
4. Czar Nicholas and his wife Alexandra often saw their little boy in terrible pain!
5. A phony monk named Rasputin eased the child's pain, but was he a gifted healer or just a con man.

12 Commas

A **comma** (,) is used to separate parts of a sentence from one another. Commas, when you use them correctly, make your sentences clear and help readers understand your meaning.

12a Use a comma before a coordinating word (*and, but, for, nor, or, so, yet*) that joins two independent clauses.

An **independent clause** contains a subject and verb and can stand alone as a sentence.

▶ The ball flew past the goalie‸but the score did not count.

▶ Her dog was enormous‸so many people found it threatening.

12b Use a comma to separate three or more items in a series.

A **series** is a list of three or more items—words, phrases, or clauses.

▶ Dancing, singing, and acting are just a few of her talents.
▶ Sunflowers grew on the hillsides, along the roads, and in the middle of every pasture.

Some writers omit the comma before the coordinating conjunction (such as *and, or*) in a brief series when using a casual or journalistic style. Occasionally this omission can create confusion, so it is better to include the final comma.

Confusing   She insured her valuable heirlooms, watches and jewelry.

            Do her heirlooms consist entirely of watches and jewelry, or did she insure three kinds of items?

Clear   She insured her valuable heirlooms, watches, and jewelry.

A comma is not used after the last item in a series.

See also 13c on when to use semicolons to separate items in a series.

▶ Aphids, slugs, and beetles⁄ can severely damage a crop.

12c Use a comma to separate two or more adjectives that modify the same noun when they are not joined by a coordinating word.

▶ Rescue workers found the frightened, hungry child.

To be sure a comma is needed, try reversing the two adjectives. If the phrase still sounds correct when the adjectives are reversed, a comma is needed. If the phrase sounds wrong, a comma is not needed.

▶ The airy, open atrium makes visitors feel at home.

The phrase *open, airy atrium* sounds right, so a comma is needed.

▶ Local businesses donated the bright red uniforms.

> The phrase *red, bright uniforms* sounds wrong because *bright* modifies *red uniforms* in the original sentence. A comma is not needed.

12d Use a comma to separate introductory words, phrases, and clauses from the rest of a sentence.

Introductory Word	Above, the sky was a mass of clouds.
	Without the comma, this sentence would be confusing.
Introductory Phrase	At the start of the project, the researchers were optimistic.
Introductory Clause	When alcohol was outlawed, many solid citizens broke the law.

Exception: A comma is not needed after a single word or short phrase or clause when there is no possibility of confusion.

▶ Then a rainbow appeared.

12e Use a comma to set off a nonrestrictive word group from the rest of the sentence.

A **nonrestrictive word group** describes or modifies a word or phrase in a sentence, but it does not change the meaning of the word or phrase. To decide whether a comma is needed, read the sentence without the word group. If the basic meaning is unchanged, a comma is needed.

▶ Most people either love or hate fruitcake, *which is a traditional holiday dessert.*

> The meaning of *fruitcake* is not changed by the relative clause *which is a traditional holiday dessert,* so the word group is **nonrestrictive** and a comma is needed.

▶ The child *wearing a tutu* delights in ballet lessons.

> The phrase *wearing a tutu* identifies which child delights in ballet lessons, so the word group is **restrictive**—necessary to explain what the word it modifies means—and a comma is not needed.

12f Use a comma to set off parenthetical expressions.

A **parenthetical expression** provides extra information. It can also be a transitional word or phrase (*however, for example, at the beginning*) that is not essential to the meaning of the sentence.

▶ *Furthermore,* his essay had not been proofread.
▶ Islamic countries were, *in fact,* responsible for preserving much classical scientific knowledge.

12g Use commas with dates, addresses, titles, and numbers.

▶ She graduated on June 8, 2014.

When you give only a month and year, a comma is not needed.

▶ She graduated in June 2014.

Place a comma after the date when it appears before the end of the sentence.

▶ The 2014 Winter Olympics began on February 7, 2014, in Sochi, Russia.

When you give an address within a sentence, do not place a comma between the state and the ZIP code.

▶ Send the package to PO Box 100, McPherson, Kansas 67460.

Separate a name from a title with a comma.

▶ The featured speaker was Kate Silverstein, Ph.D.

Use commas in numbers that have more than four digits.

▶ Estimates of the number of protesters ranged from 250,000 to 700,000.

In a number with four digits, the comma is optional: 1500 or 1,500.

A **direct quotation** gives a person's *exact* words, either spoken or written, set off by quotation marks.

12h Use a comma to separate a direct quotation from the words that explain it.

▶ She asked, "What's the score?"

Place the comma before the closing quotation mark.

See also 15b and 15e.

▶ "Wait and see," was his infuriating response.
          ∧

12i Use commas to set off the name of someone directly addressed, to set off an echo question, and with a "not" phrase.

Direct Address	"James, answer the question concisely." "Bail has not been granted, your honor."
Echo Question	More development will require a more expensive infrastructure, won't it?
"Not" Phrase	Labor Day, not the autumnal equinox, marks the end of summer for most Americans.

12j Omit unnecessary commas.

As you edit and proofread your papers, watch out for the following common errors in comma usage.

Omit a comma between a subject and verb.

┌──────── subject ────────┐ ┌─ verb ─┐
▶ The poet Wilfred Owen⁄ was killed a week before World War I ended.

Omit a comma between a verb and complement.

A **complement** is a word or group of words that describes or renames a subject or object.

┌──── verb ────┐ ┌── complement ──┐
▶ The school referendum is considered⁄ very likely to pass.

Omit a comma between an adjective and the word it modifies.

adjective noun modified
┌──┐ ┌──────┐
▶ A growing family needs a large⁄ house.

Omit a comma between two verbs in a compound predicate.

compound predicate
┌──────────────┐
▶ We sat⁄ and waited for our punishment.

Omit a comma between two nouns or pronouns in a compound subject.

┌──────── compound subject ────────┐
▶ Harold Johnson⁄ and Margaret Simpson led the expedition.

Omit a comma before a coordinating word joining two dependent clauses.

┌ dependent clause ┐ ┌── dependent clause ──┐
▶ The band began to play before we arrived⁄ but after the rain stopped.

Omit a comma after *than* in a comparison.

▶ The Homestead Act made the cost of land to pioneers less than⁄ the price the government had paid.

Omit a comma after *like* or *such as*.

▶ Direct marketing techniques such as⁄ mass mailings and telephone solicitations can be effective.

Omit commas appearing next to a question mark, an exclamation point, or a dash, or before an opening parenthesis.

▶ "Where have you been?⁄" she would always ask.
▶ "Stop!⁄" the guard shouted.
▶ Keep spending to a minimum⁄—our resources are limited—and throw nothing away.
▶ Fast food⁄ (which is usually high in fat)⁄ is growing in popularity all over the world.

Omit commas around words that rename and restrict another word before them.

If the words are **restrictive**—necessary to explain what the word they modify means—do not enclose them with commas.

▶ The man/who brought his car in for transmission work/is a lawyer.

EXERCISE 12.1

Correct any errors in the use of commas in the following sentences. Some sentences may be correct as written.

▶ After slavery was abolished in New York in 1827, several black settlements were established in what is now New York City.

1. Seneca Village a crowded shantytown on the Upper West Side was the home of many poorer black New Yorkers.
2. The city of New York, bought the land where the Seneca villagers lived.
3. The land became part of Central Park and everyone, who lived there, had to leave in the 1850s.
4. Household items from Seneca Village still turn up in Central Park today and a museum exhibit was recently devoted to life in the long-gone settlement.
5. In present-day Brooklyn, there was once a middle-class black settlement, called Weeksville.
6. James Weeks, an early resident owned much of the land.
7. Another, early, landholder, Sylvanus Smith, was a trustee of the African Free Schools of Brooklyn.
8. His daughter, Susan Smith McKinney-Steward, was born in Weeksville, and was the valedictorian of New York Medical College in 1870.
9. McKinney-Steward became the first, female, African American physician in New York, and the third in the United States.
10. Weeksville was a success story, for some of the houses survived into the twentieth century and have been preserved as historical monuments.

EXERCISE 12.2

Correct any errors in the use of commas in the following paragraph. Some sentences may be correct as written.

▶ In June/1998, fifty years after Korczak Ziolkowski began sculpting the Crazy Horse monument, the face of Crazy Horse was unveiled.

A monument to the Lakota Sioux warrior, Crazy Horse, is under construction in the Black Hills of South Dakota. Korczak Ziolkowski a sculptor, who also worked on Mount Rushmore, began the project in 1948. Ziolkowski was born on September 6, 1908,—thirty-one years to the day after Crazy Horse died. A Sioux chief asked Ziolkowski, if he would create a monument to honor Crazy Horse, and other Indian heroes. Ziolkowski designed a sculpture of Crazy Horse on horseback that, when it is completed, will be the largest statue in the world. The sculpture is being shaped from Thunderhead Mountain a six-hundred-foot granite rock. Tons of rock have been blasted, from the mountain. The sculptor died in 1982 but his widow, children, and grandchildren have carried on the work. There has been no government funding so, they have paid for the work entirely with donations and admission fees. By the middle of the twenty-first century the statue should be finished, and will depict the great Sioux hero pointing at the hills he loved.

13   Semicolons

A **semicolon** (;) indicates a stronger pause than a comma but not as strong a pause as a period.

13a   Use a semicolon to join two closely related independent clauses.

Use a semicolon to join two closely related independent clauses not connected by a coordinating word (*and, but, for, nor, or, so,* or *yet*).

> ▶ In January and February, sunny days are rare and very short in northern countries; winter depression is common in the north.

An **independent clause** contains a subject and a verb and can stand alone as a sentence.

For advice on other ways to join two independent clauses, see Section 4 of the Handbook.

13b   Use a semicolon to join two independent clauses linked by a conjunctive adverb or transitional expression.

> ▶ The stunt pilot had to eject from the cockpit; nevertheless, he was not injured.

> ▶ Mass transit is good for the environment; for example, as many people can fit in a bus as in fifteen cars.

A **conjunctive adverb** is a word (such as *also, however,* or *still*) that links two independent clauses.

13c   Use semicolons to separate items in a series if commas are used within the items.

Semicolons help prevent confusion in a sentence that contains a series of items with one or more commas within the items.

> ▶ Fairy tales inspire children by depicting magical events, which appeal to their imaginations; clever boys and girls, who encourage young readers' problem-solving skills; evil creatures, who provide thrills; and good, heroic adults, who make the childhood world seem safer.

Also use a semicolon to separate a series of independent clauses that contain commas.

> ▶ He is stubborn, selfish, and conservative; she is stubborn, combative, and liberal; and no one is surprised that they do not get along.

See also 12b on when to use commas to separate items in a series.

;

13d Do not use a semicolon to introduce a list or to separate a phrase or dependent clause from the rest of the sentence.

For more on introducing lists, see 14a.

▶ A growing number of companies employ prison inmates for certain jobs;: selling magazines, conducting surveys, reserving airplane tickets, and taking telephone orders.

▶ On the other hand; taking risks can bring impressive results.

▶ I'll always wonder; if things could have been different.

EXERCISE 13.1

Correct any errors in the use of semicolons in the following sentences. Some sentences may be correct as written.

▶ Myths and stories about vampires have been around for centuries;; however, Bram Stoker's 1897 novel *Dracula* is probably the most famous fictional account of these monsters.

1. In the years since Stoker's novel, vampires have become a movie fixture; in America and throughout the world.
2. Silent versions of the vampire tale include *Les Vampires* (1915), a French film, *Nosferatu* (1921), a German film, and *London After Midnight* (1927), an American film.
3. Actor Bela Lugosi played Count Dracula as more of a romantic figure than a monster in the 1931 film *Dracula*; this depiction provided the standard image of the vampire as a sexy fiend.
4. The vampire tale has several standard traits; yet it remains remarkably versatile.
5. The vampire tale was adapted to the American movie western; for example, in *Billy the Kid vs. Dracula* in 1966.
6. The popular *Blacula* (1972); which recast the vampire as an African prince in 1970s Los Angeles; inspired a series of black-themed "blaxploitation" horror movies.
7. In the 1980s and 1990s, filmmakers used the vampire theme in teen films like *Fright Night* (1985); *The Lost Boys* (1987); and *Buffy the Vampire Slayer* (1992).
8. In the late 1990s, *Buffy the Vampire Slayer* was revived as a popular TV series; starring Sarah Michelle Gellar.
9. Now, the *Twilight* books and films have introduced vampires to a whole new generation of readers and movie goers; who remain fascinated by this ancient character.
10. Perhaps vampires do live forever; if only in books and on screen.

EXERCISE 13.2

Correct any errors in the use of semicolons in the following paragraph. Some sentences may be correct as written.

▶ The word *placebo* is Latin for "I will please;"; placebos have long been used in medical experiments.

In medicine, a placebo is a substance; often a sugar pill, that has no medicinal use. Placebos alone cannot cure any medical problem, nevertheless, many patients improve when taking them. Because patients who receive placebos do not know that the pills are useless, they think they are getting help for their condition; and they get better. This strange but true fact—recognized by doctors; pharmacists; and other professionals—is called the placebo effect. Chemically, a placebo does nothing, theoretically, the patient should not respond, but somehow this trick works on many people. The placebo effect is often seen in patients; but it is not widely understood. Since the Middle Ages, people have considered the mind and the body as separate; the placebo effect indicates that this separation may not really exist. The mind can play tricks on the body, for example, the brain produces phantom-limb pain in amputees. Doctors wonder; if the mind can also help to heal the body. If the answer is "yes," then the advances in medical knowledge could be enormous.

14 ▶ Colons

You can use a **colon** (:) to introduce a list, an explanation, an example, or a further thought within a sentence. The information following the colon should clarify or offer specifics about the information that comes before it.

14a Use a colon to introduce a list or a series.

When you use a **colon** to introduce a list, make sure the list is preceded by a complete sentence.

▶ The archaeologists uncovered several items: pieces of pottery, seeds, animal bones, and household tools.

common childhood illnesses

▶ All students must be immunized against: measles, mumps, and rubella.
   ^

14b Use a colon to introduce an explanation, an example, or a summary.

▶ In many ways Hollywood is very predictable: Action movies arrive in the summer, dramas in the fall.
▶ One tree is particularly famous for its spectacular autumn colors: the sugar maple.
▶ Disaster relief efforts began all over the country: Volunteers raised forty million dollars.

Note: If the group of words following a colon is a complete sentence, the first word can begin with either a capital or a lowercase letter. Whichever option you choose, be consistent throughout your paper.

14c Use a colon to introduce a word or phrase that renames another noun.

▶ A hushed group of tourists stared at the most famous statue in Florence: Michelangelo's *David*.

:

14d Use a colon to introduce a lengthy or heavily punctuated quotation.

A quotation that is more than one or two lines long or that contains two or more commas can be introduced by a colon.

▶ Without pausing for breath, his campaign manager intoned the introduction: "Ladies and gentlemen, today it is my very great privilege to introduce to you the person on whose behalf you have all worked so tirelessly and with such impressive results, the man who is the reason we are all here today—the next president of the United States."

▶ The instructions were confusing: "After adjusting toggles A, B, and C, connect bracket A to post A, bracket B to post B, and bracket C to post C, securing with clamps A, B, and C, as illustrated in figure 1."

14e Use a colon to separate hours and minutes, in salutations for business letters, between titles and subtitles, and in ratios.

Hours and Minutes	9:15 a.m.
Salutations	Dear Professor Sung:
Titles and Subtitles	*American Sphinx: The Character of Thomas Jefferson*
Ratios	7:1

14f Use a colon only at the end of an independent clause.

An **independent clause** contains a subject and a verb and can stand alone as a sentence.

A colon should always follow an independent clause, which could stand on its own as a complete sentence. Do not use a colon between a verb and its object; between a preposition and its object; or before a list introduced by such words as *for example, including, is,* and *such as.*

▶ A medieval map is hard to read: The top of the map points to the east, not the north.

A medieval map is hard to read is an independent clause.

▶ Even a small garden can produce⁄beans, squash, tomatoes, and corn.

▶ My cat had hidden a ball of twine under⁄the sofa.

▶ Bird-watchers are thrilled to spy birds of prey such as⁄peregrine falcons, red-tailed hawks, and owls.

EXERCISE 14.1

Correct any errors in the use of colons in the following sentences. Some sentences may be correct as written.

▶ Young, impeccably dressed couples participated in the latest craze⁚swing
   dancing.
   ^

1. The ceremony is scheduled for precisely 10.00 a.m.
2. The proposed zoning change was defeated by a margin of 2/1.
3. On early rap records, listeners heard percussion from unusual sources such as: turntables, microphones, and synthesizers.
4. To find out whether a film is historically accurate, consult *Past Imperfect: History According to the Movies.*
5. He believes that the most American of all sports is: baseball.
6. As the entourage rushed past, the star's press agent snapped her orders: "No questions, no photos, no comment, no kidding!"
7. Travel advisories are in effect for the following areas, the northern Rocky Mountains and the upper Great Plains.
8. The neon lights gleamed: above stores and in diner windows.
9. We were not hungry, we had just eaten lunch an hour earlier.
10. Some music historians claim that the American songwriting tradition reached its peak in: the 1930s.

15 ▷ Quotation Marks

Quotation marks (" ") are used to indicate **direct quotations** or to mark words used as words in your sentences. Quotation marks are always used in pairs. The opening quotation mark (") appears at the beginning of a word or quoted passage, and the closing mark (") appears at the end.

A **direct quotation** gives a person's *exact* words, either spoken or written, set off by quotation marks.

15a Place quotation marks around direct statements from other speakers or writers.

Be careful to include the *exact* words of the speaker or writer within the quotation marks.

▶ Lincoln recalled that the United States was "dedicated to the proposition that
^

all men are created equal."
^

> Because *dedicated to the proposition that all men are created equal* repeats Lincoln's exact words, quotation marks are required.

                                                        proposition

▶ Lincoln recalled that the United States was "dedicated to the ~~idea~~ that all men
^
are created equal."

> Words in quotation marks must be quoted *exactly* as they appear in the original source.

In dialogue, place quotation marks around each speaker's words. Every time a different person speaks, begin a new paragraph.

> He said, "Sit down."
> "No, thank you," I replied.

With longer passages, indent prose quotations of more than four lines and verse quotations of more than three lines if you are following MLA style; do not use quotation marks. Indent the quotation half an inch from the left margin. When you quote a poem, follow the line breaks exactly.

> In "A Letter to Her Husband, Absent upon Public Employment," Anne Bradstreet
>
> poignantly longs for him to return:
>
> > My chilled limbs now numbed lie forlorn;
> >
> > Return, return, sweet Sol, from Capricorn;
> >
> > In this dead time, alas, what can I more
> >
> > Than view those fruits which through thy heat I bore?
> >
> > Which sweet contentment yield me for a space,
> >
> > True living pictures of their father's face. (11–16)

For more on the MLA and APA styles of documentation, see Chapter 23 (pp. 603–44).

Note: If you are following APA style, indent quotations of forty or more half an inch from the left margin.

15b Place a comma or period that follows a direct quotation *within* the quotation marks.

▶ "Play it, Sam," Rick tells the piano player in *Casablanca*.

▶ Willie Sutton robbed banks because "that's where the money is."

15c Place colons and semicolons *outside* of quotation marks.

▶ The marching band played "Seventy-Six Trombones"; the drum major's favorite song.

▶ A new national anthem should replace "The Star-Spangled Banner"; no one can sing that song.

15d Place question marks and exclamation points according to the meaning of the sentence.

If the quotation is a question or exclamation, place the question mark or exclamation point *within* the closing quotation mark. If the punctuation mark comes at the end of a sentence, no other end punctuation is needed.

▶ "How does the bridge stand up?" the child wondered.

▶ Poe's insane narrator confesses, "It is the beating of his hideous heart!"

If the entire sentence, of which the quotation is part, is a question or exclamation, the question mark or exclamation point goes *outside* the closing quotation marks at the end of the sentence.

▶ Was Scarlett O'Hara serious when she said, "Tomorrow is another day"?

15e Use a comma to separate a short quotation from an introductory or identifying phrase such as *he replied* or *she said.*

▶ "Video games improve eye-hand coordination," he replied.

▶ "The homeless population," she reported, "grew steadily throughout the 1980s."

15f Use single quotation marks (' ') to indicate a quotation or a title within a quotation.

▶ The mysterious caller repeatedly insists, "Play 'Misty' for me."

15g Place quotation marks around the titles of short works.

Section of a Book	Chapter 1, "Ozzie and Harriet in Spanish Harlem"
Poem	"Ode on a Grecian Urn"
Short Story	"The Yellow Wallpaper"
Essay or Article	"Their Malcolm, My Problem"
Song	"Bad Romana"
Episode of a Television Program	"Larry's Last Goodbye"

15h Do not use quotation marks to call unnecessary attention to words or phrases.

▶ The manager who was originally in charge of the project ⟨jumped ship⟩ before the deadline.

Quotation marks can be used to mark words used as words (as an alternative to italics).

▶ The word "receive" is often misspelled.

EXERCISE 15.1

Correct any errors in the use of quotation marks in the following sentences. Some sentences may be correct as written.

▶ The hotel has an excellent restaurant specializing in ⟨fresh⟩ fish.

1. Her essay was entitled, " "To Be or Not to Be": Shakespeare and Existentialism."
2. Why did the professor assign "To an Athlete Dying Young?"
3. A movie line many teenagers imitated was "Hasta la vista, baby".
4. After September 11, 2001, President Bush said he was going to "fight terror".
5. "I have a dream," Martin Luther King Jr. told the civil rights marchers.
6. Come live with me and be my love, pleads the speaker in Marlowe's poem.
7. The grand jury was not "completely" convinced of the need for a trial.
8. It turned out that the pianist could play only Chopsticks.
9. O'Brien originally published the chapter called "Speaking of Courage" as a short story.
10. Our waitress announced, "The special is prime rib;" unfortunately, we are vegetarians.

16 Ellipsis Marks

An ellipsis mark (. . .) is written as three equally spaced periods. It is used within a direct quotation to indicate where you have left out part of the original quotation. You use an **ellipsis mark** to shorten a quotation so that it includes just the parts you want or need to quote.

Original Quotation	"The prison, a high percentage of whose inmates are serving life sentences, looked surprisingly ordinary."
Shortened	"The prison . . . looked surprisingly ordinary."
	Notice that the two commas were also omitted when the quotation was shortened.

However, when you shorten a quotation, be careful not to change the meaning of the original passage. Do not omit any parts that will alter or misrepresent the writer's intended meaning.

Original	"Magicians create illusions, but sometimes audience members want to believe that magic is real."
Meaning Altered	"Magicians . . . want to believe that magic is real."

When you omit the last part of a quoted sentence, add a sentence period, for a total of four periods (a period plus the ellipsis mark).

Original Quotation	"In the sphere of psychology, details are also the thing. God preserve us from commonplaces. Best of all is to avoid depicting the hero's state of mind; you ought to try to make it clear from the hero's actions. It is not necessary to portray many characters. The center of gravity should be in two persons: him and her."
	Anton Chekhov, Letter to Alexander P. Chekhov
Shortened	"God preserve us from commonplaces. Best of all is to avoid depicting the hero's state of mind. . . . It is not necessary to portray many characters. The center of gravity should be in two persons: him and her."

An ellipsis mark is not needed to indicate that the quoted passage continues after the sentence ends.

▶ He is modest about his contributions to the abolitionist cause: "I could do but little; but what I could, I did with a joyful heart⌢" (Douglass 54).

Do not use an ellipsis mark at the beginning of a quotation, even though there is material in the original that comes before it.

Original Quotation	"As was the case after the recent cleaning of the Sistine Chapel, the makeover of the starry ceiling in Grand Central Station has revealed surprisingly brilliant color."
Shortened	"[T]he makeover of the starry ceiling in Grand Central Station has revealed surprisingly brilliant color."

Note: The first word of a quoted sentence should be capitalized. If you change from a lowercase to a capital letter, enclose the letter in brackets (see 18d).

For more on MLA style for ellipsis marks, see Chapter 23, pp. 598–99.

EXERCISE 16.1

Shorten each of the following quotations by omitting the underlined portion and adding an ellipsis mark where appropriate.

▶ "Some people who call themselves vegetarians still eat ~~less cuddly creatures such as~~ chicken and fish."

1. "The structure of DNA, as Watson and Crick discovered, is a double helix."
2. "Although African Americans had won Academy Awards before, Halle Berry was the first African American woman to win the Academy Award for Best Actress."
3. Hamlet muses, "To be or not to be, that is the question."
4. "Many Americans do not realize that people of all classes receive financial help from the government."
5. "Cole Porter cultivated a suave, sophisticated urban persona even though he came from a small town in Indiana."
6. "From an anthropological perspective, Zora Neale Hurston's collections of folklore proved to be valuable."
7. "We take modern conveniences for granted today, but two hundred years ago households even had to make their own soap."
8. "Folic acid, doctors now believe, can help prevent certain birth defects."
9. "Although saltwater aquariums are beautiful, they are difficult and expensive to maintain."
10. "She wrote rather doubtful grammar sometimes, and in her verses took all sorts of liberties with the metre" (Thackeray 136–37).

17   Apostrophes

An **apostrophe** (') has three functions: to show ownership or possession, to indicate omitted letters in contractions, and to form some plurals.

17a Use an apostrophe to indicate possession or ownership.

Add -'s to make a singular noun possessive, including nouns that end with s or the sound of s and **indefinite pronouns** (*anyone, nobody*).

▶ The *fox's* prey led it across the field.
▶ Whether she can win the nomination is *anybody's* guess.

Note that the possessive forms of personal pronouns do not take apostrophes: *mine, yours, his, hers, ours, theirs, its.*

An **indefinite pronoun** does not refer to a specific person, place, or object. It refers to people, places, or things in general (*anywhere, everyone, everything*).

▶ Each bee has it's function in the hive.

The possessive form of *who* is *whose* (not *who's*).

> ▶ Marie Curie, *whose* work in chemistry made history, discovered radium.

Add an apostrophe to a plural noun to make it possessive, or add -'s if the plural noun does not end in *s*.

> ▶ Both *farms'* crops were lost in the flood.
> ▶ Our *children's* children will reap the benefits of our efforts to preserve the environment today.

To show individual possession by two or more people or groups, add an apostrophe or -'s to each noun.

> ▶ Sam is equipment manager for both the *boys'* and the *girls'* basketball teams.
>
> Sam works for two different teams.

To show joint possession by two people or groups, add an apostrophe or -'s to the last noun.

> ▶ The *coaches and players'* dream came true at the end of the season.

Add -'s to the last word of a compound noun to show possession.

> ▶ My *father-in-law's* boat needs a new engine.
> ▶ We were ushered into the *chairman of the department's* office.

17b Use an apostrophe to indicate the omitted letter or letters in a contraction.

> ▶ *I've* [I have] seen the answers.
> ▶ Jason *didn't* [did not] arrive last night.

17c Use an apostrophe to form the plural of a number, letter, symbol, abbreviation, or word treated as a word.

> ▶ There are three 5's on the license plate.
> ▶ She spells her name with two *C*'s.
> ▶ The *?*'s stand for unknown quantities.
> ▶ Using two *etc.*'s is unnecessary.
> ▶ Replace all *can*'s in the contract with *cannot*'s.

For more on italics, see Section 23.

In the sentences above, note that numbers, letters, and words used as themselves are in italics. The -*s* ending should not be italicized, however.

When referring to the years in a decade, no apostrophe is used.

> ▶ The fashions of the 1970s returned in the 1990s.

Apostrophes are used, however, to signal the omission of the numerals that indicate the century.

the class of '03   music of the '90s

17d Avoid using apostrophes to form plurals and to form possessives for personal pronouns.

▶ The trapper's came to town to trade.
▶ She paid for my lunch as well as her's.

EXERCISE 17.1

Correct the errors in the use of apostrophes in the following sentences. Some sentences may be correct as written.

▶ As newer forms of communication like Twitter, Facebook, and text messaging take over our lives, we should ask whether we're becoming more connected or less connected with other people.

1. Our's is a society almost too willing to share.
2. We probably know more about the day-to-day lives of other's than ever before, as the details of our many friend's days are recorded in online status report's.
3. Its unclear, however, whether anyone is truly benefiting from all this sharing of private information, even as the various social networking sites privacy settings reveal more and more about user's.
4. Todays parents' can find out about their sons and daughters personal live's online, but they have less face-to face contact with their children.
5. Of course, theyll have to figure out the meaning of all the LOLs', BTWs, and other shorthand slang in their kids online and text messages.

18   Parentheses and Brackets

Parentheses

Parentheses—( )—are used to separate nonessential information from the rest of a sentence or paragraph.

18a Use parentheses to add words, phrases, or sentences that expand on, clarify, or explain material that precedes or follows.

▶ The EPA (Environmental Protection Agency) is responsible for developing water-pollution standards.

▶ The application fee for the four-day workshop (a total of $500, including the registration fee) is due Friday.

Be sure to use parentheses sparingly; they can clutter your writing.

18b Use parentheses to insert dates or abbreviations.

▶ Elizabeth Cady Stanton (1815–1902) helped organize the first American women's rights convention.
▶ Guidelines for documenting research papers in the humanities are published by the Modern Language Association (MLA).

18c Check the placement of other punctuation used with parentheses.

Parenthetical information that appears at the end of a sentence should be inserted before the period that ends the sentence.

▶ Ballroom dancing has become popular in the United States (probably because of the success of *Dancing with the Stars*).

When parenthetical information appears after a word that would be followed by a comma, the comma is always placed after the closing parenthesis.

▶ He called when his plane landed (or so he said), but no one answered.

When a complete sentence appears within parentheses, punctuate the sentence as you would normally.

▶ Timber companies propose various uses for national forests. (Public land can be leased for commercial purposes.)

Exception: If the material within the parentheses is a question, it should end with a question mark.

▶ A few innocent-looking plants (have you heard of the Venus flytrap?) capture and eat insects and animals.

Brackets

Brackets ([ ]) are used within quotations and within parentheses.

18d Use brackets to add information or indicate changes you have made to a quotation.

▶ Whitman's preface argued, "Here [the United States] is not merely a nation but a teeming nation of nations."

The explanation tells where *here* is.

▶ "Along came a spider and sat down beside [Miss Muffett]," who apparently suffered from a phobia.

The bracketed name replaces *her* in the original.

Use brackets to enclose the word *sic* when signaling an error in original quoted material.

▶ The incumbent's letter to the editor announced, "My opponent's [sic] claims regarding my record are simply not true."

The Latin word *sic* lets your readers know that the misspelled word or other error in the quoted material is the original author's error, not yours.

18e Use brackets to enclose parenthetical material in a group of words already enclosed in parentheses.

▶ The demonstrators (including members of the National Rifle Association [NRA]) crowded around the candidate.

EXERCISE 18.1

Correct the errors in the use of parentheses or brackets in the following sentences. Some sentences may be correct as written.

▶ Typhoid Mary would probably not have infected so many victims if she had stopped working (she was a cook*/*).
   ^
1. Nathan Hale regretted that he had "but one life to give for (his) country."
2. The Committee for Scientific Investigation of Claims of the Paranormal (CSICOP) tests claims of supernatural abilities.
3. Malcolm X [1925–1965] was an American political figure assassinated in the 1960s.
4. The invention of anesthesia made possible many advances in medicine (including lengthy surgery.)
5. Children believe what they see on television, (at least most of it) and therefore parents should monitor their children's viewing.

19 ▶ Dashes

Use a **dash** (—) to separate parts of a sentence. A dash suggests a stronger separation than a comma, colon, or semicolon does. To type a dash, hit the hyphen key twice (- -), with no spaces before, between, or after the hyphens. Some word-processing programs automatically convert the two hyphens to a dash (—).

—

19a Use a dash or dashes to emphasize a sudden shift or break in thought or mood.

▶ Computers have given the world instant communication—and electronic junk mail.

19b Use a dash or dashes to introduce an explanation, an example, or items in a series.

▶ The tattoo artist had completed a large body of work—Fred's!
▶ The tattoo artist had seen everything—a full-size bear claw on a back, bleeding heart on a bicep, even an Irish cross on the tip of a nose.

When the added thought appears in the middle of a sentence, use two dashes to set it off.

▶ The tattoo artist—who would prefer to remain nameless—thinks tattoos are a waste of money.

19c Use dashes sparingly.

Dashes are emphatic. Do not overuse them, or they will lose their effectiveness. Also be careful not to use a dash as a substitute for a **conjunction** or transition.

A **conjunction** is a word or words used to connect clauses, phrases, or individual words.

▶ Einstein's job in Switzerland was dull—it offered him plenty of time to
think—he came up with the theory of relativity.
(handwritten edits: ", but" replacing first dash; "; while working there" replacing second dash)

EXERCISE 19.1

Add a dash or pair of dashes where they might be effective, and correct any errors in the use of dashes in the following sentences.

▶ Food/who eats what and why?/is now a subject studied by academics.
(handwritten dash marks around "who eats what and why?")

1. One issue particularly concerns scholars of food; why are certain foods acceptable in some cultures but not in others?
2. Some foods were once popular, but today—hardly anyone has heard of them.
3. In the 1990s, people in Great Britain were alerted to a new danger, mad cow disease.
4. In the 1960s, frozen foods—icy blocks of corn, peas, and string beans—were popular—and convenient—alternatives to fresh produce.
5. Today fresh fruits and vegetables are valued once again, unless a busy cook has no time for peeling and chopping.

Manage Mechanics and Spelling

20 ▷ Capitalization

Capitalize the first word of a sentence, **proper nouns**, and the pronoun I.

A **proper noun** names a particular person, place, thing, or group.

20a Capitalize the first word in a sentence and in a direct quotation.

▶ ʳRevision is important.

Capitalize the first word in a direct quotation unless it is incorporated into your own sentence or it continues an earlier quotation.

▶ The union representative said, "ᵀThat meeting did not take place."

▶ Sam Verdon complained that "ⁿNo one takes college athletes seriously."

▶ "I prefer not to interpret my paintings," replied the famous watercolorist, "ᵇBecause they should speak for themselves."

20b Capitalize proper nouns, including the names of specific people, places, things, and groups.

People and Animals	Franklin Roosevelt, his dog Fala
Cities, States, Nations	St. Paul, Minnesota, the United States
Geographic Regions	the Gulf Coast, the U.S. Southwest
Government Offices, Departments, Buildings	the Pentagon, the Supreme Court, the Puck Building
Organizations (Cultural, Political, etc.)	League of Women Voters, National Basketball Association
Months, Days, Holidays	February, Thursday, Labor Day
Chapter or Section Titles in Books	"Why America Has Changed"
Nationalities and Languages	Ethiopian, Dutch
Religions and Sacred Books	Judaism, the Koran
Trade Names	Coca-Cola, Brillo
Historic Events	the Treaty of Versailles, Reconstruction
Specific Course Titles	Organic Chemistry 101

20c Do not capitalize common nouns.

Family Members	my uncle, his father
General Areas of the Country	southwestern United States

cap

Subjects	my chemistry class
Centuries	seventeenth-century England
Geographical Areas	the lake in the park

20d Capitalize the titles of literary and other works, such as books, articles, poems, plays, songs, films, and paintings.

Capitalize the first and last words of the title, the first word following a colon, and all other words except **articles**, **coordinating conjunctions**, and **prepositions**.

Articles are the words *a, an,* and *the.*

Coordinating conjunctions (*and, but, for, nor, or, so, yet*) connect sentence elements that are of equal importance.

Prepositions (such as *before, on,* and *to*) are used before a noun or pronoun to indicate time, place, space, direction, position, or some other relationship.

Book	*The Fault in Our Stars*
Article	"Making History at Madison Park"
Poem	"Aunt Jennifer's Tigers"
Play	*A Raisin in the Sun*
Song	"Hello"
Film	*La La Land*
Painting	*The Starry Night*

20e Capitalize a personal title only when it directly precedes a person's name.

▶ Vice President Maria Washington briefed the stockholders.
▶ Maria Washington was hired from a rival company to be the new vice president.

It is acceptable to capitalize the titles of certain high government officials regardless of whether they precede a name: *the President of the United States.*

EXERCISE 20.1

Correct the capitalization errors in the following paragraph.

▶ The ʋnited ɴations meets at its headquarters in New York City.
    U   N

     During world war II, the governments of twenty-six countries pledged their willingness to continue fighting on behalf of the Allies. United States president Franklin Roosevelt came up with a name for the group: the united nations. The "Declaration By United Nations" promised the support of those twenty-six governments for the war effort. The Nations signed this document on New Year's day of 1942. By 1945, the number of countries involved in the united nations had grown to fifty-one. From April through June of that year, fifty Representatives attended the united nations Conference on International Organization in San Francisco. There, the Nations debated the contents of a charter. Although the War was nearing an end, the governments foresaw a need to continue international cooperation. The charter was ratified on October 24, 1945, by China, France, The Soviet Union, The United Kingdom, The United States, and a majority of the other Nations. Every year since then, October 24 has been known as united nations day.

21   Abbreviations

Abbreviations are shortened forms of words and phrases. It is acceptable to use abbreviations for some personal titles, names of organizations, time references, and Latin expressions. Most abbreviations use periods, but those composed of all capital letters often do not.

21a Abbreviate titles before and after a person's name.

Ms. Susan Orlean   Arthur Rodriguez, M.D.

St. Mary   Deborah Tannen, Ph.D.

Dr. Gregory House   Martin Luther King Jr.

21b Abbreviate names of familiar organizations, corporations, and countries.

Use common abbreviations such as *PBS*, *CIA*, and *HIV* when you are certain that your readers will recognize them.

ABC	FBI	NATO
UNICEF	USA	DVD

21c Abbreviate time references that precede or follow a number.

▶ The meeting will begin at 10:15 a.m. and end at 12 p.m.

▶ The statues were carved in about 300 BCE.

> The letters *BCE* stand for "before the common era." An alternative is *BC* ("before Christ").

▶ Alfred became king in AD 871.

> The letters *AD* stand for the Latin term *anno Domini* and precede the date. The alternative *CE* ("common era") follows the date.

21d Use common abbreviations for Latin terms in parentheses, footnotes, or references.

It is acceptable to use abbreviations for Latin terms in parenthetical comments as well as in source notes or citations. Avoid using these abbreviations outside of parentheses in the text of your essay; use the English equivalent instead.

e.g.	for example
et al.	and others
etc.	and so forth
i.e.	that is
vs. *or* v.	versus

▶ Edison invented the light bulb, the motion picture camera, sound recording devices, etc.

(editing marks: "such items as" inserted before "the light bulb"; "and" inserted before "sound recording"; "etc." struck through and comma changed)

21e Do not abbreviate certain words and phrases when they are used in sentences.

Some abbreviations that are acceptable in scientific or technical writing should be spelled out in most other kinds of writing.

Units of Measurement	ten inches [*not* ten in.]
Parts of Written Works	chapter 6 [*not* ch. 6]
Days, Months, and Holidays	Thursday [*not* Thurs.]
Names of Subject Areas	biology [*not* bio]
Personal Titles Used without a Proper Name	doctor [*not* Dr.]
Geographical or Place Names	I live in New York City [*not* N.Y.C.]. (*Exceptions: Washington, D.C.; U.S.* when it is used as an adjective, as in *U.S. Senate*)

EXERCISE 21.1

Correct the misused abbreviations in the following sentences.

  ▶ Students of ~~poli sci~~ know that public opinion often moves in cycles.
       political science

1. According to Washington Irving's story, Rip van Winkle fell asleep in the Catskill Mts. for twenty years.
2. The average American woman is five ft. four in. tall.
3. Since it is only ninety pp. long, the text is really a novella, not a novel.
4. The Great Depression began with the stock-market crash on Black Mon.
5. The Coen brothers have a reputation for creating unorthodox films: e.g., *Fargo* and *Inside Llewyn Davis?*

22   Numbers

As a general rule, use numbers according to the rules of your field of study. Be sure to represent numbers as numerals or as words consistently.

22a Spell out numbers that begin sentences.

  ▶ ~~210~~ students attended the lecture.
     Two hundred ten

22b Spell out numbers that can be written in one or two words.

twenty-six checks   two hundred women
sixty students   one thousand pretzels

Use numerals for numbers that cannot be spelled out in one or two words.

> ▶ There are ~~three hundred seventy-five~~ ³⁷⁵ students enrolled this fall.

Use numerals for all numbers in a sentence if one of the numbers needs to be written in numerals.

> ▶ Of the 420 students in my school, only ~~twenty-eight~~ ²⁸ have a driver's license.

When two numbers appear in succession, spell out one and use numerals for the other.

> ▶ Each counselor is in charge of nine ~~three~~ ³-year-olds.

22c Use numerals according to convention.

Dates	January 10, 2017; the 1990s
Decimals, Percentages, Fractions	56.7, 50% or 50 percent, 1¾ cups
Exact Times	9:27 a.m.
Pages, Chapters, Volumes	page 27, chapter 12, volume 4
Addresses	122 Peach Street
Exact Amounts of Money	$5.60, $1.3 million
Scores and Statistics	23–6 victory, a factor of 12

EXERCISE 22.1

Correct the errors in the use of numbers in the following sentences. Some sentences may be correct as written.

> ▶ The quotation you're looking for is on page ~~seventy-seven.~~ ^{77.}

1. 77% of those responding to the poll favored increased taxes on cigarettes.
2. The estimated cost was too low by eighty-seven dollars and fourteen cents.
3. Each window is composed of 100s of small pieces of colored glass.
4. All traffic stopped as a 90-car train went slowly past.
5. February twenty-two is George Washington's birthday, but Presidents' Day is always celebrated on a Monday.

23 Italics

Italic or *slanted type* is used for emphasizing particular words or phrases. It is also used to set off titles of longer works or works that contain other works (such as anthologies, Web sites, and magazines), names of vehicles, non-English words, and words deserving special emphasis. Most word-processing programs provide italic type on the font or format tabs.

23a Italicize titles of works published separately.

Books	*Great Expectations*
Plays and Musicals	*Hamilton*
Long Poems	*The Iliad*
Magazines and Journals	*Entertainment Weekly*; the *New York Review of Books*
Newspapers	the *Columbus Dispatch*
Movies and DVDs	*The Twilight Saga: Eclipse*
Long Musical Works, Recordings	*Exile on Main St.*
Television and Radio Series	*The Walking Dead*
Works of Art	*Birth of Venus*; *The Starry Night*
Blogs and Web Sites	*Gen Y Girl*; *Spotify*

The titles of shorter works, such as the titles of articles, short stories, and songs, should be enclosed in quotation marks (see 15g).

23b Italicize the names of ships, trains, aircraft, and spacecraft.

Titanic	*Spirit of St. Louis*
Orient Express	space shuttle *Challenger*

23c Italicize non-English words not in everyday use.

Words from other languages should be italicized unless they have become a part of the English language, such as "chic" or "burrito." If you are unsure, check an English dictionary. If the word is not listed, it should be italicized.

▶ Our instructor lectured on the technique of *Verstehen*.
▶ Tacos are now as much a part of American cuisine as pizza.

23d Italicize numbers, letters, words, or phrases called out for special emphasis.

Use italics for numbers, letters, or words used as terms.

▶ Every bottle has *33* on the label.
▶ Hester Prynne is forced to wear a scarlet *A*.
▶ Today, *ain't* is listed in most dictionaries.

Italicize a word or phrase that is being defined or emphasized.

▶ *Alliteration*—the same sounds repeated at the beginning of each word in a group—can be an effective literary device.

Use italics for emphasis sparingly. When you italicize too many words in a sentence or paragraph, the emphasis is lost.

(no italics)

▶ The U.S. National Park system is *extremely important* because it protects some of

(no italics)   (no italics)

the most *beautiful* and *unusual* parts of this country.

EXERCISE 23.1

Correct the errors in the use of italics in the following sentences. Some sentences may be correct as written.

▶ *Oedipus*, written by Sophocles in the fifth century BC, is possibly the most famous play of the classical period.

1. The exchange student greeted everyone with a hearty *"Bonjour!"*
2. His professor insisted that Soap Opera Digest was not an acceptable research source.
3. Cartoons like The Simpsons have become surprisingly popular with adult audiences.
4. The first European settlers at Plymouth arrived on the Mayflower.
5. His book is discussed in depth in the article *Africa: The Hidden History*.

---

24 Hyphens

A **hyphen** (-) is used to join compound words, to connect parts of words, and to split words at the end of typewritten lines of text.

24a Use a hyphen to join words that function as a unit.

Some compound nouns and verbs are spelled as one word (*download*), some are spelled as two words (*washing machine*), and some are spelled using hyphens (*foul-up*). Check a dictionary when you are unsure; if you do not find the compound listed in your dictionary, spell it as two words.

Use a hyphen to join words that together modify a noun.

▶ An *icy-fingered* hand tapped her shoulder.

However, when the first word of the compound ends in -ly or when the compound adjective follows the noun it modifies, no hyphen is used.

▶ The guard found a *clumsily hidden* duplicate key.
▶ Her voice was *well trained*.

24b Use a hyphen with some prefixes (*all-, ex-, great-, self-*) and suffixes (*-elect*).

▶ Most Americans' parents, grandparents, or *great-grandparents* came from another country.

> ▶ The *governor-elect* made a stirring victory speech.

Use a hyphen for clarity to prevent confusion with certain combinations of prefixes and base words.

> ▶ She wants the taxpayers to approve the funding for her ~~recreation~~ re-creation of the demolished town hall.
>
> *Recreation* has a different meaning from *re-creation*.

24c Use a hyphen when spelling out fractions and the numbers *twenty-one* to *ninety-nine*, in word-number combinations, and to indicate inclusive numbers.

two-thirds finished   *twenty-two* sources

> ▶ The *675-yard* path winds through a landscaped garden.
> ▶ Pages *99–102* cover the military campaigns.

24d Use a hyphen between syllables to split a word at the end of a typewritten or handwritten line.

Although most word-processing programs automatically break the line before a long word and move the word to the next line, in typewritten or handwritten text, you should use a hyphen to divide any words that fall at the end of a line. Divide words between syllables; never break a one-syllable word. Divide a compound word between its parts. Words can also be divided between a prefix and root or between a root and suffix. Check your dictionary if you are uncertain about where to break a word.

> Viking invaders failed to conquer Ireland because the country was governed by a number of petty kings rather than by a central authority that could be effec-tively overthrown; however, by the tenth century this situation began to change.

EXERCISE 24.1

Correct the errors in the use of hyphens in the following sentences. If you are not sure about a word, check your dictionary. Some sentences may be correct as written.

> ▶ Does any ~~teen-ager~~ teenager really need liposuction?

1. Adolescents today who are unhappy with their looks can turn to the increasingly-popular option of plastic surgery.
2. For many selfconscious teens and young adults, surgery seems to be the perfect solution.
3. Until recently, very few sixteen year olds considered making permanent surgical changes.
4. But as more adults pay for nose-jobs and tummy tucks, more teens are expressing interest.
5. Are images of people with apparently perfect bodies and faces unduly influencing less-than-perfect young Americans?

25 ▸ Spelling

Misspelled words are among the most common errors for many student writers. Be sure to pay attention to spelling as you edit and proofread your papers, and keep a dictionary close at hand. Misspellings can make your paper appear carelessly written. Use the tips in the accompanying box and the basic spelling rules that follow to help improve your spelling.

Tips for Improving Your Spelling

- **Purchase a collegiate dictionary and take the time to look up the correct spellings of unfamiliar words.**
- **Use your word processor's spell-checker function.** Be sure to take advantage of the spell-checker as you edit and proofread your drafts. However, keep in mind that this function will not catch all spelling errors; for example, it cannot detect the incorrect use of *it's* versus *its* or of homonyms such as *there* versus *their* and *weather* versus *whether*. (See 25d for a list of homonyms.)
- **Proofread your drafts for spelling errors.** To avoid being distracted by the flow of ideas in your essays, proofread them backward, from the last word to the first, looking only for misspellings. For words that sound alike but have different spellings (*to/too/two, their/there*), stop to check their use in the sentence and determine whether you have used the correct word.
- **Keep a list of words you commonly misspell.** Whenever you catch spelling errors in a draft or see misspellings marked by your instructor in papers returned to you, add the words to your list. Use your dictionary to locate the correct spelling and pronunciation of each word in the list. Review your list of words periodically, and practice pronouncing and writing the words until you master their correct spellings and usage.
- **Develop a spelling awareness.** As you read and write, pay attention to words and how they are spelled. When you encounter a new word, pronounce it slowly and carefully while taking note of its spelling. Try to create a mental image of each word, especially words with silent letters or unusual spellings.

25a Remember to put *i* before *e* except after *c* or when pronounced as an *a*, as in *neighbor* and *weigh*.

i before *e*: achieve, thief
except after *c*: conceive, receive
or when pronounced as an *a*: freight, their

Memorize the exceptions, such as *either, foreign, height, leisure, neither, seize*, and *weird*.

25b Add -*s* or -*es* to form the plural of most nouns.

Singular common nouns ending in -*s*, -*ch*, -*sh*, or -*x* form the plural by adding -*es*. Nouns ending in -*o* usually form the plural by adding -*s* when the -*o* follows a vowel or -*es* when the -*o* follows a consonant.

| **Add -s:** | professor, professors | zoo, zoos |
| **Add -es:** | sandwich, sandwiches | hero, heroes |

To form the plural of common nouns ending in -y, change the y to i and add -es when the y is preceded by a consonant. Add only -s when the y is preceded by a vowel.

| story | stories | day | days |
| baby | babies | key | keys |

Compound nouns form the plural by adding -s or -es to the most important word or, when all the words are equally important, to the last word of the compound.

mother-in-law	mothers-in-law
passerby	passersby
stand-in	stand-ins

Proper nouns form the plural by adding -s or -es without changing the noun's ending.

| Thursday | Thursdays |
| Mr. and Mrs. Jones | the Joneses |

A **proper noun** names a particular person, place, thing, or group.

▶ The Gunderson's met us for dinner last night.

25c Drop, keep, change, or double the final letter when adding endings to some words.

Drop the silent e when adding an ending that begins with a vowel (a, e, i, o, u). Keep the silent e when adding an ending that begins with a consonant.

hope	hoping	care	careful
force	forcing	encourage	encouragement
advise	advisable	love	lovely

For words that end in y, change the final y to i before adding an ending when the y follows a consonant. Keep the final y when the y follows a vowel, when the ending is -ing, or when y ends a proper name.

study	studies	buy	buyer
marry	married	marry	marrying
		Fahey	Faheys

Exception: Drop the final y whenever you add -ize.

| memory | memorize |
| category | categorize |

When adding an ending to one-syllable words, double the final consonant if the ending starts with a vowel and the final consonant follows a single vowel. Do *not* double the consonant when two vowels or a vowel and another consonant precede it.

hop	hop*ped*	pair	pair*ed*
trek	trek*ked*	rent	rent*ed*

When adding an ending to words with two or more syllables, double the final consonant if a single vowel precedes it and the stress falls on the last syllable.

transmit	transmit*ted*
refer	refer*ral*

Do *not* double the final consonant when two vowels or a vowel and another consonant precede it.

react	react*ed*
redeem	redeem*ing*

Do *not* double the final consonant if the ending starts with a consonant.

commit	commit*ment*
regret	regret*fully*

25d Watch out for homonyms, groups of words that sound the same but are spelled differently.

The following list includes some commonly confused groups of words.

Homonyms	Examples of Usage
accept (to take or receive)	Most stores *accept* credit cards.
except (other than)	Everyone has arrived *except* Harry.
affect (to influence)	The new law will *affect* us.
effect (the result, outcome)	The *effect* of the storm was frightening.
allusion (a reference to)	The poem contained an *allusion* to Greek mythology.
illusion (a fantasy)	Josette is under the *illusion* that she is famous.
already (by now)	Marguerite is *already* in class.
all ready (fully prepared)	Geoffrey is *all ready*.
cite (to refer to)	Be sure to *cite* your sources.
sight (vision, or a tourist attraction)	Her *sight* is failing.
site (a place)	We visited the *site* of the accident.
complement (to complete, a counterpart)	The side dishes *complement* the main course.
compliment (praise)	Allison received numerous *compliments*.
elicit (to bring out)	The film *elicits* an emotional response.
illicit (illegal)	The sale of *illicit* drugs is prohibited on campus.

Homonyms	Examples of Usage
its (possessive of it)	The show has found *its* audience.
it's (contraction of *it is*)	*It's* too late to go back.
lead (verb: to guide or direct)	Professor Hong will *lead* the discussion group.
led (past tense of verb *lead*)	Professor Hong *led* the discussion group.
lead (noun: a heavy metal)	*Lead* poisoning is dangerous.
loose (not securely attached)	The button was *loose*.
lose (to fail to keep)	I often *lose* my keys.
principal (most important, or a head of a school)	The citizens' *principal* concern is educational costs.
principle (a basic rule or truth)	This *principle* should govern all of your actions.
their (possessive of *they*)	The students brought *their* books to class.
there (in that place, opposite of *here*)	*There* is the bus.
they're (contraction of *they are*)	*They're* early.
to (toward)	Please move *to* the front of the class.
too (also, or excessively)	Sal is coming *too*.
two (following *one*)	The *two* speeches were similar.
who's (contraction of *who is*)	*Who's* taking a cab?
whose (possessive of *who*)	*Whose* book is this?
your (possessive of *you*)	*Your* experiment is well designed.
you're (contraction of *you are*)	*You're* passing the course.

25e Watch out for commonly misspelled words.

absence	ascend	conceive	efficient
accept	athlete	conscience	eighth
accessible	attendance	conscious	eligible
accidentally	beginning	convenience	embarrass
accommodate	believe	criticism	emphasize
accuracy	benefited	criticize	environment
achievement	boundary	curiosity	especially
acquaintance	Britain	deceive	exaggerate
acquire	bureaucracy	decision	excellence
amateur	business	definitely	exercise
analysis	calendar	descendant	existence
analyze	cemetery	disappearance	experience
apologize	changeable	disappoint	explanation
apparent	characteristic	disastrous	familiar
appearance	column	discipline	fascinate
argument	committee	efficiency	February

foreign	loneliness	prejudice	seize
forty	maintenance	preparation	separate
fulfill or fulfil	maneuver	prevalent	sergeant
government	marriage	privilege	several
grammar	mathematics	probably	similar
guarantee	miniature	proceed	sincerely
harass	mischievous	professor	sophomore
height	necessary	pronunciation	succeed
humorous	niece	psychology	successful
hypocrisy	ninety	quantity	summary
imagination	noticeable	quiet	surprise
immediately	occasionally	receive	tendency
incredible	occurrence	recognize	thorough
inevitable	omission	recommend	through
intelligence	originally	reference	tragedy
interest	parallel	referred	truly
irresistible	particularly	relieve	unanimous
judgment	permissible	repetition	usually
knowledge	physical	restaurant	vacuum
laboratory	picnicking	rhythm	vengeance
leisure	pleasant	ridiculous	villain
length	possible	roommate	weird
library	practically	sacrifice	writing
license	precede	schedule	
lightning	preference	secretary	

25f Be alert for words that are formed from the same root (they may have different spellings) and for words with silent letters.

heir/heredity
aisle
pneumonia

Correct the spelling errors in the following paragraph. If you are not sure about a word, check the list of commonly misspelled words in 25e or your dictionary. Some sentences may be correct as written.

▶ After two ~~centurys~~ of isolation, Japan modernized very quickly.
       ^centuries^

    In 1542, the first European visiters arrived in Japan. Traders and missionarys from the West brought firarms, tobacco, and Christianity to the island nation, which was suffring from internal strife. Japanese rulers welcomed Christianity at first, seing it as a way to reunify the country. However, after large numbers of Japanese converted, some official intolerance toward Christianity appeared.

Finally, the rebellion of a Catholic Japanese community ensured that the government would act to prevent Western missionaries and merchants from joining forces with Japanese dissidents. In 1640, a policy of isolation took affect. No foreiners were aloud to enter Japan, and no Japanese were permitted to travel abroad. This policy was finaly relaxed in 1853, and a new era began in 1868, with the arrival of a new imperial government. The new leaders were youthful and visionary, and they wanted to bring their country up to date. Although some Japanese who had enjoied privileges in the old society lost them during modernization, most people where delighted with the country's new direction.

Avoid ESL Troublespots

26 ▶ Nouns and Articles

The two primary types of nouns in English are proper nouns and common nouns. A **proper noun** names a specific, unique person, place, thing, calendar item, or idea and is always capitalized.

Sarah Palin	Lake Erie	Toyota	Tuesday	Marxism

A **common noun** refers to a person, place, thing, or idea in general and is not capitalized.

writer	lake	car	day	ideology

Common nouns are classified as either count nouns or noncount nouns. A **count noun** names items that can be counted.

artists	books	towns

Count nouns have both singular and plural forms.

Singular Form	Plural Form
one artist	three artists
every book	most books
each town	all towns

A **noncount noun** names items that cannot be easily counted.

rain	traffic	mail

Most noncount nouns do not have a plural form.

Incorrect	Correct
advices	advice
informations	information
vocabularies	vocabulary

This chapter will help you use these categories—proper noun versus common noun, count noun versus noncount noun—to avoid errors in your writing, especially in your use of articles (*a*, *an*, and *the*).

26a Keep the following guidelines in mind for recognizing and using noncount nouns.

Nouns in the following categories are likely to be noncount nouns.

Abstractions	advice, courage, grief, information, knowledge, love, satisfaction, wealth
Fields of Study or Research	chemistry, law, medicine, pollution, sociology, weather
Sports and Games	chess, football, soccer, tennis
Liquids	milk, water
Things That Cannot Be Easily Counted	rice, sand, snow

▶ He offered some good advice~~s~~.

Do not use numbers or plural quantity words before noncount nouns.

▶ ~~Many~~ ~~r~~ain~~s~~ hit the windowpane.

(R) (s)

Do not use the article *a* or *an* with noncount nouns.

▶ The horses were covered with ~~a~~ mud.

Noncount nouns are used with singular verbs.

▶ The milk ~~were~~ sour.

was

Some nouns can be noncount or count, depending on whether they refer to something considered as a whole.

Noncount	*Bread* is a staple in almost every cuisine. [*Bread* considered as a kind of food]
Count	Some *breads* are made without yeast. [Particular types of bread, such as rye or whole wheat]

26b Use an article or a demonstrative pronoun (*this, that, these, those*) with a count noun.

▶ Her client sent her fax.

a

▶ I found fax on my chair.

this

26c Use *a* or *an* before a singular count noun that does not refer to a specific person, place, object, or concept.

▶ A laptop is *a* useful tool.
▶ She was excited to order *an* electric car.

When using the articles *a* and *an*, remember that *a* is used before words beginning with a consonant sound and *an* is used before words beginning with a vowel sound.

a baby	an eagle
a city	an hour
a fish	an island
a hope	an orange
a unicycle	an outrage

26d Use *the* before a noun that refers to something specific.

▶ Mohammad pointed out *the* planets in *the* evening sky.
▶ *The* lamp on my desk is an antique.

Be sure not to omit the article.

> the
▶ He was awake before ᴧalarm rang.

26e Use *a, an,* or *the* with most singular count nouns considered as general examples; no article is necessary for plural count nouns considered as general examples.

▶ A bird feeder is an entertaining addition to any yard.
▶ *The* cat is among the most agile creatures on earth.
▶ *Plants* add a cheery note to any room.

26f Use *the* with plural proper nouns (*the United States, the Joneses, the Koreans*) and certain types of singular proper nouns.

Some singular proper nouns use *the*.

Common Noun Plus *Of*	*the* Arch of Triumph, *the* state of Vermont, *the* University of Florida
Buildings	*the* Eiffel Tower, *the* White House
Countries Named with a Phrase	*the* Dominican Republic, *the* United Kingdom
Highways	*the* Kensington Expressway
Hotels, Museums	*the* Hilton Hotel, *the* Guggenheim Museum
Parts of the Globe	*the* Equator, *the* Northwest, *the* South Pole
Historical Periods, Events	*the* Renaissance, *the* Industrial Revolution

Seas, Oceans, Gulfs, Rivers, Deserts	*the* Red Sea, *the* Atlantic Ocean, *the* Gulf of Mexico, *the* Missouri River, *the* Sahara
Groups of Islands	*the* Hawaiian Islands
Mountain Ranges	*the* Alps

26g Do not use an article with most other singular proper nouns.

▶ The houses are beautiful on ~~the~~ Maple Street.

EXERCISE 26.1

For each of the following sentences, choose the correct article. Note that X = no article.

▶ For many Americans, (a/(the)) civil rights movement began when ((X)/the) Rosa Parks refused to give up her seat on a bus to a white man.

1. Rosa Parks, (an/the) African American woman living in Montgomery, Alabama, was riding (a/the) bus with sections reserved for white passengers.
2. (X/The) back of the bus, where African Americans were supposed to sit, was crowded.
3. Parks sat in (X/the) front of the bus, which took tremendous courage.
4. (A/The) bus driver forced her to get off (a/the) bus, but (X/the) incident set off the Montgomery bus boycott.
5. (X/The) people all over the United States heard (a/the) story of Rosa Parks, and the civil rights movement had its first hero.

27 ▶ Verbs

A **verb** shows an action, an occurrence, or a state of being. ESL writers need to pay special attention to their use of verb tenses, helping or modal verbs (also called *auxiliary verbs*), and verbs followed by an infinitive or a gerund.

27a Use the appropriate verb tense to express time accurately.

Verb tenses express time. They indicate when an action occurs, occurred, or will occur. The following sections will help you understand and form the simple, perfect, and progressive tenses.

The simple tenses. The simple tenses are used to show clear and simple time relationships. The first box on page 800 summarizes how each of the simple tenses is formed and used.

The perfect tenses. The perfect tenses are also used to show time relationships. A verb in one of the perfect tenses indicates an action that was or will be completed by

The **past participle** of regular verbs is formed by adding -d, -ed, or -en to the verb's base form. It can be used as an adjective.

The **base form** is the form of a verb as it appears in the dictionary.

or before some specified time. The perfect tenses are constructed by using a form of *have* along with the verb's **past participle**. The box at the bottom of this page summarizes how each of the perfect tenses is formed and used.

The Simple Tenses

Tense	How It Is Formed	Examples
Simple present		
Expresses an action or condition occurring at the time of speaking or writing, a statement of fact, or a habitual action	First- and second-person singular and plural, third-person plural: base form Third-person singular: base form + -s or -es	I *cook* for five people. They *cook* many unusual dishes. He *cooks* for a family of five.
Simple past		
Indicates that an action occurred in the past and was completed in the past	Regular verbs: base form + -d or -ed Irregular verbs: Forms vary; check the list in section 1c or a dictionary.	We *played* roller hockey yesterday. He *became* agitated when the doctor approached.
Simple future		
Indicates that an action will take place in the future	*will* or form of *be* + *going to* + base form	His doctor *will try* a new approach. Ron *is going to find* a way out.

The Perfect Tenses

Tense	How It Is Formed	Examples
Present perfect		
Indicates that a past action took place at an unspecified time or is continuing to the present	*has* or *have* + past participle	The landlord *has offered* to repair the damage. I *have worked* in this office for two years.
Past perfect		
Indicates that an action was completed in the past before some other past action	*had* + past participle	Rafika *had offered* to babysit, but she got sick.
Future perfect		
Indicates that an action will take place before some specified time in the future	*will* + *have* + past participle	By Monday, the team *will have offered* him a new contract.

The progressive tenses.   The simple progressive tenses describe actions in progress, indicating that an action did, does, or will continue. They are formed by using a form of *be* along with the **present participle**.

The perfect progressive tenses are used to describe actions that continue to the present or until another action takes place. They are often used to emphasize the length of time involved. The box below summarizes how the progressive and perfect progressive tenses are formed and used.

The **present participle** is the *-ing* form of a verb; it shows an action that is in progress or ongoing. It can be used as an adjective.

The Progressive and Perfect Progressive Tenses

Tense	How It Is Formed	Examples
Present progressive		
Indicates that an action began in the past, is happening now, and will end sometime in the future	form of *be* + present participle	Consultants *are changing* the workforce.
Past progressive		
Indicates that an action was in progress at a specified time in the past	*was* or *were* + present participle	He *was changing* a lightbulb when the ladder collapsed. They *were driving* to the beach when their car stalled.
Future progressive		
Indicates that an action will begin and continue in the future. The time is often specified.	*will be* + present participle, or present tense of *be* + *going to be* + present participle	New parents *will be changing* diapers for at least two years. Exams *are going to be changing* under the new principal.
Present perfect progressive		
Emphasizes the ongoing nature of an action that began in the past and continues into the present	*has* or *have been* +present participle	Her secretary *has been running* errands all morning. They *have been planning* this party for several weeks.
Past perfect progressive		
Emphasizes the duration of an action that began and continued in the past and was completed before some other past action	*had been* + present participle	He *had been running* two miles a day until he broke his toe.
Future perfect progressive		
Emphasizes the duration of an action that will continue in the future for a specified amount of time before another future action	*will have been* + present participle	When she takes over, her family *will have been running* the company for four generations.

EXERCISE 27.1

Choose the correct verb tense in the sentences below.

▶ Throughout most of American history, women (have had/will have) relatively few career opportunities.

1. Over the last several decades, however, women (had been/have been) making great strides in education and the workplace.
2. Now, for every two men who (were receiving/receive) a college degree, three women (earn/have been earning) the same academic credential.
3. Many manufacturing jobs that (have been relying/relied) on the physical strength of men have disappeared over the last several years.
4. As of 2010, women (become/have become) a majority of the United States work force for the first time in history.
5. These gains have led some to predict that soon women (will surpass/will be surpassing) men in economic and social power.

27b Use helping verbs to form tenses and express your meaning precisely.

Helping verbs are used before main verbs to form certain tenses. Some helping verbs—*have, do,* and *be*—change form to indicate tense (see 27a). The helping verb *do* indicates tense in questions, inverted phrases, and negative sentences. *Do you know her? Little did I realize what would happen. She does not like him.* It is also used for emphasis: *The sentence does need a comma.* The forms of these helping verbs are as follows.

have, has, had
be, am, is, are, was, were, being, been
do, does, did

Other helping verbs, called *modals,* do not change form. Modals include *can, could, may, might, must, shall, should, will,* and *would.* They are used to express ability, necessity, permission, intention, and so forth. See the box below for a summary.

How to Use Modals

Meaning	Present or Future Time	Past Time
Ability	*can*	*could* + *have* + past participle
	Most five-year-olds *can* tie their own shoes.	Jim *could have registered* early if he wanted to.
Necessity	*must* or *have to*	*had to*
	International travelers *must* carry passports.	The governor *had to* work with other officials.
	must or *have to*	*had to*
	Students *have to* read critically.	

Meaning	Present or Future Time	Past Time
Permission	*may, can*	*might* + *have* + past participle
	Anyone with a ticket *may see* the film.	*could* + *have* + past participle
	You *can* come in now.	You *might have waited* inside, out of the rain.
		We *could have gone* to the movies.
Intention	will	*would* + *have* + past participle
	He *will* encourage real estate development.	I *would have hiked* last weekend, but it rained.
Advisability	*should, had better*	*should* + *have* + past participle
	Everyone *should* get an education.	The trainee *should have read* the manual.
	She *had better* buy a ticket.	
Possibility	*may, might*	*may* or *might* + *have* + past participle
	An accountant *may* work long hours during tax season.	*could* + *have* + past participle
		The burglar *might have entered* through the window.
		They *could have lost* their keys.
Speculation	*would*	*would* + *have* + past participle
	He *would* like her.	No one *would have recognized* him without his moustache.

EXERCISE 27.2

In each sentence, fill in the blank with a modal from the list. In most cases, more than one modal will work in the sentence. Use each modal only once.

can	may	should	would
could have	might	will	would have

▶ Busy professionals who are looking for a husband or wife __can__ try online dating.

1. Other people feel that they _____ meet their potential mate in person.
2. Speed dating _____ be another way to find romance.
3. In the past, few _____ imagined such uses for technology.
4. Now people fear that technology _____ soon make many human activities obsolete, including matchmaking.
5. Human matchmakers _____ become obsolete if online dating remains popular.

An **infinitive** is a verb form made up of *to* plus the base form (*to run, to see*).

A **gerund** is an *-ing* form of a verb that functions as a noun (*complaining, jogging*).

27c Use gerunds or infinitives following verbs according to convention.

Often, you will need to use an **infinitive** or a **gerund** as the object of a verb in a sentence, as in the following examples.

▶ Mustafa needs *to find* his lecture notes.

▶ Lara avoids *studying* in her dormitory.

When you use an infinitive or a gerund as an object, you need to remember that some verbs are followed by infinitives, some verbs are followed by gerunds, and some can be followed by either form without a change in meaning. The following guidelines will help you determine which form to use.

Verbs followed by infinitives.   Some verbs, including the verbs listed here, are usually followed by an infinitive in English.

agree	claim	manage	promise
ask	decide	need	refuse
beg	expect	offer	venture
bother	fail	plan	want
choose	hope	pretend	wish

In general, use these verbs with an infinitive, not a gerund.

▶ Kristen managed ~~finishing~~ to finish the project.

Some verbs are followed by a noun or a pronoun and then by an infinitive. These verbs include *allow, cause, convince, hire, instruct, order, remind, tell,* and *warn*.

▶ The bank *reminded your office to send* proof of employment.

When using a negative word (such as *no* or *not*) in a sentence containing a verb followed by an infinitive, place the word carefully; its position in the sentence often affects meaning.

▶ Bella did *not* claim to know.

   She never mentioned it.

▶ Bella claimed *not* to know.

   She said she did not know.

The causative verbs *have, let,* and *make* are followed by a noun or a pronoun and the base form of the verb (without the word *to*).

▶ The noise made her *lose* her concentration.

▶ The hotel lets visitors *bring* pets.

▶ Have your assistant *type* those letters.

Verbs followed by gerunds.   The following verbs are often followed by a gerund.

admit	dislike	postpone
appreciate	enjoy	practice
avoid	finish	recall
consider	imagine	resist
delay	keep	risk
deny	mention	suggest
discuss	miss	tolerate

Use these verbs with a gerund, not an infinitive.

> ▶ The zoning committee considered ~~to approve~~ approving the proposal.

In a sentence containing a gerund, place a negative word (such as *no* or *not*) between the verb and the *-ing* form.

> ▶ Some vacationers consider *not* returning to work.

Verbs followed by infinitives or gerunds.   Some verbs (such as *begin, continue, like,* and *prefer*) can be followed by an infinitive or a gerund with little or no change in meaning.

Infinitive	Anita likes to jog.
Gerund	Anita likes jogging.

Other verbs (such as *forget, remember, stop,* and *try*) can be followed by either an infinitive or a gerund, but the meaning of the sentence changes.

Infinitive	Dien remembered to answer the letter.
	He remembered that he had an obligation to do something.
Gerund	Dien remembered answering the letter.
	He remembered (the action of) doing something.

EXERCISE 27.3

Correct the errors in the use of gerunds and infinitives in the following sentences. Some sentences may be correct as written.

> ▶ Archaeologists hope ~~discovering~~ to discover when the first Americans arrived.

1. Many archaeologists have considered to change the date they estimate that humans arrived in the Americas.
2. Until recently, scientists didn't expect finding evidence of human inhabitants older than 11,000 years, the age of stone tools found in Clovis, New Mexico, in the 1930s.
3. Recently, however, after discovering older evidence in Monte Verde, Chile, and other sites, some scientists have suggested to change this date.
4. Archaeologists began to reexamine their assumptions after it was established that Monte Verde was older than the Clovis site.
5. One site in Virginia may be over 15,000 years old, and archaeologists who keep to dig deeper may find even older evidence.

28 The Prepositions *In*, *On*, and *At*

These three common prepositions are used before nouns or pronouns to indicate time or location.

Time

Use *in* with

Months: *in* April

Years: *in* 2011

Seasons: *in* the winter

Certain parts of the day: *in* the morning, *in* the afternoon

Use *on* with

Days of the week: *on* Tuesday

Dates: *on* June 20, 2011

Use *at* with

Specific times: *at* 8 p.m., *at* noon

Other parts of the day: *at* night, *at* dawn, *at* dusk

Location

Use *in* with

Geographic places: *in* San Francisco, *in* rural areas

Enclosed areas: *in* the stadium

Use *on* with

A surface: *on* a shelf

Forms of public transportation: *on* the bus

Street names: *on* Main Street

Floors of buildings: *on* the fourth floor

Some areas of the country: *on* the Gulf Coast

Use *at* with

Specific addresses (number and street): *at* 130 Washington Street

Named locations: *at* Juanita's house

General locations: *at* the college

Locations with specific functions: *at* the library

For more on prepositions, see 1g.

EXERCISE 28.1

In the following sentences, fill in the blank with *in*, *on*, or *at*:

▶ Every year __in__ the spring, filmmakers gather in Hollywood for the Academy Awards ceremony.

1. The Academy Awards ceremony was first televised _____ 1953.
2. The participants gathered in the RKO Pantages Theater _____ Hollywood, California.
3. In 2002, the ceremony moved from its previous location _____ the Dorothy Chandler Pavilion _____ Los Angeles to its new location _____ the Kodak Theatre _____ Hollywood.

4. The participants have to arrive _____ the middle of the afternoon because the show is timed for evening _____ the East Coast.
5. The ceremony appears on television around the world, and many members of the audience watch it very late _____ night or early _____ the morning.

---

29 Adjectives

When using **adjectives**, ESL writers need to pay special attention to how adjectives are arranged when they modify the same noun and how adjectives are combined with prepositions.

> An **adjective** modifies a noun or pronoun.
>
> For more on adjectives, see 1d and Section 9 of the Handbook.

29a Follow the conventional order when two or more adjectives modify the same noun.

Possessives come before numbers.

> ▶ *Anita's three* papers were accepted.

Ordinal numbers (*first, second*) come before cardinal numbers (*one, two*).

> ▶ James's *first three* requests were denied.

Descriptive adjectives should appear in the following order.

1. Article or possessive noun: *an, Dr. Green's, these*
2. Opinion: *favorite, hideous, lovely*
3. Size: *big, enormous, tiny*
4. Shape: *circular, rectangular, round*
5. Age: *elderly, teenaged, three-year-old*
6. Color: *black, blue, maroon*
7. National origin: *English, Nigerian, Vietnamese*
8. Religion: *Christian, Jewish, Muslim*
9. Matter or substance: *crystal, onyx, tweed*
10. Noun used as an adjective: *book* (as in *book jacket*), *picture* (as in *picture frame*), *record* (as in *record producer*)
    - *beautiful large white* horse
    - *Juan's old* coat
    - *a valuable new red British* car
    - *small oval* table

29b Combine adjectives with specific prepositions to express your meaning precisely.

Keep a list of adjective-**preposition** combinations that you hear in conversation or notice in your reading. Consult an ESL dictionary when you are not sure whether a particular combination expresses the meaning you intend. Here are some common adjective-preposition combinations.

> **Prepositions** (such as *before, on,* and *to*) are used before a noun or pronoun to indicate time, place, space, direction, position, or some other relationship.

afraid of	responsible for (thing or action)
ashamed of	responsible to (person)
full of	satisfied with
grateful for (thing)	sorry for
grateful to (person)	suspicious of
interested in	tired of
proud of	

EXERCISE 29.1

Correct the errors in the order of adjectives and in adjective-preposition combinations in the following sentences.

> insane Roman emperor
> ▶ The ~~emperor Roman insane~~ Caligula succeeded his uncle, the emperor Tiberius.

1. Caligula made favorite his horse a Roman senator.
2. He was also responsible to declaring war on the sea god Neptune.
3. Brief Caligula's violent reign made many Roman citizens afraid for their emperor.
4. The emperor's notorious temper led to the deaths of unfortunate those Romans who angered him.
5. Upstanding many citizens were relieved when assassins left Caligula dead.

30 Common Sentence Problems

As you edit and proofread your writing, watch out for the following problems involving word order, relative pronouns, and negatives.

30a Place sentence elements in the correct order.

Place words and phrases that indicate time or place at the beginning or at the end of a clause. Do not place them between the verb and its direct object (DO).

Incorrect We did this afternoon our homework.

Correct We did our homework this afternoon.

Place the indirect object (IO) after the verb and before the direct object (DO).

- Ramon bought his sister a videotape.

- Ramon bought her a videotape.

Exception: When a prepositional phrase takes the place of an indirect object, the phrase should follow the direct object.

```
   ┌ verb ┐┌── DO ──┐ ┌prep. phrase┐
```
• Ramon bought a videotape for his sister.

Some verbs (such as *describe, explain, illustrate, mention, open,* and *say*) cannot be followed by an indirect object.

Incorrect   Lu described us the figurine.

Correct   Lu described the figurine to us.

EXERCISE 30.1

Correct the errors involving the placement of sentence elements in the following sentences. Some sentences may be correct as written.

▶ A park ranger explained ~~the visitors~~ the habits of the cave's bats⸓ to the visitors.

1. Every evening at sunset, thousands of bats hunt from the entrance of Carlsbad Caverns in New Mexico mosquitoes.
2. Bat experts tell people that bats are actually helpful to humans.
3. One bat can eat in a single night a huge number of insect pests.
4. At the cave entrance at dusk, the bats provide to curious onlookers a spectacular show.
5. They give the crowds who come to see them when they fly out of the cave a thrilling experience.

30b Do not omit a relative pronoun when it is the subject of a relative clause or the object of a verb or preposition within a relative clause.

A **relative clause** is a **dependent clause** that begins with a **relative pronoun** (such as *that, which, who, whom,* or *whose*) and modifies a noun or pronoun. Sometimes a relative clause begins with a preposition followed by a relative pronoun (the reason *for which* I am writing).

Incorrect   The firefighter rescued the child was given a hero's welcome.

Revised   The firefighter *who* rescued the child was given a hero's welcome.

Incorrect   Juanita found the book for she had been searching all morning.

Revised   Juanita found the book for *which* she had been searching all morning.

Exception: The relative pronoun and the verb *be* are often omitted in relative clauses when the clause is restrictive (essential to the meaning of the word or phrase it modifies); they should usually be included in a nonrestrictive clause (not essential to the meaning of the word or phrase it modifies).

A **relative pronoun** is a noun substitute that relates groups of words to nouns or other pronouns: *the patient <u>who</u> injured her leg.*

A **dependent clause** contains a subject and a verb but does not express a complete thought.

For more on nonrestrictive word groups, see 12e.

Restrictive	Michael grabbed the newspapers [that were] on the table.
	That were is optional because the clause is restrictive; it tells which newspapers are meant.
Nonrestrictive	Michael tripped over the stack of day-old newspapers, which were ready to be recycled.
	The clause supplies additional but nonessential information about the newspapers. It is nonrestrictive, so *which were* should be included.

Use the relative pronoun *whose* to show possession with a relative clause.

Incorrect	The committee sat at a table that its surface was scratched.
Revised	The committee sat at a table *whose* surface was scratched.

Use relative pronouns, not personal pronouns, to introduce relative clauses.

Incorrect	Computer terminals, they are scarce at certain times of the day, are an obsession for many students.
Revised	Computer terminals, *which* are scarce at certain times of the day, are an obsession for many students.

EXERCISE 30.2

Correct the errors in the use of relative pronouns in the following sentences. Some sentences may be correct as written.

> ▸ The United States is a nation ^that^ was founded by settlers from other lands.

1. Immigration in the United States is a controversial subject that its implications have been debated for years.
2. Early laws, they were sometimes discriminatory, restricted immigrants from certain countries.
3. Both legal and undocumented immigrants who come to the United States often seek employment.
4. Some Americans want to limit immigration fear that new arrivals will compete for scarce jobs.
5. New immigrants, their dreams and wishes resemble those of many previous generations of Americans, continue to arrive.

30c Make a sentence negative by adding *not* or a negative adverb such as *never* or *seldom*.

Place *not* after the first helping verb.

> ▸ The speech will *not* begin on time.

In questions, the helping verb should be followed by *not* or the contraction for *not* (*-n't*). Place the helping verb and *not* before the subject and the main verb.

▶ *Didn't* I read that story in the newspaper yesterday?

Place negative adverbs before the main verb. In a sentence with a helping verb, place the negative adverb after the first helping verb.

▶ Arthur *seldom forgets* an assignment.
▶ Eva *may never play* the violin again.

If a negative adverb is used at the beginning of a clause, the helping verb *do* is needed.

▶ *Rarely* does one see a bald eagle.

EXERCISE 30.3

Correct the errors in the use of negatives in the following sentences. Some sentences may be correct as written.

                                                      not
▶ Most reports of UFO sightings and aliens ~~not~~ are believed.

1. Reputable scientists have confirmed never a UFO sighting.
2. A simple explanation for a sighting is difficult seldom to find.
3. People who believe aliens have contacted them offer convincing proof almost never.
4. Isn't it possible that many people simply want to convince themselves that humans are not alone?
5. Aliens may exist, but they not have arrived on earth yet.

SUMMARY EXERCISE FOR SECTIONS 26–30

Review Sections 26–30, and then correct the errors in standard English usage in the following paragraph.

                    are
▶ Many people ~~am~~ worried about obesity in America.

    Between the 1980 and the 2008, the obesity rate among Americans to increase from 15 percent to 34 percent. According to studies recent, over 30 percent of childrens in United States are now either overweight or obese. These studies also suggest that most overweight teenagers will overweight adults become. All these excess weight will cause harms to their healths, including a increased risk of cancer and heart disease. While most people agree that obesity am a real problem, they are disagreeing about its causes. Some claiming that Americans make food choices bad, eat too much, and exercise too little Those with point of view want overweight people take more responsibility for their own healths. On the same time, others see obesity as an economic, social, and cultural problem. They point to popularity of fast-food restaurants, junk food, and sugary soft drinks, especially among younger people. In fact, companies that sell unhealthy products appeal to that children in their advertisings. People with this view also argue that healthy foods are often more expensive than unhealthy foods. Whatever its causes, widespread obesity having enormous social and financial effects. According to a study by Cornell University, the annual cost of treating obesity and obesity-related illnesses is $168 billion. Clearly, Americans not should ignore this problem.

SECTION 3

EXERCISE 3.1, P. 729

Possible Revisions

2. In the United States, for example, colleges and universities provide education to Americans of all classes and backgrounds.

4. During the nineteenth and early twentieth centuries, graduates of state universities played a key role in America's development as an industrial and economic power.

6. Federal funding from the 1944 GI Bill made it possible for millions of returning veterans to attend college.

8. Now, about two-thirds of high school graduates will attend college because those with bachelor's degrees earn $20,000 more a year on average than do people with only high school diplomas.

10. However, as education costs continue to rise, some wonder whether a traditional four-year college is always worth the expense.

SECTION 4

EXERCISE 4.1, P. 734

Possible Revisions

2. Shopping through online bookstores is convenient, but some people miss the atmosphere of a traditional bookstore.

4. In the 1960s some Americans treated Vietnam veterans disrespectfully, a situation that has changed dramatically since that time.

6. With large bodies and tiny wings, bumblebees have long been a puzzle. How do they fly?

8. The Supreme Court often makes controversial decisions because the justices must decide how to interpret the Constitution.

10. Restoring a painting is, indeed, delicate work, and too much enthusiasm can be dangerous.

SECTION 5

EXERCISE 5.1, P. 738

Answers

2. A student in most non-English-speaking industrialized nations expects to spend six or more years studying English.

4. Working for laws that require all Americans to speak English is a fairly common U.S. political tactic.

6. Some linguists joke that a person who speaks two languages is called "bilingual," while a person who speaks one language is called "American."

8. Correct

10. Everyone who studies a foreign language is likely to benefit.

SECTION 6

EXERCISE 6.1, P. 742

Answers

2. Cuba, an island that lies ninety miles off the Florida coast, provided them with an excuse to do so.

4. In addition, many people in the United States had wanted to take over Spain's territories for a long time.

6. Cuba was allowed to take control of its own affairs right away.

8. Correct

10. Many Puerto Ricans are worried that statehood would destroy the native culture of their island, and none of them wants that to happen.

SECTION 7

EXERCISE 7.1, P. 744

Possible Revisions

2. Because of the importance of the information, it often must be transmitted secretly.

4. "Invisible ink," which cannot be seen until the paper is heated, was once a popular way to communicate secretly.

6. During World War II, U.S. government code specialists hired Navajo Indians because Navajo is a difficult and little-studied language.

8. Because these cryptograms are so simple, they are no longer used to transmit messages.

10. Alan Turing, a British civil servant and mathematical genius, finally solved the Enigma code.

EXERCISE 7.2, P. 746

Answers

2. A team of researchers might disagree on their conclusions about the disappearance of the dinosaur.

4. In one way, animals resemble plants: Some are "weeds" because they have the ability to thrive under many conditions.

6. When a "weed" and a delicate native species compete for their survival, the native species usually loses.

8. People should be more concerned about the extinction of plants and animals than they seem to be.

10. The earth has experienced several mass extinctions in its history, but another would take its toll on the quality of human life.

EXERCISE 7.3, P. 749

Answers

2. Correct

4. Following the success of Mammoth Cave, many Kentucky cavers hoped to make a fortune from their spelunking.

6. In January 1925, a falling rock trapped Collins, who was spelunking in a narrow passage in Sand Cave.

8. For several days, the most famous man in Kentucky was he. [Or: For several days, he was the most famous man in Kentucky.]

10. Their failing to save Collins was a terrible tragedy for his family and the rescuers.

SECTION 8

EXERCISE 8.1, P. 753

Possible Revisions

2. We wondered whether our professor knew of the new theory and whether she agreed with it.

4. Most parents think they have a major influence on their children's behavior.

6. Children strongly desire peer acceptance, and they want to be different from adults.

8. Most adults recall that, in childhood, their friends' opinions were extremely important to them.

10. Anxious parents would be greatly relieved if this hypothesis were proven.

EXERCISE 8.3, P. 755

Possible Revisions

2. Surveys show that college graduates who intern receive higher salary offers than their classmates who do not.

4. The most important qualities are curiosity and a good work ethic.

6. Some companies provide little guidance so interns do not learn much from the experience.

8. Correct

10. Some worry that strict federal guidelines will cause companies to eliminate internship programs rather than risk any legal problems.

SECTION 9

EXERCISE 9.1, P. 759

Answers

2. *Wikipedia* has many advantages that reflect well on it as a source.

4. In a way, encyclopedias are unique because Web sites can grow to include any subject that anyone finds interesting.

6. The site has some real downsides too.

8. Many teachers and professors don't allow students to use *Wikipedia* for research.

10. If they choose to use the site, students should make it clear to their professors that they have researched their subjects thoroughly.

SECTION 10

EXERCISE 10.1, P. 761

Possible Revisions

2. So far, no proof of the existence of life forms on other planets has been found.

4. Astronomers carefully monitor signals coming from other parts of the solar system.

6. Most of the signals received so far have been caused by cell phone and satellite interference.

8. The message, containing information about earth, is on its way to other parts of our galaxy.

10. A signal sent to earth would take a similarly long time to reach us.

SECTION 11

EXERCISE 11.1, P. 763

Answers

2. Correct
4. Czar Nicholas and his wife Alexandra often saw their little boy in terrible pain.

SECTION 12

EXERCISE 12.1, P. 768

Answers

2. The city of New York bought the land where the Seneca villagers lived.
4. Household items from Seneca Village still turn up in Central Park today, and a museum exhibit was recently devoted to life in the long-gone settlement.
6. James Weeks, an early resident, owned much of the land.
8. His daughter, Susan Smith McKinney-Steward, was born in Weeksville and was the valedictorian of New York Medical College in 1870.
10. Correct

SECTION 13

EXERCISE 13.1, P. 770

Answers

2. Silent versions of the vampire tale include *Les Vampires* (1915), a French film; *Nosferatu* (1921), a German film; and *London After Midnight* (1927), an American film.
4. The vampire tale has several standard traits, yet it remains remarkably versatile.
6. The popular *Blacula* (1972), which recast the vampire as an African prince in 1970s Los Angeles, inspired a series of black-themed "blaxploitation" horror movies.
8. In the late 1990s, *Buffy the Vampire Slayer* was revived as a popular TV series starring Sarah Michelle Gellar.
10. Perhaps vampires do live forever if only in books and on screen.

SECTION 14

EXERCISE 14.1, P. 772

Answers

2. The proposed zoning change was defeated by a margin of 2:1.
4. Correct
6. Correct
8. The neon lights gleamed above stores and in diner windows.
10. Some music historians claim that the American songwriting tradition reached its peak in the 1930s.

SECTION 15

EXERCISE 15.1, P. 775

Answers

2. Why did the professor assign "To an Athlete Dying Young"?
4. After September 11, 2001, President Bush said he was going to "fight terror."
6. "Come live with me and be my love," pleads the speaker in Marlowe's poem.
8. It turned out that the pianist could play only "Chopsticks."
10. Our waitress announced, "The special is prime rib"; unfortunately, we are vegetarians.

SECTION 16

EXERCISE 16.1, P. 777

Answers

2. "Halle Berry was the first African American woman to win the Academy Award for Best Actress."
4. "[P]eople of all classes receive financial help from the government."
6. "Zora Neale Hurston's collections of folklore proved to be very valuable."
8. "Folic acid . . . can help prevent certain birth defects."
10. "She wrote rather doubtful grammar sometimes, and in her verses took . . . liberties with the metre" (Thackeray 136–37).

SECTION 17

EXERCISE 17.1,   P. 779

Answers

2. We probably know more about the day-to-day lives of others than ever before, as the details of our many friends' days are recorded in online status reports.
4. Today's parents can find out about their sons and daughters' personal lives online, but they have less face-to-face contact with their children.

SECTION 18

EXERCISE 18.1,   P. 781

Answers

2. Correct
4. The invention of anesthesia made possible many advances in medicine (including lengthy surgery).

SECTION 19

EXERCISE 19.1,   P. 782

Answers

2. Some foods were once popular, but today hardly anyone has heard of them.
4. In the 1960s, frozen foods — icy blocks of corn, peas, and string beans — were popular and convenient alternatives to fresh produce.

SECTION 21

EXERCISE 21.1,   P. 786

Answers

2. The average American woman is five feet four inches tall.
4. The Great Depression began with the stock-market crash on Black Monday.

SECTION 22

EXERCISE 22.1,   P. 787

Answers

2. The estimated cost was too low by $87.14.
4. All traffic stopped as a ninety-car train went slowly past.

SECTION 23

EXERCISE 23.1,   P. 789

Answers

2. His professor insisted that TV *Guide* was not an acceptable research source.
4. The first European settlers at Plymouth arrived on the *Mayflower.*

SECTION 24

EXERCISE 24.1,   P. 790

Answers

2. For many self-conscious teens and young adults, surgery seems to be the perfect solution.
4. But as more adults pay for nose jobs and tummy tucks, more teens are expressing interest.

SECTION 26

EXERCISE 26.1,   P. 799

Answers

2. The
4. The; the; the

SECTION 27

EXERCISE 27.1,   P. 802

Answers

2. Now, for every two men who receive a college degree, three women earn the same academic credential.
4. As of 2010, women have become a majority of the U.S. work force for the first time in history.

EXERCISE 27.2,   P. 803

Answers

2. may *or* might
4. will, may, *or* might

EXERCISE 27.3,   P. 805

Answers

2. Until recently, scientists didn't expect to find evidence of human inhabitants older than 11,000 years, the age of stone tools found in Clovis, New Mexico, in the 1930s.
4. Correct

SECTION 28

EXERCISE 28.1,   P. 806

Answers

2. in

4. in; on

SECTION 29

EXERCISE 29.1,   P. 808

Answers

2. He was also responsible for declaring war on the sea god Neptune.

4. The emperor's notorious temper led to the deaths of those unfortunate Romans who angered him.

SECTION 30

EXERCISE 30.1,   P. 809

Answers

2. Correct

4. At the cave entrance at dusk, the bats provide a spectacular show to curious onlookers. [*Or*: At the cave entrance at dusk, the bats provide curious onlookers with a spectacular show.]

EXERCISE 30.2,   P. 810

Answers

2. Early laws, which were sometimes discriminatory, restricted immigrants from certain countries.

4. Some Americans who want to limit immigration fear that new arrivals will compete for scarce jobs.

EXERCISE 30.3,   P. 811

Answers

2. A simple explanation for a sighting is seldom difficult to find.

4. Correct

Acknowledgments

Morris, Toby. "On a Plate." From *The Wireless*, 2015. Copyright © 2015 by Toby Morris. Used with permission.

Moss, Michael. "The Language of Junk Food Addiction." Joe Fassler interview with Michael Moss. From *The Atlantic*, April 30, 2013. Copyright © 2013 by Joe Fassler. Used with permission.

Mullainathan, Sendhil. "The Mental Strain of Making Do with Less." From *The New York Times*, September 21, 2013. Copyright © 2013 The New York Times. All rights reserved. Used by permission and protected by the Copyright Laws of the United States. The printing, copying, redistribution, or retransmission of this Content without express written permission is prohibited.

Nelson, Marilyn. "How I Discovered Poetry." From *Fields of Praise*. Copyright © 1997 by Louisiana State University Press. Used with permission.

Newman, Jerry. "My Secret Life on the McJob: Fast Food Managers." From *My Secret Life on the McJob: Lessons from Behind the Counter Guaranteed to Supersize Any Management Style*. Copyright © 2007 by McGraw-Hill. Used with permission.

Oremus, Will. "Superhero or Supervillain? If Science Gives People Superpowers, Will They Use Them for Good or Evil?" From *Slate*, May 3, 2013. Copyright © 2013 by Will Oremus. Used with permission.

Orner, Peter. "Writing about What Haunts Us." From *The New York Times*, December 1, 2013. Copyright © 2013 The New York Times. All rights reserved. Used by permission and protected by the Copyright Laws of the United States. The printing, copying, redistribution, or retransmission of this Content without express written permission is prohibited.

Palmer, Brian. "Tipping Is an Abomination." From *Slate*, July 9, 2013. Copyright © 2013 by The SlateGroup. All rights reserved. Used by permission and protected by the Copyright Laws of the United States. The printing, copying, redistribution, or retransmission of this Content without express written permission is prohibited.

Paul, Annie Murphy. "The New Marshmallow Test: Students Can't Resist Multitasking." From *Slate*, May 3, 2013. Copyright © 2013 The Slate Group. All rights reserved. Used by permission and protected by the Copyright Laws of the United States. The printing, copying, redistribution, or retransmission of this Content without express written permission is prohibited.

Quinones, Sam. "Dreamland, Portsmouth, Ohio." Preface, *Dreamland: The True Tale of America's Opiate Epidemic*. Copyright © 2015 by Bloomsbury Publishing. Used with permission of Bloomsberry Press, an imprint of Bloomsbury Publishing Inc.

Rashkin, Sara. "What Kind of H_2O Should You Drink?" From *LA Weekly*, September 10, 2015. Copyright © 2015 by Sara Rashkin. Used with permission.

Rivers, Ian. "Empower Pupils to Beat the Bullies." From *Times Literary Supplement*, May 11 2012. Copyright © 2012 by Times Literary Supplement Limited. Used with permission.

Safire, William. "Abolish the Penny." From *The New York Times*, June 2, 2004. Copyright © 2004 The New York Times. All rights reserved. Used by permission and protected by the Copyright Laws of the United States. The printing, copying, redistribution, or retransmission of this Content without express written permission is prohibited.

Schwartz, Todd. "American Jerk: Be Civil, or I'll Beat You to a Pulp." From *Oregon Humanities*, Fall/Winter 2008. Copyright © 2008 by Oregon Humanities. Used with permission.

Shire, Emily. "Dating on the Autism Spectrum." From *The Atlantic*, August 2013. Used with permission from the author.

Silk, Susan, and Barry Goldman. "How Not to Say the Wrong Thing." From *The Los Angeles Times*, April 7, 2013. Used with permission from the author.

Staples, Brent. "Black Men and Public Space." From *Harper's Magazine*, December 1, 1986. Copyright © 1986 by Brent Staples. Used with permission.

Sukrungruang, Ira. "Chop Suey." From *Brevity*, 19, Fall 2005. Copyright © 2005 by Ira Sukrungruang. Used with permission.

Tannen, Deborah. "'What's That Supposed to Mean?' as it originally appeared in *Reader's Digest*, July 2001," from *I Only Say This Because I Love You: How the Way We Talk Can Make or Break Family Relationships throughout Our Lives*. Copyright © 2001 by Deborah Tannen. Used by permission of Random House, an imprint and division of Penguin Random House LLC. All rights reserved.

Thompson, Gabriel. "Underground Lair: Inside a Chicken Processing Plant." Originally published as "Speaking Quiche in the Heart of Dixie," *Working in the Shadows: A Year Doing the Jobs (Most) Americans Won't Do*. Copyright © 2011 by Gabriel Thompson. Reprinted by permission of Nation Books, a member of the Perseus Books Group.

Thurston, Baratunde. "How to Be the Black Employee." Excerpt from pp. 147–54 [includes figure on p. 152: "The Inter-Negro Spectrum of Hostility"] from *How to Be Black*. Copyright © 2012 by Baratunde Thurston. Reprinted by permission of HarperCollins Publishers.

Vitale, Alex S. "Why the Police Are Rarely Indicted for Misconduct." From *Aljazeera America*, November 1, 2014. Copyright © 2014 by Aljazeera America LLC. Used with permission.

White, Alton Fitzgerald. "Right Place, Wrong Face." Originally published as "Rag Time, My Time," *The Nation*, November 10, 1999. Copyright © 1999 by The Nation. Used with permission.

Original cartoon caption (p. 138): "Class of 2008, never let the excuse 'I can't find my pants' stand in the way of your dreams."

Index

Revision Symbols

The numbers and letters refer to chapters and sections in the Handbook. Page numbers are provided for references to sections outside of the Handbook.

abbr	Faulty abbreviation **21**		no ⌃	No comma **12j**
ad	Misuse of adjective or adverb **1d, 1e, 9, 29**		;	Semicolon **13**
agr	Faulty agreement **5, 7e–7g**		:	Colon **14**
appr	Inappropriate language *pp. 205–10*		⌄	Apostrophe **17**
art	Article **26**		" "	Quotation mark **15**
awk	Awkward **7, 8, 10**		. ? !	End punctuation **11**
cap	Capital letter **20**		—	Dash **19**
case	Error in pronoun case **7h–7m**		( )	Parentheses **18a–18c**
cliché	Cliché *pp. 210–11*		[ ]	Brackets **18d, 18e**
coh	Coherence *pp. 149–50*		. . .	Ellipsis mark **16**
cs	Comma splice **4**		ref	Reference, pronoun **7a–7d**
coord	Coordination *pp. 198–99*, **1f**		run-on	Run-on sentence **4**
dm	Dangling modifier **10c**		sexist	Sexist language **7e**
ESL	ESL problem **26–30**		shift	Shift **8a–8g**
exact	Inexact word *pp. 205–10*		sl	Slang *pp. 206–7*
frag	Fragment **3**		sp	Spelling **25**
fs	Fused sentence **4**		sub	Subordination *pp. 197–201*, **1f, 2c, 2d**
hyph	Error in use of hyphen **24**		t	Error in verb tense **1c, 6e, 6f, 27a**
irreg	Error in irregular verb **1c**		trans	Transition *pp. 149–50*
ital	Italics **23**		v	Voice **1c, 6d**
lc	Lowercase letter **20**		var	Sentence variety *pp. 197–203*
mix	Mixed construction **8h–8j**		vb	Verb error **6, 27**
mm	Misplaced modifier **10a, 10b**		wrdy	Wordiness *pp. 195–97*
num	Number **22**		//	Faulty parallelism *pp. 203–4*
para, ¶	New paragraph *p. 140*		⌣	Close up
pass	Ineffective passive *pp. 204–5*, **6d**		^	Insert
p	Punctuation **11–19**		X	Obvious error
,	Comma **12**			

Handbook Contents